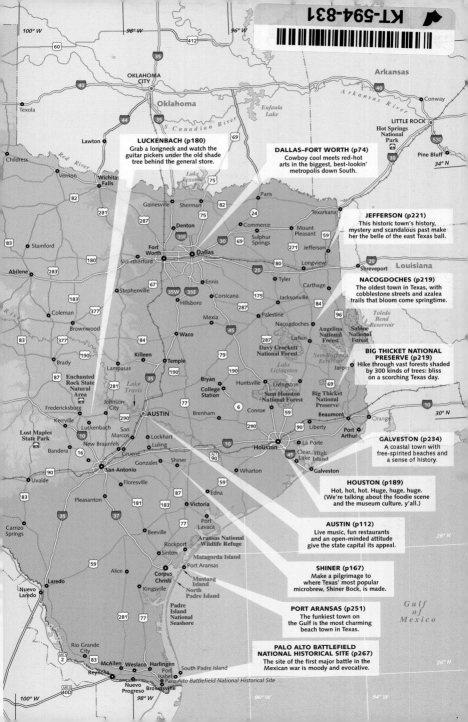

LUCKENBACH (p180)
Grab a longneck and watch the guitar pickers under the old shade tree behind the general store.

DALLAS–FORT WORTH (p74)
Cowboy cool meets red-hot arts in the biggest, best-lookin' metropolis down South.

JEFFERSON (p221)
This historic town's history, mystery and scandalous past make her the belle of the east Texas ball.

NACOGDOCHES (p219)
The oldest town in Texas, with cobblestone streets and azalea trails that bloom come springtime.

BIG THICKET NATIONAL PRESERVE (p219)
Hike through vast forests shaded by 300 kinds of trees: bliss on a scorching Texas day.

GALVESTON (p234)
A coastal town with free-spirited beaches and a sense of history.

HOUSTON (p189)
Hot, hot, hot. Huge, huge, huge. (We're talking about the foodie scene and the museum culture, y'all.)

AUSTIN (p112)
Live music, fun restaurants and an open-minded attitude give the state capital its appeal.

SHINER (p167)
Make a pilgrimage to where Texas' most popular microbrew, Shiner Bock, is made.

PORT ARANSAS (p251)
The funkiest town on the Gulf is the most charming beach town in Texas.

PALO ALTO BATTLEFIELD NATIONAL HISTORICAL SITE (p267)
The site of the first major battle in the Mexican war is moody and evocative.

On the Road

MARIELLA KRAUSE COORDINATING AUTHOR

The quantity of cow skulls on this wall might seem excessive – until you realize that together they make up the shape of a much larger cow skull. This was at the Gage Hotel (p300) in Marathon, last stop before Big Bend National Park.

RYAN VER BERKMOES Padre Island National Seashore (p253) is not just a gem of Texas but of the nation as well. Where many of the Gulf beaches are lined with condos, oil refineries or even SUVs, the 65 miles of brilliant white sand here is as natural as it's been for millennia – seaweed and all. I wandered for hours, pausing to gaze out to sea with my back resting on the sun-warmed dunes. The only sound: the breeze.

SARAH CHANDLER On our east Texas adventure my sister and I found ourselves in Kilgore (p226), a 1930s oil boom town and home to the Kilgore Rangerettes – the world's first women's precision drill team. I'm in front of the museum, channeling my best Rangerette pose. Then it was off to the Country Tavern for barbecue, of course.

For full author biographies see p363.

Best of Texas

With a state as big as Texas, you never have to worry about running out of things to do: it's more a question of where to start. There's a neverending cavalcade of activities to choose from – surprisingly few of which require cowboy boots. We've rounded up some of our favorites to give you a little inspiration and help you make the most of your visit to the Lone Star State.

PATRICK BYRD/ALAMY

1 LIVE MUSIC IN AUSTIN

It's midnight, the cocktail in my hand is sweating, and it's Dale Watson's Monday spot at the legendary Continental Club (p136). Old-timers, rockabilly chicks, hippies and country boys are all two-stepping their hearts out. With its party-like-there's-no-tomorrow energy, Austin has a beguiling way of making Mondays feel like Saturdays. Dale takes a swig of his longneck Lone Star and sings 'Whiskey or God.' If I rock out every night like this, how will I make it to Friday? Hey, it's Austin. I can sleep when I'm dead.

Sarah Chandler, Lonely Planet Author, USA

RICHARD CUMMINS

TEXAS WILDFLOWERS

Every March, the roadsides of central Texas erupt with color: red Texas paintbrushes, yellow and red Indian blankets, pink evening primrose, yellow brown-eyed Susans… But the bluebonnet is Texas' state flower, and it's easy to see why. Entire fields turn a vibrant bluish-purple for a couple of weeks (p60), sending families flocking to the fields to take pictures of their kids among the blossoms.

Mariella Krause, Lonely Planet Author, USA

RICHARD CUMMINS

3

2

SIXTH FLOOR MUSEUM, DALLAS

The 6th floor of the old Texas School Book Depository (p81), looking down on Dealey Plaza. Lee Harvey Oswald stood here almost 50 years ago and fired the shot that killed JFK. Or did he? I'm no conspiracy theorist, but this museum awakens the dark ambiguities that swirl at the heart of this tragedy. Walking through the exhibits, I live moment-to-moment through the seconds that led to the fatal climax. History – powerful and bittersweet – is alive here.

Sarah Chandler, Lonely Planet Author, USA

WITOLD SKRYPCZAK/ALAMY

4

HILL COUNTRY & THE DEVIL'S BACKBONE

My favorite drive in the Hill Country is the Devil's Backbone (p186). Sound like a blues song? It drives like one too: steep up to the vistas, fast down the hills, wicked around the curves. But the views – lush, rolling hills covered in live oaks, with a ranch or vineyard always around the next bend – are pure heaven. We blast music and coast the razor-backed ridges. The sunset blazes, the bluebonnets are the color of twilight. Am I in love, or is this just cedar fever? Welcome to paradise, with a rugged edge.

Sarah Chandler, Lonely Planet Author, USA

BIG BEND NATIONAL PARK

On our second day in Big Bend (p282) we set out for an early morning hike. We'd heard rumors that a bear had been spotted – a rare sight in the Chisos Basin. A passing hiker told us, 'No bears down there, just butterflies.' About two hours later, on our return trip, we looked up just in time to see…a bear. We froze in our tracks and fished for our camera, but before we were able to get it out, the bear ambled away.

Mariella Krause, Lonely Planet Author, USA

5

HOLGER LEUE

TEXAS FOOTBALL

Chanting and cheering on your feet as the '12th man' on the Texas A&M football team (p215) is a true Texas experience (damn noisy too!).

Lisa Dunford, Lonely Planet Author, USA

AARON M. SPRECHER/GETTY IMAGES

6

2TH MA

HOLGER LEUE

7

THE ALAMO

I'm not sure what's more intriguing – the story of outnumbered revolutionaries guarding the Alamo from Mexican troops, or the location of this tiny, crumbling fortress (p147), right next to downtown high-rises).

Suki Gear, Lonely Planet Staff

BARBECUE

Central Texans know their meat (p52) – mosey through Lockhart or the Hill Country for rib-stickin' brisket and piping hot links (with white bread, never wheat).

Jay Cooke, Lonely Planet Staff

WITOLD SKRYPCZAK

8

STEPHEN SAKS

9

GALVESTON

Hurricanes can't blow out the lights at this beguiling bit of the Old South on the Gulf Coast. The charm and culture of the century-old Strand (p235) mixes with the unbridled pleasures of East Beach (p239).

Ryan Ver Berkmoes, Lonely Planet Author, USA

RICHARD CUMMINS

10

AUSTIN'S SOUTH CONGRESS

South Congress Ave is the epitome of the 'Keep Austin Weird' movement (p127). A heady mish-mash of everything we love about Austin, the street is lined with funky stores, locally owned restaurants, cool food trailers, lively bars and a cool, locally owned hotel – without a single Borders, Chili's or Starbucks in sight.

Mariella Krause, Lonely Planet Author, USA

FORT WORTH STOCKYARDS

Wander into the Old West at the Fort Worth Stockyards (p97), where you can belly up to the saloon bar after a mini–cattle drive comes through town.

Lisa Dunford, Lonely Planet Author, USA

STEPHEN SAKS

11

COWBOY BOOTS

Even if you've never worn a pair in your life, cowboy boots are the ultimate Texas souvenir. I couldn't resist the rows of elaborately designed art pieces at Allen's Boots (p140) in Austin (hello, pointy-toe eagle design!). Four years later my boots are still kicking.

Suki Gear, Lonely Planet staff

PETER ADAMS PHOTOGRAPHY LTD/ALAMY

12

SAN ANTONIO RIVERWALK

When I was in junior high, my parents took me to San Antonio. I remember them asking if I wanted to go down and see the Riverwalk (p148). Having never seen it before, and because I was a teenager, my answer was, 'not really.' I was picturing a river just like every other river, with muddy banks and murky water and nothing to do. If you have kids, show them this picture and maybe they'll consent to join you.

Mariella Krause, Lonely Planet Author, USA

RICHARD CUMMIN

13

DEL RIO

The most atmospheric town (p275) on the Mexican border and Rio Grande River combines a fine old downtown with Wild West history, bucolic springs and even a winery.

Ryan Ver Berkmoes, Lonely Planet Author, USA

STEPHEN SAI

14

JACKSON MYERS

15

MONTROSE NEIGHBORHOOD, HOUSTON

Montrose (p199) is a Janet Joplin song sung by a drag queen at two in the morning in a *taquería*. It's an antique store full of old cowboy boots. It's Marlon Brando white T-shirts on muscled boys under strobe lights. It's gorgeous bungalows in the hot summer shadows. It's champagne in the morning and breakfast at midnight. It's mothers in vintage dresses peddling bicycles under the oaks. It's girls who like boys who like girls who like girls. It's pin-up-girl sultry. It's Houston's dark secret, love letter, soul.

Sarah Chandler, Lonely Planet Author, USA

GARY TODOROFF

RICHARD CUMMINS

PORT ARANSAS

The funkiest port on the coast is also a jammin' beach town (p251). Park on the beach, splash in the Gulf and end up playing pirate in a bar.

Ryan Ver Berkmoes, Lonely Planet Author, USA

17

PORT ARANSAS'
MOST UNIQUE S

16 **ROUTE 66**

The Texas stretch of the Mother Road (p338) packs a lot into 178 miles. Amarillo is a worthy guardian of the route with timeless roadside attractions such as the Big Texan Steak Ranch and Cadillac Ranch.

Ryan Ver Berkmoes, Lonely Planet Author, USA

RICHARD CUMMINS

18 **GRUENE**

Right on the Guadalupe River sits this tiny German settlement (p174) that, according to the T-shirts, has been 'gently resisting change since 1872.' There's not much there, but it's concentrated goodness. You can: hunt for treasures in two huge antique stores that are as likely to have rusted farm implements and vintage cowboy comics as sideboards and highboys; have dinner on the river at the Gristmill; dance the two-step at Texas' oldest dancehall; and bunk down for the night in a beautifully renovated barn.

Mariella Krause, Lonely Planet Author, USA

DAVE G. HOUSER/ALA

19 WORLD BIRDING CENTER

More than a dozen splendid sites for watching birds roost under this moniker (p64) in the Rio Grande Valley. How many of the state's 600 bird species will you spot?

Ryan Ver Berkmoes, Lonely Planet Author, USA

INDEX STOCK IMAGERY/PHOTOLIBRA

20 PADRE ISLAND NATIONAL SEASHORE

Wander 65 miles of unspoiled blinding white sand and shell beaches (p253). Find your own acre of dune and find yourself.

Ryan Ver Berkmoes, Lonely Planet Author, USA

Contents

Regional Map Contents

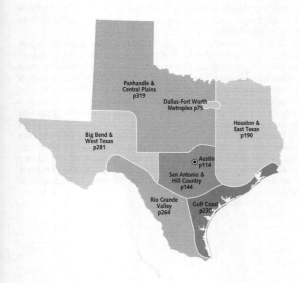

Panhandle &
Central Plains
p319

Dallas-Fort Worth
Metroplex p75

Houston &
East Texas
p190

Big Bend &
West Texas
p281

Austin
p114

San Antonio &
Hill Country
p144

Rio Grande
Valley
p264

Gulf Coast
p230

Destination Texas

Cue the theme music, and make it something epic: this is Texas, as big and sweeping a state as can be imagined. If it were a country, it would be the 40th largest, with over 268,000 sq miles to explore. And as large as it is geographically, it is equally large in people's imaginations.

Cattle ranches, pickup trucks, cowboy boots and thick Texas drawls – all of those are part of the culture, to be sure. Texas plays up the stereotype with 100-year-old dancehalls, saloons, and cowboy-themed bed and breakfasts. But an Old West theme park it is not. With a state this big, there's room for Texas to be whatever you want it to be.

There will probably always be a little bit of a maverick spirit ingrained in the culture of the Lone Star State. After all, Texas doesn't take kindly to being told what to do. Once part of Mexico, Texas declared its independence in the Texas Revolution. Then it was the Republic of Texas for a while before joining the USA. Any state that served under its own rule is bound to have some issues with authority. Although there's some dispute as to whether Texas is allowed to secede from the USA if it wants, there's a tacit satisfaction among Texans in believing they can.

You'll see 'Don't mess with Texas' emblazoned on everything from T-shirts to coffee mugs to bumper stickers throughout the state. But that's not bragging, and it's not a threat, as some people imagine: it was actually created as part of an antilitter campaign – and a highly successful one at that. Not that taking pride in the state's appearance was a hard sell. Texans take pride in just about everything.

The Texas flag is a statewide icon, as is the very state itself: the curvy silhouette of Texas, defined more by rivers and coastline than by straight lines and narrow thinking, stands out as much for its size as its easily identified shape, which is copied on everything from cookie cutters to cattle brands. (Take that, rectangular Colorado.)

But if state pride is what unites Texas, there are few other generalities you can make about a state this massive. Conservative Houstonians look askance at quirky Austinites, who have so little in common with Dallas that you'd think one of them was adopted. The Panhandle and west Texas are so remote they're a day's drive from most of the state. There are different climates, different cuisines, different accents, different attitudes.

You can pretty much choose your own adventure, from the sprawling cowboy country of west Texas to the beaches of the Third Coast, from a glitzy metropolis to the rolling hills of central Texas. You can find theme parks, citified shopping and nightlife, well-preserved historical monuments and a vibrant music scene. And the nearly year-round warm weather makes it ideal for outdoor activities such as rock climbing, cycling, hiking and rowing.

So saddle up for whatever adventure suits you best: the Lone Star State is ready to ride.

FAST FACTS

Capital city: Austin

Population: 24.8 million

Width: 773 miles

Length: 790 miles

State flower: bluebonnet

Miles of coastline: 367

Largest city: Houston

Smallest town: Luckenbach

Highest point: Guadalupe Peak (8749ft)

Number of cars at Cadillac Ranch: 10

Getting Started

Texas truly is a huge state. Seeing it all in one trip is an ambitious endeavor, especially since there are cities in Texas that are nearly 900 miles from each other. Unless you have a good amount of time, the state is best conquered in regions. Reasonable clusters to tackle: the Dallas area; Austin, San Antonio and the Hill Country; Houston, Galveston and the Gulf Coast; and west Texas and Big Bend.

You don't need much advance planning unless you're traveling during the peak summer season or attending one of the state's major events, such as Austin's SXSW music and media extravaganza, the Houston Livestock Show and Rodeo or the Texas State Fair, in which case you'll need to make arrangements months ahead. At other times it's easy to travel solo, with a couple of friends or as a family. Texas is big enough to accommodate everyone.

Most of the major cities have fairly good public transportation networks, but sprawling Texas is a driving state, and it's always easier to get around with a car or motorcycle.

WHEN TO GO

Texas' generally mild climate makes it *possible* to visit year-round, but keep in mind that it's in the southern part of the country, where the summers get hot during the day and stay hot at night. In winter, temperatures can dip below freezing at night but usually stay rather moderate. Winter is definitely the off-season in Texas, and some of the larger theme parks, for example, are closed.

See Climate Charts (p346) for more information.

The best times to visit may be from April to early June and from September to November, when temperatures are more moderate and most attractions are open. These are also the months when most festival planners throw their events. If you do visit in high summer – June to August – it will be stiflingly hot outside, but you can find easy respite indoors: there's air-conditioning almost everywhere you go.

COSTS & MONEY

Big cities such as Dallas and Houston have luxury hotels and first-class restaurants, but you don't need to be rich to enjoy Texas. In this guide, we emphasize the middle ground, while providing plenty of options for travelers who want to spend a little more or conserve their cash, as they like.

If you're camping and making most of your own meals, you could spend under $50 a day. If you're two people staying in budget motels and eating

---

DON'T LEAVE HOME WITHOUT...

- Strong sunscreen and high-quality sunglasses
- A bathing suit, even if just for the hotel
- Cowboy boots if you've got 'em; cash to buy some if you don't
- A great road map
- Your MP3 player loaded with driving tunes
- Copies of your passport, driver's license and credit-card numbers
- Your résumé, just in case you, like everyone, fall in love with Austin

out (even cheaply), budget at least $100 per person. Whether you rent a car is the wild card; without one, your expenses plummet, but you'll probably want a car, since the state is very big and public transportation isn't that great. That's at least $40 a day for a rental car, then.

For comfortable midrange travel, budget $150 to $200 per person a day. 'Comfort' is relative, but with this budget you can mix up a nicer B&B with a budget hotel and balance days at expensive destinations (say, one of Texas' many theme parks) with days at free ones (rivers, parks and the Gulf Coast beach).

Going in high season also significantly affects your costs; if you're hitting Austin during the SXSW music festival or Houston during the rodeo. And of course, if you spend all your time in Dallas' fancy hotels and hitting the nightclubs, who knows how much cash you'll drop.

If you plan ahead, check the web, call and ask, and are a little flexible, you'll find numerous opportunities to trim your costs here and there.

HOW MUCH?

Plate of Tex-Mex $8-12

Cowboy boots in Houston $100+

Bob Bullock Texas State History Museum admission $7

Vehicle admission to Big Bend National Park $20

Dallas boutique hotel room $150-200

TRAVELING RESPONSIBLY

Texas is a private-property state, but the Texas Parks & Wildlife Department does what it can to promote habitat conservation and build public support for wildlife conservation programs. One such effort provides wildlife-viewing trails like the Great Texas Coastal Birding Trail and Great Texas Wildlife Viewing Trails; see www.tpwd.state.tx.us for information.

You can do what you can by helping to keep the state clean ('Don't mess with Texas') and packing out whatever you pack in when hiking or camping.

Texas has several self-governing Native American reservations. Be aware the native communities may have different rules and regulations than the rest of the state; for example, you may need special permission or licenses to fish, hike or hunt. Watch for posted signs, or check with reservation officials.

TRAVEL LITERATURE

What's Texas really like? Glad you asked.

In small-town (and big-town) Texas, football is a religion. *Friday Night Lights* (2000), by HG Bissinger, chronicles a year in the life of the Permian High School Panthers in Odessa, where the fate of the town is inextricably tied to the fate of the team. The movie and TV series based on the book give an even more realistic look at just how many Texans talk, live and feel.

Calling Texas Home (2000), by Wells Teague, has interesting tidbits of Texas history, from its Spanish legacy and struggle for independence all the way to the modern day, interspersed with personal anecdotes that are entertaining and enlightening.

Rick Vanderpool visited all 254 counties in Texas photographing the word 'Texas' on belt buckles, theater signs, tumbledown buildings and every surface imaginable. His book *Looking for Texas* (2001) is a journal of his trip, with essays about his experiences and encounters throughout the state.

In *Texas Hill Country* (2003), by John Graves, you'll find stories of the land and its people and how they influenced each other, from the German pioneers who settled this part of the state to the modern-day settlers calling it home.

In *A Natural State* (1994) nature writer Stephen Harrigan evokes the landscape of Texas with vivid essays covering the natural wonders of Texas, from the beaches to the deserts to the Hill Country's Enchanted Rock.

Larry McMurtry is famous for *Lonesome Dove,* but in 1968 he published a classic book of essays on what it means to come from Texas. The second edition of *In a Narrow Grave* (2001) is still a timeless look into the past.

TOP 10

FESTIVALS & EVENTS

From quirky regional festivals to major events that draw thousands of visitors, Texas knows how to throw a good party.

1 Texas State Fair in Dallas, home of Big Tex (late September to early October; p85)

2 Luling Watermelon Thump (late June; boxed text, p174)

3 Mardi Gras in Galveston (February; p239)

4 Terlingua Chili Cookoff is two simultaneous events (November; boxed text, p290)

5 National Cowboy Symposium and Celebration, in Lubbock (September; p330)

6 San Antonio's Night, the late-April highlight of Fiesta (p159)

7 Austin City Limits Music Festival, a SXSW challenger (October; p125)

8 Marfa Lights Festival (Labor Day Weekend; p298)

9 Sand Castle Days showcases sand art in South Padre Island (October; p259)

10 Houston Livestock Show and Rodeo, three weeks in March (p201)

COOL SMALL TOWNS

Most visitors focus on the major cities, but Texas' small towns are an essential part of any road trip.

1 Marfa, in central west Texas, boasts minimalist art and mystery lights (boxed text, p295)

2 Round Top, west of Houston, hosts a massive antiques fair (p220)

3 Rockport, up the coast from Corpus Christi, has a pedestrian-friendly waterfront (p244)

4 Fredericksburg in Hill Country is popular when wildflowers are in bloom (p177)

5 Del Rio, west of San Antonio, is one of our favorite border towns (p275)

6 Shiner, southeast of Austin, is where Shiner Bock beer is brewed (p167)

7 Port Aransas, near Corpus Christi, is easily Texas' most charming beach town (p251)

8 Brenham, between Houston and Austin, is home to bluebonnets and Blue Bell Ice Cream (p214)

9 Port Isabel is the last stop before South Padre Island (p256)

10 Jefferson (p221) has a 19th-century feel

MUSEUMS

Art, history, taxidermy, soda pop... Texas has museums to commemorate them all.

1 Wouldn't you like to be a pepper, too? Visit the Dr Pepper Museum in Waco (p108)

2 Wander through the beautiful gardens at the Nasher Sculpture Center in Dallas (p85)

3 The Museum of Fine Arts in Houston is considered by many to be the finest art museum in the state (p198)

4 Those famous glasses are proudly on display at the Buddy Holly Center, in Lubbock (p329)

5 Republic of the Rio Grande Museum, in Laredo, is housed in the 1840 capitol of the short-lived Republic of the Rio Grande (p272)

6 The Museum of the Gulf Coast in Beaumont offers a glimpse of the natural, cultural and geological history of the region (p232)

7 Ride a bronco and see how the West was *really* won at the National Cowgirl Museum and Hall of Fame, in Fort Worth (p100)

8 Bob Bullock Texas State History Museum, in Austin, is a glitzy, high-tech presentation of how Texas got that way (p117)

9 El Paso Holocaust Museum is a hidden gem, with moving and artful displays (p304)

10 The Buckhorn Saloon & Museum, in San Antonio, has pure camp value and a ridiculous collection of horns (p149)

INTERNET RESOURCES

Lonely Planet (www.lonelyplanet.com) Get fellow travelers' advice, post questions and much more.

Texas Monthly (www.texasmonthly.com) The national magazine of Texas, with great information and wonderful writing.

TourTexas (www.tourtexas.com) Information broken down by regions, plus access to lots of free travel brochures.

TravelTex (www.traveltex.com) The state's official tourism website, where you can order the huge *Texas Travel Guide* and search for tons of info.

Wild Texas (www.wildtexas.com) A guide to Texas parks, travel and outdoor recreation, with an active forum where you can get advice from other travelers.

Itineraries
CLASSIC TRIPS

COASTAL TEXAS
One Week/Port Arthur to Corpus Christi

Start your Third Coast adventure in the Golden Triangle – **Beaumont** (p229), **Port Arthur** (p232) and **Orange** (p232) – visiting the area's museums, including the excellent **Museum of the Gulf Coast** (p232).

Head to Port Bolivar and catch the **Galveston–Port Bolivar ferry** (p242) to historic **Galveston** (p234). Spend a day or two exploring **Galveston Island State Park** (p242), ogling the mansions in the **Silk Stocking Historic Precinct** (p237), and wandering the stores, restaurants and attractions of the **Strand** (p235).

Continue around the coast, stopping at the **Sea Center Texas** (p243) in Lake Jackson to check out the aquarium and fish hatcheries. Then make your way down to **Aransas National Wildlife Refuge** (p244), the best bird-watching site on the Texas coast.

Take the loop around **Corpus Christi Bay** (p252), and be sure to stop by **Port Aransas** (p251) with its pedestrian-friendly waterfront. Finish your trip in **Corpus Christi** (p246), spending some time at the Museum of Science and History, the Texas State Aquarium, and the Art Museum of South Texas.

Follow this route, which shirks Houston in favor of 300 miles' worth of sunny beaches, interesting small museums, historical towns and some of the state's best bird-watching. The lazy pleasures of the Third Coast await.

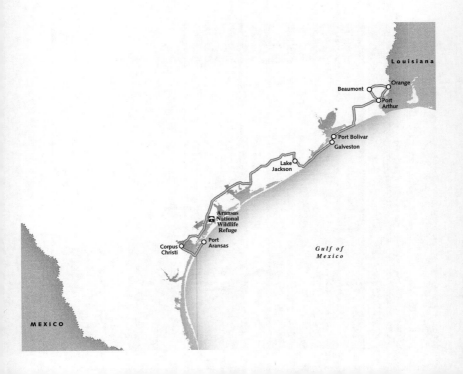

WEST TEXAS & BIG BEND LOOP   One Week/El Paso and Back

Spend a day in **El Paso** (p301), where you can tour the thoroughly enjoyable **El Paso Museum of Art** (p304) and the nearby **El Paso Museum of History** (p304). See some of that history in real life by visiting the **Mission Trail** (p305).

The next day, head to **Fort Davis** (p292) to see the remarkably well-preserved frontier **military post** (p292) that gave the town its name. Try to time your trip so you can catch a Star Party at **McDonald Observatory** (p293), 19 miles northwest of town.

In the morning, drive through **Marathon** (p300) to check out the fabulous **Gage Hotel** (p300) and pick up supplies for your drive into **Big Bend National Park** (p282). Check in to the **Chisos Mountain Lodge** (p289) or set up your tent for camping. Then it's up early for two or three days of hiking, probably the **Window Trail** (p286) the first day, the **Lost Mine Trail** (p286) the second, and your choice of hikes to see the **Rio Grande** (p286) on the third.

The next day, for a change of scenery, make your way to **Terlingua** (p289) and its ghost town, slipping in a visit to the **Starlight Theater** (p291). Spend the night in **Alpine** (p292), then visit its **Museum of the Big Bend** (p298) to learn the history of the region you just hiked.

Drive to **Marfa** (p295) and check out the gorgeous **Presidio County Courthouse** (p297) and all the **art galleries** (p296). After dinner, hit the **Marfa Lights Viewing Area** (p296) and look for the mystery lights on the horizon after dark. Spend the whole next day exploring minimalist art at the **Chinati Foundation** (p295) before heading back to El Paso.

Ditch your cell phone, your laptop and maybe even your watch as you ease into west Texas, starting with bicultural El Paso then taking a slow, 650-mile loop through small towns and Texas' best national park.

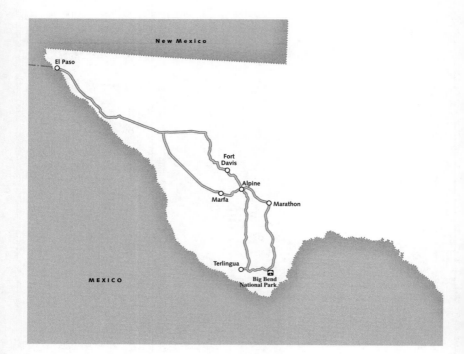

SOUTH CENTRAL TEXAS

One Weeks/Austin To San Antonio

Start with two days around **Austin** (p112), focusing on sights **downtown** (p117), around the **UT campus** (p120) and the oasis of **Zilker Park** (p123). Don't miss the **Bob Bullock Texas State History Museum** (p117), a splash in **Barton Springs Pool** (p123) or the **bat colony** (p120) under the Congress Ave bridge. Quirky **South Congress** (p113) is wonderful for people-watching, noshing and shopping. After dark, visit Austin's **live music clubs** (p135).

Next, head out to the Hill Country, stopping at **Johnson City** (p176) to see the **LBJ Ranch** (p176). Then spend two or three nights in **Fredericksburg** (p177) or **Kerrville** (p181). Activities around the former include a visit to the Texas **wine country** (p179), a climb up **Enchanted Rock** (p180) and a musical pilgrimage to **Luckenbach** (p180). Meanwhile, Kerrville is the place for **tubing** (p182) on the Guadalupe River, **cowboy art** (p181) and **dude ranches** (p184) in nearby Bandera.

On the way down to San Antonio, go hunting for antiques in **Comfort** (p183) or caving in **Boerne** (p185) or get off the beaten path on the **Waring-Welfare Rd** (p185).

Start your **San Antonio** (p144) visit with the **Alamo** (p147) and the **Mission Trail** (p153). Around sunset, stroll along the **Riverwalk** (p148) to catch live jazz at the **Landing** (p168).

The next morning, drop by the historic **King William District** (p151), then spend the afternoon museum-hopping at the **San Antonio Museum of Art** (p154) and the **McNay Art Museum** (p155). Families with energetic kids may want to head to **Natural Bridge Caverns** (p173) or spend the day at **SeaWorld** (p155) or **Six Flags Fiesta Texas** (p155).

Wildflowers, back roads and charming small towns are bookended by two of Texas' most interesting cities on this 300-mile road trip deep in the heart of Texas.

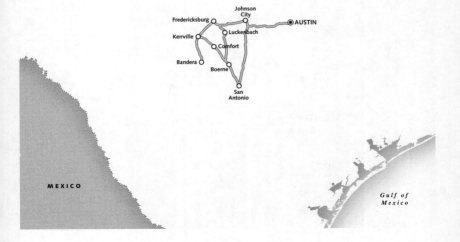

GRAND TEXAS TOUR

One Month/Austin to El Paso via Houston

So you want to do it all? Get ready for some serious driving. Spend your first week exploring **Austin** (p112), **San Antonio** (p144) and the **Hill Country** (p176) as outlined in the South Central Texas itinerary (p23). Then head west to **Houston** (p189) for a few days of big-city life. Don't miss the stellar **Museum of Fine Arts** (p198) and the **Houston Museum of Natural Science** (p198), and spend some time wandering the eclectic **Montrose** (p199) neighborhood, known for its restaurants and shops. If you have the time, drive down for an overnight in **Galveston** (p234).

Swing up to **Dallas** (p76) for more museum-hopping in the enormous **Arts District** (p83). Downtown, **Dealey Plaza** (p81) and the **Sixth Floor Museum** (p81) are fascinating for anyone with even the slightest interest in the Kennedy assassination. Heading to **Fort Worth** (p95), don't miss the world-class **Kimbell Art Museum** (p99) and take the opportunity to go dancing at the world's largest honky-tonk, **Billy Bob's** (p105).

It's now time to settle in for a looong day of driving and wide-open spaces as you head west toward **Big Bend National Park** (p282). Spend several days hiking and maybe floating down the Rio Grande. As you head back out of the park, stop in the small town of **Marfa** (p295) and check out the minimalist art of the **Chinati Foundation** (p295). Further along, don't miss the **McDonald Observatory** (p293) in **Fort Davis** (p292). Finish up in **El Paso** (p301), where you'll find some of the best Mexican food around and most of the museums are free. Congratulate yourself, because you grabbed this huge state by the horns and took it down.

> Nearly 1500 miles is what it takes to see all the best Texas has to offer, and we're probably leaving some out. You could shave some time by flying, although you'd be missing out on a lot of wonderful small towns along the way.

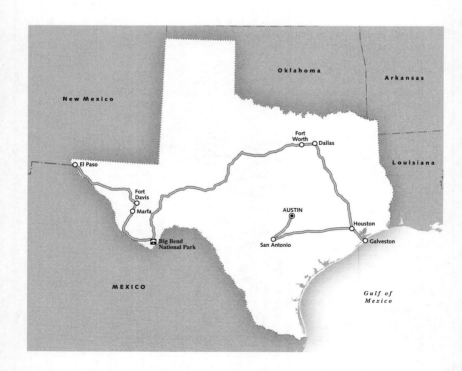

TAILORED TRIPS

TEXAS FOR KIDS

Whether your kids gravitate toward theme parks, museums or outdoor adventures, you're in luck. Texas is made for family fun.

In Austin, start out at the **Austin Children's Museum** (p124). Zip over to Zilker Park for wading in **Barton Springs Pool** (p123), **miniature train rides** (p124) and the wonders of the **Austin Nature & Science Center** (p124). Downtown, don't miss the nightly egress of Austin's own **bat colony** (p120).

Aquatic fun awaits in **San Marcos** (p173) or **New Braunfels** (p173), and San Marcos' **Wonder World** (p175) offers adventure for junior spelunkers. In San Antonio, take a cruise along the **Riverwalk** (p148), visit the **San Antonio Children's Museum** (p157), then head to Brackenridge Park (p157) for the excellent **Witte Museum** (p157), old-fashioned carnival rides and more. You could easily spend a whole day at **SeaWorld** (p155) or **Six Flags Fiesta Texas** (p155).

In Houston, be sure to catch the **Children's Museum of Houston** (p201) and the **Johnson Space Center** (p214) in Clear Lake. Galveston is home to family-friendly **Stewart Beach** (p239), or, if you need to up the wow factor, take the family to **Schlitterbahn Beach Waterpark** (p258).

If you're in Dallas in September/October, visit Big Tex at the **Texas State Fair** (p85). Over in Arlington, **Six Flags Over Texas** (p106) is great for little ones and teenagers alike.

QUIRKY TEXAS

In central Texas, locals try to **'Keep Austin Weird'** (p127), and one of our favorite embodiments of that movement is the exceedingly nontraditional **Christmas lights** (p126) on 37th Street each December. Down in San Antonio, the **Buckhorn Saloon & Museum** (p149) is a kitschy monument to taxidermy with a two-headed calf thrown in for good measure.

Houston is more conservative, but a couple of local mavericks keep the freak flag flying with two local attractions: **Orange Show** (p199) and the **Beer Can House** (p199). Kilgore is the home of the sassy **Rangerette Museum** (p226), an ode to the famous Rangerettes drill team who enlivened Kilgore College football games starting back in 1939.

West Texas has its share of oddities, including the mysterious **Marfa Mystery Lights** (p296) that appear on the horizon outside of Marfa after dark, and the little town of **Terlingua** (p289), which is actually a new town being built on top of the ruins of a ghost town.

Over in Amarillo, don't miss **Cadillac Ranch** (p336), Texas' answer to Stonehenge, and finish with a meal at the monument to excess that is the **Big Texan Steak Ranch** (p339). And tiny McLean is where you'll find the only-in-Texas **Devil's Rope Museum** (p338), with its many displays involving barbed wire.

HONKY-TONKIN'

Dancehalls, honky-tonks – call 'em what you will, but a spin or two around a well-scuffed wood floor to the sounds of live country music is an essential Texas experience. Texas' oldest continually operating dance hall is **Gruene Hall** (p174) in tiny Gruene. Built in the 1880s, this barnlike building was – and still is – the social center for the town.

If you're lucky you can catch a weekend dance at the old-old-timer **Luckenbach Dance Hall** (p181). It was established in 1849, abandoned for a while, then rescued by Hondo Crouch in the 1970s.

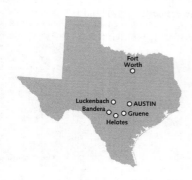

North of San Antonio in Helotes, the **John T Floore Country Store** (p168) goes back to 1942 and has an impressive roster of former guests including Hank Williams, Bob Wills and Willie Nelson. Head to nearby **Bandera** (p184), the 'Cowboy Capital of Texas,' for two historic halls from the 1930s: **Arkey Blue's Silver Dollar Bar** (p184) and **Bandera Cabaret Dance Hall** (p184).

In Austin, folks gather at the **Broken Spoke** (p137), a relative newcomer that's only been around since the 1960s but is still a great place to practice your Texas two-step. Least historic but still noteworthy, **Billy Bob's** (p105) in Fort Worth is the world's largest honky tonk, with 40 bars, live music and live bull riding.

FOR HISTORY BUFFS

Texas has some excellent historical sites and museums for anyone who wants to experience the past without the help of a history book. One of the best known is the **Alamo** (p147) in San Antonio – a must-stop on your tour. While you're remembering the Alamo, don't forget **Goliad** (p246), another significant Texas revolution site.

San Antonio is also home to the **Mission Trail** (p153), with four beautifully preserved missions. El Paso's **Mission Trail** (p305) has two missions and a chapel that form the oldest settlements in Texas.

Texas has several ties to presidential history. You don't have to be a history buff to appreciate the significance of Dallas' **Dealey Plaza** (p81), where President John F Kennedy was assassinated, or the **Sixth Floor Museum** (p81),

created from the perch where Lee Harvey Oswald hid. There's also the **Lyndon Baines Johnson (LBJ) Presidential Library & Museum** (p121) in Austin, **LBJ Ranch** (p176) in Johnson City and the **George Bush Presidential Library** (p216) in College Station.

If military history is more your style, try **Fort Davis National Historic Site** (p292), a scenic and well-preserved frontier military post, or **Fort McKavett State Historical Park** (p325), southeast of San Angelo.

The **Museum of Printing History** (p200) in Houston is a fascinating repository of old newspapers from significant historical events from around the nation.

History

History is always someone's version of what happened, and Texans can spin larger-than-life stories with the best of them. Just say the words 'Alamo' or 'JFK assassination' and you're bound to hear a hundred versions of the same story, all with gleaming bits of truth among the assorted fictions and perspectives. The Lone Star State has always been a cultural, political and geographical hotbed – and you'd think all that land would make everyone just peacefully coexist and mind their own business! Nope. From the fight for Texas independence to the border wars, Texas seems to stay at the front of the action: loud, proud and a subject of heated controversy. One thing's for sure: in the course of its history, you can say Texas has been loved and hated, but you can't say it's been ignored.

You'll find more versions of Texas history than recipes for barbecue sauce. In other words, swallow a Texas tale like you would a margarita: with a grain or two of salt.

The word 'Texas' goes back to 1691. Spanish explorers found the Caddos so friendly that they began to call their new territory *tejas* ('tay-has'), a corruption of the Caddo word for 'friend.'

IN THE BEGINNING...

Texas hasn't always been Texas. Or Mexico, for that matter. Or the United States, or Spain, or France…or any of the six flags that once flew over this epic state in its eight changes of sovereignty. The earliest evidence of humans in what is now Texas exists in the *llano estacado* ('staked plain') section of Texas and New Mexico. Little is known about the various indigenous peoples, but by the time the first Europeans arrived in the 16th century, several distinct groups of Native Americans were settled in the region.

One of these tribes, the Caddos, still figures strongly both as a namesake and cultural influence in east Texas, particularly in places like Caddo Lake and around Nacogdoches, where the Caddo Mounds State Historic Site commemorates their unique history.

Lone Star Junction (www.lsjunction.com) has ebooks and fascinating historical archives.

SPANISH EXPLORATION

In 1519, Alonzo Álvarez de Piñeda mapped the coast of the Gulf of Mexico from Florida to Mexico, creating the first maps of present-day Texas. He camped at the mouth of the Rio Grande (which he called the 'river of palms').

The Spanish planned a settlement along the Rio Grande, but after battles following disagreements between settlers and tribespeople, the Spanish withdrew.

In 1542 Luis de Moscoso led an exploration of present-day east Texas. He was frantically looking for gold – Indians would always tell him it was

The Texas State Historical Association maintains an enormous handbook of Texas history at www.tshaonline.org.

TIMELINE

1519	1539	1598
Alonzo Álvarez de Piñeda maps the coast of the Gulf of Mexico from Florida to Mexico, creating the first maps of present-day Texas.	Franciscan friar Marcos de Niza leads a greed-fueled expedition to Texas. After Indian attacks wipe out half the expedition, the friar flees back to Mexico – after hastily claiming the ground he'd covered for Spain, of course.	Nearly a quarter century before pilgrims and Indians party at Plymouth Rock in Massachusetts, Native Americans and Spanish explorers feast on the banks of the Rio Grande. Many Texans believe it to be the first real Thanksgiving.

located somewhere else – but he never found any. What he and his men did notice was that the whole place was covered in black stuff that was slimy, smelled bad and burned easily – oil, aka 'black gold.' They used the material to caulk ships and for other pedestrian applications, but apparently did not consider using it as fuel.

MISSION IMPOSSIBLE

By 1600, Spain controlled Florida and nearly all of present-day Mexico and Central America, among other lands. While the conquest of new lands was brutal, Spain's conquistadores considered their objectives not just economic and political but moral: winning over new Christian souls.

By the mid-17th century, the Spaniards' had embarked on the construction of a series of *misións* (missions) and *presidios* (forts) from Florida across the continent all the way to California in an effort to convert the Native Americans to Christianity and, not incidentally, into Spanish subjects.

More than 30 missions were constructed in Texas. The missions at their best were fully self-reliant outposts where missionaries taught local Native Americans Spanish, as well as European building and farming techniques. During the heyday of the missions, from 1745 to 1775, they became successful enough to attract the attention of Apache and Comanche Indians, who began a series of crippling attacks.

THE FRENCH THREAT

Meanwhile, the French were also exploring North America. In the 1680s, they laid claim to the territory they called Louisiana and to a piece of Texas. This hardly amused the Spanish, and it spurred them to begin their mission-building in Texas.

In 1690, construction of Spain's first mission in east Texas, Misión San Francisco de los Tejas, began. It was completed in 1691, failing only two years later. Over the next 20 years, the Spanish continued to settle east Texas, but many of the missions designed to fortify the east Texas border fell to disease, incompetence, skirmishes with Native Americans and French troops, and other disasters. In 1718, the Spanish began building missions and forts in south-central Texas to reduce the distances crossed by supply trains.

Misión San Antonio de Valero, which later became known as the Alamo, and the present-day Mission Trail were constructed around this time. In 1731, the settlement of Villa de Bexar was established by Spanish colonists imported from the Canary Islands, and a civil government was set up in the area.

The Spanish finally gave up control in 1821, and Texas became a state of newly independent Mexico. Under Mexican rule the missions were discontinued.

In the early 1500s, hapless explorer Cabeza de Vaca wrote diaries documenting his experiences as a shipwrecked prisoner in Texas, and Texas' written history – part truth, part fiction, all fascinating – was born.

THE SIX (COUNT 'EM!) FLAGS OF TEXAS

Spanish – 1519 to 1685; 1690 to 1821

French – 1685 to 1690

Mexican – 1821 to 1836

Republic of Texas – 1836 to 1845

United States – 1845 to 1861

Confederate States – 1861 to 1865

United States – 1865 to the present

From 1680	1800	1810
More than 30 missions are constructed in Texas alone. The earliest of them can be seen near what is now El Paso.	Napoléon Bonaparte forces the Spanish to cede Louisiana to France. Yet three years later France turns around and, in the best real-estate deal since the Dutch bought Manhattan, sells the entire Louisiana Territory to the USA for $15 million.	Miguel Hidalgo y Costilla, parish priest of the town of Dolores, issues his now-famous call to rebellion, the *Grito de Dolores*, demanding 'death to bad government.'

EL CAMINO REAL

No, not your daddy's El Camino. These so-called 'King's Highways' exist all over the world, and Texas is no exception. The historic El Camino Real (the King's Highway) was a well-traveled trail during the Spanish colonial era and later was used by waves of settlers from the east. Lovers of historical markers can spend a day hitting the brakes on the 34 miles of Hwy 21 between the cute town of Alto and Crockett National Forest; a marker pops up every few hundred yards. Typical is one remembering a Daniel McClean, who built a cabin on the marker's site in 1813 and was killed by Native Americans in 1837.

AMERICANS HORN IN

Before 1820, settlers moving to Texas from the USA were mainly 'resettled' Native Americans, who were being forcibly removed from newly acquired US territories in the southeast.

The first large group of Anglo-American settlers in Texas arrived as the result of a deal brokered by Moses Austin. He negotiated for the Spanish government to allow him and 300 families from the USA to move into central Texas, but he died before the move could begin. His son, Stephen Fuller Austin, who is credited in Texas folklore as being the 'Father of Texas,' carried out his father's plans in 1821.

Over the next several years, Austin's settlements extended to the Colorado River, the Camino Real and the Gulf Coast, attracting more than 5000 Americans and a bustling trade with Mexico. The word 'Texian' was coined to describe the region's residents, who were beginning to form a separate identity. In 1826, a short-lived attempt at a nation within Texas, the Republic of Fredonia, foreshadowed Texian demands for independence from Mexico.

Earlier settlers in Texas called for the region to be admitted to the USA. By 1830, with more than 30,000 settlers in the Texas territory, the situation was becoming, well, revolting. In that year, a Mexican decree banned further American settlement and limited the importation of slaves. By 1833, political unrest in Mexico led to the imposition of martial law in many Mexican territories, including Texas.

> Newly independent Mexico administratively grouped Texas with the Mexican state of Coahuila. To the north, Mexico stretched as far as New Spain once had, and included much of what is now Southwestern USA.

TEXAS WAR FOR INDEPENDENCE

Stephen Austin traveled to Mexico City to plead the settlers' case for independence, but after being faced down by Mexican government bureaucrats, he wrote back to the Texian settlers, telling them to forget about permission and go ahead and set up an independent government. Austin was arrested and detained in Mexico until 1835. Meanwhile, William B Travis led a group of hotheaded Texians who took up arms to keep reinforcements of Mexican troops from arriving in Texas. This led to a direct confrontation with General Martín Perfecto de Cós, who would later be transferred to San Antonio.

1819	March 2, 1836	By 1825
The USA acquires Florida in exchange for Spanish control over Texas; the USA will control all territory east of it. When Spain gives up Florida in 1821, Texas becomes a state of newly independent Mexico.	A group of citizen delegates meet at Washington-on-the-Brazos (now just known as Washington) to declare their independence from Mexico.	The word 'Texian' has been coined to describe residents of the region, who are beginning to form a separate identity – at this time it has nothing to do with football, oil or trucks.

Armed skirmishes throughout 1835 sparked the Texas War for Independence, which officially ran from September 30, 1835, to April 21, 1836. Those who died at the Alamo became heroes, and the battle itself is now considered a pivotal point in Texan – and American – history. Perhaps because of losses suffered and supplies used at the Alamo and Goliad, Mexican general Antonio López de Santa Anna's troops simply were not prepared when, on April 21, they ran into Texian troops under the command of Samuel Houston, a former major general in Tennessee's militia and 'Indian fighter' under US general Andrew Jackson. At the Battle of San Jacinto, Santa Anna's troops were routed.

History buffs should visit the Daughters of the Republic of Texas Library online at www.drtl.org.

THE LONE STAR REPUBLIC

While Texas had declared itself an independent republic, neither the USA nor Mexico recognized it as such. In its early years the new republic's main business was maintaining its viability as a republic, forging trade and political ties with neighbors and trying hard to establish a governmentlike capital city.

The Alamo (1960) was John Wayne's paean to Texas heroism; he directed and financed the film, which left him in debt for the rest of his life. Final battle scenes redeem much of the early speechifying.

In 1839, the central Texas village of Waterloo was renamed Austin, in honor of Stephen F, and the capital was established there. That same year, the Republic of Texas' policy toward the Native Americans who lived within its borders changed drastically, and a ruthless campaign of removal began. Later, President Sam Houston and the republic lobbied Washington for annexation as a territory in order to gain assistance in ridding Texas of Native Americans and to settle the border dispute with Mexico. After a state constitutional convention in 1845, Texas was annexed to the USA as a state.

This led directly to the Mexican-American War (1846–48), a total rout in which US troops captured Mexico City from the indefatigable Santa Anna, who had lost and been restored to power several times since the Texas War for Independence.

CIVIL WAR & RECONSTRUCTION

The US Civil War (1861–65) was brought on by a number of issues, but a few stand in the foreground, especially the profound moral and economic debate over slavery. Settlers poured into Texas from slave-owning states in the South, but Governor Houston was firmly against the South-favored secession. Popular opinion and a referendum defeated him, and he was forced to resign as governor.

Texas is unique in the USA as the only state that once was a republic (1836–45).

Texas seceded from the USA and joined the Confederate States of America on March 16, 1861. Aside from providing an estimated 80,000 troops, Texas' role in the Civil War was mainly one of supplying food to the Confederate war machine. There were very few battles fought on Texas soil, but the Civil War was one of the bloodiest conflicts in the history of modern warfare, and wounds ran incredibly deep for years afterward.

December 1835	1836	1844
At the outbreak of war, Texian troops (composed of Americans, Mexicans and Europeans) capture San Antonio from General Cós. The Texians also occupy and fortify a little building you may have heard of: the Alamo.	Santa Anna decrees that all foreigners in Texas who bear arms will be treated as pirates and shot. Times have certainly changed.	The first German immigrants arrive in central Texas to settle along the Guadalupe. Today, New Braunfels' German heritage lives on at its big water park with the very German name: 'Schlitterbahn.'

THE ALAMO

'You may all go to hell, and I will go to Texas.' – Davy Crockett, in 1835

It's hard to tell the story of the Battle of the Alamo – there is hot debate about almost every fact. For instance, it's difficult to verify with exact certainty the number of defenders, Mexican troops and casualties, among many other details. This is a volatile issue because Texans are touchy about people challenging the legends of their heroes.

Objective accounts are hard to find. Consider, for example, how the Alamo defenders are described in text reprinted in dozens of city-produced manuals and histories: '[They fought] against Santa Anna's intolerable decrees. Other [defenders] were Volunteers such as Davy Crockett and his "Tennessee Boys" who owned nothing in Texas and owed nothing to it. Theirs was a fight against tyranny wherever it might be.'

It is generally agreed that on February 23, 1836, Mexican general Antonio López de Santa Anna led anywhere from 2500 to 5000 Mexican troops in an attack against the Alamo. The 160 or so men inside the fortress included James Bowie (of knife fame), who was in command of the Alamo until pneumonia rendered him too sick; William B Travis, who took command of the troops after Bowie's incapacity; and perhaps most famous of all, David Crockett, called 'Davy' by everyone. Crockett, a three-time US congressman from Tennessee with interesting taste in headgear, first gained fame as a frontiersman and then for his public arguments with President Andrew Jackson over the latter's murderous campaigns of Indian 'removal' in the southeastern USA. Less well known were Bowie's and Travis' black slaves, who fought alongside their masters during the battle and survived.

Travis dispatched a now-famous letter to other revolutionaries pleading for reinforcements, saying that his men would not stand down under any circumstances – his call was for 'Victory or Death.' Because of slow communications, the only reinforcements that arrived in time were a group of about 30 men from Gonzales, Texas, bringing the total number of Alamo defenders up to 189, according to literature from the Daughters of the Republic of Texas (DRT), which lists the names of all but one, an unidentified black man.

Santa Anna's troops pounded the Alamo for 13 days before retaking it. Mexican losses were devastating; estimates run as low as 1000 and as high as 2000. When the Alamo was finally recaptured, the advancing troops executed almost all of the surviving defenders. The few who were spared, mostly women, children and slaves, were interrogated and released.

The Battle of the Alamo was pivotal in the war because during the two weeks Santa Anna's army was distracted in San Antonio, Texas troops were gathering strength and advancing, fueled by what they called the wholesale slaughter of their brothers in arms, under the battle cry 'Remember the Alamo!'

President Andrew Johnson, a Southerner and former slaveholder who succeeded Lincoln, devised a Reconstruction plan. While his plan granted many concessions, it was absolutely firm that the states' constitutions ratify the 13th Amendment, abolishing slavery, before re-admittance. The Texas Constitution of 1866, hastily drawn up to assure re-admittance

after 1844	1846	1848
Baron Ottfried Hans Freiherr von Meusebach, a leader of the New Braunfels Germans, seizes the laid-back spirit of Texas when he changes his name to the breezier John O Meusebach. Not Billy Ray Mosely, but it's a start.	Texas' annexation by the USA leads directly to the Mexican War, also known as the Mexican-American War, a total rout in which US troops capture Mexico City from Santa Anna.	At the end of the Mexican-American War, Mexico cedes modern Texas, California, Utah, Colorado and most of New Mexico and Arizona to the USA. ¡Ay, caramba! Talk about a major loss.

to the Union, granted blacks some measure of civil rights, but it did not give them the right to vote until martial law imposed it. Hyper-restrictive Black Codes, later to be expanded to what became known as Jim Crow laws, were introduced, making it illegal for blacks to be unemployed, restricting freedom of movement and segregating much of Southern life into white and black camps.

The Searchers (directed by John Ford, 1956) is definitely John Wayne's finest role. A pioneer family is murdered on their Texas ranch, and their daughter Natalie Wood is kidnapped, setting off a decade-long search by her uncle, the Duke.

ON THE CATTLE TRAIL

During the Civil War, the Confederate forces' need for food had increased Texas cattle production. Ranching in Texas became an enormous business, and cattle drives – the herding of up to 200,000 head of longhorn steers northward – were born.

Of all the trails that ran through Texas, it was the Chisholm Trail – from San Antonio to Abilene, Kansas, at the western terminus of the Kansas Pacific Railroad – that really spurred the business of bringing Texas cattle to market. San Antonio boomed as a cattle town. European settlers, including vast numbers of Germans and Czechs, moved to the area, and the Germans built the city's King William District, named for Kaiser Wilhelm I of Prussia. In 1879, the US Army established Fort Sam Houston.

Austin also began to boom after the arrival of the Houston and Texas Central Railroad in 1871. By 1900, the city was as cosmopolitan as many in the East, with electricity, telephones, theaters, opera houses and the Moonlight Towers – 165ft streetlights unique to Austin that illuminated the city by night. Seventeen towers remain operational and are designated historic landmarks.

BLACK GOLD

As early as 1866, oil wells were striking in east Texas. At the time, oil was being put to a number of uses, including the sealing of dirt roads. But speculators bet that oil, found in sufficient supply, could replace coal as an energy mainstay.

ON THE FENCE

With the exception of the discovery of oil, no single event has affected life in Texas as much as the invention of barbed wire. By the early 1880s, fences stretched across Texas, and a series of disputes over rights-of-way (as some ranchers fenced over access to watering holes) turned into an antifence campaign. Cowboys and ranchers would travel throughout the countryside cutting down fences, and shots were fired more and more frequently.

In 1883, Texas passed a law banning the cutting of fences, legislating a new way of life throughout the state. The Texas Rangers, once mere border guards, were reinstated as a state police force to enforce the new law. This was, effectively, the end of what most of us think of as the cowboy era.

1850s	1909	1913
Dallas gets arty: a group of French artists and intellectuals prove instrumental in the early settlement of Dallas in the 1850s.	After being jailed for six weeks at Fort Sam Houston, Apache leader Goyathlay (aka Geronimo) dies a prisoner of war. The US military has still not repatriated his remains.	Mexican revolutionary Pancho Villa is a darling of the American media, portrayed as a dashing freedom fighter. Eventually, the US turns against him. Villa is assassinated (by whom is still a mystery) in 1923.

RECONCILIATION BARBECUE

October 29, 1923, was one of the most important days in Brenham, Texas' history. At the time, this prosperous town between Austin and Houston was mostly composed of European immigrants from England, Scotland, Ireland, Holland, France and Germany, along with African Americans. On the eve of WWI Brenham was heavily German, and kids of different heritages all studied German in the public school. That all changed when the Ku Klux Klan rode into town, tarring and feathering those of German descent, beating up prominent town businesspeople, and torching the German newspaper print shop.

Out of fear of violence, people began avoiding the mean streets of Brenham. Businesses withered. As the Klan stalked and harassed German speakers, people avoided speaking German in the streets and were afraid to even go to church.

Enter barbecue to the rescue. The city of Brenham decided to solve this problem Texas-style: by throwing a giant barbecue to which they would invite all sides, thereby calling a truce. On the day of the festivities, more than 10,000 people – German speakers, African Americans, Czechs, Mexicans, you name it – gathered at the firefighters' park to eat barbecue cooked over giant pits, plus German potato salad and peach cobbler with Brenham Creameries' (later Blue Bell) ice cream. And while the German community vowed to stop publicly speaking or teaching in their native tongue in exchange for an antiviolence truce with the KKK, rumor has it that the real reconciliation was born over neighbors cooking and sharing big old plates of smoked meat. Soon after that the KKK – at least in Brenham – disbanded.

Everything changed on January 10, 1901, when a drilling site at Spindletop, east of Houston in Beaumont, pierced a salt dome, setting forth a gusher of oil so powerful that it took days to bring it under control. Spindletop began producing an estimated 80,000 barrels of oil per day. As the automobile and railroads turned to the oil industry for fuel, discoveries of 'black gold' financed the construction of much of modern Texas.

San Antonio's early-20th-century growth was also due to the military; Fort Sam Houston was joined by Kelly Air Force Base, now the nation's oldest air force base, in 1917, followed by Lackland, Randolph and Brooks Air Force Bases.

THE GREAT DEPRESSION

Following the end of WWI in 1918, Texas' economic machine, as well as the nation's, was humming right along. The surge in private automobiles made for an enormous Texas oil boom, and people were dancing the Charleston in the streets.

Then, on Black Thursday, October 24, 1929, the New York Stock Exchange hiccupped, and the bottom fell out of the economy. The crash, the result of unchecked Wall Street trading practices, led the country and the world into the Great Depression. Northern Texas was part of the region that became

The city of Austin was called Waterloo until 1839. (It's still the name of Austin's best-known music shop, Waterloo Records; p139.)

pre-Prohibition	WWI	1930s
Twenty-eight bars and two breweries line the party-hearty streets of Brenham, Texas. When Prohibition comes to town, the bars close down, the bootleggers move in and the parties move behind closed doors.	Four major military bases are established in Texas for training – Camp Travis (San Antonio), Camp Logan (Houston), Camp MacArthur (Waco) and Camp Bowie (Fort Worth).	Texas goes gaga for President Franklin Delano Roosevelt. As part of FDR's New Deal, the Works Progress Administration (WPA) and Civilian Conservation Corps (CCC) are created.

known as the 'dust bowl,' former farmland destroyed by overuse and lack of rain. Increased oil production caused a market glut that further depressed prices.

As part of Roosevelt's New Deal, the Works Progress Administration (WPA) and Civilian Conservation Corps (CCC) were created. The CCC worked to restore state and national parks, and the WPA sent armies of workers to construct buildings, roads, dams, trails and housing.

WWII & POSTWAR

New Deal or not, some felt what the country really needed to break out of Depression was a good war. The Japanese attack on Pearl Harbor, Hawaii, on December 7, 1941, finally brought the USA into the fighting that had been going on throughout the world since 1939.

The Texas war machine was brought back to full capacity, with the activation of all its bases, the creation of more than a dozen new ones and more than 40 airfields, Texas became a major training ground for WWII soldiers – almost 1.5 million were trained in the state.

The economic prosperity in the USA after WWII was unprecedented. The wartime economy had created a powerhouse, and when the fighting stopped in 1945, industry didn't want to stop with it. For the next 15 years, the US economy surged, fueled by low consumer credit rates and a defense-based economy that plowed money into manufacturing military hardware (as well as ever more automobiles and household appliances). Most people were feeling pretty good. So good, in fact, that a whole passel of Texans was born in this period: the baby boomers.

1960S

Native son Lyndon Baines Johnson was from Stonewall, east of Austin, in south-central Texas. Johnson, affectionately known as LBJ, had a well-deserved reputation for being a hard-nosed Southern Democrat. He was as stubborn as a barnfull of mules, as dirty a political fighter as he needed to be and fiercely loyal to Texas in the fight for pork-barrel government contracts. As majority leader of the US Senate, Johnson accepted the vice-presidential nomination in 1960.

On November 22, 1963, President John Fitzgerald Kennedy and Vice President Johnson rode in separate open limousines through downtown Dallas. At 12:30pm, JFK was shot. Texas governor John M Connally, riding in the seat in front of the president, was also injured by gunfire. The president died at 1pm; Connally survived. Later that day, as Kennedy's body was being transported to Washington, DC, Vice President Johnson took the oath of office aboard Air Force One, the presidential airplane, with Jacqueline Kennedy standing at his side.

Texas has the largest population of Czechs outside of the Czech Republic.

Germans introduced Texas to something for which we can all be grateful: Texas barbecue. The method of smoke-curing meats for storage in such a way that it remained soft and tender has its origins, locals say, in local German shops.

1930s	1939	WWII
WPA workers begin to restore and renovate San Antonio's old Spanish missions, which have fallen into disrepair since Texas' independence from Mexico.	If you build it, the tourists will come: WPA workers build 17,000ft of walkways and two bridges on the river in downtown San Antonio. The name of this massive project? The Paseo Del Rio (River Walk).	The government creates a dozen new military bases and activates more than 40 airfields in Texas. Almost 1.5 million soldiers train here (and hopefully get some good barbecue) before they ship out.

RIP ANN RICHARDS

Contrary to what some outsiders think, not everyone in Texas is a Republican. In fact the Lone Star State has a long history of political opposition to the conservative mainstream.

The nickname 'Yellow Dog Democrats' refers to die-hard Democrats who'd vote for an old hound before voting Republican. With a stronghold in east Texas, their voter base is increasingly Latino. Among the candidates they've managed to elect over the years is Ann Richards, who was governor from 1990 to 1994. Incidentally, when Richards was elected state treasurer in 1982, she became the first woman to hold statewide political office in Texas in more than half a century. But she was not Texas' first female governor; Miriam 'Ma' Ferguson twice successfully ran for the office in the early 20th century.

Texas' 1990 gubernatorial race was one of the messiest in state history. Richards' Republican opponent, rancher and oil millionaire Clayton Williams, started out with TV ads portraying him as a traditional Texas cowboy. Richards took up the gauntlet and painted herself as a tough-but-tender frontierswoman. Later the two candidates began muckraking – alcoholism, divorce, illegal drugs and more got thrown into the mix – but the race wasn't over until Williams made a joke about rape in front of reporters. All told, the two candidates spent $50 million on the race.

After Richards won, she spent her term as governor getting the state's finances back on track, passing stricter law enforcement measures and reforming the state's educational system in favor of local initiative. She was defeated during her 1994 re-election bid by George W Bush; mainstream voters decided they wanted a change. As Molly Ivins put it, 'The issues were God, gays and guns,' and Dubya's conservative platform won voters over.

Though Ann Richard passed away in 2006, her inimitable Texas spirit and contributions to the state ensures she won't be forgotten. Her legacy also presents an alternative version of Texas politics to the Bush dynasty's. For years she gave keynote addresses at national Democratic conventions and lectures around the country, having achieved renown for her folksy wit. She will also be remembered for her strong personality and flamboyance (she once posed on a motorcycle in full biker gear for a political photo op). Meanwhile, back in the Lone Star State, the Yellow Dog Democrats continue to voice their dissent on the Texas political scene, especially in recent virulent debates over political redistricting.

LBJ defeated Barry Goldwater in the presidential election of 1964, and his administration oversaw some of the USA's most tumultuous, tragic, and socially catalysing events. The USA's role in the Vietnam War escalated in 1964, while at home LBJ signed the landmark Civil Rights Act in response to rampant racial discrimination and the demands of the burgeoning Civil Rights Movement. By 1968, massive student protests and plummeting US support for the war had sent the country into civil unrest, only worsened by the assassinations of Martin Luther King, Jr, and Robert Kennedy. By this time, the USA was fully at war – and perhaps most of all with itself.

1960s	**1978**	**1970s**
LBJ's administration sees the USA through the invasion of North Vietnam to civil protest at home. The Johnson Administration also shepherds in 'the Great Society,' an unprecedented flurry of social legislation.	*Dallas,* the prime-time soap opera following the hijinks of that wacky, oil-rich Ewing clan, premieres.	Gas prices quadruple. Texans – who are the biggest domestic oil supplier and have many of the nation's largest refineries – profit and profit some more.

DOUBLE FEATURE

In January 2001, Republican George W Bush became only the second son in American history (after John Quincy Adams in 1824) to follow his father to the White House. Bush, born in 1946, grew up in Midland and Houston, Texas, where his father was in the oil business. Despite never before having run for office, Bush won the Texas governorship in 1994 and again in 1998.

By then Bush's eyes were on the US presidency. He took office in 2001 after a bitterly contested election and a landmark Supreme Court case, *Bush v Gore*. Though Al Gore received 543,895 more popular votes than Bush, he came in second in electoral votes. After the Supreme Court effectively halted Florida's ballot recount, that state's 25 electoral votes went to Bush, making him the electoral winner. Americans had watched as the election's televised voting controversy unfolded and this result was for a long time a hotly debated topic across the nation.

Bush's first months in the White House were marked by a slowing economy, soaring energy prices and other domestic concerns. Then the terrorist attacks of September 11, 2001, thrust the once isolationist president onto the world stage. More than 2700 people died in the attacks, and Bush suddenly found himself presiding over a nation reeling from the worst violence on US soil since the Civil War. Bush vowed to lead a long-term, international coalition against terrorism.

On March 20, 2003, coalition forces entered Iraq, and on April 9, US forces seized Baghdad. Initially Bush enjoyed wide domestic support for his 'war on terrorism' but after a time the uncertain results of the war in Afghanistan and the ongoing occupation of Iraq took a toll on his approval ratings. In September 2004, the US death toll in Iraq reached 1000 and as Bush sought a second term, the war became fodder for a plethora of candidates who challenged him – including Massachusetts senator John Kerry, the eventual Democratic nominee. Bush defied his critics by winning a second term.

Three aspects of George W Bush's presidency may prove to be his legacy: he was the president who oversaw the first great crisis of the 21st century, September 11; he became the nation's first 'Accidental President,' as *Newsweek* writer David A Kaplan dubbed him in his book on the controversial 2000 election; and he finished his second term just as the global financial crisis developed.

THE ENERGY CRISIS

The energy crisis in the 1970s brought Sultan-of-Bruneian wealth to Texas. The crisis began when members of the Organization of the Petroleum Exporting Countries (OPEC) imposed a major reduction in oil sales to the USA and its allies to punish the country for its pro-Israel policy. Texans found themselves the biggest domestic suppliers of oil, and laughed all the way to the bank.

At the same time, the USA was searching for new sources of oil and developing new types of energy. While OPEC nations argued, the price of oil halved, and Texas started hurting. Oil extraction and exploration became unprofitable.

It took another war – this time, the 1991 Persian Gulf War – to drive oil prices back up by several bucks a barrel.

1970s–early 1980s	**1984**	**1986**
Newly wealthy Texans buy British titles from debt-ridden members of the British aristocracy, creating legions of Lady Jane Billy Bobs and Duke Zachary Jims. Ranches became practically passé in the move to bigger spreads for oil barons.	PC revolutionary Michael Dell creates a little ol' computer company from his University of Texas dorm room. He drops out of school to focus full-time the Dell Computer Corporation. The billions come later.	Bust: the price of oil hits rock bottom at $10 a barrel. A worldwide glut devastates the oil industry. Offices vacate, and downtown Houston suddenly looks like a ghost town – or a post-apocalyptic nightmare.

TEXAS TODAY

During the 1990s the Texas economy grew strongly, and trade with Mexico has boomed since the 1994 passage of the North American Free Trade Agreement (Nafta). Technology was another big story in the 1990s; Austin, with its highly educated populace, became a powerhouse of high-tech companies and innovation. To top it off, Texas Governor George W Bush entered the White House in 2000.

Those still involved in the oil industries had long joked: 'Lord, give me just one more boom and I promise I won't piss it away.' Crude oil prices rose dramatically in the early 2000s, and it looked like their dreams just may have come true – until the global economic crisis began in the late 2000s.

While Texas took a hit along with the rest of the nation, the state economy remained one of only 10 outperforming the country as a whole, according to an April 2009 study by the Nelson A Rockefeller Institute of Government. Today the Texas economy is based on several breadwinners, and oil is surprisingly low on the list. The state now has the second-largest economy in the nation (just behind New York's) and the 12th-largest economy in the world. It may come as no surprise to learn that out of the 400 richest Americans, 42 are Texans.

At press time, Houston, Dallas and Austin continued to be ranked as some of the best places in the country to find a job, buy a house or start a business. As Texas learned with the oil business, what goes up must come down. Still, the Lone Star State is unusually resilient and resourceful – no matter how many hurricanes continue to batter its southeastern coast. If any state can get by on an inexhaustible supply of pride and moxie, Texas is the one.

Shrub: The Short but Happy Political Life of George W Bush is a tongue-in-cheek, occasionally scathing look at the career of one of Texas' most controversial politicians – written by Lou Dubose and the late syndicated columnist Molly Ivins, one of Texas' most beloved humorists.

Late 1990s	1990s	2005 & 2006
The dot-com boom hits. The laid-back college town and capitol, Austin, becomes a hotbed for technology companies, earning the nickname 'Silicon Hills.'	US control tightens along the Texas–Mexico border. Agents employ an array of surveillance and enforcement methods, including helicopters, airplanes, radar, floodlights, motion detectors, informants, dogs and walls. Oh, and blimps.	Longhorn quarterback Vince Young leads the University of Texas to two back-to-back Rose Bowl victories. The streets of Austin 'bleed orange' – the school's colors.

The Culture

While 'Don't mess with Texas' was the bumper-sticker slogan of a famous antilitter campaign, it's become an unofficial state motto that speaks volumes about the fiercely independent spirit of Texas. After all, this is the only state in the union that was once its own republic – and locals from Longview to Laredo won't let you forget it. Don't worry, though: they'll probably just remind you with a friendly smile, a glass of iced tea and a knowing wink. (And don't worry too much about the shotgun in the pickup: it's mostly for show.)

When you drive through Texas, you might see another bumper sticker on the back of a truck: 'Texas: It's bigger than France.' Texas is not only bigger than France, it's larger than Germany, England, Scotland, Ireland, Northern Ireland, Belgium and the Netherlands combined. Some Texans even swear that when you cross the Oklahoma border into Texas, the sky itself gets bigger. If this all sounds like bragging, it probably is. Though as they say here, 'it ain't braggin' if it's true.'

This state is so vast, with so many personalities and ethnic identities (they don't call the amusement park 'Six Flags Over Texas' for nothing) that all combine to make Texas, well, Texas. The culture's a contradiction. Picture more millionaires (and a passel of billionaires) than you can shake an oil rag at, but rural and urban poverty that's just as extreme. There's high culture in spades, but the low culture gets more press. Just the word 'Texas' conjures sleepy small towns and glittering cities, polluted beaches and pristine open prairies, rush-hour traffic and lonesome roads, outlaw country singers and conservative churchgoers. If your head's spinning, it should be: this place is a paradox.

So you want to experience Texas culture? Buckle your belt as it's not for the faint of heart. The 'best' of Texas is everywhere and it's ripe for the picking, whether you're seeking breakfast tacos or bluebonnets. Pull on some boots, get in the truck, cruise the Farm to Market (FM) roads, eat hole-in-the-wall barbecue, jump in a swimming hole, buy someone a beer, sweet-talk your waiter, burn your tongue off with salsa, witness the madness of a high-school football game, say 'ma'am' to young girls and old ladies alike, 'howdy' a stranger, curse in Spanish, two-step all night in a honky-tonk, and let a blues singer break your heart. In other words, live it.

REGIONAL IDENTITY

If the USA were a high school, Texas would be the captain of the football team: big, loud, good-looking, strong, street-smart and funny as hell – just don't mess with him. He'd steal your prom date if you let him, and then shake your hand afterwards with his maddening grin. That's the Lone Star

Many Texans don't have garages. So where do they keep their precious trucks? The answer is a carport, a simple structure – usually attached to a house – that shelters vehicles from the elements. In defense of carports, Frank Lloyd Wright once said, 'A car is not a horse, and it doesn't need a barn.'

In *How to Be Texan* Michael Hicks has an entire section discussing 'How to Stay Alive in Texas.' Rule number one? 'Never tell a Texan his dog is too skinny.'

UNDER THE INFLUENCE

Signs advertising bail bonds – services that post bail for criminal offenses for a hefty fee – are as ubiquitous on Texas roads as barbecue joints. Yes, it's ironic, but these businesses often advertise suspiciously close to bars. With Texas winning the dubious prize for the highest rate of alcohol-related arrests and fatalities in the country, it's perhaps not surprising that these get-out-of-jail-quick businesses are flourishing. In College Station, we found one local bail bondsperson who promoted his services with the question 'Having more fun than the law will allow?' Hmm. Last time we checked, it wasn't exactly 'fun' to graduate with a BA *and* a DUI (Driving Under the Influence) charge.

WHAT THE LOCALS SAY ABOUT TEXAS

- 'Hot, hot, hot! And I mean that in a good way.'
- 'Austin's a great town to never grow up in.'
- 'In Houston, if you own a truck and have 100 bucks in your pocket, you're somebody.'
- 'The high-school quarterback in a small Texas town is more important than the mayor.'
- 'I can't leave Texas. The women here are just too damn good looking.'
- 'Growing up in San Antonio and not learning Spanish is like growing up in Paris and not learning French.'
- 'In Dallas the money's new, and everyone flaunts it. In Houston the money's old, and nobody gives a damn.'
- 'Dallas is the LA of Texas. Houston is…well, that's a good question!'
- 'I'm from east Texas, that's why.'
- 'I'm from west Texas, that's why.'
- 'Austin is a velvet rut – it feels too good to leave.'
- 'Houston is the kind of town where the guy in old cowboy boots drinking a Lone Star at the bar might be an oil millionaire. Or he might just be a guy in old cowboy boots.'
- 'There is an armpit of Texas. Just no one agrees on which town it is.'

State for you – charming, but with an obnoxious streak; larger than life; undeniably vivacious. Visitors find Texas equally confounding and enchanting, and the natives (and quite a few recent transplants, too) wouldn't have it any other way.

And so the Wild West lives on here, but mostly in attitude. The state's got a serious love-it-or-leave-it attitude, with personality to spare, and it's full of people who can't imagine living anywhere else. Is Texas really the center of the world? When you're in Texas, it is. In a country where the distinct identities between states and cities often blur together, Texans won't let you ever forget, for better or worse, that you're deep in the heart of Texas.

That said, trying to typify Texas is like trying to wrestle a pig in mud – it's slippery. In vast generalization, Austin is alternative Texas, prizing environmental integrity and quality of life. Dallasites are the shoppers and the socialites. In conservative, casual Houston, oil-and-gas industrialists dine at clubby steakhouses. San Antonio and El Paso are the most Tex-Mexican of the bunch – showplaces of Hispanic culture. These days, outside of the rural areas, computer-geek millionaires and fashionistas outnumber rich cattlefolk and ranch hands, though nine-to-five professionals and blue-collar workers outnumber both; when it comes down to it, you might see any one of them knocking back a Lone Star in the same dive. All across the state, you'll notice several themes: Spanish is spoken, country music is played, football is sacred, barbecue is eaten, summer is scorching, and for boys and men, peeing outdoors is a God-given right and privilege.

Texans are notoriously friendly. Smiles, laughter, and 'have a nice day' are mandatory – and this is one place you get the sense they mean it. Small talk with strangers is a daily pleasure here. Yet a straightforward and conservative approach to life in much of the state means outward displays of emotion are looked upon as indiscreet. Texans are highly respectful in conversation. 'Sir' and 'ma'am' are used by almost everyone, so it's nice to get into the spirit of things by joining in. Ladies, don't be surprised to be called 'honey,' 'doll' (yes, still!) or 'sugar-pie' by either gender (most people are just being friendly.)

J Frank Dobie, a remarkable folklorist and newspaper columnist who helped save Texas Longhorn cattle from extinction, was instrumental in defining the myth of Texas in the American imagination.

CONCEALED HANDGUNS

The rifle rack is as much a Texas tradition as the pickup truck. Most gun owners are law-abiding citizens, but it's also true that Texas has seen more than its share of gun-related disasters – the JFK assassination in Dallas and the shootings from the University of Texas Tower in Austin among them.

On October 16, 1991, a man opened fire on customers in a Luby's Cafeteria in Killeen, Texas. After the shooting, a survivor remarked that if only she'd been armed she could have stopped the carnage. As a direct response to the massacre, surviving victims and gun-rights advocates pushed through a 1995 Texas state law – signed by ex-president (and then-governor) George W Bush – that granted a concealed weapon permit to any Texan: that is, one who's over 18, hasn't been convicted of a felony or domestic violence, and who has passed a course in handgun safety. While that Luby's location went out of business, the gun trade in Texas is booming.

Sugar-pie them right back – as long as you're sincere. (In case you haven't already guessed, we don't recommend brown-nosing in Texas.)

LIFESTYLE

Football games. Barbecues. Tailgate picnics. Tubing down lazy rivers. Fishing. Hunting. Camping. And every kind of urban activity you can imagine, from museum-going to shopping-till-dropping. Let's not forget church. Oh, and did we mention football?

With all of this hanging out and having fun, does anyone have time to have a *job* here? Sure – Texas is a play-hard, work-hard state: but not necessarily in that order. In general, Texans work as hard as or harder than the rest of the country – is it only an illusion that they seem less put-upon than the average stressed-out American? In most of the state, it goes against the cultural grain to flaunt jobs, money, college degrees or status, or seem like you're trying too hard.

Although a Texan's house is not necessarily her castle (sometimes her car or truck is just as nice, or nicer), Texans take pride in their little parcel of home, whether it's a ranch in west Texas or a ramshackle bungalow in Austin. After the kitchen, the porch is sometimes the most important room in the house; in most parts of the state, porch-sitting is a legitimate activity, and you'll find the humblest of bungalows with a porch swing made for swinging in the shade or strumming a guitar. As in the rest of the United States, family is important – and the abundance of traditionally family-oriented Hispanics throw this value into even higher relief.

Land and home prices in Texas can be downright cheap compared to similarly populous areas of the USA (such as Southern California), yet many workers are paid rock-bottom wages: Texas has the highest proportion of minimum-wage workers in the USA. Even with lots of cheap land, home ownership ain't easy on just over $7 an hour. What's more, areas of the state with the highest numbers of Hispanics are often the poorest and tend to lack sufficient social services.

So while for some, Texas is a wide-open land in which to chase the American dream, to others this dream is a bitterly distant reality. On one hand, Dallas ranks ninth worldwide for its number of *billionaires*. On the other hand, Texas ranks dead last nationwide on more widespread measures of social wellbeing: it has the worst air quality, the lowest percentage of health-insured children, and the lowest percentage of citizens who hold a high-school diploma.

In case you're hungry for a positive statistic, we'll throw this one at you: in recent years, Texas has been consistently voted the best place in the country for business. So, Texas may be a great place to make money, but it's a bad

Dallas residents spend more money on breast implants than anywhere else in the USA besides LA. Guess everything really is bigger in the 'Big D.'

place to lose it – or to be poor at all. Just one caveat: those who want to get rich quick here should be warned to keep their business above board: in a country with the highest rate of incarcerated people in the world, Texas ranks second for throwing its citizens in jail…

ECONOMY

No, that's not the smell of petrochemical emissions: Texas is stinkin' rich. Texas' economic output (GSP) ranks second in the USA – just behind California and ahead of New York. If Texas were still an independent country, it would have the 12th-largest economy in the world. Texas has created more private-sector jobs than any other state over the past decade; of the 10 largest states, it also has the lowest unemployment rate. Texas' success in seeming to escape the late nationwide economic downturn largely unscathed is attributed to a variety of factors – a lack of state income tax, business incentives, a large service economy and high-tech sector, and the fact that strong consumer-protection laws may have prevented the 'housing bubble,' which has devastated other high-population states like Florida, from bursting here.

Houston's legendary arts patron Dominique de Menil not only funded one of the finest small art museums in the nation, she also used her influence to push for desegregation in Houston and highlight human-rights abuses worldwide.

So what's the dark side of all this wealth? Poverty. It's rampant and it tends to affect minority groups, women and children most strongly. Texas ranks uncomfortably high in state poverty rankings – currently at eighth. More disturbingly, every year since 1980 the state's poverty levels have exceeded the nation's as a whole. In Texas, you're more likely to be poor if you live in rural, isolated, or sparsely populated areas. The other places where Texans are suffering? Urban centers. Also, according to the Brookings Institute, there's been a recent rise in 'suburban poverty' in cities such as Houston, where 56% of the poor live in suburbs. What to make of this disparity of wealth, other than just to write it off as just the Texan – not to mention the American – way? Some criticize the state's lack of income tax (and the inadequacy of state-funded services) as one contributing factor, while others champion it as a way to let the working-poor Texans keep a higher share of the money they make. Others criticize high numbers of illegal immigrants. Others blame the Republicans. Or the Democrats. Or the public education system…

The point is, Texas is impressively rich – and, to many visitors, surprisingly poor.

POPULATION

Texas was the fastest-growing state in the USA during the 2000s, adding four million people during the decade for a 2009 population of 24,782,302. That makes it the second-most populous state after California. Despite the

---

TRUCK IT

Explaining why he prefers a truck to a car, salty-tongued Ronald McCowan, in SR Bindler's hilarious, must-see 1997 documentary *Hands on a Hard Body* deadpans, 'Trucks make money. Cars don't make money.' While the phrase hardly explains the Texas obsession with trucks, as with the origin of many Texas traditions, it acknowledges a hard-nosed bottom line that puts business before pleasure. Originally, it was Texas' long distances, bumpy country roads and rural traditions that made trucks a necessity – but now they're a way of life. Texans buy 14% of trucks sold in the nation, far more than their fair share. Here, a truck isn't just transportation – it's an extension of one's ego, a symbol of freedom and independence, and a status symbol. For instance, a souped-up, customized truck gets the nickname 'Texas Cadillac.' A tip: if Texans approach you on a country road in a truck, they'll likely give you a two-finger wave and nod their head (or even tip their hat). That's code for 'Howdy,' so wave back and smile.

THE COWBOYS

Perhaps no other figure in literary or cinematic history has been so romanticized as the cowboy. The image has become a symbol of the freedom of the plains and the industrious and untamable nature of the American people themselves.

Normally reticent visitors will drop all pretense of superiority and giggle delightedly given the chance to throw on spurs, chaps and gloves and take to the trail at a dude ranch. And the image of the American West – the one Hollywood exported through Western films – is engraved in the minds of people from Delhi to Denmark.

The origins of the American cowboy extend to 16th-century Spain and from there to Mexico. Cattle in those countries were allowed to graze freely over large tracts of land. Mexican vaqueros, or wranglers, brought their methods to Texas and passed them on to Texans, who mispronounced the Spanish and corrupted the word to 'buckaroo.'

With westward expansion and capture of new lands from Native Americans, cattle drives became common. Cowboys, under the direction of a foreman, would begin to herd the thousands of cattle to be driven north. The cowboys caught calves, using a 'lariat' (from the Spanish *la reata*), and imprinted them for identification using the heated-iron design of the owner's brand.

During cattle drives, the pack was led by a scout and chuck wagon, which would prepare food in advance of the arrival of the herd. Cowboys would ride in packs at the front, sides and, if they were unlucky, the rear of the herd (eating dust the whole way). To filter the dust, cowboys used bandanna handkerchiefs tied over their noses and mouths.

While horses would be changed in relays along the trail, the cowboy always kept his own saddle. Masterfully crafted and as comfortable as possible to allow rides often of 24 hours or more, a cowboy's saddle was his most important tool, and the last thing he sold in hard times.

---

notable absence of Native Americans (due to many factors, but chiefly because of mistreatments by American settlers, from forced exile to murder) and a fairly small number of Asian Americans, Texas' citizenry is a model of the 'melting pot' cliché. In 2009, about 47% percent of the population was white, 37% was Hispanic and 12% was African American. Illegal immigrants, mostly from Latin America, account for 6% of the population – a fact that sparks heated debate across the state – and have become an integral part of the Texas workforce. Some critics claim they're a drag on services, resources, or even Texas' very identity, while pro-immigration reformers cite the United States' historical and humanistic tradition of immigration. Words like 'deport' or 'legalize' can send normally polite Texans over the edge: of all the red-hot issues regarding population, this is the one.

Tailgating is a tradition in Texas – especially before a football game or a concert. It's an outdoor picnic that's set up on the open tailgate of a truck in the parking lot. Grilling food is optional; beer is usually mandatory.

Hispanic people have had perhaps a greater influence on Texas life than any other group in terms of language, culture, architecture and food. The state's Hispanic population has soared in the past 20 years, and the proximity to Mexico (where many of the state's Hispanic people have roots and, in many cases, relatives) keeps the ties strong. In some areas of Texas, Hispanics are now a majority of the population, and a working knowledge of Spanish is an asset statewide.

There are three formally recognized Native American tribes still living in Texas, though only two live on State of Texas–approved reservations. The best known is the Alabama-Coushatta Reservation. Other formally recognized tribes include the Ysleta del Sur Pueblo and the Kickapoo tribes.

SPORTS

What's the official religion in the state of Texas? Football.

Say it and the word alone will incite passion, a smile and plenty of opinions in many Texans. Boys in Texas are raised to play football when they're barely out of the cradle. In fact, Texan parents are known to delay their sons' school enrollment by a year (or even two) when they begin school; by the time these boys graduate from high school, logic goes, they'll be older – but most importantly, bigger and brawnier – than their grade-level cohorts. This highly controversial, but widely practiced, tradition occurs in cities and small towns alike. While 'red-shirting,' as it's called, happens in other states, it's legendary in Texas. Kids as old as eight are known to show up on the first day of kindergarten a full three years older (and inches taller) than everyone else. Does it guarantee that these boys will be NFL stars? No. But don't tell that to the football-crazed. (See, we said it was a religion.)

The bitterest rivalry in Texas college football? Hands down, it's the University of Texas (UT) Longhorns and the Texas A&M Aggies. Second place: the University of Oklahoma Sooners and the UT Longhorns.

The Dallas Cowboys are the most famous football team – not only in Texas but the USA as a whole; in fact, their nickname is 'America's Team' and is only reinforced by the blue-and-white star-spangled outfits of their nearly equally famous cheerleaders. Houston's current NFL team is the Texans.

Keep in mind, though, that college football is what makes Texas tick. Many rabid fans of the University of Texas (UT) Longhorns or Texas A&M Aggies never set foot in a classroom on these campuses, but that doesn't mean they can't 'bleed orange,' as UT fans claim, in reference to the school colors. College football's not all fun and games, either: it's a serious industry here, and when UT coach Mack Brown got a 2009 raise that upped his salary to over a cool $5 million, few balked.

Football aside, plenty of Texans go crazy for the San Antonio Spurs – an NBA basketball team that has won four NBA championships, giving them a perfect record unmatched by any team except for the Chicago Bulls. Along with pro NBA teams in both Houston and Dallas, they prove there's more to life in Texas than football.

HIGH SCHOOL FOOTBALL   *Ryan Ver Berkmoes*

'Ref! You suck!' erupts an otherwise mild-mannered man, who could be an insurance salesperson. Shouted several decibels above the already raucous crowd noise, it soars above the partisan cacophony near the end of the first half of a high-school football play-off game.

Far from being admonished by those around him, the shouter – dressed in a custom-made, red-and-black jumpsuit emblazoned with the team's snarling logo – sees many heads nod in agreement. And a few other adults make much more profane judgments on the referees, their bloodlines and cognitive abilities.

Texas high-school football has taken on mythic proportions and meanings throughout the state. On autumn Friday nights fans gather to cheer their local teams at brightly lit stadiums in every town. At stake are local pride, reputations and other intangibles that fuel the mania.

The focus of this raw emotion is teams of teenagers – many barely shaving – who do battle within the complex strictures that govern American football. The coaches at larger schools – who often make more money than the teachers – endeavor to train 16- and 17-year-olds to perform as facsimiles of the pros who play on Sunday afternoons.

How seriously these games are taken can be seen by the trappings that surround the game. The players are merely at the apex of a huge pyramid. There are legions of student assistants and trainers; handpicked varsity cheerleaders who ascend to these prima-donna spots through competitions as ruthless as those on the field; junior cheerleaders plotting their own rises; vast marching bands; dancing and drill teams; honor guards for the flags; and many, many more. All of these students are backed by the legions of parents who cheer, scream, raise money and more.

If you are in Texas on a Friday night from September to November, you should absolutely attend a high-school football game.

RELIGION

See all those evangelical churches? They're not for show. Known for its conservative religious attitudes, Texas is considered to be the 'buckle' in the Bible Belt – a swath of states across the Southern USA associated with fundamentalist and evangelical Christianity.

Surprisingly, Catholicism is the largest denomination due to the significant Hispanic population, but this being the South, Baptists are loud and proud (especially in the churches with great choirs).

The strangest Texas religious fact? Atheists are forbidden to hold public office. Even though the American Civil Liberties Union contests that this section of the Texas Bill of Rights violates the US Constitution, it's the law: would-be senators or judges must 'acknowledge the existence of a Supreme Being.'

Seven-time Tour de France champion and Austin cyclist Lance Armstrong is Texas' most celebrated athlete worldwide. Just don't tell that to the UT Longhorns or the Dallas Cowboys.

ARTS

Literature

Writing has deep roots in the region. In the 1880s, famed short-story writer William Sidney Porter, whose pen name was O Henry, lived and wrote in a Victorian cottage in Austin that's now the O Henry Museum. Twenty miles south, Pulitzer Prize–winner Katherine Anne Porter grew up in Kyle; the Katherine Anne Porter house is now a national literary center. Further south still, San Antonio's Sandra Cisneros became one of the most important bicultural writers of the 20th century. And the list goes on.

UT Austin is a major center for writing and literature, from the acclaimed Michener Center for Writers to its impressive Harry Ransom Humanities Research Center – a treasure trove of original manuscripts, letters and memorabilia from virtually every major Western author. A faculty member at the Michener Center, Stephen Harrigan, wrote an acclaimed, suspenseful 2000 novel, *The Gates of the Alamo,* a must-read for those interested in exploring that most epic of Texas enigmas.

Of all Texas' literary stars, a transplant seems to loom largest in the public imagination: James A Michener, who relocated to Texas after his work on a book of the same name. Michener is best known for his fictionalized histories of regions and countries, including *Chesapeake, Hawaii, The Caribbean* and, of course, *Texas.* He's also fondly regarded as a philanthropist.

The best-known homegrown superstar of Texas literature is Larry McMurtry, the Wichita Falls–born icon whose books and screenplays have entered into classic territory; his novels include *Lonesome Dove, The Last Picture Show* and *Terms of Endearment.*

Don't miss El Paso–born Cormac McCarthy's *Border Trilogy,* winner of national awards and acclaim, and made up of brooding, dark and masterfully crafted coming-of-age stories involving young men from Texas who, for various reasons, head off to Mexico.

Until her death in 2007, nobody beat Molly Ivins on pure acerbic wit and the exposure of Texisms big and small. Mary Karr's shoot-from-the-hip bestseller *The Liar's Club* brought her hardscrabble Texas girlhood to vivid life. And we can't forget Texas-born novelist Ann Rice, of vampire-tale fame, who now lives in New Orleans.

Wim Wenders' 1984 film *Paris, Texas* put this town on the map – which is funny, since the film doesn't take place in Paris at all.

Cinema

Welcome to the Third Coast – headquarters, Austin. Filmmaking has blossomed locally into a mini-industry spearheaded by directors Richard Linklater, Robert Rodriguez and Quentin Tarantino, and actor Sandra Bullock, all of whom either live or own property in Austin.

ICONIC TEXAS FILMS – A SHORT LIST

Giant (1956) This film's as sprawling as the King Ranch that was the film's inspiration. Elizabeth Taylor, Rock Hudson and James Dean are superb in this big-ticket yarn tracing the life of an oil and ranching family.

The Last Picture Show (1971) This engaging film is based on a Larry McMurtry novel that traces the coming of age of two high-school football players in a deader-than-dirt small Texas town in the 1950s.

The Thin Blue Line (1988) Director Errol Morris' documentary is one of the most powerful films ever made. It tells the story of Randall Adams, who was given a life prison sentence for murdering a Dallas policeman but who, in fact, was innocent. The film got Adams released – no small feat – and captured the confession of the real killer.

El Mariachi (1992) Robert Rodriguez' little movie shot on the Texas–Mexican border for $7000 became an icon for film school students everywhere when it was shown across the USA. It made Rodriguez a bundle and received much critical acclaim. Legends aside, it is a charming fable about an unlucky traveling mariachi.

Lone Star (1996) A compelling drama set against the unsettled racial atmosphere of a Texas border town. A sheriff (Chris Cooper) has to confront the misdeeds committed by his father (Matthew McConaughey) decades before.

Traffic (2000) Filmed in part on the El Paso–Juárez borderlands, Steven Soderbergh's multilayered thriller explores the uphill battle the USA faces in continuing its war on drugs.

No Country for Old Men (2007) Cormac McCarthy's bleak Western landscapes meet the Coen Brothers' morbid humor in the rapturously terrifying flick. It's a harrowing, tightly paced film about a welder in west Texas who finds a bundle of drug money and decides to keep it. (Guess what? *Bad* idea.)

Through their efforts, hangars at Austin's old airport have been transformed into high-tech sound stages, and the Austin Film Society (AFS) is a major center for indie filmmakers. Of the state's many film festivals, Austin boasts two of the heavy hitters: the Austin Film Festival in October and the South by Southwest (SXSW) Film Festival in March (congruent with the SXSW music festival).

More than 100 movies in recent decades have been shot here, including the cult favorites *Dazed and Confused* and *Office Space,* and the original slasher flick, *Texas Chainsaw Massacre.*

Music

And then there's the music. Though Austin has both street cred and the moniker of the 'Live Music Capital of the World,' the entire state is bursting with local country, blues, roots, rock and roll, and Tejano delights, often in the most unlikely of places.

Tejano music dates to the mid-1800s, when central European immigrants brought their folk music to south Texas, where it mingled with Spanish influences. In the 1990s, Selena became the first Tejano superstar, a status that mushroomed after her 1995 murder by the president of her fan club.

It's not a stretch to say that Texas musicians have had wider influence on American music than those from any other state; more than 100 Texas artists have won a whopping nearly 300 Grammy Awards. Sure, there's great classical and opera in the big cities, but popular music's king here.

Texas has played a pivotal role in the evolution of blues and jazz. While blues music developed throughout the South, Texas contributed several early key players. Along with Leadbelly, Blind Lemon Jefferson played clubs and brothels in Deep Ellum, Dallas, starting around 1912. He later made the earliest known recordings of any Texas blues singer.

Texas wasn't the birthplace of country and western, but many argue it's where it was perfected. The original singing cowboy, Gene Autry, hails from Texas. Austin's Armadillo World Headquarters was a concert space in which the outlaw-country movement first drew wide attention, and *Austin City Limits*, a public TV program, first brought country-and-western music a

Film fanatics should check out know-it-all Austinite Harry Knowles' snarky yet spot-on film reviews and industry news at www.aintitcool.com.

TEXAS ROAD TRIP SOUNDTRACK: TOP 25 ESSENTIALS

Want to rock out across Texas? Here's your list.

- 'Piece of My Heart,' Janis Joplin
- 'New San Antonio Rose,' Bob Wills and his Texas Playboys
- 'If I Needed You,' Townes Van Zandt
- 'Black Snake Moan,' Blind Lemon Jefferson
- 'She's About a Mover,' Sir Douglas Quintet
- 'Everything Hits at Once,' Spoon
- 'Crying,' Roy Orbison
- 'Nobody Knows Me,' Lyle Lovett
- 'Cowboy Take Me Away,' Dixie Chicks
- 'Luckenback, Texas,' Waylon Jennings
- 'She's Got Legs,' ZZ Top
- 'Survivor,' Destiny's Child
- 'On the Road Again,' Willie Nelson
- 'I Wish I Was Crazy Again,' Dale Watson
- 'When You Leave, Don't Slam the Door,' Tex Ritter
- 'That'll Be the Day,' Buddy Holly and the Crickets
- 'Side of the Road,' Lucinda Williams
- 'Blue Eyes Crying in the Rain,' Willie Nelson
- 'Stormy Monday Blues,' T-Bone Walker
- 'Source Tags and Codes,' …And You Will Know Us By the Trail of Dead
- 'All My Exes Live in Texas,' George Strait
- 'The Gambler,' Kenny Rogers
- 'Me and Bobby McGee,' Kris Kristofferson
- 'Amor Prohibido,' Selena
- 'Tighten Up,' Archie Bell and the Drells

national audience. Since then, Texas has long had a reputation for producing singer-songwriters who don't quite fit the country mold.

While country and western can be traced to Anglo-Irish folk songs, Texas' most original contribution to modern music is western swing, a hodgepodge of styles that came together when Bob Wills and his Texas Playboys began recording the genre in the 1920s.

Did Lubbock, Texas–born icon Buddy Holly invent rock and roll? Maybe, but either way it's true that Texan musicians have been at the forefront of rock since its inception. Texas has definitely rocked out ever since, from Roy Orbison to ZZ Top. Two iconic female artists include Janis Joplin and Houston's R & B pop diva Beyoncé, who proved the biggest-selling female music artist of the 2000s (and won an armful of Grammys with her 3½-octave range.)

Texas also has proven a hotbed for indie-rock talent, and the best place to see it – other than every night of the week at clubs throughout Austin, Denton, and Dallas – is at the SXSW and Austin City Limits festivals.

Food & Drink

Texas food kicks ass. It's as simple as that. If American cooking could be summed up as combining generous portions of homegrown foods with foreign sensibilities and techniques, Texas spins this into a cuisine that is uniquely its own. If you're expecting bland, starchy American meals, you'll be shocked at the variety and quality on offer, anything from fire-engine-red chili and spicy jalapeño corn bread to chilled Hill Country wine. From its humble origins in a chuck wagon's iron skillet, Texas cooking has come a long way. Highlights include Texas-style barbecue, authentic Mexican fare, creative Tex-Mex cooking, down-home Southern comfort food and Gulf Coast seafood. Vegetarians have more options than ever, too, even in this beef-loving state.

Some say the origins of the term 'barbecue' may be French, meaning to cook an animal from *barbe* (chin) to *queue* (tail).

STAPLES & SPECIALTIES
Barbecue
If you're even remotely carnivorous, Texas barbecue is heavenly, and when done well (as in tiny Lockhart), it's divine. There are endless debates over barbecue sauces: what kind, how much or whether you need it at all. Find out all about it on p52.

Mexican & Tex-Mex
While Californians may disagree, many people feel that Texas has the best Mexican food in the USA. Considering the miles and miles of border Texas shares with Mexico, it's no surprise that the culinary influence is widespread throughout the state. A regional variation on Mexican food, Tex-Mex includes Americanized versions of Mexican dishes, as well as American dishes with a Mexican twist. Don't spend too much effort trying to sort the two; there's a lot of overlap and, unless you're eating at a restaurant that serves 'authentic' or 'interior Mexico' dishes, you're probably going to have some Tex sneak into your Mex.

Nuevo Tex-Mex: Festive New Recipes from Just North of the Border by chef David Garrido and food critic Robb Walsh is an inspiring reinvention of the Tex-Mex genre (with creative margarita recipes, too).

Mexican and Tex-Mex staples are often variations on a theme: take some sort of tortilla, soft or deep fried, and put meat on it or in it, whether chicken, beef, pork or seafood. Then top it with cheese, melted or not, and maybe some lettuce, sour cream, salsa and guacamole. The result? Burritos, tacos, enchiladas, nachos, fajitas and tostadas. Almost universally, a Tex-Mex main dish will be served with beans and rice on the side.

Some dishes diverge from the standard formula for success: a *chile relleno* is a mild pepper stuffed with a ground-beef mixture and then fried. Empanadas are small pastries with savory or sweet fillings. Tamales are corn dough stuffed with meat, beans, cheese, chiles or nothing at all, wrapped in corn husks or banana leaves and then steamed, while gorditas are fried corn dough filled with refried beans and topped with sour cream, cheese and lettuce.

If you've had your fill of the usual suspects, there's always more to whet the imagination and appetite. A common soup course, *caldo,* includes chunks of cabbage, carrot and the meat of the day, usually chicken or beef. Nopalitos, the pads of native cactus, are plucked clean, sliced thin and stuffed into tacos. Most Tex-Mex restaurants also serve menudo, the traditional Mexican hangover cure. It's a heady stew of jalapeños, hominy and tripe (beef stomach). According to hard-drinking experts, one bowlful will make you think twice before pounding another dozen tequila shots.

Secrets to Cooking Tex-Mex offers what it promises at www.texmex.net.

TASTES BORN IN TEXAS

Corn dogs Cornbread batter–dipped hot dogs on a stick were created in 1948 by Neil Fletcher for the State Fair of Texas (see p87). Fletcher's still sells them there; now available with jalapeño corn bread too.

Shiner Bock The state's favorite amber ale came to be when Kosmos Spoetzl brought Bavarian brewing to Shiner, Texas, in 1914. Available countrywide, it's still brewed at **Spoetzl Brewery** (☎ 361-594-3383; www.shiner.com; 603 E Brewery St, Shiner; admission free; 🕑 gift shop 9am-5pm Mon-Fri, 10am-3pm Sat, tours 11am & 1:30pm).

Chicken-fried bacon You've heard of steak coated and deep-fried like chicken, but the taste (and heart-attack factor) was taken to new heights when **Sodolak's** (☎ 979-272-6002; 9711 FM 60 E, Snook; mains $6-15; 🕑 11am-10pm), near Bryan-College Station, started cooking bacon the same way in the early 1990s.

Dr Pepper A pharmacist in a Waco drugstore/soda shop invented this aromatic cola in the 1880s. Taste the original sugarcane formula at the first bottling plant, **Dublin Dr Pepper** (☎ 888-398-1024; www.olddocs.com; 105 E Elm St, Dublin; museum free, tours adult/child $2.50/2; 🕑 10am-5pm) Don't forget to pick up some Dr Pepper cake mix at the gift and ice-cream shop.

Many Mexican restaurants offer combination breakfasts for under $5, typically composed of juice, coffee, and *huevos* (eggs), which are served in a variety of ways, including *huevos fritos con jamón o tocino* (fried eggs with ham or bacon); *huevos mexicanos* (eggs scrambled with tomatoes, chiles and onions); and *huevos rancheros* (fried eggs on tortillas, covered in salsa). Salsa is Spanish for 'sauce,' and it's made with chopped tomatoes, onions, cilantro and chiles. Many Texans get rolling on breakfast burritos, usually eggs and either refried beans or bacon rolled in a soft tortilla. *Migas* (meaning 'crumbs') are extremely popular – they're a mishmash of eggs scrambled with broken tortilla strips and a variety of savory toppings.

Cornbread Nation 1: The Best of Southern Food Writing, edited by John Egerton, is a delightful collection of essays that'll go straight to your heart and get your stomach rumblin'.

Southern

Southern cuisine is heavy on fat and meats. Typical specialties include buttermilk biscuits, collard greens (served with hot-pepper-infused vinegar) and black-eyed peas, which may be prepared with chunks of pork or ham. Main courses include fried chicken, roasted ham, pork in a variety of ways (including that favorite light snack, pickled pig's feet) and gravies with cakelike corn bread.

Another home-style Southern standard is chicken-fried steak, a tenderized slab of beef that's double-dipped in egg and flour batters, fried up crisp and golden-brown and served drenched in gravy – which readily explains how just one chicken-fried steak can account for almost an entire day's worth of calories.

Where's the beef? The Texas Beef Council has it, and it provides recipes and more at www. txbeef.org.

If you're here on New Year's Day, have a plate of black-eyed peas for good luck in the coming year. Every restaurant will be serving them; it's a Southern tradition. Grits, a corn-derived white glop that's peculiar to the South (though similar to German *griesbrei*), can be eaten as a hot cereal with cream and sugar or treated as a side dish and sprinkled with salt and pepper. Grits are often served in lieu of potatoes at breakfast.

Seafood

Lovers of fresh shrimp will be in heaven all along the Texas coast, where shrimp makes up more than 80% of the commercial catch. The ubiquitous sea critters come boiled, fried, sautéed, barbecued, in the shell and out, and in all sizes. Platters heaping with shrimp prepared in a variety of ways are a common menu item and should put your cholesterol at a level that, if nothing else, will give the mosquitoes a good case of heart disease. Other locally caught seafood items widely found on menus include scallops, oysters and red snapper.

DRINKS

Texas summers demand refreshing drinks. Luckily, there's a lot to slake your thirst.

Nonalcoholic Drinks

The quasi-official soft drink of Texas is iced tea. It's served unsweetened and with fresh lemon slices, sometimes in flavors including hibiscus or mango. If you want hot tea, specify that or you'll probably wind up with iced tea instead.

Commercially available soft drinks in Texas are the same as everywhere in the world, but a local favorite is Dr Pepper, a caffeine-heavy, sweet, carbonated drink invented in Waco, just north of Austin, where there's an official Dr Pepper museum.

Bottled drinking water is widely available, and you can get a gallon of filtered drinking water (bring your own jug) from dispensers at supermarkets for about 25¢. Tap water in Texas is usually fine to drink.

Alcoholic Drinks

The strictly enforced drinking age in Texas is 21, and it's illegal to drive with a blood-alcohol level over 0.08%. Carry a driver's license or passport as proof of age. Servers have the right to ask to see your ID and may refuse service without it. Minors are not allowed in bars and pubs, even to order nonalcoholic beverages.

BEER

Unlike many parts of the USA, Texas has been a little slow in building up its microbrew culture, though there is one excellent and widely available commercial brand, Shiner. But you will find a good selection of out-of-state microbrews and specialty brews in larger cities, where pubs routinely have dozens of beers on tap. Styles you'll likely encounter are Witbier or Weissbier, two wheat-based beers brewed in Belgian and southern-German styles, respectively; Kölsch, a slightly dry, fermented ale; lagers, including the sweetish Helles Bier; and strong bock beer. 'Ice beer' is a brew that's been frozen, then partly drained of water to concentrate its alcohol content. You'll often hear Texans order a 'long-neck.' That's a standard 12oz beer, but the neck of the bottle is longer.

Threadgill's: The Cookbook by Eddie Wilson is not just a compendium of homespun Texas cooking, with plenty of green vegetables to boot. It's also an entertaining trip through Austin's musical history.

WINE

When the Spanish settled in Texas, one of the first things they did – as they did in California – was set up wine production. But at the beginning of the 20th century, only a handful of wineries were operating. Prohibition wiped out most of these, except for the few that managed to eke out a living producing sacramental wine or grape juice. Since the 1970s, Texas wine production has boomed, and there are now more than three dozen wineries in the state. Texas has two major viticultural areas: the High Plains surrounding Lubbock and the Hill Country west of Austin and San Antonio. Texas wines are available throughout the state in liquor stores and upscale supermarkets, but prices will generally be a few dollars higher than a corresponding vintage from California. Popular varietals are cabernet sauvignon, merlot, chardonnay and pinot noir.

TEQUILA

Tequila, manufactured only in Mexico but available throughout the USA, is something with which many travelers to this region may find themselves forced to contend. By Mexican law tequila can only be made from blue agave plants from the Mexican states of Jalisco, Guanajuato, Michoacan, Nayarit or Tamaulipas. Blue agave, a spiky succulent related to the lily, is split and cooked to produce the fermentable sugars from which tequila is made.

There are four types of tequila. *Blanco* (silver) is bottled within 60 days of distillation; *joven* or *abocado* (gold) is unaged and has color and flavor added to it; *reposado* is aged from two months to one year and *añejo* is aged for at least a year in oak barrels. By the way, the stuff that has a worm at the bottom of the bottle is *mezcal,* not tequila.

Tequila can be exquisitely expensive or extraordinarily cheap. The most popular tequila in the USA is José Cuervo, though that doesn't say anything about its quality. To really taste fine tequila, ask for an excellent (and expensive) brand, such as El Tesoro de Don Felipe, Patron Añejo or Sauza Hornitos. Them's sippin' tequilas and mightily worth the extra expense.

The Texas Hill Country Cookbook by Scott Cohen features recipes from a rising-star chef who moved to the Hill Country to take advantage of the region's untapped bounty for food lovers.

Margaritas, the most popular tequila cocktails, are made with tequila, lime juice and triple sec, either served on the rocks or frozen and in a glass with a salted rim. A few restaurants stake their reputations on specialty flavors, such as mango or watermelon. Don't knock 'em till you've downed at least one.

WHERE TO EAT & DRINK

Major Texan cities offer food to match any mood, even the global cuisine you'd find on the West Coast or in NYC. But you didn't come all the way to Texas to eat sushi or foie gras, did you? We've included a few ethnic eateries in each destination chapter, as long as they have a lively local scene. Otherwise, focus is on authentic regional cooking.

The slower pace of life in the South means that service, while generally good, may not be exactly snappy. For a quick meal, shop the deli or take-out sections of grocery stores. Museum cafes and bakeries are great for a fast bite, as well as for solo diners. For those dining alone, some restaurants have counter stools, sometimes facing an open kitchen. At top-end restaurants, you can sometimes order a full meal at the bar, which is an especially convivial place during happy hour (usually 5pm to 7pm weekdays), when appetizers may be half price. Families and large groups are welcome almost everywhere, but if there are six or more of you, call ahead.

Some restaurants serve breakfast, usually between 6am and 10am on weekdays. Weekend brunch is typically served from 10am until 2pm. Some cafes and diners offer breakfast all day, every day. Lunch is usually served from 11:30am until 2pm on weekdays, with a few places staying open for light meals throughout the afternoon. Because lunch is the neglected family member of US meals, many fine restaurants offer drastically reduced prices at lunchtime. Also in this category are early-bird dinners, offered from around 4pm to 6pm, which try to lure customers for early trade by offering similar discounts. Regular dinners are usually served from 5pm until 9pm, later on weekends. If restaurants take a day off, it's typically Monday.

www.texascook.com is a people's encyclopedia of tried-and-true recipes.

VEGETARIANS & VEGANS

Vegetarianism has caught on big time in the USA, even in cattle country such as Texas. Austin in particular is bursting with vegetarian- and vegan-friendly eateries. Like any major city, San Antonio also has plenty of options for vegetarians. In rural areas, though, it can be more difficult, with meat playing a key role in most Southern cooking. Ask twice if something contains meat – some people don't consider things like sausage seasoning or bacon bits to be meat, and you may hear tell of someone serving 'beef for everyone, and chicken for the vegetarians.' Also inquire about cooking with lard, which many restaurants do even with so-called 'vegetarian' menu items.

Otherwise, salad bars are a good way to stave off hunger, and many restaurants serve large salads as main courses. Even at barbecue joints, you can often cobble together a decent meal with a number of 'sides' such as potato salad, beans, corn bread, and banana pudding for dessert. Throughout this book, we've mentioned good vegetarian options in restaurant reviews wherever possible.

EATING WITH KIDS

Families are welcome almost anywhere in Texas, especially at Mexican restaurants. Eating barbecue is another experience that kids can really dig their paws into – and it's fun! Plenty of open-air eateries (which operate year-round) and cafe patios are ideal places for families to dine. A few restaurants attached to bars may not accept minors; we've mentioned this in our restaurant reviews whenever possible. If you're unsure whether a particular establishment allows children or not, call ahead. Many restaurants in all price ranges have special kids' menus, which offer smaller portions at steeply discounted prices. Booster seats are on hand, except at cheap hole-in-the-wall joints and truly fine-dining establishments. Baby food and healthy snacks are widely available at grocery stores.

Mary Faulk Koock's *The Texas Cookbook* (1965) was penned by the owner of Austin's Green Pastures restaurant. Her recipes and tall tales of Texan life are now decidedly retro, but still delicious.

HABITS & CUSTOMS

The first thing you may notice is the incredible quantity of food served in Texas restaurants. Light eaters may do perfectly well to order an appetizer and a salad as a meal, or to share a main course (also called an entrée), for which restaurants may charge a 'split plate fee,' usually about $2. At tapas-style eateries, diners can order as many (or as few) shared dishes as they like. Many barbecue joints let you order meat by weight and skip the side dishes, if you prefer.

If you're looking for a lively meal, search out restaurants that also operate as live-music venues or bars. At top-notch restaurants, serious foodies may opt for the chef's tasting menu, which often comes with wine pairings for each of several courses, including dessert.

Many cities in Texas have passed bans on smoking inside public restaurants, with smoking allowed only at outdoor tables. Before you light up, be sure to ask.

Texas Barbecue

Make no bones about it – Texas barbecue is an obsession. It's the subject of countless newspaper and magazine articles, from national press including the *New York Times* to regional favorite *Texas Monthly*. Some of central Texas' smaller towns – Lockhart and Elgin, to name only two – maintain perennial reputations for their smokehouse cultures, and routinely draw dedicated pilgrims from miles around.

No self-respecting Texan would agree with another about who has the best barbecue, since that would take the fun out of it. But most do see eye to eye on a few things: brisket is where a pit master proves his or her reputation; seasoning is rarely much more than salt, pepper and something spicy; and if there's a sauce, it's probably made from ketchup, vinegar and the drippings of the wood-smoked meat.

> Barbecue is so popular in Texas it got its own documentary – *Barbecue: A Texas Love Story*.

However you like it – sliced thick onto butcher paper, slapped on picnic plates, doused with a tangy sauce or eaten naturally flavorful right out of the smokehouse barbecue pit – be sure to savor it…and then argue to the death that your way is the best way. Like a true Texan.

HISTORY

The origins of central Texas barbecue can be traced to 19th-century Czech and German settlers, many of whom were butchers. These settlers pioneered methods of smoking meat, both to better preserve it (before the advent of refrigeration) and also to tenderize cuts that might otherwise be wasted.

Credit also goes to Mexican *vaqueros* (Spanish-speaking cowboys), especially in Texas' southern and western borderland regions, who dug the first barbecue pits in about the 16th century, then grilled spicy meats over mesquite wood. African Americans who migrated to Texas brought with them recipes for a 'wet' style of barbecue, which involved thick marinades, sweet sauces and juicier meats.

Somewhere along the way, slow-smoked barbecue crossed the line from simple eating pleasure to statewide obsession. Maybe it's the primal joy of gnawing tender, tasty meat directly from the bone, or the simplistic, sloppy appeal of the hands-on eating experience. Whatever the reason, dedicated barbecue eaters demonstrate nearly religious devotion by worshipping at the pits of Texas' renowned smokehouses.

INGREDIENTS
The Meat

In today's Texas, barbecue recipes are as varied as central Texas summers are long. Most folks agree on the basics: slow cooking over a low-heat fire. A cooking time of up to 12 or 16 hours isn't unheard of – anything less and you're just too durn impatient. It allows the meat to be infused with a rich smoky flavor of usually hickory or pecan in the eastern part of the state, oak in central Texas and mesquite out west. (Mesquite was considered all but a weed until someone realized how nice a flavor it lent to wood chips.)

> One trade group estimates that nearly 20 million grills and smokers are sold each year.

Texas barbecue leans heavily toward beef – a logical outgrowth of the state's cattle industry – and most signature dishes come straight from the sacred cow. The most common is beef brisket, a cut often seen as corned beef. With a combination of patience, experience and skill, a seasoned pit boss can transform this notoriously tough meat into a perfectly smoked, tender slab of heaven. Even tougher cuts of meat enter the smokehouse and emerge hours later, deeply flavorful and tender to the tooth. Sliced thin and internally moistened by natural fat, a well-smoked brisket falls apart with the slightest touch and can rival more expensive cuts for butter-smooth consistency.

Carnivores seeking a more toothy challenge can indulge in beef ribs – huge meaty racks that would do Fred Flintstone proud – or relax with a saucy chopped-beef sandwich. Word to the wise: if you need to stay presentable, think twice about the ribs, which tend to be a full-contact eating experience (even as part of a three-meat sampler plate).

Lone Star cattle worship stops short of excluding other meats from the pit. The noble pig makes appearances in the form of succulent ribs, thick buttery chops and perfect slices of loin so tender they melt on the tongue. In recent years, chicken has shown up on the menu boards, mainly to provide beginners with a nonhoofed barnyard option. Traditionalists, however, stick with the good stuff – red meat and plenty of it. If there's something more unusual on the menu, such as barbecued boar or venison, we suggest you go for it: if the chef is breaking from tradition, there's usually a good reason for it, and you are probably in for a treat.

Every self-respecting barbecue joint will also serve sausage. Texas hot links, the peppery sausage of regional renown, is created with ground pork and beef combined with pungent spices. Although it's not technically in the barbecue family, sausage is cooked over the same fire so has the same smoky flavor. If nothing else it makes an excellent meat side dish to go alongside your meaty main dish. Because of the variations in everything from the meat mix to the seasonings to the cooking method, sausages can be as unique an experience as any rub mixture might bring, and almost everyone claims theirs are the best.

The Republic of Barbecue, by Elizabeth Engelhardt, provides a wonderful portrait of Lone Star barbeculture.

The Rub

Everyone knows that the word 'barbecue' is usually followed by the word 'sauce.' But not so fast, there. Good barbecue is more than just meat and sauce. The other key component is the rub, which is how the meat is seasoned before it's cooked. There are wet rubs and dry rubs. A dry rub is a mixture of salt, pepper, herbs and spices sprinkled over or painstakingly rubbed into the meat before cooking. A wet rub is created by adding liquid, which usually means oil, but also possibly vinegar, lemon juice or even mustard. Applied like a paste, a wet rub seals in the meat's natural juices before cooking. This key step is just as important as the slow cooking in getting the flavor just right.

Authentic Texas barbecue is beef brisket, dry rubbed instead of cooked with a sauce.

The Sauce

And then there's the sauce. Wisdom about barbecue sauce varies widely from region to region and sometimes joint to joint. There's huge debate over what kind, how much or whether you need it at all. In Lockhart, Kreuz Market's meat is served without any sauce at all, and it's so naturally juicy and tender you'll agree it's not necessary. But excellent sauce-heavy barbecue is divine as well. We'll leave it up to you to make up your mind.

Texas barbecue sauce has a different flavor from other types – that's why it's *Texas* barbecue, y'all. It's not as sweet as the kind you'll find gracing the tables of barbecue joints in Kansas City and Memphis – more a blend of spicy and slightly sweet. There are thousands of variations and no two sauces are exactly alike, but recipes are usually tomato-based with vinegar, brown sugar, chili powder, onion, garlic and other seasonings.

Stubb's Barbecue (☎ 512-480-8341; www.stubbsaustin.com) in Austin has made quite a venture of selling its sauce, and if it isn't in your local grocery store, you can have them send you a bottle.

Learn about every possible way to barbecue, and why it's different from grilling, at www.texasbarbeques.com.

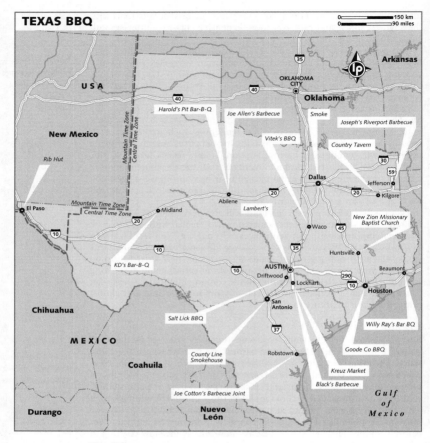

TEXAS BBQ

Arkansas

USA

OKLAHOMA CITY

Oklahoma

New Mexico

Harold's Pit Bar-B-Q

Joe Allen's Barbecue

Smoke

Joseph's Riverport Barbecue

Vitek's BBQ

Country Tavern

Rib Hut

Mountain Time Zone
Central Time Zone

Dallas

Jefferson

El Paso

Mountain Time Zone
Central Time Zone

Midland

Abilene

Lambert's

Kilgore

New Zion Missionary
Baptist Church

Waco

KD's Bar-B-Q

AUSTIN
Driftwood   Lockhart

Huntsville

Beaumont

Houston

Chihuahua

San
Antonio

Salt Lick BBQ

Willy Ray's Bar BQ

MEXICO

Goode Co BBQ

Coahuila

County Line
Smokehouse

Robstown

Kreuz Market

Joe Cotton's Barbecue Joint

Black's Barbecue

Gulf
of
Mexico

Durango

Nuevo
León

The Sides

Side dishes naturally take second place to the platters of smoked meat. Though most barbecue restaurants pile their wares on Styrofoam plates, certain old-style joints still serve in the traditional 'meat-market style' – wrapped in a generous swath of thick butcher paper. (The better to soak up the juices, my dear.) Restaurant-style side dishes usually include pinto beans, potato salad or coleslaw, while markets sometimes opt for simpler accompaniments like onion slices, dill pickles, cheese slices or whole tomatoes. (Not to worry, if your meat is served on butcher paper, the sides will come in a bowl or on a plate.)

COOK-OFFS

There are people who will travel the entire state of Texas to sample all the various permutations of barbecue. But if your time's a little more limited, you can always time your visit for one of the many (many, many) organized cook-offs around the state. Amateurs and pros alike come together for the noble joint causes of barbecue perfection and, if they're lucky, bragging rights. Cook-offs generally start on Friday afternoon so the pit masters have plenty of

Robb Walsh's *Legends of Texas Barbecue Cookbook* has recipes and recollections from Texas pit bosses.

TEXAS BBQ – LISTINGS

West Texas & Panhandle
Harold's Pit Bar-B-Q (p327; ☎ 325-672-4451; Abilene)
Joe Allen's Barbecue (p327; ☎ 325-672-6082; Abilene)
KD's Bar-B-Q (p321; ☎ 432-683-4013; Midland)
Rib Hut (p309; ☎ 915-532-7427; El Paso)

Central Texas
Black's Barbecue (p133; ☎ 512-398-2712; Lockhart)
County Line Smokehouse (p164; ☎ 210-229-1941; San Antonio)
Kreuz Market (p133; ☎ 512-398-2361; Lockhart)
Lambert's (p130; ☎ 512-494-1500; Austin)
Salt Lick BBQ (p133; ☎ 512-894-3117; Driftwood)
Smoke (p90; ☎ 214-393-4141; Dallas)
Vitek's BBQ (p109; ☎ 254-752-7591; Waco)

East Texas
Country Tavern (p226; ☎ 903-984-9954; Kilgore)
Joseph's Riverport BBQ (p224; ☎ 903-665-2341; Jefferson)
New Zion Missionary Baptist Church (p218; ☎ 936-295-2349; Huntsville)

Gulf Coast
Goode Co BBQ (p205; ☎ 713-522-2530; Houston)
Joe Cotton's Barbecue Joint (p254; ☎ 361-767-9973; Robstown)
Willy Ray's Bar BQ (p232; ☎ 409-832-7770; Beaumont)

---

time to get their meat juuuuust right before the judging on Saturday, even if it means staying up all night. (You can't rush these things.) Once the judging is complete, the public is invited to swoop in and judge for themselves. After trying the different recipes, you may not be an expert, but you'll definitely have some basis for comparison for all future barbecue you might eat.

One of the largest events is the **Taylor International Barbeque Cook-off** (www.taylorjaycees.org), held in late August in Taylor (northeast of Austin), with up to 100 contestants competing in divisions like beef, ribs, pork, poultry, lamb, seafood and wild game. If you can't make that one, a quick search on www.tourtexas.com will lead you to events such as the Good Times Barbecue Cook-off in Amarillo or the Wildfire Barbecue Cook-off, Car Show & Festival in Bowie. Or check out the calendar on the Central Texas Barbecue Association website (www.ctbahome.com), where you can also read the incredibly detailed rules that competitions must follow ('CTBA recommends the use of a Styrofoam tray with a hinged lid and without dividers or the best readily available judging container that is approximately 9 inches square on the bottom half').

It's possible to find good barbecue in large cities, but the best examples of the art form usually come from the country. Small trailers reborn as makeshift smoking shacks dot Texas back roads, with handmade signs advertising 'Real BBQ Today.' These informal roadside gems, complete with fragrant, belching smokestack and outdoor picnic seating, represent the rural answer to franchise fast food and a lasting state obsession.

The best Texas barbecue often comes from famous family dynasties that have been dishing up the same crowd-pleasing recipes for generations. Telltale signs that you've located an authentic barbecue joint include zero decor, smoke-blackened ceilings, and laidback table manners (silverware

See gorgeous photographs of Texas barbecue joints by Wyatt McSpadden in his book *Texas BBQ*.

The National Barbecue Association has a calendar of barbecue festivals, tastings and events at www.nbbqa.org.

MEAT BY MAIL

Can't get enough of Texas barbecue? Not to worry: several places ship beef brisket, sausage, ribs – even smoked turkeys – right to your door. Many also sell dry rubs, dipping sauces and the all-important apron.

To Texans who have moved away, the prospect of having meat shipped from home doesn't seem particularly excessive, especially after they've sampled out-of-state barbecue. Once you've visited, you might find that you have a similar hankering. Luckily, the ones who ship are also some of the best purveyors of meat:

Black's Barbecue (☎ 512-398-2712; www.blacksbbq.com)
County Line BBQ (☎ 210-229-1941; www.airribs.com)
Kreuz Market (☎ 512-398-2361; www.kreuzmarket.com)
Salt Lick BBQ (☎ 512-894-3117; www.saltlickbbq.com)

---

optional). At most places, you can order a combination plate or ask for specific meats to be sliced by the pound right in front of you. Of course, there are variations on this nowadays, but in Texas, where barbecue baiting is a bit of a pastime, some swear this down-home style is the only way.

BARBECUE ETIQUETTE

The first question that comes to most people's mind is, 'How do I eat this without making a mess?' You don't. Accepting the fact early on that barbecue is a messy, messy venture will give you the attitude you need to enjoy your meal. One coping mechanism is to make a drop cloth of your napkin. Bibs haven't exactly caught on in the barbecue world – this is a manly meal, after all – but tucking your napkin into your shirt is never frowned upon, especially if you didn't come dressed for it.

Follow the Smoke: 14,783 Miles of Great Texas Barbecue, by John DeMers, is the definitive guide to independent barbecuers, divided by region.

Which leads to another question: How does one dress for barbecue? First off, don't wear white. Or yellow, or pink, or anything that won't camouflage or coordinate with red. At 99% of barbecue restaurants (the exception being uppity, nouveau 'cue) you will see the most casual of casual attire, including jeans (harder to stain) and shorts, and maybe even some trucker hats.

Whether you eat with your hands or a fork depends on the cut of the meat. Brisket and sausage are fork dishes, while ribs are eaten caveperson-style. (It also depends on the restaurant. Kreuz Market doesn't offer forks. As the owner famously says, 'God put two of them at the end of your arms.')

Texas Monthly (www. texasmonthly.com) does a 'best Texas barbecue' feature every few years.

If you're eating with your hands, grab extra napkins. Ah, heck, grab extras anyway. You might also be provided with a small packet containing a moist towelette, which will at least get you clean enough to head to the restrooms to wash up.

A final thought on etiquette. If you're at a restaurant that uses a dry rub and you don't see any sauce, it's probably best not to ask: it would be a bit like asking for ketchup to put on your steak.

Environment

THE LAND

Texas, as everyone here will tell you, is big, but it's not the biggest. It's the second-largest state in the union, with an area of 268,601 sq miles. While that's less than half the size of Alaska, Texas is larger than all of Germany, the UK, Ireland, Belgium and the Netherlands combined. The old cowboy movies lie: Texas is not all dry desert, tumbleweeds and oil wells. In fact, with the natural boundaries of the Gulf of Mexico at the east and the Rio Grande at the west and south, Texas ranks as the ninth-largest state for total water area. It's a gross understatement to say that there's plenty of room here: its population density ranks in the lower half of US states, which makes it perfect for sprawling ranches, farms and vineyards, or just plain wandering by your lonesome under the big Texas sky.

Throw out your notions that all of Texas is flat as a tortilla baked by the hot sun. The land here is many things: hot and flat, hilly and green, rugged and mountainous, parched and foreboding, subtropical and palm-lined, hurricane-ravaged and white-sand pristine. We could go on. In fact, what ecosystem *doesn't* Texas have? Eleven major natural regions of Texas cover an epic range of terrain, from the Gulf coastal marshes, to the High Plains spreading north into America's heartland, to the Trans-Pecos, an extension of the Rocky Mountains, found in the far west of the state. The Rio Grande forms the southern border with Mexico in the region known as the Valley; there palm trees, citrus and vegetables grow in the tropical heat. Famous for spring-break partying and summer storms, the Gulf of Mexico's coastal climate and sugar-sand beaches typify the semi-arid southeast. Verdant hills and meandering rivers make up central Hill Country. There are pine forests and swamps in the northeast, and wide, flat desert valleys alternate with mountain ranges (Guadalupe Peak, at 8749ft, is the highest) in the way-far west. South of the Guadalupe mountain range, the Big Bend region follows the Rio Grande through dramatic canyons and sheer mountain walls.

Phew. And we haven't even gotten to what's underneath. Don't worry, we haven't forgotten about that famous three-letter word: oil. (See the boxed text, p58.)

WILDLIFE

Texas' sheer size and environmental diversity mean that it's home to a startling array of flora and fauna: over 5000 species of plants, 600 different birds (more than any other state) and 125 vertebrate animals are found here.

Animals

To the eternal shame of early settlers, American bison, or buffalo, were hunted to the brink of extinction and today exist only in remnant populations. These days, the two most famous Texas animals are the armadillo and longhorn steer, respectively the state's official smallest and largest mammals. The armadillo, whose bony carapace is unique among mammals, resembles an armored vehicle. Many homeowners are annoyed when the armadillo digs up their lawns in its search for grubs. Speeding drivers are a hazard for the armadillo, which you may first encounter as an inevitable sight on a long Texas drive: road kill.

Once the most common mammal found in west Texas, another (unofficial) mascot of the state is the black-tailed prairie dog – essentially a fat, friendly squirrel that lives off prairie grasses. Highly sociable, the prairie dog

Kids love it if you carry Darwin Spearing's *Roadside Geology of Texas* in the car. Designed for driving tours, it's a beautifully yet simply written geological guide to the state.

Texas Parks & Wildlife (www.tpwd.state.tx.us) offers environmental news and encyclopedic outdoor activity guides.

When prairie dogs meet, they 'kiss' by touching their bared teeth together.

lives in large colonies called 'towns' and hibernates in winter. Natural and human-caused environmental changes have vastly reduced the prairie-dog population over the years, but protected prairie-dog towns can be found in west Texas and the Panhandle Plains.

BATS

Don't duck (they can hear you!). Thirty-two species of bats – those blind flying mammals that populate horror movies, Halloween decorations and attics – call Texas home. You'll hear references to 'Mexican free-tailed bats'; this is a migratory subspecies of Brazilian free-tailed bats (*Tadarida brasiliensis*). For you bat nuts out there, *Tadarida brasiliensis cynocephala* is the nonmigratory subspecies of Brazilian free-tailed bats, which live primarily in the eastern US.

Sadly, the endangered Mexican longnosed bat has its only US home in the Chisos Mountains, where it summers. Yet a total 20 bat species live at Big Bend, ranking it tops among national parks in bat diversity.

Texas' official flying mammal is the Mexican free-tailed bat. The most popular spot for viewing them is in Austin at the Congress Ave bridge, where a colony summers (see the boxed text, p120). Go at dusk.

BIRDS

An image in many a traditional and blues song, the mockingbird – a long-tailed gray bird that can mimic other birds' songs – is the official Texas state bird.

Texas has over 600 documented bird species – over 75% of all species reported in the US – and bird-watching is one of the state's most popular activities. Nearly two-thirds of those species found in Texas can be spotted within an hour's drive of Austin, which is on the Central Flyway for annual migrations. The endangered golden-cheeked warbler, which exclusively nests in central Texas, is best identified by the male's distinctive song heard during late spring.

STRIKIN' IT RICH

The most exciting geological aspect of Texas – to Texans, of course – is why there's oil underneath it. The sticky black stuff sits beneath Texas, southern Mississippi and Alabama, and Louisiana; there is heaps of it under the Gulf of Mexico near all these states, as well as the Mexican states of Tamaulipas, Veracruz and Tabasco – all areas surrounding the huge sedimentary basin that forms the Gulf of Mexico.

Evolving for more than 100 million years, the basin consists of a thick sequence of sedimentary rocks. As the sedimentary material makes its way deeper into the earth, it's subjected to a great deal of pressure and heat – enough to convert much of the organic debris (the remains of plants and animals that are always part of sedimentary material) into petroleum. You know, to refine for gasoline, to fill up those ubiquitous Texas trucks needed to traverse these great distances... See, every issue here comes back, inexorably, to the land.

Petroleum flows freely under the earth, but it tends to collect into large masses that migrate into traps – so named because rocks or other impermeable materials catch the oil – where it forms pools. Pools are what oil explorers are after. Under Texas, salt domes (which are just what they sound like) act as traps; when they're pierced, oil that has been trapped beneath gushes forth. Gushers, however, are rare these days, as oil exploration has become extremely sophisticated.

In 1922 prospectors found oil outside of San Antonio in Luling. The very next year a gusher was discovered beneath Austin's University of Texas (UT) campus. The 'black gold' not only floated the university through the Depression years, but also financed the building of a top-notch institution. In 1940 UT's original oil rig, Santa Rita No 1, was moved to the northwest corner of MLK Jr Blvd and San Jacinto St, but the well continued to flow for another 50 years. You can still visit it there today.

ANIMAL HOUSE, WEST TEXAS STYLE

It's a big old mammal party over at Big Bend National Park: a whopping 75 mammal species call the Big Bend region in west Texas home. Among them, the black bear, all but gone from the region by the mid-20th century, made an amazing comeback about 20 years ago. More than 200 sightings are now reported in a typical year, most in the Chisos Mountains.

Timid campers will be relieved to know that the notoriously fierce mountain lions (often called panthers) are seen fairly rarely, but about two dozen live in the Chisos Mountains. Another well-known Big Bend mammal, the collared peccary or javelina (hav-uh-leen-a) ranges all over the park, from the mountains to the desert.

And that blur you just saw streaking across the desert? No, it's not a lost Austin hippie running towards a mirage. It's probably a jackrabbit. Big Bend's full of the critters – and they'll leave you in the dust before you can say 'Bugs Bunny.'

Birders, take note: the 70,504-acre Aransas National Wildlife Refuge is the premier birding site on the Texas Gulf Coast – more than 500 species of birds migrate through here every year. The refuge is attractive mainly to birders trying to catch a glimpse of the endangered whooping crane, the tallest bird in North America – males approach 5ft in height and have a 7ft wingspan. Other birds commonly found in east Texas include various species of spoonbill, ibis, heron, egret, warbler and of course ducks and geese.

Audubon Texas (☎ 512-306-0225; tx.audubon.org), has information about bird-watching areas throughout the state. With the popularity of bird-watching growing, almost every local tourist office in the main birding areas has information on local conditions.

Want to see something really dramatic? Check out the Austin capitol at midnight, where nighthawks can be seen circling around the dome.

DOLPHINS, MANATEES & FISH
You don't have to drag the kids to SeaWorld in San Antonio to spot dolphins. Several species of dolphin call the Gulf of Mexico home, including rough-toothed, common, bottle-nosed, striped, pantropical, Atlantic spotted and Risso's dolphins.

The endangered West Indian manatee is found, albeit exceedingly rarely, in rivers and bays, and only a tad less rarely in the Gulf of Mexico. And guess what? It has no natural enemies except people.

Game fish are common throughout the state, especially bass and trout, and sport fishing is very popular in the gulf; see the Gulf Coast chapter for more information. Most of the Big Bend region's native fish are tiny. One species, the Big Bend mosquito fish, lives in only one pond inside Big Bend National Park and nowhere else in the world. At one time, the population sadly had dwindled to two males and one female.

AMERICAN ALLIGATOR
The name 'alligator' derives from the Spanish *el lagarto,* 'the lizard,' and you'll find these reptiles in east Texas swamps and along the Gulf Coast. That's right: they're not just in Louisiana! As several B-movies have gratuitously shown, gators are carnivorous: even hatchlings eat insects, frogs, small fish, snails and the like. As they grow, alligators prefer prey that they can swallow whole, such as fish, birds and snakes; they're not above trying to swallow an entire deer, sheep, cow or (gulp!) human. They are usually (but not exclusively) found in freshwater – shallow lakes, marshes, swamps, rivers, creeks, ponds and human-made canals. They are warm-weather fans and will rarely feed when the temperature dips below 68°F – cold comfort to anyone who likes to swim the bayous come winter. Their metabolism slows considerably in cold weather, but gators are cold-blooded and can die when the temperature is

Mandatory references for naturalists include the famous Peterson's *Field Guide to the Birds of Texas and Adjacent States.* For bluebonnets and a lot more, see Peterson's completely illustrated *Field Guide to Southwestern and Texas Wildflowers.*

more than 100°F. To cool themselves, they sit on riverbanks or in the shade with their mouths wide open, which dissipates heat.

Horror movies aside, alligators generally eat only when they're hungry, not as a punitive measure – unless they're feeling attacked. A great place to catch a gator sighting is Caddo Lake (p225).

SNAKES

Spider phobia? Tarantulas are common in rural Texas, as are scorpions – 11 species of stinging scorpions live in the Big Bend region. Spot one? Give it room.

'Are there snakes in Texas?' visitors sometimes ask with the tone of voice that makes it clear they hope the answer is a resounding 'No.' But we're not gonna lie. Bad news first: there are more than 100 (yep, 100!) species of snakes in Texas. The good news is that only 16 are poisonous: the southern, broad-banded and Trans-Pecos copperheads; the Texas coral snake; the western cottonmouth; and 11 kinds of rattlesnake, of which the Mojave and the very common western diamondback are most dangerous. The diamondback rattlesnake is the largest (and most dangerous) of the pit vipers; it injects venom that destroys the red blood cells and the walls of blood vessels. Diamondbacks can grow to be 8ft long and have a big, heavy, brownish body marked with dark (almost black) diamond shapes, set off by yellowish white borders. Listen up: they usually rattle before they attack.

The coral snake, a relative of the cobra, is small and deadly: its poison is the most potent of any North American snake. It looks very pretty – its slim body has sections of black and red divided by thin orange-yellow stripes – and it can easily be mistaken for the harmless scarlet king snake. To tell them apart, remember this cheerful little rhyme: 'Red touch yellow, kill a fellow; red touch black, good for Jack.' Fortunately, the coral snake is very shy and generally nocturnal, and on the whole it rarely bites people. When it does, it rarely (because of its size) injects enough venom to cause major damage.

In addition to the copperheads and four species of rattlesnakes, Big Bend has lots of nonpoisonous varieties, including the western coachwhip, bullsnake, Big Bend patchnose snake, black-hooded snake, Trans-Pecos blind snake and Mexican milk snake.

Based on old Texas law, it's still illegal to shoot a buffalo from a 2nd story of a hotel. It's also illegal to milk someone else's cow.

See p349 for information on treating snakebites. When traveling in high-risk areas, such as Big Bend or any place where there are tall grasses or shrubs, you can reduce the risk of being bitten by practicing basic common sense.

- Wear high leather boots and long, preferably sturdy cotton or canvas, pants.
- Don't gather firewood in the dark.
- Don't reach into holes.
- Stick to cleared paths as much as possible through grass, brush or rocky areas.
- Make noise as you walk, so snakes have time to get away from you lest they attack out of sheer panic.
- Always bring a flashlight and use extreme caution at night – rattlers are nocturnal.
- If you hear a rattle, freeze – snakes are far more likely to attack a moving target.
- Watch your hands; handling firewood or rocks may inadvertently uncover (and annoy) a snake.

Plants

WILDFLOWERS

Wildflowers are to Texas what fall foliage is to Vermont: they're a way of life. Wildflower tourism is so entrenched in the state that the highway visitor centers can help you plan entire trips around watching them bloom. So

A TALE OF TWO CITIES...

Houston, We Have a Problem

At 8778 sq miles, the Greater Houston area covers more ground than any other major city in America. It's as big as the entire countries of Israel and El Salvador, and larger than New Jersey. Such vast distances mean one thing: lots and lots of cars. And trucks. And SUVs. While the city has made an effort in recent years to improve public transportation, high amounts of traffic, coupled with petrochemical emissions and proximity to the ocean (which, accordingly to geophysicists, only exacerbates the problem) create one hot mess of smog. Smog is basically ground-level ozone, which gives the city skyline, on high ozone days, that filmy, yellowish, not-so-fresh sheen.

Are things getting better? Yes, thank goodness. In 1999, Houston claimed the title of the most polluted city in the US (a title for which Los Angeles had become infamous), and retained the crown in 2000. Luckily, strict federal orders forced Houston to clean up its act, and the city went into high gear; the METRORail light rail system, created in 2004, was one encouraging step. Unfortunately, it's been criticized for lack of use – not surprising when Houstonians love their vehicles so dearly. Other local green initiatives include everything from vegetable gardens at City Hall to new recycling facilities; more notably, Houston buys more green energy than any other city in the nation – a fitting choice for the city known as 'the energy capital of the world.'

Fortunately, Houston's no longer riding the top of the most polluted list. In 2010, that honor went to Pittsburgh. Houston's seventh, and hopefully dropping. To check on Houston's progress, take a peek at the city's official 'Green' website, www.greenhoustontx.gov.

Austin Goes Green

Austin is environmentally progressive, winning national and international awards for its **Green Building Program** (☎ 512-482-5300), which offers practical workshops on sustainable building practices for homeowners and developers. The grassroots **Save Our Springs Alliance** (☎ 512-477-2320; www.sosalliance.org) is a watchdog organization that works to protect the Edwards Aquifer zone from pollution caused by development. It monitors compliance with existing laws and ensures the protection of the endangered Barton Springs salamander.

Exciting things are happening smack in the middle of town: the former Mueller airport is now home to a mixed-use community that is Texas' first Leadership in Energy & Environmental Design (LEED)–certified neighborhood, featuring energy-efficient public art, recycled materials, and residences built within 600ft of communal open spaces with trails and parklands. Talk about a hot town keeping things cool. More local residents are beginning to practice a long-held Austin tradition of growing their own produce, and even the City Council is getting green: since 2000, all new municipal buildings in Austin are built to LEED standards.

Greenbelts and greenways (areas of protected natural habitats within and around urban areas) are the focus of hot debates within the state, especially in Austin. There, as in other places, local and state government agencies are under intense pressure from developers to ease restrictions on development. So far the greenies have held out. Is it only a matter of time before money wins out over the earth in these valuable, fast-growing areas, or are green practices so part of Austin's culture that the city will only get healthier? We hope so.

what's the best time to see the crimsons and the blues in all their glory? Diehard wildflower enthusiasts would tell you that the time to see the best and widest range is from mid-March to mid-April, when roadsides and fields throughout central and west Texas, and especially the Hill Country, become explosions of color – blankets of wonderful reds, rusts, yellows and blue.

A sighting of Texas' official state flower, the bluebonnet, means that spring has officially sprung. While this wildflower—whose namesake comes from its small, blue, bonnet-shaped petals—comes in several species of North American lupine, the most beloved and iconic in Texas culture is the *lupinus texensis*: that's right, the Texas bluebonnet. Other beloved wildflower species include Indian blankets, also known as fireweels, the petals of which possess a red-orange-yellow pattern that looks almost woven. Indian paintbrushes share the same palette, but are shorter and often grow in fields of bluebonnets. Mexican hats, which belong to the sunflower family, do resemble nodding sombreros, and they're easily found growing alongside highways. The pink-blossomed stalks of horsemints have a hula skirt of green leaves underneath.

Cedar fever: two of the most dreaded words across Texas, especially in the Hill Country. Cedar's a pollen that grows throughout the state and turns many allergic Texans and visitors into sniffling, sneezing, wheezing wrecks from December to February.

Flower-crazed tourists make the epic drive to Big Bend region specifically to see the wildflowers. The blooms peak in March and April in the lowlands and May to July in the Chisos, but it's possible to find flowers year-round; there's often a second bloom in late summer after the season's heavy rains. Big Bend bluebonnet, a relative of the Texas state flower, blooms from December through June in the lowlands. Other varieties you may see include prickly poppy, sweet William, snapdragon, cardinal flower, silverleaf, bracted paintbrush, rock-nettle and desert verbena.

DESERT PLANTS

The creosote bush is among the most prevalent desert species in Texas, with dark-green leaves and a 30ft taproot that searches for underground water. The ocotillo, sometimes called coachwhip, is a woody shrub with long, slender wands that produce scarlet flowers. Lechuguilla, a fibrous-spined agave, is unique to the Chihuahuan Desert and may grow 15ft tall. Candelilla has long been used by the area's indigenous people to produce wax.

MAJOR PARKS & NATURAL AREAS

Park/natural area	Features
Aransas National Wildlife Refuge	the Texas coast's premier wildlife site; wild boars, alligators, armadillos; rare whooping cranes
Bentsen-Rio Grande Valley State Park	headquarters of the World Birding Center; 300 types of birds
Big Bend National Park	like three parks in one (mountain, desert, river), spectacular canyons, waterfalls
Big Thicket National Preserve	biodiverse area with virgin pine forests and cypress swamps, carnivorous plants; over 300 species of birds
Davis Mountains State Park	most extensive mountain range in Texas; cool pueblo lodge
Enchanted Rock State Natural Area	the biggest pink boulder you can imagine, considered haunted by Tonkawa Indians
Franklin Mountains State Park	largest US urban park – instant city getaway; birds, reptiles, eagles
Galveston Island State Park	coastal dunes, salt marshes, bayous, mudflats, white-sand beach; birds, ducks, marsh rabbits
Guadalupe Mountains National Park	world's finest fossilized reef; canyons and springs; diverse flora and fauna such as desert coyotes
Hueco Tanks State Historical Park	large natural rock basins, or *huecos;* Native American rock paintings
Palo Duro Canyon State Park	vast, multihued canyon; aoudad sheep, white-tailed mule deer, turkeys
Padre Island National Seashore	65 miles of white-sand and shell beaches, grass dunes; coyotes, sea turtles, birds
Sam Houston National Forest	forests, bayous, creeks; deer, squirrels, red-cockaded woodpecker

Prickly pear is the most common kind of cactus, with several varieties: Engelman, purple-tinged, brown-spine and blind (so-called because it looks like it has no thorns – but it does, so beware). Other cactus species include fishhook, cholla, claret cup, rainbow, eagle's claw and strawberry pitaya. One species you *won't* find is the saguaro cactus, which – although often used by New York City ad agencies as a symbol for west Texas – actually is found in the Sonoran Desert of Arizona.

NATIONAL & STATE PARKS

Texas has two national parks (check out www.nps.gov) as well as dozens of state parks and wildlife refuges (listed at www.stateparks.com/tx.html). Some of the best are listed in the box below.

ENVIRONMENTAL ISSUES

Since the 1970s, a growing level of awareness about ecology and the environment, plus the value in 'green' tourism, means that many natural areas increasingly enjoy varying degrees of protection and management by local, state, federal government agencies and private agencies. As well as providing opportunities for recreational activities, many public lands act as preserves for wildlife and offer interpretive activities and educational programs. Outside of Austin, the Lower Colorado River Authority oversees a vast conservation district that stretches from the Highland Lakes to the Gulf of Mexico.

The Azalea Trail is not a hippie band on tour, it's a springtime ritual in east Texas towns when the azaleas bloom. Good places to catch azalea fever include Nacogdoches (p219) and Tyler (p226). Wild for wildflowers? Check out the Lady Bird Johnson Wildflower Center in Austin (p122).

Activities	Best time to visit	Page
bird-watching, boat tours, wildlife walks, hiking, cycling	Nov-Mar; dawn & dusk	p244
nature walks, bird-watching, cycling, camping	late fall to early spring	p270
hiking, tubing, canoeing, cycling, birding, river rafting, climbing, scenic drives, horseback riding, camping	spring, late fall	p282
hiking, nature walks, wildflower-viewing	Mar-Oct	p219
scenic drives, hiking, mountain biking, horseback riding, stargazing	spring to fall	p293
hiking, rock climbing, birding, picnicking,	anytime it's under 85°F	p180
hiking, rock climbing, horseback riding	fall to spring	p305
swimming, nature hikes, fishing, mountain biking, picnicking, camping	spring	p242
hiking, stargazing, horseback riding, nature photography, bird-watching	fall	p314
winter rock climbing, pictograph tours, hiking	winter	p312
hiking, horseback riding, mountain biking	fall & winter'	p341
hiking, windsurfing, swimming, fishing, wildlife-watching, four-wheel driving, camping	spring, summer	p253
hiking, fishing, off-road driving, mountain biking, swimming, canoeing	spring to fall; hikers should avoid deer-hunting season	p219

WINGS AROUND THE WORLD

Given the huge popularity of bird-watching in the Rio Grande Valley, it's not surprising that the myriad sites have formed an umbrella association called the **World Birding Center** (WBC; www. worldbirdingcenter.org), which helps locations to avoid having to wing it. The WBC website has vast amounts of feathered friend facts nesting in various menus.

The following WBC locations are found in this book:

■ **Bentsen-Rio Grande Valley State Park** The WBC headquarters and one of the largest locations for birding in the valley (p270).

■ **Resaca de la Palma State Park** A newish state park in a beautiful subtropical setting (p268).

■ **Roma Bluffs** An observation deck looking across the Rio Grande (p271).

■ **South Padre Island Birding and Nature Center** A natural outpost amid the holiday excitement (p257).

Oil drilling creates its own environmental challenges in Texas, and some serious oil spills have occurred in the Gulf of Mexico – including the highly publicized, internationally condemned and ecologically disastrous BP oil spill in 2010. Economics and the potential for bad press dictate that oil companies are usually far more careful than ever before. The largest marine oil spill in history has also been deemed 'the worst environmental disaster America has ever faced' by US president Barack Obama. To get a sense of the epic proportion of the April 2010 drilling-rig explosion, imagine that for 86 days, an estimated 200 million gallons of crude oil spewed into the Gulf of Mexico, creating an oil slick that at its peak was the size of Kansas. Devastation effects on marine and wildlife habitats, as well as fishing and tourism industries, continue to be far-reaching in the Gulf.

Golf courses can be found everywhere, especially around cities such as San Antonio, Dallas and Houston, but they waste colossal amounts of water for irrigation, and runoff from the fertilizer and pesticides used on them poisons the environment; conservationists charge that the damage to local flora and fauna is irreparable. Golf courses also take up huge tracts of land, and the development associated with them – like condos and resorts – adds to the damage. Government and conservation groups have in the past decade started to employ incentive-based programs to persuade club-owners to adopt sustainable environmental practices.

Texas Outdoors

Texas has a long outdoors tradition. The cowboy custom of sleeping under the stars may not be as widespread as it was 100 years ago, but there are still plenty of ways to get out in the open. National and state park campgrounds are cheap and easy to find, and there are wonderful hiking and biking trails throughout the state. Horseback riding is very popular in Texas, and there are many opportunities to get out on the trail for a day or longer. But Texas also offers much more. White-water rafting, kayaking, tennis, golf, surfing, windsurfing and rock climbing are all easily arranged.

The best information comes from the Texans who pursue outdoor activities with a passion. Check with **REI** (www.rei.com), a member-owned outdoor retailer, for advice and gear. Stores are located in Austin, Dallas and Houston. Also check the Activities sections in each regional chapter for local specialty outfitters.

HIKING & BACKPACKING

There is perhaps no better way to appreciate the beauty of Texas than on foot and on the trail. Texas' preeminent wilderness experiences are at Big Bend and Guadalupe Mountains National Parks (p282 and p314, respectively), both in the state's western half. They are especially well suited to multiday backpacking treks, but each also has abundant day-hiking options.

Padre Island National Seashore (p253), on the Gulf Coast, stretches for 80 of the 113 miles of Padre Island. The entire park is open to hikers; hardy souls favor the sparsely visited southern 60 miles, where the camping is as free as the inhibitions of those who make it that far. However, proper preparation is essential, since there is no shade and no freshwater available.

In south central Texas, the entire Austin greenbelt is lined with hiking and mountain-biking trails, and the Texas Hill Country offers some great opportunities for hikes, especially at Lost Maples State Natural Area (p157) and Enchanted Rock State Natural Area (p180).

In east Texas, dozens of miles of hiking trails wend through the Big Thicket National Preserve (p219). Many of them pass through rural pockets of relatively unspoiled wilderness, but they also run close to logging operations, trailer parks and other human-made distractions that are prevalent throughout this less-than-preserved preserve.

The Texas Mountaineers website at www.texas mountaineers.org lists places to climb, classes and more.

National Parks

Unless you have a few days to get into the backcountry of a national park or are visiting during the off-season, expect hiking in national parks to be crowded. Trails are most heavily used May through September and during spring break in March.

Travelers with little hiking experience will appreciate the well-marked, well-maintained nature trails or self-guided interpretive trails in national parks, most of which often have toilet facilities at either end and interpretive displays along the way. These hikes are usually no longer than 2 miles and give access to the parks' natural features for the casual observer who isn't prepared to hike several miles over rugged terrain.

Most national parks require overnight hikers to carry backcountry permits. Available from visitor centers or ranger stations, the permits require hikers to follow a specific itinerary and may need to be obtained ahead of time. The best idea is to start at the website of the **National Park Service** (www.nps.gov) and search for your specific park.

Treading Lightly

Backcountry areas are composed of fragile environments and cannot support an inundation of human activity, especially insensitive and careless activity. Treat the backcountry like you would your own backyard – minus the barbecue pit.

Most conservation organizations and hikers' manuals have their own set of backcountry codes, all of which outline the same important principles: minimizing the human impact on the land, leaving no trace and taking nothing but photographs and memories. Above all, stay on the main trail, stay on the main trail and, finally, even if it means walking through mud or crossing a patch of snow, stay on the main trail.

If you go to South Padre Island, look for the Point Isabel Lighthouse, just across the Laguna Madre Bay. It's on the smallest state park in Texas.

Packing

If you're a backpacker, you probably know what to pack. But here are some specific things to think about when backpacking in Texas.

- Orange clothing – if you're hiking during hunting season (September to January) in a place where hunting is allowed, embrace this universal symbol for 'I am not a deer so please don't shoot me.'
- Shorts, light shirt – since Texas can be hot, these are good for everyday wear; remember that heavy cotton takes a long time to dry and is very cold when wet.
- Long-sleeved shirt – parts of Texas leave you exposed to the sun for hours at a time, so a long-sleeved shirt made from light cotton, wool or polypropylene is best. One with a button-down front makes layering easy and can be left open when the weather is hot and your arms need protection from the sun.
- Long pants – heavy denim jeans take forever to dry. Sturdy cotton or canvas pants are good for hiking through brush, and cotton or nylon sweats are comfortable to wear around camp.
- Canvas sneakers or Teva-style sandals – these will protect your feet when crossing rivers and keep you from sloshing around in wet boots for the rest of your hike.
- Compass, maps and GPS – Texas is really, really big, so each person should have his or her own compass and maps.
- Sundries – this is the South, so sunscreen and sunglasses are a must; lip balm, unscented moisturizing cream and moleskin for foot blisters are all worth considering.

Training for a ride? The Pedal Hard Training Center in Austin makes sure you're ready by replicating some of the toughest courses around. Book a session at www.mellowjohnnys.com/training.

Maps

A good map is essential for any hiking trip. National Park Service and United States Forest Service ranger stations usually stock topographical maps that cost $2 to $6. In the absence of a ranger station, try the local stationery or hardware store.

Longer hikes require a general map and the appropriate United States Geological Survey (USGS) Quadrangles (also known as 7.5 minute maps). The best place to get USGS topo maps is through its online store at topomaps.usgs.gov.

Find some of Texas' best organized bicycle rides at www.bicycletexas.com.

Safety

The major forces to be reckoned with while hiking and camping are the weather, which you can't control, and your own frame of mind, which you can; a positive attitude is helpful in any situation. Ask yourself: is this for me? If a hot shower, a comfortable mattress and clean clothes are essential to your well-being, don't head out into the wilderness for five days.

WILDERNESS CAMPING

Camping in undeveloped areas is rewarding for its peacefulness, but it presents special concerns. Take care to ensure that the area you choose can comfortably support your presence, and leave the surroundings in better condition than they were on your arrival. The following list of guidelines should help.

- Bury human waste in cat holes dug 6in to 8in deep and a good distance away from streams or lakes. Camouflage when finished. The salt and minerals in urine attract deer, so use a tent-bottle (funnel attachments are available for women) if you are prone to middle-of-the-night calls by Mother Nature and don't want to venture outside.

- Use soaps and detergents sparingly or not at all, and never allow them to enter streams or lakes. When washing yourself (a backcountry luxury, not a necessity), lather up with biodegradable soap and rinse yourself with cans of water as far as possible away from your water source. Scatter dishwater after removing all food particles.

- It's recommended that you carry a lightweight stove for cooking and use a lantern for light, rather than building a campfire.

- If building a fire is allowed and appropriate, dig a hole and build it in there. On islands or beach areas, build fires below the high-tide line. Gather sticks no thicker than an adult's wrist from the ground. Use only dead and downed wood; do not twist branches off standing trees, whether they're living or dead. Pour wastewater from meals around the perimeter of the campfire to prevent the fire from spreading, and thoroughly douse it before leaving or going to sleep.

- Designate special clothes for cooking, then store them with the food, away from your tent, so the aroma won't attract bears.

- Burn cans to get rid of their odor, then remove them from the ashes and pack them out.

- Pack out what you pack in, including all trash – yours and others'. Leave a site better than you found it.

Carry a rain jacket at all times. Backpackers should have a pack-liner (heavy-duty garbage bags work well), a full set of rain gear and food that does not require cooking. Experts suggest backpackers never hike alone, but if you decide to try it, the important thing to remember is always to let someone know where you are going and how long you plan to be gone. Use sign-in boards at trailheads or ranger stations. Travelers looking for hiking companions can inquire or post notices at ranger stations, outdoor-equipment stores, campgrounds and youth hostels.

Fording rivers and streams is another potentially dangerous but often necessary part of being on the trail. In national parks and along maintained trails in national forests, bridges usually cross large bodies of water, but that is not the case in designated wilderness areas, where bridges are taboo. Upon reaching a river, unclip all of your pack straps – your pack is expendable, but you are not.

Using a staff for balance is helpful, but don't rely on it to support all your weight. Don't enter water higher than midthigh – your body would give the current a large mass to work against. If you do get wet, wring your clothes out immediately, wipe off all the excess water on your body and hair and put on any dry clothes you (or your companion) might have.

People with little hiking or backpacking experience should not attempt to do too much too soon, or they might end up becoming nonhikers for the wrong reasons. Know your limitations, know the route you are going to take and pace yourself accordingly. Remember, there is absolutely nothing wrong with turning back or not going as far as you originally planned.

Based in Austin, Mountain Madness (www.mtmadness.com) is the oldest climbing school in Texas, and offers classes, clinics and private lessons at top locations across the state.

CYCLING & MOUNTAIN BIKING

Despite this being Tour de France champ Lance Armstrong's home state, car-crazy Texas is only friendly to road cyclists in some places. Cities such as Austin (Armstrong's hometown) and Fort Worth have developed good bike trails, but in many instances road riders will be sharing space with crowded surface-street traffic, and extreme caution is necessary.

For a good variety of road cycling under not-too-crowded conditions, head for Fort Davis (p294). Also note the 64-mile Caprock Canyons Trailways (p335), an excellent multiple-use trail with many bridges, fenced railroad trestles and a 1000ft tunnel.

Texas has a growing network of excellent off-road cycling trails. Examples include the DORBA Trail at Cedar Hill State Park (p87), southwest of Dallas; Cameron Park (p108) in Waco; Big Bend National Park (p282) and its vicinity; and Caprock Canyons State Park (p335).

National parks require that all riders younger than 18 wear a helmet.

The **League of American Bicyclists** (LAB; ☎ 202-822-1333; www.bikeleague.org; 1612 K St NW, Suite 800, Washington, DC 20006) and the **Adventure Cycling Association** (☎ 800-755-2453; www.adventurecycling.org; PO Box 8308, Missoula, MT 59807) can help when you plan long-distance bike treks throughout the US.

On www.biketexas.net are detailed trail descriptions, maps, pictures and stories about some of the best mountain-bike trails in Texas.

HORSEBACK RIDING

Few images are more Texan than riding on horseback across the open plains. The state offers many opportunities for riding, with stables located everywhere from big cities to state parks. Some are listed in this book; for others, check with local visitors bureaus.

Stables typically offer a range of services, from one- to two-hour trail rides, to sunset picnic rides, to extended, multiday pack trips. Riders will be

---

GLOBAL POSITIONING SYSTEM

The Global Positioning System (GPS) was developed by the US military. It involves 24 satellites, operating in six orbital planes at an altitude of 12,500 miles, putting out coded signals to be received by small units on earth. With the magic of computer chips these small instruments can determine their absolute location with surprising precision. In English, they can tell you:

■ where you are on earth (within about 55yd to 109yd, or 50m to 100m)

■ where you've been

■ where you're going (bearing, distance from any specific destination)

■ how fast you're going

■ when you'll get there

■ what your altitude is above sea level

■ and, of course, the time.

A GPS will come in handy for those traveling in remote areas without roads – say, if you're hiking, biking, canoeing, flying or parasailing. If you're heading anywhere off the beaten track, these gizmos are choice gear. Just don't depend on them as your only orienteering tool – unless you've spent a lot of money or had a lot of experience with them, bring along a good compass as well, for critical measurements.

Prices for GPS units, like most electronic gear, have plummeted in recent years. A handheld unit that cost $329 in the late 1990s now sells for half that much, and you can even find a few name-brand models for about $100 (though it's also possible to spend $400 or more for units with extra features). Look for GPS units at sporting-goods retailers or online at such sites as www.thegpsstore.com or www.amazon.com.

given a horse matched to their level of riding experience, so don't be afraid to mention if it's your first time on a horse and you need a gentle steed, or if you're a more experienced rider who wants a horse who's not an automaton.

It should be noted that while both of Texas' national parks – Big Bend and Guadalupe Mountains – have trails suitable for horseback riding, neither has horses available for rent.

Dude ranches – often called guest ranches – may be working cattle ranches, or they may not. They are plentiful throughout Texas, and you can find everything from a working-ranch experience with rustic accommodations (smelly chores and 5am wake-up calls included) to luxurious ranch retreats, some with spas (if you don't mind that the cowboys are laughing at you). Although the centerpiece of a ranch vacation is usually horseback riding, many ranches also feature swimming pools, mountain biking, tennis, golf, skeet-shooting and side trips to nearby attractions. Bandera (p184), a cowboy town outside of San Antonio, has several to choose from.

The *Birds of Texas Field Guide* (2004) by Stan Tekiela fits in your hand, is organized by color of bird and features photos instead of illustrations, making it one of the easiest-to-use field guides around.

BIRD-WATCHING

Texas has nearly 600 documented bird species – over 75% of all species reported in the US – and bird-watching is one of the state's most popular activities. Hot spots include Big Bend National Park (p287), the Rio Grande Valley (p64) and the Gulf Coast (especially Laguna Atascosa National Wildlife Refuge, p255 and Aransas National Wildlife Refuge, p244). Birding is excellent throughout the year, but peak times are the migrations in spring (March through June) and fall (September through November).

WATER SPORTS
Surfing

For many, 'Texas surfing' is an oxymoron. But local aficionados will argue that it is not as bad in Texas as surfers elsewhere have heard. Long-board surfers, in fact, will have a fun time here on most days; the longer the board, the more rideable the Gulf's mush. The key to riding the waves is timing, luck and patience.

For much of the year the Gulf of Mexico produces surf along the Texas coast that averages an underwhelming 3ft or lower. Conditions are better during the stormy season, which runs from September through February. Surf may be nonexistent one day, but reach six feet or higher the next. Hurricanes can be good news for surfers, who gleefully ride the storm-surge-driven waves until they are blown off their boards.

Although surfers patiently wait for the right conditions all along the coast, the best waves – when they occur – are found south of Galveston to the Mexican border. Mustang Island State Park (p253), on Padre Island near Corpus Christi, is an especially popular spot. The best surfing is at South Padre Island (p249), where there is the best chance of finding waves with good ground swell.

Texas Parks and Wildlife runs the Great Texas Birding Classic – one of the biggest bird-watching tournaments in the USA – every April. Learn more and download your own bird checklist at www.tpwd.state.tx.us.

Given the unreliability of Texas surf, few surfers will want to bring their boards to the coast. But the larger towns along the Gulf Coast usually have one or more surf shops. They often specialize in windsurfing gear, but they have a selection of surfboards, wax and other critical items as well. Rentals average $40 to $50 a day. See the Gulf Coast chapter for locations and more information.

See surf-cams, forecasts, surf reports and the latest Texas surfing news at www.thirdcoastsurf.com.

Windsurfing

If Texas waves are unreliable, the wind is not. The constant coastal breezes, coupled with the large bodies of water sheltered by the barrier islands, make for great windsurfing conditions.

Corpus Christi is an especially popular windsurfing spot, with national and international championships held there regularly. Laguna Madre (p249), the large body of water stretching from Corpus Christi south almost to the Mexican border, is good for windsurfing anywhere along its length. Corpus Christi Bay, some 10 miles across, is accessible to campers on beaches, day-trippers in local parks and even downtown office workers, who are known to disappear from work a bit early on days when the conditions are especially good.

South Padre Island (p258) is also popular. Several shops and bars catering to windsurfers and their groupies line the lagoon side of the island; you can rent boards and gear for about $75 a day. Windsurfing stores are common in the larger towns and cities on the Gulf Coast.

If you have your own board, you can count on being able to windsurf anywhere along the Intracoastal Waterway, an inland canal that runs from the tip of Texas at Brownsville all the way up the Gulf coast and onward to Florida.

For more information on surfing, windsurfing or even kitesurfing, surf on over to www.texasout side.com/surflanding.

Diving & Snorkeling

Diving in the Gulf of Mexico is challenging and not recommended for beginners. The most interesting sites are located 40 or more miles offshore, where the water is very deep and divers are subjected to open-water waves and weather conditions.

Muddy water and heavy plankton growth make the coastal areas of Texas no good for snorkeling, despite the shallow waters and calm conditions. The best areas are in the Laguna Madre south of Corpus Christi; the grass beds along the inner shore of Padre Island are home to blue crabs, flounder, redfish, sponges and stingrays. In July and August, millions of scallops line the bottom.

Some 110 miles southeast of Galveston lie the Flower Gardens, a wild array of coral gardens growing atop underwater salt domes at the edge of the continental shelf. At a depth ranging from 50ft to 80ft, the coral heads form their own underwater metropolis, home to more than 500 species of fish and other sea creatures. The gardens are widely regarded as the premier dive spot in the Gulf of Mexico. Boats to the **Flower Gardens** (☎ 409 621-5151; http://flowergarden.noaa.gov/) typically leave Gulf Coast ports at night for the eight-hour journey. After a full day of diving, they then make a night journey back.

ROCK CLIMBING

Rock climbing has become very popular in Texas, and perhaps the best Texas rock climbing is at Hueco Tanks State Historical Park (p312), near El Paso, although the park has started curbing access to preserve its prehistoric rock art. The Hill Country west of Austin is another popular area, especially Enchanted Rock State Natural Area (p180) north of Fredericksburg. Indoor climbing gyms are in most major Texas cities; they are a good place to learn the sport before attempting to climb real rock outdoors.

Climbing is a potentially hazardous activity. Climbers should be aware of hazards that might prompt a fall, causing serious injury or death. Weather is always an important factor to consider, as rain makes rock slippery and lightning can strike an exposed climber. Hypothermia is an additional concern – be sure to dress appropriately for the conditions in which you'll be climbing. In dry weather, lack of water can lead to dehydration, so make certain you've got enough water with you.

Many climbers follow guidelines similar to those established for hikers to preserve the resource on which their sport relies. They include concentrating one's impact in high-use areas by using established roads, trails and routes for access; dispersing one's use in areas infrequently used to avoid the creation of new routes; refraining from creating or enhancing handholds; and eschewing the placement of bolts whenever possible. Climbers should also take special care to respect archaeological and cultural resources, such as rock art, and refrain from climbing in such areas.

WET SUITS

Water temperatures in the Gulf of Mexico range from a chilly January low of 55°F (12°C) to a comfortable August high of 80°F (27°C). In the winter, windsurfers can get away with a 3/2 wet suit, but surfers will probably need a 4/3, because waves are few and far between, requiring long waits in the water for the next swell. Divers will want to wear a full 7mm wet suit.

For details on Texas diving and snorkeling, **www.divetexas.com** is a good information source.

Kayaking & Canoeing

The lagoons and canals of the long Intracoastal Waterway system are ideal for sea kayaking. Various estuaries, streams and rivers are ripe for exploration, and numerous parks make good bases from which to set off.

One of the most popular places for sea kayaking is Galveston Island State Park (p242), which hosts three paddling trails: the 2.6-mile Dana cove trail, the 4.8-mile Oak Bayou trail and the 2.8-mile Jenkins Bayou trail. **Texas Parks & Wildlife** (www.tpwd.state.tx.us) has information on where to launch your own kayak, or take a guided tour with **Artist Boat** (☎ 409-770-0722; www.artistboat.org; per person $25-50). Check the website for a tour schedule.

Goose Island State Park (p244), north of Corpus Christi, offers excellent access to the Aransas National Wildlife Refuge, which provides habitat for over 300 species of birds. Rentals are available in Corpus Christi, 40 miles away, for $35 to $65 per day; try **Coastal Bend Kayak** (☎ 361-537-8668; www.coastal-bendkayaking.com), which is a happy medium at $50 per day. You can also find kayaking nearby in Matagorda Bay Nature Park (p243).

Not headed for the ocean? There are still some prime inland spots you can put in, including New Braunfels (p173), Kerrville (p182) and the Barton Creek Greenbelt (p123).

For canoeing, you can hardly beat Big Bend National Park (p287). Also try Guadalupe River State Park and the Big Slough Canoe Trail in Crockett National Forest.

Caddo Lake (p224) is the largest lake in the state that wasn't created with the help of a dam. Often fog-shrouded, with Spanish moss draped from every cypress tree, it is a moody and beautiful place that is perfectly explored in a kayak or a canoe. The waters weave in and out of islands, swamps and bayous.

Rental is usually not a problem. If a place has good kayaking and canoeing conditions, there is usually some savvy entrepreneur around to rent you the gear. Prices tend to be around $25 to $35 a day.

Note that the Rio Grande below Laredo to the gulf is heavily polluted by industrial wastes and sewage from the factories on the US–Mexican border. Although the river is pretty, locals strongly advise against dipping so much as a toe into its murky flow, and doctors regularly treat people who have gotten sick swimming across.

Tubing & White-Water Rafting

From the classic Rio Grande trips at Big Bend (p287) to lazy tubing on the Guadalupe River near New Braunfels (p173), Texas offers plenty of wild and mild river adventure.

There is no specific season for tubing or white-water rafting in Texas; you can go year-round, weather and river conditions permitting. Local visitor centers are good sources of information; or try the extensive Texas section in the website of **RiverFacts** (www.riverfacts.com), which lets you compare white-water sections of Texas rivers to find ones that match your skills.

In the March 2010 issue of *Texas Monthly* (www.texasmonthly.com), #9 on the Bucket List is to float a Texas river in an inner tube. If that doesn't float your tube, there are 62 other things they think every Texan must do before they die.

Caddo Lake, in northeast Texas, is home to 71 species of fish, making it the state's most diverse lake in aquatic life.

> **RAFTING SAFETY**
>
> Although white-water trips aren't without danger and it's not unusual for participants to fall out of the raft in high water, serious injuries and drownings are rare, and the huge majority of trips are without incident. It's important to keep your feet and arms inside the raft. For other safety concerns, outfitters usually give orientation and safety lectures before heading off, and trips will have at least one guide experienced in safety procedures and lifesaving techniques. You don't have to be able to swim to participate, but you must wear a US Coast Guard–approved life jacket and should be in reasonably good physical condition.

Tubing is popular on smaller streams and rivers, especially the Guadalupe River near New Braunfels. Generally, you rent a tube – the inner tube of a truck tire – which may or may not be outfitted with luxuries such as handles or seats. Then, much like white-water rafters, you 'put in' at a designated spot on the river and float downstream. Make sure you arrange shuttle service or a ride to pick you up at the other end – most places that rent tubes will do this for you at no extra fee.

Commercial outfitters provide white-water experiences ranging from short, moderately priced morning or afternoon trips to expeditions of a week or more. Trips take place in either large rafts seating a dozen or more people or smaller rafts seating half a dozen; the latter are more interesting and exciting, because the ride over the rapids can be rougher and everyone participates in rowing (or, sometimes, bailing water out of the boat). Most trips are suitable for novice rafters, but some may have age, weight or experience restrictions.

Outfitters on state or federal public lands operate with permits from the appropriate agency. If you plan to rent gear or float your own boat, you, too, should check on whether permits are necessary.

Stephen Daniel's Texas Whitewater *(2004) includes maps, gradients, drainage and difficulties of some of Texas' best runs.*

Boating

The same winds propelling windsurfers are also ready to fill canvas. Corpus Christi (p249) is the sailing center for the coast, and schools at the many marinas offer lessons and rentals.

Boating ramps for launching motorboats are common all along the Intracoastal Waterway, which is very popular with recreational boaters, who enjoy the sheltered waters. However, the various locks can slow down the journey on busy days, and there are always the huge barges to contend with. Most of the towns along the gulf have harbors where you can rent a slip by the night or longer.

Jet skis are quite popular, and you'll see lots of them zipping around the Gulf Coast waters and various inland lakes, but they exact a heavy toll on the environment. They can kill fish and other marine animals, rip sea plants and protected sea grass from the bottom, scare swimmers and disrupt a peaceful visit to the beach for all concerned. They also have resulted in several deaths – Gulf Coast waters in particular are shallow and tricky to navigate.

Doin' Texas with Your Pooch *(2004) by Eileen Barish features a wide variety of pet-friendly Texan beaches, hiking trails, parks and more.*

FISHING
Offshore

With the fortunes of the commercial fishing industry battered by reduced catches and stagnant prices, many fishing-boat owners have turned to offering charters and day trips for their livelihoods. Galveston (p239), Rockport (p245), Port Aransas (p251), and South Padre Island (p258) each have dozens of boats offering trips to the rich fishing grounds in the gulf. As with diving, the best time for offshore fishing is when the waters are free of storm-related silt.

Onshore

From the scores of piers and jetties along the coast you can catch redfish, flounder, and speckled and sand trout. Surf fishing from the beaches can yield the same fish, as well as the occasional hapless stingray or small shark. Although there is always some sort of fish in peak season throughout the year, autumn is best, because the most popular species for eating – including redfish, flounder and pompano – are more likely to land on your hook then. Seafood restaurants near concentrations of charter boats often will prepare a lucky vacationer's catch.

Licenses

A fishing license is required for all nonresident anglers older than 17. A one-day license is $11; for $30, make it good for the entire year. Special stamps that allow you to fish for trout or in saltwater are extra.

Licenses are sold at sporting goods stores, tackle shops and at some park offices and convenience stores. For more information, call the **Texas Parks & Wildlife Department** (☎ 800-792-1112; www.tpwd.state.tx.us).

GOLF

Golf courses can be found all over Texas, and we have included some of the larger courses in this book. Practically every pamphlet handed out by convention and visitor bureaus or chambers of commerce lists all the golf courses in the immediate area. You also can look in the *Yellow Pages*.

HOT-AIR BALLOONING

Floating above the state in a wicker gondola has its attractions, given the scenery, but it's not cheap: one-hour flights for two people typically cost $225 to $275 or more per person. Most flights leave at dawn or at sunset and rise 1000ft to 2000ft above the ground. Generally speaking there's ballooning in every major city. The best place to check for balloonists in a given area is at the local convention and visitor bureau or at the airport.

SKYDIVING

If jumping out of a plane and falling at a speed of 150mph before opening your parachute 3000ft above the ground sounds fun to you, Texas won't disappoint. Skydiving companies have set up shop at airports around the state – just check the *Yellow Pages* or drive into any airport and ask at the information desk or tower.

For first-timers, lessons are easily arranged. The cost of a first-time static line jump (no free fall, just the kind of static line you see in old army movies, where a rope yanks the pin on your chute when you're clear of the plane) is about $175. Tandem skydiving, where you free fall with an instructor, costs about the same, while accelerated free-fall jumps run about $275 for first-timers.

Fishes of the Texas Laguna Madre (2008) by David McKee is an expert's guide to the more than 100 kinds of fish that live in Laguna Madre, a shallow lagoon along the south Texas coast that has some of the best fishing in the gulf.

The Texas chapter of the United States Tennis Association has everything – and we mean everything – you could possibly want to know about tennis in Texas. Visit its website at www.texas.usta.com.

Dallas–Fort Worth Metroplex

Dallas and Fort Worth may be next-door neighbors but they're hardly twins – or even kissing cousins. Long regarded as divergent as a Beemer-driving sophisticate and a rancher in a Dodge pickup truck, these two cities have starkly different facades, but beyond appearances share a love of high (and low) culture and good old-fashioned Texas fun. So get ready to bust up plenty of preconceived notions of the proverbial city slicker and country cousin. Sure, you'll find cowboys in Fort Worth and socialites in Dallas, but these days you might exchange howdies with a socialite in cowboy boots in either city.

The Big D rocks an ego to match its nickname. Its very identity is Texas-sized: big hair, big SUVs, big guns and big malls. The reality is not far off. Hairstyles may have tamed, but the city remains image-conscious, with plenty of sophisticates and corporate types projecting a take-no-prisoners, outta-my-way confidence that's only softened by that friendly Southern drawl. Fort Worth isn't shy either, but like a cowgirl who can shoot from 30 paces and look good doing it, she doesn't need to brag. (Though there's plenty to brag about.)

Just 30 miles apart, the two towns anchor the biggest metropolitan area in the South – more than six million people and growing – known as the Metroplex. So ooh and aah at the excesses of the Big D and then cowboy up to unsung Fort Worth for at least a weekend – the Western sights and museums there may just be the state's best-kept secrets.

HIGHLIGHTS

Best Place to Get Country
Bull-riding and two-steppin' at the biggest honky-tonk on earth, the Stockyards' Billy Bob's Texas (boxed text, p105)

Best Place to Ride 'em, Cowgirl
Giddy-up to the National Cowgirl Museum & Hall of Fame (p101)

Best Place to Loosen Yer Britches
Eat your way through Fort Worth's foodie-paradise Magnolia Street (p103) or chichi Uptown (p89) in Dallas

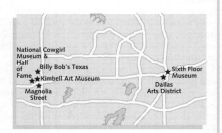

Best Lil' Museum
The oldest museum in Texas, the Kimbell Art Museum (p99) packs a world-class punch in Fort Worth

Most Historical Moment
Relive the tragic day of JFK's fateful assassination at the Sixth Floor Museum (p81)

Best Place to Blow Your Mind
The Dallas Arts District (p83) inspires with top-notch museums, music, theatre and stunning modern architecture

DALLAS–FORT WORTH METROPLEX

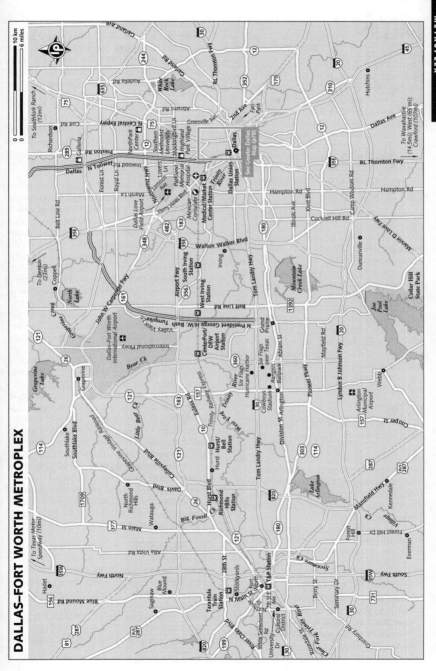

DALLAS

pop 1.2 million

Austin makes fun of her and Houston competes with her, but c'mon, they're just jealous: you can't say Dallas ain't the belle of the Texas ball. This is Texas' most mythical city, with a past and present rich in the stuff of which American legends are made. The 'Big D' is famous for its contributions to popular culture – notably the Cowboys and their cheerleaders, and *Dallas,* the TV series that for a time was a symbol of the USA to people worldwide. An upscale ethos makes for an amazing dining scene (you can tell which place is hot by the caliber of cars the valet leaves out front) and the nightlife's not too shabby either. The museums are not only excellent, but unique – history buffs should not miss the memorials to President John F Kennedy's assassination. The most impressive addition to Dallas' cultural landscape in recent years is the massive 68-acre performing-arts district, now the largest in the country. Don't worry, though: all this high-falutin' culture doesn't mean that Dallas isn't still a paragon of conspicuous consumption. With more malls per capita than anywhere else in the US (and the second-highest debt per resident), shopping is definitely this city's guiltiest pleasure. So if you feel the urge to take your credit card, throw frugality to the winds and say 'When in Dallas…', you're not alone.

HISTORY

In 1839, John Neely Bryan, a Tennessee lawyer and Indian trader, stumbled onto the three forks of the Trinity River, a site he thought had the makings of a good trading post. Dallas County was created in 1846, and both city and town were probably named for George Mifflin Dallas, US vice president under James K Polk; the two were elected on a platform favoring Texas statehood.

Dallas grew slowly for 30 years, though from its start the city had a flair for self-promotion: Bryan saw to it that Dallas was placed on maps even before there was much of a town. In the 1870s, the state decided Dallas would be the junction of the north–south Missouri, Kansas and Texas Railroad and the east–west Texas and Pacific Railroad. It worked like magic: merchants from New York, Chicago, Boston and St Louis invested heavily in the city.

Cotton created another boom. In 1885, farmland sold for $15 an acre. By 1920, with cotton prices soaring, land values had risen to $300 an acre. And when the East Texas Oil Field was struck 100 miles east of town in 1930, Dallas became the financial center of the oil industry.

In the post-WWII era, Dallas continued to build on its reputation as a citadel of commerce. But its image took a dive when President John F Kennedy was assassinated during a November 1963 visit to the city. This tragic incident, coupled with the ensuing turmoil of the 1960s, badly battered Dallas' self-esteem. Gradually, however, the city reclaimed its Texas swagger with help from a few new chest-thumping sources of civic pride: the Dallas Cowboys won the first of five Super Bowl titles in 1972, and their success on the field, along with the popularity of the skimpily attired Dallas Cowboys cheerleaders, helped earn the Cowboys the unofficial title of 'America's Team.' And then there was that little ol' TV show, the top-rated series in the US from 1980 to '82. Dallas was back, louder and prouder than ever.

Soon after, Dallas hit rock bottom again with the mid-1980s Savings & Loan crisis that killed its real-estate boom: from 1985 to 2005, nary a high-rise building was erected on what had been one of the most rapidly expanding skylines in the nation and a national symbol of big-business affluence. Finally, in 2005 construction started up again, this time with residential projects that promise to ensure the city center continues to thrum with life: go downtown and you'll feel Dallas repolishing its shiny image once more.

INFORMATION
Bookstores

Borders Books Highland Park (Map p84; ☎ 214-219-0512; 3600 McKinney Ave; 🕙 10am-10pm) Greenville Ave (Map p78; ☎ 214-739-1166; 5500 Greenville Ave; 🕙 10am-10pm)

Dicho's Books & Café (Map p78; ☎ 214-946-9422; www.dichosbooks.com; 500 N Bishop Ave) Children's, fiction, art, cooking and saucy greeting cards in the Bishop Arts District.

DRIVING DISTANCES

Dallas to Houston 242 miles, 4 hours
Dallas to Waco 100 miles, 2 hours
Fort Worth to Austin 187 miles, 3 hours
Fort Worth to San Antonio 265 miles, 4½ hours

NAVIGATING DALLAS

Although not as sprawling as Los Angeles or even Houston, Dallas covers a whole lotta ground.

Downtown Dallas is east of the junction of I-30 and I-35 E; take the Commerce St exit off I-35. Trendy Uptown lies just north of downtown; follow N Akard St to McKinney Ave. Northeast of downtown, local bars and restaurants line Greenville Ave; the Knox-Henderson area begins where N Henderson Ave intersects the lower end of Greenville, and turns into Knox where it crosses I-75.

To reach Deep Ellum, follow Commerce St just east of downtown; Elm St, another main artery of the neighborhood, runs parallel to it two blocks north. The Bishop Arts District is west of downtown and south of I-30, which connects to Fort Worth, 30 miles to the west.

Paperbacks Plus (Map p78; ☎ 214-827-4860; www.luckydogbooks.com; 6115 La Vista Dr; ☾ 10am-9pm Mon-Sat, noon-7pm Sun) Local fave for used books in Lakewood.

Emergency

For non-emergencies, the info number is ☎ 311.

Central Police Station (Map p78; ☎ 214-670-4413; 334 S Hall St, Deep Ellum)

Rape Crisis Center of Dallas County (Map p82; ☎ 214-653-8740; 899 Stemmons Fwy)

Suicide Prevention of Texas (☎ 214-828-1000)

Internet Access

Many local coffee shops (see Drinking, p90) feature free wi-fi. **Starbucks** (www.starbucks.com) also offers wi-fi free of charge. The downtown (Map p82; 1401 Commerce St), Uptown (Map p84; 3699 McKinney Ave) and Knox-Henderson (Map p78; 3216 Knox St) locations offer shaded patios for web-surfing. For those without laptops, the public library is your best bet.

Internet Resources

Dallas.com (www.Dallas.com) A comprehensive site for locals and tourists alike, featuring everything from nightlife to real estate.

EATS blog (http://eatsblog.dallasnews.com) This blog, from the *Dallas Morning News,* dishes on 'dining, sipping and shopping.'

Side Dish (http://sidedish.dmagazine.com) Follow the hot food scene with *D Magazine's* 'Side Dish' blog.

Visit Dallas (www.VisitDallas.com) The Dallas Convention & Visitors bureau site features helpful transportation info and an events calendar along with standard tourist stuff.

Libraries

Central Library (Map p82; ☎ 214-670-1400; www.dallaslibrary.org; 1515 Young St; ☾ 10am-6pm Tue, Fri & Sat, noon-8pm Wed & Thu, 1-5pm Sun) This cool downtown library offers free public-access computers and wi-fi.

Check out the copies of the US Declaration of Independence and the first complete printing of Shakespeare's works from 1623, both on display.

Dealey Library at the Dallas Historical Society (Map p78; ☎ 214-239-8141; www.dallashistory.org; 3939 Grand Ave; ☾ 1-5pm Wed-Fri, by appt only) In the Hall of State at Fair Park, the library has more than 10,000 volumes on Texas history.

Media

D Magazine (www.dmagazine.com) The glossy city monthly: good restaurant reviews and a window into all things elite and upscale in Dallas.

Dallas Morning News (www.dallasnews.com) The city's daily newspaper.

Dallas Observer (www.dallasobserver.com) Culture, dining, entertainment, reviews and news.

Dallas Weekly (www.dallasweekly.com) News from the African American community.

KERA (90.1 FM) The local NPR affiliate, with local and national programming.

Medical Services

Baylor University Medical Center (Map p78; ☎ 214-820-0111, physician referral 800-422-9567; www.baylorhealth.com; 3500 Gaston Ave)

Parkland Memorial Hospital (Map p78; ☎ 214-590-8000; www.parklandhospital.com; 5201 Harry Hines Blvd)

Prima Care (Map p78; ☎ 972-591-0851; www.primacare.com; 6350 E Mockingbird Lane, Lakewood; ☾ 8am-9pm Mon-Fri, to 5pm Sat & Sun) Ten locations treat walk-in patients with minor illnesses and injuries; travel medicine services, too.

Money

Bank of America (Map p82; ☎ 214-209-1370; www.bankofamerica.com; 901 Main St) Foreign currency exchange and ATM.

Travelex (Map p84; ☎ 214-559-3564; 2911 Turtle Creek Blvd; ☾ 9am-5pm Mon-Fri, to 1pm Sat) Foreign-currency exchange.

GREATER DALLAS

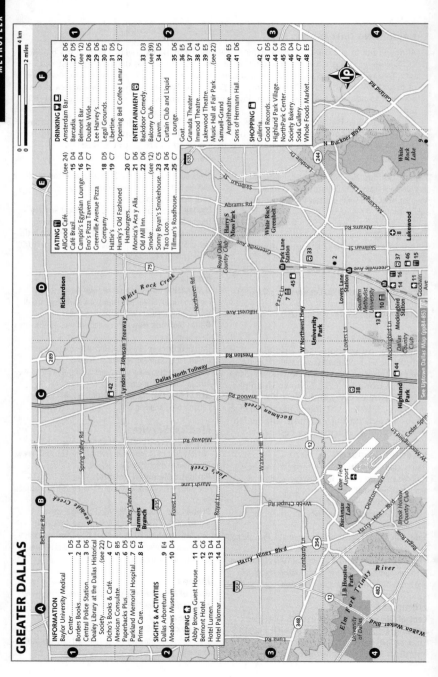

0 — 4 km
0 — 2 miles

INFORMATION
Baylor University Medical
  Center.................................**1** D5
Borders Books.........................**2** D4
Central Police Station..............**3** D6
Dealey Library at the Dallas Historical
  Society.............................(see 22)
Dicho's Books & Café................**4** C7
Mexican Consulate...................**5** B5
Paperbacks Plus......................**6** D5
Parkland Memorial Hospital......**7** C5
Prima Care.............................**8** E4

SIGHTS & ACTIVITIES
Dallas Arboretum.....................**9** E4
Meadows Museum...................**10** D4

SLEEPING
Abby Brown Guest House........**11** D4
Belmont Hotel........................**12** C6
Hotel Lumen..........................**13** D4
Hotel Palomar........................**14** D4

EATING
AllGood Café........................(see 24)
Café Brazil.............................**15** D4
Campisi's Egyptian Lounge......**16** D4
Eno's Pizza Tavern...................**17** C7
Greenville Avenue Pizza
  Company.............................**18** D5
Hattie's.................................**19** C7
Hunky's Old Fashioned
  Hamburgers.........................**20** C7
Monica's Aca y Alla.................**21** D6
Old Mill Inn............................**22** D6
Smoke................................(see 12)
Sonny Bryan's Smokehouse......**23** C5
Taco Loco.............................**24** D6
Tillman's Roadhouse................**25** C7

DRINKING
Amsterdam Bar......................**26** D6
Barcadia................................**27** D5
Belmont Bar.........................(see 12)
Double Wide...........................**28** D6
Lee Harvey's...........................**29** D6
Legal Grounds........................**30** E5
Libertine................................**31** D5
Opening Bell Coffee Lamar......**32** C7

ENTERTAINMENT
Backdoor Comedy...................**33** D3
Balcony Club........................(see 39)
Cavern..................................**34** D5
Curtain Club and Liquid
  Lounge................................**35** D6
Goat.....................................**36** E5
Granada Theater......................**37** D4
Inwood Theatre.......................**38** C4
Lakewood Theatre....................**39** E5
Music Hall at Fair Park...........(see 22)
Samuell-Grand
  Amphitheatre........................**40** E5
Sons of Hermann Hall..............**41** D6

SHOPPING
Galleria.................................**42** C1
Good Records.........................**43** D5
Highland Park Village...............**44** C4
NorthPark Center.....................**45** D3
Society Bakery........................**46** D4
Soda Gallery..........................**47** C7
Whole Foods Market................**48** E5

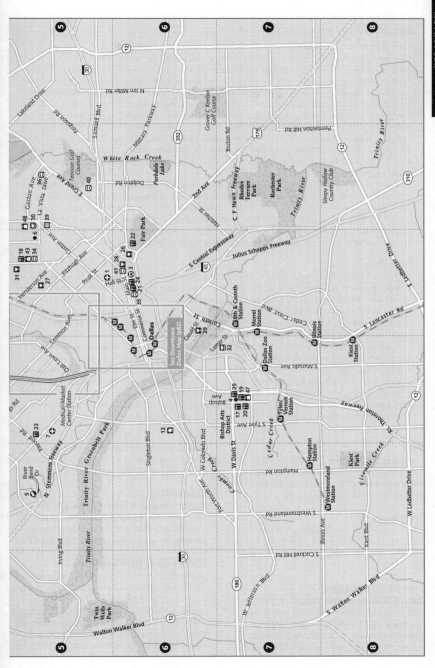

DALLAS & FORT WORTH IN...

Two Days

It's time to get your history on (yep, Dallas has a serious side). Relive the epic events of the early 1960s by taking a stroll through **Dealey Plaza** (p81), the site where JFK was shot in 1963. After chatting with various conspiracy theorists on the **Grassy Knoll** (p81), take a deep breath and head up to the moving **Sixth Floor Museum** (p81). After a stop in the **Old Red Museum** (p81) for a peek into Dallas' past, head over to the **Kennedy Memorial** (p81) to pay your respects. Lunch at the **Zodiac** (p88) will give you a vivid window into a classic Dallas tradition (and feel free to shop at the original **Neiman Marcus** – p94 – while you're at it). You're probably in a reflective mood, so wander over to **Thanks-Giving Square** (p82). (Shoppers, skip the reflection and go to the **West Village**, p94.) Evening, chill out in **Deep Ellum** – start at spicy **Monica's Aca Y Alla** (p89) before immersing yourself in Dallas' old-school musical roots at one of the many **nightclubs** (p92).

If you've only got two days, spend the morning in Dallas' **Arts District** (p83) and check out either the **Nasher Sculpture Center** (p85) or the **Trammell & Margaret Crow Center for Asian Art** (p85) before dashing off to Fort Worth's **Stockyards** (p97). Grab a burger and a shake at the **Love Shack** (p103) and check out the 4pm **cattle drive** (p97). Walk around and soak up the cowboy action before hitting **Sundance Square** (p101) for steak at **Reata** (p102) and a beer at the **Flying Saucer** (p105). Foodies, check out the heavenly cafes on **Magnolia Street** (p103) instead.

Four Days

Rest your head in **Fort Worth** (p95) so that come morning, y'all can gallop over to the **National Cowgirl Museum & Hall of Fame** (p101), and then pile up your plate at the **Buffet at the Kimbell** (p104) after which you're right there to explore the fabulous **Kimbell Art Museum** (p99). Stroll around the **Cultural District** (p99) to see what else intrigues you, and head back to Dallas to spend the evening wining and dining in **Uptown** (p89) at **Toulouse** (p89) or **Fearing's** (p89) with the beautiful people.

Day four, refresh with a walk on the **Katy Trail** (p86) before breakfast at **Bread Winners** (p89). Spend the morning in the **Arts District** (p83) (assuming you missed the museums on day two) and then break for lunch in either the **cafe** at the **Dallas Museum of Art** (p83). Journey across town to the funky **Bishop Arts District** (p90) to poke around the shops. Dinner's either Southern at **Hattie's** (p90) or barbecue at **Smoke** (p90). Up for a play or an opera at the stunning **AT&T Performing Arts Center** (p93)? If not, have a final nightcap at Greenville Ave's **Libertine** (p92) or Knox-Henderson's **Old Monk** (p92), two local bars with serious heart.

Post

Commerce St post office (Map p82; ☎ 800-275-8778; 1100 Commerce St; ◷ 8:30am-1pm & 2-5pm Mon-Fri)
Downtown post office (Map p82; ☎ 800-275-8778; 400 N Ervay St; ◷ 8:30am-5pm Mon-Fri)

Telephone

Three area codes overlap within the Dallas area: ☎ 214, 972 and 469. You'll need to dial all 10 digits no matter where you're calling from.

Tourist Information

Dallas CVB Visitor Center (Map p82; ☎ 214-571-1300, 1-800-232-5527; www.visitdallas.com; Old Red Courthouse, 100 S Houston St; ◷ 9am-5pm) Free 20-minute internet access. A handsome Romanesque building, 'Old Red' was built in the early 1890s, making

it one of the oldest structures downtown and among the city's most historic and picturesque. A helpful events hotline (☎ 214-571-1300) runs 24 hours.

Universities

Southern Methodist University (Map p78; ☎ 214-768-2000; www.smu.edu; 6425 Boaz Lane) This is the city's best known four-year school, with more than 10,000 students attending classes on a pretty campus in tony Highland Park.

DANGERS & ANNOYANCES

Throughout most of the 2000s, Dallas held the dubious accolade of having the highest crime rate among major US cities. Fortunately, things are looking up: reported crime dropped 6.4% in 2009. Follow common sense, and head home well *before* the bars close (usually at 2am). For solo travelers, the West End

Marketplace is among the city's safest areas after dark, with visible police patrols.

SIGHTS

Most of Dallas' major sights are blissfully compact, which you'll appreciate all the more on hot days: **downtown** museums and **Arts District** attractions are in areas easily traversed by either walking or taking the McKinney Ave trolley – in fact, there's no reason to drive between them. Outside of these areas, the major cultural attractions lie in **Fair Park**, 3 miles east of downtown.

Downtown

Downtown's the epicenter of Dallas' interesting – and tragic – history, with museums that both commemorate and celebrate. It's also growing into an admirable live-work community, with scores of condos popping up and pedestrian traffic defying downtown's previous image as 'dead after dark.'

Fortunately or not, Dallas will forever be known as the city where President John F Kennedy was shot, and the sites associated with his death are among Dallas' most visited attractions. Most travelers make sober pilgrimages to the museums and monuments; others congregate at Dealey Plaza, eager to swap conspiracy theories with other skeptics. JFK sites lie near the DART Rail West End station.

On N Market St you'll see the **Kennedy Memorial** (Map p82), where you can pay your respects to the fallen ex-president. Designed by architect Philip Johnson, the roofless room with a view of the sky and the carved words 'John Fitzgerald Kennedy' is a cenotaph, or open tomb, meant to evoke a sense of freedom that JFK epitomized.

Nearby, the 1892 Old Red Courthouse that houses the **Old Red Museum** (Map p82; ☎ 214-745-1100; www.oldred.org; 100 S Houston St; adult/child/student & senior $8/5/6; ⊙ 9am-4pm, to 5pm Sat & Sun) is almost as interesting as the museum's interactive exhibits on Dallas county history. Entry includes the free building tour (daily, call for times).

SIXTH FLOOR MUSEUM

President John F Kennedy's downtown assassination sent the city reeling in November 1963. The shooting was followed by a chaotic manhunt and gunman Lee Harvey Oswald's eventual assassination. The fascinating and highly audiovisual **Sixth Floor Museum** (Map p82;

☎ 214-747-6660; www.jfk.org; Book Depository, 411 Elm St; adult/under 5yr $13.50/free; ⊙ 10am-6pm Tue-Sun, noon-6pm Mon) narrates in excruciating, minute-by-minute detail what happened and where. Eyewitness photos, video and audio clips add a vivid depth to the experience. Even the myriad twisted assassin conspiracy theories are succinctly summarized. From Dealey Plaza, walk along Elm St beside the infamous grassy knoll, and look for the white 'X' in the road that marks the exact spot where the president was shot. Turn around and look up at the top floor of the Texas School Book Depository – now the museum – where Oswald pulled the trigger. Don't miss the audio tour (included in admission), which provides a thoughtful context to the exhibits and is offered in seven languages, including a simplified children's version.

Perhaps the most evocative exhibit is the corner window overlooking Dealey Plaza, the grassy knoll and the triple underpass. No one who was alive in November 1963 can fail to become choked up by the view: the same vista suspected sniper Lee Harvey Oswald had on that fateful day. The somber faces of many museum patrons, including foreign tourists and those born long after 1963, show how this historical event still holds an emotional impact.

DEALEY PLAZA & THE GRASSY KNOLL

Now a National Historic Landmark, this rectangular **park** (Map p82) is south of the former Book Depository. Dealey Plaza was named in 1935 for George Bannerman Dealey, a longtime Dallas journalist, historian and philanthropist. The grassy knoll is the hillock that rises from the north side of Elm St to the edge of the picket fence separating Dealey Plaza from the railroad yards. While some witnesses to the assassination claim shots came from this area, investigators found only cigarette butts and footprints on the knoll after the shooting. The House Select Committee on Assassinations, investigating from 1976 to 1978, concluded via acoustical analysis that a sniper did fire from behind the picket fence but missed. That bolstered the belief that Kennedy's assassination was part of a conspiracy. We may never know the truth. For a guide to the Dealey Plaza and other JFK assassination sites, take the interesting one-hour, self-guided **Cell Phone Walking Tour** ($5, or $2.50 with museum admission) available at the Sixth Floor Museum.

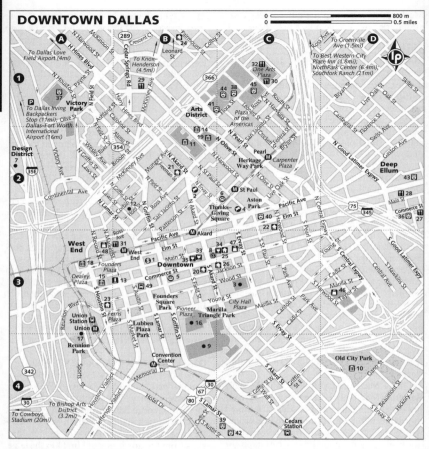

THANKS-GIVING SQUARE

For all its din, drive and shopping malls, Dallas has a surprisingly quiet side where even credit cards are rendered powerless – a triangular piece of prime downtown real estate set aside for spiritual renewal and reflection. **Thanks-Giving Square** (Map p82; ☎ 214-969-1977, 888-305-1205; www.thanksgiving.org; bounded by Bryan St, Pacific Ave & Ervay St; admission free, donations accepted; ☒ buildings 9am-5pm Mon-Fri, from 10am Sat & Sun) was established by the Thanks-Giving Foundation as a 'place where people can use gratitude as a basis for dialogue, mutual understanding and healing.'

Designed by Philip Johnson, the tranquil center includes a meditation garden, a Wall of Praise, an interdenominational Chapel of Thanksgiving and a museum of gratitude.

DALLAS HERITAGE VILLAGE AT OLD CITY PARK

This 13-acre **museum of history and architecture** (Map p82; ☎ 214-421-5141; www.oldcitypark.org; 1515 S Harwood St; adult/3-12yr/senior $7/4/5; ☒ 10am-4pm Tue-Sat, noon-4pm Sun), set on a wooded property south of downtown, shows what it was like to live in North Texas from about 1840 to 1910. The modern skyline makes for a striking backdrop for the living history exhibits, comprised of 38 historic structures including a tepee and a Civil War–era farm.

Convention Center & Reunion Area

If it seems like downtown Dallas come evening is full of roaming businesspeople looking to burn off the stress of their workday but not entirely sure where to go, you're right. Dallas is one of the world's biggest convention cities, with a **convention center** (Map p82; www.dallasconventioncenter.com) boasting more than a million square feet of exhibit space. All these conventioneers lend a work hard, play hard air to the area, which means bidness by day and packed bars by night. Everything's a short walk from either DART Rail's Convention Center Station or Union Station.

For a Texas-sized photo op or just a sight of the largest bronze monument on earth, head to **Pioneer Plaza** (cnr S Griffin & Young Sts) near the Convention Center: its showpiece is a collection of 40 bronze larger-than-life **longhorns**, amassed as if they were on a cattle drive. The **Pioneer Cemetery**, between the plaza and convention center, is the resting place of many early Dallas settlers, with gravestones from the 1850s through the 1920s.

What's 50 stories high, with a three-level spherical dome flashing with 260 lights? No, it's not a spaceship, it's **Reunion Tower** (Map p82; ☎ 214-571-5744; 300 Reunion Blvd), the unofficial symbol of Dallas. Get a workout by taking the steps up to the observation deck, or enjoy the sky-high panoramic view from the stunning celebrity-chef restaurant and lounge **Five Sixty by Wolfgang Puck** (☎ 214-5741-5560; www.wolfgangpuck.com; 5-course tasting menu $85; ⏱ dinner Mon-Sat). An underground pedestrian **tunnel** connects Reunion Tower with Union Station.

West End

Big-expense-account hotels nearby mean a big business crowd in the **West End** (www.dallaswestend.org). While the crowd might be a little one-note, it's not completely stuffy: a mix of corporate execs types, families and tourists flock to the lively restaurant patios. Come early evening, the scene turns to free-flowing happy hours with (mostly) appropriate behavior reigned in by white-collar decorum. Major thrills aside, it's a pleasant, walkable area.

After the recession killed off several attractions here, one of the only survivors remains the kid-favorite **Dallas World Aquarium** (Map p82; ☎ 214-720-2224; www.dwazoo.com; 1801 N Griffin St; adult/child $21/13; ⏱ 9am-5pm; ♿), where the flora and fauna of 14 countries (think the watery Mayan cenote swimming with sharks and rays) come alive.

Arts District

In one word: wow. True to the 'everything's bigger in Texas' ethos, this is the biggest (and one of the best) **arts district** (www.thedallasartsdistrict.org) in the nation, with 68 acres of arts, entertainment and culture. Whether you're an opera fanatic or go gaga for abstract sculpture, this urban oasis has something for you.

DALLAS MUSEUM OF ART

This **museum** (Map p82; ☎ 214-922-1200; www.dm-art.org; 1717 N Harwood St; adult/student/child $10/5/free; ⏱ 11am-5pm Tue-Sun, to 9pm Thu; ♿ 📶) is a high-caliber world tour of decorative and fine art

UPTOWN DALLAS

INFORMATION
Borders Books.............................1 D4
Resource Center Dallas...........2 B4
Starbucks – Knox-Henderson...3 F1
Starbucks – McKinney............4 D4
Travelex..............................(see 6)

SLEEPING
Best Western City Place Inn.....5 F3
Rosewood Mansion on
    Turtle Creek.......................6 C4

EATING
Bread Winners...........................7 D4
Café Madrid..............................8 E1
Cosmic Café..............................9 C4
Dream Café.............................10 C5
Highland Park Pharmacy.......11 E1
S&D Oyster Company...........12 D6
Toulouse..................................13 E1

DRINKING
Blackfriar Pub..........................14 D6
Crooked Tree Coffeehouse....15 D6
Ginger Man..............................16 D5
JR's Bar & Grill.........................17 B3
Sue Ellen's...............................18 B3
Old Monk................................19 F2
Victor Tango's.........................20 F2

ENTERTAINMENT
Kitchen Dog Theater..............21 D5
Magnolia Theatre...................22 D4

SHOPPING
Ahab Bowen............................23 D5
eatZi's Market & Bakery..........24 C3
Froggie's 5 & 10.....................25 F1

To I-635

Westway Ave

Armstrong Ave

Hawthorne Ave

Prescott Ave

Herschel Ave

Wycliff Ave

Newton Ave

Avondale Ave

Irving Ave

Turtle Creek

King's Rd

Hartford St

Raleigh St

Congress Place

Balfour Place

Cotton Belt Ave

Vandelia St

Cedar Springs Rd

Dickason Ave

Wycliff Ave

N Hall St

Herschel St

Knight St

Douglas Ave

Throckmorton St

Holland Ave

Reagan Ave

Gilbert Ave

Oak Lawn Ave

Blackburn St

Lucas Drive

Arroyo Ave

Hondo Ave

Wycliff Ave

Maple Ave

Congress Ave

Rawlins St

Lemmon Ave

N Haskell Ave

Sylvan Ave

N Hall St

William B
Dean Park

Travis St

Sylvester St

Vagas St

Douglas Ave

Knight St

Brown St

Fairmount St

Throckmorton St

Shelby St

Reagan St

Welborn St

Gillespie St

Dickason Ave

Cedar Springs Rd

Sale St

Lee Parkway

Robert E
Lee Park

Carlisle St

Cole Ave

Lemmon Ave E

Lemmon Ave

Noble Ave

McKinney Ave

Throckmorton St

Reagan St

Harry Hines Blvd

Dallas North Tollway

Oak Lawn Ave

Welborn St

Hood St

Oak
Lawn

Turtle Creek Blvd

Sneed St

Cole Ave

N Hall St

Greenwood
Cemetery

To I-635

N Stemmons Freeway

Turtle Creek Blvd

Routh St

Fairmount St

Maple Ave

Cedar Springs Rd

Lucile St

Howell St

The
Quadrangle

McKinney Ave

Allen St

Clyde Ln

Woodside St

Clark St

Worthington St

Reverchon
Park

Turtle Creek

Bookhout St

Wolf St

Randall St

Bull St

Turtle Creek Blvd

Oak Hi Line Drive

Goat Hill Rd

Edison St

Slocum St

Market Center Blvd

Dragon St

Alamo St

N Harwood St

Hunt St

Mc Kinnon St

N Pearl St

Crescent Ct

Mahon St

Routh St

Fairmount St

Colby St

Bull St

See Downtown Dallas Map (p82)

To Downtown

To I-35E

289

354

35E

289

289

354

289

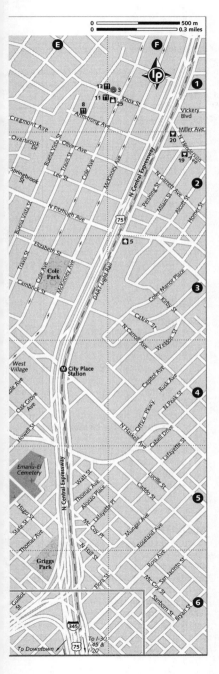

befitting a big city. Our faves include Edward Hopper's enigmatic *Lighthouse Hill* and Rodin's *Sculptor and his Muse*. The Spanish Colonial art section is extraordinary. Also, check out the stunning pair of jade screens from North India. Kids (and parents) will appreciate the Young Learners Gallery, with fun projects for young 'uns.

TRAMMELL & MARGARET CROW CENTER FOR ASIAN ART

Enter another world in this calm, pagodalike oasis of a **museum** (Map p82; ☎ 214-979-6430; www.crowcollection.com; 2010 Flora St; admission free; ☿ 10am-9pm Tue-Thu, 10am-6pm Fri-Sun, public tours 6:30pm Thu & 1pm Sat) that's nearly as remarkable for its ambience as for its rich collection of artworks from China, Japan, India and Southeast Asia, dating from 3500 BC to the early 20th century. Don't miss the gorgeous sandstone facade from North India.

NASHER SCULPTURE CENTER

Modern-art installations shine both inside and out at the fabulous glass-and-steel **Nasher Sculpture Center** (Map p82; ☎ 214-242-5100; www.nashersculpturecenter.org; 2001 Flora St; adult/child/student $10/free/5; ☿ 11am-5pm Tue-Sun). The Nashers started collecting art in the 1950s and accumulated what might be one of the greatest privately held sculpture collections in the world, with works by Calder, de Kooning, Rodin, Serra and Miró. Enter the light-filled atrium and your senses will be intrigued by the shape, light and color. The divine sculpture garden is one of the best in the country; don't miss the ethereal 'sky frame' in the garden. This is a wonderful place to while away an afternoon.

Fair Park

Created for the Texas Independence–themed 1936 Centennial Exposition, the art-deco buildings of **Fair Park** (Map p78; ☎ 214-421-9600; www.fairpark.org; 1300 Cullum Blvd; passport adult/child $24/14) today contain several interesting museums. While the grounds themselves are safe, the surrounding area – particularly to the east and south – is best avoided due to high crime. Outside of the State Fair, on-site parking is plentiful and free.

Fair Park is at its busiest during the annual three-week **State Fair of Texas**, one of the largest in the US; it takes place in the park in September and October, and more than three million people attend. For a lunch break

> **DALLAS ARCHITECTURE**
>
> The Dallas skyline has long been one of the most recognizable in the USA, and it's getting more interesting all the time. Some features to look out for:
>
> The **Magnolia Building** (Map p82; 1401 Commerce St) – the red neon Pegasus became a symbol of Dallas when it first flew atop this building in 1934. It disappeared for decades before re-emerging atop the newly renovated building, now a hotel, in 1999.
>
> **Bank of America Plaza** (Map p82; 901 Main St) – one of the tallest buildings in Texas, this modernist skyscraper is outlined each night in cool green argon tubing.

without leaving the park, seek some respite at the **Old Mill Inn** (Map p78; ☎ 214-426-4600; 3611 Grand Ave; meals $6-12; ⏰ lunch Tue-Sun), known for blue-plate specials and banana pudding. Kids' meals ($4.75) placate the young and museum-weary.

HALL OF STATE

Fair Park is full of superb 1930s art-deco architecture, none of it quite as inspired as this tribute to all things Texan. The **Hall of Heroes** (☎ 214-421-4500; admission free; ⏰ 9am-5pm Tue-Sat, 1-5pm Sun) pays homage to such luminaries as Stephen F Austin and Samuel Houston; the Great Hall of Texas features huge murals of Texas history from the 16th century on. As you leave the Hall of State, stop by the reflecting pool outside of the entrance: the golden Greek-inspired statues will thrill art-deco buffs.

TEXAS DISCOVERY GARDENS

These pretty indoor-outdoor **gardens** (☎ 214-428-7476; www.texasdiscoverygardens.org; butterfly house $4-8, garden $2-4; ⏰ outdoor gardens always open, indoor gardens 10am-5pm Tue-Sat, 1-5pm Sun) include a tropical conservatory, a fragrance garden and a butterfly garden. Don't miss the native Texas plants.

MUSEUM OF NATURE & SCIENCE

This educational, hands-on **museum** (☎ 214-428-5555; www.natureandscience.org; adult/senior & 3-12yr $10/7, planetarium $3.50, IMAX shows $7/6; ⏰ 10am-5pm Mon-Sat, noon-5pm Sun) includes a children's museum, a paleontology lab, an interactive DNA exhibit and fossils from the Ice Age. High marks for the planetarium and the IMAX theater.

AFRICAN AMERICAN MUSEUM

This **museum** (☎ 214-565-9026; www.aamdallas.org; admission free; ⏰ 11am-5pm Tue-Fri, 10am-5pm Sat) has exhibits of more than 1000 objects that richly detail the art and history of African American people from precolonial Africa through the present. Its black folk-art collection is one of the best nationwide.

WOMEN'S MUSEUM

Fascinating exhibits that share the accomplishments of famous and little-known women throughout history and across cultures are the focus of this **museum** (☎ 214-915-0860; www.thewomensmuseum.org; adult/senior & student/child $5/4/3; ⏰ noon-5pm Tue-Sun). Don't miss the 'Funny Women' video, or the poetry and music listening room.

Elsewhere in Dallas

On the shores of White Rock Lake, the gorgeous **Dallas Arboretum** (Map p78; ☎ 214-515-6500; www.dallasarboretum.org; 8525 Garland Rd; adult/6-12yr/senior $10/7/9, parking $7; ⏰ 9am-5pm) showcases plants and flowers in theme gardens such as the Sunken Garden and the Woman's Garden.

Located on the Southern Methodist University campus, the **Meadows Museum** (Map p78; ☎ 214-768-2516; www.smu.edu/meadowsmuseum; 5900 Bishop Blvd; adult/student $8/4, after 5pm Thu free; ⏰ 10am-5pm Tue-Sat, to 8pm Thu, noon-5pm Sun, closed Wed) exhibits perhaps the best and most comprehensive collection of Spanish art outside of Spain, including masterpieces by Velázquez, El Greco, Goya, Picasso and Miró.

ACTIVITIES

It's not just malls, y'all: Dallas has more than 50,000 acres of public **parks** (☎ 214-670-4100; www.dallasparks.org). The biggest and most popular surrounds **White Rock Lake** (Map p78) northeast of downtown, where there's a 9-mile **hiking** and **cycling** trail. For see-and-be-seen **running** and **cycling** with plenty of Uptown eye candy, hit the tree-lined **Katy Trail** (www.katytrail dallas.org) that runs from Highland Park to the American Airlines center in Uptown.

TOURS

Dallas Arts District Tours (☎ 214-744-6642; www.thedallasartsdistrict.org/dallas-events/tours; adults/child/senior & student $10/free/5; ☉ 10am 1st & 3rd Sat of each month, advance online reservations required) Walking tours of the arts district, sponsored by the Dallas Center for Architecture.

Dallas Segway Tours (☎ 972-821-9054; www.dallassegwaytours.com) Glide through city highlights and nature trails. Several types and lengths of tours available; reservations required.

Discover Dallas Tours (☎ 214-521-3737; www.DiscoverDallasTours.com) Arts, museum, culinary and shopping tours.

FESTIVALS & EVENTS

The 52ft Big Tex statue towers over Fair Park from late September to October, during the massive **State Fair of Texas** (☎ 214-565-9931; www.bigtex.com; Fair Park, 1300 Cullum Blvd). Come ride one of the tallest Ferris wheels in North America, eat corny dogs (this is where they were invented) and browse among the prize-winning cows, sheep and quilts.

To experience Dallas at its most bohemian, diverse and relaxed, head down to the live-music stages and eclectic arts booths at the **Deep Ellum Arts Festival** (☎ 214-855-1881; www.meifestivals.com/deepspr.html) in April. Pinch yourself: no, you're not in Austin.

SLEEPING

Staying Uptown is pricey, but you're closest to restaurants and nightlife. Upscale downtown hotels often offer good online deals, especially on weekends. The further you get from the center, the cheaper the chain motels.

Budget

Cedar Hill State Park (Map p75; ☎ 972-291-3900, reservations 512-389-8900; 1570 W FM 1382 Park; per person over 12yr $5, campsites $7-20; ⚐) Easily the best place to camp near Dallas, this park has activities galore, including mountain biking and hiking. Some sites sport views of Joe Pool Lake.

Dallas Irving Backpackers Stop (☎ 214-682-9636; 214 W 6th St, Irving; dm $23; ℗ ⊠ ▯ ⊚) Twenty minutes by bus from Dallas in Irving (Map p75), this big, clean, family-run house is a pleasant place to stay: big kitchen, living room, four-bed rooms, super owners.

 ourpick **Abby Brown Guesthouse** (Map p78; ☎ 214-264-4804; www.abbybrownguesthouse.com; 5417 Goodwin Ave; r $65; ℗ ⊠ ▯ ⊚ ⚐) This bright

and cheerful garden cottage is within walking distance of great cafes and bars on Upper Greenville Ave; with a full kitchen and sunny private patio, it's a total steal.

Best Western City Place Inn (Map p84; ☎ 214-827-6080; www.bestwestern.com; 4150 N Central Expwy; r incl breakfast $56-99; ℗ ▯ ⊚ ▣) A funky 24-hour diner on-site gives soul to this otherwise standard motel. The McKinney Ave trolley to Uptown is just a 15-minute walk away.

Midrange

Hotel Lawrence (Map p82; ☎ 214-761-9090; www.hotellawrencedallas.com; 302 S Houston St; r $89-169; ⊠ ▯ ⊚) Neoclassical earth-tone designs, a fitness center and a breakfast buffet keep this 1925 downtown hotel modern.

Hotel Indigo (Map p82; ☎ 214-741-7700; www.hotelindigo.com; 1933 Main St; r from $109-149; ⊠ ⊚) After a hot day of sightseeing, this downtown hotel pampers the senses with fresh colors, soothing scents and sweet-dreams bedding.

Hotel Lumen (Map p78; ☎ 214-219-2400; www.hotellumen.com; 6101 Hillcrest Ave; r $99-209; ℗ ⊠ ▯ ⊚) This ultramodern concrete hotel across from SMU doesn't completely live up to the hype. Yet we love the parade of poodles and shih tzus through the lobby, the DVD library and the strong coffee in the morning.

 ourpick **Belmont Hotel** (Map p78; ☎ 214-393-2300; www.belmontdallas.com; 901 Fort Worth Ave; r $99-209; ℗ ⊠ ▯ ⊚ ▣) You could just imagine Marlene Dietrich walking down the terra-cotta stairs in this stylish 1940s bungalow hotel. The garden rooms, with soaking tubs, Moroccan-blue tile work, kilim rugs and city views, will make you positively languid. Ask about B-movie night by the heated saltwater pool.

SOUTHFORK RANCH

Who shot JR? Locals certainly no longer care (the TV drama *Dallas* was canceled in 1992), but that doesn't stop interstate and international visitors from driving 20 miles north from Dallas to tour **Southfork Ranch** (off Map p75; ☎ 972-442-7800; www.southfork.com; 3700 Hogge Rd/FM 2551, Plano; adult/child $9.50/7; ☉ 9am-5pm). If you are expecting to see Miss Ellie's kitchen or JR's bedroom, don't. The ranch was used for exterior filming only; interior shots were filmed on a Hollywood set.

Magnolia Hotel (Map p82; ☎ 214-915-6500; www.magnoliahotel.com; 1401 Commerce St; r from $109; P X ⬚ 🛜 🏊) We're still dreaming about the delish breakfast, the cookie and milk buffet, and the nightly happy hour in front of the fireplace on those comfy chairs. A sleek downtown hotel that actually feels homey sounds like a paradox, but this is it.

Top End

Adolphus (Map p82; ☎ 214-742-8200; www.adolphushotel.com; 1321 Commerce St; r from $139; P X ⬚ 🛜) Feel like royalty – yes, even Queen Elizabeth has stayed here – the old-fashioned way. The Adolphus takes us back to the days when gentlemen wore ties and hotels were truly grand, not bastions of ascetic minimalism. Sip a martini ($12) in the dark wood-paneled bar.

Fairmont Hotel (Map p82; ☎ 214-720-2020; www.fairmont.com/dallas; 1717 N Akard St; r from $159; P X ⬚ 🛜 🏊) Within easy walking distance of the Arts District, this classy hotel has one of the largest and most lush hotel pool areas we've seen, with herb gardens and couches for lounging in the sun.

Joule (Map p82; ☎ 214-748-1300; www.thejouledallas.com; 1530 Main St; r from $149; P X ⬚ 🛜 🏊) A moving cog-and-wheel sculpture in the stylish lobby hints at the building's Industrial Revolution–era beginnings. Urbane elegance continues throughout. Don't miss the breathtaking, cantilevered rooftop pool area.

⟨ourpick⟩ Hotel Palomar (Map p78; ☎ 214-520-7969; www.hotelpalomar-dallas.com; 5300 E Mockingbird Lane; r from $169; P X ⬚ 🛜 🏊) Across from Mockingbird Station, the Palomar combines dramatic flair (zebra robes, Hollywood-esque infinity pool area, chichi spa) with eco-conscious policies and enough freebies, like the nightly wine and cheese happy hour, to make you feel good about being spoiled.

Hotel Za Za (Map p82; ☎ 214-468-8399; www.hotelzaza.com; 2332 Leonard St; r from $229; P X ⬚ 🛜 🏊) Hip, over-the-top, eclectic rooms and a tragically hip bar, Dragonfly. The sexy pool is reason alone to get in shape.

Rosewood Mansion on Turtle Creek (Map p84; ☎ 214-559-2100; www.mansiononturtlecreek.com; 2821 Turtle Creek Blvd; r $245-595; P X ⬚ 🛜 🏊) *The* definitive five-star Dallas hotel, and worth it if you've got it. Its eponymous restaurant (☎ 214-526-2121, lunch tasting menu $32, dinner $35 to $55) in a 1925 marble-clad Italianate villa is an opulent place to celebrate.

EATING

Downtown, Deep Ellum and the Arts District have their share of interesting eclectic spots, but head to **Uptown** (www.uptowndallas.net) for blow-your-mind choices: from the slick cafes at West Village to the converted old houses on McKinney serving everything from empanadas to escargots.

Funky restaurants with happenin' bars make their home on Knox-Henderson Sts and Greenville Ave. The Bishop Arts District in diverse Oak Cliff is a hot new dining destination: stop by on First Thursdays to sample dishes from local joints. Watch for a soon-to-be-running **trolley** (www.oakcliffta.com) that will connect Oak Cliff and downtown.

Downtown

⟨ourpick⟩ Zodiac (Map p82; ☎ 214-573-5800; 1618 Main St; meals $14-23; ☽ 11am-3pm Mon-Sat; ♿) For more than 50 years, the classic downtown lunch spot for Dallas ladies who shop – and anyone else who wants to experience the tradition. Attentive waiters bustle about, soothing and pampering diners with hot consommé, popovers with strawberry butter and elegant salads. This is legit old-school Dallas, and it doesn't need to put on airs.

Sonny Bryan's Smokehouse (Map p82; ☎ 214-744-1610; www.sonnybryans.com; 302 N Market St; meals $6-13; ☽ lunch & dinner; ♿) Sonny Bryan's barbecue has been around in some form or another since 1910. Locals aren't ashamed to admit they come all the way just for the onion rings, made fresh daily with Pearl beer. There's also a branch at 2202 Inwood Rd (Map p78).

French Room (Map p84; ☎ 214-742-8200; www.hoteladolphus.com; Adolphus Hotel, 1321 Commerce St; tasting menus $110 & $150; ☽ dinner Tue-Sat; V) With glittering chandeliers and drop-dead opulence, this is the top-rated hotel restaurant in the country. Gilt-tinged arches, marble columns and ornately painted ceilings set the scene for the classical French twist on modern American cuisine. The four-course afternoon tea ($38) is lovely.

Arts District

One Arts Plaza, at 1722 Routh St, hosts five restaurants (Italian, Southern, Japanese and wine bars); swanky **Tei-An** (Map p82; ☎ 214-220-2828; www.tei-an.com; mains $11-20; ☽ 11am-2pm & 5:30-10pm Tue-Sun) specializes in laboriously handmade Japanese soba-noodle dishes. **Screen Door** (Map p82; ☎ 214-720-9111; www.

screendoordallas.com; lunch $10-24, dinner mains $21-38; ☻ lunch & dinner Mon-Fri, dinner Sat, brunch Sun) serves an artistic interpretation of Southern mainstays.

The Dallas Museum of Art (p83) offers a casual cafe and an elegant restaurant, both terrific. At **Seventeen Seventeen** (Map p82; ☎ 214-880-0158; cnr Ross Ave & Hardwood St; lunch $10-19; ☻ lunch Tue-Fri) the seasonal menu changes frequently; on the lower level, the child-friendly Atrium Café (lunch $7 to $8; open lunch Tuesday to Sunday, dinner 5pm to 8pm Thursday) offers bistro fare for the art weary. On Thursday nights, free jazz lures diners for drinks and dinner.

Uptown & Knox-Henderson

Highland Park Pharmacy (Map p84; ☎ 214-521-2126; 3229 Knox St; ☻ lunch & dinner; ♿) Since 1912, this classic soda fountain has been serving up malts ($3.99) and grilled-cheese sandwiches to the generations.

Café Madrid (Map p84; ☎ 214-528-1731; 4501 Travis St; tapas $4-7; ☻ 5-10:30pm Mon-Thu, 11:30am-12:30am Fri & Sat) The rustic Spanish decor – wine barrels, warm saffron walls – comes to life with live flamenco guitar music. Tasty tapas at decent prices.

Cosmic Café (Map p84; ☎ 214-521-6157; www.cosmic cafedallas.com; 2912 Oak Lawn Ave; dishes $5-12; ☻ lunch & dinner; ♥) Cosmic Café serves delicious international vegetarian fare in wildly colorful surroundings.

Dream Café (Map p84; ☎ 214-954-0486; 2800 Routh St; mains $6-15; ☻ 7am-9pm Sun-Thu, to 10pm Fri & Sat; ♿ ♥) Imagine a healthy, organic diner – one with quirky decor, a huge patio, a serene fountain and a playground for kids.

our pick Bread Winners (Map p84; ☎ 214-754-4940; www.breadwinnerscafe.com; 3301 McKinney Ave; breakfast & lunch $9-15, dinner $11-19; ☻ breakfast & lunch daily, dinner Tue-Sun; ♿ ♥) If sipping a peach Bellini in a lush courtyard atrium is the rewarding reward for the agony of choosing what to order for brunch, then bring on the pain. Veggie Benedict or breakfast casserole? Bananas Foster waffle or raspberry cream-cheese-stuffed French toast? Lunch and dinner offer similar, though less tortuous, conundrums.

S&D Oyster Company (Map p84; ☎ 214-880-0111; www.sdoyster.com; 2701 McKinney Ave; mains $12-20; ☻ 11am-10pm, closed Sun) An Uptown staple for ages – the no-frills decor and great fried seafood keep 'em coming back.

Toulouse (Map p84; ☎ 214-520-8999; 3314 Knox St; breakfast & meals $11-22; ☻ lunch & dinner to midnight Fri & Sat, brunch Sat & Sun) This charming, angu-

lar cafe and bar transports us to France. Sit on the Euro-style patio and gloat over your bouillabaisse and chenin blanc at sunset as the gorgeous runners en route to the Katy Trail look on with envy.

Fearing's (Map p82; ☎ 214-922-4848; www.fearings restaurant.com; Ritz-Carlton Hotel, 2121 McKinney Ave; lunch mains $16-24, dinner mains $30-50; ☻ breakfast & dinner daily, lunch Mon-Sat, brunch Sun) Press accolades keep pouring in for chef Dean Fearing's four-star sensation. Choose to sup in the lively open-kitchen room, a glass-enclosed conservatory, a tropical courtyard or the white-table-clothed 'gallery.'

Deep Ellum

Just east of downtown, 'deep' up Elm St gets its name from the Southern-drawl pronunciation of 'Elm.'

Taco Loco (Map p78; ☎ 214-748-8226; 3014 Main St; ☻ 6am-10pm Mon-Thu, to 3am Fri & Sat) A fried catfish taco with avocado is $4.25, which is good, because it's 2am, the bars have just closed and you've got five bucks left. Addictive breakfast tacos and tamales.

Angry Dog (Map p82; ☎ 214-741-4406; www.angrydog. com; 2726 Commerce St; mains $5-9; ☻ 11am-midnight Mon-Thu, to 2am Fri & Sat, noon-10pm Sun) Workers crowd in at lunchtime for the unbeatable burgers at this saloon, whose pedigree includes best wings, hot dogs, bar food and hangover therapy for several years running.

AllGood Café (Map p78; ☎ 214-742-5362; 2934 Main St; breakfast $2.50-6, lunch & dinner $5-9; ♥) A postmodern cafe with Tex-Mex grace notes and tattooed waitresses, the AllGood is cozy as all get out. Families and rocker types all chow down on King Ranch chicken casserole and other comfort foods.

our pick Monica's Aca y Alla (Map p78; ☎ 214-748-7140; www.monicas.com; 2914 Main St; lunch $4-8, dinner $6-18; ☻ closed Mon; ♥) Try the Mexican lasagna ($5) at lunch or the tilapia Veracruz ($15) for dinner at this always social, Deep Ellum favorite that rocks a glam Mexico City vibe. $1 mimosas at brunch? Sign us up.

Deep Sushi (Map p82; ☎ 214-651-1177; www.deep sushi.com; 2624 Elm St; dinner main $13-40, 2-for-1 sushi at lunch; ☻ lunch Mon-Fri, dinner daily, to midnight Fri & Sat, happy hour 5-7pm) Red lights, black lacquer, cool people and fresh, well-priced sushi.

Greenville Avenue

Greenville Avenue Pizza Company (Map p78; ☎ 214-826-5404; 1923 Greenville Ave; big slice $3.50-5; ☻ 11:30am-2am

Tue-Sun, to 4am Fri & Sat) Fresh, hot slices to keep you raging late into the night on Greenville Ave.

Café Brazil (Map p78; ☎ 214-841-0900; 2900 Greenville Ave; meals $7-10; ☺ 7am-3pm Mon-Thu, 24hr Fri & Sat, 7am-11pm Sun; Ⓥ) This is the definitive 24-hour dining destination, whether you're recovering from the late shift at the ER, a night of clubbing or a broken heart. Ten locations, all with strong coffee and homemade desserts.

Campisi's Egyptian Lounge (Map p78; ☎ 214-827-0355; 5610 E Mockingbird Lane; pizzas $7-18) Just off Upper Greenville, this Dallas institution has a throwback mafia vibe and good, thin pizza. But more interesting are the legends and conspiracies that surrounds this place: one, that the original Campisi had ties to Jack Ruby, who killed Lee Harvey Oswald. Two, that the two ate here together the night before Kennedy was assassinated.

Bishop Arts District & Oak Cliff

Hunky's Old Fashioned Hamburgers (Map p78; ☎ 214-941-3322; 32 N Bishop; burgers $3-6; ☺ 11am-9pm Mon-Thu, to 10pm Fri & Sat, 11:30am-9pm Sun; ♿ Ⓥ) Reclaim your innocence (or at least get a damn good malt) in this throwback diner that's a far cry from those themed places where waitresses named 'Trixie' snap their gum. No, it's just an authentic neighborhood hangout with great burgers that make us nostalgic for good times in general.

Eno's Pizza Tavern (Map p78; ☎ 214-943-9200; 407 N Bishop Ave; large pizza $14-18; ☺ lunch Sat & Sun, dinner Tue-Sun) We like the old Adirondack chairs, the stacks of firewood and the get-your-own-mug beer club in this summer-cabin-esque neighborhood pizza joint. Oh, and the pizza's pretty wonderful, too.

WHAT THE...? PENGUIN

No, you haven't walked into a surrealist painting: that dude is really wearing a penguin suit. One of the kookiest bar gags we've ever seen, it's worth coming to **OE Penguin** (Map p82; ☎ 214-901-2112; 1404½ Main St; mains $5-9; ☺ 5pm-2am) to say 'I drank Jameson in a penguin suit in downtown Dallas.' Or, like most people, you could just come for the tiki-bar ambience, the good jukebox, the pool table and an until-11pm happy hour that ensures the penguin suit seems like a better idea as the night wears on.

---

ourpick Hattie's (Map p78; ☎ 214-942-7400; www.hatties.com; 418 N Bishop Ave; lunch $8-13, dinner $13-30; ☺ lunch daily, dinner Tue-Sun, brunch Sun) Upscale Southern comfort food with a mod twist? Yes, ma'am. Dig into fried green tomatoes, low-country shrimp and grits, and pecan-crusted catfish. Amid butter-colored walls, glamazons in Louboutins get down and dirty with classic cocktails like grasshoppers and juleps.

Smoke (Map p78; ☎ 214-393-4141; 901 Fort Worth Ave; ☺ 11am-midnight Sun-Thu, to 2am Fri & Sat) A barbecue joint that grows its own veggies and smokes its own meats gets enough street cred to claim the motto 'Raisin' Hell from Scratch.' The Northwoods-cozy dining room, featuring old barn walls and a fireplace nook, proves that ecofriendly can be drop-dead stylish.

Tillman's Roadhouse (Map p78; ☎ 214-942-0988; 324 W 7th St; dinner $17-29; ☺ lunch Tue-Sat, dinner Tue-Sun, brunch Sun) A mod hunting lodge for stylish cowboys features shotguns for door handles, faux stag heads, antler chandeliers and a gorgeous log bar. With all this offbeat charm, the wink-wink comfort food – chicken-fried hanger steak, white-cheddar mac 'n' cheese, tableside s'mores – is surprisingly good.

DRINKING

Those seeking a mix of high and low culture will dig the numerous pubs (usually with outdoor patios) that line Greenville Ave and Knox-Henderson. Deep Ellum is dive-bar central. Want to get dressed to the nines and knock back a martini or two? Head Uptown.

Downtown & Deep Ellum

City Tavern (Map p82; ☎ 214-745-1402; 1402 Main St; ☺ 11am-midnight Sun-Thu, to 2am Fri & Sat) Every city needs an old classic like this, with pressed-tin ceilings, live music and a low-key, feel-good, throw-back-a-beer vibe that chains only wish they could manufacture.

Double Wide (Map p78; ☎ 214-887-6510; 3510 Commerce St, Deep Ellum; ☺ 7am-2am Mon-Sat, noon-2am Sun) Are these rednecks pretending to be hipsters or hipsters pretending to be rednecks? In any case, everyone and their mom seems to be coming to Deep Ellum to drink PBRs on toilet seats and gaze at naked-lady paintings while they revel in being 'trailer trash,' if only for an hour. Live music keeps the irony from killing the fun.

Iron Cactus (Map p82; ☎ 214-749-4766; 1520 Main St; ☺ 11am-midnight Sun-Thu, to 2am Fri & Sat) With

A DARK DAY IN NOVEMBER

In the early 1960s, the USA was fascinated with its young president, his little children at play in the Oval Office and his regal wife. They seemed the perfect family, and the USA – still awash in postwar prosperity – considered itself a place where justice and amity prevailed.

But beneath the glossy surface, the USA was heading into its most divisive decade since the Civil War. By no means universally popular, Kennedy had won election over Richard Nixon by fewer than 120,000 votes from among 69 million cast. His 1961 Bay of Pigs invasion of Cuba was a foreign-policy disaster, and he escalated the US presence in Vietnam from 5000 military 'advisors' to 17,000 troops (though before his death he'd announce a cutback to 1000 troops).

In the eyes of many, Kennedy redeemed his presidency in the fall of 1962, when he stood up to Soviet premier Nikita Khrushchev after US intelligence services discovered Soviet offensive missile sites in Cuba. Yet in the nine months prior to his Dallas appearance, Kennedy had received more than 400 death threats, from critics on both the left, who felt him guilty of warmongering during the Cuban missile crisis, and the right, who charged he was soft on communism. The president's advisors were seriously concerned about the trip to Dallas, where right-wing groups including the John Birch Society and the Indignant White Citizens Council held powerful sway. Just before his death, only 59% of the nation supported his policies, yet Kennedy remained wildly popular among the moderate masses. Even in Dallas, the most conservative city on JFK's itinerary, nearly a quarter-million people lined the streets on November 23, 1963, to greet him.

What happened next has been endlessly debated and dissected by conspiracy theorists, but the events as officially recorded took place like this: Kennedy, his wife, Jacqueline, Texas governor John Connally and the rest of the motorcade left Love Field at 11:50am and arrived downtown under sunny skies. Kennedy's open-air limousine made its way down Main St to Dealey Plaza, where three streets – Main in the middle, Commerce to the south and Elm to the north – converged under a railroad bridge known as the triple underpass. The limo made a one-block jog on Houston St, turning onto Elm St beneath the Texas School Book Depository building. Just as the limousine completed its turn at 12:30pm, one shot rang out, then another. Both Kennedy and Connally appeared wounded, and then a third shot was heard, and part of the president's head exploded. Jacqueline Kennedy cradled her husband's body as the limo raced up the Stemmons Fwy toward Parkland Memorial Hospital. They arrived at 12:36pm, but doctors could not save Kennedy, who had a bullet wound in his neck in addition to the massive head wound. He was pronounced dead at 1pm.

Even before the announcement, Dallas and the nation were thrown into turmoil. Dallas police officer Marrion Baker, who had seen pigeons fly off the Book Depository roof as the shots were fired, entered the building and found a man in the employee lunchroom at 12:32pm. Depository superintendent Roy Truly identified the suspect as Lee Harvey Oswald – an employee hired five weeks earlier – so Baker let him go. Soon after, police found the sniper's perch on the 6th floor, together with spent cartridges and finger- and palm prints later identified as Oswald's. Meanwhile, Oswald was arrested at 1:50pm in the Oak Cliff section of town, a suspect in the shooting of Dallas police officer JD Tippit. He was later charged with the murder of Kennedy, but the next morning – as Oswald was being transferred from the city to the county jail pending trial, denying both murders – Dallas nightclub owner Jack Ruby shot him in the basement of Dallas police headquarters. Kennedy was buried the following day at Arlington National Cemetery, outside Washington, DC.

Amid a country in mourning, the phrase 'Where were you the moment you found out that JFK had been shot?' became a touchstone question for an entire generation.

over 80 selections of Mexican tequila, this bubbly downtown party spot is oft-rated the best happy hour in Dallas. It's certainly the breeziest patio, with a multitiered deck overlooking fountains below. Try the deadly cactus juice.

Uptown & Knox-Henderson

Barcadia (Map p78; ☎ 214-821-7300; 1917 N Henderson Ave; ☾ 4pm-2am Mon-Thu, from 3pm Fri & Sat, from 11am Sun) Come for the games, stay for the drinks. Great for making meaningful eye contact with cute strangers to whom you have nothing to say and share nothing in common, except for a love of Connect Four.

Blackfriar Pub (Map p84; ☎ 214-953-0559; 2621 McKinney Ave; ☺ 3pm-2am Mon-Fri, from noon Sat & Sun) Young professionals try their best to look perfectly carefree on the bustling patio; a great beer selection helps them (almost) succeed.

Crooked Tree Coffeehouse (Map p84; ☎ 214-953-1142; 2414 Routh St; ☺ 6am-11pm Mon-Thu, to midnight Fri & Sat, 8am-9pm Sun; ☞) Curl up with a book or your laptop in this old cottage. Good smoothies, teas and coffees for adults; highchairs and cookies for the kids.

Ginger Man (Map p84; ☎ 214-754-8771; 2718 Boll St; ☺ 11am-2am Wed-Fri, 1pm-2am Sat-Tue) A spice-colored bungalow is home to this cozy neighborhood pub. International craft beers and a great front (and back) porch.

our pick **Old Monk** (Map p84; ☎ 214-821-1880; 2847 N Henderson; ☺ 4pm-2am Mon-Thu, 3pm-2am Fri, 11am-2am Sat & Sun) The dimly lit patio on a starry night! The perfect cheese plate! The Belgian beers! We'll admit it – this is one of our favorite pubs in Texas.

Quarter Bar (Map p78; ☎ 214-754-4941; 3301 McKinney Ave; ☺ 4pm-2am daily, from noon Sat & Sun) Attached to Bread Winners in Uptown, this fun New Orleans–style bar captures the vintage ambience of the French Quarter while avoiding its obnoxious streak.

Victor Tango's (Map p84; ☎ 214-741-4406; 3001 N Henderson; ☺ 11am-midnight Sun-Thu, to 2am Fri & Sat) In Knox-Henderson, get down with the bitters, egg whites and 'what the hell is that in my glass?' vintage-cocktail craze.

Greenville Avenue

Pay close attention to signs: although free on-street parking exists, towing is rampant here.

our pick **Libertine** (Map p78; ☎ 214-824-7900; 2101 Greenville Ave; ☺ 4pm-2am Mon-Fri, from noon Sat, from 11am Sun) Any Austinite hipster who dares to call Dallas uncool should be forced to drink a single beer in this bar. We like how the sophisticated pub food and convivial neighborhood vibe, all wrapped up in a sultry retro setting, make us feel just slightly cooler than we actually are.

Lee Harvey's (Map p78; ☎ 214-428-1555; 1807 Gould St; ☺ 3pm-2am Mon-Sat, from 1pm Sun) A kitschy dive bar with a killer – sorry, pun intended – name, Lee Harvey's has really nothing to do with JFK or (thankfully) assassinations in general.

Bishop Arts District, Lakewood & Elsewhere

Belmont Bar (off Map p78; ☎ 866-870-8010; Belmont Hotel, 901 Fort Worth Ave) Sip your adult beverage on a stylish terrace overlooking the city. Sometimes the bar screens B-grade flicks on the white stucco wall in the garden.

Legal Grounds (Map p78; ☎ 214-823-7001; 2015 Abrams Rd, Lakewood; ☺ 6:30am-2pm Mon-Fri, from 7am Sat & Sun; ☞) This combination coffee shop and law office has to be the most unusual java joint in town.

Amsterdam Bar (Map p78; ☎ 214-827-3433; 831 Exposition Ave; ☺ 2:30pm-2am; ☞) By Fair Park, this bar has a beloved following for its happy hour, eclectic beers and patio jazz nights.

Opening Bell Coffee Lamar (Map p78; ☎ 214-565-0383; 1409 S Lamar St; ☺ 7am-10pm Mon-Thu, to midnight Fri, 9am-midnight Sat, 9am-3pm Sun; ☞) This cafe multitasks gracefully: sip fair-trade coffee, watch the financial markets and hear some of the best acoustic music in Dallas.

ENTERTAINMENT

High culture, low culture, country culture… Dallas has it in spades.

Cinemas

The **Landmark Theatres** (Map p78; ☎ 214-764-9106; www.landmarktheatres.com) operate two historic cinemas in town: the **Inwood** (5458 W Lovers Lane), and the **Magnolia** (Map p84; 3699 McKinney Ave) in the West Village. Both show foreign and independent films.

Another local fave is the beloved **Lakewood Theater** (Map p78; ☎ 214-821-7469; www.lakewoodtheater.com; 1825 Abrams Rd), a 1938 restored art-deco palace that shows films, music and other diversions like trivia, karaoke and burlesque.

Live Music & Nightclubs

Check the *Scene & Heard* blog (http://sceneblog.guidelive.com) for the scoop on local music happenings. Though it's been through several cycles of downturns and upswings, Deep Ellum remains Dallas' unofficial headquarters for live music.

Adair's Saloon (Map p82; ☎ 214-939-9900; www.adairssaloon.com; 2624 Commerce St) The regulars call it 'Aayy-dares.' Down-to-earth patrons and infectious country and redneck rock bands go down well with cheap beer and shuffleboard.

Granada Theater (Map p78; ☎ 214-824-9933; www.granadatheater.com; 3524 Greenville Ave) This converted

---

GAY & LESBIAN DALLAS

Dallas' gay and lesbian scene centers on Cedar Springs Rd and Oak Lawn Ave, north of Uptown. There's also a good-sized gay enclave in Oak Cliff across town. Check the **Resource Center Dallas** (Map p84; ☎ 214-528-0144; www.resourcecenterdallas.com; 2701 Reagan St) for GLBT resources and info. The *Dallas Voice* newspaper (www.dallasvoice.com) is the town's gay and lesbian advocate.

Want to get your drink on? Just walk around Cedar Springs for plenty of cutie-shopping. **Caven Enterprises** (www.caven.com) owns half of the bars, so check the website for ideas. You've got to love that the top gay and lesbian bars in Dallas are named JR's and Sue Ellen's, respectively, after the two lead (and presumably straight) characters in *Dallas*.

JR's Bar & Grill (Map p84; ☎ 214-528-1004; www.caven.com; 3923 Cedar Springs Rd, Uptown; ⊙ 11am-2am) One of the busiest bars in Texas, JR's serves lunch daily and boasts a variety of fun entertainment at night.

Sue Ellen's (Map p84; ☎ 214-559-0707; 3014 Throckmorton; ⊙ 4pm-2am) Chill out in the 'lipstick lounge' or on the dancefloor at Dallas' favorite lesbian bar.

---

old movie theater, often praised as the best live music venue in town, books popular rock and country bands like Of Montreal and Junior Brown that appeal to an older, hip crowd.

Sons of Hermann Hall (Map p78; ☎ 214-747-4422; www.sonsofhermann.com; 3414 Elm St) For 95 years, this classic Texas dancehall has been a chameleon: equal parts pick-up bar, live music venue, honky-tonk and swing-dancing club.

Cavern (Map p78; ☎ 214-828-1914; www.the caverndallas.com; 1914 Lower Greenville Ave; ⊙ 6pm-2am) A homage to the Beatles' old venue, this tiny indie spot books good alternative acts. Don't miss the Frank Sinatra cover night on Sunday, a local institution.

Curtain Club and Liquid Lounge (Map p78; ☎ 214-742-2336; www.curtainclub.com; 2800 Main St) Both clubs, under the same roof in Deep Ellum, are steady venues for local and national rock and roll acts.

Gilley's Dallas (Map p82; ☎ 888-445-5397; www.gilleysdallas.com; 1135 S Lamar St; ⊙ 8pm-2am Fri & Sat) Boot-scoot around the floor or ride the mechanical bull from the movie *Urban Cowboy* at this longtime country-and-western fave.

our pick **Balcony Club** (Map p78; ☎ 214-826-8104; 1825 Abrams at La Vista) This mysterious upstairs hideaway feels like a secret even though it's not. Emerald walls, a tiny stage and a cozy nook of a patio above the Landmark Theater draw all ages for nightly live music – mostly jazz – and sassy drinks like moonlight martinis and three-way tropical punch.

Poor David's Pub (Map p82; ☎ 214-565-1295; www.poordavidspub.com; 131 S Lamar St) Texas music legends Ray Wylie Hubbard, Kelly Willis, Guy Forsyth and Steve Earl have all graced the

stage at this venerable old club near Gilley's. For most shows, buy tickets at the door.

Goat (Map p78; ☎ 214-317-8119; www.myspace.com/goatblues; 7248 Gaston Ave, Lakewood; ⊙ 7am-2am Mon-Sat, noon-2am Sun) Open at the crack of dawn for those impromptu morning pub crawls, the Goat's a divey neighborhood bar with live blues four nights a week.

Trees (Map p82; ☎ 214-741-1122; www.treesdallas.com; 2709 Elm St, Deep Ellum) As the host for a lot of touring bands, this club is legendary for a 1991 incident in which Nirvana's Kurt Cobain tangled with a bouncer.

Sports

The **Dallas Cowboys** (www.dallascowboys.com) got the nickname 'America's Team' after they won three US football championships in the 1990s. Their snazzy, new, retractable-roof home, **Cowboys Stadium** (Map p75; ☎ 817-892-8687; http://stadium.dallascowboys.com; 925 N Collins St, Arlington; stadium tours adult/child $15/12; ⊙ 9am-6pm Mon-Sat, 11am-6pm Sun; ♿), opened in 2009.

The **American Airlines Center** (Map p82; ☎ 214-222-3687; www.americanairlinescenter.com; 2500 Victory Ave) in Victory Park hosts megaconcerts and is home to the **Dallas Stars** (☎ 214-467-8277; www.dallasstars.com) ice-hockey team and the **Dallas Mavericks** (☎ 214-747-6287; www.dallasmavericks.com) pro basketball team.

Classical Music & Dance

With the opening of the multibillion-dollar **AT&T Performing Arts Center** (Map p82; ☎ 214-880-0202; www.attpac.org, www.dallasperformingarts.org; 2403 Flora St) in October 2009, Dallas now has several new architecturally noteworthy performance venues.

The stunning crimson **Winspear Opera House** (Map p82; 2403 Flora St) is where the acclaimed **Dallas Opera** (☎ 214-443-1000; www.dallasopera.org) performs in a 2000-seat phenomenon of a venue.

The vertically stacked, 12-story **Wyly Theatre** (Map p82; 2400 Flora St) broke the architectural mold by challenging traditional theater designs. Worth seeing just for the building, it's the headquarters of the **Dallas Theater Center** (☎ 214-526-8210; www.dallastheatercenter.org). This is a major American regional theatre, producing classic dramas, musicals and edgy new works.

Renowned architect IM Pei designed the **Morton H Meyerson Symphony Center** (Map p82; ☎ 214-670-3600; www.meyersonsymphonycenter.com; 2301 Flora St) where the **Dallas Symphony Orchestra** (☎ 214-692-0203; www.dallassymphony.com) performs.

Theatre & Comedy

Music Hall at Fair Park (Map p78; ☎ 214-565-1116; www.liveatthemusichall.com; 909 1st Ave, Fair Park) Hosts summer performances of the Broadway blockbuster-style Dallas Summer Musicals (www.dallassummermusicals.org).

Majestic Theatre (Map p82; ☎ 214-880-0137; www.liveatthemajestic.com; 1925 Elm St) This grand old Downtown theater presents a year-round schedule of touring Broadway musicals.

Samuell-Grand Amphitheatre (Map p78; 1500 Tenison Parkway, Samuell-Grand Park) This is the setting for the summertime Shakespeare Festival of Dallas (☎ 214-559-2778, www.shakespearedallas.org), a series of free outdoor performances of the Bard's works.

Kitchen Dog Theater (Map p84; ☎ 214-953-1055; www.kitchendogtheater.org; 3120 McKinney Ave) You'll get professional theater with attitude from Kitchen Dog, in Uptown.

Backdoor Comedy (Map p78; ☎ 214-328-4444; www.backdoorcomedy.com; 8250 N Central Expressway) A short drive from downtown, at the Doubletree Hotel, this is Dallas' original stand-up comedy venue, featuring several comics each night.

SHOPPING

Have we mentioned that Dallas is a shopper's nirvana? That being said, it's easy to get lost in, well, the merchandise.

For quirky and one-of-a-kind, like vintage Fiestaware plates, funky chandeliers and DIY crafts, head to the **Bishop Arts District** (Map p78; www.bishopartsdistrict.com). Check the website for periodic festivals where local artists showcase their wares, such as the Oak Cliff Art Crawl held in April. Other good places to browse

for those seeking all things arty and antique-y include Uptown and Henderson St west of Greenville Ave, while Deep Ellum sports tattoo shops and Vespa stores abreast with design stores.

On the northern end of Uptown (at Lemmon and McKinney Aves), the **West Village** (www.westvil.com) neighborhood sports a distinctly So-Cal outdoor mall vibe with a vast collection of pricey chains and one-off boutiques. Kids will adore **Froggie's 5 & 10** (Map p84; ☎ 214-522-5867; www.froggies5and10.com; 3211 Knox St), an old-fashioned toy store with a smart-alecky edge: wash-off tattoos, retro candy, books and silly stuff.

Greenville Ave is home to one of Dallas' only indie record stores, **Good Records** (Map p78; ☎ 214-752-4663; www.goodrecords.com; 1808 Lower Greenville Ave; ☯ 10am-11pm Mon-Thu, to midnight Fri & Sat, 11am-9pm Sun). According to the store philosophy, they carry whatever's 'good.'

Mall devotees, rejoice. **NorthPark Center** (Map p78; ☎ 214-361-6345; www.northparkcenter.com; 1030 NorthPark Center, Northwest Hwy at US75) is gargantuan. The **Galleria** (Map p78; ☎ 972-702-7100; www.galleriadallas.com; 13355 Noel Rd) is a favorite with out-of-towners – maybe it's the ice-skating rink?

The finale: for an eye-rolling, gasp-inducing and credit card–maxing experience, head to Spanish Mission–style **Highland Park Village** (Map p78; ☎ 214-528-9401; www.hpvillage.com; Douglas Ave & Mockingbird Lane) in upper-crust Highland Park, which claims to be the oldest suburban shopping center in the world. If Jimmy Choo and Harry Winston are among your intimate acquaintances, you'll feel at home. If they're not, it's still worth a look around to see Dallas money in action (or just to see who wins when an Escalade and a Jaguar face off for a prime parking spot).

Clothing & Western Wear

Neiman Marcus (Map p82; ☎ 214-741-6911; www.neimanmarcus.com; 1618 Main St) A downtown landmark, this was the first Neiman Marcus store in the country.

`our pick` **Ahab Bowen** (Map p84; ☎ 214-720-1874; 2614 Boll St; ☯ 11am-6pm Mon-Sat, 1-5pm Sun) Tucked away on a leafy street in Uptown, this green cottage is bliss for vintage-lovers. You'll find an immaculate, well-curated selection of authentic but eminently wearable clothes, accessories and shoes, with cocktail dresses to coax out your inner Audrey Hepburn.

Wild Bill's Western Store (Map p82; ☎ 214-954-1050; www.wildbillswestern.com; 311 N Market, West End) Bill's motto is 'from the affordable to the extravagant,' and we like that you can grab a $15 T-shirt or blow your bonus on a pair of handmade and -measured snakeskin boots just like Eric Clapton's – he is but one of the many celebrities who've made their feet happy here. While you're here, enjoy a cold beer while you shop.

Food & Drink

Dallas Farmers Market (Map p82; ☎ 214-670-5880; www.dallasfarmersmarket.org; cnr Marilla Blvd & S Harwood St; ⏲ 7am-6pm) Buy produce directly from the growers, or shop for flowers and antiques at this multibarn market.

Whole Foods Market (Map p78; ☎ 214-824-1744; www.wholefoodsmarket.com; 2118 Abrams Rd) Feeling a bit run-down by the Big D? Haul your carcass to the juice or salad bar here.

eatZi's Market & Bakery (Map p84; ☎ 214-526-1515; www.eatzis.com; 3403 Oak Lawn Ave; ⏲ 7am-10pm) A Dallas staple, this market has a veritable bounty of every kind of prepared food you've ever dreamt about. Eat in or out.

ourpick Society Bakery (Map p78; ☎ 214-827-1411; www.societybakery.com; 3426 Greenville Ave; cupcake $2.95) Dallas' version of bakery heaven features from-scratch, all-butter cupcakes in banana chocolate chip, Italian cream and red velvet, among others.

Soda Gallery (Map p78; ☎ 214-946-7632; www.thesodagallery.com; 408 N Bishop Ave; ♿) A unique soda shop featuring old-fashioned brews, where you can curl up on a red leather sofa with a homemade ginger ale and a board game on a blistering afternoon.

GETTING THERE & AWAY

American Airlines' home port is **Dallas–Fort Worth International Airport** (DFW; Map p75; ☎ 972-973-8888; www.dfwairport.com), 16 miles northwest of the city via I-35 E. The UK and Mexico are among the nonstop international destinations. Southwest Airlines uses the smaller **Dallas Love Field Airport** (DAL; Map p75; ☎ 214-670-6073; www.dallas-lovefield.com), just northwest of downtown.

Greyhound buses make runs all over the country from the **Greyhound Bus Terminal** (Map p82; ☎ 214-655-7085; www.greyhound.com; 205 S Lamar St).

Amtrak's San Antonio–Chicago *Texas Eagle* stops at downtown's **Union Station** (Map p82; ☎ 214-653-1101; www.amtrak.com; 401 S Houston St).

GETTING AROUND
To/From the Airport

From Monday to Saturday you can ride the **Trinity Railway Express** (www.trinityrailwayexpress.org) between downtown's Union Station and the Center Port/DFW Airport stop ($2.50 one way), which is actually in a parking lot; free shuttle buses take you to the terminals. Daily, DART bus 39 ($1.50) travels between downtown's **West End Transit Station** (Map p82; 800 Pacific Ave) and Dallas Love Field, but service is limited on weekends.

It's often easiest to take a shared-ride shuttle: **SuperShuttle** (☎ 817-329-2000; www.supershuttle.com) runs from DFW or Dallas Love Field to downtown for $19. A taxi between either airport and central Dallas should cost about $40 to $50.

Every major rental-car company has an office at DFW, and many are at Dallas Love Field too.

Bus & Light Rail

Dallas Area Rapid Transit (DART; ☎ 214-979-1111; www.dart.org) operates buses and an extensive light-rail system that connects Union Station and other stops downtown with outlying areas (single trip $2.50). Day passes ($5) are available from the store at **Akard Station** (Map p82; 1401 Pacific Ave; ⏲ 7:30am-5:30pm Mon-Fri). Travel to Uptown from downtown on the free **McKinney Ave Trolley** (☎ 214-855-0006; www.mata.org; ⏲ 7am-10pm Mon-Thu, to midnight Friday, 10am-midnight Sat, to 10pm Sun), which runs from the corner of Ross Ave and St Paul St (Map p82), near the Dallas Museum of Art, and up McKinney Ave to Hall St.

Car & Motorcycle

Most major car-rental companies can be found at the airports. If you do rent a car, be warned that rush-hour freeway traffic is bad and there's little free parking downtown.

FORT WORTH

pop 653,000

Yee-haw! Oft-called 'Where the West Begins,' Fort Worth is one Texas town that still has its twang.

The place first became famous during the great open-range cattle drives of the late 19th century, when more than 10 million head of cattle tramped through the city on the

DALLAS–FORT WORTH METROPLEX

Chisholm Trail. Today you can see a mini–cattle drive in the morning and a rodeo on Saturday night.

Don't forget to scoot into Billy Bob's, the world's biggest honky-tonk. Down in the Cultural District, tour the Cowgirl Museum and others, including three amazing art collections. Then, after you've meditated on minimalism, Sundance Sq's restaurants and bars call you to the kick-up-your-heels downtown.

Whatever you do, don't mistake Fort Worth for being Dallas' sidekick. This city's got a headstrong spirit of its own, and it's a lot more user-friendly than Dallas (not to mention greener and cleaner). Bottom line? There's a lot to do here – without a whole lot of pretense.

HISTORY

Fort Worth got its start in 1849 as Camp Worth, one of a string of military forts on the Texas frontier, and later found fame during the great open-range cattle drives, which lasted from the 1860s to the 1880s. Millions of cattle trooped through the city on the Chisholm Trail. Most of the time, the herds moved on to the end of the trail in Kansas. Yet after the railroad arrived in 1873 and stockyards were established at Fort Worth, many drovers chose to end their trek here.

The late 19th century and early 20th saw rampant lawlessness in Fort Worth. Robert LeRoy Parker and Harry Longabaugh – better known as Butch Cassidy and the Sundance Kid – spent a lot of time hiding out in a part of downtown known as Hell's Half Acre, and Depression-era holdup artists Bonnie Parker and Clyde Barrow kicked around the city too.

Yet most of the mayhem in Fort Worth came not from celebrity ne'er-do-wells but from rank-and-file cowboys with too much pent-up energy from the trail. They were the ones who boozed and brawled their way down Exchange Ave, giving Fort Worth a far different image than that of Dallas.

Museums put the city on the high-culture map back in 1892 when the Kimbell became the first museum in Texas (imagine – the state itself was only 47 years old!).

Since then, the nationally renowned Cultural District continues to expand, and Sundance Sq has became one of the most

successful downtown-revitalization projects in the US. All this pretty much solidifies Fort Worth's legit claim to the somewhat paradoxical title 'City of Cowboys and Culture.'

ORIENTATION

Fort Worth is fairly compact and easy to drive around: I-30 runs east–west through downtown, and I-35 W runs to the south.

Downtown, the Cultural District and the Stockyards form a lopsided triangle. North Main St runs between downtown and the Stockyards, 7th St connects downtown to the Cultural District, and University and Northside Drs connect the Cultural District to North Main St near the Stockyards.

INFORMATION
Bookstores

Barnes & Noble Booksellers (Map p100; ☎ 817-332-7178; www.bn.com; 401 Commerce St) With few independent bookstores in town, this downtown store with its lively cafe is your best bet.

Emergency

Crisis Intervention (☎ 817-927-5544) Handles suicide prevention.
Women's Center of Tarrant County (☎ 817-927-2737) Runs a rape-crisis hotline.

Libraries

Fort Worth Public Library (Map p100; ☎ 817-871-7701; 500 W 3rd St; ☻ 10am-6pm Mon, Wed, Fri & Sat, noon-8pm Tue & Thu, 1-5pm Sun) This pretty downtown library offers free internet access and free 2½-hour garage parking; validate your ticket at the circulation desk.

Medical Services

Planned Parenthood (Map p98; ☎ 817-822-1175; www.plannedparenthood.org; 301 S Henderson St, Suite A; ☻ 8am-4pm Thu, to 3pm Fri & Sat) Sexual-health services for women.
Texas Health Harris Methodist Fort Worth Hospital (Map p98; ☎ 817-250-2000; 1301 Pennsylvania Ave) This 710-bed hospital offers emergency and women's services.

Media

Fort Worth Star-Telegram (www.star-telegram.com) The city's major daily newspaper.
FW Weekly (www.fwweekly.com) The free, local alternative paper: good listings for dining and the arts.
KFWR The Ranch plays 'The Sound of Texas' at 95.9 FM.
KTFW Country Legends at 92.1 FM.

Money

Bank of America (Map p100; ☎ 817-390-6161; 500 W 7th St; ☺ 9am-4pm Mon-Fri, drive-through 8am-6pm Mon-Fri)
Chase Bank (Map p100; ☎ 817-884-4105; www.chase.com; 420 Throckmorton St; ☺ 9am-5pm Mon-Thu, to 6pm Fri)

Post

Downtown post office (Map p98; ☎ 1-800-ASK-USPS; www.usps.com; 251 Lancaster Ave; ☺ 8:30am-6pm Mon-Fri)

Telephone

All Fort Worth numbers take either area code ☎ 817 or 682. You must dial the entire 10-digit number.

Tourist Information

Fort Worth Convention & Visitors Bureau (www.fortworth.com) Cultural District (Map p98; ☎ 817-882-8588; 3401 W Lancaster Ave; ☺ 10am-5pm Mon-Sat); Downtown (Map p100; ☎ 817-698-3300; 508 Main St; ☺ 10am-6pm Mon-Sat); Stockyards (Map p103; ☎ 817-624-4741; 130 E Exchange Ave; ☺ 9am-6pm Mon-Sat, noon-4pm Sun) The most together tourist board in the state; check out the Heritage Trails walking tours, and the giant iPhone at the downtown location.

SIGHTS

The Stockyards are cowboy central; most of the area's museums call the leafy Cultural District home.

Stockyards National Historic District

Sure, you'll spot cowboys on horseback roaming around, but wander the dusty streets of the Stockyards and you'll be soon mingling with a mix of families, bikers, curious European tourists and novelty-seeking college kids. This place puts fun first, with equal parts authentic

history and camera-ready tourism thrown into the pot.

Western-wear stores and knickknack shops, saloons and steak houses occupy the Old West–era buildings of the **Stockyards** (www.fortworthstockyards.org; Exchange Ave). Stop into the **visitor center** (Map p103; ☎ 817-625-9715; www.stockyardsstation.com/More-Information.html; 130 E Exchange Ave; ☺ 8:30am-6pm Mon-Fri, 9am-6pm Sat, 11am-5pm Sun) for info; it also offers a self-guided audio **walking tour** of the Stockyards in five languages.

First things first: don't miss the **cattle drive** (admission free; ☺ drives 11:30am & 4pm daily). While it's more surreal than spectacular, it's still interesting to watch a cowboy drive a small herd of Texas longhorns down the block in front of the visitor center. It's a goll-dang Kodak moment, pardner. For more intense rootin'-tootin' action, catch a real live **rodeo** at **Cowtown Coliseum** (Map p103; ☎ 817-625-1025; www.stockyardsrodeo.com; 121 E Exchange Ave; adult/child $15/10) at 8pm on Friday and Saturday nights year-round.

Do you know your rodeo clowns from your cowboys? Learn this important distinction at the **Texas Cowboy Hall of Fame** (Map p103; ☎ 817-626-7131; www.texascowboyhalloffame.org; 128 E Exchange Ave; adult/child/student & senior $5/3/4; ☺ 10am-6pm Mon-Thu, to 7pm Fri & Sat, 11am-5pm Sun), which features booths of medals and video footage of each cowboy inductee.

Inside the historic 1903 **Fort Worth Livestock Exchange** building, the truly curious will want to venture into a live **cattle auction** (☎ 800-422-2117; www.superiorlivestock.com) held every other Friday in a totally high-tech atmosphere: the heifers strut their stuff on flat-screen TVs and cowboy-hat-wearing ranchers make phone bids on the spot. Don't be intimidated by the

---

RODEO CLOWNS

While it sounds like a particularly cruel cowboy insult, it's an actual profession, and one of the most notoriously dangerous in the rodeo industry. A performer who works in bull-riding events, a rodeo clown's function is to protect a rider from being gored by the bull should they fall off the horse. But how? By distracting the bull, of course, which accounts for their colorful clothes. Before you decide this is the job for you, keep in mind that being a good (ie alive) rodeo clown requires serious agility, foot-speed and instinct. Sometimes the clowns jump in and out of a barrel, which offers minimal protection but requires even more agility, and sometimes the clowns entertain the crowd between events. If this all sounds similar to what a bullfighter does, you're right: 'bullfighter' is one type of rodeo clown, although some bullfighting events (notably in Spain and Latin America) also involve attempting to actually kill the bull as part of the sport.

FORT WORTH

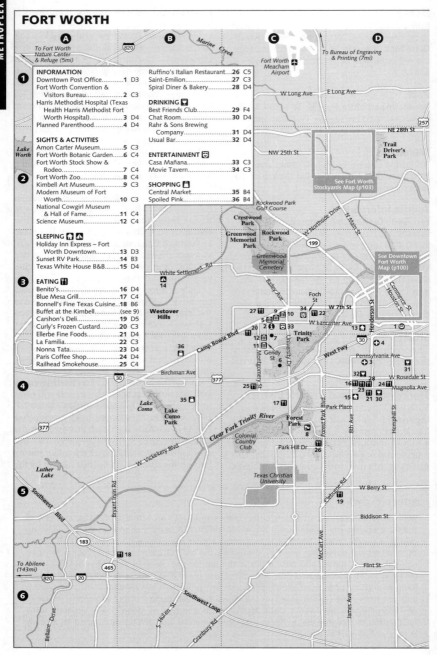

INFORMATION
Downtown Post Office............1 D3
Fort Worth Convention &
   Visitors Bureau...................2 C3
Harris Methodist Hospital (Texas
   Health Harris Methodist Fort
   Worth Hospital).................3 D4
Planned Parenthood...............4 D4

SIGHTS & ACTIVITIES
Amon Carter Museum............5 C3
Fort Worth Botanic Garden.....6 C4
Fort Worth Stock Show &
   Rodeo................................7 C3
Fort Worth Zoo......................8 C4
Kimbell Art Museum...............9 C3
Modern Museum of Fort
   Worth...............................10 C3
National Cowgirl Museum
   & Hall of Fame.................11 C4
Science Museum...................12 C4

SLEEPING
Holiday Inn Express – Fort
   Worth Downtown..............13 D3
Sunset RV Park.....................14 B3
Texas White House B&B........15 D4

EATING
Benito's................................16 D4
Blue Mesa Grill.....................17 C4
Bonnell's Fine Texas Cuisine..18 B6
Buffet at the Kimbell........(see 9)
Carshon's Deli.......................19 D5
Curly's Frozen Custard..........20 C3
Ellerbe Fine Foods.................21 D4
La Familia.............................22 C3
Nonna Tata..........................23 D4
Paris Coffee Shop.................24 D4
Railhead Smokehouse...........25 C4

Ruffino's Italian Restaurant....26 C5
Saint-Emilion........................27 C3
Spiral Diner & Bakery............28 D4

DRINKING
Best Friends Club...................29 F4
Chat Room...........................30 D4
Rahr & Sons Brewing
   Company..........................31 D4
Usual Bar.............................32 D4

ENTERTAINMENT
Casa Mañana.......................33 C3
Movie Tavern.......................34 C3

SHOPPING
Central Market......................35 B4
Spoiled Pink.........................36 B4

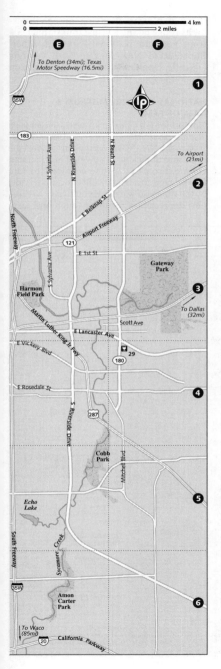

fast-talkin' auctioneer: visitors are welcome to observe. For a less interactive but no less eye-opening glimpse into cow culture, check out the unique historic artifacts at the **Stockyards Museum** (Map p103; ☎ 817-625-5082; 131 E Exchange Ave; admission free; ⏰ 10am-5pm Mon-Sat) just down the hall.

In addition to all the shops here, there and yonder, the former sheep and hog pens of **Stockyards Station** (Map p103; www.stockyardsstation. com; 140 E Exchange Ave) house a (mostly mediocre) mall of sorts. Wander from the action to find more authentic Western-themed antique shops lining **Main Street**.

Most parking lots offer $3 all-day parking, otherwise park on E Exchange Ave, or in the free lot on the northeast end of Stockyards Station.

Cultural District

Fort Worth has some of the best museums of any city in Texas. Period. In fact, some collections rival – or surpass – those at even museum-heavyweight cities Dallas and Houston. Translation? Don't skip this good stuff: it's easy to museum-hop around the parklike **Cultural District** (www.fwculture.com) on Bowie Ave, west of Downtown.

KIMBELL ART MUSEUM

Some art aficionados say this is the country's best 'small' **art museum** (Map p98; ☎ 817-332-8451; www.kimbellart.org; 3333 Camp Bowie Blvd; general admission free; ⏰ 10am-5pm Tue-Thu & Sat, noon-8pm Fri, noon-5pm Sun) while some say it's one of the unqualified best. Take your time perusing: the stunning architecture lets in natural light that allows visitors to see paintings from antiquity to the 20th century the way the artists originally intended. European masterpieces include works by Caravaggio, El Greco and Cézanne, and Michelangelo's first painting, *The Torment of St Anthony*.

MODERN MUSEUM OF FORT WORTH

Entering this **museum** (Map p98; ☎ 817-738-9215; www.themodern.org; 3200 Darnell St; adult/child/student & senior $10/free/4; ⏰ 10am-5pm Tue-Sat, 11am-5pm Sun), you round a corner from womblike, concrete galleries to be confronted by a two-story wall of glass looking out at the city skyline. One of the largest gallery spaces for modern art in the world, it houses an incredible number of provocative and mind-expanding works by luminaries such as Mark Rothko and

Picasso. Can't-miss pieces include Anselm Kiefer's *Book with Wings,* Martin Puryear's *Ladder for Booker T Washington* and Andy Warhol's eponymous *Twenty-Five Colored Marilyns.* The museum restaurant, Café Modern, is drop-dead gorgeous, seeming to float on the water of the surrounding reflecting pools.

AMON CARTER MUSEUM

Pre-1945 American art shines at this **museum** (Map p98; ☎ 817-738-1933; www.cartermuseum. org; 3501 Camp Bowie Blvd; admission free; ☺ 10am-5pm Tue-Sat, to 8pm Thu, noon-5pm Sun), including iconic works by John Singer Sargent, Winslow Homer and Alexander Calder, and an impressive collection of Western artist Frederic

Remington's work. Walking through the exhibits is like taking a visual tour of the US – from Yosemite National Park with Albert Bierstadt to New Mexico with Georgia O'Keeffe. Don't miss the amazing collection of photographs.

NATIONAL COWGIRL MUSEUM & HALL OF FAME

Not just for girls, this airy, impressive **museum** (Map p98; ☎ 817-336-4475; www.cowgirl.net; 1720 Gendy St; adult/child $10/8; ☺ 10am-5pm Tue-Sat) explores the myth and the reality of cowgirls in American culture. From rhinestone costumes to rare film footage, this is a fun and educational ride: by the time you walk out, you'll have a whole new appreciation for these tough and sassy

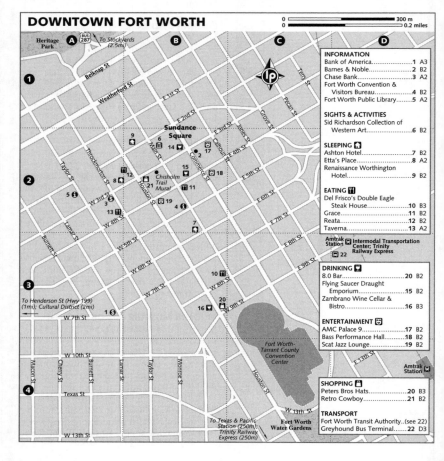

DOWNTOWN FORT WORTH

0 ————— 300 m
0 ————— 0.2 miles

INFORMATION	
Bank of America	1 A3
Barnes & Noble	2 B2
Chase Bank	3 A2
Fort Worth Convention & Visitors Bureau	4 B2
Fort Worth Public Library	5 A2

SIGHTS & ACTIVITIES	
Sid Richardson Collection of Western Art	6 B2

SLEEPING	
Ashton Hotel	7 B2
Etta's Place	8 A2
Renaissance Worthington Hotel	9 B2

EATING	
Del Frisco's Double Eagle Steak House	10 B3
Grace	11 B2
Reata	12 B2
Taverna	13 A2

Amtrak Station / Intermodal Transportation Center; Trinity Railway Express 22

DRINKING	
8.0 Bar	20 B2
Flying Saucer Draught Emporium	15 B2
Zambrano Wine Cellar & Bistro	16 B3

ENTERTAINMENT	
AMC Palace 9	17 B2
Bass Performance Hall	18 B2
Scat Jazz Lounge	19 B2

Amtrak Station

SHOPPING	
Peters Bros Hats	20 B3
Retro Cowboy	21 B2

TRANSPORT	
Fort Worth Transit Authority	(see 22)
Greyhound Bus Terminal	22 D3

ladies. If you're cowgirl enough, film yourself riding the bucking bronc.

SCIENCE MUSEUM
Kids will be all smiles in this **museum** (Map p98; ☎ 817-255-9300; www.fwmuseum.org; 1600 Gendy St; adult/child $14/10; ♿), which brims with fossils, dinosaurs and exciting stuff like a planetarium and an Omni IMAX theater.

Downtown
One of the best pedestrian downtowns in the nation? Seriously…in Texas? The point is, it's a passel of fun (and not much hassle) to hang out in the 14-block **Sundance Square** (www.sundancesquare.com), near Main and 3rd Sts. Colorful architecture, art galleries and a host of bars and restaurants make this one supremely strollable, friendly 'hood. Bonus: parking garages are free after 5pm and on weekends.

If the Stockyards didn't sate your hunger for all things Western, pop into downtown's **Sid Richardson Collection of Western Art** (Map p100; ☎ 817-332-6554; www.sidrichardsonmuseum.org; 309 Main St; admission free; ☺ 9am-5pm Mon-Thu, to 8pm Fri & Sat, noon-5pm Sun).

Elsewhere in Fort Worth
A highly regarded American zoo, the **Fort Worth Zoo** (Map p98; ☎ 817-871-7050; www.fortworthzoo. com; Forest Park off S University Dr; adult/senior & child $12/9, half-price Wed, parking $5; ☺ 10am-5pm Mon-Fri, to 6pm Sat & Sun) has about 5000 inhabitants representing 650 species, including many endangered species. Check out the Komodo dragons and the Great Barrier Reef exhibit.

A Japanese garden with a koi pond and a tropical conservatory are the highlights at the **Fort Worth Botanic Garden** (Map p98; ☎ 817-871-7686; www.fwbg.org; southwestern section, Trinity Park; admission free; conservatory adult/senior & child $1/50¢; ☺ 10am-9pm Mon-Fri, 10am-6pm Sat, 1-6pm Sun Apr-Oct, closes 4pm Sat & Sun Nov-Mar).

ACTIVITIES
Fort Worth has more than 200 **parks** (www.fort worthgov.org/pacs): you'll find ample opportunity to hike, bike, skate or stroll.

The **Trinity Trails** (www.trinitytrails.org) network of hiking, biking and equestrian trails covers 35 miles along the Trinity River, by some of Fort Worth's major parks.

The popular **Fort Worth Nature Center and Refuge** (off Map p98; ☎ 817-237-1111; www.fwnc.org;

Hwy 199; admission free; ☺ grounds 9am-5pm, visitor center 9:30am-4:30pm Tue-Sat, 12:30-4:30pm Sun, closed major holidays) has 25 miles of hiking and nature trails and an interpretive center.

FESTIVALS & EVENTS
Catch the rodeo craze with nearly a million other people at the **Fort Worth Stock Show & Rodeo** (Map p98; ☎ 817-877-2400; www.fwssr.com), which is held in January for several weeks each year at **Will Rogers Memorial Center** (1 Amon Carter Sq) in the Cultural District.

One of the Southwest's biggest arts festivals, the April **Main Street Arts Festival** (www.mainstreetartsfest.org; admission free) turns Sundance Sq into a festive epicenter of live music, juried art and food booths.

SLEEPING
Budget motels cluster near highway interchanges and along the Jacksboro Hwy (Hwy 199), northwest of downtown. You'll find decent chains along S University Dr, near the Cultural District.

Campers head to **Sunset RV Park** (Map p98; ☎ 817-258-0567; 4921 White Settlement Rd), west of downtown, for plenty of shady lots with laundry and showers.

Downtown
Holiday Inn Express – Fort Worth Downtown (Map p98; ☎ 817-698-9595; www.hiexpress.com; 1111 W Lancaster Ave; r $100-150; ▣ ▣ ☜) A retro vibe pervades the newish HI Express, just southwest of downtown. What surprising stylishness from a chain.

Texas White House B&B (Map p98; ☎ 817-923-3597; www.texaswhitehouse.com; 1417 8th St; r incl breakfast $125-235; ☒ ☜) Relax in this large, contemporary Texan-style home, convenient to downtown.

ourpick Etta's Place (Map p100; ☎ 817-255-5760; www.ettas-place.com; 200 W 3rd St; r incl breakfast from $150, ste from $185; ☒ ☜) A grand piano and a comfy library are among the cozy pleasures at this Sundance Sq hideaway that has the feel of a private Texas club. Breakfasts, like scrambled egg pizza with poblano pepper grits, can be taken on the airy patio.

Renaissance Worthington Hotel (Map p100; ☎ 817-870-1000; www.marriott.com; 200 Main St; r $150-220; ☒ ℗ ▯ ☜ ▤) Massive deep red couches, waterfalls and tropical plants lend a lush feel to this grand, Western-feel hotel where Carol Burnett and Robert Duvall have been recent guests. The athletic club's got all the bells and whistles, including a tanning deck.

Ashton Hotel (Map p100; ☎ 866-327-4860; www.theashtonhotel.com; 610 Main St; r $209-290, ste $239-300; ☒ ☜) This 39-room boutique hotel in a turn-of-the-century building off Sundance Sq offers hush-hush elegance without an ounce of snootiness. Indulge in the formal tea ($29, 2pm to 4pm Thursday to Saturday).

Stockyards

Hotel Texas (Map p103; ☎ 817-624-2224; 2415 Ellis Ave; r $89-99; ℗ ☒) This 1939 'cattleman's home away from home' is a good deal, smack in the center of the Stockyards action: simple, clean rooms decorated with framed Western art.

Miss Molly's Hotel Bed & Breakfast (Map p103; ☎ 817-626-1522; www.missmollyshotel.com; 109 W Exchange Ave; r incl breakfast $100-200, Sun-Thu $50-100; ☒) Set in the heart of the Stockyards, Miss Molly's occupies a 101-year-old house that was a bordello for 50 years. Its heavily atmospheric, almost claustrophobic vibe will feel authentic to some, eerie to others, but probably at least a little charming either way.

Stockyards Hotel (Map p103; ☎ 817-625-6427; www.stockyardshotel.com; 109 E Exchange Ave; r $189-229; ☒ ☜) First opened in 1907, this place clings to its cowboy past with Western-themed art, individual cowboyed-out rooms, a grand Old West lobby with lots of leather, and a steak house on-site. Hide out in the Bonnie and Clyde room, actually occupied by Clyde Barrow during his 1932 Fort Worth stay (the faux bullet holes and boot jacks only add to the mystique). Downstairs, you can drink a beer sitting on a real saddle at the bar.

EATING

Put on the feed bag and grab some Texas-style fixins' in Sundance Sq and in the Stockyards.

Head to West 7th and Magnolia Sts for new-fangled additions to the dining scene. PS: you're in Fort Worth – have a steak.

Downtown & West 7th

Curly's Frozen Custard (Map pp98; ☎ 817-763-8700; 4017 Camp Bowie Blvd; waffle cone $2.75) Creamy frozen custard in lemon, chocolate, sugar-free and flavor-of-the-month varieties.

La Familia (Map p98; ☎ 817-870-2002; 841 Foch St; meals $7-15; ☽ lunch & dinner Mon-Sat; ☺ Ⓥ) The kind of family-run Mexican joint that locals miss when they move away, La Familia offers gracious personal service and excellent Mexican classics. Don't skip the flaming frozen margaritas.

Taverna (Map p100; ☎ 817-885-7502; 450 Throckmorton St; meals $10-21; ☽ lunch & dinner, weekend brunch; Ⓥ) Young professionals rave about the quality pasta and the hand-tossed pizza in the bar during the lively happy hour.

Reata (Map p100; ☎ 817-336-1009; www.reata.net; 310 Houston St; lunch $9-13, dinner $16-42; ☽ lunch & dinner) The proprietors also own their own cattle ranch, so the sizable steaks are worth their weight. But you might also try the Texas specialties such as tenderloin tamales, jalapeño-cheddar grits and the $49.95 billionaire margarita made with vintage 1942 tequila.

Del Frisco's Double Eagle Steak House (Map p100; ☎ 817-877-3999; 812 Main St; steaks $22-50) The grand-daddy of Fort Worth steak houses, with a clubby atmosphere and faultless service, where steak-lovers won't mind splurging and vegetarians have been known to sin.

Grace (Map p100; ☎ 817-877-3388; 777 Main St; meals $28-49; ☽ 5:30-9:30pm Mon-Thu, to 10:30pm Fri & Sat) Yep, even modest Fort Worthians occasionally strut their stuff, and there's no better place to do it than at Grace, where local luminaries hold court (and martinis) on the couch-strewn outdoor patio. In the stunning dining room, a seasonal menu features, say, sweet-corn ravioli and diver scallops on potato cakes.

Stockyards & Around

ourpick Love Shack (Map p103; ☎ 817-740-8812; 110 E Exchange Ave; burgers $4-7; ☽ 11am-10pm Sun-Wed, to 11pm Thu, to 1am Fri & Sat) Native son and Food Network iron chef Tim Love gets accolades for his burgers (try the amore caliente) and double-thick shakes-of-the-day. A fun patio hosts live local music.

FORT WORTH STOCKYARDS

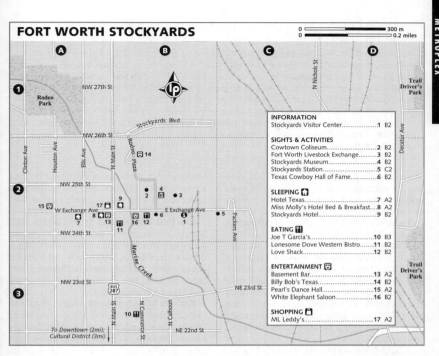

0 — 300 m
0 — 0.2 miles

INFORMATION
Stockyards Visitor Center....................1 B2

SIGHTS & ACTIVITIES
Cowtown Coliseum..........................2 B2
Fort Worth Livestock Exchange.........3 B2
Stockyards Museum...........................4 B2
Stockyards Station.............................5 C2
Texas Cowboy Hall of Fame..............6 B2

SLEEPING
Hotel Texas......................................7 A2
Miss Molly's Hotel Bed & Breakfast...8 A2
Stockyards Hotel..............................9 B2

EATING
Joe T Garcia's.................................10 B3
Lonesome Dove Western Bistro.......11 B2
Love Shack.....................................12 B2

ENTERTAINMENT
Basement Bar.................................13 A2
Billy Bob's Texas............................14 B2
Pearl's Dance Hall..........................15 A2
White Elephant Saloon....................16 B2

SHOPPING
ML Leddy's......................................17 A2

Joe T Garcia's (Map p103; ☎ 817-626-4356; 2201 N Commerce St; lunch & brunch meals $9-18; ☺ lunch & dinner daily, brunch Sat & Sun; ♿) The most famous restaurant in Fort Worth, this fourth-generation place takes up a city block. Dinners (choose between fajitas or a family-style combo plate) in the candlelit walled courtyard are magical, as Mexican-tile fountains bubble among the acres of tropical foliage. On weekends the line (no reservations!) often stretches around the block.

Lonesome Dove Western Bistro (Map p103; ☎ 817-740-8810; 2406 N Main St; dinner $24-36; ☺ lunch Tue-Sat, dinner Mon-Sat) At Tim Love's mod-Western dining experience, even the chefs wear cowboy hats. Start with a jalapeño–cucumber margarita, move on to a lamb-belly BLT or a roasted garlic-stuffed beef tenderloin, and keep your eyes peeled for a Dallas Cowboy or a country star feasting on the seared-ostrich nachos.

Magnolia Street & Around

Just walk down Magnolia and breathe in the foodie revolution.

Carshon's Deli (Map p98; ☎ 817-923-1907; 3133 Cleburne Rd; sandwich $5-9; ☺ 9am-3pm Mon-Sat)

Since 1928, Fort Worth's only kosher deli has served up classic New York sandwiches (what do you want, chopped liver?). Half the fun's in watching local movers and shakers make and break deals in between bites of corned beef on rye.

Paris Coffee Shop (Map p98; ☎ 817-335-2041; www.pariscoffeeshop.net; 700 W Magnolia Ave; lunch $4-8; ☺ 6am-3pm Mon-Fri, to 11am Sat) The venerable, Depression-era Paris is an old-school 'coffee shop,' which means it's really a diner: cheap prices, reliable classics, homemade pie and salty-tongued regulars at the counter.

Spiral Diner & Bakery (Map p98; ☎ 817-332-8633; 1314 W Magnolia Ave; meals $7-10; ☺ 11am-10pm Tue-Sat, 11am-5pm Sun; ♿ Ⓥ) One of the most inventive organic vegan restaurants in the South, this retro-feel diner actually draws sheepish meat eaters who rave about blue plate specials like a fig-and-fennel sandwich. All-you-can-eat pancakes on Sundays.

ourpick Buffet at the Kimbell (Map p98; ☎ 817-332-8451; 3333 Camp Bowie Blvd; small/large plate $8/10; ☺ lunch Tue-Sun, dinner Fri; Ⓥ) Lunching in the tranquil courtyard remains one of Cowtown's not-so-secret pleasures (and deals). Pick your

plate size, and then assemble your ideal meal
from a consistently delicious range of fresh
salads, soups, quiches and desserts. Live music
on Friday nights.

Benito's (Map p98; ☎ 817-332-8633; 1415 W Magnolia
Ave; meals $6-14; ☒ 11am-9pm Mon-Thu, to 2am Fri &
Sat, 10am-9pm Sun; ⑤) The friendly Gonzalez
family has been here for 30 years, offering a
good mix of familiar and adventurous items,
like Mexican-style pork chops and *tamal
oaxaqueno* (cornmeal baked in a banana
leaf with chicken and red mole). We like the
Spanish lesson on the menu, so you can say
'*Mas cerveza por favor*' (more beer please)
with aplomb.

our pick **Nonna Tata** (Map p98; ☎ 817-332-0250; 1400
W Magnolia Ave; lunch $9-12, dinner $13-23; ☒ 11:30am-
8pm Sun-Wed, to 11pm Thu, to 1am Fri & Sat; Ⓥ) This is
as authentic as Italian gets in Texas. Try the
gnocchi alla Romana with butter and sage,
and the fruit-laden, rustic desserts. Hope that
the elegant owner might serve you herself.
Cash only, euros accepted.

Ellerbe Fine Foods (Map p98; ☎ 817-926-3663; 1501
Magnolia Ave; lunch $10-18, dinner $21-27; ☒ lunch & dinner
Tue-Sat) Fresh, seasonal and local are the key-
words in this serene, light-filled cafe. How to
decide between Gulf shrimp and grits, green-
onion cheddar tart or scallops with spring-pea
risotto?

Saint-Emilion (Map p98; ☎ 817-737-2781; 3617 W
7th St; prix-fixe dinner $45) Perfect for capping off
a day at the museums, this quaint Cultural
District charmer serves rustic French food.
The 'menu classique' dinner includes appetizer, main and dessert; try the lamb chops
with French herbs and the fresh raspberry
tarte.

Elsewhere in Fort Worth
Railhead Smokehouse (Map p98; ☎ 817-738-9808; 2900
Montgomery St; meals $6-10) Railroad is, to some,

the legendary barbecue of Fort Worth. It's a
no-frills rustic place, where you holler your
order and in return get a big ole mess of brisket or ribs.

Blue Mesa Grill (Map p98; ☎ 817-332-6372; 1600 S
University Dr, University Park Village; meals $8-17; ☒ lunch
& dinner daily, brunch Sun) Known for its free quesa-
dillas and nachos at happy hour and fantastic
brunch, this grill and tequila bar features tasty
Santa Fe–style eats like the delish adobe pie
and blue-corn enchiladas.

Ruffino's Italian Restaurant (Map p98; ☎ 817-923-
0522; 2455 Forest Park Blvd; lunch $10-12, dinner $15-29;
☒ lunch & dinner Mon-Fri, dinner Sat, brunch Sun) A lovely
mimosa brunch and Italian classics, like egg-
plant involtini and roasted chicken *picatta*,
shine at this family-owned restaurant.

Bonnell's Fine Texas Cuisine (Map p98; ☎ 817-738-
5489; 4259 Bryant Irvin Rd; meals $10-42; ☒ lunch Tue-Fri,
dinner Tue-Sat) This is totally Texan fine dining,
featuring products from local farms and
ranches: pepper-crusted buffalo tenderloin,
'oysters Texasfeller' and a local Texas cheese
plate grace the interesting menu. Try the *tres
leches* crème brûlée.

DRINKING
8.0 Bar (Map p100; ☎ 817-336-0880; 111 E 3rd St) A large
patio and live music under the tree makes this
a favorite place to kick back.

Rahr & Sons Brewing Co (Map p98; ☎ 817-810-9266;
701 Galveston Ave, at S Main St; admission $5; ☒ tours 1pm
& 3pm Sat) Keep the pint glass after sampling
some Ugly Pug or Buffalo Butt as you burp
your way through this fun tour.

our pick **Flying Saucer Draught Emporium** (Map
p100; ☎ 817-336-7470; 111 E 4th St; ☒ 11am-1am Mon-
Wed, to 2am Thu-Sat, noon-midnight Sun) You definitely won't go thirsty: the bar inside this old
brick building is made for craft-beer-lovers
(80 brews on tap). How can you not love a
bar whose jam-packed patio is called 'Half-

Acre Hell?' The waitresses slinging beers in Catholic-schoolgirl outfits are kinda weird, but hey, this is a funky old place that flips the bird to political correctness – if the old-fashioned cigarette machine is any indication.

Zambrano Wine Cellar & Bistro (Map p100; ☎ 817-850-9463; 910 Houston St; ✆ 5-10pm Mon-Thu, to midnight Fri & Sat) With 50 wines by the glass that change bimonthly, this modern wine bar – all velvet curtains, amethyst colors and candlelight – is approachably appealing.

The **Usual Bar** (Map p98; ☎ 817-810-0114; 1408 W Magnolia Ave; admission $5; ✆ nightly) serves up debonair drinks like 'Jimador's revenge' and 'taxation & representation', so you know the retro craft-cocktail craze has come to Fort Worth. Its low-key bar, the **Chat Room** (☎ 817-922-8319; 1263 W Magnolia Ave; ✆ nightly; 🛜), has cheaper drinks, a great jukebox and free computers for surfing just down the street.

ENTERTAINMENT
Toward the weekend, you'll hear live country music wafting from the Stockyards District. Sundance Sq kicks a more diverse beat.

Live Music
our pick **Pearls Dance Hall** (Map p103; ☎ 817-624-2800; www.pearlsdancehall.com; 302 W Exchange Ave) On the edge of the stockyards, this raucous old brothel once owned by Buffalo Bill Cody is an atmospheric place to hear traditional country music with an edge. Texas luminaries like Dale Watson are known to rock out here.

Basement Bar (Map p103; ☎ 817-458-1803; www.lolasfortworth.com; 105 W Exchange St; ✆ 3pm-2am) This dark, intimate bar tucked underneath the Stockyards hosts eclectic local music. Pluses: it's usually all-ages, and there's free parking.

Scat Jazz Lounge (Map p100; ☎ 817-870-9100; www.scatjazzlounge.com; 111 W 4th; ✆ 5pm-2am Tue-Fri, from 6pm Sat, 7pm-1am Sun) Tucked into an alley, this subterranean jazz spot is low-key, with just a touch of smoky glamour.

White Elephant Saloon (Map p103; ☎ 817-624-8273; www.whiteelephantsaloon.com; 106 E Exchange Ave; ✆ 2pm-midnight Mon-Thu, to 2am Fri, noon-2am Sat, noon-midnight Sun) Stockyards cowboys have been belly-ing up to this raucous bar since 1887. Local songwriters, along with the likes of Jimmie Dale Gilmore and Ray Wylie Hubbard, play nightly.

Cinemas
AMC Palace 9 Theater (Map p100; ☎ 1-888-AMC-FUN; www.amc.com; 220 E Third) Downtown.

Movie Tavern (Map p98; ☎ 682-503-8101; www.movietavern.com; 2872 Crockett St) Munch on panini and sip on drinks like the 'matrix mojito' while you watch first-run films.

Theater & Performing Arts
The stunning, acoustically dazzling **Bass Performance Hall** (Map p100; ☎ 817-212-4280; www.basshall.com; 525 Commerce St) recalls a classic European opera house, with over 2000 seats beneath a dome of painted sky. Along with touring artists, it's also home to the **Fort Worth Symphony** (☎ 817-665-6000; www.fwsymphony.org), the **Fort Worth Opera** (☎ 817-731-0726; www.fwopera.org) and the **Texas Ballet** (☎ 817-763-0207; www.texasballettheater.org), plus plenty of touring shows.

In the Cultural District, **Casa Mañana** (Map p98; ☎ 817-332-2272; www.casamanana.org; 3101 W Lancaster Ave) presents high-quality Broadway musicals and children's theater.

SHOPPING
As you drive down Camp Bowie Blvd toward the Cultural District, don't be put off by the endless strip malls (c'mon, it's Texas after all!) –

BILLY BOB'S TEXAS
The 100,000-sq-ft building that is now the world's largest honky-tonk, called **Billy Bob's** (Map p103; ☎ 817-624-7117; www.billybobstexas.com; 2520 Rodeo Plaza, Stockyards; ✆ 11am-2am Mon-Sat, noon-2am Sun), was once a barn housing prize cattle during the Fort Worth Stock Show. After the stock show moved to the Will Rogers Memorial Center, the barn became a department store so big that the stock keepers wore roller skates.

Now Billy Bob's can hold more than 6000 people and has 40 bars to serve the thirsty masses. The most bottled beer sold in one night was 16,000 bottles, during a 1985 Hank Williams Jr concert. Top country-and-western stars, house bands and country DJs play on two stages. On Friday and Saturday nights a live bull-riding competition takes place at an indoor arena. Pool tables and games help make this a family place; under 18s are welcome with a parent.

behind their nondescript facades you'll find good local boutiques. Head to the Stockyards for Western gear and antiques.

Central Market (Map p98; ☎ 817-377-9307; www. centralmarket.com; 4651 W Fwy; ☺ 8am-10pm) This hey-it's-actually-fun-to-shop-here supermarket features a coffee and gelato bar, great to-go salads and a sprawling patio with a kids' playground.

ML Leddy's (Map p103; ☎ 888-565-2668; www.led dys.com; 2455 N Main St, Stockyards) Ah, that smell of leather that unmistakably says 'new boots.' Check out the bank ledgers, which contain the foot measurements of rock stars and presidents. If you still don't feel like kicking up your heels, the selection of hats, buckles and clothes might fit the bill.

our pick **Spoiled Pink** (Map p98; ☎ 817-737-7465; www.spoiledpink.com; 4824 Camp Bowie Blvd; ☺ 10am-6pm Mon-Sat) It's girls gone wild, but in a good way: fancy tank tops, high heels, jeans and jewelry, all locally owned and diva-worthy. Check out the outrageous martini glasses in back.

Peters Bros Hats (Map p100; ☎ 817-335-1715; www. pbhats.com; 909 Houston St) Get your Stetson on at this downtown hat shop, in business since 1911.

Retro Cowboy (Map p100; ☎ 817-338-1194; 410 Houston St) Cool cowboy-themed stuff that screams 'perfect Fort Worth souvenir!' for even skeptical Yankees.

GETTING THERE & AWAY

Most visitors to Fort Worth arrive at DFW International Airport (Map p75), 17 miles east of Fort Worth.

The *Texas Eagle* stops at the **Amtrak Station** (Map p100; ☎ 817-882-9762; www.amtrak.com; 1001 Jones St) en route to San Antonio or Chicago.

Monday to Saturday the **Trinity Railway Express** (TRE; off Map p100; ☎ 817-215-8600; www.trinity railwayexpress.org; T&P Station, 1600 Throckmorton St) connects downtown Fort Worth with downtown Dallas ($3.75, 1¼ hours).

Several buses a day make the one-hour trip from the downtown Fort Worth **Greyhound Bus Terminal** (Map p100; ☎ 817-429-3089; www.greyhound. com; 901 Commerce St) to Dallas.

GETTING AROUND

Fort Worth's coolest transportation option is **Molly the Trolley** (☎ 817-215-8600; www.mollythe trolley.com), a vintage trolley system that serves passengers traveling around downtown (free,

10am to 10pm) or between downtown and the Stockyards ($1.50, 9am to 10:30pm Saturday).

The **Fort Worth Transit Authority** (The T; Map p100; ☎ 817-215-8600; www.the-t.com) runs bus 1N to the Stockyards and bus 2W to the Cultural District, departing from the Intermodal Transportation Center (ITC) at Jones and 9th Sts. The single fare is $1.50.

BEYOND DALLAS–FORT WORTH

Can't decide which small town to visit outside of the Metroplex? Check out the **Texas Highways** (www.texashighways.com) listings to find one that suits you.

ARLINGTON
pop 367,197
Six Flags over Texas
The oldest of the Six Flags franchise and 20 minutes' drive from the downtowns of Dallas and Fort Worth, this **amusement park** (Map p75; ☎ 817-530-6000; www.sixflags.com; I-30 & Hwy 360; 1-day tickets adult/child under 48 inches $52/33, season pass $70, parking $15; ♿) can be either a blast or a wretched drag – it all depends on whether or not the place is supercrowded when you go. Roller coasters rule: there are 13 of them, including two of the old-fashioned (wooden) kind.

Keep things simple by stowing valuables and bags in lockers at the entry mall just inside the park gate, where strollers, and wheelchairs can also be rented. Even pets can be boarded for $10 a day. In the children's section, Looney Tunes Land, you'll find a baby-care and nursing center. ATMs throughout the park mean you can access cash whenever the urge for another funnel cake or foot-long corn dog strikes. Finally, remember that height restrictions vary per ride and may be anywhere from 42in to 54in; to avoid crestfallen looks and disappointment, check before you get in line.

Plan to hit the most popular rides either first thing in the morning or in the evening, when lines are shortest. Aside from the mighty, scream-inducing roller coasters such as Batman the Ride, Mr Freeze, and Shock Wave (once the world's tallest coaster), other reliable thrills include the adrenaline-charged Superman: Tower of Power, which shoots brave souls up into the sky at 45mph (cape not included) and La Vibora, a bob-sled ride that gives riders a fun taste of the Olympic sport. Coaster addicts should watch for the return of the legendary Texas Giant in 2011, which promises to be a thrilling ride: Six Flags brags that it'll have the steepest drop (79 degrees!) of any wooden coaster in the world.

Six Flags Hurricane Harbor

Across I-30 from Six Flags you can get soaked at **Six Flags Hurricane Harbor** (Map p75; ☎ 817-265-3356; adult/senior & child under 48in $26/20, parking $10; ⏰ 10:30am-7pm or 8pm late May–mid-Aug, to 6pm weekends mid-Aug–early Sep), an over-the-top water park with a good mix of thrills-and-chills and family-friendly rides. The adventurous can surf at the Surf Rider, free-fall six stories on the Geronimo, or brave the dubiously named Mega Wedgie (no explanation needed). Of course, nothing beats just chilling out in the Surf Lagoon (a pool with 4ft-high waves) or gliding on an inner tube down the Lazy River. For kids, the Hook's Lagoon Treehouse is loads of fun.

Rangers Ballpark

From April to October, the **Texas Rangers** (☎ 972-726-4377; www.rangers.mlb.com; tickets $6-215) play at the old-fashioned **Rangers Ballpark** (Map p75; ☎ 817-273-5222; access from I-30 via exits 28 or 30), which features replicas of the Fenway Park scoreboard and the right-field home-run porch from Tiger Stadium. Guided **stadium tours** (☎ 817-273-5098; adult/youth/student & senior $10/5/8; ⏰ off-season 9am-4pm on the hour Mon-Sat, on-season 9am-4pm on the hour Mon-Sat, from 11am Sun) are better off-season: they include a peek into the ballplayers' inner sanctum.

WACO
pop 121,496

No, it's not Wacko – it's Waco. Don't feel bad if you associate this unassuming town with its unlucky past: it's probably best known for the infamous 'Waco Siege' (see the boxed text, p110) that didn't even take place here. While lacking any major thrills, this is a pleasant little city with a few fun museums (Dr Pepper, anyone?). Waco is home to the biggest Baptist university on earth (the well-

respected Baylor University) and college legend claims that students can ostensibly attend a different-area Baptist church every weekend during their four years. (It's true – there are a whopping 97 of them.) Churchgoing aside, the bars are packed full of friendly residents and students who will quickly convince you that Waco's probably a little cooler than you realized.

Information

Bank of America (☎ 254-750-6000; 514 Austin Ave) Drive-in tellers and ATMs.

Barnes & Noble (☎ 254-741-9495; www.barnesandnoble.com; 4909 W Waco Dr; ⏰ 11am-10pm Mon-Sat, to 9pm Sun) This chain outlet is in the Circuit City Plaza, southwest of downtown.

Hillcrest Baptist Medical Center (☎ 254-202-2000; www.hillcrest.net; 100 Hillcrest Medical Blvd) Southwest of downtown, where Hwy 6 and I-35 meet.

Waco Convention and Visitors Bureau's office (☎ 254-750-5810; www.wacocvb.com; 100 Washington Ave) Lots of brochures; for face-to-face advice, the Tourist Information Center is your best bet.

Waco Post Office (☎ 254-754-4188; 424 Clay Ave)

Waco Tourist Information Center (☎ 254-750-8696, 800-922-6386; www.wacocvb.com; ⏰ 8am-5pm Mon-Sat, 9am-5pm Sun, closed major holidays) At the western end of Fort Fisher Park, off University Parks Dr. There's free coffee, and the friendly staff will help with hotel reservations and other advice.

Waco Tribune-Herald (www.wacotrib.com) The local daily; read it online or purchase the hard copy for 59¢ ($1.69 Sunday). NPR is on KWBU at 103.3 FM.

Waco-McLennan County Library (☎ 254-750-5941; www.waco-texas.com/cms-library; 1717 Austin Ave; ⏰ 10am-9pm Mon-Thu, 10am-6pm Fri & Sat, 1-5pm Sun) Free wi-fi, plus several internet-connected computers available.

DETOUR: GRAPEVINE

Although it's right next to DFW International Airport, **Grapevine** (Map p75; www.grapevinetexasusa.com) is as quaint a town as you'll find in the Metroplex. Its classic Main St oozes history and charm, and begs a stroll. Almost as big as Minnesota's Mall of America, the **Grapevine Mills Shopping Center** (☎ 972-724-4900; www.grapevinemills.com) is a big draw with tons of stores and restaurants and a whopping 30-screen movie theater.

FUNKIEST LITTLE TOWNS OUTSIDE THE METROPLEX

What? There's more to life in this part of Texas than shopping malls, suburbs and big-name attractions? Yes.

- A bastion of college cool and indie cred, **Denton** has a great **music scene** (www.mydenton music.com). Rock out at **Dan's Silver Leaf** (☎ 940-320-2000; www.danssilverleaf.com; 103 Industrial St) or two-step with gay cowboys at perhaps the best-named bar in Texas, **Mable Peabody's Beauty Parlor and Chain Saw Repair** (☎ 940-566-9910; www.mablepeabodys.com; 1125 E University).

- Architecture fans dig south-of-Dallas **Waxahachie** (☎ 972-937-2390; www.waxahachiechamber. com) for its Victorian, Greek Revival and Queen Anne architecture.

- Bikers had great advice for us about pit stops, and we took it. They sent us to tiny **Edom** (www.edomtexas.com) to the **Shed Café** (☎ 940-566-9910; 8337 FM 279; ⏰ 7am-8pm). Yep, it's the perfect break between Dallas and east Texas, with stellar chicken-fried steak and coconut-cream pie.

- West of Waco, **Crawford** (off Map p75) has become synonymous with ex-president George W Bush, whose **ranch** is about 8 miles from town. Just keep in mind that there's really nothing to see – and that the Secret Service doesn't look kindly on parked cars outside the ranch (don't even *think* about trespassing).

- Czech it out: stopping for kolaches off I-35 at the **Czech Stop** is a ritual for many on the drive between Dallas and Austin. It's in historic **West** (off Map p75), the Czech Heritage Capital of Texas.

Dangers & Annoyances

You'll find Waco city streets – excepting the Baylor campus – fairly deserted by nightfall. Exercise caution crossing the I-35 underpass on foot, and avoid Cameron Park after dusk.

Sights & Activities

Spend the morning checking out Waco's unique museums, and then take a leisurely stroll through Cameron Park. Bicycle enthusiasts should consider taking advantage of the great rides in the area – see the **Waco Bicycle Club** (www.wacobicycleclub.com) for information on trails.

Make sure to visit the stately 475ft pedestrian-only **Waco Suspension Bridge**, built from 1868 to 1870 and the first to cross the Brazos.

ARMSTRONG BROWNING LIBRARY

On the Baylor campus, this peaceful refuge of a **museum** (☎ 254-710-3566; www.browninglibrary. org; 710 Speight Ave; admission free; ⏰ 9am-5pm Mon-Fri, 10am-2pm Sat) houses a beautiful collection of stained glass, as well as the world's largest collection of original manuscripts and personal effects of the romantic English poets Robert and Elizabeth Barrett Browning. Don't miss the 'sunrise-sunset' windows in the gorgeous Foyer of Meditation.

DR PEPPER MUSEUM

The Dr Pepper soft drink was invented by Waco pharmacist Charles C Alderton in 1885. This **museum** (☎ 254-757-1025; www.drpeppermuseum. com; 300 S 5th St; adult/student/senior $7/3/5; ⏰ 10am-4:15pm Mon-Sat, noon-4:15pm Sun, noon-6pm summer) celebrates his creation.

Don't miss the soda fountain (admission free) where the soda jerk behind the counter will shoot you a cold Dr Pepper or an ice-cream soda the old-fashioned way, with syrup and charged water.

CAMERON PARK & ZOO

Hills, limestone cliffs and 20 miles of trails make this park a great place for hiking and mountain biking. Kiss your paramour – or just bitterly contemplate your breakup – at the clifftop, rather morbidly named Lovers' Leap.

At the eastern end of the park, the **Cameron Park Zoo** (☎ 254-750-8400; 1701 N 4th St; adult/4-12yr/senior $9/6/8; ⏰ 9am-5pm Mon-Sat, 11am-5pm Sun; ♿) features 52 acres of natural habitat. A Texas section with about 30 native species balances an impressive range of African animals, including elephants, white rhinos and giraffes.

OTHER ATTRACTIONS

In 1978, two Waco arrowhead hunters found a bone in a ravine. Not just any bone – it turned out to belong to a Columbian mammoth that had perished there about 68,000 years ago. Now open to the public, the **Waco Mammoth Site** (☎ 254-750-7946; www.wacomammoth. com; 6220 Steinbeck Bend Rd; adult/4-12yr/senior $7/5/6; ☼ 11am-5pm Tue-Fri, 9am-5pm Sat) features, after 30 years of excavation, the nation's only recorded discovery of a herd of Pleistocene mammoths.

All manner of Texas sports legends are saluted at the **Texas Sports Hall of Fame and Museum** (☎ 254-756-1633; www.tshof.org; 1108 S University Parks Dr; adult/student/senior $7/3/6; ☼ 9am-5pm Mon-Sat, noon-5pm Sun).

As one museum fan told us upon exiting the **Texas Ranger Museum and Hall of Fame** (☎ 254-750-8631; www.texasranger.org; Fort Fisher Park; adult/child $6/3; ☼ 9am-5pm), 'I could spend five hours here just salivating over the guns and knives.' Explore the history of the notorious Rangers, from their early-19th-century origins through their days fighting cattle rustlers, Indians and Mexicans, to the Rangers' present-day role as Texas' most elite state police unit.

Sleeping

Rooms get scarce during Baylor University events. You'll find plenty of chain motels and hotels off I-35.

Best Western Old Main Lodge (☎ 254-753-0316; fax 254-753-3811; I-35 & S 4th St; r incl breakfast $60-100; Ⓟ ⊠ 🛜 🛋) Adjacent to the Baylor campus, on the Baylor side of I-35, this hotel is a surprisingly good deal. We dig the English-hunting-lodge decor, the courtyard pool and the free breakfast.

Judge Baylor House B&B (☎ 254-756-0273, 888-522-9567; www.judgebaylorhouse.com; 908 Speight Ave; r incl breakfast $87-120; Ⓟ ⊠ 🛜) On a quiet residential street next to Baylor, this relaxing B&B has four rooms and one suite. Friendly innkeepers Bruce and Dorothy Dyer serve healthy breakfast fare like yogurt and granola.

Cotton Palace Bed & Breakfast (☎ 254-753-7294; www.thecottonpalace.com; 1910 Austin Ave; r incl breakfast $120-150; Ⓟ ⊠ 🛜) Find big breakfasts (think crème-brûlée French toast) and a lovely sun porch at this grand old Arts and Crafts–style house.

ourpick Livingston at Heritage Square (☎ 254-722-5721; www.the-livingston.com; 330 Austin Ave; ste $169-255; Ⓟ ⊠ 🛜) Mod luxury and great amenities (i-Pod docking stations, full kitchens, gourmet coffee, washer-dryers, HDTVs) are the standard in these downtown suites. Owner Mary Baskin's style (she's an interior designer) comes through in the details. The poshest place in town, yet totally down to earth.

Eating

Waco's restaurant scene in three words: tasty, cheap and lively. The **Shops of River Square Center** (☎ 254-757-0921; www.shopsofriversquarecenter. com; Franklin Ave & S 2nd St; ☼ 10am-6pm Mon-Sat, noon-5pm Sun), an area of converted warehouses near downtown, is a good bet for lively dining, drinking and shopping.

ourpick Lolita's (☎ 254-755-7301; 1911 Franklin Ave; meals $3-9; ☼ breakfast & lunch, closed Mon) Lolita's exudes that family-run, small-town spirit that can't be manufactured. We love the all-day breakfasts – tacos, *huevos rancheros, migas* (a signature Texas dish: think eggs scrambled with corn tortillas, onions, tomatoes, peppers and often cheese) and the 'elephante', a massive breakfast burrito with six fillings. Locals swear by the fresh salsa and queso.

Vitek's BBQ (☎ 254-752-7591; 1600 Speight Ave; meals $4-11; ☼ 10:30am-6pm Tue-Fri, 11am-4pm Sat) Since 1915, Vitek's has drawn the hungry crowds for takeout orders in its combo restaurant–store. Whatever your carnivorous pleasure, it's all homemade and excellent. Big appetite? Order the legendary Gut Pak, a monster of a sandwich with Fritos, cheese, chopped beef, beans, sausage, pickles, onions and jalapeños.

simply good eatery (☎ 254-754-1555; 213 Mary Ave; meals $5-8; ☼ lunch Mon-Fri) Vegetarians and salad cravers should head to this spacious cafe on

---

WHAT THE...? SKYSCRAPER

No, that's not the set of a postapocalyptic sci-fi film: that's Waco's skyline. The view of Waco from I-35 has long puzzled many freeway passersby unfamiliar with Waco. The historic 22-story **Alico Building** towers above the rest of the flat downtown grid and can be seen from miles away. After a 1954 tornado wiped out most of the other buildings in downtown, this building – the first skyscraper west of the Mississippi – was left standing all by its lonesome. Aw, shucks.

STANDOFF

The Branch Davidians were an offshoot of a radical sect of Seventh Day Adventists. The original group, the Davidians, set up shop in Waco in 1935 but moved outside the city in 1959 to establish a compound called New Mt Carmel, near the town of Elk. Fighting between internal factions led to splits and drama, and in 1987 Vernon Howell, who had joined the group in 1981, took control and changed his name to David Koresh.

Koresh's platform involved, among other things, arming the compound to defend it against the apocalyptic nightmare the world would become after the second coming of Christ. Believing that Koresh was buying, selling and storing illegal weapons, the federal Bureau of Alcohol, Tobacco and Firearms (ATF) staged a shamefully understaffed, poorly planned raid, rife with decisions that a 1993 US Treasury report deemed 'tragically wrong.' The agents were fired on; four ATF agents and five cult members were killed in the ensuing firefight. The resulting standoff lasted 51 days.

As local authorities and FBI hostage negotiators surrounded the compound with hundreds of police cars and even a tank, the international media had a field day; viewers around the world were treated to images of the dead ATF agents and the standoff, as well as interviews with officers from a host of government agencies.

The standoff ended on April 19, 1993, when officers fired tear gas bombs into the compound. Within hours, the buildings were completely engulfed in flames fueled by the tear gas canisters' ignition. Nine cult members survived; of the dead, most were found to have been shot, perhaps by Branch Davidian members themselves. The government's handling of the incident is still the subject of controversy. For more information on the siege, including interviews and photos, check out PBS's fascinating site, www.pbs.org/wgbh/pages/frontline/waco.

What's left of the former Branch Davidian compound stands 14.5 miles east of Waco. A trickle of visitors still makes its way here each year, some out of curiosity, others – including law-enforcement buffs, conspiracy theorists and antigovernment sympathizers – on something of a pilgrimage.

The Waco Tourist Information Center (p108) can provide free maps to the compound for the irrepressibly curious. Exercise discretion.

the 2nd floor of River Square Center. The lunch special, with a daily main, side, dessert and drink, is a steal at $5.

Kitok Restaurant (☎ 254-754-8008; 1815 N 18th St; meals $4-15; ◷ 11am-8pm Tue-Sat) Since 1975, this lovable dive has gained a loyal following for its fusion of greasy spoon and Korean food. The 'lip locker' double meat burger ($3.99) has been written up in the *New York Times*. Yeah, it's that good. Try the addictive oriental fries.

Diamond Back's Restaurant & Bar (☎ 254-757-2871; 217 Mary Ave; dinner $16-31) Best happy hour in Waco? Hands-down. Professionals and students alike flock here for tasty 'Texas-bistro' meals in a stylish, fun environment.

Drinking

The college kids may be mostly Baptist, but Waco's a drinkin' town nonetheless.

Common Grounds (☎ 254-757-2957; 1123 S 8th St; ◷ 7am-11pm, from 9am Sun; ☎) Tucked across from the Baylor University campus, this feel-good coffeehouse packs in students, professors and everyone else with live music, light

meals and a killer outdoor patio. We dig the rustic cabin feel and the 'sleep is overrated' espresso drinks like the quadruple shot 'nervous breakdown'.

Cricket's Grill (☎ 254-754-4677; 221 Mary Ave; sandwiches $6-8, pizza $7-12; ◷ 11am-2am) A cavernous beer hall with fine pizzas, lots of beers on tap and tons of games, including darts, pool and shuffleboard.

our pick Dancing Bear (☎ 254-753-0025; 1117 Speight Ave; ◷ 5pm-midnight Sun-Fri, 4pm-1am Sat) A few blocks from the Baylor campus, you'll find 16 microbrewery selections on tap, along with helpful advice and beer samples for neophytes and connoisseurs alike. A hundred bottles of craft beers, including the Southern Star Bombshell Blonde, promise to drown the most pesky of troubles.

George's 0 (☎ 254-753-1421; 1925 Speight Ave; meals $6-15; ◷ 6:30am-midnight Mon-Sat) Ah, the legendary home of the big O. What's that you say? Well, it's an 18oz beer (or margarita, if you prefer) in a round, O-shaped glass. Sit at 'The Table of Knowledge' and order the 'crazy wings' (chicken, cheese and jalapeños, wrapped in bacon and deep fried) to help wash down the beer – everyone else at this all-ages party does.

Getting There & Around

Waco is easy to reach by car: it's right on I-35, about halfway between the Dallas–Fort Worth Metroplex and Austin and nearly two hours from both. There are about seven

Greyhound (☎ 254-753-4534; www.greyhound.com; 301 S 8th St) buses a day ($23, 1¾ hours) between Dallas and Waco.

Local buses are run by **Waco Transit** (☎ 254-753-0113; www.waco-texas.com/bus.htm). Rides cost $1.50, and run weekdays until 7:30pm and Saturdays until 8:15pm. Taxi service is available from **Yellow Cab** (☎ 254-756-1861); for town car and airport shuttle service, use **Waco Streak** (☎ 254-772-0430; www.waco-streak.com).

Austin

You'll see it on bumper stickers and T-shirts throughout the city: 'Keep Austin Weird.' And while old-timers grumble that Austin has lost its funky charm, the city has still managed to hang on to its incredibly laid-back vibe. Though this former college town with a hippie soul has seen an influx of tech types and movie stars, it's still a town of artists with day jobs, where people try to focus on their music or write their novel or annoy their neighbors with crazy yard art.

Along the freeway and in the 'burbs, big-box stores and chain restaurants have proliferated at an alarming rate. But the neighborhoods still have an authentically Austin feel, with all sorts of interesting, locally owned businesses, including a flock of food trailers – a symbol of the low-key entrepreneurialism that represents Austin at its best.

The one thing everyone seems to know about Austin whether they've been there or not is that it's a music town, even if they don't actually use the words 'Live Music Capital of the World' (though that's a claim no one's disputing). The city now hosts two major music festivals, South by Southwest and the Austin City Limits festival, but you don't have to endure the crowds and exorbitant hotel prices to experience the scene, because Austin has live music all over town every night of the week.

HIGHLIGHTS

Coolest Place to Chill Out
When the heat is too much, jump into the icy waters of Barton Springs Pool (p123) for instant relief

Oddest Store Selection
Booth after booth of oddities, treasures, memorabilia and tchotchkes invite browsing at Uncommon Objects (p140)

Tastiest Margarita
Frozen or on the rocks, plain or with a sangria swirl, the margaritas at Trudy's Texas Star (p132) are practically perfect

Tallest State Capitol
It's not just the tallest one in town; the Texas State Capitol (p117) is the tallest in the USA

Best Place for Dinner and a Movie
Alamo Drafthouse Cinema (p137), because you can get them both in the same place

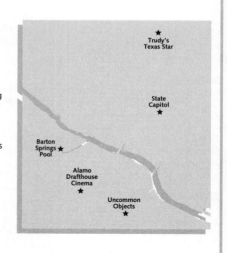

ORIENTATION

Austin is bordered by highways. The main thoroughfare is I-35, running all the way from Dallas to the north, through the east side of downtown, and south to San Antonio. The other major north–south route is MoPac Expressway (locals just call it 'MoPac') on the west edge of town. Lamar Blvd runs parallel between the two and is a handy way to get around town. What most folks consider 'in town' is bounded by Hwy 183 to the north and Hwy 290 (also known as 'Ben White Blvd') to the south.

The destinations most favored by visitors are downtown, South Congress and the University of Texas area. Sprawling East Austin, on the opposite side of I-35 from downtown, is comprised of historically African American and Spanish-speaking neighborhoods. Other outlying areas of the city also take commonsense geographical designations, such as West Austin (west of MoPac) and Westlake (by Lake Austin). Austin-Bergstrom International Airport is 8 miles southeast of downtown near the junction of Hwys 183 and 71 (E Ben White Blvd).

Downtown

Downtown Austin is an orderly grid. The main north–south artery is Congress Ave, with Cesar Chavez St running east–west. Most downtown streets are one way, including 6th St, a major westbound thoroughfare, and southbound Guadalupe St (pronounced *guad*-ah-*loop* locally, despite what you might have learned in Spanish class). Downtown is chock-full of entertainment options, including the bars of 6th St, music venues on Red River, and the more upscale Warehouse District.

South Congress

South of downtown and Lady Bird Lake, South Congress is an offbeat and oh-so-Austin neighborhood that was pretty marginal just 25 or so years ago. Tourism types nicknamed it SoCo, which has somewhat stuck, but the locals mostly still call it South Congress. S Congress Ave is the main thoroughfare and the epicenter of the action; most of the rest is residential.

UT & Hyde Park

The University of Texas cuts a huge swath of land through the area north of downtown, beyond Martin Luther King Jr Blvd and west of I-35. Where Guadalupe St borders the campus, it's called the Drag. Hyde Park, a

DRIVING DISTANCES
Austin to Dallas 200 miles, 3½ hours
Austin to Fredericksburg 80 miles, 1 hour and 40 minutes
Austin to Gruene 45 miles, 55 minutes
Austin to Lockhart 30 miles, 40 minutes
Austin to San Antonio 80 miles, 1 hour and 20 minutes

century-old enclave noted for its architecture, lies just northeast in the alphabet avenues found between Guadalupe and Red River Sts, roughly north of 38th St.

Maps

Available at visitors centers (p116), the color tear sheet *Downtown Austin* map will help you get around the city center, especially since it shows CapMetro's free 'Dillo shuttle-bus routes. The glossy foldout *Austin Street Map & Guide* gives much wider coverage of the entire city and outlying districts, with a detailed street index. *Streetwise Austin* is relatively accurate and very easy to carry in its five-fold laminated pocket-size edition.

INFORMATION

The bulletin boards found outside coffeehouses, cafes and grocery stores are a great source of news about local events, special activities and classified ads.

Bookstores

BookPeople (Map p118; ☎ 512-472-5050, 800-853-9757; www.bookpeople.com; 603 N Lamar Blvd; 9am-11pm daily) Get your maps and 'Keep Austin Weird' T-shirts at Texas' biggest and best independent bookstore.
Half Price Books, Records & Magazines (Map p114; ☎ 512-451-4463; www.halfpricebooks.com; 5555 N Lamar; 9am-10pm Mon-Sat, 10am-9pm Sun) A broad selection of excellent new and used books, with multiple locations around town.
MonkeyWrench Books (Map p114; ☎ 512-407-6925; 110 E North Loop Blvd; 11am-8pm Mon-Fri, noon-8pm Sat & Sun) A radical bookstore and community events space. Punk 'zines, feminist treatises and political bumper stickers are sold by the world's friendliest anarchists.

Emergency

Emergency (☎ 911)
Emergency Animal Hospital & Clinic (☎ 512-899-0955, South Austin; ☎ 512-331-6121, Northwest Austin)
Police (☎ 311 or ☎ 512-974-5000)

AUSTIN

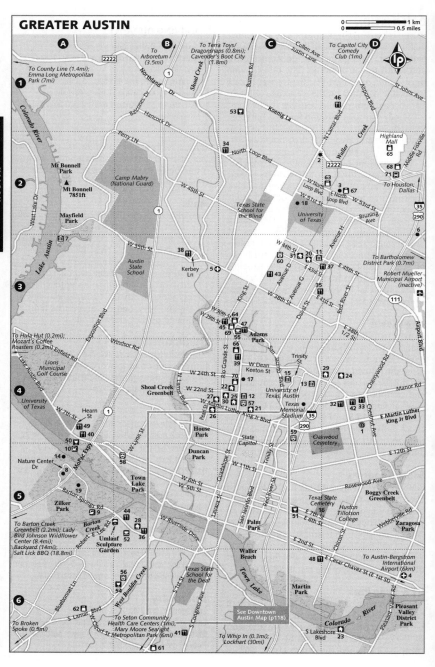

GREATER AUSTIN

Internet Access

Free public internet access is available at any public library branch; call ☎ 512-974-7301 for hours and locations. Downtown, **Faulk Central Public Library** (Map p118; ☎ 512-974-7400; 800 Guadalupe St; ☼ 10am-9pm Mon-Thu, 10am-6pm Fri & Sat, noon-6pm Sun) has dozens of wired terminals.

Many coffee shops around town have free wi-fi. Try **Hideout Coffee House & Theatre** (Map p118; ☎ 512-443-3688; 617 Congress Ave; ☼ 7am-11pm Mon-Thu, 7am-1am Fri & Sat, 8am-10pm Sun) right downtown, or join the mass of UT students at the 24-hour **Bennu** (Map p114; ☎ 512-478-4700; 2001 E Martin Luther King Jr Blvd; ☼ 24hr).

Internet Resources

Austin Chronicle (www.austinchronicle.com) Austin's local alternative weekly newspaper archives news and articles online, including comprehensive guides to live-music venues, restaurants, outdoor activities and the arts.
Austin City Links (www.austinlinks.com) The mother lode of Austin-related links covers everything from honky-tonk dancehalls to Shakespearean theater festivals.
Austin360 (www.austin360.com) Inside the Austin American-Statesman's encyclopedic city guide, search for absolutely anything Austin-related (watch out for occasionally obsolete information).

Media
NEWSPAPERS & MAGAZINES
Austin American-Statesman (www.statesman.com) The respected daily newspaper. Publishes *XLent*, a supplemental what's-on guide with restaurant and entertainment reviews, every Thursday.
Austin Chronicle (www.austinchronicle.com) Free alternative weekly with independent coverage of local politics and the lowdown on the Austin music, food and performing-arts scenes.

RADIO
Most of the following stations do live streaming broadcasts online, so you can eavesdrop on Austin before you arrive.
KGSR 107.1 FM (www.kgsr.com) 'Radio Austin' is an eclectic station that airs lots of local talent; check out the 'Lone Star State of Mind' broadcasts from 10pm until midnight every Friday.
KLBJ 590AM Local news, talk and traffic.
KOOP 91.7 FM (www.koop.org) Austin's community radio station has excellent local flavor and multicultural programming; Jay Robillard's ever-popular *The Lounge Show* spins 'hi-fi kitschy fun' from 10am until noon on Saturday.
KUT 90.5 FM (www.kut.org) A local NPR affiliate. *Eklektikos*, with music and performing arts, is on from 9am to 2pm weekdays.

AUSTIN

AUSTIN IN...

Two Days

Start your day at the **Bob Bullock History Museum** (p117), then visit the **Blanton** (which is just across the street; p121) or some of the other art museums and galleries around town. In the afternoon cool off at **Barton Springs** (p123) or **Deep Eddy Pool** (p123) and check out the **Zilker gardens** (p120) while you're there. After dark, plug into Austin's live-music scene at bars and clubs along **Red River** (p135) or in the **Warehouse District** (p136).

On day two, visit the interesting **LBJ Library** (p121) and check out the **UT campus** (p120) if you feel so inclined. Then head to South Congress for people-watching, shopping, and lunch at **Güero's Taco Bar** (p131) and a little shopping. If it's summer, make your way towards the Congress Ave bridge to witness the nightly exodus of America's largest urban **bat colony** (p120). End your evening with dinner and a movie at the **Alamo Drafthouse Cinema** (p137), or get your Texas two-step on at the **Broken Spoke** (p137).

Four Days

Follow the two-day itinerary then, on day three, it's time for a little road trip. Head out of town to **Lockhart** (p133) for some awesome barbecue then go on to **Gruene** (p174) for antique shopping and an evening at Texas' oldest dancehall. If you're feeling ambitious, take the Spoetzl Brewery tour in **Shiner** (p167) or hit the outlet malls in **San Marcos** (p175), in between Lockhart and Gruene.

Start day four back in Austin with a tour of the **Texas State Capitol** (p117), then head to the Sixth and Lamar area for some ice cream at **Amy's Ice Cream** (p130) and pick up some local music at **Waterloo Records** (p139). If you're feeling energetic, pass the afternoon rowing along the **Barton Creek Greenbelt** (p123) or cycling **Lady Bird Lake** (p123) or, for a more low-key appreciation of the outdoors, head south to the **Lady Bird Johnson Wildflower Center** (p122).

KVRX 91.7 FM (www.kvrx.org) The UT student radio station shares its bandwidth and sensibilities with KOOP.

Medical Services

Check the *Yellow Pages* for dentists offering emergency care; some keep extended office hours or stay on call overnight.

Brackenridge Hospital (Map p118; ☎ 512-324-7000; 601 E 15th St) Downtown Austin's central emergency room.

Seton Community Health Care Centers (Map p114; ☎ 512-324-4930; 2811 E 2nd St; ☎ 512-324-4940; 3706 S 1st St) Both of Seton's nonemergency clinics charge sliding-scale fees.

Seton Medical Center (Map p114; ☎ 512-324-1000; 1201 W 38th St) A major hospital near the UT campus.

Walgreens (Map p114; ☎ 512-452-9452; 5429 N I-35, at Cameron Rd; ☑ 24hrs) Has a 24-hour pharmacy.

Money

ATMs accepting most network and credit cards are easily found, except in the most popular nightlife areas, where privately owned ATMs (look for them inside convenience stores or often right on the street) charge exorbitant transaction fees. **Bank of America** (Map p118; ☎ 512-542-9799; 515 Congress Ave; ☑ 9am-4pm Mon-Thu,

9am-5pm Fri) exchanges foreign currency and traveler's checks. There are exchange booths at the airport, too.

Post

Downtown Austin Post Office (Map p118; 510 Guadalupe St; ☑ 8:30am-5:30pm Mon-Fri) Call ☎ 800-275-8777 to locate other branches.

Tourist Information

Austin Convention & Visitors Bureau (CVB; Map p118; ☎ 512-478-0098, 866-462-8784; www.austintexas.org; 209 E 6th St; ☑ 9am-5pm Mon-Fri, 9:30am-5:30pm Sat & Sun) Near the convention center, the Austin CVB has helpful staff, free maps, extensive racks of informational brochures and a sample of local souvenirs for sale.

Capitol Visitors Center (CVC; Map p118; ☎ 512-305-8400; www.texascapitolvisitorscenter.com; 112 E 11th St; ☑ 9am-5pm Mon-Sat, noon-5pm Sun) Get oriented with self-guided-tour booklets for the state capitol and grounds at this office on its southeast corner. It also has Austin information and maps of the entire state.

DANGERS & ANNOYANCES

Common sense and awareness usually ensure problem-free travel in Austin. Some folks may tell you that anywhere east of I-35 is dangerous, but while there is some truth to that, overt or covert racism – this is a predominantly African American and Latino part of town – may exaggerate claims of danger.

One major complaint is drunken college students letting it all hang out on Sixth St. It's a party atmosphere (imagine a small-scale Mardi Gras happening every weekend), and if you're drunkenly counting your cash and appraising your jewelry in an alley at 2am, you're as likely to encounter interest here as anywhere else. Generally speaking, Red River St is as far east as most people go after dark. Transients and panhandlers congregate downtown near Congress Ave, especially from 4th through 7th Sts. Keep your wits about you when returning to your car at night, or hail a taxi (or a pedicab).

Austin natives claim they live in the allergy capital of America, and at any time of year visitors are likely to sneeze and wheeze along with the rest of the city's denizens. If you're at all susceptible, especially to pollen or mold, bring proper medication. Local TV news weather segments on KVUE, Austin's ABC affiliate, include allergy forecasts, or get them instantly at www.austin360.com by clicking on the allergy report link.

SIGHTS

Most of Austin's major sights are around downtown, Zilker Park and the UT campus area. Many sights are accessible via CapMetro's free 'Dillo shuttle buses (www.capmetro. org). For advice on finding parking around the city, see p142.

Downtown
TEXAS STATE CAPITOL
One of Austin's most distinctive landmarks, the striking **state capitol** (Map p118; ☎ 512-463-0063; 1100 Congress Ave; admission & tours free; ❂ 7am-10pm Mon-Fri, 9am-8pm Sat & Sun) was built in 1988 from sunset-red Texas granite. Everything's supposedly bigger in Texas, so it should come as no surprise that this is the largest state capitol in the USA, with a dome that's taller than the US capitol building's. If you do nothing else, go inside and join the other people staring up at the lovely rotunda, the curved ceilings of which echo even the faintest noises, creating a whispering gallery that lets you hear the slightest noise from all the way across the room.

Self-guiding brochures of the capitol building and grounds are available inside the tour guide office on the ground floor. From here you can also take one of the interesting 45-minute guided tours offered daily (schedules vary; call first or show up and try your luck). The green sprawl of the **capitol grounds** and its monuments are worth a stroll before or after your tour.

Want to see government in action? Take a seat in the 3rd-floor **visitor balconies** overlooking the House of Representatives and Senate chamber galleries, which are open to the public when the state legislature is in session (from the second Tuesday of January through May or June, but only in odd-numbered years). Free two-hour parking is available inside the Capitol Visitors Parking Garage, entered from either 12th St or 13th St.

BOB BULLOCK TEXAS STATE HISTORY MUSEUM
This is no dusty old historical **museum** (Map p118; ☎ 512-936-8746, 866-369-7108; www.thestoryoftexas.com; 1800 N Congress Ave; adult/5-18yr $7/4; ❂ 9am-6pm Mon-Sat, noon-6pm Sun). Big, glitzy and still relatively new, it shows off the Lone Star State's history, all the way from when it used to be part of Mexico up to the present.

Allow at least a few hours for your visit. Ground-floor exhibits re-imagine the Native

---

BEWARE OF GODDESS

She stood atop the Texas State Capitol for nearly 100 years, a star in one hand, a sword in the other. When the **Goddess of Liberty** was removed from her perch and lowered by helicopter as part of a capitol restoration project in 1985, no one had seen her up close since 1888. And, well, *wow*. How to put this? She was not a handsome woman.

Not only was she badly weathered, she was just drop-dead ugly, with hideously exaggerated features meant to be appreciated from 300ft below. She was also 16ft tall, so no one had the nerve to tell her. After making a cast for her replacement, they restored her to her former, er, beauty and put her on display at the **Bob Bullock Texas State History Museum** (p117), where you can have a face-to-face with the woman people for decades could only admire from afar.

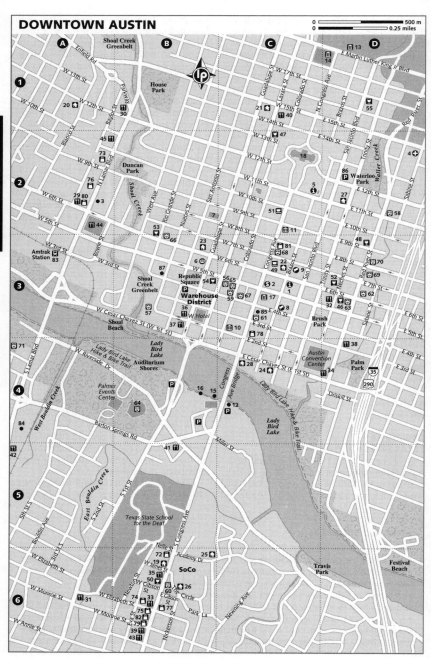

DOWNTOWN AUSTIN

0 _____ 500 m
0 _____ 0.25 miles

AUSTIN

Shoal Creek Greenbelt

House Park

Duncan Park

Shoal Creek

Waterloo Park

Amtrak Station 83

Shoal Creek Greenbelt

Republic Square

Warehouse District

W Hotel

Shoal Beach

Brush Park

Austin Convention Center

Palm Park

Lady Bird Lake Hike & Bike Trail

Lady Bird Lake

Auditorium Shores

Palmer Events Center

West Bouldin Creek

Barton Springs Rd

East Bouldin Creek

Texas State School for the Deaf

SoCo

Travis Park

Festival Beach

Enfield Rd
Shoal Creek Parkway
Baylor St
Blanco St
W 13th St
W 12th St
W 10th St
N Lamar Blvd
W 9th St
W 6th St
W 5th St
Bowie St
W 3rd St
S Lamar Blvd
W Riverside Dr
1st St
S 2nd St
S 3rd St
Bouldin Ave
W Elizabeth St
W Monroe St
W Annie St
West Ave
Rio Grande St
Nueces St
San Antonio St
Guadalupe St
Colorado St
Congress Ave
Brazos St
San Jacinto Blvd
Trinity St
Neches St
Red River St
Sabine St
E 15th St
E Martin Luther King Jr Blvd
E 14th St
E 12th St
E 11th St
E 10th St
E 9th St
E 8th St
E 7th St
E 6th St
E 5th St
E 4th St
E 3rd St
W Cesar Chavez St (W 1st St)
E Cesar Chavez St (E 1st St)
E 2nd St
Driskill St
Lady Bird Lake Hike & Bike Trail
Ave Bridge
Miller St
Congress Ave
S Congress Ave
Academy Dr
Nellie St
W James St
Newton St
Gibson St
E Gibson St
Live Oak Circle
Park La
Newning Ave
Nickerson St
W 17th St
W 15th St
W 14th St
W 13th St
W 12th St
W 11th St
W 10th St
W 9th St
W 8th St
W 7th St
W 6th St
W 5th St
W 4th St
Lavaca St
N Congress Ave
Waller Creek
Red River St

AUSTIN

American experience and the later arrival of French Jesuits, Spanish conquistadores and other frontier settlers. Upstairs, visitors trace the revolutionary years of the Republic of Texas, its rise to statehood and economic expansion into oil drilling and space exploration, and even Western movies and home-grown music from Bob Wills to Buddy Holly to the Big Bopper.

The museum also houses Austin's first **IMAX theater** (www.thestoryoftexas.com/showtimes/imax_theatre.html; adult/5-18yr $7/5), and the **Texas Spirit Theater** (adult/5-18yr $5/4) where you can see *The Star of Destiny*, a 15-minute special-effects film that's simultaneously high-tech and hokey fun. Both theaters offer discounted tickets when combined with museum admission.

Museum parking is $8.

AUSTIN MUSEUM OF ART
The museum's main **downtown gallery** (Map p118; ☎ 512-495-9224; www.amoa.org; 823 Congress Ave; adult/

under 12yr/student & senior $5/free/4; ☻ 10am-5pm Tue-Fri, 10am-8pm Thu, 10am-6pm Sat, noon-5pm Sun) has changing exhibitions as well as a small permanent collection of 20th-century paintings, sculpture, photographs, prints and drawings. The museum expects to build a more spacious downtown headquarters –eventually.

Meanwhile, check out the museum's original home at **Laguna Gloria** (Map p114; ☎ 512-458-8191; 3809 W 35th St; suggested donation $3; ☻ noon-4pm Tue & Wed, 10am-4pm Thu-Sun) out on Lake Austin. The Italianate villa built in 1916 was the former home of Texas legend Clara Driscoll and still serves as a rotating exhibition space, plus the grounds are nice for a wander.

MEXIC-ARTE MUSEUM
This wonderful, eclectic downtown **museum** (Map p118; ☎ 512-480-9373; www.mexic-artemuseum.org; 419 Congress Ave; adult/under 12yr/student $5/1/4; ☻ 10am-6pm Mon-Thu, 10am-5pm Fri & Sat, noon-5pm Sun) features works from Mexican and Mexican

American artists in exhibitions that rotate every two months. The museum's holdings include carved wooden masks, modern Latin American paintings, historic photographs and contemporary art. Don't miss the back gallery where new and experimental talent is shown. The museum's gift shop is another draw, with killer Mexican stuff that's pricey if you're heading south of the border but reasonable if you're not.

South Austin

Most of what's going on in South Austin centers on Zilker Park, a mecca for outdoor activities and kids of all ages.

ZILKER BOTANICAL GARDEN

These lush **gardens** (Map p114; ☎ 512-477-8672; www.zilkergarden.org; 2220 Barton Springs Rd; admission free; ☽ 7am-5:30pm, to 7pm during daylight savings) cover 31 acres on the south bank of the Colorado River, with displays including natural grottoes, a Japanese garden and a fragrant herb garden. You'll also find some interesting historical artifacts sprinkled about the site – kind of like an outdoor architectural museum – including a 19th-century pioneer cabin, a cupola that once sat atop a local schoolhouse, and a footbridge moved from Congress Ave.

UMLAUF SCULPTURE GARDEN

If the weather's just too perfect to be inside a climate-controlled building, stroll the open-air **Umlauf Sculpture Garden** (Map p114; ☎ 512-445-5582; www.umlaufsculpture.org; 605 Robert E Lee Rd; adult/under 6yr/student $3.50/free/1; ☽ 10am-4:30pm Wed-Fri, 1-4:30pm Sat & Sun), located near Zilker Park. Within the sculpture garden and the indoor **museum**, there are more than 130 works by 20th-century American sculptor Charles Umlauf, who was an art professor at UT for 40 years.

UT Campus Area

Look for the main tower and you'll know you've arrived. Even if you're not an alum or a Longhorn at heart, the area is home to several worthwhile museums.

UNIVERSITY OF TEXAS AT AUSTIN

Whatever you do, don't call it 'Texas University' – them are fightin' words, usually used derisively by Texas Agriculture & Mining students and alum to take their rivals down a notch. Sorry, A&M, but the main campus of the **University of Texas** (www.utexas.edu) is kind of a big deal. Established in 1883, UT (and no, don't call it 'TU,' either) has the largest enrollment in the state – about 50,000 students hailing not just from around Texas, but from all over the USA and more than 100 foreign countries.

The **Texas Union** (Map p114; ☎ 512-475-6636; 24th & Guadalupe Sts) is a good place to get oriented; the front desk sells tickets for the tower tours, and there's also the Cactus Cafe (p137), a few places to eat and an underground bowling alley.

The several notable buildings on campus include the LBJ Library and the Texas Memorial Stadium, home of the Longhorns football team. But none define the UT campus as much as the **UT Tower**. Standing 307ft high, with a clock over 12ft in diameter, the tower looms large on campus and in Austin history. It's infamous as the perch that shooter Charles Whitman used during a 1966 shooting spree but, on a more cheerful note, serves as a beacon of victory when it's lit orange to celebrate a Longhorn victory or other achievement.

The tower's **observation deck** (☎ 512-475-6633 for reservations; tour $6) is accessible only by guided tours, which are offered frequently in summer but only on weekends during the school

---

THE SWARM

Looking very much like a special effect from a B movie, a funnel cloud of up to 1.5 million Mexican free-tailed bats swarms from under the **Congress Avenue Bridge** nightly from late March to early November. Turns out, Austin isn't just the live-music capital of the world; it's also home to the largest urban bat population in North America.

Austinites have embraced the winged mammals – figuratively speaking of course – and gather to watch the bats' nightly exodus right around dusk as they leave for their evening meal. (Not to worry, they're looking for insects, and they mostly stay out of your hair.)

There's lots of standing around parking lots and on the bridge itself, but if you want a more leisurely bat-watching experience, try the TGI Friday's restaurant by the Radisson Hotel (p128) on Lady Bird Lake, or the Lone Star Riverboat or Capital Cruises for **bat-watching tours** (p124).

year. Advance reservations are recommended, although standby tickets may be available. To get on the waiting list, stop by the Texas Union's front desk.

Oh, and don't be alarmed if you are greeted with a friendly 'Hook 'em' while on campus – it's just what Longhorns do.

LYNDON BAINES JOHNSON (LBJ) LIBRARY & MUSEUM

History buffs aren't the only ones who can find something of interest at the **LBJ Library & Museum** (Map p114; ☎ 512-721-0200; www.lbjlibrary. org; 2313 Red River St; admission free; ⏰ 9am-5pm daily). There are some fascinating mementos from the 36th US president, including his presidential limo, a moon rock, and gifts from heads of state ('Why, thank you Chiang Kai-shek, for this lovely Chinese tomb sculpture!').

Johnson presided over the USA in the 1960s – one of the most exciting, angst-filled decades in US history – and the events are well represented here: the Vietnam War, the Cuban Missile Crisis, and the assassinations of President Kennedy, Martin Luther King Jr and Robert Kennedy.

Don't miss an elevator trip to the 8th floor for a look at a near-actual-size replica of Johnson's Oval Office, and an exhibit on Lady Bird Johnson, the president's wife, who found success on her own through promoting environmental causes.

HARRY RANSOM HUMANITIES RESEARCH CENTER

The fascinating **Ransom Center** (Map p114; ☎ 512-471-8944; www.hrc.utexas.edu; 21st & Guadalupe Sts; admission free; ⏰ 10am-5pm Tue, Wed & Fri, 10am-7pm Thu, noon-5pm Sat & Sun) is a major repository of historic manuscripts, photography, books, film, TV, music and more. Highlights include a complete copy of the Gutenberg Bible (one of only five in the USA) and what is thought to be the first photograph ever taken, from 1826. Check the website for special online-only exhibitions and the center's busy events calendar of author readings, live music, lectures and more. All in all, this jewel of a place should be a must-see on anyone's itinerary.

BLANTON MUSEUM OF ART

A big university with a big endowment is bound to have a big art collection, and now, finally, it has a suitable building to show

WHAT THE...? LAMPS

Keep an eye out for Austin's **moonlight towers**. All the rage in the late 1800s, these 165ft-tall street lamps were designed to give off the light of a full moon. Austin is the only city in which these historic triangular metal towers topped by a halo of six large bulbs towers still operate. Fifteen burn bright around the city: how many can you spot?

it off properly. Ranking among the best university art collections in the USA, the **Blanton** (Map p118; ☎ 512-471-7324; www.blanton-museum.org; 200 E Martin Luther King Blvd at Congress Ave; adult/under 12yr/youth $9/free/5; ⏰ 10am-5pm Tue-Fri, 11am-5pm Sat, 1-5pm Sun) showcases a variety of styles. It doesn't go very in-depth into any of them, but then again you're bound to find something of interest. Especially striking is the installment of *Missao/Missoes [How to Build Cathedrals]* – which involves 600,000 pennies, 800 communion wafers and 2000 cattle bones.

TEXAS MEMORIAL MUSEUM

We all know how kids feel about dinosaurs, and this **natural history museum** (Map p114; ☎ 512-471-1604; www.utexas.edu/tmm; 2400 Trinity St; admission free; ⏰ 9am-5pm Mon-Fri, 10am-5pm Sat, 1-5pm Sun) is the perfect place for them to indulge their fascination. Look up to see the swooping skeleton of the Texas Pterosaur – one of the most famous dino finds ever. This impressively humongous Cretaceous-era flying reptile has a wingspan of 40ft and was recovered at Big Bend in 1971.

There are other exhibits, too, focusing on anthropology, natural history, geology and biodiversity. Upstairs, you can glimpse taxidermic examples of a Texas soft-shell turtle, a Mexican beaded lizard and other critters, but most of the exhibits are like something you'd find in the dusty attic of an eccentric great aunt.

ELISABET NEY MUSEUM

A spirited German-born sculptor and trailblazer, Elisabet Ney made her home in Austin in the early 1880s, and her reconstructed studio is a serene little **museum** (Map p114; ☎ 512-458-2255; www.ci.austin.tx.us/elisabetney; 304 E 44th St at Ave H; donations welcome; ⏰ noon-5pm Wed-Sun).

One of the oldest museums in Texas, it contains more than 100 busts and statues of political figures and heads of state. It's an untrammeled oasis, and interesting not only to art lovers. Three of Ney's better-known works reside in the state capitol, but the artist considered her greatest legacy to be a sculpture of Lady Macbeth. The Smithsonian owns the original, but you can see a replica of it here.

East Austin

East Austin is on the rise, and although it has traditionally seen few visitors, it has a rich history as an African American neighborhood, with roots stretching back to the 19th century.

Revitalized in the 1990s, the state's official cemetery, **Texas State Cemetery** (Map p114; ☎ 512-463-0605; 909 Navasota St; ⏱ 8am-5pm daily, visitor center 8am-5pm Mon-Fri), is the final resting place of key figures from Texan history. Interred here are luminaries including Stephen F Austin, Miriam 'Ma' Ferguson (the state's first female governor), writer James Michener and Lone Star State flag designer Joanna Troutman, along with thousands of soldiers who died in the Civil War, plus more than 100 leaders of the Republic of Texas who were exhumed from other sites and reburied here. Self-guided-tour brochures are usually available from the visitor center. The cemetery is just north of E 7th St.

Greater Austin

Anyone with an interest in Texas' flora and fauna should make the 20-minute drive to the wonderful gardens of the **Lady Bird Johnson Wildflower Center** (off Map p114; ☎ 512-232-0100; www.wildflower.org; 4801 La Crosse Ave; adult/child 5-12yr/student & senior $8/3/7, higher during peak spring flowering; ⏱ 9am-5:30pm Tue-Sun Apr–mid-Mar, daily mid-Mar–Apr), southwest of downtown Austin. The center, founded in 1982 with the assistance of Texas' beloved former first lady, has a display garden featuring every type of wildflower and plant that grows in Texas, separated by geographical region, with an emphasis on Hill Country flora. The best time to come is in the spring (especially National Wildflower Week in May), but there's something in bloom all year.

SLACKER *Sarah Chandler*

When Richard Linklater's *Slacker,* a documentarylike manifesto for the country's meandering youth, appeared in 1991, it put the Austin film scene on the map and the word 'slacker' in the dictionary. Linklater got a bunch of his shiftless Austin friends together and made a wonderful little film about a bunch of dreamers in Austin. Intricately interwoven, the film is a series of biting vignettes whose strength can be judged by the fact that you want to see more of everybody you meet. Linklater's sophomore film, *Dazed and Confused* (1993), became a cult classic with a similarly chilled-out, stoned-out-of-its-mind ethos, only solidifying Austin's bohemian cinematic image to the rest of the country.

Austin became known as a loser-chic place with a 'whatever, man' attitude, populated by gadabouts with body piercings, long hair and an odd predilection for philosophical discourse at any hour of the day. At first the slacker spotlight was embraced: Linklater had helped define a generation and that generation's hometown became Austin. Several years later, when outsiders began to discredit all of those living in the Capitol City as lazy dreamers and, well, slackers, that same spotlight began to chafe.

These days Austin is booming, condos going up, and luxury hotels replacing hole-in-the-wall venues downtown. Most Austinites no longer think of themselves as slackers, nor do they consider their town Slacker Central – although both myth and reality prevail in many pockets of town.

That said, the change from Slacker Central to Silicon Hills has left Austin's longtime residents longing for the weirder days of yore before BMWs and Mercedes started clogging the streets and hair styles went from purple punk to purposeful. Bumper stickers and T-shirts have started appearing all over town embossed with the logo 'Keep Austin Weird' (www.keepaustinweird.com), a plea to locals and newcomers alike to show respect for Austin's oddities. Several local businesses have co-opted the phrase and many residents are taking note and repatriating their freak flags with renewed vigor. It's just one more thing that makes Austin, well, Austin.

ACTIVITIES

If there's an epicenter to outdoor recreation in Austin, it's **Zilker Park** (Map p114; ☎ 512-391-0402; Barton Springs Rd; admission free; ☼ 5am-10pm daily), just south of the Colorado River about a mile west of I-35. This 350-acre park is a slice of green heaven, lined with hiking and biking trails. The park also provides access to the famed Barton Springs natural swimming pool and Barton Creek Greenbelt.

Austin has quite a few other places to play outside, including Lady Bird Lake, Lake Austin and creekside parks, riverine nature preserves and spreading greenbelts throughout the city. You can get just about any information you might need from the **City of Austin Parks & Recreation Department** (☎ 512-974-6700; www.ci.austin.tx.us/parks; ☼ 8am-5pm Mon-Fri). Check out its website to find everything from municipal golf courses to tennis complexes to cemeteries.

Swimming & Boating
BARTON SPRINGS POOL

Hot? Not for long. Even when the temperature hits 100, you'll be shivering in a jiff after you jump into this icy-cold **natural spring pool** (Map p114; ☎ 512-476-9044, 24hr hotline ☎ 512-867-3080; 2101 Barton Springs Rd; adult/under 11yr/junior mid-Mar—Oct $3/1/2, Nov—mid-Mar free, parking $3; ☼ 5am-10pm, closed for cleaning 9am-7pm Thu).

Austinites hold this place dear in their hearts, and after one visit you'll see why. The Edwards Aquifer pumps 32 million gallons of very cold but very clear water into the 1000ft-long pool, which is a constant 68°F year-round. Draped with century-old pecan trees, the area around the pool is a social scene in itself, and the place gets packed on a hot summer day.

BARTON CREEK GREENBELT

Paddling along the waterways in the Barton Creek Greenbelt – an environmentally sensitive area constantly under pressure from developers who think Austin needs more condos and golf courses – is one of the highlights of a trip to the city. Check out the *Austin Chronicle's* **Barton Creek Guide** (www.auschron.com/guides/bartoncreek) for more information.

Zilker Park Boat Rentals (Map p114; ☎ 512-478-3852; www.zilkerboats.com; per hour/day $10/40; ☼ 11am-dusk Mon-Fri, 9am-dusk Sat & Sun Mar-Oct; closed weekends in winter), just downstream from Barton Springs Pool, rents 17ft canoes and open-deck ocean kayaks. It also has maps and will describe the best routes. The price includes paddles and life jackets; arrive early on the weekends before the boats are all gone.

LADY BIRD LAKE

Named for former first lady Lady Bird Johnson, this in-town lake kind of looks like a river. And no wonder: it's actually a damned-off section of the Colorado River that divides Austin into north and south. Enjoy it from dry land on the hike-and-bike trail, or get out on the water at the **Rowing Dock** (Map p114; ☎ 512-459-0999; www.rowingdock.com; 2418 Stratford Dr; ☼ 6:30am-8pm Mon-Fri, 7am-7pm Sat & Sun), which rents kayaks for $10 to $20 per hour and water cycles for slightly more.

DEEP EDDY POOL

With its vintage 1930s bathhouse built as part of the Works Progress Administration, Texas' oldest **swimming pool** (Map p114; ☎ 512-472-8546; www.deepeddy.org; 401 Deep Eddy Ave; adult/under 11yr/junior $3/1/2; ☼ 8am-8pm) is fed by cold springs and surrounded by cottonwood trees. There are separate areas for waders and lap swimmers.

Disc Golf

Disc golf is big in Austin, and at the time of research the city had just announced plans to close the too-well-loved Pease Park course because of the environmental impact it had on the Shoal Creek Greenbelt. Plans were afoot to build a new, state-of-the-art course at the Roy G Guerrero Colorado River Park. Other places to putt include the **Mary Moore Searight Metropolitan Park** (off Map p114; 907 Slaughter Lane), a South Austin fave just over a mile west of I-35 (exit Slaughter Lane), and **Bartholomew District Park** (off Map p114; 5201 Berkman Dr), a hilly course north of downtown near the old airport.

Cycling & Hiking

See p141 for bicycle rental, sales and repair shops.

Lady Bird Lake, lined with over 10 miles of hiking and biking trails, is the most popular spot for biking. A trail runs most of the way along the lake's northern side, which is the south edge of downtown Austin. You can also hike or mountain bike for almost 8 miles along the Barton Creek Greenbelt, which can be entered near Barton Springs Pool.

If you head out to the Lady Bird Johnson Wildflower Center, plan some extra time to ride or skate the great 3.2-mile **Veloway track** (www.veloway.com; 4898 La Cross Ave; admission free; ☉ dawn-dusk daily) nearby. The track runs clockwise, and no walking or running is permitted.

AUSTIN FOR CHILDREN

Austin is absolutely kid-friendly, thanks to the casual south-central Texas lifestyle. Zilker Park (p123) is a wonderland of family-themed fun, and think about visiting the Texas Memorial Museum (p121) on the UT campus, too. For kid-centered shopping, see p140.

Austin Children's Museum

This downtown **museum** (Map p118; ☎ 512-472-2499; www.austinkids.org; 201 Colorado St; adult & youth/under 2yr $6.50/4.50; ☉ 10am-5pm Tue-Sat, 10am-8pm Wed, noon-5pm Sun) offers lots of interactive and educational fun. Kids can try their hands at running a ranch, ordering a meal at the Global Diner and hanging upside down beneath a bridge, just like the real Austin bats.

Zilker Zephyr

Trains on the Zilker Zephyr **miniature railroad** (Map p114; ☎ 512-478-8286; adult/senior & under 12yr $3/2; ☉ 10am-5pm Mon-Fri, 10am-dusk Sat & Sun) make the 25-minute, 2-mile ride along Barton Creek and Town Lake year-round. They leave the depot near the playground every hour on the hour weekdays and every 30 to 40 minutes on weekends.

Austin Nature & Science Center

In the northwestern area of Zilker Park, this **center** (Map p114; ☎ 512-327-8181; www.ci.austin.tx.us/ansc; 301 Nature Center Dr; donations requested; ☉ 9am-5pm Mon-Sat, noon-5pm Sun) has exhibitions of native Texan mammals, birds, reptiles, amphibians and arthropods that have been injured and nursed back to health here. There are also outdoor nature trails lined with native plants, where you'll see bats, butterflies and birds.

TOURS

The Austin CVB (p116) downtown has information and brochures for many of the following city tours.

Boat Tours

With a dock on the south shore of Lady Bird Lake near the Hyatt, **Lone Star Riverboat** (Map p118; ☎ 512-327-1388; www.lonestarriverboat.com) runs one-hour cruises on its double-decked paddle-wheel riverboat at 3pm each Saturday and Sunday, March through October. The company also offers nightly sunset bat-watching trips on its 32ft electric cruiser from March through October. See its website for parking tips.

Between March and November, **Capital Cruises** (Map p118; ☎ 512-480-9264; www.capitalcruises.com; adult/child/senior $10/5/8) offers competitively priced lake excursions and bat-watching trips that depart from a dock near the Hyatt at 208 Barton Springs Rd.

Austin Duck Adventures (☎ 512-477-5274; www.austinducks.com; adult/3-12yr/senior & student $26/16/24; ☉ check website for schedule) utilizes amphibious British Alvis Stalwarts, which parade around the state capitol, roll down Congress Ave and 6th St, then splash into Lake Austin. Tour guides provide a few entertaining historical tidbits along the way.

Driving Tours

For an interesting alternative to your stereotypical, run-of-the-mill bus and van tours, try **Texpert Tours** (☎ 512-383-8989; www.texperttours.com; adult $80), led by an affable public radio host, Howie Richey (aka the 'Texas Back Roads Scholar'). Historical anecdotes, natural history and environmental tips are all part of the educational experience. A three-hour tour of central Austin takes visitors to the state capitol, Governor's Mansion and to the top of Mt Bonnell.

Train Tours

The **Austin Steam Train Association** (☎ 512-477-8468; www.austinsteamtrain.org; adults $17-43, child $12-27, senior $14-39) runs seasonal weekend day trips. The *Hill Country Flyer* (six-hour round-trip) and *Bertram Flyer* (three-hour round-trip) steam trains go from Cedar Park north of Austin into the Texas Hill Country, with special themed entertainment runs, such as murder mysteries.

For a shorter, cheaper miniature train ride, check out the Zilker Zephyr (p124) in Zilker Park.

Walking Tours

One of the best deals around is the free walking tour of downtown Austin, which leaves from the capitol's south steps at 9am Thursday, Friday and Saturday and at 2pm Sunday, weather permitting. Other free walking tours concentrate on the capitol grounds (9am Saturday and 2pm Sunday) or the historic Bremond Block (11am Saturday and Sunday). Tours last between 60 and 90 minutes and are available March through November. Make reservations online at www.austintexas.org or call ☎ 866-GO-AUSTIN.

Austin Ghost Tours (☎ 512-853-9826; www.austinghosttours.com; adult $20) take visitors on tours of haunted buildings and streets in areas including the Old Pecan St District or Warehouse District. Downtown ghost tours last 90 minutes, usually departing around 8:30pm from the Moonshine Patio Bar & Grill (p130), on Red River St.

FESTIVALS & EVENTS
Following are some special events worth planning a trip around. For a complete list, check with the Austin CVB (p116).

January
Red-Eye Regatta (☎ 512-266-1336; www.austinyachtclub.org; Jan 1) An annual New Year's Day race of 50 1st-class keel boats held on Lake Travis and sponsored by the Austin Yacht Club.

February
Carnival Brasileiro (☎ 512-452-6832; www.sambaparty.com; date & venue vary) Started by Brazilian foreign-exchange students in 1975, this euphoric one-night bash features samba, carnival drumming and bare skin galore. Buy tickets early.
Mardi Gras (date varies) Celebrate downtown on Sixth St, Austin's version of Bourbon St. Expect Cajun food, a masquerade ball, parades and beads for exhibitionists.

March
Zilker Park Kite Festival (☎ 512-448-5483; www.zilkerkitefestival.com; early Mar) This 80-year-old festival sometimes changes its date to take advantage of the best winds. It's a rite of spring.
South by Southwest (p138; www.sxsw.com; mid-Mar) Among the world's top music-industry gatherings, SXSW features dozens of venues packed with record company execs, gaggles of critics and wannabe critics, producers and hundreds of bands. There's also a film and interactive component. The town goes absolutely nuts.
Jerry Jeff Walker's Birthday Weekend (www.jerryjeff.com; late Mar) This 1970s outlaw country icon's birthday party inspires a series of live shows and dances in Austin clubs and the Hill Country. Buy tickets online way, way early.

April
Old Settler's Music Festival (☎ 888-512-7469; www.oldsettlersmusicfest.org; mid-Apr) This homegrown bluegrass and acoustic American music festival happens at Salt Lick BBQ Pavilion and Camp Ben McCulloch in Driftwood, a short drive southwest of Austin.
Eeyore's Birthday Party (☎ 512-448-5160; www.eeyores.com; Pease Park, 1100 Kingsbury St; late Apr) Perhaps no other annual event proves Austin's offbeat flavor so completely. This event, started during the hippy-dippy 1960s, has maypole dancing, live music and even a birthday cake for the namesake melancholy Winnie-the-Pooh character. You'll feel silly if you *don't* wear a costume.

May
Old Pecan Street Spring Arts Festival (☎ 512-825-2634; www.oldpecanstreetfestival.com; early May) A downtown arts-and-crafts street fair with live rock, country, Latin and world music and kids' carnival rides along E 6th St.
Cinco de Mayo Festival (www.cincodemayoaustin.com; Fiesta Gardens, 1901 Jesse Segovia Ave; early May) This event ostensibly celebrates the Mexican cavalry victory at the Battle of Puebla in 1862, but it's really an excuse to drink lots of tequila and dance to the music.

June
Austin Pride Parade (early Jun) Austin's gay pride celebration is one of Texas' largest, with block parties, music and a parade.

July
4th of July Celebration (☎ 512-476-6064; www.austinsymphony.org; Jul 4) Nearly 100,000 people come out to watch the Austin Symphony perform a free one-hour concert in Zilker Park, followed by fireworks over Lady Bird Lake.

August
Austin Chronicle Hot Sauce Contest (www.austinchronicle.com; date varies) Currently held in Waterloo Park, this summer contest has been going strong since 1990. Beer, music and all sorts of spicy delights accompany an enthusiastically judged hot-sauce competition.

September
Austin City Limits Music Festival (☎ 888-512-7469; www.aclfestival.com; late Sep to early Oct) Everyone from Phish to the Strokes to the Flaming Lips turns out at Zilker Park for this festival, named after the acclaimed public TV show. Fast becoming the locals' fave alternative to SXSW madness, the festival also features food and art shows. Three-day passes cost $185, but cheaper single-day tickets are also available (Waterloo Records sells tickets).

AUSTIN

GAY & LESBIAN AUSTIN

With a thriving gay population – not to mention pretty mellow straight people – Austin is arguably the most gay-friendly city in Texas. The **Austin Gay & Lesbian Chamber of Commerce** (☎ 512-472-4422; www.aglcc.org) sponsors the Pride Parade in June, as well as smaller events throughout the year. The *Austin Chronicle* (www.austinchronicle.com) runs a gay event column among the weekly listings, and the glossy *L Style/G Style* (www.lstylegstyle.com) magazine has a dual gal/guy focus.

Austin's gay and lesbian club scene is mainly in the Warehouse District, though there are outposts elsewhere.

Charlie's (Map p118; ☎ 512-474-6481; 1301 Lavaca St; ☯ 2pm-2am) Up near the state capitol, Charlie's is the oldest gay bar in town. Friendly staff, a laid-back atmosphere, pool tables, $5 steak nights and free parking are just some of the perks. On some nights DJs spin progressive house music.

Oilcan Harry's (Map p118; ☎ 512-320-8823; www.oilcanharrys.com; 211 W 4th St; ☯ until 2am) Oh, yes, there's dancing. And oh, yes, it's packed. (And how are you supposed to dance with all those people in there?) As much as the girls wish it were a mixed crowd, this scene is all about the boys. Sweaty ones.

Rainbow Cattle Company (Map p118; ☎ 512-472-5288; www.rainbowcattleco.com; 303 West 5th St; ☯ until 2am) You'd think that lesbians and country-and-western line dancing wouldn't really go together. But this place will prove you wrong.

Old Pecan Street Fall Arts Festival (late Sep) A repeat of E 6th St's May shindig.

October

Austin Film Festival (☎ 512-478-4795, 800-310-3378; www.austinfilmfestival.com; mid-Oct) Hollywood and independent filmmakers and screenwriters flock to this multiday event held at various venues.

Halloween (Oct 31) Downtown's Sixth St is the scene of a huge bash that attracts as many as 60,000 costumed partygoers.

November

El Día de los Muertos (Nov 2) Fanfare surrounding the Day of the Dead may include a parade and special exhibitions at the Mexic-Arte Museum.

Thanksgiving Day (4th Thu) The annual football game between UT and Texas A&M makes this traditional holiday an even bigger event.

December

Christmas Lights All of Austin gets decked out in holiday lighting, with Zilker Park among the most scenic spots. Keeping Austin weird is 37th St east of Lamar, where the lights are riotously installed alongside other creative exhibits.

SLEEPING

Chain motels and hotels dominate accommodations in Austin; only the most noteworthy are reviewed here. Hotel prices tend to be high in and near downtown, though a few bargains can be found. There's no shortage of rooms until major events, such as SXSW, the Austin City Limits festival and the Thanksgiving Day

football game between UT and Texas A&M, come to town. At these peak times prices skyrocket and rooms are booked months in advance. At other times, choose accommodations as close to downtown as you can afford. If you're staying at least a week, many outlying motels and all-suite hotels offer discounted rates; some extended-stay options offer a large suite (bedroom with a living area, bathroom and kitchen) starting at $25 per night. Many hotels and motels offer special deals via their own websites, or through www.orbitz.com and other online travel discounters.

Budget

Try **College Houses Cooperatives** (☎ 512-476-5678, 800-880-2676; www.collegehouses.org; r per person $20), which has five different student co-ops that can be rented by the night when space is available, usually when all the students have gone home for the summer. With dinner included, it's a bargain, but this isn't a drop-in kind of place. They request that you go to the website and request a room in advance.

Emma Long Metropolitan Park (off Map p114; ☎ 512-346-1831; 1600 City Park Rd; tent/RV site with hookup $6/15, plus entrance fee per car Mon-Thu/Fri-Sun $5/8; ☯ gates open 7am-10pm daily; Ⓟ Ⓡ) The only Austin city park with overnight camping, 1000-acre Emma Long Metropolitan Park (aka 'City Park') on Lake Austin, 16 miles northwest of downtown, has good swimming, sunbathing, fishing and boating. Get there early as it fills quickly and doesn't take reservations.

Austin Hostel (Map p114; ☎ 512-444-2294, 800-725-2331; www.hiaustin.org; 2200 S Lakeshore Blvd; dm members/nonmembers $21.85/24.85; 🗶 🖳 🛜) Just 2.5 miles from downtown, this 42-bed hostel has an ideal location down a shady street right on the shore of Lady Bird Lake. No hostel clutter here; the facilities are clean, tidy and cheerful. And with 24-hour access you can enjoy it at your leisure – although they do ask that all jam sessions end by 11pm (this is a music town).

Goodall Wooten (Map p114; ☎ 512-472-1343; 2112 Guadalupe St; s & d $30-40, stay 6 nights, get 7th free; 🗶 🖳) A private dorm near the University of Texas, 'the Woo' generally has rooms available mid-May to mid-August, and sometimes has space for travelers at other times of the year. Each room has a small refrigerator.

Pecan Grove RV Park (Map p114; ☎ 512-472-1067; 1518 Barton Springs Rd; RV sites with full hookups daily $30, weekly $195; 🅿) The name says it all. Located in a shady grove of pecan trees, this pleasant RV park is exceedingly well located. It's smack dab in the middle of town and just steps away from the ever-popular Shady Grove Restaurant. Your RV never had it so good.

Days Inn Austin University (Map p114; ☎ 512-478-1631, 800-329-7466; www.daysinn.com; 3105 N I-35; s & d from $59-99; 🅿 🐾) Be sure to ask for a room toward the back of this motel, since the freeway traffic noise can be bad up front. Star Seeds, the all-night diner next door, has long been a late-night favorite among bleary-eyed UT students.

Rodeway Inn University/Downtown (Map p114; ☎ 512-477-6395, 877-424-6423; www.rodewayinn.com; 2900 N I-35; d $70-90; 🅿 🐾) This place right on noisy I-35 isn't really a bargain, relatively speaking, but it is one of the less-expensive rooms in town. The digs are modest, but it's an option.

our pick **Austin Motel** (Map p118; ☎ 512-441-1157; www.austinmotel.com; 1220 S Congress Ave; r $69-110, ste $120-155; 🅿 🛜 🐾) 'Garage-sale chic' is the unifying factor at this wonderfully funky motel that embodies the spirit of the 'Keep Austin Weird' movement. Each room is individually decorated with whatever happened to be lying around at the time, with varying degrees of success. Take your chances, or hand-pick your room from the website, which has a picture of each and every one. Poolside suites are huge, and room 138 is especially cheery.

Midrange

Austin Folk House (Map p114; ☎ 512-472-6700, 866-472-6700; www.austinfolkhouse.com; 506 W 22nd; d $85-225; 🗶 🅿 🛜) One part gallery, one part B&B, the Austin Folk House has colorful and whimsical folk art in every room and up and down the halls. The rooms are comfortable and unfussy, and it's right in the bustling West Campus area.

Star of Texas Inn (Map p114; ☎ 512-477-9639; www.staroftexasinn.com; 611 W 22nd St; r $85-225; 🗶 🅿 🛜) A sister property of the Austin Folk House, this inn is the slightly more upscale of the two. The buttercup-yellow neoclassical Victorian building started as a private residence, spent

---

KEEP AUSTIN WEIRD

Bumper stickers and T-shirts insist upon it, but are they succeeding? We were saddened to hear about the closure of the Cathedral of Junk – a definite loss of weird points. So who's carrying the torch? Check out **www.keepaustinweird.com** to find out what's odd right now. In the meantime, here's a sampling of the things that set Austin apart:

- Eccentric storefronts on S Congress Ave and North Loop Blvd
- Eeyore's Birthday Party (www.eeyores.com), an annual festival where weirdness reigns supreme
- Leslie, the bearded, cross-dressing, on-the-streets-living local celebrity who ran for mayor
- The homegrown Museum of Natural & Artificial Ephemerata (www.mnae.org), open eight days a year
- Master Pancake Theater or any other offbeat event at Alamo Drafthouse (p137)
- Chicken-shit bingo at Ginny's Little Longhorn (p134)
- December's crazy Christmas lights on 37th St east of Lamar
- A disproportionate but well-deserved local obsession with dive bars

some time as a fraternity house, and has now been rescued from keggers and outfitted with antique clawfoot tubs and Victorian furnishings. The wraparound porches might sag a bit, but they're a gracious place to sit a spell.

Adams House (Map p114; www.theadamshouse.com; 4300 Ave G; d $99-110, ste $150; ✗ ℗ 🛜) On a quiet corner in historic Hyde Park, the Adams House has a homey vibe that will have you feeling like a local resident in no time. During the week, guests can help themselves to a continental breakfast, and on the weekends get a full breakfast served in the dining room. Although there's no pool on-site, it's just down the street from a city pool that's open during the summer months.

Woodburn House (Map p114; ☎ 512-458-4335, 888-690-9763; www.woodburnhouse.com; 4401 Ave D; d $90-140, ste $140-180; ℗ 🛜) This gracious Hyde Park hostelry is well removed from the bustle of the Drag. The house itself is nearly a century old, and its unique mix of architectural styles places it on the National Register of Historic Places. Relax on the wraparound porches – both up- and downstairs – and enjoy a hot, gourmet breakfast seven days a week.

Hotel San José (p118; ☎ 512-444-7322, 800-574-8897; www.sanjosehotel.com; 1316 S Congress Ave; d $160-260, without bathroom $95-105; ✗ ℗ 🛜 🖳) Local hotelier Liz Lambert revamped a 1930s-vintage motel into a chic SoCo retreat with minimalist rooms, native Texas gardens, and a very Austin-esque hotel bar in the courtyard that's known for its celebrity-spotting potential.

Extended StayAmerica (Map p118; ☎ 512-457-9994, 800-398-7829; www.exstay.com; 600 Guadalupe St; d $100-110, per night $80-90 weekly, $60-70 monthly; ✗ ℗ 🛜) This extended-stay hotel has an excellent downtown location, walking distance to tons of bars and restaurants. Rooms are bland but include a kitchenette stocked with utensils, and the weekly rates are a great excuse to hang out in Austin a while.

La Quinta Inn Austin Capitol (Map p118; ☎ 512-476-1166, 800-753-3757; www.laquinta.com; 300 E 11th St; d $99-149; ✗ ℗ 🛜 🖳) The downtown location is not the most serene, but you can't get any closer to the handsome state capitol building (you practically share a lawn). We're not sure why a midrange motel insists on valet parking – at $13 a night, no less – unless it's to keep state legislators from snagging a free spot. But we do give them extra points for the Texas-shaped waffles they serve at breakfast.

Doubletree Guest Suites Austin (Map p118; ☎ 512-478-7000, 800-222-8733; www.doubletreehotelaustin.com; 303 W 15th St; ste from $115; ℗ 🛜 🖳) Just northwest of the capitol and within walking distance of UT, the all-suites Doubletree feels remarkably corporate, but it does offer a little extra space, with accommodations featuring a sleeper sofa, full kitchen, dining area and balcony. Parking is $17.

Inn at Pearl Street (Map p114; ☎ 512-478-0051; 800-494-2261; www.innpearl.com; 1809 Pearl St; d $115-155; ✗ ℗ 🛜) This B&B is a preservationist's dream come true. The owners picked up this run-down property, dusted it off and – well, they more than dusted it off. They completely restored it and decorated it in a plush, European style that makes it a cozy place to shack up for a few days.

Brava House (Map p118; ☎ 512-478-5034; www.bravahouse.com; 1108 Blanco St; d $129-175, ste $159-225; ✗ ℗ 🛜) One of the only nonhotel options in the city center, this boutique B&B has lovely rooms and suites, with a canopy bed in the Moroccan-style Casablanca Room, a clawfoot bathtub in the Garbo Suite and tons of space in the 650-sq-ft Monroe Suite.

Mansion at Judge's Hill (Map p114; ☎ 512-495-1800, 800-311-1619; www.mansionatjudgeshill.com; 1900 Rio Grande St; d $129-399; ℗ 🛜) You want luxury? You got it. This place is hands-down the most gorgeous B&B in town. Weekend guests might have to fight their way through wedding parties or bridal photos – an unavoidable side effect of staying in a historic mansion with beautiful grounds. (A bit of hard-to-believe trivia: this place was once a drug and alcohol rehab center.)

Radisson Hotel & Suites (Map p118; ☎ 512-478-9611, 800-395-7046; www.radisson.com/austintx; 111 E Cesar Chavez St; d $140-219; ✗ 🛜 🖳) Bats? Yes, bats. This is a great place from which to watch their nightly exodus from under the Congress St Bridge. It puts you right on the water and upstairs from the hike and bike trail around Lady Bird Lake. It's also walking distance to tons of downtown bars and restaurants. This place has certainly got location.

Top End
AT&T Executive Education & Conference Center (Map p114; ☎ 512-404-1900; www.downtownaustinhotel.com; 1900 University Ave; d $189-249; ✗ 🛜) OK, so the name of this hotel has all the romance of a mandatory training workshop. This swanky newcomer right on the UT campus is perfect

for alum who want to relive their college days but still want to be kept in the style to which they've (perhaps) become accustomed. References to UT abound, but the motif is so subtle that nonalums would never notice – think burnt-orange accent walls, historical campus photos and leather headboards (sorry, Bevo).

Driskill Hotel (Map p118; ☎ 512-474-5911, 800-252-9367; www.driskillhotel.com; 604 Brazos St; r $185-275, ste $300-900; ✕ Ⓟ �) Every city should have a beautiful old historic hotel made out of native stone. And it doesn't hurt if it was built in the late 1800s by a wealthy cattle baron, at least if it's in Texas. No generic hotel decor here; this place is pure Texas, from the leather couches to the mounted longhorn head on the wall. (Not to worry, the elegant rooms are taxidermy-free.) A bit of trivia? LBJ and Lady Bird had their first date here.

Kimber Modern (Map p118; ☎ 512-912-1046; www.kimbermodern.com; 110 The Circle; r incl breakfast $250-295; ✕ Ⓟ) Staying in one of the five rooms at the architecturally adept Kimber is like staying in a minimalist art museum, with lots of white space accented by splashes of color. But the patio – now that's a different story altogether. If the rooms feel sterile, just step outside and relax under the insanely sprawling live oak.

Hotel St Cecilia (Map p118; ☎ 512-852-2400; www.hotelsaintcecilia.com; 112 Academy Dr; d $295-350, ste $295-610; ✕ Ⓟ) Local hotelier Liz Lambert has a knack for ubercool design, and she's put it to good use here. Choose from a Victorian-style house (c 1888) furnished with the perfect blend of modern, vintage and artistic touches, or one of the sleek poolside bungalows. The hustle and bustle of South Congress melts away the moment you cross over onto the serene lawn graced by a 300-year-old live oak.

Four Seasons Austin (Map p118; ☎ 512-478-4500; www.fourseasons.com/austin; 98 San Jacinto Blvd; d midweek/weekends from $295/395; ✕ Ⓟ) Four Seasons luxury done Texas style means leather chairs, cowhide couches and native limestone. It's like staying on a really swanky ranch, except it's right downtown on the shores of Lady Bird Lake (views cost extra). Check the website and you might be able to score one of the 'Voluntourism' packages that lets you volunteer in exchange for a discounted room rate. Parking is $27.

EATING
Barbecue and Tex-Mex are the mainstays, but Austin also has many fine-dining restaurants and a broadening array of world cuisines. For hot tips on new restaurants, pick up the free alternative weekly *Austin Chronicle*, or *Xlent*, both published on Thursday.

Downtown eateries are a real mixed bag, serving tourists, business folks, politicians, artists and night-owl clubbers. Over the bridge in South Austin, there are some long-running favorites that justify any trip. Other neighborhoods, such as West End and Hyde Park, also boast a few eclectic restaurants. Around the UT campus area, prices drop – but often so does food quality.

Central Austin & Downtown
BUDGET
Texas Chili Parlor (Map p118; ☎ 512-472-2828; 1409 Lavaca St; mains $5-11; 11am-2am) Ready for a triple X–rated meal? When ordering your chili, keep in mind that 'X' is mild, 'XX' is spicy, and 'XXX' will melt your face off. There's more than just chili on the menu; there's also Frito pie, which is chili over Fritos. Still not feeling it? There's also burgers, enchiladas and, of course, more chili.

MIDRANGE
Whole Foods Market (Map p118; ☎ 512-476-1206; 525 N Lamar Blvd; 8am-10pm daily) Austinites remember Whole Foods back when it was just a low-key hippie grocer, and look at it now, with more than 140 stores nationwide focusing on healthy, natural and organic groceries. There's a great selection of takeout at this enormous flagship store, perfect for stocking a picnic.

Austin Java Company (Map p118; ☎ 512-476-1829; 1206 Parkway; burgers & mains $5-10; breakfast, lunch & dinner Mon-Fri, 8am-10pm Sat & Sun) Uniquely Austin, this restaurant disguised as a coffee shop has a relaxed atmosphere and tons and tons of good, cheap food to choose from. There are three other locations in town but only this one has a large bug on the roof, left over from the building's days as a Terminix office.

Iron Works BBQ (Map p118; ☎ 512-478-4855; 100 Red River St; mains $6-13; 11am-9pm Mon-Sat) Follow the deliciously smoky aroma to this rustic former ironsmith's shop near the convention center for smoked pork loin, huge beef ribs and an all-you-can-eat salad bar.

I SCREAM, YOU SCREAM

Even if it means pushing away the free basket of tortilla chips that come with your dinner, save room for **Amy's Ice Creams** (Map p118; ☎ 512-480-0673; www.amysicecreams.com; 1012 W Sixth St; ☻ 11:30am-midnight Sun-Thu, 11:30am-1am Fri & Sat). Short of jumping in Barton Springs, there's no better way to cool off than at this locally owned store, which is an Austin classic.

It's not just the ice cream itself, which, by the way, is smooth, creamy and delightful. It's the toppings – pardon us, *crush'ns* they call 'em – that get pounded and blended in, violently but lovingly, by the staff wielding a metal scoop in each hand. Mexican vanilla bean with fresh strawberries, dark chocolate with Reese's Peanut Butter Cups, or mango with jelly beans if that's what you're into. With 15 flavors (rotated from their 300 recipes) and dozens of toppings, ranging from cookies and candy, to fruit or nuts, the combinations aren't endless, but they number too high to count.

Look for other locations on Guadalupe St north of the campus and on South Congress near all the shops.

TOP END

La Condesa (Map p118; ☎ 512-499-0300; 400 W 2nd St; small plates $7-14, mains $18-32; ☻ dinner Mon-Wed, 5-11pm Thu & Fri, 11am-11pm Sat, lunch & dinner Sun) Here in slacky Slackerville, decor is often an afterthought, but La Condesa came along and changed all that with an eye-poppingly gorgeous space that's colorful, supermodern and artsy, with a dazzling mural taking up an entire wall. If you find their dinners to be a little spendy, come for brunch in the $10 to $14 range.

Lambert's (Map p118; ☎ 512-494-1500; 401 W 2nd St; mains $14-34; ☻ lunch Mon-Sat, 11am-2pm Sun, dinner Sun-Wed, 5:30-11pm Thu-Sat) Torn between barbecue and fine dining? Lambert's serves intelligent updates of American comfort-food classics – some might call it 'uppity barbecue' – in a historic stone building run by Austin chef Lou Lambert.

Moonshine Patio Bar & Grill (Map p118; ☎ 512-236-9599; 303 Red River St; lunch $9-14, dinner $11-21; ☻ lunch & dinner Mon-Thu, 11am-11pm Fri & Sat, 10am-2:30pm & dinner Sun) Dating from the mid-1850s, this historic building is a remarkably well preserved homage to Austin's early days. Within its exposed limestone walls, you can enjoy upscale comfort food, half-price appetizers at happy hour, or a lavish Sunday brunch buffet ($16.95).

Chez Nous (Map p118; ☎ 512-473-2413; 510 Neches St; lunch $8-20, dinner mains $20-35, three-course dinner $26.50; ☻ lunch 11:45am-2pm Tue-Fri, dinner 6-10:30pm Tue-Sun) This classic Parisian-style bistro has been quietly serving excellent food since 1982. Low-key and casual, Chez Nous is as unpretentious as they come, and has made many a French food lover *trés heureux*.

Wink (Map p118; ☎ 512-482-8868; 1014 N Lamar Blvd; mains $15-32; ☻ 6-10:30pm Mon-Wed, 6-11:30pm Thu-Sat) At this gem hidden behind Whole Earth Provision Co, diners are ushered to tables underneath windows that are screened with Japanese *washi* (rice paper), then presented with an exceptional wine list. The chef-inspired fare takes on a nouveau fusion attitude that is equal parts modern French and Asian.

South Austin

With more variety than any other neighborhood in the city, South Austin is a sure-fire choice for any appetite.

BUDGET

Jo's (Map p118; ☎ 512-444-3800; 1300 S Congress Ave; sandwiches $5; ☻ 7am-9pm Sun-Fri, breakfast, lunch & dinner Sat) Walk-up window, shaded patio, plus great people-watching…throw in breakfast tacos, gourmet deli sandwiches and coffee drinks. Stick it in the middle of hopping South Congress, and you've got a classic Austin hangout.

Bouldin Creek Coffee House (Map p118; ☎ 512-416-1601; 1501 S 1st St; meals $3-7; ☻ 7am-midnight Mon-Fri, 9am-midnight Sat & Sun; Ⓥ) Vegetarian meals (mmm, veggie chorizo) are made from scratch right in the kitchen, and breakfast is served all day. A 'Slacker's Banquet' of beans over rice and 'Cosmic Sloppy Joes' should clue you in about the clientele.

Magnolia Cafe South (Map p114; ☎ 512-445-0000; 1920 S Congress Ave; mains $5-9; ☻ 24hrs) This outpost of the original Westlake cafe (p132) attracts a mix of artists, surfers and bleary-eyed club-hoppers.

Green Mesquite BBQ & More (Map p114; ☎ 512-479-0485; 1400 Barton Springs Rd; mains $6-10, kids' plates $4; 🕙 11am-10pm Sun-Thu, to 11pm Fri & Sat) As its T-shirts say, it's been 'horrifying vegetarians since 1988.' This inexpensive, low-key spot has lots of meat, pecan pie, cold beer, and a shady outdoor area that's lovely on cool days.

MIDRANGE

ourpick Güero's Taco Bar (Map p118; ☎ 512-447-7688; 1412 S Congress Ave; mains $6-15; 🕙 11am-11pm Mon-Fri, 8am-11pm Sat & Sun) Oh, Güero's, how we love you. Why must you make us wait? Well, clearly it's because of the three million other hungry people crammed into your bar area. Still, we'll try to be patient, because we love the atmosphere lent by the century-old former feed-and-seed store, and because we have an obsessive craving for your chicken tortilla soup.

Shady Grove Restaurant (Map p114; ☎ 512-474-9991; 1624 Barton Springs Rd; mains $7-12; 🕙 lunch & dinner Sun-Thu, 11am-11pm Fri & Sat) 'Do you want inside or out?' Really, what kind of question is that? We came for the shady patio, like everyone else. The lodgelike stone building is fine if it's raining, or if you're too hungry to wait, but outdoors under the pecan trees is prime real estate for enjoying everything from chili cheese fries to the vegetarian Hippie Sandwich.

Threadgill's World Headquarters (Map p118; ☎ 512-472-9304; 301 W Riverside Dr; mains $8-15; 🕙 lunch & dinner Mon-Sat, 10am-9:30pm Sun) Taking home cooking to a gluttonous new level, Threadgill's lets you choose from a ridiculously long list of vegetable sides – something you just don't get at home. Pair your meatloaf or chicken-fried steak with spinach casserole, butter beans, mac and cheese (not technically a vegetable, but still) and classic mashed potatoes and gravy.

TOP END

Reservations are recommended for these restaurants.

Uchi (Map p118; ☎ 512-916-4808; 801 S Lamar Blvd; sushi from $3, appetizers & mains $5-18; 🕙 dinner Mon-Thu, 5-11pm Fri & Sat) When East meets West, they collide beautifully at this top-notch South Austin sushi joint. The sleek interior would feel right at home in LA, and the sushi is every bit as fresh as what you'd get there.

South Congress Cafe (Map p118; ☎ 512-447-3905; 1600 S Congress Ave; mains $12-28; 🕙 10am-4pm Mon-Fri, 9am-4pm Sat & Sun, dinner daily) The stylish side of Tex-Mex can be found at this hoppin' little cafe, which seamlessly combines a vintage space with modern architecture. Come for half-price appetizers at happy hour from 3pm to 6pm weekdays; stay for dinner.

Vespaio (Map p118; ☎ 512-441-6100; 1610 S Congress Ave; mains $17-29; 🕙 from 5:30pm) This cozy Italian restaurant gets high marks for its fresh, authentic, seasonal menus. You can always go the pizza or pasta route, but the critic's favorites are usually found among the *specialitas della casa*.

MEALS ON WHEELS

Food trailers are here to stay – even if they can move around at whim. We haven't listed any of these rolling restaurants because of their transient nature, but instead invite you to explore some of the areas where they congregate. Wander from trailer to trailer till one strikes your fancy, or make a progressive dinner out of it. Look for clusters of airstreams and taco trucks in some of these likely spots:

■ **South Congress** (btwn Elizabeth & Monroe Sts) At time of research, a parking lot across from the main drag of SoCo had several trailers, but there was talk of someone building a permanent structure there. If it's still there, look for the awesome **Mighty Cone**.

■ **South Austin Trailer Park & Eatery** (1311 S First) This seems to be a rather settled trailer community, with a fence, an official name, a sign and picnic tables. Cross your fingers that there's still a **Torchy's Tacos** trailer.

■ **South Lamar** (1219 S Lamar Blvd) If you're lucky, you'll find **Gourdoughs** in this parking lot cluster. The gourmet doughnuts are expensive but provide a full dessert for two.

■ **Flip Happy Crepes** (☎ 512-552-9034; 🕙 10am-2:30pm Wed-Fri, 9am-3pm Sat, 10am-2pm Sun) There's only one trailer here, parked behind 400 Josephine St, but it was one of the (if not *the*) first, so we thought it deserved a mention.

UT Area & Hyde Park

There are some spicy exceptions to the generally bland, student-oriented fare that crowds Guadalupe St (aka the Drag).

BUDGET

Freebirds World Burrito (Map p114; ☎ 512-451-5514; 1000 E 41st St; burritos $5-8; ☺ lunch & dinner Sun-Thu, 11am-11pm Fri & Sat) Burritos – and nothing but – are why you come to Freebirds. Each one is custom-made under your watchful eye, with a boggling number of combinations of tortilla, meat and toppings. For a place with kind of a rock-and-roll atmosphere, the staff is surprisingly friendly and helpful.

New World Deli (Map p114; ☎ 512-451-7170; 4101 Guadalupe St; sandwiches $5-8; ☺ 9am-9pm Mon-Wed, 9am-late Thu-Sat, 9am-6pm Sun) Fans of the sandwich will be delighted with the offerings at New World, whether they're after a sloppy joe, pastrami on rye, or curried chicken salad on wheat – all of which are made with New World's amazing, fresh-baked bread, and all of which will raise the bar on what you'll expect from any future sandwiches you encounter.

Texas French Bread (Map p114; ☎ 512-499-0544; 2900 Rio Grande St; lunch $7-10, dinner $14-21; ☺ 7am-6pm Mon, breakfast, lunch & dinner Tue-Sat, 8am-5pm Sun) Forget the French bread; you want the yummy pastries, or perhaps one of the lunch specials followed by a yummy pastry. This place has been perfecting its ginger cookies, chocolate cake and hobbit bread for decades, so they're pretty much perfect. Now serving dinner in the evenings.

Kerbey Lane Café (Map p114; ☎ 512-451-1436; 3704 Kerbey Lane; breakfast $4-8, lunch & dinner $6-11; ☺ 24hr) Located in a former home, the original Kerbey Lane is a longtime Austin favorite, fulfilling round-the-clock cravings for anything from gingerbread pancakes to black-bean tacos to mahimahi. Vegetarians will find plenty to choose from. There's another branch closer to campus, at 2606 Guadalupe St (Map p114; ☎ 512-477-5717).

Trudy's Texas Star (Map p114; ☎ 512-477-2935; 409 W 30th; mains $6-11; ☺ 4pm-midnight Mon-Thu, 9am-2am Fri & Sat, 9am-midnight Sun) Get your Tex-Mex fix here; the menu is consistently good, with several healthier-than-usual options. But we'll let you in on a little secret: this place could serve beans and dirt and people would still line up for the margaritas, which might very well be the best in Austin.

MIDRANGE & TOP END

Hyde Park Bar & Grill (Map p114; ☎ 512-458-3168; 4206 Duval St; mains $5-16; ☺ 11am-late) Look for the enormous fork out front to guide you to this homey neighborhood haunt. The diverse menu has plenty of options, but no matter what you choose, consider an order of batter-dipped french fries, which is what this place is famous for.

East Austin

East Austin's ethnic eateries are worthy of notice, especially if you're already sightseeing in the neighborhood. This area is majorly up-and-coming, especially on 6th and 7th Sts. Look for new bars and restaurants in the blocks just east of I-35.

El Chilito (Map p114; ☎ 512-382-3797; 2219 Manor Rd; tacos/burritos $2-5; ☺ breakfast, lunch & dinner Mon-Fri, 8am-10pm Sat, 8am-9pm Sun) If you want quick, cheap and easy, this walk-up taco stand (with a big deck for your dining pleasure) can't be beat. You've got to try breakfast tacos, and this is a good place to get them.

Your Mom's Burger Bar (Map p114; ☎ 512-474-MOMS; 1701 E Cesar Chavez St, Suite B; mains $6-8; ☺ 11am-11pm Mon-Sat) How very Austin: these guys pawned an amp to start their burger biz (which faces Chalmers St, even though the address is on Cesar Chavez). And we're glad they did, because these stuffed burgers are really rather excellent. Rock on!

Mi Madre's (Map p114; ☎ 512-322-9721; 2201 Manor Rd; tacos $2-4, mains $6-10; ☺ 6am-2pm Mon-Sat, 8am-3pm Sun) Barbacoa, chorizo and adobado are just a few of the authentic Mexican specialties here. In fact, it was recommended by a friend who said the barbacoa was just like his grandma used to make. Praise doesn't come much higher than that.

El Chile (Map p114; ☎ 512-457-9900; 1809 Manor Rd; mains $10-14; ☺ 11am-9pm Sun-Mon, 11am-10pm Tue-Sat) Let the comfy red chairs on the patio scoop you up for half-price appetizers at happy hour (all night on Monday!) and grab a spicy, orange-infused Chilango Margarita, or stay for enchiladas and other *especialidades*. Visit its other location at 1025 Barton Springs Rd.

Greater Austin

BUDGET

Magnolia Cafe (Map p114; ☎ 512-478-8645; 2304 Lake Austin Blvd; mains $5-9; ☺ 24hr) In Westlake, opposite Deep Eddy Cabaret (p134), this casual, all-night cafe serves American and Tex-Mex standbys such as *migas*, enchiladas, pancakes and potato scrambles. It gets absurdly crowded on weekends.

Whip In (off Map p114; ☎ 512-442-5337; 1950 S IH 35; mains $5-9; ⏰ 10am-midnight) It started as a convenience store on a frontage road. Then the beer and Indian food started to take over. Now it's half Indian restaurant and half beer store, with a few groceries still hanging around to keep it confusing. Would we mention it if the food (breakfast naan and 'panaani' sandwiches) wasn't awesome? We would not.

MIDRANGE

Threadgill's Restaurant (Map p114; ☎ 512-451-5440; 6416 N Lamar Blvd; mains $6-18; ⏰ lunch & dinner Mon-Sat, 11am-9pm Sun) Kenneth Threadgill's original restaurant and hootenanny palace in North Austin is where Janis Joplin once performed. See the more centrally located Threadgill's World Headquarters (p131) for a full review.

Salt Lick BBQ (off Map p114; ☎ 512-894-3117; 18300 FM 1826, Driftwood; mains $7-15, kids menu $5; ⏰ 11am-10pm) Many people say the Salt Lick is well worth the drive for the vast Hill Country horizons seen from its rustic outdoor tables. The family-style meal includes all-you-can-eat beef, sausage, pork ribs and sides. There's also live music on weekends.

County Line (off Map p114; ☎ 512-346-3664; 5204 FM 2222; mains $8-20; ⏰ 11am-9pm Sun & Mon, lunch & dinner Tue-Sat) Unless you have an enormous appetite, there's no need to splurge on the all-you-can-eat meals. Most of the combos and platters of delicious ribs, brisket and sausage are – truly – all you can eat. We love the lakeside location

(enjoy a beer on the dock while you wait) and the lake-lodge decor.

TOP END

Reservations are essential at the following places.

Fonda San Miguel (Map p114; ☎ 512-459-4121; 2330 W North Loop Blvd; mains $16-25; ⏰ from 5:30pm Mon-Sat, last seating at 9:30pm, 11am-2pm Sun) The gorgeous building is drenched in the atmosphere of old Mexico, with folk-inspired art, and this place has been serving interior Mexican cooking for over 25 years. The Sunday brunch buffet is an impressive event but, at $39 per person, you'd better come hungry to make it worthwhile.

Zoot (Map p114; ☎ 512-477-6535; 509 Hearn St; mains $17-25; ⏰ 6-10pm Tue-Thu, dinner Fri-Sun) In a charming early-20th-century bungalow off Lake Austin Blvd, this unpretentious New American bistro turns out some of Austin's finest cuisine, as it has for years despite many changes in ownership. Expect surprisingly good New American fare, for instance halibut with grilled mango relish. A French influence is also apparent, not least in the wine list.

DRINKING

There are bejillions of bars in Austin, so what follows is only a very short list. The legendary 6th St bar scene has spilled onto nearby thoroughfares, especially Red River St. Many of the new places on Sixth St are shot bars aimed at party-hardy college students and tourists, while the Red River establishments retain a harder local edge.

DETOUR: LOCKHART

In 1999 the Texas Legislature adopted a resolution naming Lockhart the barbecue capital of Texas. Of course, that means it's the barbecue capital of the *world*. You can eat very well for under $10 at these places:

Black's Barbecue (☎ 512-398-2712; 215 N Main St; ⏰ 10am-8pm Sun-Thu, 10am-8:30pm Fri & Sat) A longtime Lockhart favorite since 1932, with sausage so good Lyndon Johnson had Black's cater a party at the nation's capital.

Kreuz Market (☎ 512-398-2361; 619 N Colorado St; ⏰ 10:30am-8pm Mon-Sat) Serving Lockhart since 1900, the barnlike Kreuz Market uses a dry rub, which means you shouldn't insult it by asking for barbecue sauce. Kreuz doesn't serve it, and the meat doesn't need it.

Chisholm Trail Bar-B-Q (☎ 512-398-6027; 1323 S Colorado St; ⏰ 11am-8:30pm Mon-Sat) Like Black's and Kreuz Market, Chisholm Trail has been named one of the top 10 barbecue restaurants in the state by *Texas Monthly* magazine.

Smitty's Market (☎ 512-398-9344; 208 S Commerce St; ⏰ 7am-6pm Mon-Fri, 7am-6:30pm Sat, 9am-3pm Sun) The blackened pit room and homely dining room are all original (knives used to be chained to the tables). Ask to have the fat trimmed off the brisket if you're particular about that.

AUSTIN

COFFEE CULTURE

Austin's a laid-back kind of town, and there's no better way to cultivate your slacker vibe than hanging out, sipping coffee and watching everyone else doing the same. Most places offer light meals in addition to caffeinated treats. Here are a few of our favorites:

Bouldin Creek Coffee House (Map p118) Very representative of the South Austin scene, it has outdoor tables by creaky old fans, punk music, vegetarian food and tattoos galore.

Flipnotics (Map p114; ☎ 512-322-9750; 1601 Barton Springs Rd; ☽ 7am-7pm Mon, 7am-midnight Tue-Fri, 7am-1am Sat, 8am-11pm Sun) This is a good place to nurse a hangover or just chill with a cigarette on the back porch.

Hideout Coffee House & Theatre (p137) Despite its downtown location, it has a very near-campus vibe, and damn fine brews.

Little City (Map p118; ☎ 512-476-2489; 916 Congress Ave; ☽ 7am-midnight Mon-Fri, 9am-midnight Sat, 9am-10pm Sun) Less funky, more modern, with strong espresso and great iced-coffee drinks.

Mozart's Coffee Roasters (off Map p114; ☎ 512-477-2900; 3825 Lake Austin Blvd; ☽ 7am-midnight Mon-Thu, 7am-1am Fri, 8am-1am Sat, 8am-midnight Sun) Out on Lake Austin you'll find a great waterfront view and a sinful dessert case.

Spider House (Map p114; ☎ 512-480-9562; 2908 Fruth St; ☽ 8am-2am) North of campus, Spider House has a big, funky patio bedecked with all sorts of oddities. It's open late and also serves beer and wine.

Downtown

Scholz Biergarten (Map p118; ☎ 512-474-1958; 1607 San Jacinto Blvd) Near the capitol complex, this enormous 19th-century German pub was one of O Henry's hangouts back in the day. It's a low-key spot, and is equally popular with politicians, UT students and European expats.

Malverde (Map p118; ☎ 512-705-0666; 400 W 2nd St; ☽ Wed-Sat) Handcrafted specialty cocktails and DJs set the tone for this swanky upstairs bar, which is right above La Condesa (p130). The outdoor patio with artful plant formations is a great place to watch the city below.

Opal Divine's Freehouse (Map p118; ☎ 512-477-3308; 700 W 6th St) Named for the owner's grandmother, a woman who supposedly enjoyed 'good drink and a good card game,' this breezy and spacious pub serves microbrews, imported lagers and almost 20 types of tequila.

Red River

Club de Ville (Map p118; ☎ 512-457-0900; 900 Red River St) Before Red River was even a scene, Club de Ville was there serving cheap drinks in a space decorated with mismatched retro furniture. And that's not to mention its cool, leafy patio – one of downtown's best places to imbibe outdoors.

Casino El Camino (Map p118; ☎ 512-469-9330; 517 E 6th St) With a legendary jukebox and even better burgers, this is the spot for serious drinking and late-night carousing. If it's too dark inside, head for the back patio.

Lovejoy's (Map p118; ☎ 512-477-1268; 604 Neches St) Basically a bar with an eclectic coffeehouse vibe, this is a comfortable yet cool place to hang out, assuming you don't mind a little (or a lot of) cigarette smoke. It's got quirky touches like a table made out of a coffin, alongside standard bar amenities like a jukebox and pool table.

Around Austin

Get out of downtown to enjoy a wide variety of tippling opportunities.

Deep Eddy Cabaret (Map p114; ☎ 512-472-0961; 2315 Lake Austin Blvd) This great little neighborhood bar is known for its excellent jukebox, loaded with almost a thousand tunes in all genres. Yep, it's a dive, but a top-rate one.

Hula Hut (off Map p114; ☎ 512-476-4852; 3825 Lake Austin Blvd) The hula theme is so thorough that this restaurant feels like a chain, even though it's not. But the bar's sprawling deck that stretches out over Lake Austin makes it a popular hangout among Austin's nonslackers.

Ginny's Little Longhorn Saloon (Map p114; ☎ 512-458-1813; 5434 Burnet Rd; ☽ Mon-Sat) This funky little cinder-block building is one of those dive bars that Austinites love so very much – and did even before it became nationally famous for Chicken-Shit Bingo on Sunday nights.

Hotel San José (Map p118; ☎ 512-444-7322, 800-574-8897; 1316 S Congress Ave) Transcending the hotel-bar genre, this one is actually a cool, Zen-like outdoor patio that attracts a chill crowd, and it's a nice place to hang if you want to actually have a conversation.

East Side Showroom (Map p114; ☎ 512-467-4280; 1100 E 6th St) With an ambience that would feel right at home in Brooklyn, this bar on the emerging east-side scene is full of hipsters soaking up the craft cocktails and bohemian atmosphere.

ENTERTAINMENT

Austin calls itself the 'Live Music Capital of the World,' and you won't hear any argument from us. Music is the town's leading nighttime attraction, and a major industry as well, with several thousand bands and performers from all over the world plying their trade in the city's clubs and bars. Most bars stay open till 2am, while a few clubs stay hoppin' until 4am.

You can get heaps of information on the city's whole entertainment scene in the *Austin Chronicle* or the *Austin American-Statesman*'s *XLent* section, both out on Thursday. *XLent* has an ultrastreamlined 'Club Listings' chart that lets your plan your evening's entertainment at a glance, but the *Chronicle*'s night-by-night encyclopedia of listings often includes set times (handy if you'd like to hit several venues in one night), plus music critics' picks and local gossip to really plug you into the scene.

Advance tickets (which may be cheaper) for major venues are sold through **Star Tickets** (☎ 800-585-3737; www.startickets.com); it also handles some performing arts and sports events.

Live Music

Music is a proud tradition in this part of the state, where you can see any kind of musical performance, from a four-piece bluegrass band kicking out jug tunes to a lone DJ spinning the latest trance grooves. The area's unique prominence on the country's musical stage can be traced all the way back to the German settlers who immigrated to the area in the mid-1800s, as well as to the rich musical heritage Texas has always shared with Mexico. Austin's modern sound first took shape in the early 1970s at a barnlike venue known as the Armadillo World Headquarters (see p136).

Today, most live-music bars and clubs have a mix of local and touring bands. On any given Friday night there are several hundred acts playing in the town's 200 or so venues, and even on an off night (Monday and Tuesday are usually the slowest) you'll typically have your pick of more than two dozen performances. Generally there are two to three bands per venue each night. Cover

charges ranges from $3 for local bands to $15 or more for touring acts. Music shows often start late, with the headliner starting anywhere from 9pm to midnight, though a few clubs offer music as early as 4pm, and doors almost always open half an hour to an hour before showtime. Showing up at the last minute or fashionably late may result in not getting in. If you want to get started early, most places have a happy hour (4pm to 7pm).

Many of the venues we recommend are longtime Austin institutions. If you want to experience Austin's music scene but aren't sure where to start, any of these are good bets.

DOWNTOWN – RED RIVER STREET
Stubb's Bar-B-Q (Map p118; ☎ 512-480-8341; www.stubbsaustin.com; 801 Red River St) Stubb's has live music almost every night, with a great mix of premier local and touring acts from across the musical spectrum. Many warm-weather shows are held out back along Waller Creek. There are two stages, a smaller stage indoors and a larger backyard venue.

Emo's (Map p118; ☎ 512-474-5370; www.emosaustin.com; 603 Red River St) Long one of Austin's great punk-rock clubs, the expanded Emo's still has some of the cheapest cover charges in town. Alternative bands rule here, including quite a few touring acts. There are at least three or four bands nearly every night with punk, alternative rock and heavy-metal tendencies, and two stages along with outdoor tables. Shows are all ages unless explicitly stated otherwise.

Red Eyed Fly (Map p118; ☎ 512-474-1084; www.redeyedfly.com; 715 Red River St) On Waller Creek near Stubb's is the Fly, an anchor on the Red River scene. There's live music nightly, plus pool tables, a jukebox and extreme neon that bathes everyone in a creepy red glow.

DRUNK DIALING

If you plan on driving in Austin, and if you've been known to enjoy some adult beverages of the margarita persuasion – quick, program ☎ 512-848-4553 into your phone and file it under **Tipsy Taxi** (www.tipsytaxiaustin.com).

These designated drivers for hire show up in pairs: one to escort you safely home, and one to follow in your car so you don't have to figure out where you left it the next day.

BACK TO THE ARMADILLO *Sam Martin*

In 1970 the Armadillo World Headquarters opened, and catapulted the Austin music scene into the national spotlight it still enjoys today. The club's owners included Eddie Wilson, former band manager for Shiva's Head Band, and Jim Franklin, a local muralist and poster artist – together they turned the building into a hippie haven. The Armadillo quickly became known as the new counterculture hangout, and it attracted antiestablishment hipsters from all over.

The new 'Austin sound' emerged at the Armadillo when Willie Nelson made his debut in 1972. Instead of doing straight-up country tunes, he began mixing blues, rock and Tejano influences into his songs. The result was a curious mix of styles that brought rednecks and hippies cozily together under the Armadillo's singular roof.

The music and the scene were an immediate hit, and the progressive country sound took off. Musicians and bands who heretofore had been hard-pressed to find an audience for their country-rock songs now began to flock to the Armadillo. Marcia Ball, Commander Cody, Doug Sahm, Joe Ely, Asleep at the Wheel and Kinky Friedman all regularly played to packed crowds.

With the success of the Armadillo, other clubs like the Hole in the Wall, near the UT campus, began drawing bigger crowds and more famous bands. *Austin City Limits* debuted in 1976 with Willie Nelson playing on the pilot episode. Big-name bands and musicians took notice of Austin's appreciative audiences and added the city to their tour lists; the Armadillo soon saw such luminaries as Frank Zappa, Bruce Springsteen, Van Morrison, Iggy Pop and the Clash.

The last show at the Armadillo World Headquarters was on New Year's Eve in 1980. In the decade it was open, thousands of bands played there, some of whom became famous because of it and some of whom were already famous and simply wanted to experience the legendary atmosphere. In 1996, Wilson opened Threadgill's World Headquarters (p131) in a building next door to where the Armadillo once stood, and today the restaurant continues to book live local acts five nights a week.

DOWNTOWN – WAREHOUSE DISTRICT

West of Congress Ave, the Warehouse District is more about sexy salsa spots and swingers' drinks, but you'll also find a couple of decent live-music venues.

Lucky Lounge (Map p118; ☎ 512-479-7700; www.theluckylounge.com; 209A W 5th St) Head for this no-pretense spot for early shows (usually starting around 8pm) with no cover charge. And check out that neon sign and mod '60s decor.

Cedar Street Courtyard (Map p118; ☎ 512-495-9669; www.cedarstreetaustin.com; 208 W 4th St) Forget the dark and crowded club scene; this sophisticated courtyard venue serves martinis along with jazz and swing.

Elephant Room (Map p118; ☎ 512-473-2279; www.elephantroom.com; 315 Congress Ave) This intimate, subterranean jazz club has a cool vibe, and live music almost every night. The cover charge stays low (it's mostly free except on weekends), and there are happy-hour shows at 6pm weekdays.

DOWNTOWN – SIXTH STREET

Although the part of Sixth St between I-35 and S Congress Ave has become more of a frat-boy-and-tourist scene, there are still a few venues for dependably great live shows, especially as you head west of Congress.

Flamingo Cantina (Map p118; ☎ 512-494-9336; www.flamingocantina.com; 515 E 6th St) Called 'the last place with soul on Sixth,' Austin's premier reggae joint prides itself on its good rasta vibes and bouncy dancefloor. Seat yourself on the carpeted bleachers for good views of the stage.

MoMo's (Map p118; ☎ 512-479-8848; www.momosclub.com; 618 W 6th St) Named after a very different Las Vegas club, MoMo's has a great rooftop patio and eclectic mix of bands, making it a casual, fun place. Often there's no cover before the end of happy hour.

Donn's Depot (Map p114; ☎ 512-478-0336; http://donnr.home.texas.net; 1600 W 5th St; ✆ Mon-Sat) Austin loves a dive bar, and Donn's combines a retro atmosphere inside an old railway car with live music six nights a week, including Donn himself performing alongside the Station Masters.

SOUTH AUSTIN

Continental Club (Map p118; ☎ 512-441-2444; www.continentalclub.com; 1315 S Congress Ave) No passive toe-tapping here; this 1950s-era lounge has a dancefloor that's always swinging with some of the city's best local acts.

Saxon Pub (Map p114; ☎ 512-448-2552; www.thesax-onpub.com; 1320 S Lamar Blvd) The superchill Saxon Pub, presided over by 'Rusty,' a huge knight who sits out the front, has music every night, mostly Texas performers in the blues-rock vein. A great place to kick back, drink a beer and discover a new favorite artist.

Dance Clubs
We can't tell you the best dance club in town, because on any given day, it just closed down last week. (Its clientele was probably too busy seeing live music.) Your best bet is to pick up the free *Austin Chronicle* for fresh listings, or wander Sixth St or the Warehouse District and follow the thumping beat.

That said, if you are ready for a little Texas two-steppin', there is only one place you should dream of going: the **Broken Spoke** (off Map p114; ☎ 512-442-6189; 3201 S Lamar Blvd; ☺ live music Tue-Sat evenings). This is country-and-western nirvana – a totally authentic Texas dancehall that's been in business since 1964. Here you'll find dudes in boots and Wranglers two-stepping around a crowded dance floor alongside hipsters, college students and slackers; many consider it an essential Austin experience. (You'll know you've arrived when you spot a big old oak tree propping up an old wagon wheel out front.)

Comedy Clubs
Hideout Coffee House & Theatre (Map p118; ☎ 512-443-3688; www.hideouttheatre.com; 617 Congress Ave; tickets $5-10; ☺ shows usually Thu-Sat) The hipsters'

Hideout is a small coffeehouse/theater space that rubs shoulders with the big theaters on Congress Ave. Shows here feature live improv with plenty of audience participation. The box office usually opens half an hour before showtime.

Esther's Follies (Map p118; ☎ 512-320-0553; www.esthersfollies.com; 525 E 6th St; tickets $18-20; ☺ shows 8pm Thu-Sat, plus 10pm Fri & Sat) Drawing from current events and pop culture, this long-running satire show has a vaudevillian slant, thanks to musical numbers and, yep, even a magician. Good harmless fun.

Capitol City Comedy Club (off Map p114; ☎ 512-467-2333; www.capcitycomedy.com; 8120 Research Blvd, Ste 100; ticket prices vary; ☺ shows 8pm daily, plus 10:30pm Fri & Sat) Far from downtown, Capitol City hosts national headliner comics. Mondays are often reserved for local talent.

Cinema
Check the free *Austin Chronicle* weekly for movie reviews and cinema showtimes.

Alamo Drafthouse Cinema (Map p114; ☎ 512-476-1320; www.originalalamo.com; 1120 S Lamar Blvd; admission $1-12) Easily the most fun you can have at the movies: sing along with *Grease*, quote along with *Princess Bride*, or listen to professional hecklers skewer whatever movie they feel like mocking as part of the Master Pancake series. All that, and you can have food and drink delivered right to your seat.

Austin Film Society (AFS; ☎ 512-322-0145; www.austinfilm.org) Frequent classic and independent

---

LIVE IN AUSTIN

Major places to catch live touring acts include the following:
Austin Music Hall (Map p118; ☎ 512-263-4146; www.austinmusichall.com; 208 Nueces St) A grown-up venue at the edge of downtown, with a capacity of 3000 seated or 4400 general admission.
Backyard (off Map p114; ☎ 512-263-4146; www.thebackyard.net; 13472 W Hwy 71, just west of RM620) A pleasant, open-air amphitheater shaded by trees, a half-hour drive southwest of town. Seats up to 5000 people.
Cactus Cafe (Map p114; ☎ 512-475-6515; www.utexas.edu/student/txunion; Texas Union, 24th & Guadalupe Sts) Inside the UT student union, this tiny venue has seen a stellar array of performers, including Lyle Lovett and Shawn Colvin, since it opened in the 1970s. Seating starts 45 minutes before showtime, but people start lining up even earlier. The focus is on the music, mostly acoustic.
Frank Erwin Center (Map p114; ☎ 512-477-6060; www.uterwincenter.com; 1701 Red River St) Known as 'The Drum' among UT students, this major venue for concerts and UT sports can hold up to 17,000 screaming fans.
Paramount Theatre (Map p118; ☎ 512-472-5470; www.austintheatre.org; 713 Congress Ave) An early-20th-century art-deco theater that stages a little bit of everything, from alt-country to comedy to choral music.
Stubb's Bar-B-Q (p135) A small indoor stage looks onto the main backyard concert venue, which rocks the Red River scene. Excellent acoustics.
Antone's (Map p118; ☎ 512-320-8424; www.antones.net; 213 W 5th St) A key player in Austin's musical history, Antone's has attracted the best of the blues and other popular local acts since 1975. All ages, all the time.

AUSTIN

MUSIC FESTIVALS

For five nights in mid-March tens of thousands of record-label reps, musicians, journalists and rabid fans from around the country descend on Austin for the **South by Southwest Music & Media Conference** (SXSW; ☎ 512-467-7979; www.sxsw.com), a musical extravaganza that attracts a couple thousand groups and solo artists from around the world to 90 different Austin venues.

Though SXSW started out as an opportunity for little-known bands and singers to catch the ear of a record-label rep, it has since become more of an industry showcase for already-signed bands that need some exposure. With all the media attention it gets, the festival is also drawing bigger names into the fray: Tom Waits, Johnny Cash and Tony Bennett have all played at SXSW in recent years.

So that's where music lovers go in the spring, but what do they do in autumn? Now there's a second festival that, while not as big as SXSW, has been swiftly gaining on it in terms of popularity: the **Austin City Limits Festival** (ACL; ☎ tickets 888-512-SHOW; www.aclfestival.com; 1-/3-day pass $85/185). The three-day festival held each October on eight stages in Zilker Park books more than 100 pretty impressive acts and sells out months in advance.

---

film screenings at venues around town. *Slacker* director Richard Linklater was an early promoter and Quentin Tarantino is now on the board of directors.

Dobie Theatre (Map p114; ☎ 512-472-3456; www.landmarktheatre.com; Dobie Mall, 2025 Guadalupe St) Part of the Landmark chain, the Dobie is a four-screen venue for independent, foreign-language and other offbeat films.

Performing Arts

Austin's performing arts scene doesn't rival other US cities, but the number of national and touring troupes that stop off in the Capitol City is astonishing.

CLASSICAL MUSIC, DANCE & OPERA

Long Center for the Performing Arts (Map p118; ☎ 512-457-5100; www.thelongcenter.org; 701 W Riverside Dr) This state-of-the-art theater opened in late 2008 as part of a waterfront redevelopment along Lady Bird Lake. The multistage venue hosts drama, dance, concerts and comedians.

Austin Symphony (Map p118; ☎ 512-476-6064; www.austinsymphony.org; ticket office 1101 Red River St; tickets $19-48; ☯ box office 9am-5pm Mon-Fri, on performance days noon-5pm Sat) Founded in the early 20th century, the city's oldest performing arts group plays classical and pop music at numerous venues throughout the city. The main performance season runs from September to April.

THEATER

Austin has a small but active theater scene at venues all over town. Check the *Austin Chronicle* or *XLent* for performance schedules. Following are some of the best theaters.

Hyde Park Theatre (Map p114; ☎ 512-479-7529; 511 W 43rd St) This is one of Austin's coolest theaters, presenting regional premieres of off-Broadway hits and recent Obie (Off-Broadway Theater Awards) winners. Its annual FronteraFest presents more than 100 new works over five weeks at venues around town.

Paramount Theatre (Map p118; ☎ 512-472-5470; www.austintheatre.org; 713 Congress Ave; ☯ box office noon-5:30pm Mon-Sat) Dating from 1915, this old vaudevillian house has staged everything from the Ziegfield Follies to splashy Broadway shows to classic film screenings.

Zach Theatre Center (Map p118; ☎ 512-476-0541; www.zachtheatre.org; 1510 Toomey Rd; ☯ box office noon-7pm Mon-Sat) Often reprising popular Broadway and off-Broadway hits, this theatre has two venues: Whisenhunt Stage (1510 Toomey Rd) and Kleberg Stage (1421 W Riverside Drive).

Spectator Sports

The whole town turns burnt orange during University of Texas game weekends, especially during football season, when the fiercely loyal Longhorn fans are downright fanatical. (They're not flipping you off: it's probably just the two-fingered sign for 'Hook 'em Horns.') For tickets to any university-sponsored sporting event, contact the **UT ticket office** (Map p114; ☎ 512-477-6060, 800-982-2386; www.texasboxoffice.com).

SHOPPING

Not many folks visit Austin just to shop. That said, music is a huge industry here and you'll find heaps of it in Austin's record stores. Vintage is a lifestyle, and the city's best hunting grounds for retro fashions and furnishings are South Austin and Guadalupe St near UT.

On the first Thursday of the month, S Congress Ave is definitely the place to be, when stores stay open until 10pm and there's live entertainment; visit www.firstthursday. info for upcoming events. For a list of bookshops, see p113.

Music

Music is tops on the list of things to buy in Austin, and record-shop employees are usually fairly knowledgeable and will likely be in a band themselves. The best stores let you listen to just about anything before you buy, and will carry the bands you see around town.

Waterloo Records (Map p118; ☎ 512-474-2500; www. waterloorecords.com; 600A N Lamar Blvd; ☾ 10am-11pm Mon-Sat, 11am-11pm Sun) Waterloo is a landmark and the best music store in town, with a huge selection and low prices on new and used CDs and vinyl. There are sections reserved just for local bands, and listening stations featuring Texas, indie and alt-country acts.

Antone's Records (Map p114; ☎ 512-322-0660; www. antones.com; 2928 Guadalupe St; ☾ 10am-10pm Mon-Sat, 11am-8pm Sun) North of UT, legendary Antone's was founded in 1972 and has a well-respected selection of Austin, Texas and American blues music (with plenty of rare vinyl), plus a bulletin board for musicians, and vintage concert posters for sale.

Cheapo Discs & DVDs (Map p118; ☎ 512-477-4499; 914 N Lamar Blvd; ☾ 9am-midnight) Though not as much of a bargain as the name suggests, it does have racks of used CDs, including Texas and alt-country music. Free in-store performances are often scheduled for the first Friday of the month.

Clothing & Shoes
FASHION

Blackmail (Map p118; ☎ 512-376-7670; 1202 S Congress Ave; ☾ 10:30am-6pm Tue-Sat) Black is the new black at this color-challenged store that unites Goths, punks and urban sophisticates. That means gorgeous black dresses and *guayabera* shirts, black-and-silver jewelry, black beaded handbags, black shoes and even minimalist black-and-white home decor.

Emeralds (Map p118; ☎ 512-476-4496; www.hello-emeralds.com; 624 N Lamar Blvd; ☾ 10am-9pm Mon-Sat, noon-7pm Sun) Almost a minidepartment store for trendy women, Emeralds sells racks of spirited clothes that instead of being separated

by designer are grouped by color. You'll also find jewelry by Texas artisans, handbags and, oh, the shoes.

Stag (Map p118; ☎ 512-373-7824; www.stagaustin.com; 1423 S Congress Ave; ☾ 11am-8pm Mon-Sat, 11am-6pm Sun) Embrace the art of manliness at this stylish SoCo store that's just for the guys, or for girls who are shopping for guys.

Pangaea Trading Company (Map p114; ☎ 512-472-3533; 2712 Guadalupe St; ☾ 11am-6pm) Good clothes can be hard to find on the Drag, but Pangaea stands out with unique and affordable clothing, shoes and jewelry from around the world.

VINTAGE, USED & DISCOUNT
Austin loves vintage clothing. For even more options, check out www.vintagearoundtown guide.com.

Electric Ladyland (Map p118; ☎ 512-444-2002; www. lucyindisguise.com; 1506 S Congress Ave; ☾ 11am-7pm Mon-Sat, noon-6pm Sun) Colorful and over the top, this South Congress staple has been outfitting Austinites for years. You can rent or buy costume pieces, which is this place's specialty, but you can also find everyday vintage duds as well.

Amelia's Retrovogue & Relics (Map p114; ☎ 512-442-4446; www.ameliasretrovogue.com; 2213 S 1st St; ☾ noon-5pm Tue-Sat) Austin's queen of vintage high fashion, Amelia's brings together *Vogue*-worthy dresses, retro '50s bathing suits and other old-school glamour for both men and women. It's a favorite with film industry folk.

Blue Velvet (Map p114; ☎ 512-452-2583; www. bluevelvetaustin.com; 217 W North Loop Blvd; ☾ 11am-8pm Mon-Sat, noon-8pm Sun) Western wear, vintage T-shirts and even oddities such as all-American bowling wear hang on the racks at Blue Velvet, where you'll find an equal number of

---

THE HIGHBALL

We wanted to mention the **Highball** (Map p114; ☎ 512-383-8309; 1142 S Lamar Blvd; ☾ 4:30pm-2am Mon-Fri, 1pm-2am Sat & Sun) but we had no idea what to list it under. Bar? Brunch spot? Bowling alley? Karaoke? Skee-ball? Retro-swanky amusement emporium? The Highball is all of those things.

In other words, if you're not sure what you want to do, this is a good place to start. It's next door to (and owned by) the folks at Alamo Drafthouse (p137) so you're sure to find something that amuses you.

men and women eyeing the goods. Summer fashions are stocked year-round.

Buffalo Exchange (Map p114; ☎ 512-480-9922; 2904 Guadalupe St; ⏰ 11am-8pm Mon-Sat, noon-6pm Sun) The Austin branch of this nationwide used-clothing chain has an impressive selection of vintage clothes and shoes for men and women, including Texas styles and Western wear. A retro T-shirt matched with a simple skirt or jeans will instantly achieve that alternative Austin look.

WESTERN WEAR

Allen's Boots (Map p118; ☎ 512-447-1413; 1522 S Congress Ave; ⏰ 9am-8pm Mon-Sat, noon-6pm Sun) In hip South Austin, family-owned Allen's sells rows upon rows of traditional cowboy boots for ladies, gents and kids. A basic pair costs from $50, while somethin' fancy runs a few hundred dollars.

In North Austin, **Shepler's** (Map p114; ☎ 512-454-3000; 6001 Middle Fiskville Rd), just south of Highland Mall, and **Cavender's Boot City** (off Map p114; ☎ 512-451-7474; 8809 Burnet Rd) are giant chains for Western wear of all kinds.

Art & Antiques

For a complete list of art galleries and happenings around town, visit www.inthegalleriesaustin.com, or pick up an 'In the Galleries' brochure at any gallery.

our pick Uncommon Objects (Map p118; ☎ 512-442-4000; 1512 S Congress Ave; ⏰ 11am-6pm Sun-Thu, 11am-7pm Fri & Sat) 'Curious oddities' is what they advertise at this quirky antique store that sells all manner of fabulous knick-knackery. The merchandise is displayed with an artful eye that makes browsing akin to visiting a rambling museum of memorabilia, all of which happens to be for sale.

Yard Dog (Map p118; ☎ 512-912-1613; www.yarddog.com; 1510 S Congress Ave; ⏰ 11am-5pm Mon-Fri, 11am-6pm Sat, noon-5pm Sun) Stop into this small but scrappy gallery (right next door to Uncommon Objects) that focuses on folk and outsider art.

Austin Art Garage (Map p114; ☎ 512-351-5934; www.austinartgarage.com; 2200 S Lamar Blvd; ⏰ 11am-6pm Tue-Sat, noon-5pm Sun) This cool little independent… well, we hesitate to call it a 'gallery' because that would needlessly scare some people off. Anyway, it features some pretty great artwork by Austin artists. (Hey, Joel Ganucheau: we're fans.) Check out the website to catch the vibe, and definitely check out the 'gallery' if you like what you see.

Room Service (Map p114; ☎ 512-451-1057; 107 E North Loop Blvd; ⏰ 11am-5:30pm Mon-Sat, noon-5pm Sun) Whether your style is '70s moon chairs or art-nouveau fainting couches, this is the most fabulous place in the city for vintage furnishings. Plenty of smaller (and more portable) stuff is for sale, like gobstopping ashtrays, silk kimonos and more.

Gifts

University Coop (Map p114; ☎ 512-476-7211; 2246 Guadalupe St; ⏰ 8:30am-7:30pm Mon-Fri, 9:30am-6pm Sat, 11am-5pm Sun) School spirit is alive and well at this store on the UT Drag brimming with all manner of burnt-orange-and-white clothing and souvenirs sporting the Longhorn logo.

Toy Joy (Map p114; ☎ 512-320-0090; www.toyjoy.com; 2900 N Guadalupe St; ⏰ 10am-11pm Sun-Thu, 11am-midnight Fri & Sat) Just north of campus, this toy store for grownups and big kids is an exuberant repository that's packed floor to ceiling with fun.

Tesoros Trading Co (Map p118; ☎ 512-479-8377; 209 Congress Ave; ⏰ 11am-6pm Sun-Fri, 10am-6pm Sat) Browse folk art and crafts from around the world, with a heavy Latin American influence of metalwork, jewelry, colorfully painted handicrafts, the Virgin Mary, and *Día de los Muertos.*

Wild About Music (Map p118; ☎ 512-708-1700; 721 Congress Ave; ⏰ 10am-7pm Mon-Thu, 10am-9pm Fri & Sat, 10am-6pm Sun) In the downtown theater block, this store features art and gifts inspired by music and musicians – everything from caps, T-shirts and bumper stickers to Elvis cookie jars and handcrafted CD racks.

For Kids

Dragonsnaps (off Map p114; ☎ 512-445-4497; 2438 West Anderson Ln; ⏰ 10am-6pm Mon-Sat, noon-6pm Sun) Presided over by a jolly green dragon, this kids' clothing store is perfect for comfortably outfitting your young 'uns with a dash of panache. Prices may be high, but most of this well-made clothing will last a long time.

Terra Toys (Map p114; ☎ 512-445-4489; 2438 W Anderson Ln; ⏰ 9am-8pm Mon-Sat, noon-6pm Sun) Meant for zany adults almost as much as it is for kids, this toy store sells puzzles and puppets, Mad Libs books, Nunzilla wind-up dolls, bouncy balls and even kites to fly in Zilker Park.

Eco-wise (Map p118; ☎ 512-326-4474; www.ecowise.com; 110 W Elizabeth St; ⏰ 11am-7pm Mon-Fri, 10am-6pm Sat, noon-5pm Sun) Specializing in hemp, organic cotton and nontoxic goods, this store aimed at adults also carries a wealth of ecofriendly baby products, as well as cooperative games and outdoor gear for older kids.

Malls

Arboretum (off Map p114; ☎ 512-338-4437; 10000 Research Blvd; ✆ 10am-6pm Mon-Wed, Fri & Sat, 10am-8pm Thu, hours vary Sun) About 20 minutes northwest of downtown, the Arboretum is a parklike collection of high-end stores, including Sharper Image and Restoration Hardware.

Highland Mall (Map p114; ☎ 512-451-2920; 6001 Airport Blvd; ✆ 10am-9pm Mon-Fri, 10am-7pm Sat, noon-6pm Sun) Northeast of downtown off I-35, Highland Mall has your standard mall offerings.

GETTING THERE & AWAY
Air

Opened in 1999, **Austin-Bergstrom International Airport** (off Map p114; AUS; ☎ 512-530-2242; www.ci.austin.tx.us/austinairport; 3600 Presidential Blvd) is about 10 miles southeast of downtown. It's served by American, Continental, Delta, Frontier, JetBlue, Southwest and United-Lufthansa Airlines.

A nice welcome to the city, the airport features live music by local acts on some evenings near the center of the departures level. You can also sample food from Austin-based restaurants, including Amy's Ice Cream and Salt Lick BBQ, or buy some last-minute CDs from the Austin City Limits store. The airport's only big drawback is its lack of lockers, so plan to keep your carry-on bags with you.

Bus

The **main bus station** (Map p114; 916 E Koenig Lane) is served by **Greyhound** (☎ 512-458-4463; www.greyhound.com) and the **Kerrville Bus Co** (☎ 512-458-3823; www.iridekbc.com). Capital Metro bus 7-Duval (www.capmetro.org) will deliver you from the station to the UT campus or downtown. Buses leave from here for other major Texas cities frequently; there are also some rather pricey services to the nearby Hill Country.

Train

The downtown **Amtrak station** (Map p118; ☎ 512-476-5684; www.amtrak.com; 250 N Lamar Blvd) is served by the *Texas Eagle* that extends from Chicago to Los Angeles. There's free parking and an enclosed waiting area, but no staff. Fares vary wildly.

GETTING AROUND
To/From the Airport

Ground transportation from Austin-Bergstrom International Airport can be found on the lower level near baggage claim. A taxi between the airport and downtown costs about $25 to $30. Capital Metro runs a limited-stop Airport Flyer (bus 100) service between the airport and downtown and the University of Texas for just $1 each way, with departures every 40 minutes. Check with **Capital Metro** (www.capmetro.org) for exact schedules. It takes at least 20 minutes to get downtown from the airport, and 35 minutes to reach the UT campus.

SuperShuttle (☎ 512-258-3826, 800-258-3826; www.supershuttle.com) offers a shared-van service from the airport to downtown hotels for about $14 one way, or a few dollars more to accommodations along north I-35 and near the Arboretum mall.

Bicycle

A grand bicycle tour of greater Austin isn't feasible, due to interstate highways and the like, but cycling around downtown, South Congress and the UT campus is totally doable. There are also miles of recreational paths around the city that are ideal for cruisin'. Check www.austinbikeroutes.com.

You know you're in good hands when you rent a bike from Lance Armstrong. Located right downtown, **Mellow Johnny's Bike Shop** (Map p118; ☎ 512-473-0222; www.mellowjohnnys.com; 400 Nueces St; 4hr bike rental adult $20-40, child $10, 24hr adult $30-60, child $20; ✆ 8am-7pm Mon-Fri, 8am-6pm Sat, 10am-4pm Sun) is co-owned by the seven-time Tour de France winner. It rents high-performance bikes as well as commuter bikes, and offers free guided bike rides (check the website for a schedule).

WHAT THE...? JUAN PELOTA

You can't say Lance Armstrong doesn't have a sense of humor. His bike shop, **Mellow Johnny's**, is a play on the French for yellow jersey, *maillot jaune*. And the attached coffee shop is called Juan Pelota. Consider that Juan sounds like 'one,' *pelota* means 'ball,' and Lance once had a certain anatomical part removed, and the curious name that sounds like a Tex-Mex restaurant starts to make a lot more sense.

The cool thing about **Bicycle Sportshop** (Map p118; ☎ 512-477-3472; www.bicyclesportshop.com; 517 S Lamar Blvd; ☺ 10am-7pm Mon-Fri, 9am-6pm Sat, 11am-5pm Sun) is its proximity to Zilker Park, Barton Springs and the Lady Bird Lake bike paths, all of which are within a few blocks. Rentals range from $13 for a two-hour cruise on a standard bike, to $60 for a full day on a top-end full-suspension model. On weekends and holidays, advance reservations are advised.

Car & Motorcycle

Getting around Austin is easy enough, but the main consideration for drivers – other than rush-hour gridlock and what people from smaller towns consider crazy drivers – is where to leave your car when you're not in it.

Downtown, the best deal is at the **Capitol Visitors Parking Garage** (Map p118; 1201 San Jacinto Blvd). It's free for the first two hours, and only 75¢ per half-hour after that, maxing out at $6. Other downtown garages and lots are fairly abundant. They usually charge $1 to $2 per hour, with a daily maximum of $8 to $10.

The state-operated parking garage at 4th and San Antonio Sts is free after 6pm, and fills up quickly. Other downtown garages and parking lots typically charge a flat fee of around $6 or so after dark. People also park for free under I-35 at the east end of 6th St, but you can't depend on it being available (or legal).

On-street parking meters cost 25¢ for 15 to 20 minutes during the day, but are free in the evenings. Free park-and-ride lots on the outskirts of downtown sponsored by Capital Metro let you connect with free 'Dillo shuttle buses into downtown.

Day or night, finding a spot around the UT campus can take a while. Free visitor parking is available outside the LBJ Library, but from there it's a long, hot walk across campus to the UT Tower and other sights. Parking spots on Guadalupe St are both timed and metered. Otherwise, your best bet is to search

for free parking in the residential streets west of Guadalupe St.

Elsewhere around Austin, there is free on-street parking, but pay careful attention to posted permit parking and time limits. Meters are usually free after 6pm and all day Sunday.

Public Transport

Austin's handy public transit system is run by **Capital Metro** (CapMetro; ☎ 512-474-1200; www.capmetro.org). Call for directions to anywhere or stop into the downtown **Capital Metro Transit Store** (Map p118; 323 Congress Ave; ☺ 7:30am-5pm Mon-Fri) for information.

Many visitor attractions are accessible through the free 'Dillo shuttle buses that circulate through central Austin, connecting downtown with South Austin and the UT campus area. Regular city buses – not including the more-expensive express routes – cost $1 for adults, 50¢ for students and are free for seniors.

There are bicycle racks (where you can hitch your bike for free) on the front of almost all CapMetro buses, including more than a dozen UT shuttle routes.

Taxi

You'll usually need to call for a cab instead of just flagging one down on the street, except at the airport, major hotels, around the state capitol and at major entertainment areas. The flag drops at $1.75, then it's $1.75 for each additional mile. Larger companies include **Yellow Cab** (☎ 512-452-9999), **Austin Cab** (☎ 512-478-2222), **Checker Cab** (☎ 512-472-1111) and **Roy's Taxi** (☎ 512-482-0000), or check the *Yellow Pages*.

Human-powered bicycle taxis, or **p**edicabs, are available downtown on 6th St and around the Warehouse District, usually from about 9pm until after 2am from Wednesday to Saturday evenings. The drivers, who are typically young students or musicians, work entirely for tips, so please be generous.

San Antonio & Hill Country

Everyone thinks Texas is thoroughly, consistently flat. But in south central Texas, there are hills in them thar' hills. There are also caves, rivers, trees, and wildflowers lining the roadways in spring, making it a marvelous place to meander.

Fredericksburg is the most touristy Hill Country town, but the area is more about winding roads and stopping along the way than any particular destination.

San Antonio, on the other hand, is definitely a destination. The seventh-largest city in the US offers museums, the Riverwalk and, for families, two theme parks worthy of a day each. San Antonio also caters to the history buff. Of course there's the Alamo, site of the most famous battle in the fight for Texas' independence from Mexico. There are also four beautifully preserved Spanish missions, a historical church, and a military base where Geronimo was held captive.

San Antonio has a large Hispanic population, which has a significant impact on the local culture – from mariachi bands roaming downtown to colorful handicrafts available at the local *tiendas*. And there's excellent Mexican food everywhere you turn, with margaritas, cervezas and *aguas frescas* to wash it down.

HIGHLIGHTS

Best Beer in Texas
Hands down, it's Shiner Bock, and you can watch it brewed at the Spoetzl Brewery (p167) in Shiner

Easiest Place to Remember
The Alamo (p147), a historical shrine in San Antonio to the men who fought for Texas' independence

Most German Town in Texas
The unofficial capital of the Hill Country, Fredericksburg (p177) offers a hearty *wilkommen* to all

Most Taxidermy per Square Foot
The Buckhorn Saloon & Museum (p149) in San Antonio packs in mounted animals and discarded horns

Smallest Town with Nightlife
Luckenbach(p180), population three, welcomes visitors with its cold beer and daily live music

Bow-Leggiest Town
Bandera (p184), the self-proclaimed Cowboy Capital of Texas (which would make it the Cowboy Capital of the World)

SAN ANTONIO

pop 1.3 million

In most large cities, downtown is bustling with businesspeople dressed for office work hurrying to their meetings and luncheons. Not so in San Antonio. Instead, downtown is filled with tourists in shorts carrying cameras and consulting their maps. In fact, many people are surprised to find that two of the state's most popular destinations – the Riverwalk and the Alamo – are right smack dab in the middle of downtown, surrounded by historical hotels, tourist attractions and souvenir shops.

The rest of the city sprawls out around downtown, careful not to impinge on the tourist trade. And even though San Antonio is the seventh-largest city in the USA, it never feels particularly crowded.

ORIENTATION

San Antonio is daunting for drivers, and parking is no treat either. Yet the city is laid out in a grid system (albeit a little skewed at times), making navigation easier on the nerves. Pay close attention to highway signs, especially when they indicate a left-hand exit – miss one of those and you're in for a nickel tour of the surrounding suburbs.

Central San Antonio is enclosed by two concentric rings of highways. The ring closest to downtown is formed by I-35 in the west and north, Hwys 87 and 90 and I-10 in the south and west (they run along I-35 for a while),

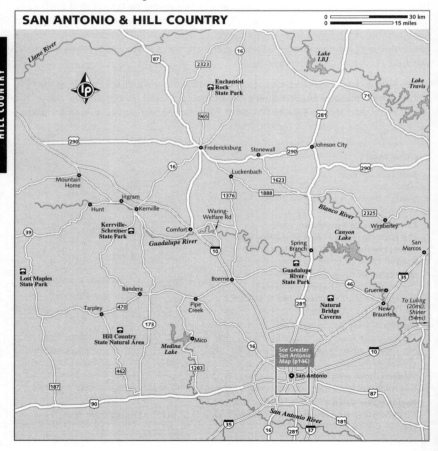

SAN ANTONIO & HILL COUNTRY

and I-37 and US 281 in the east. All these highways feed out to I-410, locally called Loop 410, which circles the city. Note that I-10, which usually runs east–west across Texas, runs north–south in most of San Antonio; directions to take I-10 west from downtown to Six Flags Fiesta Texas (which is almost due north of downtown) are accurate.

Downtown's major north–south arteries include Broadway and Main Ave. East–west thoroughfares include Commerce St, Market St and Houston St. The intersection of Commerce and Losoya Sts is the very heart of downtown and below street level is the Riverwalk, a developed canal loop off the San Antonio River.

The historic King William District lies directly south of downtown across Durango Blvd. The mainly residential district is bordered on the east by S Alamo St, which is the main drag through Southtown, an arts district of galleries, cafes and restaurants.

INFORMATION
Bookstores
Many museums, attractions and Texas-themed gift shops, including souvenir stores inside the Alamo and along the Mission Trail, stock a variety of regional-interest titles.

Borders Books, Music & Cafe (Map p146; ☎ 210-828-9496; Alamo Quarry Market, 255 E Basse Rd; ⊙ 9am-11pm Mon-Sat, 10am-9pm Sun) This chain behemoth in the Alamo Quarry Market is favored for its good general selection.

Half Price Books (Map p146; ☎ 210-822-4597; www.halfpricebooks.com; 3207 Broadway; ⊙ 9:30am-9pm Mon-Sat, 11am-7pm Sun) A broad selection of excellent new and used books. Other locations include 11255 Huebner Rd and 125 NW Loop 410.

Nine Lives Affordable Books (off Map p146; ☎ 210-647-5656; www.ninelivesbooks.com; 4919 NW Loop 410; ⊙ 10am-9pm Mon-Sat, noon-8pm Sun) Used books and cats – both up for adoption!

Twig Bookshop (Map p152; ☎ 210-826-6411; thetwig.com; 200 E Grayson; ⊙ 10am-8pm Mon-Thu, 10am-6pm Fri & Sat) This great little indie bookstore located in the Pearl Brewery development specializes in regional interest, children's books and author events.

Emergency
Police (☎ 210-207-7273)

Internet Access
SA's public library system provides free internet access, but time online may be limited

---

> **DRIVING DISTANCES**
> **Fredericksburg to Johnson City** 30 miles, 35 minutes
> **Kerrville to Fredericksburg** 24 miles, 30 minutes
> **New Braunfels to San Antonio** 33 miles, 40 minutes **San Antonio to Kerrville** 65 miles, 1 hour, 10 minutes
> **San Antonio to Johnson City** 64 miles, 1 hour, 15 minutes

---

to 30 minutes. You must sign up in person (no phone reservations) for the next available terminal. Bring a library card or photo ID. The central **San Antonio Public Library** (Map p152; ☎ 210-207-2500; www.mysapl.org; 600 Soledad St; ⊙ 9am-9pm Mon-Thu, 9am-5pm Fri & Sat, 11am-5pm Sun) is a first-rate multimedia facility with children's programs and helpful staff. Validated parking at the library garage is free for one hour.

Internet Resources
The San Antonio Convention & Visitors Bureau site (www.visitsanantonio.com) has plenty of general information on the city, but for something more in-depth, check these out:

My San Antonio (www.mysanantonio.com) This up-to-date website from the *San Antonio Express-News* covers local news and entertainment and has a calendar of events.

San Antonio Current (www.sacurrent.com) SA's alternative weekly has thumbnail entertainment listings, restaurant reviews, news and classified ads.

Virtual Tours (www.saculturaltours.com) The City of San Antonio's Office of Cultural Affairs has an excellent website that lets you explore cultural gems in different San Antonio neighborhoods.

Media
La Prensa (www.laprensa.com) A bilingual Spanish-language weekly.

San Antonio Current (www.sacurrent.com) The free alternative weekly isn't nearly comprehensive enough, but it's still the best local what's-on guide.

San Antonio Express-News (www.express-news.com) The major daily newspaper; publishes Friday 'Weekender' and Wednesday food sections; Jim Beal's 'Night Lights' column is a good guide to live music.

Medical Services
Check the *Yellow Pages* for dentists offering emergency care; some keep extended office hours or stay on-call at night.

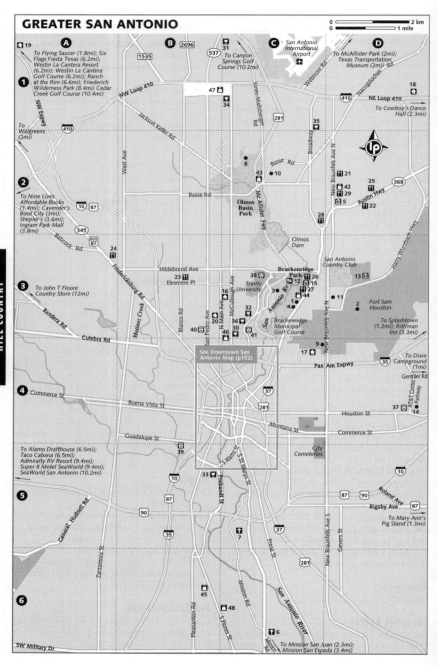

GREATER SAN ANTONIO

0 ——————— 2 km
0 ——————— 1 mile

To Flying Saucer (1.8mi); Six Flags Fiesta Texas (6.2mi); Westin La Cantera Resort (6.2mi); Westin La Cantera Golf Course (6.2mi); Ranch at the Rim (6.6mi); Friederich Wilderness Park (8.4mi) Cedar Creek Golf Course (10.4mi)

San Antonio International Airport

To McAllister Park (2mi); Texas Transportation Museum (2mi)

To Canyon Springs Golf Course (10.2mi)

To Cowboy's Dance Hall (2.3mi)

To Walgreens (2mi)

To Nine Lives Affordable Books (1.4mi); Cavender's Boot City (3mi); Shepler's (3.6mi); Ingram Park Mall (3.8mi)

Olmos Basin Park

Olmos Dam

San Antonio Country Club

To John T Floore Country Store (12mi)

Hildebrand Ave

Elesmere Pl

Trinity University

Brackenridge Park

Fort Sam Houston

To Splashtown (1.2mi); Rittiman Inn (3.3mi)

Brackenridge Municipal Golf Course

See Downtown San Antonio Map (p152)

Pan Am Expwy

To Dixie Campground (1mi)

Gembler Rd

AT&T Center Parkway

To Alamo Drafthouse (6.5mi); Taco Cabana (6.5mi); Admiralty RV Resort (9.4mi); Super 8 Motel SeaWorld (9.4mi); SeaWorld San Antonio (10.2mi)

Commerce St

Buena Vista St

Guadalupe St

Houston St

Commerce St

City Cemeteries

Montana St

To Mary Ann's Pig Stand (1.3mi)

Rigsby Ave

Roland Ave

General Hudnell Rd

SW Military Dr

To Mission San Juan (2.3mi); Mission San Espada (3.4mi)

SAN ANTONIO & HILL COUNTRY

Baptist Medical Center (Map p146; ☎ 210-297-7000; 111 Dallas St) A central hospital, just east of Navarro and Soledad Sts.
Walgreens (off Map p146; ☎ 210-614-3590; 7802 Wurzbach; 🕐 24hr) A 24-hour pharmacy north of Loop 410, near the major hospitals and medical complexes.

Money
There are ATMs that accept most network and credit cards throughout the city, including in malls, at major theme parks and in the gift shop at the Alamo. You can change foreign currency and traveler's checks at **Frost Bank** (Map p152; ☎ 210-220-4011; 100 W Houston St; 🕐 9am-4pm Mon-Thu, 9am-5pm Fri) or **Bank of America** (Map p152; ☎ 210-270-5540; 300 Convent St; 🕐 9am-4pm Mon-Thu, 9am-5pm Fri). There are also two foreign-exchange desks at the airport and one in Six Flags Fiesta Texas.

Post
United States Postal Service (USPS) Downtown Branch (Map p152; 615 E Houston St, enter off Alamo St; 🕐 9am-5pm Mon-Fri). Call ☎ 800-275-8777 to locate other branches.

Tourist Information
Check out the website for the **San Antonio Convention & Visitors Bureau** (CVB; ☎ 210-207-6700, 800-447-3372; www.visitsanantonio.com) for the online version of what you'll find at the **downtown visitors center** (Map p152; ☎ 210-207-6748; 317 Alamo Plaza; 🕐 9am-5pm, till 6pm in summer), opposite the Alamo. While the staff do not book hotel rooms, they can answer questions, provide maps and brochures and sell tickets for tours and also VIA bus and streetcar passes.

DANGERS & ANNOYANCES
The swarming-with-cops downtown is considered safe. East and west of downtown (basically, anywhere across the railway tracks) is not as well patrolled, so common sense is needed in these areas. North of downtown, Avenue B, which parallels Broadway beside Brackenridge Park, may look handy for parking, but it's often deserted after dark and not well lit. Poorer Hispanic and African American areas to the south of the city are considered dangerous but, as in Austin, some latent racism may play a part in exaggerating the actual danger.

The San Antonio River is not a toy and there are several drownings a year. Be especially careful in areas near the Riverwalk that don't have fences.

Other hazards for first-time visitors, especially during summer, are dehydration, heat exhaustion or even heat stroke. To avoid passing out in front of the Alamo (as a few tourists each year inevitably do), always maintain a good fluid intake.

SIGHTS
Downtown
ALAMO
The folks who valiantly fought for Texas' independence from Mexico would never be able to imagine the **Alamo** (Map p152; ☎ 210-225-1391; www.thealamo.org; 300 Alamo Plaza; admission free; 🕐 9am-5:30pm Mon-Sat, from 10am Sun) as it is today, sitting at the heart of San Antonio, surrounded by tacky tourist attractions and having its picture taken every 17 seconds or so.

SAN ANTONIO & HILL COUNTRY

SAN ANTONIO IN...

Two Days
Start your day off exploring the **Riverwalk** (p148), then pay your respects to the **Alamo** (p147) and any other downtown sight that tickles your fancy, perhaps the **Buckhorn Saloon & Museum** (p149) or **Market Square** (p149). Stop in the Southtown area for lunch before exploring the **Blue Star Contemporary Art Center** and historic **King William District** (p151). Return to the Riverwalk for sunset margaritas, dinner and jazz at the **Landing** (p168), then indulge in a good night's sleep at any of SA's historic downtown hotels.

On your second day, head north to **Brackenridge Park** (p154). Spend some time at the **San Antonio Botanical Gardens** (p154), then visit the divine **Marion Koogler McNay Art Museum** (p155) or the **San Antonio Museum of Art** (p154). Have dinner at eclectic **Josephine Street** (p166), then meander over to the **Strip** (p167) to catch a live show. Or, head back to **Southtown** (p167) for drinks, a fine Mexican meal and dancing.

Four Days
Those traveling with kids may want to spend a day visiting **SeaWorld** (p155) or **Six Flags Fiesta Texas** (p155). Alternatively, head out to the hill country, being sure to hit **Bandera** (p184), the Cowboy Capital of Texas, along the way. Explore **Fredericksburg** (p177) and stop into **Luckenbach** (p180) to catch a picking circle if you can. Eat at the **Hill Top Café** (p180) before heading back to San Antonio.

On your final day, explore the four missions along the **Mission Trail** (p153). In the afternoon, head over to the new **Pearl** (p155) development at the old Pearl Brewery to see what's new. Pick a restaurant and stick around for dinner.

But the Alamo is more than just a photo op. Go on in and find out why the story of the Alamo can rouse a Texan's sense of state pride like few other things. For many, it's not so much a tourist attraction as a pilgrimage, and you might notice some of the visitors getting downright dewy-eyed at the description of how a few hundred revolutionaries died defending the fort against thousands of Mexican troops. (Learn more about the history of the Alamo on p29.)

The main chapel building is now known as the **Shrine**. From here you can set off for a history talk in the Cavalry Courtyard, hearing one of many perspectives on the actual events, which are somewhat in dispute.

In addition to the chapel you can visit the **Long Barrack**, which served as a residence for the Spanish priests and later a hospital for Mexican and Texan troops, and today holds a museum. There's also a 17-minute-long film, which not only gives you another perspective on the battle, but is an excellent place to escape the heat.

Just so you're not surprised: the legend of the Alamo – along with all those glossy, closely cropped publicity stills – has inflated the size of the fort's main chapel building in our collective imaginations, so don't be taken aback when you first encounter its diminutive stature.

See p169 for a review of *Alamo: The Price of Freedom*, an IMAX film showing in nearby Rivercenter Mall.

RIVERWALK
A little slice of Europe in the heart of downtown San Antonio, the **Riverwalk** is an essential part of the San Antonio experience. This is no ordinary riverfront, but a charming canal and pedestrian street that is the main artery at the heart of San Antonio's tourism efforts.

Stroll past landscaped hotel gardens, eat at riverside cafes, stop at souvenir shops and cruise the waterway. Restaurant after restaurant, and bar after bar, vie for your tourist buck. Crowds are common, especially on weekends. The $259 million project to expand the Riverwalk to a total of 14 miles will be completed by 2014. In mid-2009 the first additional 2-mile segment opened, connecting the commercial core with peaceful paths that lead to the Art Museum and the developing Pearl Brewery shopping complex to the north.

One of the best ways to soak in the ambience all at once is on a narrated boat tour with **Rio San Antonio Cruises** (☎ 210-244-5700; www.riosanantonio.com; adult/under 5yr $8.50/2; ☼ 9am-

9pm). Tours let you soak up 2½ miles' worth of river in 35 to 40 minutes, offering a nice visual overview along with a light history lesson – plus, it's just a pleasant way to pass the time. You can buy tickets online, or get them on the spot on the waterfront at the Rivercenter Mall (corner Commerce and Bowie Sts) or across the water from the Hilton (near Market and S Alamo Sts).

MARKET SQUARE
A little bit of Mexico in downtown San Antonio, **Market Square** (Map p152; ☎ 210-207-8600; www.marketsquaresa.com; 514 W Commerce St; ☼ 10am-8pm Jun-Aug, to 6pm Sep-May) is a fair approximation of a trip south of the border, with Mexican food, mariachi bands, and store after store filled with Mexican wares. Buy a Tecate beer or a pineapple *agua fresca* and remember: this is Mexico (kind of) so be prepared to bargain.

A big chunk of the square is taken up by **El Mercado**, the largest Mexican marketplace outside of Mexico. Wander the booths and stock up on Mexican doodads such as paper flowers, colorful pottery, maracas, *papel picado* (perforated paper), onyx figurines and the Virgin Mary in every conceivable medium. Although the market has historical roots – it goes back to the 1890s – it can feel like a bit of a tourist trap at times, but you can find some beautiful handicrafts if you take time to sort through the mass-produced sombreros and serapes. The **Farmers Market** was once exactly what it sounds like, but now the fresh produce has been crowded out by even more stores, as well as a food court.

MUSEO ALAMEDA
One place we're hoping sticks around is the **Museo Alameda** (Map p152; ☎ 210-299-4300; www.thealameda.org; 101 S Santa Rosa St; adult/5-17yr $4/2, Tue free; ☼ noon-6pm Tue-Sun). The museum opened in downtown's Market Square in 2007, but had yet to find its financial footing at time of research so, well, call before you go. But do go if you can. Despite San Antonio's predominantly Hispanic population, this is the city's first art museum to showcase Mexican art and culture, as well as the largest Hispanic museum in the US. It's also the first official affiliate of the Smithsonian Museum outside of Washington, DC, which means the Museo gets to draw on the Smithsonian's extensive collections for its rotating displays. Plus, the building is just crazy-cool: the surprisingly modern exterior (no adobe here) has hot-pink walls accented with metal panels that resemble a tin luminaria.

BUCKHORN SALOON & MUSEUM
Waaaay back in 1881, the Buckhorn Saloon opened up, and the owner promised patrons a free beer or whiskey shot for every pair of deer antlers they brought. Although the location has changed a couple of times, you can still see the collection – and the bar – at the newish-fangled **Buckhorn Saloon & Museum** (Map p152; ☎ 210-247-4000; www.buckhornmuseum.com; 318 E Houston St; adult/3-11yr $18/14; ☼ 10am-5pm, 10am-8pm in summer).

An overpriced beverage is enough to buy your admission to the Saloon, which has an impressive number of deer mounts numbly watching over you. If that doesn't quench your thirst for taxidermy, pony up the slightly steep admission price for a kitsch adventure that includes such oddities as a two-headed cow and an eight-legged lamb. (For those of you who may be wondering, yes, this is the same Buckhorn Collection that occupied the Hall of Horns at the Lone Star Brewery from 1956 to 1998.)

It's not only dead animals you'll experience. There are other only-in-Texas displays, such as maps of Texas made from rattlesnake rattles and a jaw-dropping collection of Lone Star Beer paraphernalia – as well as a wax museum unconvincingly reenacting key scenes in Texas history.

LA VILLITA HISTORIC ARTS VILLAGE
History meets commerce at downtown's **La Villita** (Map p152; ☎ 210-207-8610; www.lavillita.com; 418 Villita St; admission free; ☼ most shops 10am-6pm). San Antonio's first neighborhood, this 'little village' of stone and adobe houses dates back to the early 1800s (even earlier if you count a settlement of Coahuiltecan Indians or the primitive huts that once housed Spanish soldiers).

La Villita doesn't exactly offer a portal into the past – the buildings are now a collection of touristy shops and galleries – but it's worth a stroll, especially if you pause for a walking tour (maps are available all around the village) that puts the village into the right historical context.

SAN FERNANDO CATHEDRAL
Pretty church, or historic monument? The **San Fernando Cathedral** (Map p152; ☎ 210-227-1297;

www.sfcathedral.org; 115 Main Plaza; donations welcome) is both. Established in 1731, it's the oldest active cathedral in the United States. But it was its role in the Battle of the Alamo that makes it an important local landmark.

In happier times, future Alamo hero James Bowie was married here. But as Bowie defended the Alamo just across the river, Santa Anna took over the church as an observation post, and it was from here that he raised a flag of 'no quarter' that began the deadly siege – 'no quarter' being a short way of saying 'take no prisoners.'

In 1936 some remains were uncovered and, since they included charred bones and fragments of uniforms, they were wildly purported to be those of Davy Crockett, William Travis and James Bowie. (Never mind that the Alamo defenders didn't wear uniforms.) Pay your respects to whoever they are at the marble casket at the rear of the church.

Modern-day wedding parties streaming through the cathedral doors may prevent all but the most persistent visitor from getting inside to take a peek. Your best bet may be to attend Mass.

SPANISH GOVERNOR'S PALACE

More history? Sure, why not. Built in the mid-18th century, the **Spanish Governor's Palace** (Map p152; ☎ 210-224-0601; 105 Plaza de Armas; adult/7-13yr $4/2; ☼ 9am-5pm Tue-Sat, from 10am Sun), west of city hall, was originally the quarters for the *presidio capitan* of the area's Spanish colonial troops. In 1722 it became the seat of Texas' colonial government. After Texan independence, the house was used in a variety of ways (including as a saloon), but it was bought and refurbished by the city in 1928. Today, it's a museum filled with period furniture that provides a charming foreground against the backdrop of the palace's adobe walls, brick ovens and fireplaces.

WHAT THE...? F.I.S.H.

Fish gotta swim, birds gotta fly, right? Wait – or is it the other way around? Under the I-35 overpass at Camden St, a school of larger-than-life fish floats overhead – an art installment by Donald Lipski entitled *F.I.S.H.* The fiberglass fish are lit from within, turning the unlikeliest of spaces into an upside-down aquarium.

HEMISFAIR PARK

Like Seattle's Space Needle that came six years before it, San Antonio's 750ft **Tower of the Americas** (Map p152; ☎ 210-223-3101; www.toweroftheamericas.com; 600 Hemisfair Plaza Way; adult/4-11yr $11/9; ☼ 10am-10pm Sun-Thu, 10am-11pm Fri & Sat) is a skyline-defining landmark left over from a World's Fair. From the 579ft observation deck you'll mostly see the tops of buildings – no mountains or ocean like in Seattle – but the sheer height alone might earn a few 'ooohs' and 'aaahs.' Your admission also includes **Skies over Texas**, a 3-D film with special effects presenting the history of Texas.

These things always seem to have a revolving restaurant at the top, and this one's no exception. If you want the view to last all through dinner (or if you want to skip the admission price and the film) make a reservation to dine at the Chart House (☎ 210-223-3101).

INSTITUTE OF TEXAN CULTURES

Thirty cultures, including Native American and Mexican, have made Texas what it is; explore them at the museum of the **Institute of Texan Cultures** (Map p152; ☎ 210-458-2330; www.texancultures.com; 801 E Durango Blvd in HemisFair Park; adult/3-11yr $8/6; ☼ 9am-5pm Mon-Sat, from noon Sun). The Latin-American influence is fairly prominent in San Antonio, so this museum can be an eye-opener to visitors learning about Texas' diverse background. The main exhibit, spread out over an enormous single-floor space, has sections devoted to more than two dozen ethnic and national groups of settlers in Texas, including Anglo-Americans, Germans, European Jews, Irish and African Americans.

Be sure to catch one of the daily shows in the Bluebonnet Puppet Theater or the 360-degree Dome Theater. The Back 40 Area, behind the main exhibition, has reconstructed living-history buildings such as a fort, schoolhouse, log cabin and a windmill. Don't miss the displays of footwear donated by famous Texans near the front entrance; there's everything from a pair of vanity cowboy boots once worn by Dubya to the sparkly high heels of novelist Sandra Cisneros.

SUNSET STATION

You shouldn't necessarily make a special trip, but if you happen to be in the vicinity of the Alamodome, check out the former rail depot **Sunset Station** (Map p152; ☎ 210-222-9481; www.sunset-station.com; 1174 E Commerce St). Originally

RIVERWALK

In 1921, floods destroyed downtown San Antonio; water 10ft deep from the overflowing San Antonio River gushed through the center of the city, obliterating homes and businesses and drowning as many as 50 people. As a result, the Olmos Dam was constructed to handle overflow and route the extra water around the downtown area through a canal called the Oxbow.

The fix was meant to be temporary and was intended to be submerged and turned into an enormous storm drain beneath the city. Before this happened though, some locals formed the San Antonio Conservation Society and dedicated themselves to preserving and developing the canal into an attraction.

The Works Progress Administration (WPA) in 1938 assumed control of the canal's fate, and executed a plan to develop a central business district of shops and restaurants along a cobbled walk. More than 1000 jobs were created during the construction of Riverwalk, and the project is definitely among the top 10 most beautiful results of the WPA effort.

the Southern Pacific Railroad Depot and the city's Amtrak station (which moved next door), and a stop along the Sunset Limited line between San Francisco and New Orleans, the station has been fully restored to its old glory, complete with stained-glass windows and a colorful, bold interior. Don't overlook the vintage 1916 steam engine either. The station is usually hired out in the evening for private events, but it's open to visitors during the day. Look on its website for a historical walking tour.

ARTPACE

This unique contemporary **art gallery** (Map p152; ☎ 210-212-4900; www.artpace.org; 445 N Main Ave; admission free; ✆ noon-5pm Wed-Sun) hosts temporary exhibitions by its outstanding artists-in-residence, who are selected from a pool drawn from across Texas, the USA and abroad. Inside a 1920s automobile showroom, the renovated gallery space is inspiring and the works are often experimental. ArtPace also schedules special community events, including lectures, films, artist conversations and more.

ALAMO PLAZA ATTRACTIONS

Time to throw the kids a bone? After touring historical sites all day, you can reward them with a visit to this teen-friendly trio: **Ripley's Haunted Adventure**, **Guinness World Records Museum** and **Tomb Rider 3D** (Map p152; ☎ 210-226-2828; www.alamoplazaattractions.com; adult/4-12yr $27/17; ✆ 10am-11pm Sun-Thu, 10am-midnight Fri & Sat summer, 10am-7pm Sun-Thu, 10am-10pm Fri & Sat off-season). One admission gets you into the haunted house, museum of oddities and theme-park-style ride, or you can pay a reduced admission if you only have time for one or two. It's a little

cheesy, and definitely touristy, but a good antidote to slogging around the missions all day.

King William District & Southtown

South of downtown on the banks of the San Antonio River, the charming King William District (once nicknamed 'Sauer Kraut Bend') was built by wealthy German settlers at the end of the 19th century. The architecture here is mostly Victorian, though there are fine examples of Italianate, colonial-revival, beaux arts, and even art deco styles. Most of the district's houses have been renovated and are privately owned or run as B&Bs. It's a very pleasant area for a stroll. Stop by the **San Antonio Conservation Society** (Map p152; ☎ 210-224-6163; 107 King William St) for self-guided-walking-tour brochures.

Across S Alamo St to the east is **Southtown** (www.southtown.net), a small arts district. On the first Friday of every month, galleries stay open late and restaurants host entertainment. A 1920s warehouse contains the **Blue Star Contemporary Art Center** (Map p152; ☎ 210-227-6960; www.bluestararspace.org; 116 Blue Star; admission free; ✆ noon-6pm Wed-Sun) and its fiber arts, photography and contemporary studio spaces.

VIA's Blue Line streetcars stop nearby all of the following sights.

SAN ANTONIO ART LEAGUE MUSEUM

This tiny **museum** (Map p152; ☎ 210-223-1140; www.saalm.org; 130 King William St; admission free; ✆ 10am-3pm Tue-Sat) houses art from regional 20th-century American artists. In the 1920s, the San Antonio Art League was famous for annual exhibitions of paintings of Texas wildflowers. The museum's early patron was Marion McNay, who also founded the

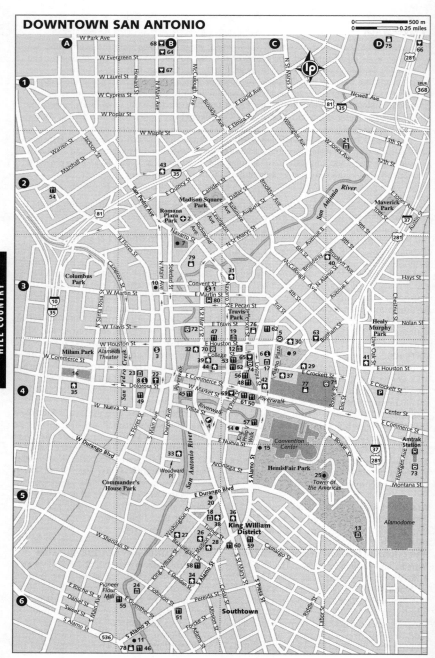

DOWNTOWN SAN ANTONIO

INFORMATION
Bank of America....1 B3
Baptist Medical Center....2 B2
Frost Bank....3 B4
Mexican Consulate....4 B4
Post Office....5 C3
San Antonio Convention & Visitors Bureau....6 C4
San Antonio Public Library....7 B3
The Twig Bookshop....(see 75)
VIA's Downtown Visitors Center..8 B4

SIGHTS & ACTIVITIES
Alamo....9 C4
Artpace....10 B3
Blue Star Contemporary Art Center....11 B6
Buckhorn Saloon & Museum....12 C4
Guiness World Records Museum....(see 17)
Institute of Texan Cultures....13 D5
La Villita Historic Arts Village....14 C4
Magik Children's Theatre....15 C5
Market Square....16 A4
Museo Alameda....(see 16)
Ripley's Haunted Adventure....17 C4
San Antonio Art League Museum....18 B5
San Antonio Children's Museum....19 C3
San Antonio Conservation Society....20 B5
San Antonio Museum of Art (SAMA)....21 D2
San Fernando Cathedral....22 B4
Spanish Governor's Palace....23 B4
Steves Homestead....24 B6
Tomb Rider 3D....(see 17)
Tower of the Americas....25 C5

SLEEPING
A Yellow Rose Inn....26 B5
Beauregard House B&B Inn....27 B5
Brackenridge House B&B....28 B5
Crockett Hotel....29 C4
Emily Morgan Hotel....30 C4
Hotel Havana....31 C3
Hotel Valencia....32 B4
Inn on the Riverwalk....33 B5
King William Manor....34 B6
La Quinta Inn Market Square....35 A4
La Villita Inn....36 C5
Menger Hotel....37 C4
Noble Inns....38 B5
Omni Mansion del Rio....39 B4
Painted Lady Inn....40 D3
Red Roof Inn San Antonio Downtown....41 D4
Riverwalk Vista....42 C4
Rodeway Inn Downtown....43 B2
Watermark Hotel & Spa....44 B4

EATING
Biga on the Banks....45 B4
Blue Star Brewing Company....46 B6
Bohanan's....47 B3
Boudro's on the Riverwalk....48 C4
Candy's Old Fashioned Restaurant....49 B4
Casa Rio....50 C4
Casbeers....51 B6
County Line Smokehouse....52 C4
Dick's Last Resort....53 C4
Green Vegetarian Cuisine....54 A2
Guenther House....55 B6
Il Sogno Osteria....(see 75)
Justin's Ice Cream Company....56 C4
Little Rhein Steak House....57 C4
Madhatters Tea House & Café..58 B6
Mi Tierra Cafe & Bakery....(see 16)
Mr Tim's Country Kitchen Cafe..59 C5
Rosario's Mexican Cafe....60 C5
Schilo's German Delicatessen....61 C4
Twin Sisters Bakery & Café....62 C3

DRINKING
Bonham Exchange....63 C3
Heat....64 B1
Mad Dog's British Pub....65 C4
Menger Bar....(see 37)
Pegasus....(see 67)
Sam's Burger Joint....66 D1
Silver Dollar Saloon....67 B1
The Saint....68 B1
Zinc Champagne & Wine Bar...69 C4

ENTERTAINMENT
Arneson River Theater....(see 14)
Majestic Theatre....70 B4
Overtime Theater....(see 11)
Rivercenter Comedy Club....71 D4
San Antonio IMAX Alamo Theatre....(see 71)
San Antonio Symphony Box Office....72 B3
Sunset Station....73 D5
The Landing....74 C4

SHOPPING
Melissa Guerra....75 D1
Paris Hatters....76 C3
Rivercenter Mall....77 C4
San Angel Folk Art Gallery....78 B6
Southwest School of Art & Craft....79 B3

TRANSPORT
Bus Terminal....80 B3

excellent McNay Art Museum. Here, the permanent collections include textiles, paintings, sculpture, furniture and photography. If you're in the neighborhood, it's worth a short visit, especially since you'll likely have the place all to yourself.

STEVES HOMESTEAD

Most of the mansions in the King William District can only be appreciated from curbside. Too bad you can't just go knock on a door and be invited in for tea. But one of them does provide guided tours: the **Steves Homestead** (Map p152; ☎ 210-225-5924; 509 King William St; adult/under 12 $6/free; 10am-4:15pm, last tour 3:30pm).

Volunteer docents from the San Antonio Conservation Society run guided tours through this Italianate villa and French Second Empire–style home that dates from 1876. Built for Edward Steves, a wealthy lumber merchant, this stately house has been restored to demonstrate the life of the affluent at the end of the 19th century. Incidentally, San Antonio's first indoor swimming pool is on the property.

Mission Trail

Spain's missionary presence can best be felt at the ruins of the four missions south of town. Together, Missions Concepción (1731), San José (1720), San Juan (1731) and Espada (1745–56) make up **San Antonio Missions National Historical Park** (☎ 210-932-1001; www.nps.gov/saan; Mission San José, 6701 San José Dr; admission free; 9am-5pm). Religious services are still held in the mission churches of San José, San Juan and Espada, and the mariachi Mass at 12:30pm on Sunday is a San Antonio tradition.

The San Antonio missions were constructed in the early 18th century as part of an effort to provide way-stations and staging areas for Spanish colonial expansion to the north. The native Coahuiltecans, already under pressure from other nomadic Native American tribes pushing down from the

north, showed a willingness to convert to
Christianity, and labored for the colonial
Spanish priests in order to receive food and
protection at the missions.

Constructed in what is now downtown, the
first and most impressive mission was what
would come to be known as the Alamo. With
the destruction by war or disease of many east
Texas missions, the Spanish quickly built four
more missions south of the Alamo, which collectively are known as the 'Mission Trail.' (Not
to be confused with the 8-mile hike-and-bike
trail that connects them.)

First along the trail is **Mission Concepción**
(Map p146; 807 Mission Rd), which features a
Spanish colonial church built in 1755. It's
a passably interesting stop for history buffs,
and essential for anyone who doesn't do
things by half.

If your interest level is 'somewhat' rather
than 'totally,' skip straight to the second
stop, **Mission San José** (Map p146; 6539 San Jose Dr),
which is also the location of the main **visitor center.** Known in its time as the Queen
of the Missions, it's certainly the largest and
arguably the most beautiful of all on the trail.
Because it's a little more remote and pastoral,
surrounded by thick stone walls, you can really get a sense of what life was like here in the
18th and 19th centuries.

Ranger-led tours cover life in the mission
and show up close the magnificent church
and its famous rose window, a stunningly
carved masterpiece attached to the sacristy.
The best time to visit? That would absolutely
be on Sundays at 12:30pm, when they hold a
mariachi Mass.

The most somber of the missions, **Misión
San Juan** (off Map p146; 9102 Graf Rd) is your next
stop if you're on the let's-see-them-all plan.
The surviving church is open, as is a small
visitor center and a quarter-mile nature trail
along the river.

And last but not least, **Misión Espada** (off Map
p146; 10040 Espada Rd) was the oldest mission in the
east Texas chain, and is the best place to check
out the historic *acequia*, or aqueduct – the
missions' irrigation system that's still in use
today and has been designated as a Historic
Civil Engineering Landmark.

From downtown, VIA transit bus 42 goes
to San José (see p172 for transit details). The
Texas Trolley tours (p158) visit San José
and Concepción. Otherwise, rent a bicycle
or drive. From downtown, take St Mary's St

south until it becomes Mission Rd, then follow the brown signs indicating the direction
to the missions.

Brackenridge Park & Around

A couple of miles north of downtown,
Brackenridge Park has been a favorite San
Antonio getaway spot for more than a century, with boat rentals, playgrounds, rides
and gardens. Its main attraction – other than
a serene green setting – is that it's the head-
spring for the San Antonio River. Many of the
park's sights are designed for children, but
may be equally interesting for adults, such as
the impressive Witte Museum (p157).

SAN ANTONIO MUSEUM OF ART

Housed in the original 1880s Lone Star
Brewery, which is a piece of artwork itself,
the **San Antonio Museum of Art** (SAMA; Map p152;
☎ 210-978-8100; www. samuseum.org; 200 W Jones Ave;
adult/4-11yr $8/3; ☺ 10am-9pm Tue, 10am-5pm Wed-
Sat, noon-6pm Sun) is off Broadway just north of
downtown. San Antonio's strong Hispanic
influence is reflected in an impressive trove
of Latin American art, including Spanish colonial, Mexican and pre-Columbian – one of
the most comprehensive collections in the US.

But it's more than just Latin America that's
represented here: the museum has a little of
everything, from Egyptian antiquities to contemporary abstracts, and in 2005 it opened a
new Asian wing to accommodate a growing
collection of Chinese ceramics, paintings,
decorative items and more.

SAN ANTONIO BOTANICAL GARDENS

This expertly tended, 33-acre **garden complex**
(Map p146; ☎ 210-207-3250; www.sabot.org; 555 Funston
Place; adult/3-13yr $7/4; ☺ 9am-5pm), northeast of
downtown, showcases native Texas flora.
There's also a fragrance garden and a wonderful conservatory, with a bit of everything
from equatorial rainforest to alpine flowers
to a tropical lagoon. The strolling garden was
designed and created by a 26th-generation
gardener and one of Japan's living national
treasures from the island of Kyūshū, specifically the city of Kumamoto, which is also
home to one of Japan's most revered traditional gardens, Suizenji-kōen. A few of that
famous garden's elements appear here. Call or
go online for a calendar of special events, anything from concerts under the stars to bonsai
workshops to summer classes for children.

JAPANESE TEA GARDENS

At Brackenridge Park's northwestern end, an eyesore of a quarry has been transformed into a Japanese-style strolling **garden** (Map p146; www.japaneseteagardensf.com; 3800 N St Mary's St; admission free; 8am-dusk), with stone bridges, floral displays and a 60ft waterfall. Popular with families and senior citizens, it's a pretty spot near the San Antonio Zoo. But it probably isn't worth a special trip, especially if you've already seen the San Antonio Botanical Gardens. The curious sign over the front entrance still says 'Chinese Tea Gardens,' lingering evidence of America's backlash against all things Japanese during WWII.

Greater San Antonio

Leaving downtown yields a greater breadth of options, including theme parks and museums. With all the firepower in the area, the city is teeming with military museums. But note that access to the bases is restricted, and for all, you'll need to get visitor's passes (obtainable only through certain gates, and even then subject to change), so bring photo ID. Sometimes the bases may be closed entirely except to military personnel and their dependents, so always call ahead.

MARION KOOGLER MCNAY ART MUSEUM

Several artistic heavy hitters are represented at the **Marion Koogler McNay Art Museum** (Map p146; 210-824-5368; www.mcnayart.org; 6000 N New Braunfels Ave; adult/under 13 $8/free; 10am-4pm Tue & Wed, 10am-9pm Thu, 10am-5pm Fri, 10am-5pm Sat, noon-5pm Sun, grounds 7am-6pm daily). Upon her death in 1950, Ms McNay left her impressive collection of European and American modern art to the city. It has since been supplemented with even more art, and the collection is now among the best in the Southwest.

In addition to seeing paintings by household names such as van Gogh, Picasso, Matisse, Renoir, O'Keeffe and Cézanne, half the fun is wandering the spectacular Spanish Colonial revival-style mansion that was the private residence of Marion Koogler McNay.

The Stieren Center for Exhibitions was added in June 2008, and, while it doesn't integrate seamlessly with the original mansion – the center describes itself as a 'translucent, two-story box' – it does add 45,000 sq ft of exhibition space for rotating shows.

SEAWORLD

A curious combination of marine mammals and roller coasters, **SeaWorld San Antonio** (off Map p146; 210-523-3000, 800-700-7786; www.seaworld.com, 10500 SeaWorld Dr; adult/3-9yr $59/50; from 10am, closes from 5-10pm depending on date) is home to both Shamu the killer whale and 'Great White,' an inverted 'heels-over-head' roller coaster. Numerous opportunities arise to get wet – which is a welcome relief during the hot summer months – including the Shamu show, three different water rides, and the **Lost Lagoon Waterpark**, which is included in your admission. Animal feedings and shows take place at scheduled times, so plan your day to make sure you don't miss out. Check the website for behind-the-scenes tours; parking is $15.

SIX FLAGS FIESTA TEXAS

You don't have to be a kid to enjoy **Fiesta Texas** (off Map p146; 210-697-5050; www.sixflags.com/fiesta Texas; 17000 IH-10 W, exit 555; adult/child under 48in tall $52/37; hours vary, weekends only Labor Day–Memorial Day). This popular theme park has plenty of rides that you must be 'this tall' to ride, for grown-ups to lose their lunch over. There are more than 25 kids' rides for the vertically

---

BUILT ON BEER

Beer isn't the only good thing to come out of breweries. San Antonio was once a brewing town, home to two of Texas' largest breweries. The Lone Star Brewery and Pearl Brewery were both established by German settlers in the late 1800s. And while both of them eventually shut down, they left behind two remarkable buildings.

The Lone Star Brewery has provided an impressive setting for the San Antonio Museum of Art (p154), which opened in 1981. And the old Pearl Brewery is in the process of getting a face-lift as part of the new Pearl development north of downtown. Rumors vary on what the future holds for the gorgeous main building (condos, museum, hotel, all of the above?) but some of the other buildings have already been turned into restaurants, such as Il Sogno Osteria (p166), and stores, such as Melissa Guerra (p171), and we can't wait to see what they do with the place.

challenged, as well as swimming pools and water rides over in the White Water Bay area (open May to September). The setting – against a limestone quarry that looks similar to the Arizona desert – is dramatic, and there's plenty of music and shows. Parking is $15.

SPLASHTOWN
San Antonio can get awfully hot and sticky in the summer, and one of the best remedies is putting on your swimsuit and heading to the **water park** (off Map p146; ☎ 210-227-1400; www.splashtownsa.com; 3600 N IH-35; adult/child under 48in tall $27/20, after 5pm all $17; ✆ 11am-8pm Sun-Thu, 11am-9pm Fri & Sat summer, 11am-7pm Sat & Sun off-season). Splashtown is where you'll find Texas' biggest wave pool, a seven-story aquatic bobsled run, and inner tubing in total darkness. There are also gentler floating rides and a special 'Kids Kove' for preschoolers. Call or check the website to find out the schedule before heading out.

FORT SAM HOUSTON
Known 'round here as 'Fort Sam,' and dating from the late 1800s, **Fort Sam Houston** (Map p146; ☎ public affairs 210-221-1151) is ready to enlist you for a little military history. Just northeast of downtown, it's home to several historic buildings with designated museums that are open to the public. Fort Sam does have a couple of claims to fame: the Apache Chief Geronimo was held here for 40 days, and it was also the site from which the first military flight in US history took off in 1910.

The oldest building at Fort Sam (and Geronimo's short-term residence) is the **Quadrangle** (Map p146; ☎ 210-221-1232; cnr E Grayson St & Liscum Rd; admission free; ✆ 8am-5pm Mon-Fri, noon-5pm Sat & Sun), built in 1876. Today, the Quadrangle is open as a museum of the history of the fort, and it leads through to a sort of petting zoo – deer have been kept here for more than 100 years, and rabbits, ducks and chickens abound. The Quadrangle is west of New Braunfels Ave; hours can change depending on the army's schedule.

In the northeast section of the grounds, the **US Army Medical Department Museum** (Map p146; ☎ 210-221-6358, 210-221-6277; 2310 Stanley St; admission free; ✆ 10am-4pm Tue-Sun) has a display of army medical gear from the US and several other countries, including Germany, the former Soviet Union, Vietnam and China,

and a cool collection of restored ambulances, helicopters and a hospital rail car. But what makes the AMEDD museum really worth the trip is the collection of Civil War surgical gear, notably the disturbing saws and portable amputation kits.

TEXAS TRANSPORTATION MUSEUM
This modest volunteer-run **museum** (TTM; off Map p146; ☎ 210-490-3554; www.txtransportation museum.org; 11731 Wetmore Rd, off Wurzbach Parkway; adult/under 13yr $8/5; ✆ 9am-3pm Thu & Fri, 10am-5pm Sat & Sun) boasts full-size, miniature and indoor scale-model railroads. On the weekends, hourly train rides are included with the price of admission, and there are special holiday events for kids.

ACTIVITIES
Apart from Brackenridge Park (p154) and the Mission Trail (p153), San Antonio is short on places to enjoy the great outdoors. You've usually got to head into the Hill Country or drive north on I-35 to the aquatic wonderlands of New Braunfels, Gruene and San Marcos, where you can go swimming and tubing to your heart's content on local rivers and at amusement parks. Golfers are in luck, however.

Golf
San Antonio is a favorite golfing vacation destination, thanks to the region's mild year-round climate. Rates vary from $35 to tote your own bag around a public course to more than $150 to play a round at a private resort.

Municipal golf courses include the following:
Brackenridge Park (Map p146; ☎ 210-226-5612; 2315 Ave B)
Cedar Creek (off Map p146; ☎ 210-695-5050; 8250 Vista Colina)
Olmos Basin (Map p146; ☎ 210-826-4041; 7022 N McCullough Ave)
Willow Springs (Map p146; ☎ 210-226-6721; 202 AT&T Parkway)

Nationally renowned public golf courses include the following:
Canyon Springs Golf Club (off Map p146; ☎ 210-497-1770, 888-800-1511; 2440 Wilderness Oak Rd)
Quarry Golf Club (Map p146; ☎ 210-824-4500, 800-347-7759; 444 E Basse Rd)
Westin La Cantera (off Map p146; ☎ 210-558-4653, 800-446-5387; 16641 La Cantera Parkway)

SAN ANTONIO & HILL COUNTRY

Hiking & Cycling

Your best options are the 12-mile paved recreational path along the Mission Trail (p153) or a visit to Brackenridge Park (p154). Or try one of two parks that are a little farther out.

For a taste of the Hill Country without venturing outside the city limits, head to the 850-acre **McAllister Park** (off Map p146; ☎ 210-207-7275; 13102 Jones Maltsberger Rd; admission free; ☉ dawn-dusk). It has about 7 miles of trails for walking and cycling; one of the trails is also wheelchair-accessible.

Close to Six Flags Fiesta Texas, the 230-acre **Friedrich Wilderness Park** (off Map p146; ☎ 210-372-9124; www.fofriedrichpark.org; 21480 Milsa, north of Loop 1604; admission free; ☉ 8am-5pm, 8am-8pm Apr-Sep) has 5½ miles of walking trails that are especially worth a detour when wildflowers are blooming in spring.

SAN ANTONIO FOR CHILDREN

San Antonio is a very popular family destination, thanks to its theme parks and mild year-round climate.

San Antonio Children's Museum

Perfect for the 10-and-under set, even kids who are barely standing have a blast at the **San Antonio Children's Museum** (Map p152; ☎ 210-212-4453; www.sakids.org; 305 E Houston St; adult/under 2yr $7/free; ☉ summer 9am-5pm Mon-Fri, 9am-6pm Sat, noon-5pm Sun, shorter hours in winter).

It has two floors of exhibits focusing on interactive play, including the Tot Spot, Art Pavilion, the Bubble Ranch and Leonardo's Lab. There's plenty for kids to do: open an account and use an ATM at the Good Cents Bank; run an airport and fly an airplane; or learn about science in PowerBall Hall.

Community volunteers and local businesses come in for workshops and special events; check the website or call for a schedule. Parking is validated for one hour at the MidCity Parking Garage at 240 E Houston St, and at the St Mary's Garage at 400 N St Mary's St.

Magik Children's Theatre

Not far from the Riverwalk, this merry **theater troupe** (Map p152; ☎ 210-227-2751; www.magiktheatre.org; 420 S Alamo St; adult/infant/child $10/2/8; ☉ box office 9am-5pm Mon-Fri, 10am-5pm Sat) stages adaptations of favorite children's books, hilarious original musicals and modern retellings of Texas legends and classic fairy tales, such as the witty (and bilingual!) *La Cinderella*. The theater's regular season runs from September to May, and includes a contemporary play series for adults, too.

Brackenridge Park

North of downtown near Trinity University, this 343-acre **park** (Map p146; ☎ 210-734-7184; 3910 N St Mary's St; ☉ 9:30am-5pm, longer hours in summer) is a great place to spend the day with your family. In addition to the San Antonio Zoo (p158), you'll find the Brackenridge Eagle **miniature train**, an old-fashioned **carousel** (adult/3-11yr $2.50/2), a modest **skyride** (adult/3-11yr $2.50/2) and the Japanese Tea Gardens (which, as a side note, were spitefully renamed 'Chinese Sunken Gardens' for a time after WWII).

Witte Museum

If your kids are a little too grown-up for the Children's Museum, they can graduate to the **Witte** (Map p146; ☎ 210-357-1900; www.wittemuseum.org; 3801 Broadway; adult/4-11yr $8/6; ☉ 10am-5pm Mon-Sat, till 8pm Tue, noon-5pm Sun, extended hours in summer), north of downtown along the eastern edge of Brackenridge Park.

SAN ANTONIO & HILL COUNTRY

The Witte (pronounced 'witty') is educational but engaging, with hands-on explorations of natural history, science and Texas history. Inside the main museum are excellent permanent exhibits on the indigenous peoples of the Lower Pecos region, including a replica of their cave dwellings. Downstairs is Texas Wild, which covers the flora and fauna of all Texas ecological regions. Especially noteworthy are special temporary exhibitions on the history, culture and peoples of the River City, aimed at both adults and children.

Don't miss the Science Treehouse, a high-tech activity center in back of the museum building. It's a hit with all ages, even the *really* big kids (read: parents). Kids begin downstairs with lots of cool physical-property displays then move on up to the more cerebral displays upstairs, which include music makers, a video-light microscope and an internet room. Outside the treehouse, a deck overlooks the San Antonio River; there's a real treehouse as well.

The museum is free on Tuesdays from 3pm to 9pm.

San Antonio Zoo

Established in 1914, the **San Antonio Zoo & Aquarium** (Map p146; ☎ 210-734-7183; www.sazoo -aq.org; 3903 N St Mary's St; adult/senior & 3-11yr $10/8; ☽ 9am-6pm) is famous for its animal breeding conservation programs, which have given it one of the largest endangered-animal collections in the country. But parts of the zoo still need renovation and expansion, so don't be surprised to find some of the exhibits looking cramped. There are more than 3500 animals here, representing some 750 species. Things to see include enormous free-flight tropical aviaries and a petting zoo and playground. A recent addition is the Conservation Research Center, which has a number of endangered species on show, including the wonderfully creepy Goliath bird-eating spider.

Kiddie Park

This 1920s-vintage kiddie **amusement park** (Map p146; ☎ 210-824-4351; www.kiddiepark.com; 3015 Broadway; s-ride tickets $2.16, 6 tickets for $10, unlimited day pass $12; ☽ 10am-7pm) has a wonderful old carousel, a tiny roller coaster, a Ferris wheel, skee-ball alleys and more. It's a slice of carni-

val atmosphere year-round. Bargain discount days are on Wednesday, which might save you a buck or two.

TOURS

The downtown visitors center (p147) has information about other possibilities.

San Antonio Trolley Tours (☎ 210-492-4144; www. sanantoniotrolleytours.com; 122 Losoya St; adult/child 1hr narrated tour $20/10, hopper pass $26/13) Get a quick overview of the town with a one-hour narrated tour, or spend a few dollars more for a two-day hopper pass that lets you get off and on at all the attractions. If you're looking to get out of town, there are also hill country tours and wine tours.

SegCity Ghost Tours (☎ 210-224-0773; www.segcity. com; 124 Losoya St; tours $65; ☽ tours 7pm) A fun twist on predictable ghost tours? Do it on a Segway. That means if you do see a ghost, it'll be easier to outrun it. This company also offers regular old nonhaunted tours of downtown and the King William District.

Alamo Ghost Hunt (☎ 210-336-7831; www.alamo cityghosttours.com; adult/5-17yr $15/10; ☽ tours 9pm) This more affordable ghost tour leaves on foot from the north wall of Ripley's Believe It or Not. Don't expect anything too serious; the jokes themselves can be kind of scary.

FESTIVALS & EVENTS

San Antonio is a city with a full calendar of festivals and events; visitors are bound to run into at least one. For a complete list, check with the downtown visitor center (p147). Advance tickets for many of the biggest events are sold through **Ticketmaster** (☎ 210-224-9600; www.ticketmaster.com).

January

San Antonio Mud Festival (☎ 210-227-4262; thesanantonioriverwalk.com) Held in mid-January, this 'dirty' celebration fetes the draining of the San Antonio River with an arts and crafts fair, live music and the annual crowning of the Mud King and Queen at the Kangaroo Court on the Riverwalk.

February

San Antonio Stock Show & Rodeo (☎ 210-225- 5851; www.sarodeo.com; 3201 E Houston St; admission $10-25) Two weeks' worth of buckin' broncos and other Western hoopla comes to the AT&T Center in mid-February; Texan rock, country and Latin music stars also perform on rodeo days.

Mardi Gras (☎ 210-227-4262; thesanantonioriver walk.com) On the weekend before Ash Wednesday, the riverfront fills up with decorated barges and all manner of local musicians playing everything from adagio to zydeco, including all the Texan twang most folks can take.

March
St Patrick's Day On the weekend closest to the 17th, the city dyes the river green and celebrates the feat by tossing back downright Irish quantities of beer. Many festivities are at downtown's La Villita and the Arneson River Theater (p169).

April
Fiesta San Antonio Held in mid-April, this is the city's biggest bash of the year, and definitely worth planning any trip around. See the boxed text, p159, for full details.

May
Cinco de Mayo In celebration of Mexico's defeat of French troops at the 1862 Battle of Puebla, food, music and dances take place around the city, especially at Market Square, on May 5.

Tejano Conjunto Festival (☎ 210-271-3151, www. guadalupeculturalarts.org) Feast on five days of the world's best *conjunto* musicianship to progressive Tejano sounds, along with plenty of Tex-Mex cooking and dancing. Held mid-May.

Culinaria Wine and Culinary Arts Festival (☎ 210-822-9555; www.culinariasa.com) Celebrity chefs, wine and food from all around the Americas, with workshops and events at top restaurants around the city.

Fiesta Noche del Rio (www.alamo-kiwanis.org/FiestaNoche.html) All summer long (late May-early Sep), the Fiesta Noche del Rio brings Latin music to the Arneson River Theater (p169) in a series of concerts and dance performances.

June
Texas Folklife Festival (www.texasfolklifefestival.org) A multicultural celebration with food, storytellers, artisans, dancers and live music held over four days in mid-June at the Institute of Texan Cultures.

Juneteenth (www.juneteenthsanantonio.com) Commemorating the date when the news of the Emancipation Proclamation freeing slaves finally reached Texas, the city comes alive on June 19 with African American cultural festivities and a multimedia Freedom Fair.

July
Contemporary Art Month (☎ 210-222-2787; www.contemporaryartmonth.com) With more than 400

GAY & LESBIAN SAN ANTONIO

Despite its conservative outlook (at least compared with Austin), the River City is one of the most tolerant places in Texas for gay, lesbian, bisexual and transgendered travelers. Although this ain't San Francisco or NYC, there's definitely a vibrant community here. One of the best times to visit is during Fiesta San Antonio (p159). June's Pridefest SA is another big event.

Out in San Antonio (www.outinsanantonio.com) is an online source of news, events calendars, advice columns, chat rooms and more. San Antonio **LGBT Chamber of Commerce** (www.sagaychamber.com) provides lists of gay-owned and gay-friendly bars, clubs, businesses and other services, as does **Q San Antonio** (www.qsanantonio.com).

King William Manor (p162) and Oge House (p162) in the King William District are especially welcoming to same-sex couples.

The River City's gay nightlife scene is concentrated along Main and San Pedro Aves, just north of downtown. Venues change, but the strips remain the same.

Bonham Exchange (Map p152; ☎ 210-271-3811; www.bonhamexchange.net; 411 Bonham St; cover varies, before 10pm some nights free; ✆ usually Wed-Sun) Nothing low-key about the Bonham; this enormous dance club is dark, loud and packed on weekends. See p168.

Bermuda Triangle (Map p146; ☎ 210-342-2276; 10127 Coachlight; ✆ Wed-Sun 8pm-2am) It's always ladies' night at this lesbian bar that proudly proclaims, 'Not responsible for lost or stolen girlfriends.' Located north of downtown near the airport.

Heat (Map p152; ☎ 210-227-2600; 1500 N Main Ave; before 11pm free; ✆ 9pm-2am or later) This 18-and-up club is frequently open after hours, catering to a late-night crowd which comes for the huge dancefloor, techno music, theme nights and drag shows. Heat also puts you in close proximity to some other gay venues, including the following:

Saint (Map p146; ☎ 210-225-7330; 1430 N Main Ave)
Silver Dollar Saloon (Map p152; ☎ 210-227-2633; 1422 N Main Ave)
Pegasus (Map p146; ☎ 210-299-4222; 1402 N Main Ave)

exhibitors at several dozen venues around town, this series of gallery events, talks and festivities is a month-long contemporary arts fair.

September

Mexican Independence Day Held on the weekend closest to the 16th, the Diez Y Sies festival is celebrated with food, music and theater all across the city, including at Market Square.

Jazz 'SAlive (☎ 210-212-8423; www.saparksfoundation .org/jazzsalive.html; admission free) A top-tier jazz festival in downtown's Travis Park and other venues, with past performances by Branford Marsalis and Sergio Mendes Brasil 2003. Held in mid-September.

October

International Accordion Festival (☎ 210-865.8578; www.internationalaccordionfestival.org) A two-day outdoor marathon in mid-October featuring dancing and accordion music of all styles, from cumbia to conjunto and zydeco to klezmer.

November

El Día de los Muertos Altars, religious services, processions and cultural activities celebrate the Day of the Dead on November 2, especially along the old Spanish colonial Mission Trail and at many museums.

December

Las Luminarias & Las Posadas Following up the feast of the Virgen de Guadalupe on the two weekends preceding Christmas, the San Antonio Conservation Society (p151) stages candlelit nativity pageant processions and bilingual caroling along the riverbanks in mid-December.

Alamo Bowl (☎ 210-226-2695; www.alamobowl. com) A college football championship of Big 10 vs Big 12 conference teams draws up to 65,000 spectators to the Alamodome. Held in late December.

SLEEPING

San Antonio has loads of places to stay that become booked solid, and much more expensive, during major NCAA games, city festivals and large conventions. Most motels and hotels raise their rates substantially during summer, too.

Even though the city has plenty of hotels, really cheap places downtown are few and far between. The downtown area does have a good selection of reasonably priced motels, and there are a multitude of choices out by the airport and along the interstates.

San Antonio also has its fair share of B&Bs, and generally speaking they are good value, ensconced in fine old homes in the more historic areas of the city, especially the King William District.

Downtown
BUDGET
Rodeway Inn Downtown (Map p152; ☎ 210-223-2951, 877-424-6423; www.rodewayinn.com; 900 N Main Ave; d $35-44; P 🛜 🐾) You could walk to the Alamo and Riverwalk, which are just 1 mile away, but you don't even have to because the downtown

---

FIESTA SAN ANTONIO

In late April, hundreds of thousands of partygoers throng the streets of San Antonio – and that's how you know Fiesta San Antonio has arrived. A nine-day series of riotous events makes for the city's biggest celebration, with general mayhem, fairs, feeds, rodeos, races and a whole lot of music and dancing. Going strong after more than 110 years, the **festival** (☎ 210-227-5191, 877-723-4378; www.fiesta-sa.org; box office & festival store 2611 Broadway) is the high point of the River City's year.

Fiesta San Antonio dates back to 1891, when local women paraded on horseback in front of the Alamo and threw flowers at each other, all meant to honor the heroes of the Alamo and the Battle of San Jacinto. Today's **Battle of the Flowers** (www.battleofflowers.org) is only a small piece of Fiesta, which has grown into an enormous party involving 75,000 volunteers, millions of spectators and more than 150 events.

At the beginning of Fiesta week, the **Texas Cavaliers' River Parade** kicks off with decorated floats drifting along the San Antonio River and a pilgrimage to the Alamo. On the final Saturday night, **Fiesta Flambeau** claims to be the largest lighted parade in the USA, with marchers carrying candles, sparklers, flashlights, torches and anything else handy.

But locals' top pick of Fiesta week is **A Night Out in Old San Antonio**, which actually runs for four nights, during which a small army of women volunteers transforms La Villita into a multiethnic bazaar of food, music, dancing, arts and much, much more.

trolley comes right to your door. Rooms are basic as can be, but you'll save some dollars, especially when you factor in free parking and continental breakfast.

Red Roof Inn San Antonio Downtown (Map p152; ☎ 210-229-9973; www.redroof.com; 1011 E Houston St; d $69-99; P 🛜 🖵) An easy walk to both the Alamo and Riverwalk, but the trade-off is the freeway location. Still, it's a good deal, and the standard rooms are huge.

MIDRANGE
La Quinta Inn Market Square (Map p152; ☎ 210-271-0001; www.laquinta.com; 900 Dolorosa St; d $69-129; P 🖵) The updated rooms have been tastefully redecorated (hooray for no more Southwestern motif!) and right downstairs is Mi Tierra Cafe & Bakery (p164), which is ideal for 3am enchilada cravings. Prices vary widely depending on when you visit; shoot for the lower end of the spectrum to feel satisfied with your choice.

Crockett Hotel (Map p152; ☎ 210-225-6500, 800-292-1050; www.crocketthotel.com; 320 Bonham St; d $119-139 P ⊠ 🛜 🖵) No wonder pictures of the Alamo are always tightly cropped. Pull back and you can see the Crockett's sign hovering just behind the fort. (In Texas, they call that 'spittin' distance.') Rooms are basic but pleasant enough, and there's an outdoor pool, Jacuzzi and rooftop sundeck.

Inn on the Riverwalk (Map p152; ☎ 210-225-6333, 800-730-0019; www.innonriver.com; 129 Woodward Pl; s, d & tr $109-300; P 🛜) Presided over by a venerable pecan tree, this B&B is in a beautiful, peaceful setting by the river. Each cheery room has its own private bath, with the more expensive digs equipped with a Jacuzzi, private porch or balcony.

Hotel Valencia (Map p152; ☎ 210-227-9700; www.hotelvalencia-riverwalk.com; 150 E Houston St; d $113-249; P 🛜) Faux-mink throws, molded concrete, light shining through perforated metal – this place is all about texture. At times it feels like it was transported from New York City, both in its minimalist-chic style and in the size of some of the smaller rooms, but it does add a hip option if you eschew chains and historic hotels.

Riverwalk Vista (Map p152; ☎ 210-223-3200, 866-898-4782; 262 Losoya St; www.riverwalkvista.com; d $120-210, ste $180-270; 🖵) Soaring ceilings with enormous windows, exposed brick walls, crisp, white bedding – this is simplicity done right. And just because the decor is simple doesn't mean you won't be pampered: there are still plenty of niceties such as flat-screen TVs, leather chairs and feather blankets.

Menger Hotel (Map p152; ☎ 210-223-4361, 800-345-9285; www.historicmenger.com; 204 Alamo Plaza; d $129-299; P ⊠ 🛜 🖵) Historic? Definitely. This place was built in the shadow of the Alamo a scant 23 years after the famous battle. Oscar Wilde, Mae West, Teddy Roosevelt – the former guest roster is impressive. Over the decades, new additions kept getting built on, so it's a bit rambling and confusing to get around. The vaguely charming 'Antique Rooms' are the same price as the refurbished rooms, which are the same price as the unrefurbished rooms from the 1960s. Be sure to be clear about what you're reserving.

TOP END
Painted Lady Inn (Map p152; ☎ 210-220-1092; www.thepaintedladyinn.com; 620 Broadway; d & ste $129-229; P 🛜) This 1920s guesthouse is on an unwelcoming stretch of Broadway, but it's worth the trip for its European-style decor, tasteful antique furnishings and fabulous breakfasts. With rooms named after Oscar Wilde, Mae West and Liberace, it's no surprise that this B&B is gay-friendly.

Hotel Havana (Map p152; ☎ 210-222-2008; www.havanasanantonio.com; 1015 Navarro St; d $149-189; 🖵) Texas design guru and hotelier Liz Lambert could make a radish look cool. Luckily she's turned her sights on fixing up a few lucky properties such as this one, judiciously adding eclectic touches – a retro pink refrigerator, for example – to her simple, clean designs.

Emily Morgan Hotel (Map p152; ☎ 210-225-5100, 800-824-6674; www.emilymorganhotel.com; 705 E Houston St; d $189-269; P ⊠ 🛜 🖵) The name sounds as though this place should be awash in floral prints and lace runners, but this historic hotel right behind the Alamo is actually pretty stylish. The boutique-style rooms are clean, large and enjoy all the luxury amenities, from Tazo teas and Aveda bath products to high-speed internet access.

Omni Mansion del Rio (Map p152; ☎ 210-518-1000; www.lamansion.com; 112 College St; d $219-399; 🖵 🖵) This is another fabulous downtown property, born out of 19th-century religious school buildings in the Spanish-Mexican hacienda style. It's on a quiet stretch of the Riverwalk, and its discreet oasis attracts stars and other notables. Enjoy in-room spa services, swim in the outdoor heated pool or unwind at the hotel's exceptional restaurant, Las Canarias.

Watermark Hotel & Spa (Map p152; ☎ 866-605-1212; www.watermarkhotel.com; 212 W Crockett St; d $279-399; ☐ ☒) If you really want to go all out, this luxurious hotel is a good place to get pampered, with top-of-the-line amenities and an on-site spa. It's ultra-serene, in stark contrast to the tourist scene waiting just downstairs, and ideally suited to people who want to just draw the blinds and enjoy some relaxation.

King William District

This historic district is known for its beautiful homes, so it's no surprise that the majority of offerings here are B&Bs.

La Villita Inn (Map p152; ☎ 210-798-1121; 736 S St Mary's St; d $69-99; ☐ ☐ ☜) Let's just get it out there: this is a weird little building where you walk through a parking garage to get to the 2nd-floor rooms. But it's also cheap and extremely well located. Although the rooms are pretty shabby, the place is not at all creepy, which is something you can't really say about most independently owned motels at this price point.

King William Manor (Map p152; ☎ 210-222-0144; www.kingwilliammanor.com; 1037 S Alamo St; d $79-165; ☐ ☒ ☜ ☒) In a neighborhood known for beautiful old houses and B&Bs, this grand, Greek Revival mansion occupying a large corner lot still manages to jump out at you and say, 'Hey, look at me!' Maybe it's the columns, maybe it's the sprawling lawn, or perhaps it's the wraparound porches. The inside lives up to the exterior, with understatedly elegant rooms, some of which are enormous.

A Yellow Rose Inn (Map p152; ☎ 210-229-9903, 800-950-9903; www.ayellowrose.com; 229 Madison St; d $89-200; ☐ ☜) True to its name, this butterscotch-colored house is a beauty. Spacious rooms are tastefully furnished, with well-thought-out amenities such as fresh flowers, snacks, sodas and juice. We love the flexible breakfast policy, which allows you to take your breakfast in your room, or skip it altogether and pay a little less.

Brackenridge House B&B (Map p152; ☎ 210-271-3442, 800-221-1412; www.brackenridgehouse.com; 230 Madison St; d $120-250, ste $145-275; ☐ ☜) This hospitable B&B likes to feed you, from the formal, three-course breakfast to sherry and chocolate treats later in the day. The rooms are of the frilly sort, with quilts, floral prints and lace, but they're also practical, with bar fridges and microwaves.

Beauregard House B&B Inn (Map p152; ☎ 210-222-1198; www.beauregardhouse.com; 215 Beauregard St; d $129-159, ste $139-199; ☐ ☒ ☜) Well, *someone's* been antique shopping, and they made off with some impressive pieces. And the understated design shirks floral prints and doodads, opting instead for a quiet, dignified style. Breakfast is no drop-by affair. It's served in the dining room at 9am, and it shouldn't be missed if your schedule allows.

Noble Inns (Map p152; ☎ 210-223-2353, 800-242-2770; www.nobleinns.com; ☐ ☒ ☜ ☒) We won't say this collection of three inns has something for everyone, but it does have something for everyone who likes antiques and Victorian style. The Oge House (209 Washington St; doubles $179 to $349) is the most elegant of the three, with lushly appointed rooms and a prime location on the residential end of the Riverwalk. The Jackson House (107 Madison St; doubles $149 to $219) is a little more traditional B&B in style, plus it has a warm swim spa in a stained-glass conservatory. And the Carriage House (202 Washington St, check in at the Oge House; suites $159 to $259) is the frilliest of all, but offers access to a pool and spa.

Brackenridge Park & Around

This neighborhood offers relief from downtown prices, but still keeps you close to the action.

BUDGET & MIDRANGE

HI San Antonio International Hostel (Map p146; 210-223-9426; hisananton@aol.com; 621 Pierce St; dm $25; ☺ office 8am-10pm) Two miles north of downtown, and situated next to a large, colonial ranch-style historic house with a swimming pool and day-only common area, this basic hostel offers a kitchen and internet access, but no laundry facilities. It's the lowest price in town, but not necessarily the best value.

Bullis House Inn (Map p146; ☎ 210-223-9426, 877-477-4100; www.bullishouseinn.com; 621 Pierce St; s & d $60-109; ☐ ☒) This national historic trust property is under the same management as the youth hostel. Take your continental breakfast on the outdoor veranda, then splash in the swimming pool. Some rooms have fireplaces and French doors, but all share a hall telephone and bathrooms.

Ruckman Haus (Map p146; ☎ 210-736-1468, 866-736-1468; www.ruckmanhaus.com; 629 W French St; d $100-170; ☐ ☒ ☜) Welcome home! It's hard to feel more at ease than you will at this homey, comfortable B&B, with lovely gardens, porches and common areas where you could hang out all day. We love the Sun Room because it has – surprise! – a sun room, as well as a private rooftop deck.

Bonner Garden (Map p146; ☎ 210-733-4222; www.bonnergarden.com; 45 E Agarita Ave; d $130-165; P ⊠ ☒) This lovely Italianate villa dates from 1910 and was built for artist Mary Bonner. Original works by Texas artists hang on the walls, and there's a fireplace with antique tiles. Our hands-down favorite is Mary Bonner's studio, a detached suite with whitewashed stone walls and Saltillo tile floors.

TOP END

Inn at Craig Place (Map p146; ☎ 210-736-1017, 877-427-2447; www.craigplace.com; 117 W Craig Pl; d $140-185; P) A quiet getaway in the historic Monte Vista neighborhood, this national-trust property is popular for weddings and honeymoons. Each of the romantic rooms has its own breakfast table, bath and telephone. Freshly baked cookies and chocolates appear in the evening, plus there's a three-course hot breakfast every morning. Peruse the library or simply relax in the antique-furnished parlor.

Greater San Antonio
BUDGET

Dixie Campground (off Map p146; ☎ 210-337-6501; 1011 Gembler Rd; tent sites with electricity $20, RV sites with full hookups $27-30; P ☒) Dixie is northeast of downtown San Antonio near the SBC Center. It's about as flashy as your typical KOA and slightly cheaper, too.

Admiralty RV Resort (off Map p146; ☎ 210-647-7878, 877-236-4715; www.admiraltyrvresort.com; 1485 N Ellison Dr; RV sites regular/luxury $36/45; P ☎ ☒) This top-notch RV park with a junior Olympic-size swimming pool and plenty of shade is convenient to SeaWorld, which runs a free shuttle service to the campground during summer. Discounts are available for weekly stays, AAA, AARP and others.

Rittiman Inn (off Map p146; ☎ 210-657-0808; www.rittimaninn.com; 6364 IH-35 N; d $49-69; P) This independently owned motel is a bit of a surprise. The outside has some quirky, faux-Bavarian touches that first got our attention, and the inside manages to pull of a look that, while it may not have been updated in ages, doesn't come off as shabby, like they just pulled the

plastic slipcovers off right before you came. It's, dare we say, kind of cute?

Super 8 Motel SeaWorld (off Map p146; ☎ 210-678-0888; 2211 SW Loop 410; winter $50-80, summer $68-100; P ☒) All right, so you're not going for luxury. You're spending most of your time at SeaWorld (which is only 1.2 miles away) anyway. This Super 8 motel is slightly nicer than the norm, with an outdoor pool, making it a decent base of operations.

MIDRANGE & TOP END

Hill Country Inn & Suites (Map p146; ☎ 210-599-4204, 800-314-3424; www.shellhospitality.com; 2383 NE Loop 410; d $59-99; P ☒ ⚐) About 15 minutes north of downtown, and less than 5 miles from the airport, this anachronistic place does feel more like it belongs in the Hill Country than off of an interstate in San Antonio, with ranch-style porches and country-style furnishings. Picnic tables and a full-fledged playscape make it a great choice for families.

Hyatt Place Northwest (Map p146; ☎ 210-561-0099; http://sanantonionorthwest.place.hyatt.com; 4303 Hyatt Place Dr; d $109-169; P ⊠ ☐ ☎ ☒) Almost everything out near Six Flags is a chain, but this awesome little Hyatt Place is one of the best. It's clean and fresh, with spacious rooms and a smartly modern decor, and it's just 6 miles from the park. Flat-screen TVs, continental breakfast and free computer access and printing make it a bargain.

Westin La Cantera Resort (off Map p146; ☎ 210-558-6500, 888-625-5144; www.westinlacantera.com; 16641 La Cantera Parkway; d $199-299 plus resort charge $15; P ⊠ ☎ ☒) This resort must be trying to break the world record for most hospitality awards ever. *Condé Nast Traveler, Golf Digest, AAA Four Diamond* are among those that have recognized the destination property. Standard rooms are elegant but on the small side, so you'll enjoy it most if you're willing to get out and take advantage of the six pools, three hot tubs, golf course, tennis courts, health club and spa. Almost outside of town, the overwhelming offerings might upstage your other sightseeing activities.

EATING

A location along the Riverwalk gives any restaurant instant atmosphere – especially when there's a patio involved. That makes it prime real estate, which means you're not going to find many bargains there. Southtown has its share of hip eateries that are better value, and north of downtown around Brackenridge Park has tons of inexpensive dining options.

Naturally, some of the best cooking is Tex-Mex and Mexican-style. Both the *San Antonio Current* and the *San Antonio Express-News*' 'Weekender' section regularly list their top pick of restaurants and are worth checking out.

Riverwalk
BUDGET

Justin's Ice Cream Company (Map p152; ☎ 210-222-1457; 510 Riverwalk; ☷ noon-11pm) Ready to stop and rest for a bit? Cool off with a dish of housemade, Italian-style ice cream, gelato or sorbet at a table overlooking the river.

Casa Rio (Map p152; ☎ 210-225-6718; 430 E Commerce St; mains $8-14; ☷ lunch & dinner) One of SA's oldest Mexican restaurants, Casa Rio has been around since 1946, and the building itself is a Spanish hacienda that dates back to the colonial period of Texas history. A colorful array of umbrellas makes this a cheerful (and affordable!) place to soak in the ambience.

MIDRANGE & TOP END
County Line Smokehouse (Map p152; ☎ 210-229-1941; 111 W Crockett St; barbecue from $5, platters $10-20; ☷ lunch & dinner) San Antonio isn't known for its barbecue – it's clearly more of a Tex-Mex kind of town – but this outpost of the Austin minichain does a decent job with heaping dishes of brisket, ribs and sausage.

Boudro's on the Riverwalk (Map p152; ☎ 210-224-8484; 421 E Commerce St; lunch $7-12.50, dinner mains $15-33; ☷ lunch & dinner) This brightly colored restaurant is hugely popular even with locals. Fresh guacamole is made right at your table. The upscale Tex-Mex menu reveals some gourmet surprises, such as black-bean soup made with sherry and white cheddar, lobster tail fajitas drizzled with pineapple *pico de gallo* and wines from Texas and California.

Dick's Last Resort (Map p152; ☎ 210-224-0026; 406 Navarro St; mains $10-20; ☷ 11am-2am) Sure, this hopping chain restaurant is touristy, but, well, so is the Riverwalk. The main reason to give in to Dick's is the purposefully and comically obnoxious service. (Let's just say its name is no coincidence.)

Biga on the Banks (Map p152; ☎ 210-225-0722; 203 S St Mary's St; mains $20-35; ☷ dinner) This is one of the most justifiably praised restaurants in town, run by Bruce Auden, who is also the chef. The menu is a wonderful mix of European,

Tex-Mex, American and Asian influences that probably don't cost as much as they should (certainly not what they could). It's stylish yet welcoming, and the wine list is impressive.

Downtown
BUDGET

Schilo's German Delicatessen (Map p152; ☎ 210-223-6692; 424 E Commerce St; meals $4-9; ☷ 7am-8:30pm Mon-Sat) Schilo's has certainly earned its ambience: this German restaurant has been around since 1917, and looks the part, down to the wooden booths and the elaborate pattern of the hexagonal floor tiles. Specialties include wonderful split-pea soup, fresh pumpernickel bread, German beer and homemade root beer.

Twin Sisters Bakery & Café (Map p152; ☎ 210-354-1559; 124 Broadway; meals $4-9; ☷ 8am-3pm Mon-Fri) 'Healthy' and 'natural' aren't words you'd attribute to many of the downtown restaurants, so this cheerful little cafe is a welcome addition to the bunch for weekday breakfast and lunch.

Candy's Old Fashioned Restaurant (Map p152; ☎ 210-222-9659; 115 S Flores St; mains $4-9; ☷ 10am-8pm Mon-Fri) This little place has a tiny dining room with a nostalgic, small-town feel. But lest that sound a bit quaint, wait till you see the whoppin' burgers and big fried catfish platters they're serving up.

MIDRANGE & TOP END
Mi Tierra Cafe & Bakery (Map p152; ☎ 210-225-1262; 218 Produce Row; meals $12-15; ☷ 24hr) Dishing out traditional Mexican food since 1941, this 500-seat behemoth sprawls across several dining areas, giving the busy wait staff and strolling mariachis quite a workout. Best of all? It's open 24 hours, which means it's always there when you need it.

Little Rhein Steak House (Map p152; ☎ 210-225-2111; 231 S Alamo St; mains $21-44, sides extra; ☷ dinner) Close to the Riverwalk and within La Villita, this historic steakhouse is located in a two-story limestone home built in the mid-1800s. It's plenty atmospheric, with an old-world charm indoors and a pleasant patio outdoors where you can enjoy steak and seafood dishes.

Bohanan's (Map p152; ☎ 210-472-2277; 219 E Houston St; mains $22-125; ☷ lunch Mon-Fri, dinner Mon-Sat, 5-9pm Sun) These people take their steaks seriously and, at these prices, so should you. Lots of people can appreciate a great steak, but you'll treasure the experience even more if you're the type of person who throws around terms such as 'Akaushi beef.' These cows were raised in a humane and healthy fashion, and probably given pedicures, too, from the sound of it.

King William District & Southtown
BUDGET
Madhatters Tea House & Café (Map p152; ☎ 210-212-4832; 320 Beauregard St; bakery $1-5, meals $6-11; ⏰ 7am-9pm Mon-Fri, 8am-9pm Sat, 9am-3pm Sun) With more than 70 types of tea on hand, this is the perfect stop for an afternoon snack. During the week, it serves club sandwiches, spinach salads and sirloin burgers; brunch brings French toast, eggs benedict with chipotle hollandaise and mimosas. And of course, you can always stop by for afternoon tea.

Guenther House (Map p152; ☎ 210-227-1061; 205 E Guenther St; mains $4-8; ⏰ breakfast & lunch Mon-Sat) Located in the Pioneer Flour Mill complex, this is the kind of place you'd choose if you were meeting up with the gals or taking your mom out to lunch. The specialty is the champagne-chicken enchiladas, but it also serves yummy sandwiches and all-day breakfast.

Casbeers (Map p146; ☎ 210-271-7791; www.casbeers.com; 1150 S Alamo St; mains $6-9; ⏰ lunch Mon-Sat, dinner Tue-Sat) Known for the enchiladas and also the Kinky Burger (named after Kinky Friedman, not some weird burger fetish), this San Antonio institution has upgraded locations and is now in a rather lovely building that used to be a Methodist Church.

MIDRANGE
Mr Tim's Country Kitchen Cafe (Map p152; ☎ 210-271-7887; 620 S Presa St; meals $6-13; ⏰ 7am-8pm) You'd think there'd be more American-style home cooking around, but this is one of a few places that serves up Texas-style comfort food: pork chops, liver and onions, and breakfast, including cinnamon rolls as big as your head.

Blue Star Brewing Company (Map p152; ☎ 210-212-5506; 1414 S Alamo St; mains $7-10; ⏰ lunch & dinner Mon-Sat, to 8pm Sun) Attracting a casual, creative crowd (thanks to its location in the Blue Star Arts Complex) this brewpub and restaurant is a relaxed place to hang out for a bite served with one of its craft brews.

Rosario's Mexican Cafe (Map p152; ☎ 210-223-1806; 910 S Alamo St; mains $9-12; ⏰ lunch & dinner Mon-Sat, to 9pm Sun) This lively restaurant is always hopping, with huge windows lining the walls that let in natural light and wistful glances from hungry onlookers. The food is nothing special,

but it's clearly good enough to keep people satisfied.

Brackenridge Park & Around
These neighborhoods are havens for some of the best-value eateries in the city. If you have a car, take advantage of the lower prices; most of these restaurants are just five to 10 minutes from downtown.

BUDGET
Taco Cabana (off Map p146; ☎ 210-733-9332; 3310 San Pedro Ave; tacos $1-3, plates $3-6; ⏰ 24hr) This Texas chain is beloved across the state for its excellent (and cheap!) breakfast tacos, fajitas and burritos, and this is the location where it all began. It's a welcome sight when you're looking for food at 3am.

Earl Abel's (Map p146; ☎ 210-822-3358; 1201 Austin Hwy; breakfast $4-10, mains $8-22; ⏰ breakfast, lunch & dinner) Earl Abel's has been feeding San Antonians since 1933. This isn't the original location, but it keeps the tradition alive, with photos and memorabilia from the original. More importantly, the homestyle meals (most less than $10) are deliciously satisfying, with breakfast staples served all day.

Chris Madrid's (Map p146; ☎ 210-735-3552; 1900 Blanco Rd; mains $5-8; ⏰ lunch & dinner Mon-Sat) Two words: tostada burgers. Topping a burger with tortilla chips and refried beans sounds weird, but it works, combining two of our favorite meals into one deliciously unholy alliance. Throw some jalapeños on for a memorable meal.

Twin Sisters Bakery & Café (Map p146; ☎ 210-822-0761; 6322 N New Braunfels Ave; meals $5-8; ⏰ 7am-9pm Mon-Fri, 7am-3pm Sat, 9am-2pm Sun) Near the McNay Art Museum, this laidback cafe is a great spot for breakfast, when you'll find a hearty selection of American and Mexican food. Vegetarians are well catered for; the vegetable sauté is an excellent choice.

Green Vegetarian Cuisine (Map p152; ☎ 210-320-5865; 1017 N Flores; mains $5-10; ⏰ 9am-9pm Sun-Fri; Ⓥ) Vegetarians all around the city must've breathed a sigh of contentment when this cafe opened up. It's the only place in town (at least at the time of research) that's 100% vegetarian, and it's 100% kosher to boot. With dishes such as basil mint pecan pesto pasta, avocado eggs Benedict, and 'neatloaf,' it's the kind of place even a meat-eater can enjoy.

Bun 'N' Barrell (Map p146; ☎ 210-828-2829; 1150 Austin Hwy; mains $6-11; ⏰ 11am-8pm Sun-Wed, 11am-9pm

Thu-Sat) 'Honk for curb service.' No really, the sign out front says so. This drive-in has been around since 1950 and, while the outside looks the part, the interior has had a recent renovation that's surprisingly spiffy. Another surprise? In addition to the expected hamburgers, the other specialty is barbecue by the pound.

Mary Ann's Pig Stand (off Map p146; ☎ 210-222-9923; 1508 Broadway St; mains $6-14; ☺ 6am-midnight Mon-Thu, 24hr Fri & Sat) The history, the ambience, the neon sign shaped like an enormous pig... it's hard to say what we love most about this place, which has been around since the 1920s. After the Pig Stand chain closed, Mary Ann, a long-term employee, brought this location back to life for San Antonians to enjoy in all its porcine glory.

MIDRANGE & TOP END

Josephine Street (Map p146; ☎ 210-224-6169; 400 E Josephine St; mains $7-15; ☺ lunch & dinner Mon-Sat) The neon signs in the front window advertise 'steak' and 'whisky.' There's a tree growing up through the floor and out the ceiling of the dining room. And the creaky hardwood floors slant more than a little. This isn't the place for fussy foodies. It is, however, the place for anyone who wants good steak and seafood – hold the fine-dining ambience and prices.

Adelante Mexican Food (Map p146; ☎ 210-822-7681; 21 Brees Blvd; mains $8-10; ☺ 11am-9pm Tue-Sat) This cute Mexican diner is a nice little secret. Located in a strip mall near the McNay Art Museum, it would be easy to overlook, but the inside has the feel of a Mexican *mercado*, with colorful handicrafts right down to the painted furniture. Plus, the food seems a little lighter than most, and doesn't leave you wanting a siesta.

Paloma Blanca (Map p146; ☎ 210-822-6151; 5800 Broadway St; lunch $8-10, mains $10-15; ☺ 9am-5pm Mon, lunch & dinner Tue-Sat, 9am-9pm Sun) In a sea of excellent Mexican food, this place sets itself apart with a sleek and stylish ambience that makes it feel just a little more special than the others – think dim lighting, exposed brick walls, and oversized artwork – with food that definitely lives up to the decor.

Little Aussie Bakery & Cafe (Map p146; ☎ 210-826-7877; 3610 Ave B; mains $9-12; ☺ 11am-5pm Tue-Thu, 11am-7pm Fri, 11am-5pm Sat, 10am-3pm Sun) Gluten-free everything! If you have celiac disease or are on a low-carb diet, that's all you need to know about this place: excellent bread and other

baked goodies, as well as tasty lunches, with nary any gluten with which to concern yourself.

Il Sogno Osteria (Map p152; ☎ 210-223-3900; 200 E Grayson St; mains $14-32; ☺ lunch & dinner Tue-Sun) Over in the new Pearl development (built on the grounds of the old Pearl Brewery), this stylish former warehouse is frequently packed with people vying for a shot at the fresh, house-made pastas. Warning: it doesn't take reservations.

Greater San Antonio

Amy's Ice Cream (Map p146; ☎ 210-832-8886; 255 E Basse Rd in the Quarry; ☺ 11am-11pm Sun-Thu, 11am-midnight Fri & Sat) Choose your ice cream, pick a topping – then watch the staff pulverize the two into a blended little cup of heaven.

Taco Cabana (Map p146; ☎ 210-822-6877; 1255 NE Loop 410; tacos $1-3, plates $3-6; ☺ 24hr) Look for the pink neon sign around town for cheap, fast and delish Mexican food (see p165). This location is near the airport; look for others at 2908 Broadway near Brackenridge Park or 543 Malone south of downtown.

DeWese's Tip Top Cafe (Map p146; ☎ 210-732-0191; 2814 Fredericksburg Rd; mains $4-16; ☺ 11am-8pm Tue-Sat, 11am-7pm Sun) Some of the best chicken-fried steak and onion rings in the known universe are at this diner, which has been around since 1938. The made-from-scratch pies – chocolate, banana meringue, apple, coconut or egg custard – are good enough to fight over.

DRINKING

A heavy concentration of the city's watering holes is downtown, but for more interesting choices, head to Southtown, which has a more independent-minded nightlife.

Downtown & the Riverwalk

There's no shortage of beverages of the adult variety around the Riverwalk. But lest you end up at a chain such as Coyote Ugly, here are a few worth trying.

Menger Bar (Map p152; ☎ 210-223-4361; 204 Alamo Pl) More than 100 years ago, Teddy Roosevelt recruited Rough Riders from this bar that, incidentally, was a replica of the House of Lords Pub in London. To complete the image, picture a mounted moose head, scant lighting and lots of wood. There probably won't be a local in sight, but the history alone makes it a worthwhile stop.

Zinc Champagne & Wine Bar (Map p152; ☎ 210-224-2900; 207 N Presa St) Head to Zinc's for an atmosphere that's nicely chilled-out, helped along by a good range of music and an array of wines, champagnes and ports that are simply stunning. There's also a nice garden bar and an extensive selection of cigars.

Mad Dog's British Pub (Map p152; ☎ 210-222-0220; 123 Losoya St) Authenticity is not in high demand along the Riverwalk, but this Britishy pub (named after the bar started by two Scots over in Hong Kong) has ales on tap, billiards, pool tables and darts. Occasionally there's live entertainment, too.

Southtown

A Latin-flavored scene that's refreshingly unpretentious is what you'll find in this neighborhood near all of the King William District's B&Bs.

La Tuna Ice House (Map p146; ☎ 210-224-8862; 100 Probandt St) When the sun starts to set over Southtown, scoot down by the railroad tracks to this back-to-basics watering hole for a few cold beers and nostalgic school-size snacks. Locals, even families, crowd around outdoor tables until well after dark, especially on weekends when there's live music.

Blue Star Brewing Company (Map p152; ☎ 210-212-5506; 1414 S Alamo St; ☽ 11am-11pm Mon-Thu, 11am-midnight Fri & Sat; 10am-8pm Sun) See those great big brewing tanks behind the bar? That's your craft beer being made. The people-watching, the relaxed vibe and the location inside the Blue Star Arts complex all invite you to linger.

Greater San Antonio

Flying Saucer (off Map p146; ☎ 210-696-5080; 11255 Huebner Rd) More than 300 beer choices, from Abita Abbey Ale to Young's Double Chocolate

Stout and everything in between, make this place a beer-lover's paradise, as does the casual, beer garden vibe. It's a bit of a schlep from downtown – around a 15 to 20 minute drive – but it's a good way to unwind after a (child-free) visit to Fiesta Texas.

ENTERTAINMENT

Although the live music scene isn't as jumping as in Austin, there's still plenty of entertainment in San Antonio. Check the *San Antonio Current* or Jim Beal's 'Night Lights' column in the 'Weekender' section of the *San Antonio Express-News* for upcoming concerts. Both publications also have comprehensive listings of art exhibitions and openings, touring shows, theater, classical music and cinema.

Most bars stay open until 2am daily (unless otherwise noted), while a few clubs stay hoppin' until 4am. Club schedules vary (as do club cover charges, which vary from $3 for local bands to $25 or more for big-name acts). Tickets for major sports and performing arts events can be purchased through **Ticketmaster** (☎ 210-224-9600; www.ticketmaster. com), which has more than a dozen city-wide ticket outlets.

Live Music

North of downtown along N St Mary's St, the **Strip** was once a very vibrant music and bar scene at the center of the university student's universe. Though not what it was, it's still a good place to start your search for live local shows (and the occasional international act) in San Antonio. There are also a few places by the Riverwalk and on the city's outskirts.

DETOUR: SHINER

The highlight of any trip to Shiner, the self-proclaimed 'cleanest little city in Texas,' is a tour of the **Spoetzl Brewery** (☎ 800-574-4637; www.shiner.com; 603 E Brewery St; tours free; ☽ tours usually 11am & 1:30pm Mon-Fri) where America's best-selling bock beer, Shiner Bock, is produced. Czech and German settlers who began making beer under brewmaster Kosmos Spoetzl (pronounced shpet-zul) founded the brewery more than 90 years ago. Today the brewery still produces several types using the same methods, including bock, blonde, honey wheat, summer stock and winter ale. You can sample the beers for free after the tour in the little bar. Shiner's 'Bocktoberfest,' featuring rock and country music concerts, is held in mid-October; admission is $30 to $35 per adult (children under 12 free).

By car from San Antonio, take I-10 past Luling to US 95 and go south right to the very doors of Spoetzl Brewery. From Austin, take US 183 south through Luling to Gonzales, then turn east (left) and follow US 90A, which brings you right into the center of town; cross the railroad tracks and make a left turn on US 95 to reach the brewery.

There are lots of places to hear Tejano bands and conjunto music, but which place is hottest tends to shift; check the Spanish-language newspapers for listings.

DOWNTOWN & SOUTHTOWN

The Landing (Map p152; ☎ 210-223-7266; www.landing.com; Riverwalk level, Hyatt Regency Hotel, 123 Losoya St) Jazz at the Landing is not just a San Antonio tradition; it's also a syndicated show on NPR. Catch a taping of *Riverwalk Jazz* on Saturday nights, when advance reservations are definitely required. The rest of the week, live jazz duos play starting at noon on the outside riverside patio, weather permitting. On many evenings, you can catch the seven-piece Jim Cullum Jazz Band.

Sunset Station (Map p152; ☎ 210-222-9481; www.sunset-station.com; 1174 E Commerce St; ☼ box office 10am-6pm Mon-Fri, show days 5-11pm) The renovated South Pacific Railroad Depot is now home to this complex, which houses a number of restaurants, clubs and music venues under one roof. Regular outdoor concerts for touring international bands are held here, under the shadow of the Alamodome. For information on future gigs, check out the website, call or go in person to the box office inside the Sunset Saloon.

Rosario's (Map p152; ☎ 210-223-1806; 910 S Alamo St) This restaurant (p165) has live music Friday and Saturday night. On Friday you'll find the small dancefloor packed with salsa, cumbia and merengue dancers, and Saturday it's all about jazz. There's no cover charge, and the bar stays open until 1:30am.

BRACKENRIDGE PARK & AROUND

The following venues are all on or near the Strip.

White Rabbit (Map p146; ☎ 210-737-2221; www.sawhiterabbit.com; 2410 N St Mary's St) This is one of the best places for indie, metal and punk sounds, with two stages, slates of several bands per night and often no cover. These days, it has diversified into a college bar scene on Thursday nights. Acoustic acts take over Tuesday nights.

Sam's Burger Joint (Map p152; ☎ 210-223-2830; www.samsburgerjoint.com; 330 E Grayson St) Its neon sign visible from the highway overhead, Sam's hosts plenty of rockabilly, ska and punk bands all week long. It's also SA's main venue for open-mic poetry slams, often held Tuesday nights.

Carmen's de la Calle Café (Map p146; ☎ 210-737-8272; 720 E Mistletoe Ave; ☼ 6pm-midnight Thu-Sat) San Antonio has Mexican down pat, but you can also indulge in a little Spanish culture with tapas, sangria and live jazz, flamenco and world music in a garden setting.

Saluté (Map p146; ☎ 210-732-5307; 2801 N St Mary's St) This tiny place looks like a dive at first, especially with its siren-red neon sign. Inside there's great live music of all stripes, from funk to soul to Latin jazz to blues-rock and beyond.

GREATER SAN ANTONIO

Martini's (Map p146; ☎ 210-344-4747; 8507 McCullough Ave) For a taste of Las Vegas in the heart of San Antonio, head to what can only be described as a kitsch lounge bar. Wayne, the owner–singer–guitarist–trumpeter–saxophonist, fronts a three-piece band. He can impersonate anyone by request, from Neil Diamond to Willie Nelson, to perfection. Located in a strip mall next to the Avon shop, the only indication of the bar's existence is a small brass plaque reading 'Martini's' screwed to the wall next to the entrance.

Re-Bar (Map p146; ☎ 210-320-4091; 8134 Broadway) Just off of Loop 410, this stylish lounge is not only a place to meet and mingle, but it also books live local bands a few nights a week. Sit on the open-air patio, if you can.

John T Floore Country Store (off Map p146; ☎ 210-695-8827; www.liveatfloores.com; 14492 Old Bandera Rd, Helotes; ☼ live music usually Wed-Sun) Northwest of town in Helotes, this dancehall has been around since the 1940s, and rivals Gruene Hall (p174) for authenticity. The hall hosts plenty of country-and-western concerts; Willie Nelson, Bob Wills, Patsy Cline and Elvis have all done shows here. Sunday is family night, with free admission and dancing after 6pm.

Dance Clubs

San Antonio doesn't have a real club scene, but some of its dance clubs are big enough to pack in half the city. Check in the local papers about schedules and drop-in classes for tango, salsa, folk and country two-step dancing.

Bonham Exchange (Map p152; ☎ 210-271-3811; www.bonhamexchange.net; 411 Bonham St; cover varies, before 10pm some nights free; ☼ usually Wed-Sun) There's plenty of room for everyone at the Bonham: although it's predominantly a gay bar, the sheer enormity of the place attracts a mixed crowd with drinking and dancing on their mind. Located in an imposing Victorian edifice built in 1892, it has huge dancefloors and five bars spread over three floors.

Atomix (Map p146; ☎ 210-733-3855; http://kaozgoth. tripod.com; 1902 McCullough Ave; cover under $5, before 10pm Fri & 11pm Sat free; ☽ to 3am Fri & Sat) Goth and industrial music is not dead. No, really, we swear. On Friday and Saturday nights, this midtown club spins '80s and '90s retro from new wave to synth-punk and electro grooves. Drinks are unbelievably cheap.

Cowboy's Dance Hall (off Map p146; ☎ 210-646-9378; www.cowboysdancehall.com; 3030 NE Loop 410, east of I-35; cover from $5; ☽ Wed-Sun) This enormous dancehall packs in a mix of people – hard to say the proportion of actual cowboys – ready to scoot their boots to country-and-western music. Check the website for drink specials, teen nights and ladies' nights festivities.

Comedy Clubs
Visiting headliners sometimes perform at the downtown Majestic Theatre and Trinity University's Laurie Auditorium (p169); check the *Current* or the *Express-News'* 'Weekender' section for more information.

Rivercenter Comedy Club (Map p152; ☎ 210-229-1420; www.rivercentercomedyclub.com; 3rd level, Rivercenter Mall, 849 E Commerce St; most tickets $15; ☽ 8:30pm Sun-Thu, 8:30pm & 10:30pm Fri & Sat) Check out the up-and-coming local funnymen and -women – as well as occasional major headliners – at this lively club in the Rivercenter. There's no cover for the open-mic show on Saturdays at 3:30pm, and you usually get what you paid for, although you never know. There's also a free adults-only 'After Midnight Madness' show on Saturday night. Three-hour parking at the Rivercenter Mall is available with validation.

Cinema
Check the *Current* or the *Express-News'* 'Weekender' section for cinemas and show times.

Alamo Drafthouse (off Map p146; ☎ 210-677-8500; www.drafthouse.com; adult/child $9/7, 3-D films $11.50; 1255 SW Loop 410) It's a bit of a drive from downtown, but you can catch both dinner and a movie at this theater that surprisingly has nothing to do with the Alamo at all. (It actually started in Austin. Go fig.) It serves a full menu including beer and wine that's brought right to your seat to enjoy during the first-run films.

San Antonio IMAX Alamo Theatre (Map p152; ☎ 210-247-4629, 800-354-4629; www.imax-sa.com; Rivercenter Mall, 849 E Commerce St; adult/child $11.50/9) Films shown here include the 45-minute award-winning film *Alamo: The Price of Freedom*, about guess what. If you've never seen a film on a six-story-high screen in six-track surround sound, this theater plays several movies in the IMAX format – it's worth the admission price just for the experience.

Spectator Sports
The big news in town is the **San Antonio Spurs** (www.nba.com/spurs), currently one of the top NBA teams in the country. The city is understandably proud, so you'll forgive them if they indulge in a little Spurs mania seven or eight months out of the year. Games held at the **AT&T Center** (Map p146; cnr Houston St & SBC Center Parkway) are exciting, action-packed spectacles. Buy your **tickets** from the Spurs **ticket office** (☎ 210-444-5819) or through **Ticketmaster** (☎ 800-745-3000; www.ticketmaster.com).

Winners of the Texas League championships in 2003 and 2007, the **San Antonio Missions** (☎ 210-675-7275; www.samissions.com; 5757 US 90 W; tickets $7-10; ☽ regular season Apr-Aug) play minor league baseball at Nelson Wolff Municipal Stadium, a short drive west of downtown.

Performing Arts
San Antonio's most historic downtown venue for the performing arts is the **Majestic Theatre** (Map p152; ☎ 210-226-3333; www.majesticempire.com; 226 E Houston St; ☽ box office 10am-5pm Mon-Fri, varies Sat), which hosts a variety of musical concerts, Broadway plays and other events year-round. In La Villita, the **Arneson River Theater** (Map p152; ☎ 210-207-8610; 418 Villita St) is an outdoor venue for anything from Latin dance to plays to festival processions. Trinity University's **Laurie Auditorium** (Map p146; ☎ 210-999-8117; One Stadium Dr) also hosts a few musical concerts and dance and theater performances year-round.

May is the month to celebrate dance in San Antonio, with recitals by local troupes, national touring companies and new choreographers' works at both indoor and outdoor venues around the city; contact **San Antonio Dance Umbrella** (☎ 210-212-6600; www.sadu.org) for details.

Visit www.satheatre.com for information on the venues below, as well as other theaters and dramatic companies performing year-round.

Overtime Theater (Map p152; ☎ 210-557-7562; www.theovertimetheater.net; 1414 S Alamo St) This up-start produces innovative shows and keeps ticket prices low. The names of some of its original shows gives you an idea of the vibe: *Sheer Bloody Lunacy!, Pirates vs Ninjas,* and *The Brain That Wouldn't Die: A New Musical.*

AtticRep (Map p146; ☎ 210-800-838-3006; www.atticrep.org; 1 Trinity Pl) This cutting-edge theater knows how to pick a great script, producing shows that are edgy, compelling and current.

San Pedro Playhouse (Map p146; ☎ 210-733-7258; box office 210-733-7258; www.sanpedroplayhouse.com; 800 W Ashby, at San Pedro Ave) The Russell Hill Rogers Theater is the performance venue for the nonprofit San Antonio Little Theatre, which stages several shows a year, usually classics. It's also home to the Cellar Theater, a 60-seat venue that holds scaled-down and experimental works.

Guadalupe Theatre (Map p146; ☎ 210-271-3151; www.guadalupeculturalarts.org; 1301 Guadalupe St, cnr Brazos St) You never know what to expect at this community arts center, whether it's a poetry reading, dance recital, contemporary drama or *ballet folklorico* performance, but it's always worth the trip.

Classical Music

The Majestic Theatre and Laurie Auditorium are the main performance venues for both local and touring orchestras and chamber groups.

San Antonio Symphony (Map p152; ☎ 210-554-1010; www.sasymphony.org; box office 5th fl, IBC Bank Bldg, 130 East Travis St, Suite 550; tickets from $16) The symphony performs a wide range of classical concerts, operas and ballets at different venues around town, including the spectacular Majestic Theatre. Tickets (which range in price wildly) can be bought from the symphony's box office or from Ticketmaster outlets.

SHOPPING

Don't overlook San Antonio's museum gift shops, especially SAMA (p154) and the McNay Art Museum (p155), which can be exceptional. Popular attractions such as the Alamo, Buckhorn Saloon and Guenther House also make for unique souvenir shopping. If you're just desperate because you forgot to get gifts until the last minute, Texas-made goods are sold at stores in both terminals of San Antonio's airport.

Markets, Art & Crafts

Many of the art galleries around town are excellent for buying crafts by contemporary Texan and Mexican artists.

Market Square (p152; ☎ 210-207-8600; 514 W Commerce St; ☼ 10am-6pm, 10am-8pm summer) A short ride from the Riverwalk, 'El Mercado' is a re-creation of a Mexican marketplace. As far as tourist traps go, you could do worse, with about 100 merchants selling blankets, handbags, rugs, craftwork, clothing and reasonable Mexican food. Prices will seem decent if you've haven't been south of the border.

Southwest School of Art & Craft (Map p152; ☎ 210-224-1848; www.swschool.org; 300 Augusta St; admission free; ☼ 10am-5pm Mon-Sat) The gallery shop exhibits and sells works by the school's artists and visiting artists, representing an eclectic mix of almost every medium imaginable.

San Angel Folk Art Gallery (Map p152; ☎ 210-226-6688; www.sanangelfolkart.com; 110 Blue Star; ☼ 11am-6pm) Located inside the Blue Star Arts Complex, this store has a fabulous collection of colorful and whimsical folk art, and is a good place to start when exploring the shops and galleries.

Clothing & Western Wear

Although you won't find many unique items, there are great bargains to be had at the factory outlets in New Braunfels and San Marcos. If you're headed to the hill country, you might want to hold off on Western wear, but if not, you can find plenty here in San Antonio.

Adelante Boutique (Map p146; ☎ 210-826-6770; Sunset Ridge shopping center, 6414 New Braunfels Ave N; ☼ 10am-5:30pm Mon-Sat) Like a romantic breath of fresh air, this shop has mix-and-match pieces in vibrant prints and fabrics you won't find anywhere else, along with designer jewelry imports.

Ranch at the Rim (off Map p146; ☎ 210-319-3001; 18007 IH-10 West; ☼ 10am-9pm Mon-Sat, noon-7pm Sun) It's a bit of a mosey from downtown, but if you want to get decked out in cowboy gear, including apparel, boots and hats, this is a great place to start.

Paris Hatters (Map p152; ☎ 210-223-3453; 119 Broadway; ☼ hours vary) A humble downtown storefront, Paris Hatters has been around a long, long time. It's one of the best places in the state to get a Stetson (or any other brand of cowboy hat).

Dave Little's Boots (Map p146; ☎ 210-923-2221; www.davelittleboots.com; 110 Division Ave; ☼ hours vary)

PAPA JIM'S BOTANICA

If you have never visited a botanica before, be sure to make a special trip out to **Papa Jim's** (Map p146; ☎ 210-922-6665; www.papajimsbotanica.com; 5630 S Flores St; 9am-5pm Mon-Fri, 10am-6pm Sat) in the southern part of the city. It's basically a religious and Santeria superstore (mixed with a bit of voodoo), selling items to rid you of the problem of your choice: Get-Rich candles, Do-As-I-Say floor wash, Jinx Removal air-freshener, Run-Devil-Run and Get-out-of-Jail oil, and Stop-Gossip soap, all for a few dollars apiece. The store also has books, herbal teas, incense, good-luck charms and other items related to Santeria, a synthesis of Catholicism and the Nigerian Yoruba folk beliefs of slaves brought to the Caribbean. Papa Jim's motto is 'Whatever Works,' and obviously it works for some: the botanica has been around since 1980.

This high-quality bootmaker's shop established in 1915 now caters to country music stars, actors and locals alike. Get your custom pair with a belt to match made from calf, crocodile, 'gator, lizard, eel, ostrich or even kangaroo skin. Allow a few months for delivery.

Affordably priced Western-wear chains around town include **Sheplers** (off Map p146; ☎ 210-681-8230; 6201 NW Loop 410; 9am-9pm Mon-Sat, 11am-6pm Sun), next to Ingram Park Mall, and **Cavender's Boot City** (off Map p146; ☎ 210-520-2668; 5075 NW Loop 410; 9am-9pm Mon-Sat, noon-6pm Sun).

Housewares
Melissa Guerra (Map p152; ☎ 210-293-3983; 200 E Grayson in Pearl Brewery; 10am-6:30pm Mon-Sat) San Antonio's answer to Williams Sonoma, Melissa Guerra has upscale kitchen implements and table settings with a Latin flavor, layered in with Mexican craft items such as *lotería* jewelry and painted pottery. It's one of the first stores in the new Pearl Brewery development; stop here and see what else has opened up around it.

Music
Hogwild Records (Map p146; ☎ 210-733-5354; 1824 N Main Ave; 10am-9pm Mon-Sat, noon-8pm Sun) With an expert selection of vinyl, Hogwild also vends tapes and CDs. If you're after alt-country, punk 'zines or rare drum 'n' bass records, this independent music store is the place. Just look for the front door, plastered with band flyers and deep layers of stickers.

CD Exchange (Map p146; ☎ 210-828-5525; 3703 Broadway; 10am-9pm Mon-Sat, noon-7pm Sun) This reliable chain music store has lots of cheap secondhand CDs, DVDs and videotapes in all genres. Call for other locations around San Antonio; this one is nearby Brackenridge Park.

Malls
The malls below all keep the same hours: 10am to 9pm Monday to Saturday, and noon to 6pm Sunday.

Rivercenter Mall (Map p152; ☎ 210-225-0000; 849 E Commerce St) It's the most accessible megamall in town, and its setting on the Riverwalk isn't bad at all. Because of the cinemas, IMAX theater, comedy club, restaurants and dozens of shops, you'll probably end up here at some point in your stay.

Alamo Quarry Market (Map p146; ☎ 210-824-8885; 255 E Basse Rd) Making fine use of an old 19th-century cement plant, this outdoor mall has plenty of top-brand stores, a multiplex cinema and restaurants. A few Austin-based chains here include Whole Foods Market for groceries, Amy's Ice Creams and the outdoors outfitter Whole Earth Provision Co.

For mall offerings such as Macys, Gap and Bath & Body Works, try **Ingram Park Mall** (off Map p146; ☎ 210-684-9570; 6301 NW Loop 410 at Ingram Rd) or **North Star Mall** (Map p152; ☎ 210-340-6627; 7400 San Pedro Ave at Loop 410).

GETTING THERE & AWAY
See the Transport chapter (p355) for toll-free contact numbers, websites, car rental and other regional transportation information.

Air
San Antonio International Airport (SAT; ☎ 210-207-3411; www.sanantonio.gov/aviation; 9800 Airport Blvd) is about 9 miles north of downtown, just north of the intersection of Loop 410 and US 281. It's served by taxis, public transportation and shuttles.

The airport offers frequent flights to destinations in Texas and the rest of the USA via the following airlines: Airtran, American, Continental, Delta, Frontier, Skywest, Southwest, United-Lufthansa and US Airways.

There are also direct or connecting air services to Mexico with Aeromexico, American, Continental and Mexicana Airlines.

Bus
Greyhound (☎ 210-270-5824; www.greyhound.com) and **Kerrville Bus Co** (☎ 210-226-7371, 800-474-3352; www.iridekbc.com) share a **bus terminal** (500 N St Mary's St) right downtown. Kerrville Bus Co has direct service to the Hill Country.

Car & Motorcycle
Downtown San Antonio is bordered by I-35, I-10 and I-37, with concentric rings of highways radiating from the center. I-35 connects Austin and San Antonio, and I-10 connects San Antonio with Houston to the east and El Paso to the west.

To get to the Hill Country, you can take I-10 north to Fredericksburg and Kerrville, or US 281, which is the northbound continuation of I-37, to Johnson City. All of the major rental-car agencies have outlets at San Antonio International Airport, and some have outlets downtown as well.

Train
Squeezed between Sunset Station and the Alamodome, the **Amtrak station** (Map p152; ☎ 210-223-3226; 350 Hoefgen St) is served by *Sunset Limited* and *Texas Eagle* trains. It's a fully staffed Amtrak station, with an enclosed waiting area and free short-term parking. VIA streetcars ($1.10) on the yellow line connect Sunset Station with the downtown Riverwalk, where you can transfer to other streetcar and bus lines.

GETTING AROUND
To/From the Airport
VIA bus 2 runs at least hourly between the airport and downtown from around 6am (8am on weekends) until 9:30pm. The regular service costs $1.10, the express service $2.50; the journey takes between 45 minutes and an hour. Slower bus 550 (clockwise) and 551 (counterclockwise) circumnavigate the city on Loop 410, taking three hours and stopping at the airport on the way.

All of the major rental-car agencies have outlets at San Antonio International Airport. Major downtown hotels have free airport courtesy shuttles; be sure to ask. A taxi ride from the airport to downtown costs between $22 and $25 for up to four people. Or, if you're traveling solo, you can save a few bucks and

take a shuttle with **Airport Express** (☎ 210-281-9900; www.saairportshuttle.com; one way/round-trip $18/32). Look on its website for a $2-off coupon.

Bicycle
Getting around by bicycle isn't very feasible in San Antonio. Downtown streets are too congested for cycling, and the spread-out nature of the city makes it even more difficult to travel. That said, cycling around Brackenridge Park and the Mission Trail are two attractive options.

To rent bicycles, try **Abel's Bicycle Repair & Rental** (☎ 210-533-9927). They rent bikes for $30 a day, and will deliver bikes free of charge to the downtown area.

Car & Motorcycle
There are plenty of public parking lots downtown, including by most of the major hotels. The lots generally cost $3 per hour, or $5 to $8 for 24 hours (go figure). Otherwise you can park for free in the residential streets of the King William District and Southtown, then walk or ride VIA's blue line streetcars (see p172) north into downtown.

Public Transport
San Antonio's public-transport network, **VIA Metropolitan Transit** (☎ 210-362-2020; www.viainfo.net), operates more than 100 regular bus routes, plus four streetcar routes. VIA passes, bus schedules and streetcar route maps are available at VIA's downtown **information center** (Map p152; ☎ 210-475-9008; 211 W Commerce St; 7am-6pm Mon-Fri, 9am-2pm Sat).

Local VIA bus and streetcar fares are $1.10 (15¢ for a transfer), and exact change is required. VIA express buses, which use interstate highways and include buses to theme parks, cost $2.50. Discount fares are available for children, seniors and the mobility impaired. Otherwise, a $4 pass allows a full day of unlimited rides on all VIA buses and streetcars.

Note that the streetcars look more like trolleys, since there is no overhead cable. The streetcar routes are occasionally served by buses, too, although the fare remains the same in that case. VIA streetcars run to and from the Alamo, Market Square, HemisFair Park, the Alamodome, Sunset Station, Southtown and the King William District. There are stops throughout downtown and at several hotels. The main transfer station for all streetcar lines is near the Rivercenter Mall.

Taxi

Taxi stands are found at major downtown hotels, the Greyhound and Amtrak stations and the airport. Otherwise you'll probably need to telephone for one. Taxi rates are $1.70 at flag fall ($2.60 between 9pm and 5am), then $1.80 for each additional mile. Bigger companies include the following:

AAA Taxi (☎ 210-599-9999; www.aaataxi.com)
San Antonio Taxis (☎ 210-444-2222; www.sataxi.com)
Yellow Cab (☎ 210-222-2222; www.yellowcabsa.com)

AROUND SAN ANTONIO

The area directly north of San Antonio is known primarily as a haven for shoppers who stream by the hundreds of thousands into the factory-outlet malls in the cities of San Marcos and New Braunfels, off I-35. It's definitely something every bargain shopper should put on his or her itinerary. But these towns are also great destinations for outdoor recreation on local rivers, perfect for families or anyone else who needs to cool off on a hot summer's day!

NATURAL BRIDGE CAVERNS

About halfway between San Antonio and New Braunfels, this **national landmark cave** (☎ 210-651-6101; 26495 Natural Bridge Caverns Rd; Hwy 3009, west of I-35 exit 175; www.naturalbridgecaverns.com; adult/3-11yr $18/10; 🕓 9am-4pm, extended hours summer) is one of the state's largest underground formations. Its name comes from the 60ft natural limestone bridge that spans the entrance, but inside (where it's always 70°F) are simply phenomenal formations, including the Watchtower, a 50ft pedestal that looks like a crystallized flower. You can only see the caverns as part of a guided tour, which includes the family-friendly Discovery Tour, the Hidden Passages Illuminations Tour, or the more challenging Adventure Tours. Attached is the Natural Caverns Wildlife Park, a small zoo with rare animals.

NEW BRAUNFELS

The richly historic town of New Braunfels (named for its Prussian founder, Prince Carl of Solms Braunfels) was the first German settlement in Texas. Today residents from Austin and San Antonio flock to New Braunfels in the summer for its main attraction: the cool and easy-flowing waters of the Guadalupe and Comal Rivers.

Visit the Greater New Braunfels **Chamber of Commerce** (☎ 800-572-2626; 390 S Seguin Ave; 🕓 8am-5pm Mon-Fri) or the highway **visitors center** (☎ 830-625-7973; 237 IH-35 N; 🕓 9am-5pm) to pick up maps, historic downtown walking tour brochures and loads more information on local attractions. The town's annual sausage festival, **Wurstfest**, is held in early November.

Sights & Activities

For a day of doing nothing but chilling in the Guadalupe River, you don't have to go far in New Braunfels. For the most part, the river is calm, with a few good rapids to make things exciting, and it's something the whole family can enjoy.

Dozens of tubing outfitters rent rafts, kayaks, canoes and tubes and arrange shuttles to pick up and drop off floaters. Most offer tubes with built-in bottoms so you won't scrape your backside on the bottom of the rocky river. (It gets rockier the longer the region goes without rain, which can be for months during the summer; check current water levels at the visitor centers.) Don't forget to bring sunscreen, a hat and drinking water, and also be sure to wear shoes or sandals that you don't mind getting wet.

The following rental agencies also provide shuttle services:

Gruene River Company (☎ 830-625-2800, 888-705-2800; www.gruenerivercompany.com; 1404 Gruene Rd; tubes $17)
Riverbank Outfitters (☎ 830-625-4928; 6000 River Rd; tubes $15-17)
Rockin' 'R' River Rides (☎ 830-629-9999, 800-553-5628; www.rockinr.com; 1405 Gruene Rd; tubes $15-17)

For a more controlled – but just as exhilarating – experience, try the Bavarian-themed **Schlitterbahn Waterpark Resort** (☎ 830-625-2351; www.schlitterbahn.com; 305 W Austin; all-day pass adult/child $40/32; 🕓 10am-6pm or later May-Sep, weekends only early May & late Sep). It's Texas' largest water park, featuring about 30 different slides and water pools all using water from the Comal River. It's one of the best places to be with kids on a hot day.

Landa Park (☎ 830-221-4350; boathouse 110 Golf Course Dr, pool 350 Aquatic Circle; park admission free, train rides $2.50, mini-golf $2, pool $4; 🕓 hours vary) has an 18-hole golf course, a miniature railroad, shady picnic facilities and an Olympic-size swimming pool, all with different opening hours, so call first. In Price Solms Park, the **City Tube Chute**

(☎ 830-608-2165; 100 Leibscher Dr; entry $5, tube rental $7, weekend parking $5; ⏰ 10am-7pm Jun-Aug, weekends only May) lets you fly down rapids in the Comal River.

Looking for family fun on dry land? Kids can explore everything from outer space to dude ranches at the **McKenna Children's Museum** (830-606-9525; www.mckennakids.org; 801 W San Antonio St; admission $5.50-7.50; ⏰ 10am-5pm Mon-Sat, noon-5pm Sun summer). The innovation center is particularly cool, with interactive graphics that respond to kids' movements.

Sleeping & Eating

With a convenient downtown location, the popular **Prince Solms' Inn** (☎ 830-625-9169, 800-625-9169; www.princesolmsinn.com; 295 E San Antonio St; d $125-175; ♿) is one of the oldest still-operating inns in Texas. Its flowery Victorian and rustic Western-themed rooms offer authentic furnishings (some also have bunk beds, a great option for families). The romantic cabin out back has a full kitchen. Wines and desserts are specialties of the house at the attached Uptown Piano Bar.

For Czech kolaches and German strudels, try **Naegelin's Bakery** (☎ 830-625-5722; www.naeglins.com; 129 S Seguin Ave; ⏰ 6:30am-5:30pm Mon-Fri, 6:30am-5pm Sat), one of the oldest continuously operating bakeries in Texas (it opened in 1868). Hearty Tex-Mex breakfast and German-style lunch/dinner is served at popular **Friesenhaus** (☎ 830-625-1040; www.friesenhausnb.com; 148 South Castell Ave; mains $7-17; ⏰ 8am-10pm Mon-Sat, 8am-9pm Sun), which also has fish mains and salads. **Huisache Grille** (☎ 830-620-9001; www.huisache.com; 303 W San Antonio St; mains $7.50-17; ⏰ 11am-10pm), just across the railroad tracks from the plaza,

serves up imaginative Southwestern cuisine, such as achiote-rubbed 'charboiled chicken Yucatan' in a cilantro cream sauce. For an eclectic upscale atmosphere and some serious steaks, try **Myrons Steakhouse** (☎ 830-624-1024; www.myronsprimesteakhouse.com; 136 N Castell Ave; mains $23-43; ⏰ 4-10pm Mon-Sat, 4pm-11pm Fri & Sat), located inside an old movie theater.

Shopping

Good deals can be had at **New Braunfels Marketplace** (☎ 830-620-7475; 621 N Business IH 35; ⏰ 10am-8pm Mon-Sat, noon-6pm Sun), a former outlet mall that's become more of a 'town center.'

GRUENE

The charming and historic town of Gruene (pronounced 'green') is just 4 miles northeast of New Braunfels. It's close to all of the Guadalupe River tubing outfitters (p173) and loaded with antiques and crafts shops. **Old Gruene Market Day** is held the third weekend of the month from February through November.

The town is best known for Texas' oldest dancehall, **Gruene Hall** (☎ 830-606-1281; www.gruenehall.com; 1281 Gruene Rd; cover $8-12, advance show tickets $15-30; ⏰ 11am-11pm Mon-Thu, 10am-1am Fri & Sat, 10am-9pm Sun). There's no air-conditioning, but it's got cold beer, great bands and a big wooden dancefloor in a barnlike environment. It seems that anyone who's anyone has played here, from Jerry Lee Lewis to Willie Nelson, and on Friday and Saturday nights it's always packed.

For a rural escape from the big city, you can't beat **Gruene Mansion Inn** (☎ 830-629-2641; www.gruenemansioninn.com; 1275 Gruene Rd; d $170-250). This cluster of buildings is practically

---

DETOUR: LULING

Luling trumpets that it's the 'crossroads to everywhere.' But pretty much the only reason to stop here these days as you whiz through on the way to Shiner (p167) is to see the annual **Luling Watermelon Thump** (www.watermelonthump.com), which has been covered in *People* magazine and the *New York Times*. The famous fruit-growing contest, complete with a crowned queen, takes place the last full weekend of June. Incidentally, Luling is also the two-time holder of the world watermelon-seed-spitting championship as documented in the *Guinness Book of World Records*.

Luling was founded as the western end of the Sunset branch of the Southern Pacific Railroad in 1874, and in 1922 oil was discovered beneath it. The downtown **Central Texas Oil Patch Museum** (421 E Davis St; admission by donation; ⏰ 9am-noon & 1-3pm Mon-Fri, noon-3pm Sat) is dedicated to Luling's history and heritage. In the same building, the Luling **Chamber of Commerce** (☎ 830-875-3214; www.lulingcc.org) has more information on the area, including its antiques shops.

Luling is on US 183 where it meets Hwys 80 and 90, just north of I-10; it's about an hour's drive from San Antonio or Austin, and is served by Greyhound.

its own village, with rooms in the mansion, the former carriage house and the old barns. Richly decorated in a style the owners call 'rustic Victorian elegance,' the rooms feature lots of wood, floral prints and pressed-tin ceiling tiles. Each room is different, but you can get a sneak peak and pick your favorite on the website.

Another option is just down the road at the **Gruene River Inn** (☎ 830-627-1600; 1111 Gruene Rd; d $159-189; 🖲). It's more of a traditional style B&B with quilts and antiques – think Grandma's house – but the real draw is the private decks overlooking the Guadalupe River.

Gruene has a couple of restaurants but the main place everyone heads to for chicken-fried steak and other Texas dishes is the **Gristmill River Restaurant & Bar** (☎ 830-625-0684; www.gristmillrestaurant.com; 1287 Gruene Rd; mains $8-15; 🕒 11am-9pm, 11am-10pm Fri & Sat, 1 hour later in summer), which is situated inside the brick remnants of an 80-year-old cotton gin behind Gruene Hall. Indoor seating affords a rustic ambience, and outdoor tables get a view of the river.

SAN MARCOS

While practically everyone of the tens of thousands who come through here daily is heading to the factory outlet malls (maybe the best around), San Marcos is also home to Wonder World, Texas' most visited cave, and natural attractions around Southwest Texas State University, including tubing on the San Marcos River.

The **San Marcos Tourist Information Center** (☎ 512-393-5930; www.sanmarcostexas.com; 617 N IH-35 exit 204B/205; 🕒 9am-5pm Mon-Sat, 10am-4pm Sun) has maps, brochures and information on trolley tours of the town's historic districts. Since San Marcos is so close to San Antonio, visitors rarely need to avail themselves of overnight accommodations.

Sights & Activities

Owned by Southwest Texas State University, the enjoyable **Aquarena Center** (☎ 512-245-7570; www.aquarena.txstate.edu; 921 Aquarena Springs Dr, west of I-35 exit 206; admission free, boat tours adult/ 4-15yr/senior $9/6/7.50; 🕒 9:30am-6pm summer, 9:30am-5pm fall) is home to family-oriented exhibitions on ecology, history and archaeology, and includes the ruins of a Spanish mission founded here on the Feast of San Marcos. This educational center also offers hour-long glass-bottom boat tours of the lake formed by the town's name-sake springs, which gush forth 1½ million gallons of artesian water every day.

Just south of the Aquarena Center, the **Lions Club** (☎ 512-396-5466; City Park, next to the Texas National Guard Armory; tubes $7-9) rents tubes to tackle the usually docile stretch of the San Marcos River from 10am to 7pm daily between Memorial Day and Labor Day, as well as on weekends in May and September. The last tube is rented at 5:30pm and the last shuttle pickup from Rio Vista Dam is at 6:45pm sharp.

A mini-theme-park has been built around the USA's largest earthquake-created cave, **Wonder World** (☎ 512-392-3760; www.wonderworldpark.com; 1000 Prospect St; combination tickets adult/ 3-5yr/6-12yr $20/7.50/15; 🕒 8am-8pm Jun-Aug, 9am-5pm Mon-Fri & 9am-6pm Sat & Sun Sep-May), which is the most-visited cave in Texas. Take a one-hour tour through the Balcones Fault Line Cave, where you can look at the Edwards Aquifer up close; tours begin every 15 to 30 minutes year-round. Outside, in the 110ft Tejas Observation Tower, you can make out the fault line itself. Other attractions include a petting park filled with Texas animals, a train ride around the park and the quaint 'Anti-Gravity House,' a holdover from family vacations of yesteryear. There's a picnic area on the grounds.

Adults may want to detour onto the university campus to visit the excellent free exhibitions at the **Witliff Collections** (☎ 512-245-2313; www.thewitliffcollections.txstate.edu), found on the 7th floor of the Alkek Library. Hours vary, so call ahead. Take Aquarena Springs Dr three-quarters of a mile west of the Aquarena Center, then turn right onto University Dr and take another right less than a half-mile later onto Guadalupe St. Follow the signs to the LBJ Student Center parking garage ($2 per hour). The library is a short walk downhill from the student center.

Shopping

There are more than 100 name-brand factory-outlet stores at **Prime Outlets** (☎ 512-396-2200, 800-628-9465; www.primeoutlets.com; off I-35 exit 200; 🕒 10am-9pm Mon-Sat, 10am-7pm Sun), an enormous shopping complex. Located off the same interstate exit, equally big **Tanger Outlets** (☎ 512-396-7446; www.tangeroutlet.com/sanmarcos; 4015 S IH-35; 🕒 9am-9pm Mon-Sat, 10am-7pm Sun) has similar offerings. Outlet shops at both malls offer at least a 30% discount on regular retail prices, and sometimes as much as 75% off brands. Stores include Calvin Klein, Tommy Hilfiger and Levi's, to name just a few.

HILL COUNTRY

New York has the Hamptons, San Francisco has the wine country, Texas has the Hill Country. Just an hour or two's drive from both Austin and San Antonio, the area is an easy day trip or weekend getaway, and its natural beauty paired with its easygoing nature has inspired more than a few early retirements.

Thanks to former First Lady Claudia Taylor Johnson – 'round here everyone calls her Lady Bird – each spring the highways are lined with eye-popping wildflowers that stretch for miles and miles, planted as part of her Highway Beautification Act.

In addition to the bluebonnets, Indian paintbrushes and black-eyed Susans that blanket the roads, the Hill Country shirks Texas' reputation as being dry and flat, with rolling hills, giant oak trees, spring-fed creeks and flowing rivers.

Information
You can spend an entire vacation in the Hill Country and not see it all. The best time to visit is spring when temperatures are mild and the wildflowers are in full bloom, but many people also enjoy visiting in December when the towns light up for the holiday season. Visit www.hill-country-visitor.com for information on special events, accommodations, outdoor recreation and other Hill Country destinations.

Orientation
Ask 10 people the boundaries of the Hill Country and you'll get 11 different answers but, generally speaking, the Hill Country is an area west of the I-35 corridor between Austin and San Antonio, with

---

U-R-B-A-N P-L-A-N-N-I-N-G

Street names in Fredericksburg appear to be a mishmash of trees, Texas towns and former US presidents. But they were actually named so their initials spell out secret codes. The streets crossing Main St to the east of Courthouse Sq are Adams, Llano, Lincoln, Washington, Elk, Lee, Columbus, Olive, Mesquite and Eagle. And the streets to the west are Crockett, Orange, Milam, Edison, Bowie, Acorn, Cherry and Kay.

Fredericksburg and Kerrville being the westernmost points and largest towns. Some people consider San Marcos, New Braunfels and Gruene to be part of the Hill Country, but you really have to leave the interstate to get the effect.

JOHNSON CITY & STONEWALL
pop 1191
Founded in the late 1800s, Johnson City was named after a town settler by the name of James Polk Johnson. The fact that James' great-grandson went on to be the 36th president of the United States was certainly convenient, since Johnson City's biggest claim to fame is being the home of Lyndon Baines Johnson.

These days, the **Lyndon B Johnson National Historical Park** (☎ 830-868-7128; www.nps.gov/lyjo; admission free; ☽ 9am-5:30pm) welcomes visitors to learn about Johnson's life from beginning to end. The park includes the Johnson birthplace, childhood home, the ranch, and even the family cemetery where LBJ and Lady Bird are both buried.

There are two visitor centers, 14 miles apart. In Johnson City you'll find **Johnson's Boyhood Home** (100 E Ladybird Lane; admission free), which Johnson himself had restored for personal posterity. Then, 14 miles to the west near Stonewall is the **LBJ Ranch** (Hwy 290; house tour $2; ☽ 9am-5:30pm, house tours 10am-4:30pm), where Johnson spent so much time during his administration that it became known as the 'Texas White House.'

There aren't many hotels or motels in town, although a few B&Bs do a solid business. In Johnson City, try **Chantilly Lace Country Inn** (☎ 830-868-2767; 625 Nugent Ave, Johnson City; ste $99-145), which isn't as lacy and countrified as its name would imply. Or, head on over to Stonewall to the exquisite **Rose Hill Manor** (☎ 877-767-3445; www.rose-hill.com; 2614 Upper Albert Rd, Stonewall; ste $155-249) a top-notch B&B with suites and cottages.

The best dining in Johnson City – and what could become some of the best in the Hill Country – can be found at the perfectly rustic **Silver K Cafe** (☎ 830-868-2911; 209 E Main St; mains $9-15; ☽ lunch 11am-3pm, dinner 5-8:30pm Sun-Fri, 5-9pm Sat). In the Old Lumber Yard, the Silver K serves up imaginative Texas-style home cookin'. Most dishes are around $10, except on Saturday nights, when the fine-dining menu kicks in.

SCENIC DRIVE: WILDFLOWER TRAILS

You know spring has arrived in Texas when you see cars pulling up roadside and families climbing out to take the requisite picture of their kids surrounded by bluebonnets – the state flower. From March to April in Hill Country, orange Indian paintbrushes, deep-purple winecups and white-to-blue bluebonnets are at their peak. To see vast cultivated fields of color, there's **Wildseed Farms** (☎ 800-848-0078; www.wildseedfarms.com; 100 Legacy Dr; admission free, botanical garden $5; ⏱ 9am-6:30pm), which is 7 miles east of Fredericksburg on US 290. Or for a more do-it-yourself experience, check with TXDOT's **Wildflower Hotline** (☎ 800-452-9292) to find out what's blooming where. Taking Rte 16 and FM 1323, north from Fredericksburg and east to Willow City, is usually a good route. Then again you might just set to wandering – most back roads host their own shows daily.

FREDERICKSBURG

pop 8900

Although we recommend meandering through the Hill Country, if you're only going to see one town, make it this one. The 19th-century German settlement packs a lot of charm into a relatively small amount of space. There is a boggling array of welcoming inns and B&Bs, and a main street lined with historic buildings that house German restaurants, *biergartens,* antique stores and shops. Many of the shops are typical tourist-town offerings (think T-shirts, fudge and faux-quaint painted signs), but there are enough interesting stores to make it fun to wander. Plus, the town is a great base for checking out the surrounding peach orchards, vineyards and natural getaways, such as Enchanted Rock and Johnson City, as well as little Luckenbach (p180), just 10 miles away.

Orientation

Most of the action on Main St happens between Washington and Adams St (the latter divides Fredericksburg addresses into east and west). Most shops and restaurants are on (or a block off) Main St, starting near the prowlike facade of the former Nimitz Hotel (now the Museum of the Pacific War) and continuing to Friedhelms Bavarian Inn, where US 290 and US 87 split.

Information

Fredericksburg Convention & Visitors Bureau (☎ 830-997-6523; www.fredericksburg-texas.com; 302 E Austin St; ⏱ 8:30am-5pm Mon-Fri, 9am-noon & 1-5pm Sat, noon-4pm Sun) has a friendly staff and a new building a block off Main St.

You'll find a 24-hour ATM at **Broadway National Bank** (☎ 830-997-7691; 204 W Main St). Internet access is free at the **Pioneer Public Library** (☎ 830-997-6513; 115 W Main St; ⏱ 9am-6pm Mon-Thu, 9am-7pm Wed, 9am-2pm Fri & Sat). The **Hill Country Memorial Hospital** (☎ 830-997-4353; 1020 S Hwy 16 via S Adams St) has 24-hour emergency services.

Sights

NATIONAL MUSEUM OF THE PACIFIC WAR

Quaint Fredericksburg seems an unlikely setting for a museum complex dedicated to WWII's Pacific Theatre. But here's how that played out: WWII Admiral Chester Nimitz was born in Fredericksburg, so a museum was built here commemorating his life. Makes perfect sense. Then, the logical next step (perhaps) was to build an enormous museum commemorating the Pacific War.

This **museum complex** (☎ 830-997-4379; www.nimitz-museum.org; 340 E Main St; adult/under 6yr/child $12/free/6; ⏱ 9am-5pm) consists of three galleries: the **Admiral Nimitz Museum**, which details the life and times of its favorite son; the **George Bush Gallery of the Pacific War**, a large, impressive building housing big planes, big boats and big artillery; and the **Pacific Combat Zone**, a 3-acre site that's been transformed into a South Pacific battle zone. History buffs can learn about (or refresh their memories on) the battles and campaigns, and kids will be awed by the enormous vehicles. If nothing else, it's an interesting contrast after a day of wildflower peeping.

PIONEER MUSEUM & VEREINS KIRCHE

Find out what life was like for the town's early inhabitants as you wander the grounds of the **Gillespie County Historical Pioneer Museum** (☎ 830-990-8441; www.pioneermuseum.com; 325 W Main St; adult/6-17yr $5/$3; ⏱ 10am-5pm Mon-Sat, noon-4pm Sun). If nothing else, this collection of restored homes and businesses from the late 1800s will help you to appreciate the modern conveniences awaiting you at your guesthouse.

Your admission includes a visit to the city's **Vereins Kirche** (100 block of W Main St; 🕙 10am-5pm Mon-Sat), which was the original town church, meeting hall and school. This tiny building doesn't add a lot to your visit, unless you want to check out the small collection of archival photos and dusty historical artifacts.

Activities

Fredericksburg is known throughout the state for its peaches, and for good reason. They're fat, juicy and nothing like what you'll find in your local produce department. Mid-May through June is peach-pickin' season around town. You can get them straight from the farm, and some will let you pick your own. For a list of more than 20 local **peach farms**, visit www.texaspeaches.com.

Right around dusk from May to October, you can watch a colony of bats emerging from an abandoned railroad tunnel for their nightly meal. Over three million Mexican free-tailed bats make their home at **Old Tunnel Wildlife Management Area** (☎ 866-978-2287; 10619 Old San Antonio Rd; 🕙 sunrise-sunset). The **upper deck viewing area** is open daily and it's free, but the **lower deck** (adult/6-16yr $5/$2), which is open Thursday to Sunday and has a charge, affords an up-close view that is decidedly more impactful.

Tours

Despite having more than its share of touristy shops, Fredericksburg's historic district has retained the look (if not the feel) of 125 years ago. Beautiful limestone-clad buildings with gingerbread-style storefronts, hand-hewn ceiling joists and longleaf pine floors line Main St from end to end. A free self-guided walking tour map of the district is available at the visitor center.

Fredericksburg is a horse-and-carriage kind of town, and you can clip-clop your way down Main St with the **Stardust Carriage Service** (☎ 830-992-0700; whole carriage per 15min $25).

Festivals & Events

Every October, Fredericksburg celebrates its German heritage in a big way with Texas' largest **Oktoberfest** (☎ 830-997-4810; www.oktoberfestinfbg.com; adult/6-12yr $6/$1). Families crowd around the Vereins Kirche for oompah bands,

endless kegs of German beer, and schnitzels and pretzels galore.

Toward the end of the month, the festivities continue with the **Fredericksburg Food and Wine Fest** (☎ 830-997-8515; www.fbgfoodandwinefest.com; admission $20), which is a tamer version of Oktoberfest.

Sleeping

Guesthouses and B&Bs are a popular choice in Fredericksburg – there are hundreds – and the following local reservations services can help you find anything from a flowery guestroom in a B&B to your own 19th-century limestone cottage:

Absolute Charm Luxury B&B Reservation Service (☎ 866-244-7897; www.absolutecharm.com; 223 E Main St)

Gastehaus Schmidt (☎ 830-997-5612; www.fbglodging.com; 231 W Main St)

Main St B&B Reservation Service (☎ 830-997-0153; www.travelmainstreet.com; 337 E Main St)

BUDGET

Dietzel Motel (☎ 830-997-3330; www.dietzelmotel.com; 1141 W US 290; d $60-96; 🐾) This family-run motel is a great budget option located at the west end of town away from the hustle and bustle. Rates are higher during special events, lower in winter; all in all, it's a good deal.

Lady Bird Johnson Municipal Park (☎ 830-997-4202; 432 Lady Bird Drive; campsites/RV sites $10/25; 🛜) This pretty country park sits 3 miles south of town on the Pedernales River. There are plenty of RV hookups but no tent sites per se, just a big field behind the park's headquarters.

MIDRANGE & TOP END

Fredericksburg Inn & Suites (☎ 830-997-0202; www.fredericksburg-inn.com; 201 S Washington St; d $79-219; 🛜 🐾) Tops in the midpriced motel category, this place was built to look like the historic house it sits behind, and it succeeds. A fabulously inviting pool with a waterslide, all-day complimentary beverages and clean, updated rooms make it great value for the price.

Bed & Brew (☎ 830-997-1646; www.yourbrewery.com; 245 E Main St; d $99-129) Here's an amenity you don't find just anywhere: beer. The 12 rooms owned by the Fredericksburg Brewing Company are right upstairs from the brewery, and each day you get a free sample of suds (which helps explain its no-kids policy). Some of the eclectic rooms have themes and some don't; the crazy Red Stallion room has

HILL COUNTRY WINERIES   *Sara Benson*

When most people think of Texas, they think of cactus, Cadillacs and cowboys...not grapes. But the Lone Star State has become the fifth-largest wine-producing state in the country (behind California, Washington, New York and Oregon). The Hill Country, with its robust Provence-like limestone and hot South African–style climate, has become the most productive wine-making region in the state. These rolling hills are home to more than a dozen wineries.

Most wineries are open daily for tastings and tours. Many also host special events, such as grape stompings and annual wine and food feasts. Local visitor bureaus stock the handy *Texas Hill Country Wine Trail* leaflet, which details the wineries and schedules of wine trail weekends (or visit www.texaswinetrail.com). You could leave the driving to someone else with **Texas Wine Tours** (☎ 830-997-8687; www.texas-wine-tours.com; tours $89-179), which runs tours in a limousine-style bus.

The largest concentration of Hill Country vineyards is around Fredericksburg. **Becker Vineyards** (☎ 830-644-2681; www.beckervineyards.com; Jenscheke Lane; ☯ 10am-5pm Mon-Thu, 10am-6pm Fri & Sat, noon-5pm Sun) is one of the state's most decorated wine producers. Located 10 miles east of Fredericksburg, just off US 290, the vineyard has 36 acres of vines and allegedly Texas' largest underground wine cellar. Its tasting room is housed in a beautiful old stone barn.

Another well-known vineyard is **Fall Creek Vineyards** (☎ 915-379-5361; www.fcv.com; 1820 CR 222; ☯ 11am-4pm Mon-Fri, noon-5pm Sat, noon-4pm Sun), located just over 2 miles north of the town post office in Tow, close to Llano and perched beautifully on the shores of Lake Buchanan. Now in its 28th year, Fall Creek churns out several different French- and German-style varietals, including a popular chenin blanc and a tasty Riesling. The winery offers a colorful, modern tasting room as well.

A smaller vineyard with wines that have begun to turn heads is unique **Dry Comal Creek** (☎ 830-885-4076; www.drycomalcreek.com; 1741 Herbelin Rd, off Hwy 46; ☯ noon-5pm Wed-Sun), located about 7 miles west of New Braunfels. Proprietor Franklin Houser gives his own tours around the tiny winery, which is constructed of stone and cedar trees.

a mural of big red mustangs stampeding toward the bed.

Hangar Hotel (☎ 830-997-9990; www.hangarhotel.com; 155 Airport Rd; d $119-169) If you didn't know better, you'd think this rounded, barnlike structure right on the tarmac of the Gillespie County Airport was a converted hangar from the 1940s, but it's actually a new building with a fun aviation shtick. The Observation Deck is a great place to watch the small aircraft buzz in and out, or you can just throw open your widows for a similar effect.

Roadrunner Inn (☎ 830-997-8555; www.theroadrunnerinn.com; 306-B E Main St; d $149-169; ☷) If you want to ensure your lodging is doily-free, check out one of the three smartly retro rooms that feature kitchenettes, Jacuzzi tubs and flat-screen TVs.

Cotton Gin Village (☎ 830-990-5734; www.cottonginlodging.com; 2805 S Hwy 16; cabins $159-179) Just south of town, this cluster of rustic cabins made from stone and timber offers guests a supremely private stay away from both the crowds and the other guests. Romantic getaway? Start packing.

Eating & Drinking

Dietz Bakery (☎ 830-997-3250; 218 E Main St; ☯ 8am until sold out, Tue-Sat) This third-generation family bakery makes some of the best pastries this side of Bavaria, from doughnuts and Danishes to breads and baguettes. Be sure to get here before noon, because they always sell out.

Mahaley's Cafe (☎ 830-997-4400; 341 E Main St; menu items $2-8; ☯ 6:30am-7pm Mon-Thu, to 8pm Fri & Sat, 7:30am-2pm Sun) Breakfast tacos are the big draw at this little cafe in a former gas station but, then again, the cupcakes and coffee drinks are pretty tasty, too.

Rather Sweet Bakery & Cafe (☎ 830-990-0498; 249 E Main St; mains $6-9; ☯ 8am-5pm Mon-Sat) Stop at Rather Sweet, Too for grab-and-go goodies, or head back through the shady patio to the cafe in back for breakfast (until 10am), lunch or some of the scrumptious bakery offerings. **Hondo's on Main** (☎ 830-997-1633; 312 W Main St; mains $6-15; ☯ 11am-10:30pm Wed, Thu & Sun, 11am-midnight Fri & Sat) Named after local legend Hondo Crouch, this hoppin' place caters to your need for both food and fun, with live music on the patio five nights a week. It's famous for its 'doughnut burger', which has more to do with the way the patty is formed than the actual ingredients.

Altdorf Restaurant & Biergarten (☎ 830-997-7865; 301 W Main St; mains $7-16; ☽ 11am-9pm Wed-Sat & Mon, 11am-4pm Sun) German food is a Fredericksburg staple, and this place is as good as any for Bavarian-style specialties, with a traditional *biergarten* where you can get your oompah on.

Silver Creek Restaurant (☎ 830-990-4949; 310 E Main St; mains $7-28; ☽ 11am-4pm & 5-9pm Wed-Mon) A great compromise when only some of you want schnitzel, this place serves both American and German dishes, and its shady patio is one of the few places to hang out on a Monday night.

Navajo Grill (☎ 830-990-8289; 803 E Main St; mains $18-33; ☽ 5:30-9pm Sun-Thu, 5:30-10pm Fri & Sat) For something more upmarket, head straight to the Navajo Grill, which boasts a lovely patio, creative Southwestern cuisine and a list of about 40 different wines to choose from.

Getting There & Around
Heading west from Austin, US 290 becomes Fredericksburg's Main St. Hwy 16, which runs between Fredericksburg and Kerrville, is S Adams St in town. The **Kerrville Bus Co** (☎ 210-227-5669, 800-474-3352; www.iridekbc.com) will get you to and from Fredericksburg from San Antonio; if you're traveling from Austin, you'll have to take Greyhound (p172) to San Antonio and transfer there. In town buses leave and depart from the Fredericksburg **bus station** (1001 Hwy 16 S).

DETOUR: HILL TOP CAFÉ

The best dining experience in town is actually out of town at the **Hill Top Café** (☎ 830-997-8922; 10661 US 87; mains $12-25; ☽ 11am-2pm & 5-9pm Tue-Sun), about 10 miles north of Fredericksburg. Inside a renovated 1950s gas station, this cozy roadhouse serves up an imaginative mix of spicy Cajun seafood, fresh Greek salads and good ol' chicken-fried steaks. On weekends there's live blues from the owner, Johnny Nicholas, a former member of the West Coast swing band Asleep at the Wheel. Trust us, this is the Texas Hill Country at its best. Reservations are recommended.

You can rent bicycles at **Hill Country Bicycle Works** (☎ 830-990-2609; 702 E Main St; ☽ 10am-6pm Mon, Tue, Thu & Fri, 10am-4pm Sat) for $28 per day.

ENCHANTED ROCK STATE NATURAL AREA
What's so enchanting about a rock, you might ask? Well, when you see the dome of pink granite dating from the Proterozoic era rising 425ft above ground – one of the largest batholiths in the US – you certainly know you're not looking at just any old rock. (And remember, that's just the part you can see; most of the rock formation is underground.) The dome heats up during the day and cools off at night, creating a crackling noise that Tonkawa Indians believed were ghost fires.

Hiking and rock climbing (duh) are two of the most popular activities at this popular **park** (☎ 915-247-3903, camping reservations 512-389-8900; 16710 RR 965; admission $5, primitive/standard campsites $8/10; ☽ 8am-10pm) that's 18 miles north of Fredericksburg off RR 965 and just south of Llano. It gets crowded on weekends, spring break and holidays, so get there early during peak times (by 11am at the latest) or risk finding the gates closed.

LUCKENBACH
pop 3
As small as Luckenbach is – there are only three permanent residents, not counting the cat – it's big on Texas charm. You won't find a more laid-back place, where the main activity is sitting at a picnic table under an old oak tree with a cold bottle of Shiner Bock and listening to guitar pickers, who are often accompanied by roosters. Come prepared to relax, get to know some folks, and bask in the small-town atmosphere.

Actually, 'small town' doesn't describe it just right: Luckenbach is more like a cluster of buildings than a town, and its permanent structures are outnumbered by the port-a-potties brought in to facilitate weekend visitors. The heart of the, er, action is the old trading post established back in 1849 – now the **Luckenbach General Store** (☎ 830-997-3224, 888-311-8990; ☽ 10am-9pm Mon-Sat, noon-9pm Sun), which also serves as the local post office, saloon and community center.

Despite the lack of amenities, there is a website where you can find the **music schedule** (www.luckenbachtexas.com). Sometimes the picking circle starts at 1pm and sometimes it's 5pm,

THE STORY BEHIND THE SONG

A famous saying in Luckenbach goes something like this: 'We have discovered that, on the globe, Luckenbach is at the center of the world.' And while today's casual visitor may question that logic over a cold beer and a lazy afternoon, not so in 1977, when the town was at the center of the world – or at least the country music world. Waylon Jennings and Willie Nelson's hit song 'Luckenbach, Texas (Back to the Basics of Love)' stayed at number one on the country music charts for nearly the entire summer.

What's odd about one of the most catchy country tunes ever recorded is that it was written by Bobby Emmons and Chips Moman, two Nashville producers who'd never been to Luckenbach. Even Jennings couldn't say he'd actually set foot in any one of the three buildings in town until the first and only time he made the trip, in 1997, 20 years after the song's original release. Still, 'Luckenbach, Texas' was and remains a well-loved tribute to the Hill Country hamlet, partly because Nelson is a Texas fixture and has held his famous 4th of July Picnic here off and on for years. Also, since Jennings' death in 2002, Luckenbach has thrown an annual mid-July tribute party to the musician, giving the town's regulars (and its three permanent residents) one more reason to call Luckenbach the center of the world.

and there are usually live-music events on the weekends in the old **dancehall** – a Texas classic. The 4th of July and Labor Day weekends see a deluge of visitors for concerts.

We'd be remiss if we didn't mention that Luckenbach was made famous in a country song by Waylon Jennings. But we figured you either already knew that, or wouldn't really care.

To get there from Fredericksburg, take US 290 east then take FM 1376 south for about 3 miles.

KERRVILLE

pop 21,700

If Fredericksburg feels too fussy for you, Kerrville makes a good base of operations for exploring the Hill Country. What it might lack in personality, it makes up for in size, offering plenty of services for travelers as well as easy access to kayaking, canoeing and swimming on the Guadalupe River. It's also home to one of the world's best museums of cowboy life and a jam-packed springtime folk festival. It doesn't turn on the charm, but it gets the job done.

Orientation & Information

Kerrville is half an hour south of Fredericksburg on Hwy 16, or just over an hour northwest from San Antonio on I-10. In town, Hwy 16 becomes Sidney Baker St, and Hwy 27 (aka Junction Hwy) becomes Main St.

Kerrville's excellent **visitor center** (☎ 830-792-3535, 800-221-7958; www.kerrvilletexascvb.com; 2108 Sidney Baker St; ☯ 8:30am-5pm Mon-Fri, 9am-3pm Sat,

10am-3pm Sun) has everything you'll need to get out and about in the Hill Country, including heaps of brochures and coupon books for accommodations.

The **Butt-Holdsworth Memorial Library** (☎ 830-257-8422; 505 Water St; ☯ 10am-6pm Mon-Sat, 10am-8pm Tue & Thu, 1-5pm Sun) provides free internet access. You can change money at **Bank of America** (☎ 830-896-3111; 741 Water St; ☯ 9am-4pm Mon-Thu, 9am-5pm Fri), which has an ATM. **Peterson Regional Medical Center** (☎ 830-896-4200; 551 Hill Country Dr) has a new facility and 24-hour emergency services.

Sights

Catch the pulse of the Hill Country art scene at the **Kerr Arts & Cultural Center** (☎ 830-895-2911; www.kacckerrville.com; 228 Earl Garrett St; admission free; ☯ 10am-4pm Tue-Sat, 1-4pm Sun). Located in the old post office, it frequently changes exhibits, which could include anything from quilts to watercolors to gourd art.

Next door, check out the opulent former residence of Charles Schreiner (the man who built half the town), which is now the **Hill Country Museum** (☎ 830-896-8633; 226 Earl Garrett St; adult/6-12yr $5/2; ☯ 10am-4:30pm Mon-Sat). The exterior stonework is impressive, and if you like historic homes, head inside to see more.

The **National Center for American Western Art** (☎ 830-896-2553; www.museumofwesternart.com; 1550 Bandera Hwy; adult/under 9yr/student $7/free/5; ☯ 9am-5pm Tue-Sat) is a nonprofit showcase of Western Americana. The quality and detail of the work – paintings and bronze sculptures mostly – is astounding; all depict scenes of cowboy life, the Western landscape or vignettes of Native American life. The museum has permanent displays of two artists' studios, the equipment of cowboy life (where kids can climb on saddles, feel a lasso and play with spurs) and a research library available to anyone interested in learning more about the frontier. The building itself is fabulous, with handmade mesquite parquet and unique vaulted domes overhead.

Activities

Three miles southeast of town, **Kerrville-Schreiner Park** (☎ 830-257-5392, camping reservations 512-389-8900; 2385 TX 173, off Hwy 16; day-use per person $4; ◷ 8am-10pm) is a beautiful place for cycling, hiking, canoeing, tubing and camping. The park's concession stand rents inner tubes (per day $4) and four-person canoes (per hour from $7) for lazy floats along the Guadalupe River.

Near the river, at the south end of downtown, the **Riverside Nature Center** (☎ 830-257-4837; 150 Francisco Lemos St; admission free; ◷ dawn-dusk) has walking trails, a wildflower meadow and Guadalupe River access. Take a refreshing swim in the river at **Louise Hays City Park** (Thompson Dr, west of Sidney Baker St S; admission free; ◷ 7:30am-11pm) and **Guadalupe Street City Park** (1001 Junction Hwy; ◷ 7:30am-11pm), behind the Inn of the Hills Resort.

Kerrville Kayak & Canoe Rentals (☎ 830-459-2122, 800-256-5873; 130 W Main St; per hr $10) rents watercraft by the hour from Kerrville Schreiner Park. You can save money with half-day or full-day rentals, and also by picking up your craft from the shop.

Festivals & Events

The Quiet Valley Ranch turns up the volume each spring during the **Kerrville Folk Festival** (☎ 830-257-3600; www.kerrville-music.com; 3876 Medina Hwy). This 18-day musical extravaganza starts right around Memorial Day and features music by national touring acts and local musicians. One-day tickets cost $25 to $40; check the website for information about camping at the ranch.

Want an encore? The **Kerrville Wine and Music Festival** is a four-day miniversion of the folk festival held on the Labor Day weekend.

Sleeping

If you're planning on heading to Kerrville during any of the festivals, book months in advance. Kerrville doesn't have the glut of charming B&Bs you'll find in Fredericksburg; the lodging here caters to practical travelers.

BUDGET

There are several chains right off the highway on Sidney Baker St. They're interchangeable, but they're there if you need them.

Kerrville-Schreiner Park (☎ 830-257-5392; 2385 Bandera Hwy; day-use per person $3, campsites/RV sites $10/15, screened shelters $16) This is a beautiful park set right on the river. Pitch a tent or hook up your RV in one of the well-tended campsites, then go enjoy the 500 acres.

Hillcrest Inn (☎ 830-896-7400; 1508 Sidney Baker St; r $48-75) The management is almost comically private: they wouldn't show us a room and finding out prices was like wresting government information from a spy. But still, this place looks cute from the outside and in this price range, it's about the only thing we could find that wasn't a chain. Good luck to you.

MIDRANGE & TOP END

Inn of the Hills Resort & Conference Center (☎ 830-895-5000, 800-292-5690; www.innofthehills.com; 1001 Junction Hwy; d $89-125; ✕ 🤶 🖭) The rooms are nothing special – one might even say 'plain' – but the common areas are nice enough. The Olympic-style pool is one of the nicest in town. Ask about the secret pool overlooking the river.

Trail's End Guesthouse (☎ 830-377-1725; www.trailsendguesthouse.com; 180 Gay Dr N; d $119-124, cabins $99-149; ✕ 🤶 🖭) Just outside of town, this guesthouse has a rustic charm that fits right into the surrounding hills, with exposed beams and plank walls in every room and cabin. Did we mention a hearty breakfast is delivered right to your door?

YO Ranch Resort Hotel (☎ 830-257-4440, 877-967-3767; www.yoresort.com; 2033 Sidney Baker St; r from $119, 1-/2-bedroom ste $170/260; 🤶 🖭 🖱) If you're one of those folks who's freaked out by taxidermy, you might want to mosey on. If you're not, this is one of the more interesting hotel lobbies you'll see, lined with trophy mounts of elk, moose and longhorns, plus a large, stuffed grizzly bear. Oh, you wanted to know about the rooms as well? They're on the bland side, but who needs 'em: the resort also has court facilities for tennis, basketball and volleyball, a walking track and a playground.

WHAT THE ...? STONEHENGE II

So **Stonehenge II** isn't the real Stonehenge. We're not real druids, so there you go. This second-string henge has much less mysterious origins than the ancient megalithic structure near Salisbury, England. Two locals built the 60% scale model out of concrete and threw in some Easter Island statues for good measure.

From Hunt, which is 12.7 miles west of Fredericksburg on Hwy 39, turn north on FM 1340 for 2 miles; the monument is on the left. You can't miss it; it's in an open field right on the highway. And even though it's private property, it's very open to visitors. Bring a picnic but watch out for the fire ants. At the time of research, the property was for sale, so let's hope the new owners have a similar sense of humor.

Eating

Hill Country Cafe (☎ 830-257-6665; 806 Main St; menu items $2-10; 🕑 6am-2pm Mon-Fri, 6-11am Sat) This tiny hole-in-the-wall diner near the historic district serves up hearty home cooking in heaping portions, including just about everything you could want for breakfast as well as sandwiches and lunch plates.

Taco To Go (☎ 830-896-8226; 428 Sidney Baker St; meals $5-7; 🕑 6am-9pm Mon-Sat, 7am-2pm Sun) You can take your tacos to go or eat inside, but don't miss out on the excellent soft tacos – including breakfast tacos served all day – made with homemade tortillas and salsa.

Francisco's (☎ 830-257-2995; 201 Earl Garret St; lunch $7-10, dinner $13-38; 🕑 11am-3pm Mon-Sat, 5:30-9pm Thu-Sat) This colorful, bright and airy bistro and sidewalk cafe is housed in an old limestone building in the historic district. It's packed at lunch, and is one of the swankiest places in town for a weekend dinner.

Classics Burgers & 'Moore' (☎ 830-257-8866; 448 Sidney Baker St; mains $7-14; 🕑 11am-3pm Mon-Sat, 5-8pm Mon-Fri) This burger joint does have sort of a classic quality to it, and its burgers and fries blow the fast-food-chain burgers out of the water.

Rails Cafe at the Depot (☎ 830-257-3877; 615 Schreiner; meals $9-18; 🕑 11am-9pm Mon-Sat) This cute cafe in the old train depot is awfully pleasant. Make a lunch of panini or salad, or splurge a bit with the osso bucco or beef tenderloin.

La Four's Seafood Restaurant (☎ 830-896-1449; 1129 Junction Hwy; mains $9-20; 🕑 11am-2pm & 4-9pm Tue-Sat, 11am-2:30pm Sun) This stucco-walled local spot is known for its excellent fried shrimp and Cajun-influenced fare such as frogs legs and spicy jalapeño hush puppies.

Cowboy Steakhouse (☎ 830-896-5688; 416 Main St; mains $12-25; 🕑 5-10pm Mon-Sat) For no-frills buffalo steaks, lobster and Texas quail, head on over to this meat-lover's paradise. Locals name it as the best steak house in town.

Getting There & Around

By car from Austin, take US 290 west to Fredericksburg, then turn south onto Hwy 16, which meets Kerrville south of I-10. From San Antonio, take I-10 north to Hwy 16, then head south. **Kerrville Bus Co** (☎ 830-257-7454; 701 Sidney Baker St) has service to both cities. In town, **Bicycle Works** (☎ 830-896-6864; 141 W Water St; full-day rental $28; 🕑 10am-6pm Mon-Fri, 10am-4pm Sat) rents bikes.

COMFORT
pop 1477

Another 19th-century German settlement tucked into the hills, Comfort is perhaps the most idyllic of the Hill Country bunch, with rough-hewn limestone homes from the late 1800s and a beautifully restored business district. Shopping for antiques is the number-one activity, but you'll also find a few good restaurants, a winery and, as the town's name suggests, an easy way of life.

One of the nicest places in town is **814-A: A Texas Bistro** (☎ 830-995-4990; 713 High St; lunch $8-14, dinner $27-29; 🕑 11am-2:30pm Wed-Sun & 6:30-9:30pm Thu-Sat). Located in the former Comfort post office and with a rustic decor, this place is pure Hill Country. There's not a cornucopia of choices: dinner offers three mains options that change weekly, so the focus is on doing just a couple of things but doing them well. Lunch is equally limited, but you can usually count on a burger.

For something more casual, head to local favorite **Los Jarritos** (☎ 830-995-4112; 1005 Hwy 87 S; mains $4-7; 🕑 7am-8:30pm Mon-Sat), next door to the Texaco station, for a dang good Mexican dinner. The place may look a bit divey, but the green-chile chicken enchiladas and homemade corn tortillas will melt in your mouth.

About halfway between Kerrville and Boerne, Comfort is on TX 27, just 2 miles west of I-10.

BANDERA
pop 1296

Bandera has the look and feel of an old
Western movie set, and that's just the effect
the locals want in order to support their claim
as the Cowboy Capital of Texas. There are
certainly lots of dude ranches around, and
rodeos and horseback riding are easy to come
by. Perhaps one of the best reasons to come
to Bandera is to drink beer and dance in one
of the many hole-in-the-wall cowboy bars
and honky-tonks, where you'll find friendly
locals, good live music and a rich atmosphere.
Giddy up!

Orientation & Information

Main St is roughly north–south through the
center of town. At the southern edge of downtown, Cypress St heads east–west, continuing
as Hwy 16 at the eastern end of town.

For more information and friendly advice,
drop by the **Bandera Convention & Visitors Bureau**
(CVB; ☎ 800-364-3833; ½ block south of Main St on Hwy 16
S; ☺ 9am-5pm Mon-Fri, 10am-3pm Sat).

Sights & Activities

The visitor center stocks a handy historical walking tour brochure covering many
of the old buildings scattered around town,
including the St Stanislaus Catholic Church
and adjacent Convent Cemetery and the
First Bandera Jail. The **Frontier Times Museum**
(☎ 830-796-3864; www.frontiertimesmuseum.org; 510
13th St; adult/6-17yr/senior $5/2/3; ☺ 10am-4:30pm Mon-
Sat) displays guns, branding irons and cowboy gear, and there are various temporary
exhibitions.

Local rodeos are held twice weekly during
summer at **Mansfield Park** (contact the CVB
for information), on Hwy 16 toward Medina,
and **Twin Elm Guest Ranch** (☎ 830-796-3628; www.
twinelmranch.com; on Hwy 470), which lets the bulls
loose on Fridays at 8pm.

The CVB knows nearly a dozen places in
and around town were you can go **horseback
riding**. There are also more than a dozen dude
ranches in the area, all with hundreds of acres,
enormous ranch houses, resort features and
heaps of riding opportunities. Most of them
also offer horseback riding to nonguests, usually for around $25 to $30 per hour, $80 for a
half-day ride with lunch or $180 for overnight
rides with meals.

The CVB can help you make reservations
at all of the following:

Dixie Dude Ranch (☎ 830-796-7771, 800-375-9255;
www.dixieduderanch.com; 833 Dixie Dude Ranch Rd)
LH7 Ranch and Resort (☎ 830-796-4314; off FM
3240, 3½ miles northwest of Bandera; cottages $80)
Silver Spur Guest Ranch (☎ 830-796-3037; www.
silverspur-ranch.com; 9266 Bandera Creek Rd)
Running-R Ranch (☎ 830-796-3984; www.rrranch.
com; 9059 Bandera Creek Rd)
Yellow Rose Ranch (☎ 210-845-7350; www.yellow
roseranch.com; in Tarpley, 22 miles northwest of Bandera)

Sleeping & Eating

Overnight stays at the dude ranches all cost
about the same; plan on spending about $130
per person per night (usually there's a two-
night minimum stay), which might include
meals or horseback riding.

At the south end of town, the friendly,
family-run **River Front Motel** (☎ 830-460-3690,
800-870-5671; www.theriverfrontmotel.com; 1003 Maple St;
cabins $74-125; ℗) offers 11 cabins on the river,
each with a fridge, coffeemaker and cable
TV. It's your best bet for the money. Another
good choice is the **River Oak Inn** (☎ 830-796-7751;
1203 Main St; d $59-120; ℗), where all of the clean
rooms have a fridge and microwave.

When it's time to eat, head to **Busbee's BBQ
& Catering** (☎ 830-796-3153; 319 Main St; mains $6-10;
☺ 10:30am-8pm Mon, Wed & Thu, 10:30am-9pm Fri & Sat),
where you can get smoked meat by the pound,
plate meals and decent burgers. Or try **OST
Restaurant** (☎ 830-796-3836; 305 Main St; mains $6-14;
☺ 6am-10pm, from 7am Sun) – the name stands for
Old Spanish Trail – which does hearty chuck-
wagon-style breakfasts, along with Tex-Mex
and the ubiquitous chicken-fried steaks at
dinner. There's an entire wall devoted to the
likeness of John Wayne.

Entertainment

If it's honky-tonkin' and beer drinkin' you're
looking for, you've come to the right place.
Arkey Blue's Silver Dollar Bar (☎ 830-796-8826; 308
Main St) is a dancehall where you can cotton-
eyed-Joe with the best of them. Look for
Hank Williams Sr's carved signature in one
of the wooden tables. **Bandera Cabaret Dance Hall**
(☎ 830-796-8166; 801 Main St; ☺ 5pm-midnight Wed &
Thu, 5pm-2am Fri, 7pm-2am Sat) is another rootin'
tootin' dance hall that's bigger than Arkey's
and has been around since 1936. Bandera
resident Robert Earl Keen and Austin yodeler
Don Walser have been known to play its stage.

The not-to-be-missed **11th St Cowboy Bar**
(☎ 830-796-4849; www.11thstreetcowboybar.com; 307

11th St), just north of Cypress St, is the 'Biggest Little Bar in Texas' with world-famous acts and, out back, the only jet-cooled dancefloor and patio in Texas. It frequently offers drink specials, steak nights, free hot dogs and hamburgers, and parties for just about every holiday on the calendar.

Getting There & Away

From Kerrville, the most direct route is Hwy 173 (Bandera Hwy). The more pleasant and scenic way – through hill and dale and past Medina – is to take Hwy 16 south.

BOERNE
pop 6178
Sights & Activities

Twenty-three miles east of Bandera on Hwy 46 is the bustling little center of Boerne (rhymes with 'journey'), settled by German immigrants in 1849. The town clings strongly to its German roots, and it's less overrun with tourists than Fredericksburg. It's a pleasant place to spend a few hours, and the **Boerne Chamber of Commerce** (☎ 830-249-8000; www.boerne. org; 126 Rosewood Ave; ☒ 9am-5pm Mon-Fri, 9am-noon Sat) has brochures covering historical markers around town. Main St seems to focus on **antique stores**; most stock a handy leaflet that will help you navigate around the plethora of shops.

East of Main St, the **Cibolo Nature Center** (City Park Rd, off Hwy 46; admission free; ☒ 8am-dusk) is a small park with rewarding nature trails that wind through native Texan woods, marshland and along Cibolo Creek. Call the park visitor center to ask about a series of live-music concerts and events held here during summer.

Natural attractions outside town include popular **Cascade Caverns** (☎ 830-755-8080; www. cascadecaverns.com; 226 Cascade Caverns Rd, off I-10 exit 543; adult/3-11yr $11/7; ☒ 10am-4pm Mon-Fri, 9am-5pm Sat & Sun, later in summer), about 3 miles south of Boerne. The caverns include a 140ft-deep cave that features giant stalagmites and stalactites and a 100ft waterfall. The only way to see the cave is by taking a 45-minute tour, which departs every 30 minutes.

Sleeping & Eating

Ye Kendall Inn (☎ 830-249-2138; www.yekendallinn. com; 128 W Blanco St; d $100-200, cabins $109-249; P) This national-landmark hotel is the nicest place to stay in Boerne. The creekside main house is made of hand-cut limestone and features a two-story, 200ft-long front porch; the building dates to 1859 and has 14 rooms. There are also three cabins and a small church, all of which date from the 1800s and were relocated to the property from various places around the state (the stunning Enchanted Cabin was built near Enchanted Rock). Prices at the inn include a three-course gourmet breakfast from the attached Limestone Grille (mains $13 to $25, open for breakfast, lunch and dinner), an upscale spot serving good food in a somewhat stuffy atmosphere.

For a fresh, delicious breakfast buffet, don't look any further than **Bear Moon Bakery & Cafe** (☎ 830-816-2327; 401 S Main St; mains $5-10; ☒ 6am-5pm Tue-Sat, 8am-4pm Sun). On weekends, be sure to arrive early – it's always packed. There are plenty of home-baked goodies to tempt you as well, along with fresh soups, salads and sandwiches for lunch. Another prime choice for early-morning coffee and tea is the **Daily Grind** (☎ 830-249-4677; 143 S Main St), a cute little spot right on the main strip.

For a tasty mix of Mexican and German fare and homemade beers in an eclectic atmosphere, head to the **Dodging Duck Brewhaus** (☎ 830-248-3825; 402 River Rd; mains $8-20; ☒ 11am-9pm Sun-Thu, to 10pm Fri & Sat). In addition to lunch and dinner, they also have plenty of shareable bar snacks.

Out on the edge of town, **Po Po Family Restaurant** (☎ 830-537-4194; 829 FM 289; mains $12-24; ☒ 11am-9pm Sun-Thu, to 10pm Fri & Sat) serves steaks and seafood – including hard-to-find frogs legs – but the main reason to come here is to see the absolutely astounding collection of souvenir plates: more than 2000 of them cover almost every inch of wall space.

WARING-WELFARE ROAD

Just up the road from Boerne on I-10 is the tiny town of Nelson City, which is notable mainly as the starting point for a drive along the Waring-Welfare Rd (SR 1621), a lazy country lane that dips and meanders past some beautiful scenery and a few hidden Hill Country escapes.

Nelson City is really just a smattering of buildings off I-10 at the Waring-Welfare Rd exit. One of these is **Nelson City Dance Hall** (☎ 830-537-3835; 825 Waring-Welfare Rd, 0.5 mile off I-10 exit 533; ☒ 5-11pm Wed & Thu, 4pm-2am Fri & Sat, 2-10pm Sun), a family-friendly honky-tonk where you can show off your new cowboy boots and do a little two-steppin'. On the weekends, live bands play everything from country and bluegrass to zydeco and Tejano.

Drive north on SR 1621 for about 3 miles to the town of Welfare. About 10 people call Welfare home, including Gaby McCormick and David Lawhorn, the chef-owners of the **Welfare Cafe** (☎ 830-537-3700; 223 Waring-Welfare Rd; mains $10-22; ☙ brunch 11am-3pm Sat & Sun, dinner 5-9pm Wed-Sun, 5-10pm Sat), a gourmet restaurant housed inside a 1920s general store and post office. American-style seafood as well as German schnitzel are on the eclectic menu; dinner reservations are recommended. The Welfare also offers a superb selection of beer and wine, as well as live music in a beautiful outdoor beer garden on Thursday and Sunday evenings.

If you're looking for the spirit of the Hill Country, it doesn't get much more spirited than the **Waring General Store** (☎ 210-434-2331; Waring-Welfare Rd). About 7 miles north of Welfare, this old-time general store has seen a lot of boots scuff across its hardwood floors over the years. There's live music under a giant old oak tree on the first Saturday of each month, and you can dine there on Wednesdays during **steak night** (www.steaknite.com).

GUADALUPE RIVER STATE PARK

Thirty miles north of San Antonio, this exceptionally beautiful **state park** (☎ 830-438-2656; 3350 Park Rd 31, Spring Branch; adult/under 12yr $4/free, campsites/RV sites $12/15; ☙ dawn-dusk) straddles a 9-mile stretch of the sparklingly clear, bald-cypress-tree-lined Guadalupe River, and it's great for canoeing and tubing. There are also 3 miles of hiking trails through the park's almost 2000 acres. Two-hour guided tours of the nearby Honey Creek State Natural Area are included in the price of admission. The tours leave at 9am on Saturday morning from the Guadalupe ranger station.

WIMBERLEY

pop 2100

It's not really on the way to or from anywhere else, so, as the locals like to say, 'You have to mean to visit Wimberley.' A popular weekend spot for Austinites, this artists' community gets absolutely jam-packed during summer weekends – especially on the first Saturday of each month from April to December, when local art galleries, shops and craftspeople set

up booths for **Wimberley Market Days**, a bustling collection of live music, food and more than 400 vendors at Lion's Field on RR 2325.

Even on nonmarket weekends, there are plenty of shops to visit, stocked with antiques, gifts, and local arts and crafts. You can also taste olive oil in one of the state's only commercial olive orchards, eat expertly baked homemade pies or simply kick back at one of the many B&Bs along the creek.

For more information on market days and other happenings around town, contact the **Wimberley Convention & Visitors Bureau** (CVB; ☎ 512-847-2201; www.visitwimberley.com; 14001 RR 12; ☙ 9am-4pm Mon-Sat, noon-4pm Sun) near Brookshires grocery store.

Sights & Activities

An unusual sight in Wimberley (and the rest of Texas, for that matter) is the only producing olive orchard in the Hill Country, found at **Bella Vista Ranch** (☎ 512-847-6514; www.texasoliveoil. com; 3101 Mt Sharp Rd, off CR 182; ☙ 10am-5pm Thu-Sat, noon-4pm Sun). There's a gift shop with free tastings as well as tours of the orchard and the olive press, one of only two in Texas.

For excellent scenic views of the surrounding limestone hills near Wimberley, take a drive on the **Devil's Backbone**. From Wimberley, head south on RR 12 to FM 32, then turn right toward Fischer and Canyon Lake. The road gets steeper, then winds out onto a craggy ridge – the 'backbone' – with a 360-degree vista. About the only establishment on this stretch of road, **Devil's Backbone Tavern** (☎ 830-964-2544; 4041 FM 32; ☙ daily) is a perfectly tattered and dusty beer joint with a country-music jukebox and live acoustic music on Wednesday and Friday.

The famous **Blue Hole** (☎ 512-847-9127; off CR 173; admission $1; ☙ 9am-8pm) is one of the Hill Country's best swimming holes. It's a privately owned spot in the calm, shady and crystal-clear waters of Cypress Creek. To get here from Wimberley, head down Hwy 12 south of the square, turn left on County Rd 173, and then after another half-mile, turn onto the access road between a church and a cemetery.

Sleeping & Eating

There are dozens of B&Bs and cottages in Wimberley; call the CVB or visit its website for more information. Close to the action and just a quarter-mile east of the square, the **Wimberley Inn Motel** (☎ 512-847-3750; www. wimberleyinn.com; 200 RR 3237; d $89-149) offers large, no-frills rooms at a fair price.

Two miles south of town, **Blair House** (☎ 512-847-1111, 877-549-5450; www.blairhouseinn.com; 100 Spoke Hill Rd; d $150-289, ste $215-289, cabins $275; ✕ ☎ ⬛) is a quiet, lovely B&B with eight rooms and two cabins. Some of the suites are knockouts, with big windows and stone fireplaces. There's also a cooking school, restaurant and spa on-site, so you can really hole up here for a while if you want.

Get out of the crowded downtown area for a relaxed lunch at the **Leaning Pear** (☎ 512-847-7327; 111 River Rd; mains $7-9; ☒ 11am-3pm Sun, Mon, Wed & Thu, 11am-8pm Fri & Sat). This cafe exudes Hill Country charm like a cool glass of iced tea, with salads and sandwiches served in a restored stone house.

You haven't eaten until you've wrapped your mouth around a pie from the **Wimberley Pie Company** (☎ 512-847-9462; 13619 RR12; ☒ 9:30am-5:30pm Tue-Fri, 10am-5pm Sat, noon-4pm Sun), a small but popular bakery that supplies many of the area's restaurants (and a few in Austin) with every kind of pie and cheesecake you can imagine, and then some. It's about a quarter-mile east of the square.

Shopping

Art galleries, antique shops and craft stores surround Wimberley Square, located where Ranch Rd 12 crosses Cypress Creek and bends into an 'S.' The best browsing is 1½ miles north of the square on Ranch Rd 12 at **Poco Rio** (15406 RR 12), a shopping center with boutique clothing stores, artists' galleries, eateries, a health spa for acupuncture and massage and an 18-hole putt-putt golf course, all set among lush gardens and tree-shaded pathways.

Getting There & Away

There is no public transportation to Wimberley. To make the 1½-hour drive from Austin, take US 290 west to Dripping Springs, then turn left onto Ranch Rd 12. From San Antonio, take I-35 north to San Marcos, where you can pick up Ranch Rd 12 headed west and then north into town.

Houston & East Texas

It's not the Southwest, it's not Tex-Mex and it's not really the Deep South, either. A holy trifecta of the three, perhaps? The easternmost notch on the nation's Bible Belt? This part of Texas is a bit of an enigma and it likes it that way. Now throw in some piney woods, the world's largest cypress forest, red-hot Houston and a little Cajun seasoning to spice things up, and you've got east Texas. When you hear 'Y'all come back now,' people actually mean it.

And then there's H-town. More country than Dallas, too conservative for Austin, Houston reeks of both money and poverty, and this city turns on a dime: bourgeois and backwards, businesslike and bohemian. Picture more than two million residents spread over an ever-swelling region that takes up twice as much land as Chicago, crank up the heat, throw plenty of stellar restaurants, culture and entertainment into the mix, and send in a torrid hurricane or two. This is one edgy place.

Outside Houston, you'll see a whole lot of churches among the pine trees. Heavily evangelical, east Texas was once known for its 'dry' counties, meaning the sale of alcohol to the public was – at least theoretically – prohibited. To the dismay of some, these counties are again drying up. Consider it a nostalgic throwback, then, if you find yourself in an east Texas 'private club' that sells booze only to 'members;' while they might charge you a few bucks for a 'temporary membership,' these days they'll likely just look the other way. Now that's the Texas spirit.

HIGHLIGHTS

Best Free Art
Form some opinions on postmodern art at Houston's Menil Collection (p199)

Best Place to Get Spooked
Tiny Jefferson (p221) is rife with ghosts and haunted hotels, but the locals are friendly as all get out

Best Place to Ditch the Sunscreen
Wander the shady trails through fragrant piney woods at the Big Thicket National Preserve (p219)

Best Drink to Chill Out
On a scorcher of a Houston afternoon, we cooled down right quick with the frozen mimosa at Onion Creek Café (p209)

Best Place to Get Lost
Glide among the mysterious cypress trees on the labyrinthine Caddo Lake (p###)

Best Place to Savor Your Freedom
Surrounded by maximum-security prisons, it's easy to feel like a free (wo)man in Huntsville (p217)

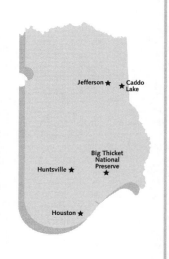

Jefferson ★   ★ Caddo Lake

Big Thicket National Preserve ★

Huntsville ★

Houston ★

Climate

The word 'hot' doesn't really begin to describe this part of Texas in the summer, but you get the picture. Neither does 'humid,' and the nearer you get to the Gulf, the more intense the humidity. 'Scorching' – yeah, that's more like it, but you need to say it as you run, screaming, into air-conditioning. After all, that's what locals do. That's right, if you plan on walking more than a block or two during the summer months, be prepared for those 'Hey, crazy!' looks. The average July high in that notorious hotbox – Houston – is 94°F (34°C); a few hours north, in Nacogdoches, it's just as sweltering.

Getting There & Around

The proverb 'the car is king in Texas' applies here. Luckily, it means that all roads in these here parts do lead to Houston, and even the smaller towns are generally easy to reach. Houston is the most convenient major airport for locales south of Lufkin, while Dallas best serves places north. Bus service primarily serves cities along the interstates. Amtrak service can be described in two words: limited and slow.

If you're driving, your trip will be much more scenic and enjoyable if you get off the interstate onto the secondary roads – either the US highways or, better yet, the bucolic Farm to Market (FM) roads.

HOUSTON

pop 2.26 million

In a state known for its outsized personality, ego and geography, Houston is the biggest bad boy on the block. Big, brash, hazy Houston may be the fourth-largest city in the US (and Houstonians are rooting for it to edge in at number three), but it's hardly one of the most celebrated – even in Texas.

Sure, Houston's got issues, but could this city be just a tad bit *underrated*? The proud locals would stop their cowboy boots (or their Jimmy Choos) and said say, 'Heck yes.' Celebrated for its arts and international flair, maligned for its air pollution, sprawl and Enron-sized scandals, Houston is a cosmopolitan metropolis to some and a big hot mess to others. An entrepreneurial business-first spirit combined with a Wild West mentality toward city planning means that Houston's stupen-

dous growth has been largely unfettered by zoning and other planning restrictions. The result? A surreal hodgepodge of strip malls, diverse residential areas and 'downtown' areas in addition to the traditional center. Yet delights abound: with a map, a little curiosity and plenty of friendly locals to give advice, you'll find that Houston's cultural scene is as rich as its oil industry.

Visitors and even residents find Houston to be a confusing sprawl. However, most of the areas of interest lie in the 6 miles between the Galleria mall and downtown. While Houston's major sights could be seen in a weekend, this city pays off to those who stop and meander through its laid-back, eclectic and downright pretty central neighborhoods.

The beauty of Houston lies in its dual personality: laid-back pickup-truck-and-boots town meets high-powered, high-cultured metropolis. During the day, chill out in your flip-flops, take in museums and shopping, and hit happy hour under a palm-shaded patio. By night, revel in culinary or operatic bliss – the burgeoning foodie scene and the Houston Grand Opera are nationally renowned.

HISTORY

The most important two words in Houston's history are not 'oil' and 'cattle' – although they have been extremely important. Rather, the two words critical to the city's spectacular growth are 'air' and 'conditioning.'

Until the 1930s, Houston was a sleepy regional center with a population under 100,000. Office workers grumpily plugged away at their desks in sweatshop conditions; during summer months, Houstonians fled the city in search of cooler coastal breezes. When air-conditioning became available on

DRIVING DISTANCES

Big Thicket Preserve to Nacogdoches 87 miles, 1¾ hours
Dallas to Jefferson 164 miles, 3 hours
Houston to Austin 161 miles, 3 hours
Houston to College Station 98 miles, 1¾ hours
Houston to Dallas 242 miles, 4 hours
Houston to Nacogdoches 145 miles, 2¾ hours
Houston to Sam Houston National Forest 58 miles, 1½ hours
Houston to Tyler 200 miles, 3¾ hours

GREATER HOUSTON

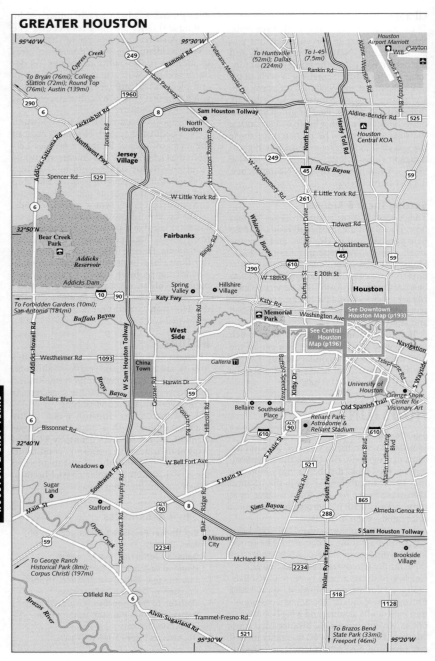

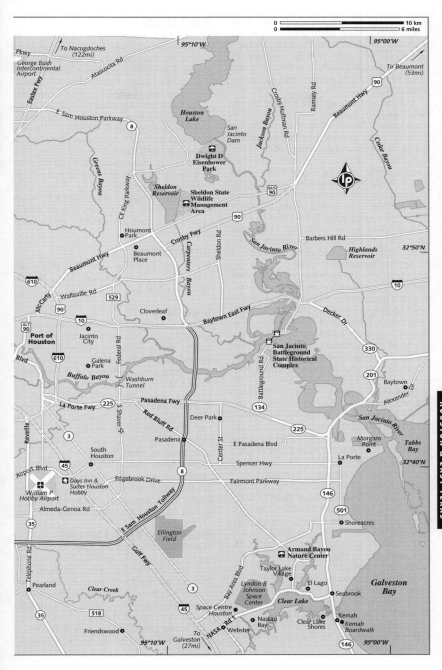

a widespread basis, it was the breath of life Houston had been waiting for. Businesses rushed to embrace the cool, and homeowners weren't far behind. By 1950 Houston's population had jumped to 600,000. By 1960 it had reached nearly one million and has never looked back.

A devotion to cheap land and fast money has shaped Houston ever since its inception as a mosquito-ridden trading post in 1824. For the rest of that century the city grew slowly, fed by the cotton and the cattle trade. In 1901 the discovery of oil – the ultimate get-rich-quick scheme – set the tone for Houston's future. By the 1970s oil was the foundation of the economy, with hundreds of firms involved in exploring, refining and selling the 'black gold.' When oil reached $40 a barrel in 1981, Houston was awash in money. Four years later, the price of oil plummeted to single digits, and – poof! – so did the dreams of many who had gambled on oil.

In the 1990s Houston's economy diversified into medical services and high tech as the city rode the country's economic boom, which reached its apex in the late 2000s. Always the trendsetter, Houston ushered in an era of corporate scandal and bankruptcy (and got plenty of international news coverage) with the Enron scandal (see the boxed text, p210). However, this spunky town bounced back like usual: the Enron sign is down and the petrochemical industry carries on. Houston was the closest and most obvious major city to shelter evacuees after nearby Hurricanes Katrina, Rita and Ike; several years later, the city has absorbed more than 90,000 hurricane refugees, which some say continues to put a strain on the city's resources. Yet throughout the nationwide recession, Houston's economic growth has remained strong, outpacing even other cities in 'recession-proof' Texas.

Home to many expats, Houston's international and multicultural vibe has only gotten stronger. In 1997, Houston's first black mayor, Lee P Brown, was elected for two terms. He was succeeded by the popular Democrat Bill White, who served for three terms before launching a campaign for the 2010 Texas gubernatorial election. Recent political developments only confirm the city's inclusive, forward-thinking streak: Houston recently surprised the nation – and probably even itself – by appointing its first lesbian mayor, Annise Parker, in 2010.

ORIENTATION
Where I-45 (northwest–southeast), I-59 (southwest–northeast) and I-10 (east–west) meet forms downtown Houston. The light-rail system line starts along Main St downtown and zooms south to the Museum District, Hermann Park, the Texas Medical Center and on to the behemoth Reliant Park. Midtown begins southwest of downtown, while eclectic Montrose is further west. Westheimer Rd runs from it to wealthy River Oaks and out to the Galleria at I-610. Tranquil Houston Heights is north of I-10 from Montrose, while the West University/Rice Village areas lie just west of the Museum District.

Houston's sprawl radiates from downtown in all directions. Within the city, the streets are laid out in a grid pattern that's fairly predictable.

INFORMATION
When making phone calls, three area codes serve the greater Houston area: ☎ 281, ☎ 713, and ☎ 832.

Bookstores
Borders (Map p196; ☎ 713-524-0200; www.borders.com; 3025 Kirby Dr; ☯ 9am-11pm Mon-Sat, 9am-10pm Sun; ☎) In the River Oaks area, with free wi-fi and a cafe.
Brazos Bookstore (Map p196; ☎ 713-523-0701; www.brazosbookstore.com; 2421 Bissonnet St; ☯ 10am-7pm Mon-Thu, 10am-6pm Fri-Sun) Independent bookseller since 1974 with many author events. Near Rice Village.
Half Price Books (Map p196; www.halfpricebooks.com; ☯ 9am-10pm Mon-Sat, 10am-8pm Sun); Rice Village (☎ 713-524-6635; 2537 University Blvd;); Montrose (☎ 713-520-1084; 1011 Westheimer Rd) Diverse used books, movies, and eclectic clientele.
Kaboom Books (off Map p196); Studewood (☎ 713-869-1700; 733 Studewood St; ☯ noon-8pm Thu-Sat, 8am-6pm Sun); Houston Ave (☎ 713-869-7600; 3115 Houston Ave; ☯ noon-8pm Mon-Sat, noon-6pm Sun) It's the city's 'most exuberantly misanthropic' used bookstore.

Emergency & Medical Services
For medical emergencies, head to the emergency room of the nearest local hospital. For less immediately threatening conditions, it's cheaper and quicker to go to an urgent-care clinic. Countless CVS and Walgreens pharmacies dot Houston, some of them with prescription services open 24 hours.
CVS Pharmacy (Map p196; ☎ 713-807-8491; www.cvs.com; 1003 Richmond Ave; ☯ 24hr) Centrally located in Montrose.

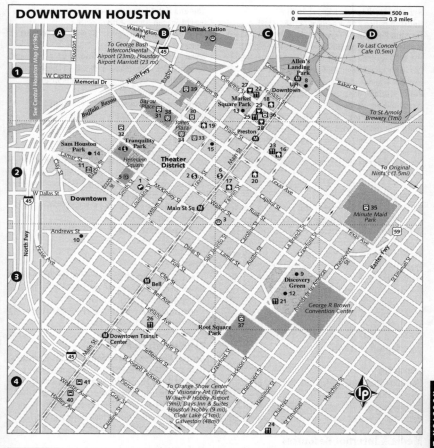

DOWNTOWN HOUSTON

0 — 500 m
0 — 0.3 miles

HOUSTON & EAST TEXAS

HIV-AIDS Hotline (☎ 800-342-2437)
Houston police (☎ nonurgent 713-884-3131)
Houston Red Cross – Travelers' Aid (☎ 713-526-8300)
Memorial Hermann Hospital (Map p196; ☎ 713-704-4000; www.memorialhermann.org; 6411 Fannin St) Part of the Texas Medical Center megacomplex, with a level-one Trauma Center for emergencies.
Police station (Map p196; ☎ 713-284-8604; 802 Westheimer Rd; ⏲ 24hr)
Rape Crisis Hotline (☎ 713-526-7273)
RediClinic (off Map p196; ☎ 713-343-2679; www.rediclinic.com; 2660 Fountain View Dr; ⏲ 8am-8pm Mon-Fri, 9am-5pm Sat, 10am-5pm Sun) This urgent-care clinic provides affordable care for minor illnesses and injuries on a walk-in basis.

Internet Access
Most hotels and motels offer wi-fi free, or for a small fee. See Drinking (p207) for Houston coffee shops that provide free wi-fi (most do). Not dragging your laptop around? Probably a good idea in this heat. Montrose's **Copy.com** (Map p196; ☎ 713-528-1201; www.houstoncopy.com; 1201F Westheimer Rd; ⏲ 7am-midnight Mon-Fri, 11am-7pm Sat) features an internet bar where you can check your email ($7.50 per hour, in five-minute increments) and print documents. You can also head to the public library (p194). At Rice University's leafy campus (p194) crack open your laptop and surf for free.

Libraries
Houston Public Library (Map p193; ☎ 713-236-1313; www.hpl.lib.tx.us; 500 McKinney St; 🛜) Free internet computers and wi-fi in a bright modern building downtown. Helpful staff, a pleasant reading area and a good travel section.

Media & Internet Resources
For additional information, check the visitors bureau (p194).
Houston Chronicle (www.chron.com) The major daily newspaper. 'Nuff said.
Houston Press (www.houstonpress.com) Alternative weekly offering political comment and loads of dining and entertainment info; widely available at cafes, bookstores and street kiosks.
Houston.Citysearch.com A searchable database of reviews and 'best of' lists.
Houston Sun (www.houstonsun.com) News from the African American community.
http://blogs.houstonpress.com/eating Houston Press' 'Eating Our Words' foodie blog features up-to-date info on new restaurants and food events.
KUHT 88.7 Classical music and National Public Radio (NPR) from the University of Houston.

Semana News (www.semananews.com) Houston's biggest Spanish-language news source.
www.Houston.com Links to city resources, from golf courses to airport info to festivals.
www.riceinfo.rice.edu/houston 'Houston: It's Cooler than You Think' is the motto for this site, a fabulous orientation to the city for the most clueless of newbie visitors. Links to all the good stuff.
www.yelp.com/houston Highly opinionated user reviews on food, bars, shopping and services.

Money
Houston's myriad banks are open at least from 9am to 4pm, with many branches open later in the evening and on Saturday. Find ATMs in banks, gas stations, convenience stores and nightspots.
Capital One (Map p193; ☎ 713-435-7025; 910 Travis St) Full-service bank with ATM.
JPMorgan Chase Bank (Map p193; ☎ 713-216-4865; 712 Main St) Full-service bank with ATM.

Post
The central **post office** (Map p193; ☎ 713-226-3161; www.usps.com; 401 Franklin St; ⏲ 7am-7pm Mon-Fri) is at the north edge of downtown.
Downtown post office (Map p193; ☎ 713-651-0112; 909 Fannin St; ⏲ 10am-4pm Mon-Fri)

Tourist Information
Greater Houston Convention & Visitors Bureau (Map p193; ☎ 713-437-5556; www.visithoustontexas.com; 901 Bagby St; ⏲ 9am-4pm Mon-Sat) A brochure-stuffed visitor center inside the art-deco City Hall. Pick up *Above & Below*, an essential tool for exploring the poorly marked subterranean maze of downtown Houston. Free one-hour visitor parking on Walker St.

Universities
One of the largest universities in Texas, the commuter-heavy **University of Houston** (Map p190; ☎ 713-743-2255, www.uh.edu; 4800 Calhoun Rd) is the major local university and boasts strong programs in the arts. While some locals roll their eyes at the reputation of elite **Rice University** (Map p196; ☎ 713-348-0000; www.rice.edu; 6100 Main St) as 'the Harvard of Texas,' as more than one Texan told us, 'It ain't braggin' if it's true.'

DANGERS & ANNOYANCES
See those crosswalk signs? The speeding SUVs ignore them, so as a pedestrian, you should, too. While Houston's made a big effort to improve its public transportation with reliable city buses and (drum roll) a light-rail system,

HOUSTON IN...

Two Days

If stuffing yourself on culture and good food for a full 48 hours makes you say 'Yee haw!' follow this plan.

The proper Texan way to start the day – with a breakfast taco, natch – is in order. Hit up **Tacos A Go Go** (p205) in Midtown, before heading downtown. Check out the historic side of Houston – **Sam Houston Park** (p198). Then it's up, way up, to the **Sky Lobby** (p197), where you can get a sense of how whopping this city really is. With kids, head to **Discovery Green** (p198) across downtown for some urban R&R. Otherwise, take the light rail over to the **Museum District** (p198). You're officially in museum heaven, but it's overload to see more than two in an afternoon. So start at the phenomenal **Museum of Fine Arts, Houston** (p###) then head over to the **Houston Museum of Natural Science** (p198), where you should head straight to the dinosaurs and the Hall of Gems and Minerals. Grab a light lunch at nearby **Tart Café** (p204), or take it to go for a picnic in **Hermann Park** (p201). Evening, head back to **Midtown** (p198) for an early dinner at **T'afia** (p204) and a glass of wine of **13 Celsius** (p208). Culture hounds should check what's on at the **Houston Grand Opera** (p209) or the **Alley Theatre** (p209), in which case your nightcap could be at candlelit **La Carafe** (p207).

Day two means an adventure in Houston's coolest neighborhood, **Montrose** (p199). After breakfast at **Baby Barnaby's** (p206), take your time strolling from the **Menil Collection** (p199) to the **Rothko Chapel** (p200). Hit **Brasil** (p206) for lunch – now you're right on Westheimer to explore its funky shops. Luckily, there's no reason to leave Montrose at sundown. After a frozen happy-hour mojito at **Boheme** (p208), hit amazing **Indika** (p206). Head to **Washington Avenue** (p209) for bar-hopping, or just stay in the 'Gayborhood' (see p208) and party with the locals at **Poison Girl** (p209) or **South Beach** (p208).

Four Days

Follow the above plan for the first 48 hours, and then fill up your tank with gas...we're hitting the road. Begin your day at the legendary **Breakfast Klub** (p204) for Southern wings 'n' waffles before hitting the **Heights** (p200) for boutique and antique cruising. If you're feeling funky, stop at the **Art Car Museum** (p199). Hit **Pie in the Sky Pie Company** (p206) or **Onion Creek Café** (p209) for a low-key lunch on the patio. Head to the **Clear Lake Area** (p214) before rush hour. Spend the evening strolling the **Kemah Boardwalk** (p214) at sunset.

Go to the moon on your final morning – or just pretend to at the **Space Center Houston** (p214). Head back to H-town and lunch among the flowers at **Tiny Boxwoods** (p207) before spending the afternoon browsing the shops of **Rice Village** (p199) – though true mall rats should split for the **Galleria** (p211). No doubt you're craving Mexican food and margaritas by now, so cap off your evening with fancy at **Hugo's** (p205) or fun at **Chuy's** (p205), before checking out local music at **Cézanne** (p211) or **Rudyard's Pub** (p210).

car traffic is a downright menace to pedestrians and cyclists. In fact, in 2008 Houston was ranked 8th-most-dangerous city for walking, based on the Pedestrian Danger Index (PDI). Look sharply.

While crime in Houston hit a 25-year low in 2008, the usual advice for American big cities applies in Houston. Lock your car, keep valuables out of sight, beware of dark and lonely streets and if an area looks dangerous, it probably is. Areas to the east and southeast of downtown Houston can be sketchy at any time, but that description is by no means universal.

Other than dangerous drivers, heat is probably the biggest danger. Summer temperatures over 100°F coupled with extreme humidity can exhaust a hardened cowboy: drink water and seek shade.

SIGHTS

Houston's huge with a capital H and plays hard to get – you gotta dig deep to get on intimate terms. Escape from its traffic-choked main drags, and you'll find several charming – heck, downright lovely – central neighborhoods full of picturesque cottages, bungalows and mansions from a mix of architectural eras,

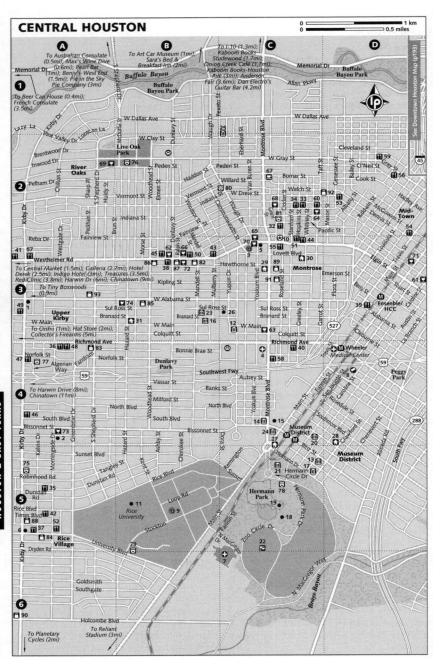

CENTRAL HOUSTON

often shaded by lush live oak trees. Although development in recent decades has favored faceless subdivisions with generic names that always seem to include the ubiquitous word 'oak,' keep in mind that treasures may lay just beyond the seemingly endless (sub) urban blight.

Downtown
With the fourth-largest skyline in the country (best seen at night), the downtown area can come off as all business by day: a monotonous thicket of high-rises interspersed with parking lots and the occasional urban park, with few pedestrians braving the hot sidewalks. No, they're not at the pool. Go underground: air-conditioned, underground pedestrian tunnels link most downtown buildings. In fact, those seeking water, snacks, and sunscreen to brave the shimmering downtown heat will more likely find these necessities within the tunnel system than in above-ground shops. (Yes, even the McDonald's is underground!)

While it doesn't possess the downtown energy of Austin or Dallas, Houston's certainly come a long way since the snarky phrase 'ghost town' was oft-used to describe downtown after dark. Aside from the longtime buzzing **Theater District** (www.houstontheaterdistrict.org), you'll find plenty of restaurants, nightlife and new hotels springing up to the delight of after-work happy-hour-seekers. Start at Congress and Travis Sts, and stroll.

You'll notice how 19th-century buildings sharply contrast with their modern surroundings in **Market Square Park** (Map p193; cnr Congress & Travis Sts), the historical center of downtown, along with **Allen's Landing Park** (Map p193; 1001 Commerce St), named after Houston's founders and the so-called 'Plymouth Rock' of Houston, right on the **Buffalo Bayou**. Get your bearings with a bird's-eye view (or at least 1002ft of it) by climbing the elevator of the JPMorgan Chase Tower to the **Sky Lobby** (Map p193; ☎ 713-223-0441; 600 Travis St; admission free;

HOUSTON & EAST TEXAS

(🕑 9am-5pm Mon-Fri). Barring smog, you can see for 20 miles – which is only a fraction of this massive city.

SAM HOUSTON PARK

The **Heritage Society** (Map p193; ☎ 713-655-1912; www.heritagesociety.org; 1100 Bagby St; museum free, hourly tours adult/child/senior $10/free/8; 🕑 10am-4pm Tue-Sat, 1-4pm Sun) has relocated several of Houston's most historic buildings to the oldest **park** in town (amid the roar of traffic, naturally). Among them, check out the **Yates House** (1870), the home of a freed slave who became a prominent black preacher, and the **Old Place** (1823), a log cabin rumored to be the oldest structure in town. A somewhat hidden free parking lot sits off Clay St west of Bagby St.

DISCOVERY GREEN

Houston's latest and greatest downtown **park** (Map p193; www.discoverygreen.com; 1500 McKinney St; 🏄) is a legitimately cool, Leadership in Energy and Environmental Design (LEED)–certified attraction for all ages. What looks bizarre from a distance – a vast swath of grass raked on a steep diagonal over a parking lot – is impressive from within, with oak-shaded walkways, sculptures, gardens blooming with native Texas plants, and a small lake which transforms into a skating rink (p201) in winter. There are plenty of diversions for kids yet adults won't feel left out: there's even a swanky restaurant, Grove (p204).

Midtown

For gentrification in action, hurry up and come to diverse Midtown. Think soul food, yogurt shops, condos, dog walkers and a distinctly chilled-out urban buzz. More urban than Montrose, more personable than downtown, and to some, cooler than both. A successful example of the live/work pedestrian neighborhoods springing up around the country, Midtown is the place to glimpse the most hopeful version of Houston's future. Head to West Gray and Baldwin Sts to find the newest epicenter of the action.

Museum District

Museum-lovers, you've hit the jackpot in Houston, and the high-stakes action is hottest in the aptly named Museum District. As one of the most extensive arts districts in the country, this area seethes with big art, big money, and big trees overhanging the streets. You'll find the major museums north and northeast of Hermann Park; to plan your route, pick up a copy of the essential *Houston Museum District* guide, available at the visitor bureau and some museums.

For a peek at where the city's legendary 'oil money' lay their heads, wander the streets: some of city's grandest old homes are sheltered in the deep shade of the draping Spanish moss. Free parking lies off the main streets, so ditch the car and museum-hop on foot.

MUSEUM OF FINE ARTS, HOUSTON

French impressionism and post-1945 European and American painting shine in this nationally renowned **palace of art** (Map p196; ☎ 713-639-7300; www.mfah.org; 1001 Bissonnet St; adult/child $7/3.50, Thu free; 🕑 10am-5pm Tue & Wed, 10am-9pm Thu, 10am-7pm Fri & Sat, 12:15-7pm Sun), which includes major works by Picasso and Rembrandt. Check out its Latin American and Photography collections, two strong areas often overlooked by institutions of this size. Across the street, admire the talents of luminaries such as Rodin and Matisse in the tranquil **Cullen Sculpture Garden** (Map p196; cnr Montrose Blvd & Bissonnet St; admission free; 🕑 dawn-dusk).

HOUSTON MUSEUM OF NATURAL SCIENCE

The tactile pleasures of this **museum** (Map p196; ☎ 713-639-4629; www.hmns.org; 1 Hermann Circle; adult/child/senior $15/10/10; 🕑 9am-5pm Mon-Sat, 11am-5pm Sun) entertain the kids; the educational and aesthetic experiences woo the adults. If you're over 16 and you find yourself thinking, 'Science museums are actually sorta cool!' you're not alone. Full-grown adults have been known to audibly ooh and aah their way from the giant diplodocus skeleton to the Gemstones and Minerals Hall. In fact, ogling precious gems in their natural (a giant aquamarine) and man-made (an exiled Russian princess's diamond tiara) forms while Ella Fitzgerald tunes are piped into the cool dark has got to be one of Houston's most thrilling secret pleasures.

CONTEMPORARY ARTS MUSEUM

An hour spent fully immersing yourself in the works of just one or two artists is one of the chief satisfactions of this modern **museum** (Map p196; ☎ 713-284-8250; www.camh.org; 5216 Montrose Blvd; admission free; 🕑 10am-5pm Tue-Sat, to 9pm Thu, noon-5pm Sun), whose strength lies in its lack of permanent collection. Check what's on the schedule: this is one of Houston's epicenters of cool, new and seriously cutting edge.

HOLOCAUST MUSEUM HOUSTON

This superbly curated **museum** (Map p196; ☎ 713-942-8000; www.hmh.org; 5401 Caroline St; admission free, suggested donation $5; ☙ 9am-5pm Mon-Fri, noon-5pm Sat & Sun, until 8pm 1st Thu of month) strikes the delicate balance of providing a sobering yet poignant homage to the casualties of the 20th century's greatest tragedy. The permanent exhibit offers an in-depth education on the context, history and aftermaths of not only the Holocaust itself but of Nazi Germany's terrifying rise to power. Other exhibits trace the lives of European Jews from before WWII through the post-Nazi era, as survivors tried to rebuild their lives.

Rice Village

Shopping for the smart set? Several square blocks with more than 300 (many unique) shops and nightspots sit west of **Rice University** (Map p196; ☎ 713-348-0000; www.rice.edu; 6100 Main St). The impressive campus, west of Hermann Park, makes for a lovely stroll. Take a break at the mod **Pavilion Coffeehouse** (Map p196; ☎ 713-348-2279; www.dining.rice.edu; ☙ 8am-6pm Mon-Fri, from 9am Sat & Sun), in the Central Quad, behind Fondren Library, where budding philosophers and rocket scientists hunker down over their laptops.

One of the few parts of town best explored on foot, the **'Village'** (www.ricevillageonline.com; cnr University Blvd & Kirby Dr) buzzes with a hip student energy. There's free two-hour parking. The surrounding homes (how much do these Rice professors make, anyway?) run the gamut from gorgeous to stunning, and the locals aren't too shabby either.

Montrose

Sure, Houston's museums kick ass, but museums alone do not a hip city make. Yet deep in the heart of town, the Montrose neighborhood has long been holding the torch of Houston cool. Recently named one of the top-10 greatest neighborhoods in the USA by the American Planning Association, Montrose simply rocks. Full of tattooed lawyers and artists by day, and drag queens by night, Montrose has long welcomed the beautiful and the damned to its superfunky mix of shops, bars, restaurants and galleries. Centered at the intersection of Montrose Blvd and Westheimer Rd, it's nicknamed 'the Gayborhood' – and while it's the heartbeat of Houston's thriving gay scene, everyone is invited to the party.

Criticize Houston all you want for its lack of city planning – the way that the Montrose area museums are tucked away in the heart of this eclectic urban neighborhood is pure genius. Stroll from modern art to meditation chapel, all under the canopy of blessedly shady trees.

MENIL COLLECTION

Abstract- and modern-art haters, be warned: we dare you to hate this **museum** (Map p196; ☎ 713-525-9400; www.menil.org; 1515 Sul Ross St; admission free; ☙ 11am-7pm Wed-Sun). Local philanthropists John and Dominique de Menil's massive private collection form the core of this adventurous whirl through the medieval to the surreal, with whole rooms devoted to mind-bending René Magritte and Max Ernst. The **park** adjacent to the Menil is great for picnicking, frolicking, and debating the

HOUSTON & EAST TEXAS

AND NOW FOR SOMETHING COMPLETELY DIFFERENT

Beer-can houses, art cars, giant welded-steel oranges and plastic flower art? Conservative Houston has a wacky creative streak, especially when it comes to its quirkiest museums. A maze-like junk-art tribute to one man's favorite citrus fruit, the **Orange Show Center for Visionary Art** (off Map p196; ☎ 713-926-6368; www.orangeshow.org; 2402 Munger St; admission $1; ☙ noon-5pm Sat & Sun) is a madcap experience. The center fosters the folk-art vision by offering children's art education and keeping up the 50,000-strong **Beer Can House** (off Map p196; ☎ 713-880-2008; www.beercanhouse.org; 222 Malone St; grounds admission $2, guided tour $5; ☙ noon-5pm Sat & Sun), off Memorial Dr.

If you're not in town for the fabulous Art Car Parade & Festival (p201) in May, the next best thing is to view the amazingly decorated vehicles at the warehouselike **Art Car Museum** (off Map p196; ☎ 713-861-5526; www.artcarmuseum.com; 140 Heights Blvd; admission free; ☙ 11am-6pm Wed-Sun). It contains more than 15 vehicles that have been tricked out into psychedelic and Mad Max–esque wonders.

merits of that surrealist painting you didn't understand.

Love it or loathe it: the adjacent **Cy Twombly Gallery** (Map p196; ☎ 713-525-9450; 1501 Branard St; admission free; ☽ 11am-7pm Wed-Sun) annex contains seriously abstract art. Some call it pretentious, some call it crazy, some call it beautiful: you can't walk out without an opinion one way or another, and isn't that the point of art in the first place?

ROTHKO CHAPEL
A temple of contemplation, a really empty yoga studio, a church or a nuclear bunker? All places you might pray, and at first glance it could be any of the above. The point is, the one and only **Rothko Chapel** (Map p196; ☎ 713-524-9839; www.rothkochapel.org; 1409 Sul Ross St; admission free; ☽ 10am-6pm) is whatever you want it to be. With 14 large paintings by American abstract expressionist Mark Rothko, it's a perfect place to sit and do something radical: just be.

BYZANTINE FRESCO MUSEUM
This **museum** (Map p196; ☎ 713-521-3990; 4011 Yupon Dr; admission free; ☽ 11am-6pm Fri-Sun) contains stunning 13th-century frescoes that came to Houston from their home in Cyprus early in the 20th century in a manner not unlike the travels of the Maltese Falcon. A tiny museum with an evocative spiritual energy, it packs a visceral punch.

MUSEUM OF PRINTING HISTORY
This carefully curated **museum** (Map p196; ☎ 713-522-4652; www.printingmuseum.org; 1324 W Clay St; adult/child $4/2, Thu free; ☽ 10am-5pm Tue-Sun) is an often-missed gem that has rare and unusual printed works such as the *Dharani Scroll*, which dates from AD 764 and is one of the oldest printed works in existence. The vast collection of daily papers printed on historical dates – the *Titanic* disaster, JFK's assassination and the invasion of Pearl Harbor – are as poignant as they are historically fascinating.

Houston Heights
Some say it's a mini-Austin, some say it's too cool for school, but whatever your impression, this neighborhood north of River Oaks is indisputably of one the oldest – and may we say, one of the best lookin' – in Houston. Take a stroll or a drive down **Heights Boulevard** to see the fine Arts and Crafts homes shaded by old oaks, then wind up on eclectic 19th and Yale Sts for some shopping. Overlooking the **Buffalo Bayou**, it's an enjoyable neighborhood to cycle around.

River Oaks
Home to many lovely trees, and a few Bushes, too – heck, you might even spot Dick Cheney. An exclusive enclave 3 miles from downtown, River Oaks in Houston is codeword for 'old money,' but (almost) no one means it in a nasty way. Anyway, the money's not all that old – it just means people made it in oil instead of dot-com. Along Gray St and Kirby Dr there are shops and restaurants galore.

Uptown/Post Oak
Grab your platinum card, and leave your frugality back at the hotel, *dahling:* the Post Oak (also known as Uptown) area was made to max out a credit card. As the largest mall in Texas, the **Galleria** (off Map p196; ☎ 713-622-0663; www.simon.com; 5075 Westheimer Rd) anchors this upscale extravaganza of a neighborhood. Whatever your views on capitalism, it's a madcap place to experience true American consumer excess in all of its dubious glory. Think chain hotels, chain restaurants and chain stores: in other words, it's the perfect place to wake up in a Hilton and throw on your Abercrombie jeans that seem tight after last night's indulgences at the Cheesecake Factory.

ACTIVITIES
A **stroll** or a **run** through expansive Memorial Park or **Hermann Park** (Map p196; ☎ 713-845-1000; www.hermannpark.org; 600 Fannin St; ♿) might give you that dose of green and air that at least *feels* fresh, even if pollution dictates it's not. Sun phobics seeking maximum shade should head out to Main St where it runs past Rice University (p194). The huge oak trees form a welcome canopy over the sidewalks. One caveat – school officials warn incoming Rice freshers that due to traffic emissions, running this loop during rush hour is the equivalent of smoking a pack of cigarettes.

Though cycling during traffic in much of Houston can be a down-and-out death wish, Houston has several parks that are ideal for **cycling**. Hit the trails at Memorial and Hermann Parks or cruise along the bayous. Need a rental? Try **Planetary Cycles** (Map p196; ☎ 713-668-2300; www.planetarycycles.com; 4004 S Braeswood Blvd; bicycle rental per day/week $25/150; ☽ 10am-7pm Mon-Fri, 10am-6pm Sat).

HOUSTON FOR CHILDREN

Young 'uns gettin' restless? Since mid-2008, there's been a new place to play – right downtown at **Discovery Green** (Map p193; www. discoverygreen.com; 1500 McKinney St; 🚼). Think playgrounds, play fountains, art and a kid-friendly restaurant.

In the museum district, **Hermann Park** (Map p196; ☎ 713-845-1000; www.hermannpark.org; 600 Fannin St; 🚼) is home to playgrounds, a lake with paddleboats, the **Hermann Park Miniature Train** (Map p196; ☎ 713-529-5216; per ride $3; 🕑 10am-5:30pm, until 6pm Sat & Sun; 🚼) and 4500 animals at the tropical, 55-acre **Houston Zoo** (Map p196; ☎ 713-533-6500; www.houstonzoo.org; 6200 Hermann Park Dr; adult/child $11/7; 🕑 9am-6pm, to 7pm Mar-Nov; 🚼).

Walking distance from the park you'll find the high-octane, stupendously fun **Children's Museum of Houston** (Map p196; ☎ 713-522-1138; www. cmhouston.org; 1500 Binz St; admission $7; 🕑 9am-5pm Tue-Sat, to 8pm Thu, noon-5pm Sun; 🚼), where little ones can make tortillas in a Mexican village, or draw in an open-air art studio. A few blocks away, future brain surgeons will like checking out the huge organs on display in the interactive **Health Museum** (Map p196; ☎ 713-521-1515; www.mhms.org; 1515 Hermann Dr; adult/senior/child $8/6/6; 🕑 9am-5pm Mon-Sat, noon-5pm Sun).

See also Tours (p201) for other ways to keep the little ones entertained.

TOURS

Discover Houston Tours (☎ 713-222-9255; www. discoverhoustontours.com) Eclectic tours include a tour of Houston's tunnel system, a barbecue-lovers tour and a ghost-walk pub crawl.

Houston Culinary Tours (☎ 281-444-8636; www. www.visithoustontexas.com/culinarytours) Foodie

---

WHAT THE...? ICE-SKATING?

Outdoor **ice-skating** in Houston? Surely a joke. Nope, downtown's Discovery Green (p198) isn't messing with you: skate from Thanksgiving through Martin Luther King day on the park's **Kinder Lake** (Map p193; ☎ 713-434-7465; 1500 McKinney St; admission incl skate rental $10; 🕑 hours vary; 🚼). In summertime, cool off on the Galleria mall's **skating rink** (off Map p196; ☎ 713-621-1500; 5015 Westheimer Rd; admission $8, skate rental $3.50; 🕑 10am-5pm & 8-10pm Mon-Thu, 10am-10pm Fri, 12:30-10pm Sat, 1-7pm Sun; 🚼). Just don't try to window-shop during that triple axel.

---

adventures feature chef tours, secret ethnic eateries and plenty of noshing.

Sam Houston Boat Tours (☎ 713-670-2416; www.port ofhouston.com) Free 90-minute tours of one of the largest ports in the USA; call ahead to reserve 24 hours in advance.

Segway Tours of Houston (☎ 713-522-1200; segway toursofhouston.com) Zip around H-town with a bunch of other brave souls who aren't afraid to geek out on these futuristic contraptions.

St Arnold Brewery (off Map p193; ☎ 713-686-9494; www.saintarnold.com; 2000 Lyons Ave; tours $7; 🕑 3-3:30 Mon-Fri, 11am-2pm Sat) Texas' oldest craft brewery offers fun group tours followed by tastings of Texas-only microbrews in the beer garden.

FESTIVALS & EVENTS

Houston likes to party, heat or no heat.

Spring

Houston Livestock Show & Rodeo (☎ 832-667-1000; www.rodeohouston.com) Yee-haw! In March, step right into Texas culture at one of the world's largest rodeo and cattle shows.

Azalea Trail (☎ 713-523-2483; www.riveroaks gardenclub.org) Six or more historic homes and gardens are opened for tours in March during this popular event, organized by the River Oaks Garden Club and named for the flowering shrubs in bloom at each location at this time of year.

Houston International Festival (☎ 713-654-8808; www.ifest.org). This multicultural celebration of food, art and music lights up the city in April. Events include WorldFest and the Houston International Film Festival (☎ 713-965-9955; www.worldfest.org).

Art Car Parade & Festival (☎ 713-926-6368; www. orangeshow.org; Allen Parkway) Wacky arted-out automobiles roll on by on the second Sunday in May.

Bayou City Art Festival (☎ 713-521-0133; www. bayoucityartfestival.com) Hundreds of artists sell their wares, and there's a festive array of musicians and food. This popular biannual festival takes places in Memorial Park each spring, and downtown each fall.

Summer

Juneteenth (☎ 832-429-4432; www.houstonculture. org/juneteenth) This celebration of African American culture, with plenty of gospel, jazz and blues, occurs around June 19 – the day in 1865 when word reached Texas that slaves had been emancipated.

Houston Shakespeare Festival (☎ 713-926-2277; www. houstonfestivalscompany.org) Star-crossed lovers and mistaken identities under the stars at the Miller Outdoor Theatre (100 Concert Dr) for two weeks beginning in late July. Reserve free tickets online to get a seat, or picnic on the lawn.

Fall
Fiestas Patrias (☎ 713-926-2636) This September 16 festival features a parade, ball and music in celebration of Mexican Independence Day.

Thanksgiving Day Parade (☎ 713-654-8808; www. heb.com) Why go to New York for Macy's version when Houston has one of its own?

SLEEPING
Funky to no frills to five star: Houston sleeps around. Find oodles of chains in nondescript neighborhoods along the freeways, especially near the airports and the Galleria.

Budget
Houston Central KOA (Map p190; ☎ 281-442-3700, 800-562-2132; www.koa.com; 1620 Peach Leaf; tent/RV sites $20/$36; ☎ ☎) This pleasant, wooded campground is 12 miles north of downtown, close to George Bush Intercontinental airport. Facilities include a store, laundry and playground.

Houston International Hostel (Map p196; ☎ 713-523-1009; www.houstonhostel.com; 5302 Crawford St; dm/r $18/23; ☒ ℗ 🖳 ☎) An easy walk to Houston's major museums and light rail makes this a steal. A mix of semipermanent residents and backpackers; friendly, eccentric staff; and worn '70s furnishings lend a hippie tour-bus feel, though it's clean and safe.

Midrange
Club Quarters (Map p193; ☎ 713-224-6400; www.clubquarters.com; 720 Fannin St; s/d from $69/89; ☒ 🖳 ☎) Business rooms at a bargain price (when club members don't fill them).

Sara's Bed & Breakfast Inn (Map p196; ☎ 713-868-1130; www.saras.com; 941 Heights Blvd; r incl breakfast $95-195; ☒ ℗ 🖳 ☎) This Queen Anne mansion in the heart of the happenin' Heights has 11 airy rooms furnished with antiques, and the kind of sprawling Southern porch that makes you want to gossip over mint juleps.

Lovett Inn (Map p196; ☎ 713-522-5224; www.lovettinn.com; 501 Lovett Blvd; r $99-160; ☒ 🖳 ☎ ☎) This classic Montrose inn set on landscaped grounds is popular with couples of all persuasions. We like the book-filled library and the tranquil pool.

our pick Modern B&B (Map p196; ☎ 832-279-6367; www.modernbb.com; 4003 Hazard St; r incl breakfast $100-200; ☒ ℗ 🖳 ☎) Close to the Menil, the solar-powered Modern is rock-star cool without the rock-star attitude. An architect's dream, the multistoried mod building is rife with

airy decks, spiral staircases and sunlight. Slate showers, in-room Jacuzzi tubs, private decks and iPod docking stations, sure – but the real draw here is the cool guests from all over the world. Unwind with them at the informal happy hour, or at breakfast over a fresh herb omelet at the sunny dining room. Families will dig the suite with adjoining rooms.

Alden Hotel (Map p193; ☎ 832-200-8800; www.aldenhotels.com; 1117 Prairie St; r $103-169, ste from $269; ☒ ℗ 🖳 ☎) This downtown boutique hotel pulls off a vibe that's sleek yet low-key. Aveda bath products, granite showers, and an all-grey color scheme in the rooms keep things cool – if a little too vanilla.

Lancaster Hotel (Map p193; ☎ 713-228-9500; www.lancasterhotel.com; 701 Texas Ave; r $119-199; ☒ 🖳 ☎) The European clientele, original marble and old-fashioned keys make this gracious hotel feel more London-esque than Houston-ish, except for the prices. Say cheers over a gimlet in the cozy Lancaster Bistro, where the old-school bartenders preside over the chatty post-theater scene.

Indigo Hotel (off Map p196; ☎ 713-621-8988; 5160 Hidalgo St; r $125-190, ste $219; ℗ 🖳 ☎ ♿) With a location convenient to the Galleria, the Indigo pulls off a relaxing seaside hotel vibe with fresh spring colors, soothing sounds of nature, and comfy rooms. Every season, the hotel changes its decor and signature scent, making it a cool place to refresh and recharge in the big hot city.

Magnolia Hotel (Map p193; ☎ 713-221-0011; www.magnoliahotelhouston.com; 1100 Texas Ave; r $125-225; ℗ 🖳 ☎ ☎) Dressed in deep woods and modern neutrals, rooms at this downtown hotel are both stylish *and* comfortable. Don't miss the free happy hour from 5pm until 7pm.

Hotel Icon (Map p193; ☎ 713-224-4266; www.hotelicon.com; 220 Main St; r $129-270; ☒ ℗ 🖳 ☎) The pleasures of this hotel begin in the to-die-for red and gold lobby, with its c-1911 bank vault reception desk and soaring, multichandeliered ceilings. With a lobby this fantastic, we expect a lot from the rooms, and they deliver.

Top End
Hotel Derek (off Map p196; ☎ 713-961-3000; www.hotelderek.com; 2525 West Loop S; s $139, d $179-199; 🖳 ☎ ☎) After shopping at the Galleria, you can lay your head fashionably thanks to a two-million-dollar 2009 Hotel Derek renovation. Frequent guests Faith Hill and Tim McGraw seem to like it.

HOUSTON & EAST TEXAS

AIRPORT HOTELS

Late arrival or early departure? Skip the hassle and stay by the airport for a night. Convenience guaranteed; charm optional.

Days Inn & Suites Houston Hobby (Map p190; ☎ 713-944-3004; www.daysinn.com; 9114 Airport Blvd; r $69-145; ✕ P ☎ ⊜ ⊛) Right near Hobby Airport, this new inexpensive property offers a free airport shuttle, breakfast and a fitness center.

Houston Airport Marriott (Map p190; ☎ 281-443-2310; www.marriott.com; 18700 JFK Blvd; rooms $149-249; ✕ P ⊟ ⊜ ⊛) This place couldn't be closer to George Bush Intercontinental Airport because it's *in* George Bush Intercontinental airport. Splash in the outdoor pool while jets roar above.

---

ourpick **Hotel ZaZa** (Map p196; ☎ 713-526-1991; www.hotelzazahouston.com; 5701 Main St; r $205-270; ✕ P ⊟ ⊜ ⊛) Strike a pose at this flamboyantly hip Museum District hotel, close to the light-rail stop. Don't be scared by the attractive staff who glide around in chic black outfits: they actually want to please you. Occupying a prime spot overlooking Hermann Park, the ZaZa is an edgy antidote to a world of chain hotels: the over-the-top themed suites, the Vegas-style poolside bar, and the wink-wink sexy rooms that bring to life your inner Hollywood starlet.

La Colombe d'Or Hotel (Map p196; ☎ 713-524-7999; www.lacolombedor.com; 3410 Montrose Blvd; r $295-525; ✕ P ⊜) Sotheby's-quality antiques and rare oil paintings fill six opulent suites (with dining rooms, no less) in a 1923 Montrose mansion. You might be two blocks south of Westheimer, but you'll feel like you're in a mansion on Paris' right bank. We like the racy Renoir suite, which will delight your inner libertine with its opium-den feel. The restaurant wins praise for its French classics such as rack of baby lamb and red snapper with lump crab.

EATING

Houston's restaurant scene is smokin' hot – and we don't just mean the salsa. In fact, Houstonians eat out more than residents of any other US city, and the *New York Times* recently called the foodie scene 'world class.' To keep abreast of what's hot and what's not, search online reviews and local food blogs. Of course, nothing beats the *Zagat Survey* (www.zagat.com) or our new fave, the razor-tongued *Fearless Critic* (www.fearlesscritic.com).

The new foodies on the block are Midtown and Washington Avenue, where joints serving everything from the humble to the high falutin' are attracting major buzz. And don't

forget the king of expense-account meals – steak. It's a bloody big deal in Houston, and most of the heavy hitters are downtown or on Westheimer Rd near the Galleria. Mexican food is ubiquitous no matter the 'hood. And despite the near-obsession with meat in Texas, remember that Houston is an ultramodern, diverse city with plenty of options for – gasp! – vegetarians.

Downtown
BUDGET

Les Givral's (Map p193; ☎ 713-547-0444; 801 Congress St; meals $3-8; ⊙ 9am-6pm Mon-Thu, until 10pm Fri & Sat) Banh mi oh my! Food bloggers and downtown office workers are going crazy for this sleek but cheap spot. They keep it simple and sweet – *pho*, a smattering of rice and meat dishes, and the to-die-for Vietnamese sammies worth braving traffic for.

Hubcap Grill (Map p193; ☎ 713-223-5885; 1111 Prairie St; mains $4-8; ⊙ lunch Mon-Sat) With a burger named 'Quadruple Heart Clogger' and double-fried fries, you might want to invite your cardiologist to dine here. Everything's homemade, from the fresh-baked buns to the hand-cut fries. Sit at an outdoor table and heckle the office workers carrying their pitifully healthy takeout salads back to work.

Zydeco Louisiana Diner (Map p193; ☎ 713-759-2001; 1119 Pease St; meals $6-9; ⊙ lunch Mon-Sat) If you see people dancing in the street, it's because this place is having one of its frequent after-work crawfish boils, complete with live zydeco music. By day, dive into authentic Louisiana classics such as oyster po'boys, jambalaya and étouffée. Great lemonade, too.

ourpick **Treebeards** (Map p193; ☎ 713-337-7321; 315 Travis St; sandwiches $7-19, mains $6-9; ⊙ lunch Mon-Fri) Since 1978, locals have flocked at lunchtime to chow down on Southern favorites such as jerk chicken, cheese grits and seafood gumbo.

MIDRANGE & TOP END
Kim Son (Map p193; ☎ 713-222-2461; 2001 Jefferson St; lunch specials $6-10, mains $10-18; ☺ 11am-11pm) Nationally renowned and a local legend for more than a quarter century, this restaurant has a dramatic past: its original location was in Vietnam before the owners fled Communist rule. The 280-item menu is a daunting thrill.

Grove (Map p193; ☎ 713-337-7321; 1611 Lamar St; sandwiches $7-19, mains $12-32; ☺ 11am-10pm) Free-range chicken potpie, pork belly sliders...the American classics get a modern metropolitan update at Discovery Green's Grove.

Hearsay (Map p193; ☎ 713-225-8079; 218 Travis St; mains $11-24, prix fixe $35-55; ☺ 11am-midnight Mon-Thu, until 2am Fri & Sat, 11am-6pm Sun) A sexy gastro-lounge where the cocktails (pomegranate gimlet, seasonal fruit mojito) taste as good (or better) as the playful food (mahimahi tacos, raspberry crème brûlée).

Midtown
Long known for its great soul food, a spanking new stretch of high-end condos on Gray St now anchors the west end of this urban hot spot, and diverse new restaurants and bars are rushing in.

BUDGET
Sweet Lola Yogurt Bar Map p196; ☎ 713-521-3222; 304 Gray St; average yogurt $4; ☺ noon-9pm Tue-Sat, 2-9pm Sun) With its comfy-chic vibe and yogurt flavors such as ginger agave and lavender, family-owned Sweet Lola is the antidote to the antiseptic Pinkberrys of the world. The topping bar seduces first-timers with peanut-butter sea-salt croutons and dark-chocolate pomegranate.

Breakfast Klub (Map p196; ☎ 713-528-8561; 3711 Travis St; mains $4-10; ☺ 7am-2pm Mon-Fri, 8am-2pm Sat) Weekends, you'll find everyone and their mother (or at least hometown girl Beyoncé and Jay-Z) lining up around the block for down-home wings 'n' waffles. When the hostess asks how you're doing today, she's really asking, so smile.

MIDRANGE & TOP END
This Is It (Map p196; ☎ 713-659-1608; 207 Gray St; meals $10-12; ☺ 11am-8pm Mon-Fri, 11am-6pm Sun) If James Brown is the 'Godfather of Soul,' then This Is It must be the godfather of Houston soul food. In fact they've been slinging the good stuff cafeteria-style since before Brown released his first album (1959). What else do you need to

know? Real Southern food cooked with heart. You'll feel good. (We knew that you would.)

Reef (Map p196; ☎ 713-526-8282; 2600 Travis St; lunch $11-19, dinner $19-29; ☺ 11am-10pm Mon-Fri, 5-11pm Sat) Gulf Coast seafood is served in a sleek and sophisticated dining room with a skyline-view raw bar. The chef has won oodles of awards.

ourpick T'afia (Map p196; ☎ 713-524-6922; 3701 Travis St; mains $15-22; ☺ 5:30-10pm Tue-Thu, to 10:30pm Fri & Sat; V) Nationally renowned chef Monica Pope brings top-quality local and organic ingredients to life in her new American cuisine. Come for the fun farmers-market Saturday mornings, or for Houston's best foodie happy hour: choose two fantabulous appetizers for every equally sublime cocktail you order.

Museum District & Rice Village
BUDGET
Croissant Brioche French Bakery Café (Map p196; ☎ 713-526-9188; 2435 Rice Blvd; meals $4-7; ☺ 7am-7pm, until 5pm Sun) Munch on a perfect éclair or an asparagus quiche at the communal table and soak up the *trés magnifique* atmosphere of this casual hangout, rife with Rice intellectuals and brioche addicts scoring a fix.

Istanbul Café & Market (Map p196; ☎ 713-526-2800; 5613 Morningside Dr; meals $6-11; ☺ 11am-10pm) Simple, satisfying Middle Eastern fare in a fun, casual atmosphere. The patio bustles on week-nights with families, casual dates, and medical students conspicuously still in their scrubs, all munching doner kabobs and tabouli. Ask for a glass of dry Turkish white wine ($7.50) – it's not on the menu.

Tart Café (Map p196; ☎ 713-526-8278; 4411 Montrose Blvd; meals $10; ☺ 11am-5pm Mon-Sat) Savory and sweet. No, we're not talking about that hot curator sitting next to you, we're talking about the tarts on offer for lunch. Corn poblano, chicken pesto and lime margarita varieties should sate your inner pastry libertine.

MIDRANGE & TOP END
Café Rabelais (Map p196; ☎ 713-520-8841; 2442 Times Blvd; sandwiches $8-10, mains $14-28; ☺ lunch Tue-Sat, dinner Mon-Sat) *Excusez-moi?* A French restaurant in Texas that actual French people say is authentic? Praised for its mussels, steak and classic desserts, this cafe knows that beauty lies in simplicity.

Bombay Brasserie (Map p196; ☎ 713-355-2000; 2414 University Blvd; lunch buffet $12.95, dinner $10-16; ☺ lunch

TACO HERE, TACO THERE, TACO EVERYWHERE

Craving Tex-Mex? Or just Mexican? Or maybe interior Mexican... Exhausted yet? Seriously, trying to navigate the myriad Mexican dining options in Houston is not for the faint of heart.

Classic Houston Tex-Mex

Don't be fooled by the countless imitations: **Original Ninfas** (off Map p193; ☎ 713-228-1175; 2704 Navigation Blvd; meals $10-20; ☺ lunch & dinner; ♿) is the one and only original, where generations of Houstonians have been coming since the 1970s for 'shrimp diablo', *tacos al carbon* (tacos cooked over charcoal), and handmade tamales all crafted with a dash of hometown pride.

Most Fun Mexican

Easy: it's Tex-Mex **Chuy's** (Map p196; ☎ 713-524-1700; 2706 Westheimer Rd; mains $7-12 ☺ 11am-10:30pm Sun-Thu, to 11pm Fri & Sat; ♿) What's not fun about burritos 'as big as yo' face,' a shrine to Elvis and a party atmosphere that's kid-friendly?

Best Interior Mexican

Chef Hugo Ortega gets raves for his inspired interior-Mexican regional cuisine at **Hugo's** (Map p196; ☎ 713-524-7744; 1600 Westheimer Rd; lunch $12-22, dinner $16-32; ☺ 11am-10pm Sun-Thu, to 11pm Fri & Sat).

Best Breakfast Taco

On a highly personal subject, many locals are willing to lay down their reputation on **Tacos A Go Go** (Map p196; ☎ 713-807-8226; 3704 Main St; breakfast tacos, $1.75; ☺ 7am-10pm Mon-Fri, to 2am Fri & Sat, 9am-3pm Sun).

Best Mod Mex

We're huge fans of sleek **Taco Milagro** (Map p196; ☎ 713-522-1999; 2555 Kirby Dr, River Oaks; mains $6-9; ☺ 11am-10pm Sun-Tue, to 11pm Wed, to 1am Thu, to midnight Fri & Sat; ⓥ) with its fresh ingredients, bountiful salsa bar, live music and gurgling fountain.

Best Late-Night Mexican

Sating 2am enchilada and Michelada cravings, **Chapultepec Lupita** (Map p196; ☎ 713-522-2365; 813 Richmond Ave; mains $5-10; ☺ 24hr), the-24 hour dive offers a staggering menu of margaritas. A great place to end the party – of course, the party here really never ends.

& dinner) Expertly crafted classic Indian at good prices for a white-tablecloth affair.

Benjy's (brunch/lunch $11-17, dinner $12-25); Rice Village (Map p196; ☎ 713-522-7602; 2424 Dunstan Rd; ☺ 11am-9pm Sun & Mon, until 10pm Tue-Thu, until 11pm Fri & Sat); West End (off Map p196; ☎ 713-868-1131; 5922 Washington Ave; ☺ 11am-3pm Sun-Fri, dinner daily) At the stylish Sunday brunch, happily munch away on the nut-crusted challah French toast ($10.95), while a luxe happy hour lets you try blood-orange margaritas, butternut-squash crepes, and pistachio-crusted goat's cheese at half the price.

Upper Kirby

Hobbit Hole Cafe (Map p196; ☎ 713-581-8483; 2243 Richmond Ave; meals $7-12; ☺ 11am-9:30pm Mon-Fri, until 10:30pm Sat, 10:30am-9pm Sun; ♿ ⓥ) You don't have to be a *Lord of the Rings* fan to geek out over this adorable woodsy hideaway with enticing veggie options. What would Frodo order? Probably the Gandalf sandwich or the curry chicken salad, guaranteed to fortify against orc attacks.

Blue Fish House (Map p196; ☎ 713-529-3100; 2241 Richmond Ave; sushi combos $7-13; ☺ lunch & dinner Mon-Sat) Fresh, well-priced sushi in an intimate environment that's a nice change of pace from all of those upscale trying-too-hard sushi joints that seem to double as minimalist techno nightclubs filled with wannabe models.

Goode Co BBQ (Map p196; ☎ 713-522-2530; 5109 Kirby Dr; meat plates $8-11; ☺ 11am-10pm) Belly up to piles of beef brisket, Czech sausage, smoked duck and gallon ice teas in a big ol' barn or out back on picnic tables at this local institution.

HOUSTON & EAST TEXAS

Montrose & Houston Heights

BUDGET

Lankford's Cafe (Map p196; ☎ 713-522-9555; 88 Dennis St; lunch $4-9; ☺ 7am-3pm Mon-Sat) A Montrose institution that has outlasted hippies, disco and grunge, and was classic before classic was cool. The burgers, topped with whimsical ingredients such as fried eggs and mac 'n' cheese, have been rated among the 100 best in the USA. Cash only.

Empire Café (Map p196; ☎ 713-528-5282; 1732 Westheimer Rd; lunch $6-14; ☺ 7:30am-10pm, to 11pm Fri & Sat; ♿ Ⓥ) A classic fixture of the Montrose neighborhood and one of the best all-day breakfasts in town, the Empire's a jack of all trades that manages to excel at everything: coffee, lunch, evening cocktails… We like to sit on the shady patio with a slice of luscious lemon poppy cake – or maybe the Chocolate Blackout. With half-price cake night on Monday, why not order both?

Ziggy's Healthy Grill (Map p196; ☎ 832-519-0476; 302 Fairview St; meals $6-14; ☺ 9am-10pm Mon-Fri, 8am-10pm Sat, 8am-9pm Sun; Ⓥ) In a cozy old house with a twinkling outdoor patio, Ziggy's succeeds with that elusive oxymoron, healthy comfort food. (Think spicy garlic turkey burgers so tasty that they may woo vegetarians to the, um, dark side.) Hell, we'd eat this stuff even if it *weren't* healthy. Delish breakfasts, too.

Pie in the Sky Pie Company (off Map p196; ☎ 713-864-3301; 631 W 19th St; meals $7-9; ☺ 7am-10pm; ♿) The magic words are: bumbleberry, Mississipi Mud, lemon cream. For the guilt-prone, the strawberry spinach salad and savory pies justify the trip to this sweet Heights cafe.

ourpick Brasil (Map p196; ☎ 713-528-1993; 2604 Dunlavy St; meals $7-12; ☺ 7:30am-midnight; Ⓥ) Fresh soups, such as sweet potato and fresh thyme, paired with salads and pizzas. Decadent cheesecakes and nightly drink specials. Oh Brasil, what *don't* you offer? Retreat to the shaded back patio for an artsy scene full of writers, professors, and bright-eyed dilettantes engrossed in their laptops, cigarettes, and red wine. Watch for offbeat movies that screen most evenings.

MIDRANGE

Baba Yega (Map p196; ☎ 713-522-0042; 2607 Grant St; meals $8-16; ☺ 11am-9:30pm Mon-Thu, until 10:30pm Fri & Sat, 10am-9pm Sun; Ⓥ) Grilled salmon and fruit blintzes overflow the Sunday buffet brunch (a bargain at $18.95) in this pretty garden bungalow cafe that's named after a witchy

character in Slavic folklore. Plenty of TLC for vegetarians – such as a veggie meatloaf with garlic mashed potatoes – balanced with good burgers and homemade peanut-butter pie mean that all appetites will happily co-exist here.

Dolce Vita (Map p196; ☎ 713-520-8222; 500 Westheimer Rd; lunch $14-19, dinner mains $18-28; ☺ 11am-10pm Sun-Thu, to 11pm Fri & Sat) The thin-crust pizza in this convivial two-story house is very good, and loyal fans sing its praises in even more superlative terms. Try the Taleggio (taleggio cheese, pears, arugula, truffle oil) or the Zucca (butternut squash, pancetta, mozzarella).

With a wait even on *weekday* mornings, we suspect that Montrosians are playing hooky from work in exchange for chicken apple sausage, pancakes and strong coffee at **Baby Barnaby's** (Map p196; ☎ 713-522-4229; 604 Fairview St; breakfast $5-8; ☺ 7am-noon Mon-Fri, 8am-2pm Sat & Sun; ♿). Or maybe it's the service: these folks remembered our order on our second visit. For lunch, **Barnaby's Café** (Map p196; ☎ 713-522-0106; meals $8-15; ☺ 11am-10pm Sun-Thu, to 11pm Fri & Sat) next door is equally beloved for its burgers and salads.

TOP END

ourpick Indika (Map p196; ☎ 713-524-2170; 516 Westheimer Rd; lunch $12-14, dinner $17-35; ☺ lunch Tue-Fri, dinner Tue-Sat, brunch 11am-3pm Sun) One of the best Indian restaurants in Texas, or maybe in the whole South. OK, we'll fess up – we have a crush on Indika. The alluring dining room sets the tone for the sublime Indian food here, a fusion of authentic tastes and adventurous preparations, such as crabmeat samosas with papaya ginger chutney. Great happy hour and Sunday brunch.

Da Marco (Map p196; ☎ 713-807-8857;1520 Westheimer Rd; lunch $14-28, dinner $16-40; ☺ lunch Tue-Fri, dinner Tue-Sat) Don't let the BMWs in the valet parking lot scare you off: Da Marco is more about food than fuss. Try the three-course business lunch, a steal at $25. Probably Houston's best Italian.

Ruggles Grill (Map p196; ☎ 713-527-9400; 903 Westheimer Rd; meals $17-32; ☺ 5-10pm) Houston's original green restaurant is a dietary-restriction-friendly Montrose phenomenon. Local, organic ingredients shine in creative dishes such as butternut hemp ravioli and agave-glazed pork chops. The answer to one of life's most agonizing questions, 'Do you want dessert?' should be a resounding 'Yes' here. (Chocolate crème brûlée, red velvet cake and a low-fat *tres leches*.)

River Oaks & Uptown/Post Oak

Oishii (off Map p196; ☎ 713-621-8628; 3764 Richmond Ave; sushi from $2; ☼ 11am-10pm Mon-Fri, from noon Sat) 'Cheap' and 'fresh' rarely go together when it comes to sushi, but Oishii delivers on that oxymoron. You – and your wallet – might get happy just looking at the menu. A $2 spicy tuna roll? Are you kidding us?

House of Pies (Map p196; ☎ 713-528-3816; 3112 Kirby Dr; mains $5-9; ☼ 24hr) Not really a house at all, unless your idea of a house is a packed counter teeming with red-eyed hipsters chowing down on pancakes and burgers. No, the food's not amazing. On the other hand, it's three in the morning, the girl with the weird tattoo is winking at you, and there's one last slice of pumpkin.

Tiny Boxwoods (off Map p196; ☎ 713-622-4224; 3614 W Alabama; lunch $10-12, dinner $13-28; ☼ 7am-10pm Tue-Sat, 9am-2pm Sun) Set among blooming flowers in a River Oaks garden shop, this lovely cafe is a natural haven for ladies who lunch. With food this good (grilled cheese and pesto sammies at noon, pumpkin gnocchi and smoky goat lamb burgers at night), guys secretly love it too.

Haven (Map p196; ☎ 713-581-6101; 2502 Algerian Way; meals $18-32; ☼ 11am-10pm Mon-Thu, until 11pm Fri, 5-11pm Sat) Houston's first LEED-certified restaurant cooks up farm-to-table cuisine that's so fresh your grandma would slap it. An adventurous menu puts a mod spin on Texas comfort foods, such as free-range devilled eggs, peanut-crusted soft-shell crab with okra and Hill Country wild-boar chili.

DRINKING

Bottom line: this town can get wicked crazy at sundown, when the corporate types abandon their office parks and come out to play with everyone else. Houston's subtropical climate means that open-air patios are practically mandatory, though the scene varies wildly: on the same street, you can experience a swankier-than-thou cocktail lounge, a kick-back-in-your boots jukebox and beer joint, and a 'pound a shot of Patron and kiss a hot stranger' party bar.

'Nobody cool goes downtown anymore,' one hipster lamented to us, 'they all go to Washington Ave.' To the youngish set, the stretch of Washington Ave bars and clubs de-

---

PICK YOUR POISON

What kind of mood are you in? Houston's got the perfect bar for you.

Best Bar to Break Up Poison Girl (p209).

Best Bar to Make Up La Carafe (p207).

Best Bar to Make Out Marfreless (p210).

Best Bar to Black Out Warren's Inn (p208) or Lola's (p209).

Best Bar to Get Down South Beach (p208).

Best Bar to Fly Solo Boheme (p208).

Worst Bar to Hit on Someone Else's Girlfriend Chances (p208).

---

fines all that is hip and happening in Houston nightlife (although lately downtown is none too shabby in that department), so feed off the high-energy vibe while it's still raging and ask around: the best new dance club was still cool five minutes ago. A great way to avoid both driving and tipsy crosswalk-surfing between bars, the **Washington Wave** (☎ 713-863-WAVE; www.thewashingtonwave.com; 1-way/all-night incl parking $5/10) is either a great capitalist venture or a community service: it's a jitney shuttle that transports partiers on a fixed route between the Washington Ave district, Midtown and the Heights. However you roll, end your night of debauchery at one of the food trucks parked along the street. We like Maya Quiche, outside of Pearl Bar (p209) at press time, with its fresh, cilantro-laden $2 tacos.

In the Heights, the corner of White Oak and Studemont is home to a few funky little bars, including a roadhouse, a tiki bar and a live-music club in an old house. Finally, walkable Montrose, Rice Village and downtown are all prime bar-hopping spots to avoid that commonest devil of Texas crimes, driving under the influence.

Downtown & Midtown

our pick **La Carafe** (Map p193; ☎ 713-229-9399; 813 Congress St) In an 1860 building (that's prehistoric in Houston), this intimate place has one of the town's best jukeboxes, well-priced wines by the glass and an ancient wooden bar lit by wax-dripping candles.

Nouveau Antique Art Bar (Map p196; ☎ 713-526-2220; 2913 Main St) Full of stunning Tiffany lamps, this is a fancy-pants hideaway in Midtown where they play Frank Sinatra and Cat Power low enough to have an actual convo. It's not stuffy, just arty.

WELCOME TO THE GAYBORHOOD

Hands down, Houston's got one of the hottest gay and lesbian scenes in the nation. **Montrose** is the Greenwich Village of Houston. What else is there to say?

To take the pulse on the Gay, Lesbian, Bisexual, Transgender (GLBT) community, check www. houstongayguide.com. *OutSmart,* online at www.outsmartmagazine.com, is the go-to news source. Every June, the **Pride Committee of Houston** (☎ 713-529-6979; www.pridehouston.org) sponsors a huge gay-pride parade.

If the book-smart gay kids from small Texas towns move to Austin, the party animals apparently move to Houston. Several clubs line Pacific St; the high-tech sound and dancefloor lights help keep **South Beach** (Map p196; ☎ 713-529-7623; www.southbeachthenightclub.com; 810 Pacific St) stay true to its namesake. **EJ's Bar** (Map p196; ☎ 713-527-9071; 2517 Ralph St) puts some hunky eye candy on display during regular amateur strip shows.

It's girls, girls, girls at popular lesbian bar **Chances** (Map p196; ☎ 713-523-7217; 1100 Westheimer Rd) with four atmospheres, including a laid-back live-music bar, a country-and-western bar, a dance club and a martini lounge. A sign on the wall warns that 'fighting' will result in arrest. Girls gone wild, indeed.

Hung up your dancin' shoes? Enjoy a tasty cup o' Joe with the boys at **Inversion Coffee House** (Map p196; ☎ 713-523-4866; 1953 Montrose Blvd; ⏱ 6:30am-10pm Mon-Fri, 7:30am-10pm Sat & Sun; 📶). For a relaxed evening, head to **Mo Mong** (Map p196; ☎ 713-524-5664; 1201 Westheimer Rd). The ubersocial Wednesday-night happy hour is a Montrose institution that welcomes people of all persuasions. Warning: frozen cosmos may turn you from a Charlotte into a Samantha. And yes, we mean you boys too.

13 Celsius (Map p196; ☎ 713-529-8466; 3000 Caroline St; ⏱ 4pm-midnight Sun-Wed, until 2am Thu-Sat) With a earthy-sexy European *enoteca* feel, it's the only bar in Houston to keep a temperature-controlled wine cellar. Knowledgeable bartenders offer friendly guidance to enophiles and the clueless alike.

no tsu oH (Map p193; ☎ 713-409-4740; 314 Main St; 📶) A favorite haunt of the alternative brigade, the name is actually 'Houston' spelled backward. As its website proclaims, 'people are here to get drunk...the place is full of liars.' If that intrigues you, check out this late-night place that features dancing, nude figure-drawing sessions and chess. Free wi-fi and plenty of weirdness. Yep, an enigma.

Warren's Inn (Map p193; ☎ 713-247-9207; 307 Travis St) The jukebox at this lovable downtown institution has been officially voted best in town, while the drinks have been unofficially voted the strongest.

Rice Village

Kelvin Arms (Map p196; ☎ 713-528-5002; 2424 Dunstan) A comfy Scottish pub, the Kelvin Arms is good for a midweek game of pool or a leisurely pint. Walk through an actual bank-vault door to canoodle on the couches with your honey, or just your Honey Lager.

Salento (Map p196; ☎ 713-528-7478; 2407 Rice Blvd; ⏱ 7am-10:30pm Mon-Thu & Sun, until 11:30pm Fri & Sat; 📶) Euro cafe by day, wine bar by night, and killer black-bean soup. Wednesday Tango Night gets saucy.

Under the Volcano (Map p196; ☎ 713-526-5282; 2349 Bissonnet St) Unwind in a tropical-island atmosphere without the obnoxious accoutrements. Yes, a classic Rice undergrad bar, but the smarty-pants mix of grad students and faculty convinces you that your third Mai Tai was a brilliant idea.

Montrose

Agora (Map p196; ☎ 713-526-7212; 1712 Westheimer Rd; ⏱ 9am-2am; 📶) A jukebox and a vast selection of wines by-the-glass in a coffee shop? Yes, please. OK, so not everyone's discussing Greek philosophy here, but the student/boho vibe is indeed old school. Sit on the front patio or on the quiet second-level balcony, where movies on a flat-screen TV woo would-be savants away from their studies.

Boheme `our pick` (Map p196; ☎ 713-52-1099; 307 Fairview St; ⏱ 8:30am-midnight Sun & Mon, until 2am Tue-Sat; 📶) Bewitching Boheme has that *je ne sais quoi* that's as appealing as it is enigmatic. Velvety sofas and old movie equipment, a lazy patio, Thursday arts nights, and minty frozen mojitos that reign among of our favorite drinks in town. Part wine bar, part coffee shop, 100% bohemian.

Black Labrador (Map p196; ☎ 713-529-1199; 4100 Montrose Blvd; ☜ 11am-11pm Mon-Thu, until midnight Fri & Sat, until 10pm Sun) English pubs in this town are commonplace, but not ones in gorgeous brick buildings with lovely patios and giant outdoor chess games. Brilliant.

Lola's (Map p196; ☎ 713-528-8342; 2327 Grant St) Punk bartenders sling shots with a vengeance. Yeah, this dive is a bit hardcore, but the drinks are strong and ridiculously cheap. That's code for 'walk or take a cab here.'

our pick Poison Girl (Map p196; ☎ 713-527-9929; 1641 Westheimer Rd) The name says it all. Seductive pinup girls stare down on hipsters drinking longneck beer and other pick-your-poisons. Add in a killer back patio, some vintage pinball games, the right combo of come-hither glances and friendly conversation, and you've got Houston's sexiest dive.

West Alabama Ice House (Map p196; ☎ 713-528-6874; 1919 W Alabama St; ☜ 10am-midnight Mon-Fri, until 1am Sat, noon-midnight Sun) Is it the free hot dogs on Friday? The dog-friendly patio? Who knows, but this rickety old place – Texas' oldest 'ice house' in fact – draws the crowds, from bikers to lawyers. Wear sunscreen, and buy someone a beer.

Houston Heights

our pick Onion Creek Café (off Map p196; ☎ 713-880-0768; 3106 White Oak Blvd; ☜ 7am-2am) As a sign on the sprawling, ultrachill patio proclaims, it's 186 miles to Austin. But why make the drive? This cafe rocks a Hill Country atmosphere: from Austin-themed specials such as the 'Hippie Hollow Burger' (yes, named after the capital's infamous nude beach) and 'Cheap Ass Beer' for $1.25. Actually, the best things here have little to do with Austin: the palm-shaded patio, the 'Bad Ass Hot Dogs' (veggie ones, too!), the bacon and cheddar waffle and the frozen mimosas.

Washington Avenue

Pearl Bar (off Map p196; ☎ 713-868-5337; 4216 Washington Ave; ☜ 2pm-2am) How does this place still manage to feel so damn chilled-out on a packed Saturday night? Is it the awesome back patio, fairly priced drinks, the ping-pong table, or that they always seem be playing that bitter love song you need to hear?

Max's Wine Dive (off Map p196; ☎ 713-526-5282; 4720 Washington Ave; ☜ 2pm-2am) A swanky retro vibe, serious comfort food and good wines by

the glass make this one of the best places to get your Washington Ave bar-hopping off to a swinging start. If you don't find the slogan, 'Fried chicken and champagne? Why the hell not?' déclassé, you'll like it here.

ENTERTAINMENT

Bursting with high-class performance venues, the mainstream heart of Houston entertainment is the downtown **Theater District** (www.houstontheaterdistrict.org). Around the intersection of Smith St and Texas Ave, it attracts the well-heeled, tourists, and other cultural mavens. Outdoor concerts are held many Tuesday, Wednesday and Thursday evenings at **Jones Plaza** (601 Louisiana St), in front of Jones Hall for the Performing Arts, spring through fall. Discovery Green (p198) also features outdoor concerts.

Cinemas

Two handy sites for checking movie times are www.houston.mrmovietimes.com and the *Houston Chronicle's* site www.chron.com/entertainment/movies.

Landmark River Oaks Theater (Map p196; ☎ 713-866-8881; www.landmarktheatres.com/market/houston/riveroakstheatre.htm; 2009 W Gray St) This fancy vintage cinema shows a mix of the indie and mainstream flicks.

Rice University Media Center (Map p196; ☎ 713-348-4882; www.ricecinema.rice.edu; 6100 Main St) Classic movies plus really offbeat stuff at bargain prices on the Rice University campus.

Angelika Film Center & Cafe (Map p193; ☎ 713-225-5232; www.angelikafilmcenter.com, Bayou Pl, 510 Texas Ave) Movie buffs will thrill over this southern outpost of Manhattan's famed Angelika, which shows art-house films in an upscale setting.

Theater & Performing Arts

Alley Theatre (Map p193; ☎ 713-220-5700; www.alleytheatre.org; 615 Texas Ave) Houston's heavy-hitter theater is one of the last in the nation to keep a resident company of actors. From classics to modern plays, the magic of this ensemble is palpable.

Hobby Center for the Performing Arts (Map p193; ☎ 713-315-2525; www.thehobbycenter.org; 800 Bagby St) is home to the acclaimed **Theatre Under the Stars** (☎ 713-558-2600; www.tuts.com), which produces big-budget, Broadway-style musicals (actually inside and in air-conditioned comfort, despite the company's name).

Jones Hall for the Performing Arts (Map p193; ☎ 713-227-3974; 615 Louisiana St) hosts the **Houston**

DOWN & DIRTY HOUSTON

Long before busty sex symbol Anna Nicole Smith wooed elderly billionaire J Howard Smith from the pole in one of Houston's notorious strip clubs, Houston's had a rep for the bawdy and the naughty. Corporate scandals? Check. Lap dances? Check. Need a gun? Check. Boob job? Some of the best surgeons are here. Here are just a few off-the-radar places to sample some of Houston's notoriety, both past and present.

Enron: it's a four-letter word. Yet long before Jeffrey Skilling became an infamous household name, the ne'er do wells of the energy-trading giant the **Enron Corporation** were racking up their corporate bonuses and a trail of massive corruption inside the old **headquarters** (off Map p193; 1400 Smith St), a 50-story, 1.3-million-sq-ft shimmering glass tower in downtown Houston. After the FBI raided Enron and exposed the fraud, the building became the sinister backdrop for TV news coverage of the event and this iconic sight became familiar to many Americans disgruntled – or more accurately, disgusted – by one of what was to be a long series of corporate scandals during the 2000s. It sold in 2003 for a cool $55 million, but you can still see it – although the trademark 'Enron' sign is gone.

Greed isn't the only sin running rampant 'round Houston. They've got lust covered pretty well too, from the torrid to the tame. Let's start with the torrid. If you've ever asked yourself, 'Is everything really bigger in Texas?' the cheeky answer is: at the strip clubs, yes. For the curious or the connoisseur, the most decadent Vegas-style joint in town is **Treasures** (off Map p196; ☎ 713-629-6200; www.treasureshouston.com; 5647 Westheimer Rd; cover $7, after 7pm $15; ☼ 11am-2am Sun-Tue, 11am-4am Wed-Sat). BMWs flood the valet and corporate types flood the VIP room, where mandatory bottle service *begins* at $150. Full lap dances ($20 per song) are legal in Texas and notoriously X-rated, though 'bottoms' (read: a string) must be worn when alcohol is served. If it looks too good to be real, it probably isn't.

For those who prefer a more sophisticated evening (that is, where dollar bills are simply tips, not g-string decorations), head to tony River Oaks. Every wonder where the corporate execs take their paramours? Behind a nameless blue door, it's easy to miss off-the-radar **Marfreless** (Map p196; ☎ 713-528-0083; 2006 Peden St), a legitimately interesting bar that plays soothing classical music in a dim, candlelit room. It also happens to harbor consenting adults seeking discreet PG-rated action in the notorious balcony area. You'll soon understand why there's no sign. Order a cocktail, kick back on the leather couches, whisper sweet nothings and keep your pants on.

Symphony Orchestra (☎ 713-224-7575; www.houston symphony.org).

Wortham Center (Map p193; ☎ 713-237-1439; www.houstontx.gov/worthamcenter/index.htm; 501 Texas Ave), built during the 1980s oil bust, is an impressive complex that is home to the **Houston Ballet** (☎ 713-523-6300; www.houstonballet.org) and the **Houston Grand Opera** (☎ 713-546-0200; www.houstongrandopera.org), both highly regarded.

Live Music

When it's time to rock out, visit www.spacecityrock.com, the online version of a local music mag.

POP, ROCK, FOLK & COUNTRY

Anderson Fair (off Map p196; ☎ 713-227-3974; 2007 Grant St) A legendary stop on the folk-music circuit since the 1960s, this is one of the oldest continuously operating original-music venues in the US.

Dan Electro's Guitar Bar (off Map p196; ☎ 713-862-8707; www.danelectrosguitarbar.com; 1031 E 24th St) This down-home joint in the laid-back Heights rocks out, but you could probably take your parents. A little gritty, a bit hippie, totally cool. It's near N Main St.

Big Easy (Map p196; ☎ 713-523-9999; www.thebigeasyblues.com; 5731 Kirby Dr; ☼ 6pm-2am Mon-Thu, 3pm-2am Fri, 6pm-1am Sun) This unpretentious place in the Village honors Houston's New Orleans connection with live blues and zydeco.

McGonigel's Mucky Duck (Map p196; ☎ 713-528-5999; www.mcgonigels.com; 2425 Norfolk St; ☼ 11am-2am Mon-Sat, 5-9pm Sun) Listen nightly to live acoustic, Irish, folk and country performers in pubby surrounds.

Rudyard's Pub (Map p196; ☎ 713-521-0521; www.rudyards.com; 2010 Waugh Dr; ☼ 11:30am-2am) Killer pub food and an upstairs venue that's host to eclectic – OK, sometimes downright kooky – theatrical and music fare, from local story-telling nights to avant-garde theatrics. Yet with these bells and whistles, the neighborhood pub vibe – it's one of the best in town – prevails.

Last Concert Cafe (off Map p193; ☎ 713-226-8563; www.lastconcert.com; 1403 Nance St; 11am-2am Mon-Fri, 5pm-2am Sat, 11am-9pm Sun) For a real local original, find your way just northeast of downtown to this homely little place. After you knock on the red door (there's no sign), you can hang out drinking cheap suds at the bar or dig into cheap Tex-Mex and live music on the patio.

Verizon Wireless Theater (Map p193; ☎ 713-230-1666; www.livenation.com; 520 Texas Ave) This massive venue's inside Downtown's Bayou Place entertainment complex, luring everyone from Erykah Badu and Elton John to the Houston Roller Derby girls.

JAZZ

For good information on the local scene, see www.jazzhouston.com.

Cézanne (Map p196; ☎ 713-522-9621; www.tiannahall.com/cezannehome; 4100 Montrose Blvd) This is simply Houston's best place to hear jazz. Above the Black Labrador this classy, intimate venue mixes some of the best pure Texas and international jazz with a very cool piano bar.

Red Cat Jazz Café (Map p193; ☎ 713-226-7870; www.redcatjazzcafe.com; 924 Congress St; 6pm-2am) This slick downtown joint attracting interest offers live music every night (except Sunday) and Sunday brunch featuring a gospel group; food's good, too.

Sports

While Houston teams of late don't get the kind of rabid following as, say, the UT Longhorns or the San Antonio Spurs, there's plenty of action to be found. It's an understatement to say that football's popular in Texas, and if you're a fan, the **Houston Texans** (☎ 877-635-2002; www.houstontexans.com) play at **Reliant Stadium** (off Map p196; ☎ 832-667-1400; www.reliantpark.com; 1 Reliant Park) and draw plenty of raucous crowds.

After a stint at the now-dubiously named Enron Field, the **Houston Astros** (☎ 713-259-8000; www.astros.com) play pro baseball downtown at **Minute Maid Park** (Map p193; ☎ 713-259-8000; 501 Crawford St).

Basketball fans can follow the NBA's **Houston Rockets** (☎ 713-627-3865; www.houstonrockets.com) at the **Toyota Center** (Map p193; ☎ 713-758-7200;

www.houstontoyotacenter.com; 1510 Polk St), which is also home to the **Comets** (☎ 713-627-9622; www.wnba.com/comets), Houston's highly regarded women's basketball team.

SHOPPING

Welcome to the Mall. To some, it's Houston's Valhalla of shopping, to others it's just a big mall with a skating rink; in any case, the **Galleria** (off Map p196; ☎ 713-622-0663; www.simon.com; 5075 Westheimer Rd) is Texas' biggest and badass-est mall in a state bursting with big malls. This place is so iconic to Houston that saying 'the Galleria' refers to the whole surrounding neighborhood, a district so densely suburban it's practically, well, urban.

For browsing in a more eclectic and locally owned stores, hit the neighborhoods. Along 19th St (between Yale St and Shepherd Dr) in the **Heights** (www.heightsfirstsaturday.com), you'll find unique antiques, clever crafts and cafes. On the first Saturday of every month, the street takes on a carnival-like air with outdoor booths and entertainment. Midtown's also popping up on the shopping radar.

In Montrose, Westheimer St's a dream for crafty fashionistas and antique-hunters alike. Start on Dunlavy Rd and work your way down the street, where you'll find a mix of used- and new-clothing stores running the gamut from vintage to punk rock to Tokyo mod, plus lots of funky old furniture.

For slightly less rebellious fashion terrain, stroll around Rice Village and let the window displays lure you in.

If you're looking for a sari, head to the Little India shops along **Harwin Drive** (off Map p196; Southwest Fwy), southwest of town off I-59. Houston's **Chinatown** (off Map p196; www.chinatownmap.com) is a scattered mix of Chinese and Vietnamese shops and restaurants on Bellaire Blvd at Beltway 8.

Clothing & Accessories

our pick **Lot 8** (Map p196; ☎ 713-807-1565; www.lot8online.com; 6127 Kirby Dr; 10am-8pm Mon-Sat, noon-7pm Sun) Try on Chloe Dao's *Project Runway* winners in this Rice Village gem that's all about local designers, looking good and having fun. Pose on the pedestal, say 'Auf Weidersehen,' and pretend you're Heidi Klum.

Buffalo Exchange (Map p196; ☎ 713-523-8701; www.buffaloexchange.com; 1618 Westheimer Rd; 10am-8pm Mon-Sat, noon-7pm Sun) Texas' definitive and

TEN-GALLONS, SIX-SHOOTERS & SH*T-KICKERS

For rootin', tootin', six-shootin' souvenirs (can you call a shotgun a souvenir?), the following stores will do nicely.

Look Ma! No waiting period! Hey, this is Texas. **Collector's Firearms** (off Map p196; ☎ 713-781-1960; www.collectorsfirearms.com; 3301 Fondren, at Richmond Ave; ☯ 10am-6:30pm Mon-Sat) is a great place to live out your Charlton Heston (but probably not your Michael Moore) fantasies: a full-service shop that's definitely not for the gun-shy. With enough cash and a clean background check, you can walk out with anything from a Civil War–era shotgun to a Gatling. Whatever your gun politics, the professional staff are happy to educate you.

For those of you who fail the background check – only kidding! – a less intimidating way to buy into the spirit of Texas is at the **Hat Store** (Map p196; ☎ 713-780-2480; 5587 Richmond Ave). This superfriendly third-generation hatmaker has outfitted everyone from Clint Black and Lyle Lovett to ZZ Top. This is one of the ultimate Texas souvenirs: they hand-shape and steam the hats here, while dispersing bits of wisdom along the way ('Ever worn 100% beaver? It feels like heaven on your head').

If you've got the hat sorted, boots are obviously the next purchase. While you can shell out big bucks on a new pair at a big boot store in the 'burbs, why not head over to the **Texas Junk Company** (Map p196; ☎ 713-524-6257; 215 Welch St) where Robert's been outfitting locals in pre-worn cowboy boots since before country got cool again? For three decades, this collection of Texas memorabilia and vintage ephemera has remained a Montrose fixture, where locals lounge outside with coffee and local advice. Be sure to call ahead in the summer months: Robert might be closed for remodeling...or off at Burning Man.

best buy-sell-trade clothing store, notorious for turning away the very outfit you believed was totally in vogue only three months ago. Yeah, they're picky, and that's a good thing.

Duo (Map p196; ☎ 713-963-8825; www.ishopaac.com; 1665 Westheimer Rd) The rare store in Montrose that showcases trendy women's and men's fashion in the same location, which makes it perfect for couples shopping together.

Couture Blowout (Map p196; ☎ 713-520-7585; www.couture-blowout.com; 1621 Westheimer Rd; ☯ 11am-7pm Tue-Sat) Fulfill those Prada dreams with only a minor dent in your credit card at this gently used, surprisingly friendly couture store. The selection changes often but always features some awe- and aah-inspiring dresses.

M2M Fashions (Map p196; ☎ 713-521-0804; www.m2mfashion.com; 3400 Montrose Blvd; ☯ 11am-8pm Mon-Thu, until 9pm Fri & Sat, noon-6pm Sun) Gay or straight, frat boy or professional: this place isn't about a demographic so much as hot fashion, pure and simple. Play it safe (Ben Sherman, Zachary Prell) or a little riskier (Diesel, Z Brand).

Whole Earth Provision Company (Map p196; ☎ 713-526-5226; www.wholeearthprovision.com; 2934 S Shepherd Dr; ☯ 10am-9pm Mon-Fri, to 8pm Sat, noon-6pm Sun) Along with lots of high-tech, thermodynamic clothes for the crunchy set, it has essential travel stuff such as guidebooks and gear.

Food & Drink

Central Market (off Map p196; ☎ 713-386-1700; www.centralmarket.com; 3315 Westheimer Rd) Practically hands-down the best supermarket chain in Texas, Central Market offers well-priced organic, fresh produce and other ready-to-eat foods.

Chocolate Bar (Map p196; www.theoriginalchocolatebar.com; ☯ 10am-10pm Mon-Thu, until midnight Fri & Sat, noon-10pm Sun); River Oaks (☎ 713-520-8599; 1835 W Alabama St); Rice Village (☎ 713-520-8888; 2521 University Blvd) Kids dream about places like this, and adults resist them. It's futile. Chocolate in all of its forms: bar, confection, cake, pie, ice cream...but don't take our word for it.

Rice Epicurean Market (Map p196; ☎ 713-621-0422; www.riceepicurean.com; 2617 W Holcombe Blvd) The name says it all: this chain of five upscale stores is for gourmets, or just Food Network–addicts jonesing for specialty ingredients.

Design & Music

our pick **Domy** (Map p196; ☎ 713-523-3669; www.domystore.com; 1709 Westheimer Rd; ☯ noon-8pm Mon-Fri, from 11am Sat, 11am-7pm Sun) In a brick Montrose cottage, this fun-spirited store features a mod mix of architecture, design, art and style – plus weird Japanese toys. After shopping, retreat to the back patio shared with Brasil cafe (p206).

HOUSTON & EAST TEXAS

Cactus Music (Map p196; ☎ 713-526-9272; www.cactus musicitx.com; 2110 Portsmouth; ☯ 10am-9pm Mon-Sat, noon-7pm Sun) Off Richmond Ave and Shepherd Dr in Upper Kirby, Houston's original indie-music store has been rocking out for more than 30 years, pleasing hippies, punks and country boys alike.

Soundwaves (Map p196; ☎ 713-520-9283; www. soundwaves.com; 3509 Montrose Blvd; ☯ 10am-9pm Mon-Sat, noon-6pm Sun; ☻) Houston's largest indie-music store is also the largest surf shop in the state, which means that along with your rock and roll you can pick up a swimsuit and flip-flops or some surf/skateboard gear. Oh, and it's got, like, free wi-fi, dude.

GETTING THERE & AWAY
Air
Houston Airport System (www.fly2houston.com) has two airports. Twenty-two miles north of the city center, **George Bush Intercontinental Airport** (IAH; off Map p193; ☎ 281-230-3100; btwn I-45 & I-59 N; ☻), home base for Continental Airlines, serves cities worldwide through many carriers. Two interterminal train systems connect passengers to all five terminals. Southeast of town, the quieter and smaller **William P Hobby Airport** (HOU; off Map p193; ☎ 713-640-3000; ☻) is a major hub for Southwest Airlines and domestic travel. Free wi-fi is available at both facilities.

Bus
Long-distance buses headed all over Texas depart from the **Greyhound Bus Terminal** (Map p193; ☎ 713-759-6565; www.greyhound.com; 2121 Main St), which is located two blocks from the Downtown Transit Center light-rail stop. **El Expreso** (Map p193; ☎ 713-926-6621; 2201 Main St) right by Greyhound, runs buses to Mexico.

Train
Ah, Amtrak. Yep, it's still a pain. The chronically late *Sunset Limited* train stops at the **Amtrak Station** (Map p193; ☎ 713-224-1577; www. amtrak.com; 902 Washington Ave) three times a week.

GETTING AROUND
To/From the Airport
The Hobby airport bus (88) connects to downtown (and to the Downtown Transit Center light-rail stop) from Monday to Saturday, 6am to 11pm ($1.25). The Airport Direct nonstop bus runs between the Downtown Transit Center and George Bush

Intercontinental ($15, 30 minutes) every half-hour from 5:30am to 8:00pm. **SuperShuttle** (☎ 800-258-3826; www.supershuttle.com) provides service from both Bush ($23) and Hobby ($19) airports.

Cabs are readily available at both airports. Airport rates are determined by zone, and you'll pay either the flat zone rate or the meter rate, whatever's less. You'll shell out $60 to get from George Bush Intercontinental to downtown; from Hobby it's about $25.

Car & Motorcycle
Houstonians drive. Period. Environmental politics aside, few people disagree that a car is the easiest way to get around greater Houston – despite the traffic. Parking is plentiful and often free. Don't be entirely put off by valet parking: even at upscale joints, it's often free for patrons.

CAR RENTAL
All major rental cars are available at both Houston airports. Decent prices make Houston an ideal departure point for a Texas road trip.

Public Transportation
BUS
The Houston area is served by **Metropolitan Transit Authority** (Metro; ☎ 713-635-4000; www.ride metro.org), a network of bus lines that cover the Houston area from north of George Bush Intercontinental south all the way to Clear Lake. Service is geared toward weekday downtown commuters.

LIGHT RAIL
Houston's **Metro** (☎ 713-635-4000; www.ridemetro. org) runs the convenient light-rail system; $1.25 gets you a one-way ride. Most of the in-town sights are along the Downtown–Museum District–Reliant Park light-rail corridor. The METRORail light-rail system links downtown with Midtown, the Museum District, Hermann Park, the Medical Center and south as far as the Astrodome along the Main St corridor.

Taxi
Although Houston's taxi rates are reasonable ($2.50 for flag-fall, 17¢ per additional mile), given Houston's sprawl, your cab tab can quickly surpass car-rental rates. With Houston's 'Six in the City' deal, you can hop

between any two downtown spots for a bargain $6 for up to 4 people.

Taxis Fiesta (☎ 713-225-2666; www.taxisfiesta.com)
United Cab (☎ 713-699-0000; www.unitedcab.com)
Yellow Cab (☎ 713-236-1111; www.yellowcab houston.com)

AROUND HOUSTON

The following sites are within a 90-minute drive of downtown Houston.

CLEAR LAKE AREA

Clear Lake, the Kemah Boardwalk and the Space Center form the greater Houston area's holy trinity of tourism: stay for a day or two and you can easily experience all three sights.

The historically important Johnson Space Center lures the NASA-crazed tourists, while the marinas of **Clear Lake** (Map p190; www.clear lakearea.com), 22 miles from downtown, serve as Houston's recreational boating port of call. While 'Clear Lake' might be an exaggeration, you can't say it isn't popular. The lake doesn't look very clear, but it's home to one of the largest concentrations of recreational boats in the US. On NASA Rd, you'll find beaches, harbors, jetties and delightful waterfront joints full of bikini-clad soccer moms and cyclists alike.

Sights & Activities

East on Galveston Bay, the **Kemah Boardwalk** (Map p190; ☎ 281-334-9880; www.kemahboardwalk.com;

cnr Bradford & 2nd Sts, off Hwy 146; all-day ride pass $20/17; ⏦) is a cartoonish carnival of commercialism to some, a family paradise to others. Whatever your take, the boardwalk's attractively garish, there's plenty to do in the waterfront entertainment complex (especially for kiddies) and it's right smack on the water. When you see the Ferris wheel, the neon and the sunburns, you know you've arrived.

The **Bay Area Houston Convention & Visitors Bureau** (☎ 281-474-9700; www.visitbayareahouston.com; 913 N Meyer Rd, Seabrook; ⏦ 9am-5pm Mon-Fri, 10am-5pm Sat & Sun) lists activities, accommodations and water-sports operators on its website.

Dream of a landing on the moon? You can't get any closer (without years of training) than at **Space Center Houston** (Map p190; ☎ 281-244-2100; www.spacecenter.org; 1601 NASA Rd 1, Clear Lake; adult/child $20/16; ⏦ 10am-5pm Mon-Fri, 10am-7pm Sat & Sun), the official visitor center and museum of NASA's **Johnson Space Center**. When the Manned Spacecraft Center (MSC) opened in 1961 it practically put Houston on the map. Despite exuding a theme-park vibe, interactive exhibits nonetheless entertain. Hope that on your NASA Tram tour you get to see astronauts training for future missions; if not, you still get to peek into several actual working areas of the Space Center, such as both the current and the historic Mission Control Center (you know, the 'Houston' of the famous *Apollo 13* line 'Houston, we have a problem') and the Neutral Buoyancy Lab. Kids will dig 'The Feel of Space' module, where they can get answers to essential questions like 'How do you eat in space?' and 'Can I access my Facebook ac-

---

DETOUR: BRENHAM

Hands-down one of the cutest damn small towns in Texas, **Brenham** is a great place to chill out between Houston and Austin. We mean that literally: since 1907 it's been the home of **Blue Bell Creameries** (☎ 979-830-2179; www.bluebell.com; Loop 577, off Hwy 290 E; adult/senior & child $5/3; ⏦ 10am-2:30pm Mon-Fri; ⏦) or what Texans like to call 'the real creamery in Brenham.' Little it's not: this is a veritable ice-cream palace, with tours given daily.

Brenham sports a walkable, compact downtown with a **Washington County Chamber of Commerce** (☎ 979-836-3695; www.brenhamtexas.com; 314 S Austin St), and oodles of shops and restaurants that beg you to poke around. At lunch, go for the delish Salade Marrakesh and homemade desserts at the aptly named **Funky Art Café** (☎ 979-836-5220; 202 W Commerce St; meals $6-10; ⏦ lunch Mon-Sat) or head to **Volare Italian Restaurant** (☎ 979-836-1514; 102 Ross St; meals $9-20; ⏦ lunch & dinner Tue-Sat) for rustic Italian served in a lovely wooden house. Come nightfall, lay your head at the **Ant Street Inn** (☎ 979-836-7393; www.antstreetinn.com; 107 W Commerce St; r incl breakfast $115-235; ⏦ ⏦ ⏦), where you'll get a full dose of 19th-century Texas elegance in the splendor of its 14 stained-glass-laden rooms.

SKI COLLEGE STATION

They say dreams can move mountains, but apparently they can also *make* mountains. At least that's the case for George Jessup, who took what some might call a harebrained scheme and turned it into this giant university's most popular club.

Describe Mt Aggie. It's a human-made ski hill on campus, made from lots of dirt and covered by a special surface called SnoPak.

How did you build it? Was this a university-sponsored project? In the beginning, I dragged big sheets of Astroturf across campus behind my Porsche, and the club ordered metal football bleachers for the height. We did this over a weekend. In the morning, the university officials weren't thrilled to discover it. It was definitely *not* university sponsored at first, but it soon became a campus landmark and a 'university tradition.' Strangely, Mt Aggie just kept getting bigger...to the college president's puzzlement, of course.

Does College Station have any natural hills or mountains? [Laughs] That would be a definite no.

What do students like best about the ski club? When A&M was mostly male in the 1970s, it was the only coed club on campus – so obviously it was the best place to meet women! Now it's about the camaraderie and the ski trips.

Any advice for someone who wants to build their own ski hill? 'Tis easier to beg forgiveness than to get permission.

George Jessup is Texas A&M's winter sports visionary and co-proprietor of the Rudder-Jessup Bed & Breakfast, retired after 38 years as a professor. He still teaches Intermediate Snow Skiing.

count in space?' IMAX fans will go gaga for the Blastoff Theater, which might be the next best thing to actually launching in space, without the side effects of zero gravity. If your personal version of hell is kids running around pretending to be astronauts, avoid visiting on school holidays.

If the Space Center or Kemah are your main destination, stay nearby and avoid Houston traffic woes. Decent-priced chain hotels congregate along NASA Rd 1. For party-hearty atmosphere and predictable tourist-trap food, the Kemah Boardwalk's chock full of the usual suspects.

Sleeping & Eating

A While Pelican Bed & Breakfast (☎ 281-538-3900; www.awhitetexaspelican.com; 408a Bay Ave, Kemah; r incl breakfast Jan-Apr $75-125, May-Dec $95-235; ✕ ☎) This place rocks a lazy beachfront vibe, with views of Galveston Bay and the Kemah Boardwalk. Like to fish? There's a private 250ft pier. Or just watch the sunset on the deck.

Beacon Hill Bed & Breakfast (☎ 281-326-7643; www.visitbeaconhill.com; 3701 Nasa Parkway, Seabrook; r incl breakfast $125-150; ✕ ☎) Just 3 miles east of the Space Center, this cozy B&B overlooks Clear Lake, and a four-course breakfast is served in the lakeside sunroom.

Aquarium (☎ 281-334-9010; 11 Kemah Boardwalk, Kemah; mains $13-32, kids meals $6-7; ⚑) If eight-year-

olds were restaurant critics, this place would get four stars. Don't come for the food – come for the 50,000-gallon aquarium. If watching sharks while you're eating fish feels surreal, then you get the point of this 'underwater dining adventure.'

Pizza Oven (☎ 281-334-2228; 10 Kemah Boardwalk, Kemah; pizza $12; ⚑) Plus: good prices, no hassle. Minus: no bells and whistles, such as swimming stingrays or hotties serving beer in tight orange shorts. But hey, the pizza and pasta ain't bad, the kids are happy, and you haven't just dropped a hundred bucks on mediocre seafood.

COLLEGE STATION

pop 74,100

Howdy! That's code for 'Welcome to Aggieland.' While College Station and neighboring Bryan hold a combined permanent population of 163,000, most of the year that number gets a boost from the whopping 46,000 students at **Texas A&M University** (☎ 979-845-5851; www.tamu.edu). And while the legendary A&M (which originally stood for Agricultural and Mechanical) football stadium is in itself the biggest visitor draw in the area, life does exist off campus. The **Bryan-College Station Convention & Visitors Bureau** (☎ 979-260-9898, 800-777-8292; 715 University Dr E; ☼ 8am-5pm Mon-Fri), off Hwy 6, offers free maps and local advice.

HOUSTON & EAST TEXAS

THE FIGHTIN' TEXAS AGGIE CORPS OF CADETS

See those guys in athletic gear running around the A&M campus yelling their heads off, while other guys run in front of them while holding what appear to be, um, *mop handles* over their heads? What might have been mistaken for a bad acid trip on a 1970s college campus is pretty much the opposite: what you're seeing is part of the many rituals and regimes of the **A&M Corps of Cadets** (☎ 1-800-8268-247; www.aggiecorps.org), the largest Reserve Officer Training Corps (ROTC) program in the nation. Oh, and those aren't mop handles being used in these grueling exercise drills – they're flagpoles. Questions about these arcane procedures? Stop any of the friendly uniformed cadets strolling around campus and ask – they're unfailingly polite.

Sights

At 5200 acres, A&M is one of the nation's largest college campuses. While the campus vibe comes off as more corporate than picturesque, the school is steeped in tradition – in fact, students claim it's more like a religion. Catching an Aggies game can be an unforgettable experience of 'maroon madness.' One note: wear orange at your own peril (that's rival University of Texas' colors).

A few unusual sights will reward those who brave a stroll around this giant of a campus. The behemoth **Kyle Field** (☎ 979-845-5129, ticket line 979-845-2311; www.aggieathletics.com/school-bio/tickets-and-venues.html; 198 Joe Routt Blvd; ☽ 8am-5pm Mon-Fri) is not only the largest football stadium in this football-crazed state, it's notorious for being intimidating to visiting teams. The Aggies historically tend to win home games – in fact, in the 1990s, they won 92.5% of them. (With that many screaming fans in the stadium, it's not hard to understand why.) At 6500lb of bronze, you can't miss the giant 'Aggie' class ring at the **Haynes Ring Plaza** (505 George Bush Dr). To avoid getting lost, snag a free campus map from the **Appelt Aggieland Visitor Center** (☎ 979-845-5851; http://visit.tamu.edu; Rudder Tower; ☽ 8am-5pm Mon-Fri, 9:30am-3:30pm Sat, 1-4pm Sun). Note: legend has it that A&M students greet passersby with an enthusiastic 'Howdy!' on campus.

Republicans and Democrats alike can probably agree on one thing: the **George Bush Presidential Library & Museum** (☎ 979-691-4000; 1000 George Bush Dr W; adult/student/senior $7/3/6, under 16yr free; ☽ 9:30am-5pm Mon-Sat, noon-5pm Sun), just off FM 2818, is a darn fine museum. Renovated in 2007 to the tune of $8 million, the well-curated exhibits paint the elder Bush statesman's rise from Texas oil prospector through his virtual tour of national politics: from Ambassador to the UN, to Republican National Committee (RNC) chairman, to CIA

director, to the White House, to becoming the first American president to see his own offspring occupy the Oval Office. (Yes, that's 'Dubya,' or America's 43rd president, George W Bush.) While exhibits paint George Sr's diplomacy in an unfailingly positive light (though we noticed any homage to Dan Quayle is notably lacking), they nonetheless serve as an interesting primer on American history from WWII through the 1990s. Museum items such as the AK-47 captured by the contras from the Sandinistas – a gift to Bush by Nicaraguan then-president Violeta Chamorro – lend a vivid perspective on the down-and-dirty American foreign policy of the Reagan-Bush era. Don't miss General Manuel Noriega's shooting-practice target – a paper figure on which Bush's own name is ominously scrawled.

Sleeping

While the city of College Station appears to be one big strip mall that exploded around the college, a few surprisingly personable sleeping and eating options stand out amid the faceless chains.

Vineyard Court Hotel (☎ 888-846-2678; www.vineyardcourt.com; 1500 George Bush Dr E; ste $109-179; ✗ 🅿 🛜 🛗) This reasonably priced tranquil hideaway (complete with gurgling fountains) seems worlds away. Luxe linens and personal touches deck out each whimsically themed suite. We like the free wine and cheese happy hour and continental breakfast, best enjoyed out in the courtyard under the fragrant wisteria arbor.

Rudder-Jessup Bed & Breakfast (☎ 866-744-2470; www.rudderbandb.com; 115 Lee Ave; incl full breakfast r $129, ste $159; ✗ 🅿 🛜 🛗) If a dose of fascinating local lore – and maybe even an invitation to dinner with your jovial hosts – sounds intriguing to you, stay here. In the old college president's stately home, hosts George and

Hillary will charm your socks off. As they wryly state, 'Children with well-behaved parents are welcome.'

7F Lodge (☎ 970-690-0073; www.7flodge.com; 16611 Royder Rd; r $169-239; P 🛜) Whimsical cottages designed to evoke, say, a French chateau or a Castilian noble's castle. Covet your own dancefloor and 1959 Wurlitzer jukebox? The Sully's Place cabin has it. Stunning woodwork and Jacuzzis (yep, even heart-shaped ones) round out the 'oohs' and 'aahs.'

Eating & Drinking

Not a college student anymore? That doesn't mean you can't drink like one! Come nightfall, head to Northgate, the most happenin' – and only walkable – stretch of restaurants and nightlife in town. A sociable area to grab a drink and dinner, it turns into a spectacle of collegiate drinking as the night wears on. Start off with dinner at the dimly lit, upscale **Café Eccell** (☎ 979-846-7908; 101 Church Ave; meals $12-27; 🕑 lunch & dinner) or grab some fun, fresh Mexican across the street at **La Bodega** (☎ 979-691-8226; 102 Church Ave; meals $7-14; 🕑 lunch & dinner daily, breakfast Sat & Sun, to 2am Wed-Sat). To cap off the evening, relive your senior-year memories by exploring Northgate's string of bars, which run the gamut from country line dancing to good old-fashioned beer swilling. Whatever your tastes, a stop at Aggieland's most notorious bar, the **Dixie Chicken** (☎ 979-846-2322; 307 University Dr; 🕑 10am-2am), is de rigueur. You might find that after the third drink, people in maroon athletic gear look a little more attractive than they did at first glance.

Don't want to hear phrases such as 'I'm so wasted' at the next table? Head to **Veritas Wine & Bistro** (☎ 979-268-3251; 830 University Dr E; 🕑 to 10pm Mon-Thu, to 11pm Fri & Sat, to 9pm Sun). For a late-night (or early-morning) caffeine buzz, locals love **Sweet Eugene's** (☎ 979-696-5282; 1702 George Bush Dr E; 🕑 6am-1am Mon-Thu, 6am-2am Fri & Sat, 7am-1am Sun) coffee.

BRYAN
pop 67,300

If you want to soak up the area's local sights but skip the college atmosphere come nightfall, Bryan is a pleasant town in which to eat and stay: don't believe the hype that College Station is the only game in town. This old-school Texas town, more attractive than not, claims bragging rights to the state's oldest **Carnegie Library** (☎ 979-209-5630; www.bcslibrary.

org; 111 S Main St; 🕑 9am-6pm, closed Wed & Sun) and a walkable downtown that just begs you to stop for lunch.

Come nightfall in Bryan, lay your head at the historic 1928 **LaSalle Hotel** (☎ 979-822-2000; www.lasalle-hotel.com; 120 S Main St; r $79-139; P 🛜) where the deep-blue and magenta colors and comfy beds exude a relaxed boutique feel. Bonus points for the free beer and wine reception and evening cookie buffet. Architecture- and design-lovers will dig the uniquely shaped **Abigaile's Treehouse** (☎ 979-823-6350; www.abigailestreehouse.com; 1015 E 24th St; r $119-199; P 🛜), offering four tranquil rooms with garden views.

For great sandwiches and salads, locals flock to **It Must Be Heaven** (☎ 979-822-7722; 100 S Main St; meals $6-10; 🕑 8am-6pm Mon-Fri, 8:30am-3pm Sat; 🪑) where the tempting homemade pies (try the mile-high Coconut Meringue) compete with a slew of Blue Bell ice-cream concoctions. For rustic elegance and gracious service, try **Madden's Casual Gourmet** (☎ 979-779-2558; 202 N Bryan Ave; meals $10-28; 🕑 lunch & dinner Mon-Sat, breakfast Sat; 🪑) inside the **Old Bryan Marketplace**. Vegetarian, gluten-free and children's-menu offerings thoughtfully balance out more adventurous items such as a chocolate-, coffee- and chile-rubbed beef tenderloin with cheddar polenta. During the day, browse the eclectic offerings at the shops inside the charming marketplace, from antiques to rare coins.

HUNTSVILLE
pop 38,000

Never thought you'd end up doing time in Huntsville? Well, welcome to the club. The club of more than 13,690, that is, which is the number of prisoners locked up in the area's seven **state prisons**. This town feels a little like a Johnny Cash song: full of hard livin' and hard knocks, but friendly and down-to-earth all the same. While the prisons' dominance in Huntsville isn't necessarily appealing, it is downright fascinating.

Sam Houston spent much of his life in Huntsville, which is now home to **Sam Houston State University** (☎ 936-294-111; www.shsu.com; 1903 University Ave). Several Houston-related buildings are part of the school's 15-acre **Sam Houston Memorial Museum Complex** (☎ 936-294-1832; www.shsu.edu/~smm_www; 1836 Sam Houston Ave; admission free; 🕑 9am-4:30pm Tue, from noon Sun), south of downtown. Looming large in the Texas imagination,

PRISON BREAK

Texas is notorious for its prison system. Huntsville is considered 'prison central' in Texas, and is home to the highest number of executions in the US. We spoke to a correctional officer at Texas State Penitentiary at Huntsville to get the lowdown on the realities of prison life.

There are seven prisons in town. How does this affect daily life here? To the locals, the prison system is just part of life here, more mundane than sensational. Except when, of course, the prison siren goes off three times in a row.

What does that mean? That mean's someone's missing. One siren signals the count. Two is for count clear – every prisoner's accounted for. Three means 'oh crap, what just happened?' They count prisoners several times during the day and night.

What happens if someone escapes? The whole system mobilizes, and every guard goes on duty. I'll get put on roadside checkpoint. [Laughs] I don't get my weekend then.

Do they give you a gun when you're out searching for the escapee? No, a flashlight.

A flashlight?! Yeah. A flashlight.

Are the locals worried that the prisoners will stay in Huntsville and commit crimes? If a prisoner escapes in Huntsville, Huntsville is the last place they're going to stay.

Can you share any secret prison lingo with us? Sure. 'Chain out' – that's when a prisoner gets released. We like to call prisoners 'Ole thang.' A 'trustee,' that's a prisoner who's earned some trust. And 'Code 20.'

What does that mean? You don't even want to know.

C Banks Barbee, correctional officer at Wynne Unit, Texas State Penitentiary, Huntsville

a 67ft-tall Sam Houston **statue** stands over the freeway on Hwy 75 just south of town (no, the giant white man looming over the highway isn't a trick of your imagination).

Huntsville is in the news every time Texas puts one of its condemned prisoners to death. Death row and the execution room are downtown at **'the Walls'** (815 12th St). When you see protesters outside this building, you'll know there's a scheduled execution.

As depressing as it is fascinating, the **Texas Prison Museum** (☎ 936-295-2155; 1113 12th St; adult/child $2/1; 🕑 noon-5pm Tue-Fri & Sun, 9am-5pm Sat) doesn't sugarcoat its exhibits, such as 'Old Sparky,' the electric chair once used in dispatching the condemned. Don't miss the exhibit on the prison rodeo: watching convicted murderers ride wild bucking broncos may seem like a bizarre way to pass the time, but hey, that was before YouTube was invented.

The **Huntsville-Walker County Chamber of Commerce** (☎ 936-295-8113; www.chamber.huntsville.tx.us; 1327 11th St; 🕑 9am-5pm Mon-Sat, 11am-5pm Sun), downtown, offers tourist information on other sights. Snag a copy of the mesmerizing *Prison Driving Tour* brochure, which outlines key prison-related sites in town, including the departure area, where about 100 ex-cons are released per day. On a sunny day, you can catch the low-security inmates playing baseball in the (fenced) prison yard.

Sleeping & Eating

Plenty of chain motels cluster at the edge of Huntsville around I-45 exit 116.

Sam Houston State University Hotel (☎ 936-291-2151; www.shsuhotel.org; 1610 Bobby K Marks Dr; r $80, ste $125-135; ⊠ P 📶 👶) In a brick dormlike building, this hotel offers spacious rooms with pedestal glass-bowl sinks and great showers. Suites feature balconies perfect for breathing in the fragrant pines that surround the hotel. Psst...that siren you hear a few times a day? Yes, 'the Walls' unit is spitting distance.

New Zion Missionary Baptist Church (☎ 936-294-0884; 2601 Montgomery Rd; all-you-can-eat $12; 🕑 11am-7pm Thu-Sat) Well sure, you can worship God here, but most people flock to worship the incredibly good and cheap barbecue cooked in a smoky shack next to the church.

our pick **Farmhouse Café** (☎ 936-435-1450; 1004 14th St; meals $7-9; 👶) The 'meat and three' blue-plate lunch specials taste more deep Deep South than Texas – but whatever – yum's the word. Don't be put off by the strip-mall location – inside it's a friendly farmhouse feel. Choosing which kind of pie is painful, but lemon icebox or chocolate mousse will equally blow your mind.

Homestead at 19th (☎ 936-291-7366; 1215 19th St; meals $15-25; 🕑 dinner Tue-Sat, brunch 1st Sun of month) A turn-of-the-century cabin nestled in the trees transports diners into the past, but the new American cuisine is entirely modern. It's hard to choose between dining in the lovely courtyard or on the front porch overlooking the shimmering pond.

Stardust Room (☎ 936-293-1295; 1115 University Ave; main $6-10) Right on the town square, this bar-restaurant lures loyal students and professors (and a few correctional officers, too) with Guinness, cheap cocktails and the kind of ironic 'dive bars make me feel surreal and glamorous' ethos that signals that yes, you're in a college town.

Getting There & Away

Other than driving to Huntsville (the most common option) there's a **Greyhound Station** (☎ 936-295-3732; www.greyhound.com; 1000 12th St) that's likely the most fascinating one in America. This is where most of the newly released inmates 'chain out': that is, it's the primary departure point every day for scores of just-released inmates who don't have a ride outta prison and are returning home. If that scares you, skip it. Otherwise, figure they've done their time and are just folks on the bus, on their way to new (and, hopefully, legal) adventures, just like you. It's 1½ hours to Houston (one-way/round-trip $21.50/43).

AROUND HUNTSVILLE
Sam Houston National Forest

Only 50 miles north of Houston but a world away, this is the largest of Texas' **national forests** (www.fs.fed.us). Recreational facilities include off-road vehicle tracks, mountain-bike trails, and the 126-mile Lone Star Hiking Trail. The trail, maintained by the **Houston Sierra Club** (☎ 713-895-9309; www.houston.sierraclub.com), is lined with magnificent flowering magnolia trees, and has several developed campgrounds. Inside the forest, the **Double Lake Recreation Area** offers swimming, canoeing and hiking. Contact the **ranger office** (☎ 936-344-6205; 394 FM 1375 W, New Waverly) for information. The gun-shy (and probably everyone else, too) should exercise caution during deer-hunting season (November to early January; call the ranger's office for exact dates).

Big Thicket National Preserve

Until the mid-19th century, the **Big Thicket National Preserve** (☎ 409-246-2337; www.nps.gov/bith; cnr Hwy 69 & Rte 420; admission free; ⊙ visitor center 9am-5pm) was a dense and mysterious forest where Civil War draft dodgers hid out. Now it's one of Texas' most interesting ecosystems: coastal

plains meet desert sand dunes, and cypress swamps stand next to pine and hardwood forests. One of the coolest trails in Texas, the **Pitcher Plant Trail** is a fully accessible half-mile boardwalk providing a good look at several of the bizarre carnivorous plants in North America. The preserve is also a prime spot for bird-watching, with more than 300 species of bird.

NORTHEAST TEXAS

Most Americans don't think 'forests' when they think of east Texas, which is too bad: despite Houston's smoggy, industrial image, just north of the city you'll find some of the country's most beautiful pine forests. Scratch that: here they call them the 'Piney Woods,' and you should too. Don't miss exploring some of the most underrated parklands south of the old Mason–Dixon line.

While the area lacks jaw-dropping 'gotta send Mom a postcard' sights, the gently rolling wooded terrain provides plenty of low-key thrills for nature-lovers. And scores of small, pretty towns charm the visitor with their classic central squares and stately brick buildings. You'll find traditional Southern and Louisiana influences creeping into dialects, architecture and food, which only deepen the closer you get to the border. (Translation: great biscuits, pie, and gumbo, y'all.)

NACOGDOCHES
pop 31,100

Whether Nacogdoches (nack-uh-*doe*-chuss) is the oldest town in Texas (as it claims) is open for debate. It dates from 1716, when a mission was established as a remote outpost of the Spanish empire. This is the cultural

---

WHAT THE...? DOUGHNUTS

As you drive through Huntsville, you may exclaim, 'Doughnuts. And more doughnuts!' No, it's not your imagination. There are indeed an inordinate number of doughnut shops: we counted six in this small town. In the USA, doughnut shops are often associated with law enforcement. Or is it that police officers are associated with doughnuts? Pssst...you can find several of the shops on Sam Houston Ave. Just look out for the police cars.

heart of east Texas, with a historic, cobble-stone downtown that exudes a remarkably genteel atmosphere balanced by a college-town buzz from **Stephen F Austin State University** (☎ 936-468-3401; www.sfasu.edu; 1936 North St). Come spring, the town's famous for its 20-mile-long **Azalea Trail** (www.nacogdochesazaleas.com), an artfully manicured stretch of flowers through pretty neighborhoods. Call ahead to see when the azaleas are predicted to bloom.

Main St runs through the historic center and is bisected by Hwy 59F, which is called North St running north of Main, and South St running south of Main.

In the middle of downtown, the **Nacogdoches Convention & Visitors Bureau** (☎ 936-564-7351; 200 E Main St; �9am-5pm Mon-Fri, 10am-4pm Sat, 1-4pm Sun) provides everything you need to know about the town and region, including a historic-walking-tour map.

Sights & Activities

The **Sterne-Hoya House** (☎ 936-560-5426; 211 S Lanana St; admission free; ☉10am-4pm Tue-Sat) was built in 1828 and is the site of Sam Houston's baptism (sites visited by Sam Houston are the Texas equivalent of 'George Washington slept here'). For a rundown on the interesting history of east Texas, check out the **Stone Fort Museum** (☎ 936-468-2408; cnr Clark & Griffith Blvds, Stephen F Austin State University; admission free; ☉9am-5pm Mon-Sat, 1-5pm Sun). North of town, **Millard's Crossing** (☎ 936-564-6631; www.millardscrossing.org; 6020 North St; adult/child $5/4; ☉9am-4pm Mon-Sat, 1-4pm Sun) is a collection

of 12 old buildings dating from 1820 to 1905, including a schoolhouse and a log cabin.

Sleeping

Hotel Fredonia (☎ 936-564-1234; www.hotelfredonia.com; 200 N Fredonia St; r from $90; P ⊛ ☒) Gurgling fountains and crooning Frank Sinatra lend an air of 1950s faded glamour to this hotel, despite its dated rooms. Our tip: ask for a remodeled cabana room out by the lushly landscaped saltwater pool.

Brick House (☎ 936-564-7428; www.thebrickhouseinn.biz; 522 Virginia Ave; r incl breakfast $112-129; ☒ P ⊛) Three comfy rooms in one of the oldest (brick, obviously) houses in town. Hope that orange pecan French toast is for breakfast.

Eating & Drinking

Java Jack's (☎ 936-559-9350; 1122 North St; medium lattes $2.50; ☉6:30am-10pm Mon-Sat, from 7am Sun) The local students totally dig this coffee shop. Grab a couch spot in the upstairs loft under the skylights.

ourpick Shelley's Bakery Café (☎ 936-564-4100; 112 N Church St; main $8-11; ☉lunch Tue-Sat) A near-perfect cafe with that certain breezy Southern charm that makes your cares, or at least your diet, fade away. With excellent salads and homemade soups, this is actually pretty healthy stuff. Splurge on the luscious éclairs.

Auntie Pasta's (☎ 936-569-2171; 211 Old Tyler Rd; lunch $5-9, dinner $8-18; ☉11am-9pm Sun-Thu, 11am-10pm Fri & Sat; ⑤) In a cavernous old warehouse, exposed brick and hanging stained-glass win-

---

ROUND TOP'S BARDS, GUITARS & ARMOIRES

Welcome to **Round Top**, population 88, which rivals Luckenbach as the cutest *tiny* town in Texas and is home to a ridiculous number of cultural festivals and events. Renowned cellists fly across half the world to play at the **Round Top Festival Institute** (☎ 979-249-3129; www.festivalhill.org; 248 Jester Rd), a year-round, international classical-music festival headquartered in a 1000-seat, acoustically phenomenal concert hall. (Amid bucolic grounds, naturally.)

Four times a year, antiques fever hits town: the **Round Top Antiques Festival** (☎ 512-237-4747; www.roundtoptexasantiques.com) is the largest in the country, drawing a staggering number of dealers, vendors, collectors and bargain-sniffers to sprawling grounds. In summer, get thee to a barn – the **Shakespeare at Winedale** (www.shakespeare-winedale.org; 3738 FM 2714; tickets $10/5) barn, that is, where loyal fans drive for miles each summer to see University of Texas students perform Shakespeare plays in a rustic setting redolent of the Bard's more ribald comedies.

Feeling lazy? Just plain hanging out works too. Find information at the **Round Top Chamber of Commerce** (☎ 979-249-4042; www.roundtop.org; 102 E Mill Street; ☉10am-2pm Tue-Sat), and explore Round Top's tiny town square with cute local shops and galleries, good food and better pie: you can't walk 20 steps without hitting all of them. The place is dripping with cozy B&Bs, too: check the city website for options. Yep, you might as well just plan to stay in Round Top all year. These superfriendly folks might even change the sign to 'Population: 89.'

dows lend a creative air to this simple pasta and pizza joint.

Flashbacks Café (☎ 936-462-9550; 109 Wettermark St; ☺ 4pm-midnight Mon-Fri) This campus-area bar welcomes all ages with a raucous edge of fun. Beware dollar drink night, unless you like drunk college girls serenading you.

Getting There & Away

Kerrville Bus Co (☎ 1-800-335-3722; www.iridekbc.com; 2915 NW Stallings Dr) serves Nacogdoches with a bus line that runs to and from Houston three times daily ($38, three hours) and daily to Tyler ($23.50, four hours).

HISTORIC SITES & PARKS

The only part of the Camino Real where Davy Crockett and Sam Houston actually walked (bad-ass, huh?), the **Mission Tejas State Park** (☎ reservations 512-389-8900, info 800-792-1112; www. tpwd.state.tx.us/missiontejas; 105 Park Rd 44, Grapeland; ☺ 8:30am-4:30am Tue-Sun) doubles as a camp-ground ($8 to $14) and historical site, with a replica of the 17th-century Mission San Francisco de los Tejas.

Notable for its Native American history – the Caddo people built a village and myste-rious ceremonial mounds here some 1200 years ago – the **Caddoan Mounds State Historic Site** (☎ 936-858-3218; www.visitcaddomounds.com; 1649 Hwy 21 W, Alto; ☺ 8:30am-4:30pm Tue-Sun; ☺) is a nice picnic spot on the way to Nacogdoches.

Ah, the golden age of rail travel. Relive it at **Rusk-Palestine State Park**, where the **Texas State Railroad** (☎ 903-683-2561, in Texas 800-442-8951; www.texasstaterr.com; Hwy 84; adult/child $40.50/23; ☺) offers fun train trips through dogwood-bloom-filled forests, powered by old steam engines. Predictably, kids dig it. Check the website for schedules.

NATIONAL FORESTS

Pining for a walk in the woods? East Texas has four large **national forests** (including Sam Houston (p219) filled with more than 300 kinds of trees, wildlife galore, camping, hik-ing, canoeing, fishing, boating…yep, they've got it all.

Detailed maps of each forest and its rec-reational areas are available for $6 each from the **US Forest Service** (☎ 936-639-8501; www.fs.fed. us/r8/texas; 415 S First St, Suite 110, Lufkin). Campsites ($4 to $20, depending on amenities) in and nearby the parks are available on a first-come, first-served basis; call the park offices listed

---

IF YOU CAN READ THIS BUMPER STICKER, YOU'RE TOO DAMN CLOSE TO MY TRUCK

Best bumper stickers in east Texas:

- 'If you ain't gonna cowboy up, go sit in the truck'
- 'Yankee by birth, Texan by choice'
- 'I don't cowboy up to win, I cowboy up to whoop ass'
- 'Texas ain't no place for amateurs'
- 'You can talk the bull, but can you ride it?'
- 'I'm not a redneck, just a Southerner with an attitude'
- 'This ain't my first rodeo'
- '73% redneck, and the rest – beer!'

---

following for specifics. A few precautions: hike with a partner and keep valuables out of sight in your car. Avoid hiking or wilderness camping during hunting season each fall and winter – call the ranger for exact dates.

With 251 sq miles, **Davy Crockett National Forest** (☎ 936-655-2299) is one of the less-developed forests and contains the **Ratcliff Lake Recreation Area**, and the picturesque, 20-mile **Four C National Recreation Trail** overlooking the Neches River. Canoers will dig the **Big Slough Canoe Trail**, part of a 3000-acre wilderness area which contains some of the biggest old-growth timber in Texas.

The smallest of the bunch, **Angelina National Forest** (☎ 936-897-1068) has the **Sawmill Hiking Trail**, a 5½-mile-long gem along the Neches River. For the area's best boating and fishing, head to the **Sam Rayburn Reservoir**.

Along the Texas–Louisiana border, **Sabine National Forest** (☎ 409-625-1940) lines the west bank of **Toledo Bend Reservoir**, where you'll find recreational, boating and camping sites on-shore. Inside the park, **Indian Mounds Recreation Site & Wilderness Area** offers several hiking trails.

JEFFERSON
pop 1900

Jefferson is the kind of town you fanta-size actually exists, but secretly believe it doesn't. Pinch yourself: you're not dreaming. Welcome to one of the most fascinating – and picturesque – towns in this humongous state. With a dose of Texas spirit, a generous help-ing of Deep South charm, plenty of gracious architecture, charismatic locals and a few

NORTHEAST TEXAS

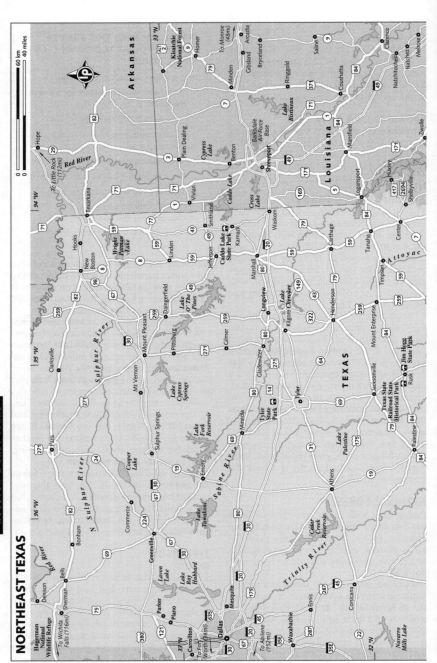

HOUSTON & EAST TEXAS

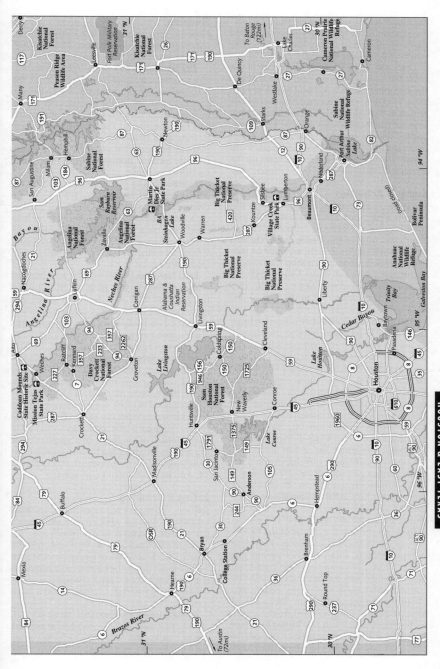

skeletons in her proverbial closet, Jefferson's a seductive Southern belle with a checkered past and a flask full of moonshine. No wonder you've fallen under her spell.

Once the largest inland river port in the USA, Jefferson was once a mini–New Orleans: the stomping grounds of a wild bunch of gamblers, riverboat men and madams. Since then, Jefferson has calmed down considerably but kept its irrepressibly fun spirit – and apparently a few ghosts, too. How could you not love a town with two old-fashioned soda fountains? Don't even think of stopping for just an afternoon – this town begs for a leisurely visit.

Sights & Activities

Listen up, y'all: the best thing to do in this town is a lazy, east-Texas-style **stroll**. So pick up a copy of the *Historic Jefferson Walking Tours* brochure at the **Marion County Chamber of Commerce** (☎ 903-665-2672; www.jefferson-texas. com; 101 N Polk St), an essential stop for friendly, expert guidance on all things Jefferson. Ghost-hunters are advised to take a midnight stroll in the town **graveyard**: when the moon's full it's a wistful, eerie place.

Rail baron Jay Gould once offered to bring the railroad to Jefferson, but the town (inauspiciously) turned him down, deciding to bet its future on river traffic. Lucky for Jefferson, Jay Gould's ultraluxe private 1888 **railroad car**, the *Atalanta*, now sits across from the Excelsior House on Austin St. This must-see is open for tours ($5); call the Excelsior (☎ 903-665-2513) for information.

For a bitty tour museum, the **Jefferson Historical Museum** (☎ 903-665-2775; 223 W Austin St; adult/child $3/1; ☉ 9:30am-5pm) is top-notch, with eye-opening exhibits on early life in east Texas, and a gorgeous display of antique clothing.

An afternoon activity in its own right, browsing the huge **Jefferson General Store** (☎ 903-665-8481; www.jeffersongeneralstore.com; 113 E Austin St; ☉ 9am-6pm Sun-Thu, until 10pm Fri & Sat) is a madcap delight: it's crammed with one of the best arrays of Texas-themed souvenirs, postcards, bumper stickers, mugs and outrageous gifts we've ever seen. Pick up your 'Don't mess with Texas Women' cowboy hat and cool off at the counter with a cherry ice-cream soda ($3.50).

Hit the river (and drink up plenty of local lore) on the hour-long narrated riverboat tours on Big Cypress Bayou, led by **Turning Basin Tours** (☎ 903-665-2222; www.jeffersonbayoutours.com; adult/child $7/5), just across Polk St bridge from downtown.

Sleeping

Historic inns and B&Bs are everywhere in Jefferson. **Classic Inn Reservations** (☎ 800-468-2627; www.classicinn.com) can help you choose one.

our pick Alley-McKay House (☎ 800-468-2627; www.mckayhouse.com; 306 E Delta St; r $79-149; ⊠ Ⓟ ⊜) A sprawling, romantic bungalow with a rustic back cottage contains the most eclectic rooms in town, filled with the right mix of comfort and funky antiques. The garden patio, overflowing with flowering vines, is a delightful place to enjoy chilled wine and a slice of the friendly owners' homemade red velvet cake on balmy evenings.

Excelsior House (☎ 903-665-2513; www.excelsior@ jeffersontx.com; 211 W Austin St; r $79-167; ⊠ ⊜) Owned and operated by the local garden club, this historic 15-room inn was built in the 1850s by a riverboat captain. Famous guests have included US presidents Ulysses S Grant and Rutherford B Hayes, as well as poet Oscar Wilde.

Delta Street Inn (☎ 903-665-2929; www.deltastreet inn.com; 206 E Delta St; r $89-139; ⊠ Ⓟ ⊜) A peaceful, gracious idyll on a dead-end street, this is the perfect antidote for anyone who has overdosed on B&B Victoriana. Amenities include a game room, flat-screen TVs, private balconies and an upstairs coffee bar.

Jefferson Hotel (☎ 903-665-2631; www.historic jeffersonhotel.com; 124 W Austin St; r $99-135; ⊠ ⊜) Fans of paranormal cable shows are advised to stay at this historic hotel, apparently the most haunted hotel in town. Rooms 19 and 20 have been known to freak out eye-rolling skeptics (even a frightened Stephen King is rumored to have checked out in the dead of night). If you dig the idea of a fetching blonde appearing at your bedside in a cloud of mist, stay in Room 14. And no, that doesn't cost extra.

Eating & Drinking

Jefferson bursts with interesting restaurants for its size. Mosey around the little downtown, and peek in wherever strikes your fancy.

Joseph's Riverport BBQ (☎ 903-665-2341; 201 N Polk St; meals $5-8; ☉ lunch & dinner) Cheap and cheerful barbecue. Order at the counter and retreat to the wooden tables with a groaning plate of brisket, turkey breast, fried okra and a huge iced tea.

Auntie Skinner's Riverboat Club (☎ 903-665-7121; 107 W Austin St; meals $6-18; ☉ lunch & dinner daily, until 2am Fri & Sat, breakfast Sat & Sun) This is the classic Jefferson bar, restaurant and social club, where everyone in town gets down to tasty pub food, beer and live music. Try the catfish and hushpuppies, and don't be a stranger.

ourpick **Austin Street Bistro** (☎ 903-665-9700; 117 E Austin St; meals $7-12; ☯ lunch Wed-Sun, dinner Wed-Sat) Amazing homemade food appears like magic out of a tiny kitchen. Everything you want a small-town restaurant to be: authentic, unpretentious and friendly.

CADDO LAKE & AROUND

Welcome to one of the most evocative, intoxicating…and OK, admit it, eerie spots in Texas. **Caddo Lake** (www.caddolake.net) is not only Texas' largest freshwater lake, the area is home to the world's largest cypress forest. Picture low-hanging, willowy trees over

moonlit labyrinthine waterways with the occasional alligator gliding by, and you've got a scene that's part Hitchcock, part Scooby-Doo, and entirely magical. If you can, rise early to watch as the steam rises off the bayous.

Nicknamed 'Spanish Beards' by the French settlers in an attempt to insult their Spanish rivals, the bald cypress trees strung with Spanish moss are hundreds of years old. If that sounds cool, it is: this area is one of the ecological – not to mention atmospheric – highlights of the Lone Star State.

Sights & Activities

The Caddo Lake's de facto headquarters are located in **Uncertain** (☎ 903-789-3443; www.cityof

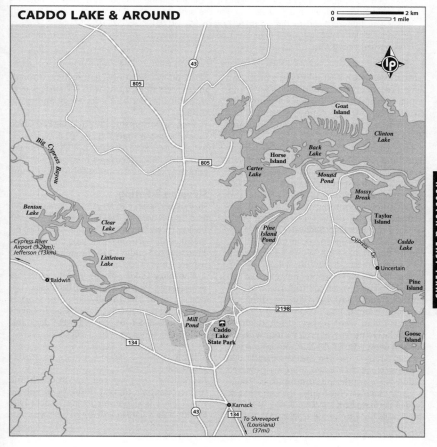

CADDO LAKE & AROUND

DRILL, BABY, DRILL!

And we don't mean just for oil. Twenty miles east of Tyler, **Kilgore** is not only home to the **World's Richest Acre**, but claims bragging rights as the home of the world's oldest women's precision drill team, the Kilgore Rangerettes. These ladies have performed at several presidential inaugurations and every Cotton Bowl since 1950. Yet what *is* a Rangerette, you ask, and what exactly do they drill? Thankfully, the **Rangerette Museum** (1100 Broadway; admission free; ☺ 9am-4pm Mon-Fri, 10am-4pm Sat) explains everything. If you're lucky, one of the original Rangerettes (no, not still in uniform) will be on hand to answer questions. Don't skip the film: it's full of fascinating footage, and there's no substitute for seeing the fringe-spangled, smiling gals in action. Speaking of action, this town had plenty in the 1950s, and not just because of the Rangerettes. Many things have made Texas Texas: the Alamo, breakfast tacos…but one thing made Kilgore, and that's oil. Trace the boom – and bust – at the **East Texas Oil Museum** (☎ 903-983-8295; www.easttexasoilmuseum.com; Kilgore College Campus, cnr Hwy 259 & Ross St; admission free; ☺ 9am-4pm Tue-Sat, until 5pm Apr-Sep). While the museum's name hardly inspires rapture, the vivid exhibits do an admirable re-creation of Kilgore's main street at the first oil boom in 1930–31. Before leaving Kilgore, take a spin around downtown. It recalls the kind of Texas that you might imagine James Dean circa *Giant* roaming around, with the old movie theater, the dusty streets, the oil wells rising in the distance… And if thinking of James Dean makes you hungry, head to the **Country Tavern** (☎ 903-984-9954; 1526 FM 2767; mains $7-26; ☺ lunch & dinner, closed Sun) just 5 miles west of town on Hwy 31, for tender and utterly mind-blowing barbecued ribs.

uncertain.com), which is a funky (some might say junky) meandering area of fishing shops, tour companies and down-home restaurants with erratic hours strung along Cypress Dr. But hey, with a name like Uncertain, you can't claim false advertising.

Hire a local guide to explore Caddo's highlights and safely live out your Indiana Jones swamp fantasies. You don't want to paddle alone through a spot nicknamed 'Hell's Half Acre,' do you? Tours include private and group tours by pontoon, steamboat and flat-bottomed swamp boats. One excellent guide service is **Caddo Outback Backwater Tours** (☎ 903-789-3384; www.caddolaketours.com; 1hr tour per pair $40), run by the affable John Wynn who grew up on Caddo; in fact, local authorities use him as a guide whenever someone gets 'lost' on the lake. (Hint: when visiting the vast and mighty Caddo, whatever you do, don't get 'lost.' We mean it.)

Those who want to keep their distance from lake creatures will prefer a tour with the **Graceful Ghost** (☎ 903-789-2238; www.gracefulghost.com; 510 Cypress Dr, Uncertain; adult/senior $20/18, child $1 per year of age; ☺ Mar-Nov), a steam-powered paddle wheeler offering 90-minute lake tours.

On the lake's western edge, the atmospheric **Caddo Lake State Park** (☎ 903-679-3351; FM 2198, off Hwy 43; admission $2, tent sites $8-12, RV sites $12-15, cabins $70-95) offers educational nature hikes through the cypress trees, along with RV sites, waterside tent sites perfect for kayakers, and rustic cabins.

From a dock inside the park, **Old Port Caddo Canoe Rentals & Tours** (☎ 903-930-0075; www.oldportcaddo.com; adult/child/senior $15/8/12) offers lake tours aboard a 24ft covered pontoon boat. The company also rents canoes for $10 per hour.

Sleeping & Eating

Shady Glade Resort (☎ 903-789-3295; www.shadygladeresort.com; 449 Cypress Dr; motel r $70, 1-bedroom cabins $60, 3-bedroom mobile homes $100) This one-stop shop on the lake offers a home-style cafe (7am to 2pm Thursday to Sunday), boat launch and guided fishing tours ($200 to $300).

Moonglow Lodge (☎ 903-789-3940; www.moonglowlodge.com; 144 N Mossy Brake Rd, Uncertain; r $120-140) A trio of charmingly rustic properties sits among the cypress trees on Caddo Lake's Taylor Island. Sit for a spell on the deck and soak up the mystery. No credit cards.

TYLER
pop 94,100

Romantics, be prepared to swoon: home to the country's biggest domestic supply of roses, Tyler is also home to the 14-acre **Tyler Municipal Rose Garden** (☎ 903-531-1212; www.texas

rosefestival.com/museum/garden.htm; 420 Rose Park Dr; admission free; ☼ dawn-dusk). Lushes, be prepared to stock up or detox: the closest liquor store in this dry county is 20 miles away (although it's legal to order a drink in a restaurant… go figure).

Flowers are the focus of two annual festivals in the 'Rose City': the **Azalea & Spring Flower Trail** (www.tylerazaleatrail.com) in late March, and the **Rose Festival** (www.texasrose festival.com) in October. Visit downtown's **Tyler Convention & Visitors Bureau** (☎ 800-235-5712; www. visittyler.com; 315 N Broadway; ☼ 8:30am-5pm Mon-Fri) for details.

Tyler's **Rosevine Inn** (☎ 903-592-2221; www.rose vine.com; 415 S Vine; r $110, ste $175; ✗ P ☎) is a gracious brick home offering bounteous breakfasts and five sweet, comfy rooms. Enjoy the outdoor hot tub and the red barn decked out as a rec room (pool players, rejoice!).

Otherwise, chain options abound on the interstate: the best among them is the **LaQuinta Inn** (☎ 903-561-2223; 1601 W Southwest Loop 323; r from $79; ✗ P ☎) a mile west of Hwy 69.

In Tyler's old downtown, we like **Rick's on the Square** (☎ 903-531-2415; 104 W Erwin St; lunch $6-12, dinner $17-45; ☼ 11am-midnight Mon-Fri, 5pm-1am Sat), an old brick building that offers comfort-food lunch specials, upscale dinner mains and homemade desserts (blackberry cobbler, $5), plus live music and dancing. For tasty Mexican, locals swear by **Taqueria El Lugar** (☎ 903-597-4717; 1726 E Gentry Parkway; meals $4-9) where you order off the menu by number (try the addictive No 3 or No 7).

LONGVIEW
pop 73,400

An easy base for the region, the **Longview Convention & Visitors Bureau** (☎ 903-753-3281; visit longviewtexas.com; 410 N Center St; ☼ 8:30am-5pm Mon-Fri) can fill you in on town events such as **Alley Fest** (www.alleyfest.org), a festive summer downtown block party and art fair, and late July's **Great Texas Balloon Race** (www.greattexas.balloonrace.com).

Since 1972, the enormous **Barron's Books** (☎ 1-800-284-6817; www.shopbarrons.com; 405 W Loop 281; ☼ 9am-9pm Mon-Sat) has been the region's go-to indie bookstore. The **cafe** (☎ 903-663-4737; meals $12-29) features dishes such as maple-roasted pecan salad and lobster ravioli in an airy, art-filled setting.

Day-trip from Longview to **Carthage**, home of the **Texas Country Music Hall of Fame & Tex Ritter Museum** (☎ 903-693-6634; www.carthagetexas.com/HallofFame/museum.htm; 310 W Panola; adult/child $5/3; ☼ 10am-4pm Mon-Sat).

Plentiful chain lodging congregates around where I-20 intersects with Hwy 281. The spiffiest midrange option is **Hampton Inn & Suites Longview North** (☎ 903-758-1113; fax 903-663-8670; 3044 N Eastman Rd; r incl breakfast $80-120, ste $120-160; ✗ P ☎ 🏊).

You'll find well-prepared New Orleans–style seafood at 60-year-favorite **Johnny Cace's Seafood & Steak House** (☎ 903-753-7691; 1501 E Marshall Ave/Hwy 80; mains $12-23; ☼ lunch & dinner Tue-Sun, dinner only Mon; �). **Mugshot Coffee House** (☎ 903-291-1077; 2655 Bill Owens Parkway; ☼ 6am-9pm Mon-Thu, until 11pm Fri, 7am-11pm Sat; ☎) offers Fair Trade coffees, live music and Friday movie nights.

HOUSTON & EAST TEXAS

Gulf Coast

America's 'Third Coast,' as it likes to call itself, is a place of many contrasts. All along the Gulf of Mexico, there's a quietude that is often surprising given the images of rowdy spring break high jinks on South Padre Island or the madcap Mardi Gras celebrations of Galveston. Yet even these towns are significantly calmer at times other than during their signature events.

Some parts of the Gulf Coast – like Port Arthur or Brazosport – have forgone any significant future from tourism in order to profit from the contemporary need for oil. Drilling rigs, refineries and related industries cover huge tracts of land. Meanwhile other areas seem to have forgotten the future altogether. Tiny coastal communities like Fulton and Rockport slumber away in solitude, and wandering coastal back roads in these areas is reason enough for a visit.

It's out on the sandy barrier islands where you find some of the greatest interest of the Gulf Coast. Galveston is built on a barrier island, and despite the very real peril from hurricanes, it has a fascinating heritage found in its old downtown and neighborhoods, while it still knows how to cut loose at the shore.

Port Aransas is another gem, with a culture that might have you donning flip-flops and staying a decade or two. Other watery delights are found in coastal highlights such as Aransas National Wildlife Refuge and the good museums of Corpus Christi. In any place along the coast, expect the best seafood imaginable (with a dash of Cajun color in the Golden Triangle).

HIGHLIGHTS

Best Single Stop
Galveston combines acres of sandy joy with the state's most historic downtown (p234)

Ideal Place to Whoop it Up
Spot majestic and rare but recovering whooping cranes at Aransas National Wildlife Refuge (p244)

Loyola Beach ★

Aransas National Wildlife Refuge ★

Mustang & Padre Islands Beaches ★

Port Aransas ★

Galveston ★

Where to Pound Sand
Mustang and Padre Islands (p253) have endless white sand beaches; some purely for fun, others carefully protected

How to Feed Like a Whale on Shrimp Tails
Join the crowds for the tasty seaside seafood at King's Inn in Loyola Beach (p255)

Best Place to Liberate Your Inner Beach Bum
Port Aransas (p251) has goofy old places to stay, goofy seafood joints for chow, and laid-back bars to be a goof in

GOLDEN TRIANGLE

The cities of Beaumont, Port Arthur and Orange make up the corners of the Golden Triangle, the southeasternmost corner of Texas. The area was first settled by French and Spanish trappers in the early 19th century, and has more in common culturally with neighboring Louisiana than it does with the rest of Texas. A large and freewheeling Cajun community and the state's largest African-American population by percentage (33%) combine to give the Triangle a culture that is as rich and spicy as the ubiquitous gumbo. This is not a part of Texas that subscribes to the abstemious notions in force elsewhere in the state.

Prior to 1901, the subsistence lives of the local trappers meant that the area could have been legitimately called the Beaver Triangle. Then oil was discovered south of Beaumont on a site called Spindletop, and the Triangle turned golden with cash. It was then the richest discovery made in the USA, and it sparked the creation of the entire US petroleum industry. Companies that later transmogrified into giants such as Chevron and ExxonMobil got their starts here. Some of the world's largest petrochemical works are found near Port Arthur and Beaumont. Pollution and a dependence on fluctuations in the price of oil are some of the legacies; oil spills – such as the massive one in 2010 – and hurricanes, some of the hazards.

Taken separately, the cities of Beaumont, Port Arthur and Orange are not compelling tourist destinations, but together they warrant a day or two of exploration. They bristle with small museums as well as fascinating sights related to the oil industry. The towns are roughly 20 miles apart and well connected by roads, meaning that it makes most sense for a visitor to treat them as one.

South of the Golden Triangle, the Texas Gulf Coast begins. The stretch curving southwest to Galveston is quiet much of the year and boasts attractive beaches and grass-covered dunes.

Orientation & Information

Beaumont is linked to Houston, 83 miles to the west, by I-10, which continues east into Louisiana. Orange is 23 miles east on I-10. Port Arthur is 17 miles south on the combined

---

DRIVING DISTANCES

Austin to Corpus Christi 192 miles, 3 hours
Corpus Christi to South Padre Island 172 miles, 3 hours
Houston to Beaumont 86 miles, 90 minutes
Houston to Galveston 50 miles, 45 minutes

US 69/96/287; the parallel TX 347 is a slower but more interesting road.

If you're entering the area from the east, you'll find a state-operated **Texas Travel Information Center** (☎ 409-883-9416, 800-452-9292; 1708 I-10 E; 🕓 8am-5pm) just over the Texas–Louisiana border in Orange. It has statewide information and a nature walk over the swamp out back.

BEAUMONT
pop 111,500

On January 10, 1901, a heretofore dry exploratory well leased by Anthony Lucas started to rumble and then blew out a fountain of oil. Soon hundreds of wildcat oil explorers had oil rigs crowded together like pine trees in a forest. The Spindletop field dried up within 10 years, but the oil industry was in the Golden Triangle to stay.

Besides the petrochemical industry, Beaumont has developed a busy port on the Neches River that services offshore oil-drilling platforms. Sights related to the oil industry are the main draws. The downtown is mostly quiet apart from a block of upscale bars.

Information

Babe Didrikson Zaharias Museum & Visitors Center (☎ 409-833-4622; 1750 I-10 exit 854, Martin Luther King Parkway; admission free; 🕓 9am-5pm) Has regional information and a room devoted to the achievements of one of the greatest female athletes of all time.

Beaumont Convention & Visitors Bureau (☎ 409-880-3749, 800-392-4401; www.beaumontcvb.com; 505 Willow St; 🕓 8am-5pm Mon-Fri) Downtown, with good regional info.

Sights & Activities
TEXAS ENERGY MUSEUM

This **museum** (☎ 409-833-5100; www.texasenergy museum.org; 600 Main St; adult/child $2/1; 🕓 9am-5pm Tue-Sat, 1-5pm Sun) is a mixed bag. Downstairs are exhibits that attempt to dazzle visitors with the science of oil drilling and a good bit of jingoism. Upstairs exhibits cover the Spindletop

GULF COAST

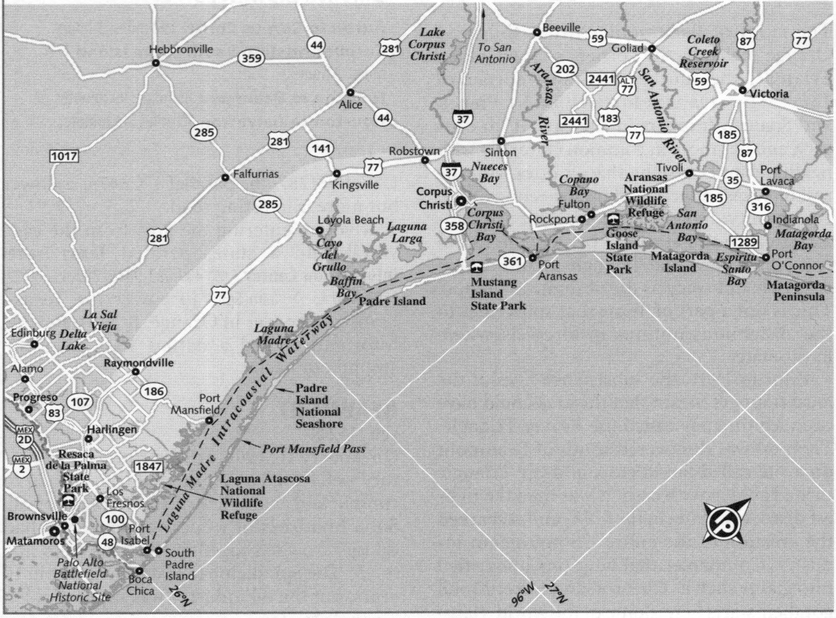

discovery and the subsequent growth of the Texas oil industry, and these are well done.

ART MUSEUM OF SOUTHEAST TEXAS

This **museum** (☎ 409-832-3432; www.amset.org; 500 Main St; admission free; 🕒 9am-5pm Mon-Fri, 10am-5pm Sat, noon-5pm Sun) has ever-changing exhibits drawn from the permanent collection and visiting shows. It is right next to the Texas Energy Museum downtown.

MCFADDIN-WARD HOUSE

If you want to see the kind of riches made possible by the Spindleton oil boom, visit this fabulous 1906 **mansion** (☎ 409-832-2134; www.mcfaddin-ward.org; 1906 McFaddin Ave, visitor center 1906 Calder St; tours $3; 🕒 10am-2:30pm Tue-Sat, 1-3pm Sun). Built before the advent of air-conditioning, it makes full use of huge overhangs and shade trees as well as awnings and transoms to let in the cool breezes. Members of the McFaddin family lived in the house until 1984, and their rich antique furnishings fill the lavish rooms.

To see more historic homes, restored and unrestored, explore the Oaks neighborhood in the blocks north and south of Calder St west of Martin Luther King Parkway.

SPINDLETOP/GLADYS CITY BOOMTOWN MUSEUM

This intriguing **museum** (☎ 409-835-0823; University Dr & north side of US 69/96/287; adult/child $3/1; 🕒 10-5pm Tue-Sat, 1-5pm Sun) is an altogether too-tidy reconstruction of part of the original boomtown – add 800,000 barrels of spilled oil and then you'd have some authenticity. Standing in a nearby field is the Lucas Gusher Monument, an imposing 58ft pink granite obelisk built in 1941 to commemorate the original well.

GATOR COUNTRY

Now that's entertainment! The name says it all at this **adventure park** (☎ 409-794-9453; www.gatorrescue.com; 21159 FM 365 at I-10 exit 838; adult/child $12/9; 🕒 10am-8pm daily Jun-Aug, 10am-6pm Sat & Sun Sep-May) run by the stars of the reality TV show *Gator 911* (aired on CMT). See dozens of huge gators munching on chickens to thrill the crowds (it's tough work) and learn all about the TV show, which proves *everybody* gets 15 minutes of fame.

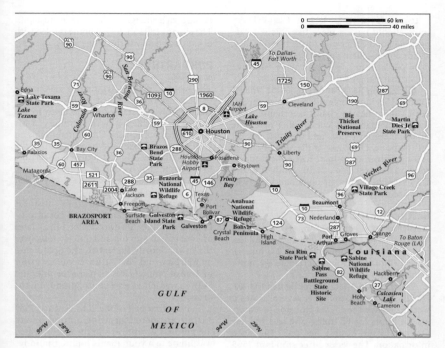

CARDINAL NECHES RIVER ADVENTURES

Gators not ready for their close-ups might be spotted on these **boat tours** (☎ 409-880-8907; www.nechesriveradventures.org; adult/child $15/10; ☷ various times Mar-Nov) of the vast ecosystem of the local river. Or you might see some of the hundreds of other plant and animal species. Call for details and reservations.

Sleeping

Most of the motels are chains along I-10. The area around the split with US 69/96/287 is especially ripe.

Village Creek State Park (☎ 409-755-7322; www.tpwd.state.tx.us; 1101 Alma Dr) This park, 10 miles north of Beaumont on US 96 near Lumberton, has nice but buggy creekside tent sites for $7 and sites with water and electricity for $15.

La Quinta Inn (☎ 409-838-9991; www.lq.com; 220 I-10 N exit at Calder; r $50-120; ☷ 🐾) A rambling place popular with utility workers and bargain hunters; a bit scarred but convenient. The rooms range from slightly small to very large. Opt for those way back, away from Interstate noise.

Best Western Jefferson Inn (☎ 409-842-0037, 800-528-1234; www.bestwestern.com; 1610 I-10 S exit 851; r $70-120; 🖳 ☷ 🐾) This comfortable older place features a pool and free breakfast bar. The 119 rooms have fridges and microwaves although the wi-fi reception in some is dodgy.

Sleep Inn & Suites (☎ 409-892-6700; www.sleepinn.com; 2030 N 11th St at I-10 exit 853B; r $80-140; ☷ 🐾) This newer reduced service motel has 53 rooms over three floors with interior halls. It's all generic but there are fridges and microwaves.

Eating & Drinking

Roam the Golden Triangle to maximize your food fun.

There's a strip of bars and clubs downtown in the Crockett St district (really one side of one short block, www.crockettstreet.com).

Dixie Dance Hall (☎ 409-833-1881; 234 Crockett St) A huge dance floor packs 'em in on weekends for country and party music.

Hub Lounge & Patio Bar (☎ 409-833-1881; 260 Crockett St) All things to all drinkers, there's decent bar food, rock music at night and lots of cold beer. The eponymous patio is the place to be on balmy evenings.

Logon Café (☎ 409-832-1529; 3805 Calder St) Every town should have a place like this – a cafe offering good coffee and meals (sandwiches, salads and excellent desserts), internet access (12¢ per minute), beer and wine, and live music many nights.

our pick **Willy Ray's Bar BQ** (☎ 409-832-7770; 145 I-10N; 🕑) Seeing people scarfing down the generic slop at nearby chains is a shame when there's such fabulous 'cue on offer here. The brisket is smoky tender and the pork ribs fall off the bone. Dirty rice is the side of choice among many fine options. It's on the frontage road on the west side of I-10, south of where US 69/96/287 splits off north, and it's near many of the motels.

Getting There & Around

Greyhound (☎ 409-832-2557; www.greyhound.com; 650 Magnolia St) is just north of downtown and has frequent buses to Houston ($18, 1½ hours). Buses within the Golden Triangle are not a viable option.

Amtrak's often-late **Sunset Limited** (☎ 800-872-7245; www.amtrak.com) runs several times a week going west to LA via Houston (a lethargic 2½ hours for 82 miles) and east to New Orleans (seven hours). See p357 for more information. The service-free stop is at 2555 W Cedar St.

ORANGE
pop 18,200

The smallest of the Triangle cities, Orange may have been named for citrus trees that once grew here or for some Dutch settlers; no one is certain. The widely scattered Cajun population lives along secluded bayous and tributaries of the Sabine River, which forms the border with Louisiana. For a year-round light show right out of *Close Encounters of the Third Kind*, drive Farm to Market (FM) 1006 at night and marvel at the blaring, multicolored factory lights of 'chemical row.'

The **Stark Museum of Art** (☎ 409-883-6661; www.starkmuseum.org; 712 W Green Ave; admission free; 🕑 10am-5pm Tue-Sat) has collections focused on artworks depicting native wildlife such as birds, including works by John J Audubon. One gallery is devoted to craftworks by Native Americans.

Across the street from the namesake museum, the carefully restored **WH Stark House** (☎ 409-883-0871; 610 W Main St; tours $5, no children under 10yr; 🕑 10am-3pm Tue-Sat) reveals the lifestyle of families rich enough to build whole museums. The elegant 1894 Victorian home is filled with ornate and heavy furnishings.

PORT ARTHUR
pop 55,600

The history of Port Arthur is a classic tale of Texan boom and bust. Railroad tycoon Arthur Stilwell established the town in the late 1890s as the southern terminus of his grandly named Kansas City, Pittsburgh and Gulf Coast Railroad, and happily named the settlement after himself. Stilwell cheerfully told people that he had designed the town based on the advice of 'brownies' – spirits that came to him in his sleep.

Unfortunately, the brownies' business advice was lacking, and Stilwell got into financial trouble. Shrewd dealer John Gates offered to bail him out and quickly took over the town. Shortly thereafter, the Spindletop oil well blew and Port Arthur became a major oil transit point. Gates reaped a fortune, and Stilwell was left to seek consolation from the brownies.

For the first half of the 20th century, Port Arthur prospered, growing around one of the prettiest downtowns in the South, which was home to a young Janis Joplin. But in recent years it has been devastated – first by residents fleeing to the suburbs and second due to hurricanes (Rita in 2005, Ike in 2008). However, the town's one great museum is always reason to visit.

Hwy 82 passes through three of the largest (and expanding) petrochemical plants in the world. Flames from exhaust towers, spewing gases and a constellation of multicolored lights make these places an arresting vision, especially at dusk. Closer to the gulf, huge deep-sea drilling rigs beached at the maintenance yards tower over the landscape.

The **Port Arthur Convention and Visitors Bureau** (☎ 409-985-7822, 800-235-7822; www.portarthurtexas.com; 3401 Cultural Center Dr; 🕑 8am-5pm Mon-Fri) is right off TX 73 and 9th Ave. Be sure to get copies of the Easy Driving Tour and Janis Joplin brochures (the latter takes you to virtually every site associated with her life here, including even the church of her baptism).

Sights
MUSEUM OF THE GULF COAST

This is a splendid **museum** (☎ 409-982-7000; www.museumofthegulfcoast.org; 700 Procter St; adult/child

$4/2; ☺ 9am-5pm Mon-Sat, 1-5pm Sun) that covers the natural, geological and cultural history of the region 'from Jurassic to Joplin.'

Allow a couple of hours to explore the two floors of exhibits in an old bank building downtown. A vast and colorful mural tracing the geologic development of the area from the time of the dinosaurs dominates the main display room.

Several musicians hail from the region, including blues great Clarence 'Gatemouth' Brown and Jiles Perry Richardson Jr, otherwise known as 'the Big Bopper.' A large area is devoted to Joplin, who remained loyal to her hometown right up until her death from an overdose in 1970. Check out her high-school yearbook photo, complete with bouffant hairdo.

HISTORIC HOMES

Lakeshore Dr near the center of Port Arthur has a few beautiful old homes from the region's glory days that have managed to survive the hurricanes as well as good views from the tall levee.

Constructed in 1900 by barbed-wire baron Isaac Ellwood, the pink, one-story **Pompeiian Villa** (☎ 409-983-5977; 1953 Lakeshore Dr; adult/child $2/1; ☺ 10am-2pm Tue-Fri) is modeled after a villa uncovered in Pompeii, Italy.

Other historic homes you'll see on this stretch include the 1915 **White Haven** (2545 Lakeshore Dr) and the 1906 **Rose Hill** (100 Wordsworth Blvd).

Sleeping

Most of the chains are north near Nederland along Memorial Blvd-US 69/96/287.

Super 8 Motel (☎ 409-722-1012; www.super8.com; 7700 Memorial Blvd; r $60-100; ☺ 🖥) A newer outlet of the ubiquitous budget chain, this Super 8 has large rooms (with microwaves and fridges) on three floors with inside halls. The small pool is indoors.

Holiday Inn Park Central (☎ 409-724-5000; fax 409-724-7644; 2929 Jimmy Johnson Blvd; Sun-Thu $84, Fri & Sat $69) This 164-room hotel is just off US 69 on a street named for the local-boy-made-good ex-football coach and broadcaster (some will like waking up on Jimmy Johnson, others will have nightmares). Ask for a room overlooking the pretty courtyard garden and pool.

Eating & Drinking

The staple of local cuisine is shrimp cooked every possible way, supplied by the scores of shrimp boats that call Port Arthur home. Some of the best eats are actually in the adjoining communities of Nederland (north) and Groves (east).

Boudin Hut (☎ 409-962-5079; 5714 Gulfway Dr; meals from $6; ☺ 11am-11pm Mon-Sat) Live zydeco and Cajun music are the main nighttime events at this lively place in a plain tin wrapper. Cheap, tasty Cajun lunches are hugely popular with gregarious refinery workers.

our pick **Larry's French Market & Cajun Restaurant** (☎ 409-962-3381; 3701 Atlantic Hwy/FM 366, Groves; meals $8-22; ☺ 11am-2pm Mon-Wed, 11am-9pm Thu,

---

CAJUN CULTURE

The Golden Triangle is also referred to as the Cajun Triangle due to the number of Cajuns living in the area. Their large numbers (approximately 30,000) and influence on the local way of life result from the region's close proximity to Louisiana's Cajun Country, officially called Acadiana. It's named for the French-speaking settlers exiled from l'Acadie (now Nova Scotia), who sought refuge in the area from the mid- to late 18th century (the term 'Cajun' is a corruption of 'Acadian'). In the early 20th century many Cajuns moved across the border to Beaumont and Port Arthur to find work in the oil fields.

Cajun culture is famed for its cuisine, music and spirited *bons temps,* and its influence is now found in many places in Texas, especially in Houston and towns along the coast. Look for menus featuring Cajun specialties such as crawfish (also called 'mudbugs' – miniature lobsters in appearance and taste), alligator meat, frog legs, gumbo, boudin and andouille sausages, 'dirty rice' (rice cooked with small quantities of chicken giblets or ground pork, along with green onions, peppers, and herbs and spices) or the classic red beans and rice. You'll also see po'boys, loaf sandwiches filled with such treats as fried oysters, soft-shell crabs or catfish.

Restaurants and bars in the Golden Triangle (including most of those listed here) have crawfish boils during the mudbug season, which peaks from March to May. The boils see crawfish cooked in a vat of boiling water laced with spices along with potatoes and corn.

to 10pm Fri, 5-10pm Sat) This fabulous, friendly place is part tasty Cajun restaurant and part Cajun dancehall. The food – local specialties include shrimp creole, fried crawfish and gumbo – is excellent and plentiful. You will be floored by the choice as you go down the serving line. From Thursday to Saturday, the low-ceilinged bar area rocks to Cajun and zydeco music.

Schooner (☎ 409-722-2323; 1507 US 69 at FM 365, Nederland; meals $10-20; 11am-10pm Mon-Sat) 'If it swims, we have it' is the policy of this traditional family-run supper club. Judging by the comprehensive menu, this is close to the truth. There's lots of shrimp, naturally, and fresh fish with Cajun flair.

Sartin's Seafood (☎ 409-721-9420; 3520 Nederland Ave, Nederland; meals $10-22; 11am-9pm Tue-Sat, 11am-3pm Sun) Barbecued crabs are found on menus all over the Triangle, but this place claims to have invented them. The large seafood platter is a Cajun feast.

SABINE PASS AREA

Driving 12 miles south from Port Arthur to Sabine Pass and beyond, along TX 87, offers a fascinating look at the area's historic past, its economy today and the perils of nature.

You may or may not see tall and massive offshore rigs docked along the Sabine Pass channel. When the world market price of oil is high, it's economically feasible for oil companies to drill exploratory wells in the gulf. When the price is low, companies can't make money, and you'll see dozens of their huge rigs stored along the waterway.

After Sabine Pass, TX 87 theoretically continues for 50 scenic miles southwest to the ferry from Port Bolivar to Galveston Island (p242), but the road has been closed as far as High Island for years because of hurricanes and a lack of bureaucratic will. Instead, you have to take the long way around via US 73 and TX 124 to the ferry, although this allows you to drive through the green carpet of Anahuac National Wildlife Refuge (p242).

Sabine Pass Battleground State Historic Site

During the Civil War, it was vital to the Confederacy that it continue its lucrative cotton trade with England and France. Weapons, supplies, medicine and more were bought with the cotton. The Union responded with a fairly effective blockade of Southern ports from Virginia all the way to the Mexican border near Brownsville.

At Sabine Pass, a small fort was built to prevent the Union Navy from gaining control of the waterway. On September 8, 1863, a lone guard, Lt Dick Dowling, saw four Union gunboats approaching. He ran 2 miles into town and summoned 46 additional troops – mostly Irish mercenaries – who were drunk in a bar. Hastening back to the fort and seeing the attacking boats loaded with 4000 Union troops proved sobering. The men used the fort's six cannons to force two of the gunboats aground, and ran off the others. It was a major victory for the Confederacy.

The site of the fort is now offshore, but detailed outdoor displays recall the battle. This 57-acre **site** (☎ 409-971-2451; www.visitsabinepassbattleground.com; admission free; 8am-5pm) offers great views of idle oil rigs and passing ships and has good picnic areas.

Sea Rim State Park

More than 15,000 acres in size, this **park** (☎ 800-792-1112; www.tpwd.state.tx.us) includes vast marshlands north of TX 87 and over 5 miles of beaches south of the road. The wetlands are popular with bird-watchers, who can use blinds that have been built at key points. The beach areas are usually popular on summer weekends but are almost deserted at other times of the year. However, as of 2010, much of the park remained closed with all services destroyed due to hurricanes. Plans call for parts to be slowly reopened for day use, so check on progress before making the drive.

GALVESTON AREA

The city of Galveston is at the heart of a region of long barrier islands, undeveloped marshes, the busy Houston ship channel, oodles of vacation homes and long ribbons of white-sand beaches.

GALVESTON

pop 59,200

A mixture of failed dreams and high hopes for the future, its history overshadowed by tragedy, sultry Galveston Island is as close as you will get to the Deep South in Texas. Along block after oleander-scented block, people in tar-paper houses one step above shacks live cheek by powdered jowl with the moneyed in their mansions. The latter have their own closed society, and if you're not a BOI – 'born on island' – you don't quite fit in, no matter how many decades you've lived in the 30 sq miles that make up the heart of town.

More than a century after the 1900 cataclysm and 2008's Hurricane Ike (see the boxed text, p235), Galveston is building on its past. For many visitors, it's just a beach town with some history. But there are better beaches elsewhere, and what makes Galveston irresistible is that it's actually a historic town with some beaches. Visitors can revel in the town's heritage and then go have a cold one while getting a tan. It's also a very popular cruise-ship port, which has been a vital boost to the economy.

Orientation & Information

Nothing more than a sandy barrier island, Galveston stretches 30 miles in length and is no more than 3 miles wide. The city itself is 100 blocks long, from the ferry dock in the east to the newest developments west of the airport. I-45 from the mainland becomes Broadway Ave, which runs through the heart of town. Seawall Blvd is just that, and it follows the gulf shore for more than 10 miles. A beach runs along the base of the seawall, and a long, wide sidewalk runs along the boulevard.

The port, the Strand historic district and the center of much of Galveston's life are on the bay side between 19th and 25th Sts.

Galveston Bookshop (☎ 409-750-8200; 317 23rd St) Has a good selection of new and secondhand books, many of local interest. Pick up a copy of *Walking Historic Galveston: A Guide to its Neighborhoods* by local writer Jan Johnson.

Galveston Island Visitors Center (☎ 409-763-4311; www.galveston.com; Ashton Villa, 2328 Broadway Ave; ☾ 9am-5pm) A model for other visitor centers. Look for the mark showing how high Ike's waters reached in 2008.

Dangers & Annoyances

Galveston is not all restored mansions and fun-filled tourist attractions. It has a bad drug problem and neighborhoods as decrepit as any you'll find in the USA. Be aware of your surroundings and use your own judgment in determining a neighborhood's safety.

Sights

THE STRAND

The center of activity on the island, this historic district is best covered on foot. Checking out the many attractions, shops, restaurants and bars can easily take a day or more. Informative historical markers identify buildings and sights all over the district. Walking around, you'll get a real appreciation for the city's glory days in the late 19th century.

A TALE OF TWO HURRICANES

Galveston boasts a long list of Texas firsts from its glory days as the leading city in Texas: the first private bank (1854), first opera house (1870), first electric lights (1883), first country club (1898) and many more.

Everything changed on September 8, 1900, when the nation's deadliest natural disaster struck. A hurricane with winds of 120mph drove a storm surge that submerged much of the island under 20ft of water. Where Galveston Island had been, there were now only the waters of the Gulf of Mexico.

Of the town's 37,000 people, at least 6000 died, but no one will ever know the exact toll. Galveston never recovered. The port business moved to Houston along with most of the banks, the stock exchange and much of the commerce.

From the 1920s through the '50s, Galveston was best known for moral turpitude. Gambling, prostitution and anything money can buy could be bought on its streets. Rock bottom for the island came in the 1960s, when even the illicit trade moved elsewhere and the most beautiful and historic parts of town, like the Strand, fell into ruin.

However, a preservation movement began just in the nick of time, and it helped restore hundreds of buildings and entire neighborhoods. At the same time, Galveston found favor with a new generation of sun-seekers.

But revitalization literally took a blow on September 13, 2008 when Hurricane Ike blew right across Galveston killing more than 100 people. The vast seawall helped deflect much of the worst of the storm but damage was still in the billions of dollars. Even two years later, damage was still evident and some attractions and services had yet to be restored.

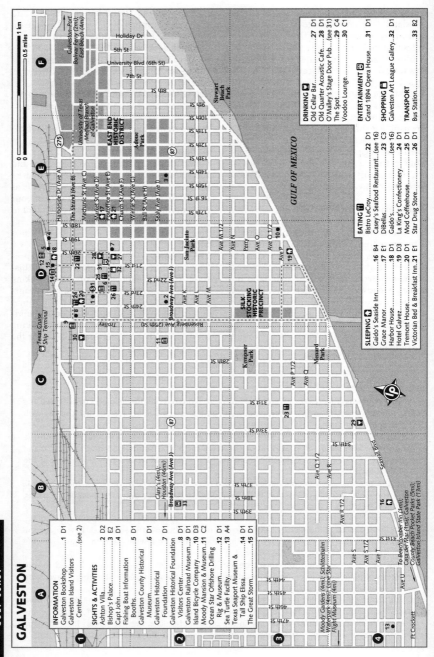

GALVESTON

GULF COAST

INFORMATION
Galveston Bookshop..................1 D1
Galveston Island Visitors
 Center..........................(see 2)

SIGHTS & ACTIVITIES
Ashton Villa...............................2 D2
Bishop's Palace..........................3 E2
Capt John..................................4 D1
Fishing Boat Information
 Booths.....................................5 D1
Galveston County Historical
 Museum...................................6 D1
Galveston Historical
 Foundation...............................7 D1
Galveston Historical Foundation
 Visitors Center..........................8 D1
Galveston Railroad Museum......9 D1
Island Bicycle Company............10 D3
Moody Mansion & Museum......11 C2
Ocean Star Offshore Drilling
 Rig & Museum...........................12 D1
Sea Turtle Facility......................13 A4
Texas Seaport Museum &
 Tall Ship Elissa.........................14 D1
The Great Storm.......................15 D1

SLEEPING
Gaido's Seaside Inn...................16 B4
Grace Manor..............................17 E1
Harbor House............................18 D1
Hotel Galvez..............................19 D3
Tremont House...........................20 D1
Victorian Bed & Breakfast Inn...21 E1

EATING
Bistro LeCroy.............................22 D1
Casey's Seafood Restaurant....(see 16)
DiBellas.....................................23 C3
Gaido's...................................(see 16)
La King's Confectionery.............24 D1
Mod Coffeehouse......................25 D1
Star Drug Store..........................26 D1

DRINKING
Old Cellar Bar............................27 D1
Old Quarter Acoustic Cafe........28 D1
O'Malley's Stage Door Pub.....(see 31)
The Spot....................................29 C4
Voodoo Lounge.........................30 C1

ENTERTAINMENT
Grand 1894 Opera House...........31 D1

SHOPPING
Galveston Art League Gallery....32 D1

TRANSPORT
Bus Station................................33 B2

The busy pier area, north of Harborside Dr at the end of Sts 19 to 22, has been converted from an old dock area and has numerous shops, restaurants and museums.

Galveston Historical Foundation

The **organization** (☎ 409-765-7834; www.galvestonhis| tory.org; 502 20th St; ☼ 8:30am-5pm) responsible for much of Galveston's ongoing preservation and renewal has information at its headquarters in the 1861 Customs House. It also has a tiny **visitor center** (☎ 409-621-2209; 2417 Strand St; ☼ 10am-4pm Wed-Sun) in an 1875 building. Be sure to get the $1 walking map of the Strand as well as discount coupons for the foundation's many attractions. Also, watch for the reopening of the foundation's Galveston County Historical Museum, which had been at 2219 Market St. Ike dealt this building a possibly fatal blow.

The Great Storm

This 30-minute multimedia **documentary** (☎ 409-763-8808; www.galvestonhistory.org; Pier 21; adult/child $4/3; ☼ on the hour 11am-6pm Wed-Mon) avoids the maudlin as it recounts the 1900 hurricane through photos, eyewitness accounts and various special effects. Even the most jaded will be able to imagine the horror that Galveston residents experienced as the hurricane submerged much of the island. A movie about Galveston's rich pirate heritage may help you talk like one.

Texas Seaport Museum & Tall Ship Elissa

This vast **museum** (☎ 409-763-1877; www.galveston history.org; Pier 21; adult/child $8/4; ☼ 10am-5pm) explains life around Galveston's port during its heyday in the 19th century. One of the best displays shows how gunpowder was smuggled through the port during the Texas Revolution.

Outside, the *Elissa*, a sailing ship built in Scotland in 1877, has been carefully restored and is a good example of the typical boat that called on Galveston harbor in the late 19th century.

Ocean Star Offshore Drilling Rig & Museum

From 1969 to 1984, this offshore drilling rig explored for oil in up to 173ft of water out in the gulf. Now moored in the Pier 19 area at the end of 19th St, it has been converted into a three-level **exhibit** (☎ 409-766-7827; adult/child $8/5; ☼ 10am-5pm) that explains offshore oil exploration for people who want to see beyond catastrophic blowouts and spills.

Galveston Railroad Museum

Ike tore up this sweet little collection and the reopening of the **museum** (☎ 409-765-5700; 25th St at the Strand), in the beautifully restored Santa Fe station, is uncertain.

HISTORIC HOMES

The **East End Historic District** has scores of pretty old buildings and is bordered by 11th, 19th and Mechanic Sts and Broadway Ave. A good driving and walking-tour guide and map is widely available. This historic district is the area just east of the Strand and it has several B&Bs.

The **Silk Stocking Historic Precinct** (www.silkstock inggalveston.org) runs along 23rd, 24th and 25th Sts between Aves N and P. It is home to some of the grandest mansions and some of the lushest oleander bushes and gardens. The area was named after the luxury items only women from here could afford.

Many historic homes in Galveston have been beautifully restored and are open at various times for tours. The Galveston Historical Foundation (p237) operates several and sells discounted tickets.

Ashton Villa (☎ 409-762-3933; www.galvestonhistory. org; 2328 Broadway Ave) The Galveston Island Visitors Center occupies part of the ground floor of this 1858 mansion, while the rest is closed for renovations.

Bishop's Palace (☎ 409-762-2475; www.galvestonhis tory.org; 1402 Broadway Ave; adult/child $8/4; ☼ tours noon-4pm) Built between 1886 and 1893, this ornate traffic-stopper has hidden back stairs and other fun features you can see on special tours.

Moody Mansion & Museum (☎ 409-762-7668; www.moodymansion.org; 2618 Broadway Ave; adult/child $7/3.50; ☼ tours 11am-3pm) The grandest mansion on the island, this place dates from 1895 and shines in its original splendor.

MOODY GARDENS

Moody Gardens (☎ 409-744-4673, 800-582-4673; www. moodygardens.com; 1 Hope Blvd; admission pass $50, individual exhibits also priced separately; ☼ 10am-6pm, to 8pm summer) is a vast complex combining an aquarium, botanical exhibits, theaters and other spectacles. It's Galveston's number-one tourist attraction, but it can also be a very expensive day out if you're not careful. It's best to get there early and scope out your choices. If you don't think you can do everything, don't buy a day pass; instead buy individual tickets (eg the Rainforest Pyramid is adult/child $11/9).

GULF COAST

The three striking pyramids filled with themed attractions are the architectural focus of the gardens.

The Aquarium Pyramid offers king penguins, fur seals and the largest display of sea horses in the world. The Rainforest Pyramid is a 10-story glass structure housing a lush tropical forest, including plants, birds, butterflies and a wonderful crawly bug exhibit. The Discovery Pyramid is home to some so-so space-related exhibits and some often excellent traveling exhibits.

Elsewhere, there are the requisite IMAX and 3-D theaters; the Ridefilm Theater is a gimmick that 'enhances' the movie by shaking you about like a paint can at the hardware store.

Palm Beach is an artificial beach that seems somewhat superfluous, given that Galveston already has 32 miles of real beaches.

The **Colonel** is a replica paddle wheeler offering one-hour tours of Offatts Bayou, an inlet on the north side of the island. Voyages depart daily at 2pm and 4pm ($10/8 adult/child), and there are also evening dinner cruises and other special voyages at higher prices.

To reach Moody Gardens, take 81st St from Seawall Blvd to Jones Rd, then turn left onto Hope Blvd.

SCHLITTERBAHN WATERPARK

Close to Moody, this ginormous, indoor-outdoor **water park** (☎ 409-770-9283; www.schlitterbahn.com; 2026 Lockheed St; adult/child $40/32; ☯ 10am-8pm summer, reduced hours other times) has slides and indoor beaches among 32 watery delights.

LONE STAR FLIGHT MUSEUM

Also close to Moody, this great **museum** (☎ 409-740-7722; 2002 Terminal Dr; adult/child $10/5; ☯ 9am-5pm) for historic airplane lovers is still recovering from Ike. Inside the hangers at Galveston Municipal Airport you can see ongoing restoration of storm damage to the collection. For just a bit more ($375) you can have a ride on one of the historic planes like the B-25, which the author's father flew on in WWII.

SEA TURTLE FACILITY

The National Oceanic and Atmospheric Administration has an often-ignored **laboratory** (☎ 409-766-3670; Sias Dr; ☯ free tours by appointment) devoted to saving the highly endangered Kemp's ridley sea turtle. Injured adults are treated and young turtles are raised for release in the gulf. The facility is off Ave U near 45th St.

BIRDERS OF A FEATHER FLOCK TOGETHER

If you associate Texas largely with the stereotypes of oil, cowboys and cattle, it may surprise you to learn that the Lone Star State offers outstanding bird-watching opportunities. Indeed, Texas has long been a favorite destination for bird-watchers, and with good reason – it has more bird species (more than 600) than any other state in the USA, and of these 600 species, more than 75% have been seen along the Gulf Coast.

Like seagulls on a beach after a community picnic, the coast is dotted with bird-watching sites and parks. Some are enhanced with boardwalks, kiosks, observation platforms or other features; many towns stage events and festivals to coincide with the local birding season and to attract visitors to their charms.

Among the more notable sites for spotting feathered friends in this chapter, are the following:

- Sea Rim State Park near Port Arthur (p234)
- Anahuac National Wildlife Refuge near Galveston (p242)
- The magnificent Aransas National Wildlife Refuge (p244)
- The nature preserves of Port Aransas (p251)
- Padre Island National Seashore (p253)
- Laguna Atascosa National Wildlife Refuge (p255)
- South Padre Island Birding and Nature Center (p257)

The Rio Grande Valley is a natural extension of a bird-watching itinerary. See the boxed text, p64 for locations.

GULF COAST

BEACHES

There are beaches all along Seawall Blvd. Usually. Storms can take away the sand, leaving little to enjoy. However, Galveston has valiantly fought back with 'beach restoration' projects that pump sand from the gulf onto the shore.

Of course, beachgoers here have to contend with the aesthetic problems posed by the 17ft-tall concrete seawalls and the 'new' beaches often wash away quickly. You'll probably find the beaches listed here more to your liking.

East Beach

Also called Apffel Park, this vast expanse of hard-packed sand is at the very eastern end of the island. On summer weekends, it has live concerts and becomes one vast outdoor party (large signs say drinking is permitted). Brewers sponsor concerts and bikini contests. Admission is $8 per vehicle and there's beach parking for a mere 7000 cars. You can also park and walk in for free.

Stewart Beach

The place for people who met on East Beach and had kids. Family-friendly activities abound; admission is $8 per car. The beach begins at the south end of 6th St.

Galveston County Beach Pocket Parks

The crescent-shaped beaches run by the county are found southwest of town off FM 3005 (the continuation of Seawall Blvd) at three roads with names taken right off an odometer: 7 Mile Rd, 9 Mile Rd and 11 Mile Rd. All have bathrooms and showers, and the latter two have concession stands.

Activities

Many stores along Seawall Blvd rent bicycles, as well as in-line skates and other gear for land and sea. Cycling is an excellent way to explore the town and historic districts. **Island Bicycle Company** (☎ 409-762-2453; www.islandbicyclecompany.com; 1808 Seawall Blvd) rents bikes ($30 per day), surfboards ($50 per day) and kayaks ($60 per day).

Red snapper is the fish most prized by people fishing offshore from Galveston, but catches are often restricted. Still there are many fish in the sea and you have your pick of party boats and charters from Pier 19. **Capt John** (☎ 409-762-8808; www.galvestonfishingboats.com;

Pier 19) has four-hour bay trips for $25 and all-day deep-sea adventures from $60.

Check with the **National Oceanic and Atmospheric Administration (NOAA)** (http://flowergarden.noaa.gov/visiting/charter_ops.html) for operators who run tours out the Flower Gardens, a premier dive spot in the Gulf of Mexico.

Tours

Tours come in many shapes and sizes.
Artist Boat (☎ 409-770-0722; www.artistboat.org; tours from $50) Creative and fascinating tours of the natural side of Galveston Island and the bay via kayak. Leaders meld science and art.
Galveston Sightseeing Train (☎ 409-221-0282; adult/child $10/5; ☒ tours 9:30am, noon, 2:30pm & 5pm Jun-Aug, reduced schedule Sep-May) One of those tractor-pulled fake affairs where the riders look slightly embarrassed; covers 17 miles of the island over 1½ hours. Tours depart from the corner of Seawall Blvd and 25th St.
Harbor Tours (☎ 409-763-1877; www.galvestonhistory.org; Pier 22; adult/child $12/10) One-hour tours of the oil-rig-filled harbor that depart from the Texas Seaport Museum (p237); dolphins often spotted.

Festivals & Events

Because tourism is the island's number-one source of revenue, Galveston schedules a succession of special events. The following are among the most notable.

February

Mardi Gras (www.mardigrasgalveston.com) For 12 days before Ash Wednesday, Galveston does its best to outdo New Orleans with parades, pageants, parties and more. Make lodging reservations far in advance.

May

Historic Homes Tour (☎ 409-765-7834; www.galvestonhistory.org) There are guided tours of some of the city's finest privately owned historic mansions for the first two weekends in May.

December

Dickens on the Strand (☎ 409-765-7834; www.dickensonthestrand.org) During this event over the first weekend in December, the Galveston Historical Foundation creates its own version of Victorian London.

Sleeping

Rates for rooms vary widely from the lows of midweek in the non-summer months to the high highs of summer weekends and special events like Mardi Gras – times when everything books up far in advance.

CAMPING

RV parks took a big hit from Ike and are rebuilding. Galveston Island State Park has excellent but limited camping facilities (p242).

MOTELS & HOTELS

Galveston's seafront budget motels are not impressive. Ask to see rooms before committing. However, there are good options near the sand that won't have you end up in a chain place around 61st St. Staying in the Strand puts you in the midst of atmosphere and nightlife.

Beachcomber Inn (☎ 409-744-7133; www.galveston inn.com; 2825 61st St; r $40-180; 🛜 📺) One block from Seawall Blvd and the beach, this indie motel should serve as a model for others. Rooms in the basic two-story building are spotless, and all have microwaves and fridges.

Gaido's Seaside Inn (☎ 409-762-9625; www. gaidosofgalveston.com; 3802 Seawall Blvd; r $60-200; 🛜 📺) This older motel behind the famous restaurant (see p241) has simple but comfortable, well-maintained rooms. Exterior corridors let you ponder the surf and make new friends.

Casa del Mar (☎ 409-740-2431, 800-392-1205; 6102 Seawall Blvd; r $80-240; 🛜 📺) This friendly, albeit starkly designed place has 150 small but comfortable condo-style units with kitchen, living room, balcony and accommodations for six (queen-size bed, foldout sofa and bunks in the hall suitable for kids).

Harbor House (☎ 409-763-3321; www.harborhouse pier21.com; Pier 21; r $90-200; 🛜 📺) An excellent Strand choice, this comfy hotel is in the Pier 21 complex. The 42 rooms are large and have good views of the harbor through small windows.

Tremont House (☎ 409-763-0300; www.wyndham tremonthouse.com; 2300 Mechanic St; r $110-300; 📺 🛜 📺) A former 1870s dry-goods store has been reborn as a luxury hotel. The 119 rooms are a mix of new and old and have high Victorian windows that let in lots of light. The best feature, however, is the rooftop bar with views of sunsets and passing ships.

Hotel Galvez (☎ 409-765-7721; www.wyndhamhotel galvez.com; 2024 Seawall Blvd; r $120-300; 📺 🛜 📺) The Galvez is a grand seafront hotel in the Spanish colonial style dating to 1911. It's a plush place offering over 200 rooms that define old-world luxe (and also old-world size: some are small). It has a renowned spa.

B&BS

The most charming option is a B&B in one of Galveston's historic neighborhoods, which are usually a short walk to the Strand. Check out www.galveston.com, which lists several options.

Victorian Bed & Breakfast Inn (☎ 409-762-3235; www.vicbb.com; 511 17th St; r $125-175) This 1899 brick house built by a concrete baron survived the 1900 hurricane. Three rooms have king-size beds and share a bathroom; three suites have private bathrooms and one or two bedrooms plus a kitchen. We like the Garden Apartment: private entry and access to gorgeous gardens.

Grace Manor (☎ 409-621-1662; www.gracemanor -galveston.com; 1702 Postoffice St; r $140-180) Built in 1905, this grand Queen Anne–style home has colonnades inside and out. The four rooms are decorated in period plush with king-size beds and either claw-foot or Jacuzzi tubs.

CONDOS

There are a lot of condominium developments on Galveston Island, especially as you go southwest, away from town. See the island website (www.galveston.com) for a long list of agents for these places.

Eating

Galveston is more than cheap beach joints serving up so-so fried fish. The discriminating locals demand quality and they get it.

La King's Confectionery (☎ 409-762-6100; 2323 Strand St; snacks from $3; 🕑 10am-7pm) This is an old-style candy factory, coffee shop and ice-cream parlor rolled into one. Watch the saltwater taffy, peanut brittle and chocolates being made by master candymaker Ernest Torres.

Mod Coffeehouse (☎ 409-765-5659; 2126 Postoffice St; meals from $5; 🕑 7am-10pm; 🛜) The de facto Strand community center, this coffeehouse has fine baked goods and swell iced teas. At tables out front you'll hear all the local gossip.

Star Drug Store (☎ 409-766-7719; 510 23rd St; meals from $6; 🕑 7am-3pm) The place in town to sit at the counter and order a banana split. Not retro because it's never changed, this old drug store has classic diner faves. Breakfasts are hearty.

Bistro LeCroy (☎ 409-762-4200; 2021 Strand St; meals $9-20; 🕑 11am-3pm Tue-Sun, 5-10pm Fri & Sat) With the arcaded sidewalk out front you could be in the French Quarter of New Orleans, but rather the Big Easy has come to you. Fine Cajun and Creole fare served in a boisterous, family-run place. Make this your Mardi Gras HQ year-round.

DiBellas (☎ 409-763-9036; 1902 31st St; meals $10-25; ☯ 11am-2pm Tue-Fri, 5-9pm Tue-Sun) This is where BOIs go when they want a family feast of the kind of tasty Italian food your grandmother might have cooked had she a) been Italian, and b) been a really good cook. Pastas with sausage, meatballs and the like are the staples, but the real star is the Placido: shrimp and crab-topped red snapper.

Clary's (☎ 409-740-0771; 8509 Teichman Rd; meals $13-30; ☯ 4:30-10pm Tue-Sat) Out west on Offatts Bayou, Clary's looks like nothing from the front but the rear has serene water views. The real excitement is the fresher-than-fresh seafood, especially the scallops, crab and shrimp.

Casey's Seafood Restaurant (☎ 409-762-9625; 3800 Seawall Blvd; meals from $14; ☯ 11am-9pm) This casual branch of Gaido's is also more fun. Sit outside overlooking the gulf and ponder the stupefying selection of seafood combos. It's all excellent, more so when you get a side of roasted garlic.

Gaido's (☎ 409-762-9625; 3800 Seawall Blvd; meals $20-35) Run by the same family since 1911, this is easily the best-known and best-loved restaurant in Galveston; it serves vast platters of no-compromise seafood (oh, the oysters…). It's all white tablecloths and hushed tones, except when someone succumbs to the amazing crustless pecan pie and explodes.

Drinking

The Strand is an excellent place for bar-hopping, with several great old boozers plus trendy clubs. Seawall Blvd has lots of classic beach bars. Find out what's on with the free weeklies: *After Hours* (www.afterhoursmag.com) and *The Parrot* (www.galvestonparrot.com).

O'Malley's Stage Door Pub (☎ 409-763-1731; 2022 Postoffice St) This pub, right next to the Opera House, is home to some very friendly young and eccentric locals who lounge about on the mismatched furniture.

our pick Old Quarter Acoustic Cafe (☎ 409-762-9199; 413 20th St) This funky place features lots of live music and is prone to festivals honoring Dylan.

Voodoo Lounge (☎ 409-515-5454; 201 26th St) Lives up to its name with a scary movie room, although you may just want to start in the 'kissing room.' The dance floor is huge and the patio is a fine break.

The Spot (☎ 409-621-5237; 3204 Seawall Blvd) This rollicking and boisterous bar overlooking the gulf is the best of many competitors (with classic names of the genre like 'the poop deck'). Burgers and sandwiches are excellent and help absorb the vast array of drinks on offer (specials dazzle). There's often live music.

Entertainment

The **Grand 1894 Opera House** (☎ 409-765-1894; www.thegrand.com; 2020 Postoffice St; tours $2; ☯ box office & tours 9am-5pm Mon-Sat) is a beautifully restored building that gives you an idea of Galveston's pre-hurricane culture and wealth. A Strand anchor, it is used for musical and theatrical performances throughout the year.

Shopping

Antique stores, galleries and kitsch merchants abound around the Strand.

Galveston Art League Gallery (☎ 409-621-1008; 2117A Postoffice St) is run by local artists and is a fine place to start exploring the vibrant local art scene.

Getting There & Around

Galveston is 49 miles southeast of Houston on I-45. There is little point in trying for scenery on the parallel TX 3. It passes the same strip malls and scrubland, and has lots of stoplights. For details on driving along the coast south of here, see the boxed text, p243. If traveling north, the Galveston–Port Bolivar Ferry is an attraction in itself (see p242).

Kerrville Bus Company (☎ 800-231-2222; www.iridekbc.com; 3825 Broadway Ave) runs a morning bus and an evening bus (from $20, one hour) to Houston.

Galveston Limousine Service (☎ 409-744-5466; www.galvestonlimousineservice.com) has van service every two hours to and from Houston Hobby Airport (adult/child $45/20, one hour) and IAH (adult/child $55/25, two hours). Call to reserve and arrange pickup.

Island Transit (☎ 409-797-3900; www.islandtransit.net; adult/child $1/50¢) operates buses from the central stop at 20th and Market Sts. The routes are mostly designed for car-less residents in the neighborhoods.

Ike knocked Island Transit's Galveston Island Trolley off the rails. Restoration has proceeded slowly, but when reopened, the two routes (linking the Strand with other historic neighborhoods and Seawall Blvd via 25th St) will be ideal for visitors.

AROUND GALVESTON
Bolivar Peninsula
The drive north along this literally windswept peninsula passes through areas that will take years to recover from Ike (although large vacation homes are like mushrooms after the rain). There are few real towns or attractions over the 30 miles of TX 87 from Port Bolivar to High Island and TX 124 which runs inland. The coast road northeast of here is closed and to reach Sabine Pass, you have to take the long way around (see p234).

GALVESTON–PORT BOLIVAR FERRY
Linking Galveston Island and the Bolivar Peninsula, the **boats** (☎ 409-763-2386) run around the clock daily and are free. On summer weekends the waits at either end can easily be one hour or longer. The 20-minute ride is an attraction in itself. You'll see a big shipwreck, freighters from all over the world, and usually dolphins.

ANAHUAC NATIONAL WILDLIFE REFUGE
Of the three national wildlife refuges along the Gulf Coast from Galveston to Louisiana, Anahuac has the best access and is therefore the most popular. In practical terms, this means that on some days you'll actually see other people. A 3-mile road leads to the often unattended **visitor station** (☎ 409-267-3337; admission free; ☼ gates open during daylight hours). There are bathrooms at the station.

Several miles of gravel and dirt roads traverse deep marsh, ponds, prairie and bayous. During the winter, up to 80,000 Canadian snow geese gather at one time, a truly spectacular sight. Other wildlife includes alligators and some of the largest mosquitoes you may ever encounter.

The refuge's main entrance is off FM 1985, 10 miles west of FM 1985's juncture with TX 124 (from the high bridge on the latter, the refuge unfolds like one vast green carpet).

Galveston Island State Park
Some 10 miles southwest of the city on the island, this **park** (☎ 409-737-1222, reservations 512-389-8900; www.tpwd.state.tx.us; 14901 FM 3005; adult/child $5/free) is still recovering from the scouring it got from Ike. It has nature trails through the coastal dunes, salt marshes, bayous and mudflats. Swimmers will find a hard-packed white-sand beach. Facilities are still few and shade is rare but it's a lovely spot, far from

the huge, ugly vacation barns that line much of FM 3005.

Most of the park's **campsites** (sites $15-25) are probably in a swamp near Houston, but 36 weren't blown away and are often reserved.

The park's campsites are suitable for tents and/or RVs and have water and electricity; they cost $12 to $20 (plus admission). Sites with screened shelters cost $18. This park is very popular in the summer, so reserve well in advance.

For details on driving along the coast south of here, see the boxed text, p243.

THE COASTAL BEND

The name 'Coastal Bend' can rather amorphously apply to communities from Galveston to South Padre Island. But its heart is the rural stretch running from the southern tip of Galveston Island to Corpus Christi. Here small towns, many forgotten by time, lie next to the water at the end of long and quiet roads. Many shelter on the profusion of inlets and bays, protected by more than 100 miles of uninhabited barrier islands. The only visitors to the islands are birds, which flock here by the score.

The region just south of Galveston, around the Brazos River, doesn't get much respect despite the clever marketing moniker that has been dreamed up for it: 'Brazosport.' Or maybe that's because of it. South of here, the lands are rural and often bucolic. Natural areas such as Aransas National Wildlife Refuge and Goose Island State Park should be your focus along with the towns of Fulton and Rockport.

It's more than possible to drive from Galveston south along the confusing maze of roads to Corpus Christi or Port Aransas in a day and still see the best sights. See the boxed text, p243.

BRAZOSPORT AREA
pop 89,000
Nine towns – Brazoria, Clute, Freeport, Jones Creek, Lake Jackson, Oyster Creek, Quintana, Richwood and Surfside Beach – are part of a confused hodgepodge crisscrossed by industry railroads, highways, creeks, lakes and channels and surrounded by chemical plants collectively known as Brazosport.

This area has been the focus of much arguing between the federal Environmental

Protection Agency (EPA) and the state of Texas. The former claims the latter allows industry to flaunt pollution regulations. The state disingenuously sidesteps the issue by claiming the feds have no right to tell it what to do.

The one attraction worth finding is **Sea Center Texas** (☎ 979-292-0100; www.tpwd.state.tx.us/seacenter; 300 Medical Dr, Lake Jackson; admission free; ☯ 9am-4pm Tue-Sat, 1-4pm Sun). It's an excellent place to learn about Texas salt marshes, the surf zone and coastal bays. A large aquarium holds gulf stars like huge groupers and slithery eels. Out back are 35 acres of fish hatcheries which you can tour at certain times. A walkway extends across 5 acres of wetlands.

MATAGORDA
pop 1900
Names in this area must have been hard to come by, because authorities decided to confuse everybody by christening a bay, a town, a county, a peninsula and an island with the same name – Matagorda. The tiny town offers a link to the peninsula (Matagorda Peninsula, not to be confused with Matagorda Island, the inaccessible state park off Port O'Connor), a popular spot for fishing.

The town still has a vintage feel to it and has a few stores. Head south on TX 60 over the grand new bridge which arches far over the busy Intracoastal Waterway (views from the top show the land seeming to dissolve into water), and drive 6 miles to the end of the road and the gulf.

There are 22 miles of lonely white-sand **beaches** out here. With a permit ($10; buy it at any gas station in Matagorda), you can drive out the beach and stake out your claim. **Matagorda Bay Nature Park** (☎ 979-863-2603; www.lcra.org; admission free; ☯ 8am-5pm) is a great resource with numerous programs where you can learn about the wetlands and barrier islands. Check for schedules; the guided kayak tours ($40 including kayak rental) are excellent.

PALACIOS
pop 5200
At a pleasant bend in TX 35, this somewhat frayed small town overlooks an inlet off Matagorda Bay.

FOLLOWING THE COAST FROM GALVESTON TO CORPUS CHRISTI

Trying to follow the Gulf Coast from Galveston or even Houston to the Corpus Christi area can be an adventure – good or bad. It's possible to do it in a day and still have time for a variety of sights and activities. Here are the key details to the journey:

After the upscale – and rebuilt – houses that extend to the southern tip of Galveston Island, the sudden lack of development after you cross the San Luis Pass bridge (toll $2) to the relative emptiness of Follets Island can be a pleasant surprise.

Surfside Beach, 13.5 miles southeast, is a workmanlike party town, where few pass the convenience store at the main crossroad without stopping for a case of beer.

Fans of oil refineries will appreciate the 11-mile drive inland on TX 332. Watch for signs for the delightful **Sea Center Texas** (p243) in Lake Jackson.

From Lake Jackson, take FM 2004, which becomes FM 2611 when it crosses TX 36. This a lovely drive through lush lands laced with rivers and peppered with wildflowers. Turn north when you hit FM 457, go 6 miles and turn west on FM 521 for 15.5 miles to TX 60, then turn south to **Matagorda** (p243) and the beaches, a total of 55 miles from Lake Jackson.

From Matagorda drive back north 9 miles to FM 521 and turn west. You make a big loop to the north around a nuclear power plant – watch out for lobsters the size of Godzilla – and after 19 miles you turn south on TX 35 for 5 miles to **Palacios** (p243).

Continue on TX 35 for 50 miles through Port Lavaca (avoiding any temptation to detour to uninteresting Port O'Connor) until just past tiny Tivoli, where you should turn southeast on TX 239. Follow the signs for 18 miles through humdrum corn farms until you reach the wonders of **Aransas National Wildlife Refuge** (p244).

Leaving Aransas NWR, take FM 774 through a series of turns 12 miles west to TX 35. Turn south and go 13.5 miles to Lamar and the charms of **Goose Island State Park** (p244).

From here, it's only 6 miles south on TX 35 to the fun twin coastal towns of **Fulton** and **Rockport** (p244). Port Aransas, a good place to bed down, is only 20 miles beyond.

It's a town with, a realtor would say, a lot of potential. This is especially true at the **Luther Hotel** (☎ 361-972-2312; 408 S Bay Blvd; r $55-130), which dates to 1904. Still operating, it's the full-time avocation of the Luther family. Just maintaining the huge place is an endless chore, as the scruffy motel-style units on one side of the crescent drive suggest. Stepping inside the main building is like stepping back a few generations. It's charming in a creaky sort of way and isn't for guests who expect everything to work (although the rockers on the front porch rock just fine, thank you).

ARANSAS NATIONAL WILDLIFE REFUGE

For bird-watchers, the 115,000-acre **Aransas National Wildlife Refuge** (☎ 361-286-3559; www.fws. gov/southwest/refuges/texas/aransas; per person/carload $3/5; ☾ 6am-dusk, visitor center 8:30am-4:30pm) is the premier site on the Texas coast. Even people who don't carry binoculars and ornithological checklists can get caught up in the bird-spotting frenzy that peaks here every March and November but is great throughout the year.

The scenery alone is spectacular – the blue Aransas Bay waters are speckled with green islets ringed with white sand. Native dune grasses blow gently in the breezes while songbirds provide choral background music.

On the ground, you may well see some of the refuge's wild boars, alligators, armadillos, white-tailed deer and many more species. Everywhere you will see some of the close to 400 bird species that have been documented at Aransas. None are more famous, more followed or more watched than the whooping cranes. Some of the rarest creatures in North America, about 200 survivors of the species summer in Canada and spend November to March in the refuge. Spotters and scientists come from all over the world to study the 5ft-tall birds.

Aransas is easily reached. See the boxed text, p243 for details. The visitor center should be your first stop. You can borrow binoculars here for free. A 40ft observation tower is 5 miles from the visitor center and overlooks much of the refuge and has free telescopes.

The auto loop covers 16 miles, so allow two to four hours. Bikes are a good way to explore the many hiking trails. There's no camping anywhere in the park, but Goose Island State Park is a good option (p244).

Boats tour the estuaries from November to March spotting whooping cranes, and this is easily the best way to get a good view of the rare birds. The tours usually leave in the mornings and afternoons for three- to four-hour tours and cost about $40. Among the operators:

Rockport Adventures (☎ 361-727-0643, 877-892-4737; www.whoopingcranetours.com; N Fulton Beach Rd & Cactus St) Leaves from Fulton, and also runs kayak tours.
Wharf Cat (☎ 361-729-4855, 800-782-2473; www.texaswhoopers.com) Leaves from Rockport and Port Aransas.

GOOSE ISLAND STATE PARK

The oldest tree on the coast is an oak in excess of 1000 years near **Goose Island State Park** (☎ 361-729-2858; www.tpwd.state.tx.us; admission $5). It lies at the end of a sweet little drive from TX 35 and the village of Lamar that passes under an entire thicket of live oaks that shade the road. Although stuck with the prosaic moniker 'the big tree' (the trunk is more than 35ft in diameter), this grand specimen is in an idyllic spot amid a sea of wildflowers, near the actual sea, and surrounded by panels with poetry.

The park is right on Aransas Bay (but there's no swimming). The namesake marshy island is a mere 140 acres, linked to another 174 acres on the mainland. The busiest times at the park are during the summer and whooping crane season (November to March). It's worth booking in advance. Walk-in sites away from RVs are $10 while sites with utilities are $16. A word of caution: the phrase 'bring insect repellent' appears more frequently in this park's official brochure than in any other.

The park is 12 miles north of Rockport, off E Main St, which runs east from TX 35, just north of bridge over Copano Bay. The old tree is 1.5 miles north of the park along the water.

ROCKPORT & FULTON
pop 11,100

A pedestrian-friendly waterfront, a couple of worthy sites, fishing boats plying their trade and a cute little downtown make the twin towns of Rockport and Fulton an enjoyable stop.

The side streets between TX 35 and Aransas Bay are dotted with numerous art galleries. Rockport and Fulton claim to be home to the state's highest percentage of artists. Coming from the north, leave TX 35 after you cross the LBJ Causeway and follow Fulton Beach

Rd south first through Fulton and then into Rockport, where Austin St is the main drag of the cute little downtown.

The **Rockport-Fulton Area Chamber of Commerce** (☎ 361-729-9952, 800-826-6441; www.rockport-fulton.org; 404 Broadway St, Rockport; ☯ 9am-5pm Mon-Fri, 9am-2pm Sat) overlooks the harbor.

Sights

ROCKPORT HARBOR
Crescent-shaped Rockport Harbor is one of the prettiest on the Gulf Coast. It's lined with shrimp boats, fishing charter boats, whooping crane tour boats, pleasure craft and a series of rustic peel-and-eat shrimp joints and bait shops. The small volunteer-run **Aquarium at Rockport Harbor** (☎ 361-729-2328; www.rockportaquarium.com; 702 Navigation Circle; admission free; ☯ 1-4pm Thu-Mon) has crabs and sea critters.

TEXAS MARITIME MUSEUM
Everything from fishing boats to offshore oil rigs to the story of the short-lived Texas Navy is covered at this fun **museum** (☎ 361-729-1271; www.texasmaritimemuseum.org; 1202 Navigation Circle, Rockport; adult/child $6/3; ☯ 10am-4pm Tue-Sat, 1-4pm Sun) on the harbor. Displays emphasize the human aspects of the Texas seacoast. Several old boats that were used to rescue people caught in storms are displayed outside.

ROCKPORT CENTER FOR THE ARTS
It's worth popping into this cheery **center** (☎ 361-729-5519; 902 Navigation Circle, Rockport; admission free; ☯ 10am-4pm Tue-Sat, 1-4pm Sun), housed partly in a charming 1890s building, to see what's going on with the lively local arts scene.

FULTON MANSION STATE HISTORICAL PARK
This imposing 1870s **mansion** (☎ 361-729-0386; www.visitfultonmansion.com; 317 S Fulton Beach Rd, Fulton; adult/child $6/3; ☯ 10am-3pm Tue-Sat, 1-3pm Sun) comes as a surprise amid other more modern – and modest – shorefront buildings. It was built by George Fulton, who was clever with the design. On the outside, it looks like an imposing French Second Empire creation, right down to the mansard roofs. Inside those walls, however, are concrete foundations and walls more than 5in thick. Although other contemporary buildings have been blown away, the mansion has withstood several hurricanes.

Sleeping & Eating
The Fulton waterfront by the mansion has a few modest motels and there is another good patch down by Rockport harbor.

Bayfront Cottages & Pier (☎ 361-729-6693; www.rockportbayfrontcottages.com; 309 S Fulton Beach Rd, Fulton; r $50-150; ☂) A nicely redone old motor court is next to the mansion and across from the water. Use its pier to catch a fish, then cook it up in the small kitchen that comes with each unit.

Hoope's House (☎ 361-729-8424; www.hoopeshouse.com; 417 N Broadway St, Rockport; r $175; ☂ ☒) This landmark mansion overlooks the Rockport Harbor and has four rooms in the main house and another four in a new wing. It's plush without being fussy and there's a large pool and a fab breakfast.

Jama's Kitchen & Famous Cheesecake (☎ 361-729-5007; 415 S Austin St; meals from $6; ☯ 7am-4pm Tue-Sat, 7-11am Sun) Amid galleries and funky shops, Jama's has a sprightly menu of breakfasts, sandwiches and salads. Baked goods include the tasty house special that's in the name.

Boiling Pot (☎ 361-729-6972; 2015 Fulton Beach Rd, Fulton; meals from $8; ☯ 4-10pm Mon-Thu, 11am-11pm Fri & Sat, to 10pm Sun) This is a rustic classic, and a lot of fun. Mountains of shellfish plus potatoes, sausage and corn are dumped in a pot full of spicy boiling water; then dumped on your paper-covered table and you dive in (no cutlery, no crockery – bibs provided).

Latitude 2802 (☎ 361-727-9009; 105 N Austin, Rockport; meals from $20; ☯ 5-10pm Tue-Sun) The finest dining locally. Look for creative takes on seafood at this stylish little place that includes an art gallery. The local special, grouper, is prepared in several ways; sides vary with the season – try the green beans with garlic.

COASTAL PLAINS

Goliad is worth a detour from the coastal bend; it's a charming small town steeped in history. You might consider a circle route that takes in the coast one way and the plains the other.

VICTORIA
pop 62,800
Victoria has some 100 historic buildings near its downtown. Many have been restored by owners drawn to deeply shaded, oak-lined streets. The **Victoria Convention and Visitors Bureau**

(☎ 361-582-4285; www.visitvictoriatexas.com; 700 Main St; ☙ 8.30am-5pm Mon-Fri) has tour information.

Victoria is at the junction of US 77 and US 59, 125 miles south of Houston and 85 miles north of Corpus Christi. It is a good base while exploring the historical parks in Goliad, 25 miles to the south on US 59. Most chain motels are found along the highways.

The granite and limestone **Old Victoria County Courthouse** (101 N Bridge St) dates from 1892, when towns took pride in such places. It fronts the picturesque DeLeon Plaza.

Dairy Treet (☎ 361-573-3104; 3808 N Laurent St; meals from $5; ☙ 11am-10pm) is an old-time soft-serve ice-cream joint with marvy burgers and hand-dipped onion rings. It's pure Americana hanging out here on a balmy evening.

GOLIAD
pop 2050

'Remember the Alamo!' is the verbal icon of the Texas revolution, but it should also be 'Remember Goliad!' where, on Palm Sunday, March 27, 1836, Mexican general Antonio López de Santa Anna ordered 350 Texian prisoners shot. The death toll was double that at the Alamo and helped inspire the Texians in their victory over Santa Anna at San Jacinto the following month (see p29).

The **Goliad Chamber of Commerce** (☎ 361-645-3563; www.goliadcc.org; 231 S Market St; ☙ 9am-5pm Mon-Fri) has a good walking tour brochure for the town. The town is 25 miles off US 77 and Victoria. It has a few small motels and cafes and is best visited on the way to someplace else.

Built in 1749 by the Spanish to deter the French who were sniffing around the eastern edges of their empire, **Presidio La Bahia** (☎ 361-645-3752; www.presidiolabahia.org; US 183; adult/child $4/1; ☙ 9am-4:45pm) played a role in six revolutions and wars. Texas revolutionaries seized the fort – now faithfully restored – in October 1835. The following year, Colonel Fannin and his men were held by the Mexican forces inside the walls for two weeks before their execution. The *presidio* is 1 mile south of Goliad.

Established in 1749, the Misión Espiritu Santo de Zuñiga has a less bloody history than the presidio just down the road. It now stands as the focal point of the lush **Goliad State Park** (☎ 361-645-3405; reservations 512-389-8900; www.tpwd. state.tx.us; 108 Park Rd 6; adult/child $3/free; ☙ 8am-5pm, gates close 10pm except to overnight guests), which has quiet hiking trails.

The mission buildings have been restored, and there is a good museum in the old school and workshop building. In the large church, look for the Door of Death, complete with skull and crossbones on the external wall.

There are well-shaded camping areas in the park, including many along the San Antonio River. Fees are $8 for primitive tent sites, $15 for sites with electricity and $20 for full hookups. Reserve in advance.

The hub of the downtown area, **Courthouse Square** features – surprise! – a grand old 1894 courthouse. Among the many stately oaks on the square is one labeled the 'Hanging Tree,' for self-explanatory reasons. A historical marker recalls the Regulators, 50 vigilantes who 'pursued criminals with vigor and often with cruelty' from 1868 to 1870.

The square has cafes; on the second Saturday of each month Market Day lures vendors of all types.

CORPUS CHRISTI AREA

Corpus Christi is the bull's-eye of its namesake region and bay. Its museums and attractions can fill a day or more while the pull of the beaches on Mustang and Padre Islands is irresistible – Port Aransas is easily the most charming beach town in Texas. But it's not all sand and sea – it can be cowboys and cattle too if you like: an easy day trip from Corpus Christi takes you to Kingsville, home of the King Ranch, one of the largest and oldest working ranches in the world.

CORPUS CHRISTI
pop 286,400

Known simply as Corpus, this city by the placid bay is a growing and vibrant place. Its attractions are worth a visit and its perpetually sunny location on its namesake bay is beguiling.

Spaniards named the bay after the Roman Catholic holy day of Corpus Christi in 1519, when Alonzo Álvarez de Piñeda discovered its calm waters. The town established here in the early 1800s later took the name as well. Growth was slow, however, due to yellow fever in the 19th century and a hurricane in 1919. Construction of Shoreline Blvd and the deepwater port between 1933 and 1941, combined with a boom brought on by WWII, caused rapid growth. Although the downtown is sleepy away from the water, the city does a good business attracting large conventions and meetings at the vast American Bank Center.

Orientation & Information

Downtown Corpus lies behind Shoreline Blvd, a wide seafront boulevard that was designed by Gutzon Borglum, the sculptor of Mt Rushmore.

North Beach, the closest beach to downtown, lies across the ship channel to the north. The huge US 181 bridge spans the channel between the downtown and beach areas. There's no good pedestrian link.

Corpus Christi Area Convention & Visitors Bureau (☎ 361-561-2000, 800-766-2322; www.visitcorpuschris titx.org; 1823 N Chaparral; ☽ 9am-5pm) Near the museums.

Sights

USS LEXINGTON MUSEUM ON THE BAY

The second sight you are likely to notice in Corpus (after the bay) is this 900ft-long **aircraft carrier** (☎ 361-888-4873; www.usslexington.com; 2914 N Shoreline Blvd; adult/child $13/8; ☽ 9am-5pm, to 6pm summer) moored just north of the ship channel. The ship served in the Pacific during WWII and was finally retired in 1991. A number of high-tech exhibits give visitors a chance to relive some of the wartime experiences, without actually dying in a kamikaze attack. During the evening, the ship is eerily lit with blue lights that recall its WWII nickname, 'the Blue Ghost.'

TEXAS STATE AQUARIUM

The **Texas State Aquarium** (☎ 361-881-1200; www. texasstateaquarium.org; 2710 N Shoreline Blvd; adult/child $16/11; ☽ 9am-5pm, to 6pm summer) is a good place to learn about marine life along the Gulf Coast. The main exhibits, on a circular course, include a huge tank replicating the environment around offshore oil rigs, complete with sharks, grouper and red snapper (but no leaks). Outside are more displays, including endangered turtles, otters, alligators and a large dolphin pool.

MUSEUM OF SCIENCE & HISTORY

Explore shipwrecks at this fun **museum** (☎ 361-883-2862; 1900 N Chaparral St; adult/child $12.50/6; ☽ 10am-5pm Tue-Sat, noon-5pm Sun), right on the south side of the ship channel. See how Texas proved to be the doom for the French explorer La Salle and see the moldering remains of reproductions of two of Columbus' ships (see the boxed text, p247).

ART MUSEUM OF SOUTH TEXAS

Rotating exhibits of contemporary art are the main feature at this dramatic **museum** (☎ 361-825-3500; www.artmuseumofsouthtexas.org; 1902 N Shoreline Blvd; adult/child $6/free; ☽ 10am-5pm Tue-Sat, 1-5pm Sun), across a plaza from the Museum of Science and History. Rotating exhibits join selections for the permanent collection of American art.

MUSEUM OF ASIAN CULTURES

This small **museum** (☎ 361-882-2641; www.asian culturesmuseum.org; 1809 N Chaparral St; adult/child $6/3;

THE CURSED COLUMBUS FLEET

In 1992, the government of Spain built replicas of Columbus' ships, the *Niña*, the *Pinta* and the *Santa María*, to commemorate the 500th anniversary of Columbus' voyage to the New World. After sailing them around the Atlantic, Spain agreed to lease them to the city of Corpus Christi for 50 years. Shortly after they arrived to huge fanfare in 1993, a rogue barge went out of control on the ship channel and rammed all three, causing huge damage. The *Niña* stayed afloat, while the *Pinta* and *Santa María* were moved to a concrete dry dock behind the Museum of Science and History, looking quite the worse for wear. Meanwhile the original group that had agreed to operate the ships went bankrupt in 1999.

The intervening years have not been kind. Petty and bureaucratic wrangling between the city, the museum, the government of Spain and volunteer organizations have been ongoing. In the meantime virtually nothing has been done to maintain the ships and all three are in bad shape. After several offers to restore them met with hassles from Corpus Christi, Spain washed its hands of the ships in 2006.

A volunteer group has now been formed to restore these ships and is hoping to gain title to them (Spain has even agreed to kick in some cash), but at the time of research the city was still to make a decision.

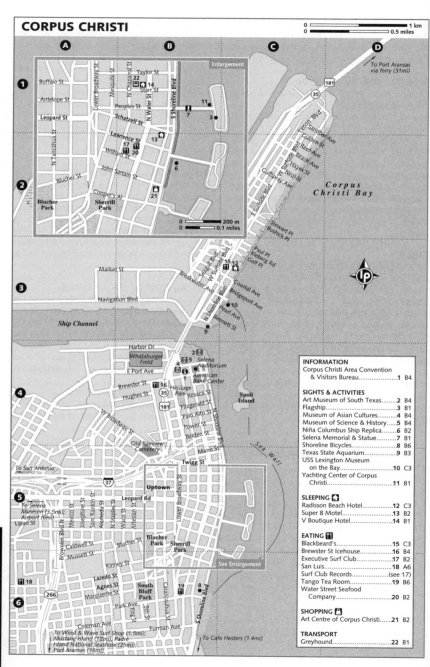

CORPUS CHRISTI

0   1 km
0   0.5 miles

To Port Aransas
via ferry (31mi)

*Corpus
Christi Bay*

A   **B**   **C**   **D**

Buffalo St
Antelope St
Leopard St

Enlargement

Taylor St
Starr St
Peoples St
Schatzell St
Lawrence St
William St
John Sartain St
Coopers Al

Blucher Park
Sherrill Park

Mesquite St
N Chaparral St
N Water St
S Shoreline Blvd
Lower Broadway St
N Tancahua St
Blucher St

0   200 m
0   0.1 miles

Timon Blvd
Sandbar Ave
Gulden St
Reef Ave
Beach Ave
Hayes St
Neal St
Gulfspray Ave
E Surface Blvd

Market St

Navigation Blvd

Ship Channel

Breakwater Ave
N Shoreline Blvd
W Surface Blvd
Coastal Ave
Bridgeport Ave
Pearl Ave
Bennett St

Stewart Pl
Busluck Pl
Paul Pl
Kleberg Rd
Golf Pl

Harbor Dr
Whataburger Field
E Port Ave
Brewster St
Hughes St

Selena Auditorium
American Bank Center
Heritage Park
Resaca St
Fitzgerald St
Palo Alto St
Power St
Belden St
Mann St

Spoil Island

Sea Wall

To San Antonio

Old Bayview Cemetery

Twigg St

Uptown

Leopard Rd

Brownlee Blvd N
Mexico St
Josephine St
San Rankin St
Alameda St
N Staples St
Waco St
Artesian St

To Selena Museum (3.5mi);
Airport (6mi)
Lipan St
Caldwell St
Mussett St
Kinney St
Laredo St
Agnes St
Marguerite St

Blucher Park
Sherrill Park

Lower Broadway St

Coleman Ave
Park Ave
5th St
Furman Ave

South Bluff Park

Caracahua St
S Shoreline Blvd

See Enlargement

To Wind & Wave Surf Shop (1.5mi);
Mustang Island (18mi); Padre
Island National Seashore (25mi);
Port Aransas (38mi)

To Cafe Hesters (1.4mi)

INFORMATION
Corpus Christi Area Convention
& Visitors Bureau...................**1** B4

SIGHTS & ACTIVITIES
Art Museum of South Texas........**2** B4
Flagship...............................**3** B1
Museum of Asian Cultures.........**4** B4
Museum of Science & History.....**5** B4
Niña Columbus Ship Replica.......**6** B2
Selena Memorial & Statue.........**7** B1
Shoreline Bicycles...................**8** B6
Texas State Aquarium...............**9** B3
USS Lexington Museum
  on the Bay........................**10** C3
Yachting Center of Corpus
  Christi.............................**11** B1

SLEEPING
Radisson Beach Hotel...............**12** C3
Super 8 Motel.......................**13** B2
V Boutique Hotel....................**14** B1

EATING
Blackbeard's........................**15** C3
Brewster St Icehouse...............**16** B4
Executive Surf Club.................**17** B2
San Luis..............................**18** A6
Surf Club Records..................(see **17**)
Tango Tea Room.....................**19** B6
Water Street Seafood
  Company.........................**20** B2

SHOPPING
Art Centre of Corpus Christi......**21** B2

TRANSPORT
Greyhound...........................**22** B1

GULF COAST

(🕑 10am-4pm Tue-Sat) is worth a look if you have an interest in Japanese and other Asian art. There are some interesting masks and kabuki figures, plus a tranquil bamboo garden.

HERITAGE PARK
Originally a neighborhood of old homes, **Heritage Park** (☎ 361-883-0639; 1581 N Chaparral St; admission free; 🕑 10am-2pm Tue-Sat, tours 10:30am Mon, Thu & Fri) has morphed into a theme park of old homes. A dozen Corpus houses dating back as far as 1851 have been moved to this area, bounded by Mesquite, N Chaparral, Hughes and Fitzgerald Sts. Tours (adult/child $6/2) depart from the 1908 Galvan House.

Activities
CYCLING
If the wind's not too fierce, a very pleasant afternoon can be spent cycling along the bayfront. **Shoreline Bicycles** (☎ 361-883-8888; 555 S Shoreline Blvd) rents bikes (from $20 per day).

FISHING
Many of the skippers who charter boats are based in Rockport or Port Aransas because it puts them closer to the gulf.

WATER SPORTS
Laguna Madre, west of Padre Island, is a prized windsurfing location thanks to the unusually calm waters and the nearly constant breezes. See p254 for details on one of the best ways to windsurf in the US.

The alphabetically shaped T and L docks downtown are home to large marinas. **Yachting Center of Corpus Christi** (☎ 361-881-8503; yachtingcc.com; 108 Peoples St, T-dock; 🕑 10am-5pm) offers an introduction to yachting ($60), which includes two hours of hands-on sailing. Kayaks are rented from $15 per hour.

South Coast Kiteboarding (☎ 361-949-3278; www.southcoastkiteboarding.com; lessons per hr from $100) Renowned pros run this shop and they know how to ride the constant local breezes. Lessons are usually given at Packery Channel Park over the JFK Causeway from town, but call to book and confirm.

Wind & Wave Surf Shop (☎ 361-937-9283; 10721 S Padre Island Dr/TX 358) is a good place to get information on local conditions. It rents boogie boards, surfboards for the terminally optimistic ($30 per day) and kayaks ($50 per day).

Tours
The **Flagship** (☎ 361-884-8306; www.captclarksflagship.com; Peoples St, T-dock; adult/child $8/5; 🕑 3pm year-round), a 400-person faux paddle wheeler, offers one-hour guided cruises of the bay. On weekends, holidays and in summer it sails more than once per day.

Sleeping
Dare we say it, you might want to opt for the beach-town charms of Port Aransas for your slumber and visit Corpus as a day trip. But there are good options near the water here.

The parks on Padre and Mustang Islands all have various camping facilities; see those sections later in the chapter.

Super 8 Motel (☎ 361-884-4815; www.super8.com; 411 N Shoreline Blvd; r $60-120; 🛜 🖳) No surprises here, but you will find decent, budget rooms in an excellent downtown location, smack bang between the T-heads and the nightlife of Water St. The pool sparkles from a refit.

Radisson Beach Hotel (☎ 361-883-9700; www.radisson.com; 3200 Surfside Blvd; r $100-200; 🖳 🛜 🖳) The 139 rooms are comfortable and have microwaves and fridges at this upscale beachfront hotel. Get a 7th-floor room facing the Lexington and imagine you're coming in for a landing.

V Boutique Hotel (☎ 361-883-9200; www.vhotelcc.com; 701 North Water St; r $160-250; 🛜) Absolutely adored by its guests, this small hotel in the heart of downtown offers a high level of service, including 24-hour concierges. Rooms come in eight styles, from studios to one-bedroom loft suites.

Eating & Drinking
Bars and restaurants cluster on the streets surrounding Chaparral and Water Sts downtown.

San Luis (☎ 361-885-0117; 2110 Laredo St; meals $5-12; 🕑 7am-9pm) A dead-simple Mexican diner, there's the requisite Selena posters plus a list of well-executed standards that are accented by fabulous, garlicky salsa.

Cafe Hesters (☎ 361-885-0558; 1714 S Alameda St; meals from $7-10; 🕑 7am-3pm Mon-Sat) Next to the market of vendors selling vintage clothing and assorted trinkets, Hesters has the kind of baked goods that make you order one to eat straightaway and another for an hour later. Sandwiches, omelettes, quiches and more highlight the fresh, creative menu.

Tango Tea Room (☎ 361-883-9123; 505 S Water St; meals from $8-10; 🕑 10am-7pm Mon-Thu, to 9pm Fri & Sat)

SELENA

Selena Quintanilla Perez, easily the most famous person Corpus Christi has produced, was almost single-handedly responsible for the crossover of Tejano music to the mainstream. She had a charismatic stage presence and since her murder in 1995, she has assumed martyr status with many. Images of her can be found behind cash registers in shops and restaurants all over town.

Selena was 23 when Yolanda Saldivar, the president of her fan club, shot her in the parking lot of the Days Inn near the Corpus Christi airport. At the trial prosecutors successfully argued that Saldivar shot the singing star because Selena had discovered that Saldivar was stealing Selena's money. Saldivar got life in prison.

In death, Selena's music still sells and many devotees make the pilgrimage to Corpus. Her story has been embraced by fans because it is one with which they can empathize. Selena's parents tried and failed at running a Mexican restaurant in Corpus, and it fell to their plucky daughter and her crowd-pleasing talents to save the family from ruin. Along the way, she ran afoul of her father, an authoritarian who objected to her revealing stage clothes. And she married her lead guitarist in a secret ceremony.

It was great melodrama as seen in 1997's *Selena,* which made a star of the then relatively unknown Jennifer Lopez.

In Corpus Christi, a memorial and statue of Selena stand at the entrance to the Peoples St T-head on Shoreline Blvd. Serious Selena fans will want to check out the **Selena Museum** (☎ 361-289-9013; www.q-productions.com; 5410 Leopard St; adult/child $2/1; ☉ 10am-4pm Mon-Fri), a charmless warehouse with memorabilia, including her awards, her red Porsche and many of her stage costumes.

Amid a coven of little alternative shops offering herbal healing and belly dancing lessons, this funky vegetarian cafe has a long menu of fresh sandwiches, salads and baked goods, plus all the tea implied by the name.

Blackbeard's (☎ 361-884-1030; 3117 Surfside Blvd; meals from $8; ☉ 11am-10pm Sun-Thu, to 11pm Fri & Sat) Near North Beach, this rollicking place serves up tasty Mexican and American cuisine. Wash it down with cheap margaritas while sitting back for the live music.

Executive Surf Club (☎ 361-884-7873; www.execu tivesurfclub.com; 309 N Water St; meals $8-15; ☉ 11am-11pm Sun-Wed, to midnight Thu-Sat) Eat a fried-shrimp po'boy from a surfboard table at this longtime fave which has tables inside and out plus live music.

Brewster St Icehouse (☎ 361-884-2739; 1724 N Tancahua St; meals $8-16; ☉ 11am-2am) Has country-fried everything, cold brews, live music (Thursday to Saturday nights) and a huge deck. This old warehouse really rocks after minor-league baseball games at nearby Whataburger Field.

Water Street Seafood Company (☎ 361-882-8684; 309 N Water St; meals $12-30; ☉ 11am-10pm Sun-Thu, to 11pm Fri & Sat) Busy all week, this high-ceilinged restaurant has a huge and changing selection of fresh seafood, much of it not deep-fried. It also has a very popular oyster bar, big with the after-work crowd.

Shopping

Art Centre of Corpus Christi (☎ 361-884-6406; 100 Shoreline Blvd; ☉ 10am-4pm Tue-Sun) Galleries and studios for local artists are housed in this grand old building downtown. The cafe is good for lunch.

Surf Club Records (☎ 361-882-2364; 309 N Water St) Part of the Water St Market, there is a great selection of hard-to-find CDs with surf music, country and rock. There's a small surfing museum area with displays on the history of surfing in Texas.

Getting There & Around

You'll find **Corpus Christi International Airport** (CRP; ☎ 361-289-0171; www.corpuschristiairport.com) 6 miles west of downtown at International Dr and TX 44. American Eagle serves Dallas–Fort Worth, Continental Express serves Houston IAH and Southwest serves Houston Hobby. Cabs from the airport to downtown cost at least $30; most motels and hotels run shuttles.

Greyhound (☎ 361-882-2516; www.greyhound.com; 702 N Chaparral St) has regular service to Houston ($32, 4½ hours), Brownsville ($32, three hours) and San Antonio ($35, 2½ hours).

The B (☎ 361-289-2600; www.ccrta.org) is the jaunty name for the local buses. Fares are cheap: 75/35¢ for adult/child; a day pass is $1.75. Buses on most routes run about 6:30am to 6:30pm, although few run on Sunday.

Useful routes for travelers are the 75 Bayfront Connector, which covers the downtown area, including N Water St and the museums, on a circular route and the 78 CC Beach Connector, which makes the jump over the ship channel via US 181 and links the downtown area with the aquarium, the Lexington and the beach.

In addition, the B sometimes operates a harbor ferry across the Channel between the museums and the Lexington, but the schedule is erratic.

PORT ARANSAS
pop 3900

Port Aransas (Ah-*ran*-ziss), or Port A, on the northern tip of Mustang Island, is in many ways the most pleasant beach town on the Texas coast. It is small enough that you can ride a bike or walk anywhere, but large enough that it has lots of activities and nightlife. The pace is very relaxed, and activities are dominated by hanging out on the beach, fishing and doing nothing.

Information

Port Aransas Chamber of Commerce and Tourist Bureau (☎ 361-749-5919, 800-452-6278; www.portaransas.org; 403 Cotter Ave; ☼ 9am-5pm Mon-Fri, 9am-3pm Sat) Has stacks of brochures, maps and information.

Sights & Activities

Port A can be the base or a stop on a looping drive around the bay. See the boxed text, p252, for details.

BEACHES

Port A has 18 miles of beaches on the gulf side of Mustang Island. You can drive and park on the sand; the main access point is via Beach St (try to remember that) to the county-run **Port Aransas Park** (☎ 361-749-6117). The park has rest rooms, the Horace Caldwell fishing pier and seasonal concession stands. You can park for free on the sand here.

PORT ARANSAS MUSEUM

Volunteers make this small **museum** (☎ 361-749-3800; www.portaransasmuseum.org; 101 E Brundrett St; admission free; ☼ 1-5pm Thu-Sun) a delightful place to learn the history of Port A, from sand (when this was just a barrier island) to sea (when the residents were professional fishers) to sand and sea (when the economy was based on fishing and beachgoing for fun).

UNIVERSITY OF TEXAS MARINE SCIENCE INSTITUTE

The tiny school's **visitor center** (Map p258; ☎ 361-749-6806; 750 Channelview Dr; admission free; ☼ 8am-5pm Mon-Fri) has views of the busy shipping channel and exhibits about dunes, sand and fish.

NATURE PRESERVES

The city runs a **birding center** (☎ 361-749-4111; Ross Ave; admission free; ☼ 24hr, free tours with guide 9am Wed), with a boardwalk over the marshes and a viewing tower. It has also opened a **nature preserve** at the lagoon end of Port St. It has over 2 miles of trails through the marshes.

SAN JOSÉ ISLAND

A privately owned island, known as St Jo to locals, is just across the ship channel from Port Aransas. This desert island is popular for fishing and beachcombing, although users are advised to bring over virtually everything they will require, including water. The **jetty boat** (☎ 361-749-5448; www.wharfcat.com; adult/child $12/6; ☼ 6am-6pm) runs many times daily from a dock off Cotter Ave.

FISHING

Fishing is big business in Port A, and there are dozens of boats offering trips and available for private charter. The tourist bureau has listings. Rates vary widely, depending on whether you're going to the bay or gulf, the length of the trip and what exactly you're trying to catch; think somewhere between $50 and $1000 or more.

Deep Sea Headquarters (☎ 361-749-5597, 800-705-3474; www.deepseaheadquarters.com) Has a name that says it all. Daily five-/eight-hour fishing trips cost $40/60, including equipment and bait. It's at the ferry landing.

Woody's Sports Center (☎ 361-749-5252, 800-211-9227; www.woodysonline.com; 136 Cotter Ave) Fishing trips, dolphin watches and nature tours.

OTHER ACTIVITIES

There are myriad places offering water adventures and gear. The following is a brief selection:

Coastal Bend Kayak (☎ 361-537-8668) Offers kayak nature tours and lessons (from $100).

Island Surf Rentals (☎ 361-749-0822; 130 E Ave G; ☼ 10am-5pm) Rents per day surfboards ($25), boogie boards ($10), bikes ($20) and kayaks ($40 to $60).

Texas Surf Camps (☎ 361-749-6956; www.texassurfcamps.com; ☼ Jun-Aug) Surf lessons in Port A for $70 per day.

Sleeping

There are more motel/condo rooms in Port A than there are permanent residents, so there are plenty of options and something to meet most budgets. Not surprisingly, summer weekends are when rooms are at their most dear; book in advance. Lots of choices let you wander the walkable part of Port A; avoid the unsightly large condo developments south of town.

CAMPING

You can camp at both Port Aransas Park (p251) and Mustang Island State Park (p253). At the former, primitive beach camping is $12 per night while a tent site with utilities costs $20. At the latter there are two main options.

MOTELS

Port A has scores of locally owned motels that are filled with character, if not characters. All the ones below are close to nightlife; rates here range from low to high season.

Captain's Quarters Inn (☎ 361-749-6005, 888-272-6727; www.captainsquartersportaransas.com; 235 W Cotter Ave; r $60-160; ☎ ☒) Right across from the harbor, this motel-style place offers comfortable rooms, all with fridge and microwave. It is close to the ferry and has a walled pool area.

Sea Shell Village (☎ 361-749-4294; 502 E Ave G; r $60-200; ☎ ☒) These bright, colorful units are close to the beach and can each sleep two to six people. Floor plans differ, but all come with kitchens or kitchenettes and are ideal for a longer stay (weekly rates are also available).

Sea Breeze Suites (☎ 361-749-1500; www.seabreezeporta.com; 407 Beach St; r $70-140; ☎ ☒) Close to both the beach and the center of town, the

building won't win any architecture awards but the 24 rooms are large and have balconies with views of the gulf and channel. Each has a full kitchen.

Tarpon Inn (☎ 361-749-5555, 800-365-6784; www.thetarponinn.com; 200 E Cotter Ave; r $90-200; ☎) Dating from 1900, this charming, rickety place has been rebuilt several times after hurricanes, most extensively after the 1919 big blow. The lobby has more than 7000 of the huge silver scales that come from tarpon, the 6ft-long namesake fish. Rooms are small and have no TVs or phones, but do have lots of character and rocking chairs on the verandah.

Dancing Dunes (☎ 361-749-3029; www.5dancingdunes.com; 1607 S 11th St; r $100-300) Five funky beach apartments in a small compound have two or three bedrooms each. Flotsam, jetsam and wrecked rowboats decorate the grounds and decor like a holiday episode of *Laverne & Shirley* and guarantee fun.

CONDOS

A large proportion of the lodging around Port A is in condos. They range from simple units in town and away from the water to imposing high-rises on the beach (11th St is known as Condo Row). Many developments are south of town, beyond walking distance. Agents include:

CCMS (☎ 361-749-4141, 800-598-2267; www.portaransas-texas.com)

Coastline Adventures (☎ 361-749-7635, 800-656-5692; www.coastadv.com)

Eating & Drinking

Port A has a great selection of bars and restaurants, almost all as casual as a bunch of sand in your shorts. Many have the kind of goofy vibe that helps make Port A the cool beach town that it is.

ourpick Shorty's (☎ 361-749-8077; 821 Tarpon St; meals from $6; ☒ 11am-late) The town's 'oldest and friendliest' watering hole is filled with real local seadogs and characters both inside and out on the battered porch. It has dartboards and pool tables, and the ceiling is adorned with hundreds of caps from around the world. You can bar-hop around the block here, by the docks.

Fins (☎ 361-749-5597; meals from $6; ☒ 10am-9pm) Next to the docks at Deep Sea Headquarters, you can overhear charter captains talk about the fish – or maybe it was the tourist – they lost overboard. Cheap beer and ultrafresh sea-

---

DRIVING THE BAY LOOP

You can do a loop of Corpus Christi Bay in two hours, without stops. In the south, Padre and Mustang Islands are joined to the mainland via the John F Kennedy Causeway across Laguna Madre. The causeway in turn is reached from Corpus Christi by either Ocean Dr from downtown or by TX 358 (S Padre Island Dr, often called just SPID), which links to the other highways and passes by an ocean of shopping malls. In the north, a car ferry links Port Aransas to TX 361, which leads to Aransas Pass where TX 35 links with US 181 and Corpus.

GULF COAST

food are served on a screened porch. If you catch something, they'll cook it.

The Gaff (☎ 361-749-5970; 323 Beach St; meals from $6; ☻ 11am-late) Out by the beach, this shacky bar is perfect for one aspiring to arrested development. Fun includes belt sander races and chicken poop bingo (come on bird, come on!). There's decent pizza and live music that includes blues and country. Most days are 'talk like a pirate day' here.

Port Aransas Brewing (☎ 361-749-2739; 429 N Alister St; meals from $8; ☻ 11am-10pm Thu-Tue) The microbrews are darn tasty at this small bar and grill in the center (we like the Island Pale Ale) and they get points for also stocking bottles of some of the best microbrews from around the US. The burgers are thick, juicy and lauded. There's a small deck out front.

Roosevelt's (☎ 361-749-5555; 200 E Cotter Ave; meals from $20; ☻ 5-10pm Wed-Sat, 10am-1pm Sun) The fine dining room at the Tarpon Inn is worth getting spiffed up for. Reserve a table on the verandah and settle back to enjoy a seasonal menu of seafood and steaks, simply and creatively prepared. Brunch will have you snoozing for the rest of the day.

Getting There & Around

A highlight of getting to Port A is the constantly running, free **ferries** (☎ 361-749-2850; ☻ 24hr) which connect with TX 361 and Aransas Pass on the mainland. The ride takes 15 minutes and the wait is usually under 10 minutes, except at busy times when it can be 45 minutes.

The lone public transit option for Port Aransas is operated by **The B** (p250; ☎ 361-289-2600; www.ccrta.org). Route 65 runs twice daily June to August from the transit mall on the south side of Corpus Christi (fare 75¢). From here you can transfer to buses to the airport and downtown.

The B runs Route 94 (25¢, every four minutes 10am to 5pm), a fake trolley shuttle, around much of Port Aransas.

MUSTANG & PADRE ISLAND BEACHES

The gulf side of Mustang and Padre Islands is one 131-mile-long beach. The notable parks, Mustang Island State Park and Padre Island National Seashore, are covered in this section. The rest of the beach is administered by Nueces County.

There are beach access roads every few miles, and most have a parking area; parts of the beach are blocked off so that yahoos in SUVs can't mow you down. Camping is permitted anywhere, but limited to three days in any one location. Sand dunes back most of the beach area. Only since the 1970s have some monstrous condo developments appeared on Mustang Island near Port Aransas, otherwise most of the sand is blissfully undeveloped.

Except for Port Aransas Park, you need a $12 permit to drive and park on the beaches.

The well-equipped **Mustang Island State Park** (☎ 361-749-5246, reservations 512-389-8900; www.tpwd. state.tx.us; admission $3; ☻ gates close 10pm except to overnight guests) covers 4000 acres and has 5.5 miles of beach.

This park is popular with surfers, but given the normally calm nature of the gulf, you may have to wait for storms to see any surfable waves. Some picnic areas have shade.

There are 300 nonreservable sites on the beach ($8) that have access to water, showers and rest rooms (a 1.5-mile hike from the furthest sites), these are good compromises for people who want to wake up to the sound of waves but don't want to dig a hole to poop. A more formal area with sites with utilities costs $16 per night.

PADRE ISLAND NATIONAL SEASHORE

One of the longest stretches of undeveloped seashore in the US, the southern half part of Padre Island is administered by the National Park Service. Its main feature is 65 miles of white sand and shell beaches, backed by grassy dunes and the very salty Laguna Madre.

The island is home to all the coastal wildlife found elsewhere along the coast and then some. There's excellent birding, of course, plus numerous coyotes, white-tailed deer, sea turtles and more. It offers a delightful day's outing for anyone who wants to try a little natural beauty, or a major adventure for anyone who wants to escape civilization.

Note that Padre Island National Seashore is separated from South Padre Island by the Mansfield Channel and there is no transport across this gap. South Padre Island, the resort town, is only accessible from the very south of the state.

The first 6 miles of road into the park are paved. After that are 5 miles of beach to the south, which has very hard-packed sand suitable for driving most cars. After milepost 5 on the beach, only 4WD vehicles can continue the trip.

The typically excellent park map is free at the entrance. Besides showing the island in great detail, it has good information about flora, fauna and various activities such as fishing and beachcombing. If you're visiting in summer, you might be able to take part in a turtle release; call the **Hatchling Hotline** (☎ 361-949-7163) for information.

Information

Entrance to the park costs $10 per vehicle, which is good for seven days.

The **Malaquite Beach Visitor Center** (☎ 361-949-8068; www.nps.gov/pais; ◷ 9am-5pm) is on the beach just before the end of the paved road. It has showers, rest rooms and picnic facilities and offers excellent information. Check the schedule for interpretive walks (there's usually one at 11am along the beach).

A small store with convenience foods and souvenirs is also here. There is very little past the visitor center except beautiful beaches and dunes where the only sounds you'll hear are the wind and water, punctuated by the occasional bird's cry.

Camping & Hiking

Reservations are not accepted for any of the facilities. Primitive camping on the beaches is free but requires a permit (available from the visitor center).

The Malaquite Campground is a developed camping area close to the beach and about half a mile from the visitor center. It's suitable for tents and RVs, but it doesn't have any hookups. It does have rest rooms and showers, and camping here costs $8 a night. Many people park their RVs and trailers along the first 5 miles of beach, where driving is fairly easy.

There is primitive camping (pit toilets only) at Bird Island Basin, on the Laguna Madre about 4 miles from the visitor center. It's suitable for RVs and tents and costs $5 a night.

The rangers advise campers and hikers of the common sense needed for a trek south on the island. Bring at least 1 gallon of water per person per day, along with sunscreen, insect repellent, good shady hats and other sensible attire. Shore fishing is permitted with a Texas state fishing license.

Windsurfing

Bird Island Basin faces the Laguna Madre and has been voted as one of the best windsurfing spots in North America. **Worldwinds** (☎ 361-949-

7472, 800-793-7471; www.worldwinds.net) has a base here, offering equipment and gear rental ($45 to $60 per day) and lessons.

Tours

Padre Island Safaris (☎ 361-937-8446; www.billysandifer. com) goes to remote parts of the park for nature-watching and fishing. Respected fisherman and unofficial local historian Captain Billy Sandifer will take you the length of the park; a four- to six-hour birding trip costs $300 for two.

CORPUS CHRISTI TO HARLINGEN

US 77 is the main southbound route from the Corpus Christi to the semitropical south. Except for a few diversions like Kingsville, there's 120 miles of scrubland before you reach Harlingen.

Robstown

Just south of where TX 44 hits US 77 from Corpus Christi you may notice cars exiting in droves. It's likely the siren song of **Joe Cotton's Barbecue Joint** (☎ 361-767-9973; 607 US 77 S; meals from $7; ◷ 10am-9:30pm Tue-Sat) has grabbed them. And for good reason, the barbecue is sublime. Hordes pass through, served by waiters with huge platters of meat, flagons of iced tea and enough bread for a factory.

Kingsville
pop 24,500

King is the name of the game in this company town that is the direct result of the fabled 825,000-acre King Ranch, the largest of its kind in the world. Former riverboat captain Richard King established the ranch in 1853 on land that others saw as a scrub-covered semidesert. King instead saw scrub-covered semidesert with the only natural springs for hundreds of miles. Today the ranch is bigger than Rhode Island, a state that the ranch's fences would reach if they were laid end to end.

Kingsville is on US 77 and the ranch makes an interesting stop while passing by or as a day trip from Corpus Christi. Information is available through the **Kingsville Visitor Center** (☎ 361-592-8516, 800-333-5032; www.kingsvilletexas. com; US 77 at Corral St; ◷ 9am-5pm Mon-Fri, 10am-2pm Sat). Sadly, the historic downtown has been decimated by chain stores on the garish strip by the highway.

Much of the **King Ranch** (☎ visitor center 361-592-8055; www.king-ranch.com; ranch tours adult/child $8/4; ◷ 9am-4pm Mon-Sat, noon-5pm Sun) is not open to the public. But there are 60,000 head of cattle, 400 horses and dozens of cowboys here – many fifth- and sixth-generation descendants of Mexicans who moved to the ranch in the 1860s. On the tour's 10-mile loop you will see the horse and cattle breeds that made the ranch famous, plus some native wildlife. You'll pass the lavish main building (33,000 sq feet), and with any luck you'll get to hear some excellent commentary and personal anecdotes from the tour guides, who are often retired ranch employees.

Tours depart from the visitor center, which is just inside the rather modest entrance to the ranch on the west side of Kingsville at the end of Santa Gertrudis Ave.

In addition to the standard tours, there are guided bird-watching and wildlife-spotting tours across the unspoiled expanses of the ranch lasting from four to nine hours ($25 to $200). Schedules change by season.

Housed in a renovated ice-storage house downtown, the **King Ranch Museum** (☎ 361-595-1881; 405 6th St; adult/child $4/2.50; ☷ 10am-4pm Mon-Sat, 1-5pm Sun) covers the history of the ranch. Be sure to follow the minor family dramas of the first generation, they are like a movie (foreman marries King daughter etc).

The upmarket **King Ranch Saddle Shop** (☎ 800-282-5464; 201 E Kleberg Ave; ☷ 10am-6pm Mon-Sat) has expensive clothing and gear branded with the distinctive King Ranch logo, which looks like a squiggly snake.

Loyola Beach

This unassuming Texas coastal village, 24 miles southeast of Kingsville, is home to another one of those restaurants that causes people to detour in droves. **King's Inn** (☎ 361-297-5265; meals from $10; ☷ 11am-10pm Tue-Sat) is a legendary place known for its vast platters of fresh seafood, onion rings, avocado salad and more. About 15 miles south of Kingsville look for FM 628 and go east 9 miles. Make reservations for dinner.

LOWER GULF COAST

Palm trees and hot humid weather are but one sign you've hit the subtropical southern Gulf Coast. Ribbons of traffic zipping along TX 100 to South Padre Island mean that you've come within the gravitational force of the state's favorite beach resort.

HARLINGEN
pop 70,800

Harlingen just isn't what it used to be, and that's a good thing. In 1910 it was called Six-Shooter Junction because of the explosive stew of lawless bands, Mexican raiders, Texas Rangers and US National Guardsmen that prowled its streets. Today, most permanent residents are more occupied with agriculture than lawlessness. Look for fields of large, spiky aloe plants, which produce the soothing substance used in lotions, shampoos and ointments. It has a couple of diversions worthy of a pit stop on your way to South Padre Island or the Rio Grande Valley. Mostly, though, this is a land for Winter Texans (see the boxed text, p64).

The excellent **Texas Travel Information Center** (☎ 956-428-4477; 2021 W Harrison St; ☷ 8am-5pm) at the junction of US 77 and US 83 has maps, brochures and other information about the region and the entire state.

Return to the days of Six-Shooter Junction at the **Harlingen Arts & Heritage Museum** (☎ 956-216-4906; Boxwood & Raintree Sts, off Loop 499; admission free; ☷ 10am-4pm Tue-Sun), which combines several museums in one. An 1870s stagecoach inn recalls the hot, dusty conditions of the old trail, where the only friend you were likely to make at the end of a long day was a bedbug. The region's colorful and violent past is extensively documented. It's near the airport.

Harlingen's best eats are at **Smokey Joe's** (☎ 956-364-1266; 102 N US Business 77, near E Harrison Ave/TX 206; meals from $8; ☷ 11am-8pm), a spectacular family-run barbecue joint on the old commercial strip. Pecan and mesquite in the smoker yield fine results.

Valley International Airport (HRL; ☎ 956-430-8600; www.flythevalley.com), on Loop 499, 3 miles east of downtown, has service from Continental Express to Houston and Southwest to and from Houston and San Antonio. It's a popular link for South Padre Island and the Rio Grande Valley.

LAGUNA ATASCOSA NATIONAL WILDLIFE REFUGE

From the moment you step out of your car at this 70-sq-mile federal **preserve** (☎ 956-748-3607; www.fws.gov; per vehicle $3; ☷ gates dawn-dusk, visitor center 8am-5pm winter, 9am-6pm summer), northwest of Port Isabel, you are surrounded by the calls of birds. You may think you've stepped into the Hitchcock movie or are trapped in a hellish version of the old Woolworth's para-keet department, but you haven't. The calls blend into a mélange of melodies that cause you to stop and just listen.

The land is a veritable avian playground (more than 400 species have been spotted); wetlands, thorn brush, trees and grasses offer something for everyone with feathers. The refuge is also home to the rare, but rather cute, ocelot, a relative of the jaguar.

The roads to the refuge are not well marked. From Harlingen, take FM 106 east 18 miles until it dead-ends, then turn left and drive 3 miles to the refuge entrance. If you're coming from the east, take FM 510 from TX 100 at Laguna Vista and then Buena Vista Rd for a total of 15 miles north to the refuge.

Strung out along TX 100, the South Padre Island road there are two good reasons to pause in **Los Fresnos**.

Bobz World at Seven Seas (☎ 956-554-4540; 36451 TX 100; ⏰ 9am-6pm, longer during holidays) is a souvenir store that is so over the top as to be literally unmissable. Outside, enormous plaster dinosaurs and sea creatures beckon. Inside, every kind of shell, trinket and beach toy imaginable await. Fudge too.

Excellent Texas barbecue awaits at **Wild Blue BBQ** (☎ 956-233-8185; 31230 TX 100; meals from $8; ⏰ 11am-9pm Mon-Sat), a splendid roadside joint where the little things matter. Even the sides are just so and the sweet potato flan is sublime.

PORT ISABEL
pop 5300
In the days before inexpensive hurricane insurance made South Padre Island viable as a town, Port Isabel was the focus of life near the southern end of Texas. Records show that Spaniards and pirates both made fre-quent landfalls here in the 16th, 17th and 18th centuries.

Today Port Isabel is a must-stop just be-fore SPI (South Padre Island). Its small old town covers the waterfront for a couple of blocks on either side of the base of the TX 100 Queen Isabella Causeway. It is served by the free Wave shuttle to/from SPI; see p262 for details.

The **Port Isabel Lighthouse** (☎ 956-943-2262; TX 100 & Tarnava St; adult/child $3/1; ⏰ 9am-5pm) was built between 1852 and 1853. A climb up its 70 steps yields great views of the surrounding area, SPI and the gulf. It is also the source of local tourist info.

Built sturdily of bricks to resist storms, the 1899 home of the **Port Isabel Historical Museum** (☎ 956-943-7602; 317 Railroad Ave; adult/child $3/1; ⏰ 10am-4pm Tue-Sat) served at various times as the town's railroad station, post office and general store. You'll find it one block south of TX 100, near the lighthouse.

Connected to the Historical Museum, **Treasures of the Gulf Museum** (☎ 956-943-7602; 317 Railroad Ave; adult/child $3/1; ⏰ 10am-4pm Tue-Sat) documents the 1554 sinking of three Spanish ships off South Padre Island and has kid-friendly marine-archaeology exhibits.

All three of the above sites are close to each other and you can buy combined tickets (adult/child $7/2).

The waterfront is predictably lined with popular seafood joints and bars with decks looking over the water. But one block west of the lighthouse is a sleeper: **Joe's Oyster Bar Restaurant** (☎ 956-943-4501; 207 Maxan St; meals from $6; ⏰ 11am-7pm) has seafood direct off the boats and makes a mean crab cake. You can get anything to go for picnics or packed fresh for cooking later in the condo.

SOUTH PADRE ISLAND
pop 3100
Covering the bottom 5 miles of South Padre Island, the town of South Padre Island (SPI) works hard to exploit its sunny climate and beaches. The water is warm for much of the year, the beaches are clean, and the laid-back locals are ready to welcome each and every tourist who crosses the 2.5-mile Queen Isabella Causeway from the mainland (the permanent population is augmented by 10,000 or more visitors at any given time). SPI is a varied mix of beach overdevelopment, charming cottages and long stretches of open sand.

Until 1962, there was no South Padre Island, only the 147-mile Padre Island, a barrier island that was the longest of its kind in the world. However, the pleas of Port Mansfield for direct access to the gulf shipping lanes were finally heeded, and a channel was cut through the island, creating 34-mile South Padre Island.

January and February, when the weather can be either balmy or a bit chilly, are the quietest months to visit SPI. The busiest (and most expensive) periods are spring break (all of March except the first week; see the boxed text, p257) and summer, when the moderating gulf breezes make the shore more tolerable than the sweltering inland areas.

Orientation

No ferry or bridge crosses Port Mansfield Pass. To reach Padre Island National Seashore from South Padre Island you must either have your own boat or make the long drive all the way around the mainland via Harlingen and Corpus Christi.

South Padre Island is only a half-mile wide at its widest point. Laguna Madre, the shallow inland waterway between the island and the mainland, is ideally suited for windsurfing (see p258).

The southern, developed end of Padre Blvd is the main traffic artery, so it tends to be crowded and noisy. In fact the stretch north from Dolphin St is a pedestrian nightmare, with families trying to cross around SUVs doing 60mph. One block west, Laguna Blvd is a more peaceful road for walking or cycling. To the east, running parallel to the beach, is Gulf Blvd, which is mostly lined with large developments.

Information
BOOKSTORES
Paragraphs (Map p261; ☎ 956-433-5057; 5505 Padre Blvd; ⏰ 10am-5pm Mon & Wed-Sat, noon-4pm Sun; 🛜) An excellent indie bookstore with a nice patio.

INTERNET ACCESS
You'll find wi-fi at many restaurants and bars (the better to post pics of yourself doing shots) and at most accommodations.
South Padre Office Center (Map p261; ☎ 956-761-1182; 2600 Padre Blvd; ⏰ 9am-6pm) Has internet access and full computer services, plus a shipping center.

TOURIST INFORMATION
South Padre Island Convention & Visitors Bureau (Map p258; ☎ 956-761-4412; www.sopadre.com; 600 Padre Blvd; ⏰ 9am-6pm Mon-Fri, to 5pm winter, 9am-5pm Sat & Sun) Near the end of the causeway, has a full range of local information.

Sights
The beach (see the boxed text, p259) is the first and last thing many visitors wish to see but there are various attractions that allow you to engage with SPI's natural beauty.

SOUTH PADRE ISLAND BIRDING & NATURE CENTER
Part of the World Birding Center (p64), this 50-acre **nature preserve** (Map p261; ☎ 956-243-8179; www.worldbirdingcenter.org; 6801 Padre Blvd; adult/child $5/2; ⏰ 9am-5pm) has boardwalks through the dunes, bird blinds, spotting towers and much

---

A PARTY FOR 100,000

Like other second-tier beach resorts, such as Florida's Panama City Beach, South Padre Island has discovered gold in spring break, the period in March when hordes of college students (and high-school students with lax parents) congregate at beaches for a week or more of completely pleasurable excess that's limited only by the capacity of their livers, loins and billfolds. Resorts such as Fort Lauderdale, in Florida, now turn up their noses at spring break, but SPI does everything possible to welcome this free-spending mob.

During the last three weeks of March, when various US colleges and universities have their breaks, more than 100,000 students descend on the island for days of drinking, swimming, sunbathing, frolicking and more, followed by nights of drinking, skinny-dipping, frolicking and more. Major sponsors, such as beer and soda companies, stage concerts and games on the beaches. MTV is usually there broadcasting live.

During spring break, it's hard to escape the mobs of students cruising the developed part of town. If the idea of spending a week at a beach party with thousands of young people on their first real bender appeals to you, you will have a wonderful time. More sedate types should avoid the island for the month.

Ground zero for SPI's spring break is the area near the end of the causeway, where the largest condos and hotels, including the Isla Grand Beach Resort and the Sheraton South Padre Beach Condominiums, are located. Major clubs catering to the spring break crowds include Chaos and Louie's Backyard. See p262 for details. Apart from these hot spots, any place on SPI that sells beer will see spring break action, with many serving locally popular drinks such as The Whammy and Charlie's Cherry.

The best accommodations – meaning those closest to the action – usually book up six months or more before March. The web is awash with offers.

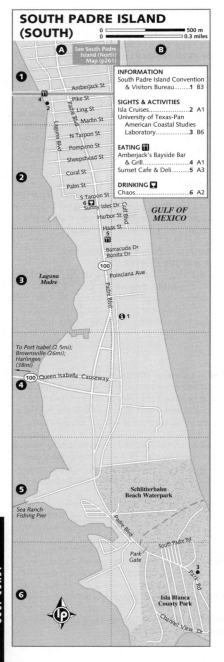

SOUTH PADRE ISLAND (SOUTH)

0 — 500 m
0 — 0.3 miles

See South Padre Island (North) Map (p261)

INFORMATION
South Padre Island Convention & Visitors Bureau.........**1** B3

SIGHTS & ACTIVITIES
Isla Cruises.....................**2** A1
University of Texas-Pan American Coastal Studies Laboratory.................**3** B6

EATING
Amberjack's Bayside Bar & Grill.......................**4** A1
Sunset Cafe & Deli.........**5** A3

DRINKING
Chaos.............................**6** A2

GULF OF MEXICO

Laguna Madre

To Port Isabel (2.5mi); Brownsville (26mi); Harlingen (38mi)

Queen Isabella Causeway

Schlitterbahn Beach Waterpark

Sea Ranch Fishing Pier

Park Gate

Isla Blanca County Park

---

more. Learn the differences between a dune meadow, a salt marsh and an intertidal flat – and there won't even be a quiz after.

SEA TURTLE, INC

The late Ila Loestcher started **Sea Turtle, Inc** (Map p261; ☎ 956-761-4511; www.seaturtleinc.org; 6617 Padre Blvd; $3 donation requested; ☼ 10am-4pm Tue-Sun) in 1977 after sea turtles had almost vanished from the Texas coast. Today more than a dozen Kemp's ridley sea turtles are nesting again on SPI and her organization is thriving thanks to a dedicated cadre of volunteers and benefactors. Visits to the center are a fascinating change from SPI's commercialism; you can see rescued turtles and learn firsthand about the slow rebirth of local turtle populations.

SCHLITTERBAHN BEACH WATERPARK

Just north of Isla Blanca County Park, this vast **water park** (Map p258; ☎ 956-772-7873; www. schlitterbahn.com; 90 Padre Blvd; adult/child $40/32; ☼ 10am-8pm summer, shorter hours other times, closed Oct-Mar) offers water slides and pools of every description.

Activities

There are so many activities on SPI that you may be exhausted before you start.

FISHING

More than 50 fishing boats leave from the piers on the lagoon. **Jim's Pier** (Map p261; ☎ 956-761-2865; 209 W Whiting St) offers scheduled four-hour trips onto the bay ($30) where you may catch flounder or speckled trout. Longer trips head into the gulf for prime game fish such as wahoo.

HORSEBACK RIDING

About a mile north of the convention center, **Island Equestrian Center** (☎ 956-761-4677; www. horsesonthebeach.com; 1hr rides from $45) rents horses for all levels of riders and leads tours of the beaches.

WATER SPORTS

You'll find outfits offering parasailing and other rides over and on the water along the beaches in the developed part of SPI. The lagoon side is renowned for wind-powered water sports like windsurfing. There are dozens of operators, two of the best (offering lessons and rental) are:

Boatyard (Map p261; ☎ 956-761-5061; www.wind surftheboatyard.com; 5514 Padre Blvd) Rents windsurf boards (half-day $45) and also kayaks and mountain bikes.

Windsurf, Inc (Map p261; ☎ 956-761-1434; www. windsurfinc.com; 224 W Carolyn Dr) Specializes in windsurfing (lessons from $45 per hour), kiteboarding, surfing, kayaking and wakeboarding.

Tours

Bottlenose dolphins love the lagoon and SPI visitors love looking at them. **Isla Cruises** (Map p258; ☎ 956-761-4752; www.islatours.com; cnr Pike St & Laguna Blvd; tours $15) offers two-hour boat rides to see the finned friends. You can bring your own beer on board, which gives you the opportunity to invent new drinking games that involve Flipper.

Festivals & Events

SPI schedules events year-round, including weekend fireworks through the summer. In addition to spring break in March, some of the major events and their usual dates include **Sand Castle Days** in mid-October and the **Kite Festival** in early November. The CVB has details.

Sleeping
CAMPING

Camping is popular on SPI. You can choose an organized park with all the amenities or a pristine, nearly deserted beach with no facilities whatsoever.

Isla Blanca County Park (Map p258; ☎ 956-761-5494; 1/2 Park Rd 100; tent sites $15, sites with amenities from $24; 🛜) Popular because of its proximity to

---

BEACH GUIDE

SPI is beaches, but there are great variations along the 34 miles of bright white, hard-packed gulf sand. You can enjoy the company of a few thousand of your best friends you haven't met yet, go for a drive, get lost in the dunes or shed virtually everything far from another soul.

SPI's spine, Padre Blvd, extends 12 miles from the south to a point where the pavement literally ends. There are several access points onto the sand where you can drive your vehicle out onto the sand. On summer weekends, many of these areas are tailgating paradises.

From south to north, here are some SPI beach highlights:

- **Isla Blanca County Park** (Map p258; ☎ 956-761-5494; 1/2 Park Rd 100; per vehicle $4) Just south of the causeway, this county park is the most popular beach on SPI thanks to various concessions and facilities.

- **University of Texas-Pan American Coastal Studies Laboratory** (Map p258; ☎ 956-761-2644; admission free; 🕑 1:30-4:30pm Sun-Fri) This working lab is open for self-guided tours of its fish tanks and various wall displays. If you can get past its meager utilitarian charms, you'll find lots of information about local marine life. Grapefruit-size conch show you how the popular fritters look while still in the water.

- **Andy Bowie County Park** (Map p261; ☎ 956-761-2639; per car $4) Across from South Padre Island Convention Center, this pleasant beach park used to mark the end of development, but as you'll see, that has changed. It's 5.5 miles north from Isla Blanca.

- **Edwin King Atwood County Park** (off Map p261; per car $3) Two miles north of Bowie, Atwood sports towering sand dunes backing the beach. This is a beautiful, unspoiled area where sand often obscures Padre Blvd, however real estate agent signs suggest a different future.

- **Beach access points** ($3 per car) Numbered through 6, these are merely breaks in the sand to allow vehicles out onto the hard sand. You can camp if you desire.

- **North End** Padre Blvd ends 12 miles north of Isla Blanca. North of here there's 20 miles of nothing all the way to the channel. Nude sunbathers, anglers, bird-watchers and other outdoorsy types can find a sandy acre to call their own, even though vehicles can drive on the beach.

Need an umbrella to shade from the energetic sun and some beach loungers to rest your weary bones? **Jim's Beach Rentals** (☎ 956-761-2130) will do the set up and take down wherever you want. The cost is $24 for one day, with weekly rates available.

the action, this park has a variety of camping facilities, including sites with beach views. Long-term rates are available. Reservations may only be made for stays of seven or more days.

MOTELS & HOTELS

Accommodations on SPI come in three broad categories: big glitzy resorts, regular chain motels and funky places with lots of beach atmosphere. Some of the resort places are nice, while others look like the result of a five-year plan. Rates vary hugely between warm-weather weekends (when it pays to seek out quiet neighbors) and the middle of January.

Flamingo Inn (Map p261; ☎ 956-761-3377; www.flamingo-spi.com; 3408 Padre Blvd; r $60-140; 🔁 🐾) It looks like a chain motel but the managers live right here and there are delightful quirks (like the colonnaded Jacuzzi suites) that make it pure indie. Needless to say, the Flamingo is painted pink. The 29 rooms have fridges and microwaves.

South Beach Inn (Map p261; ☎ 956-761-2471; www.seagrapemotel.com; 120 E Jupiter Lane; r $60-100; 🔁 🐾) This 19-unit motel is vintage 1961 but has been colorfully kept up and exudes a fun vibe. It is a half block from the beach and has a pool, barbecue area and rooms with kitchens.

Wanna Wanna Inn (Map p261; ☎ 956-761-7677; www.wannawanna.com; 5100 Gulf Blvd; r $80-180; 🔁) Much remodeled, the low-rise Wanna Wanna has but 15 rooms, some with excellent views of the gulf from this beachfront location. Units have either microwaves and fridges or kitchenettes. Murals in the rooms include one with a spunky Flipper that is bound to be inspirational. The beachside bar is fun.

Palms Resort (Map p261; ☎ 956-761-1316, 800-466-1316; www.palmsresortcafe.com; 3616 Gulf Blvd; r $100-200; 🔁 🐾) This unassuming two-story motel looks right over the grass-covered dune to the gulf. Units are large and have fridges and microwaves; some have granite wet bars and showers for two (no more dirty backs). The beachfront cafe/bar is fun.

Tiki Condominium Hotel (Map p261; ☎ 956-761-2694, 800-551-8454; www.thetiki.com; 6608 Padre Blvd; r $110-350; 🔁 🐾) It's Ginger or Mary Ann time at this wonderful Polynesian-themed veteran that plays the tiki-cliché to the max. Large, two-story blocks cover the beachfront site at

the north end of developed SPI. Units have full kitchens and range in size from one to three bedrooms.

CONDOS & COTTAGES

More than 4000 apartments are available for rent on SPI. They can be ugly – notable examples being the Saida Towers and the thoroughly god-awful Bridgepoint – or nice. They come with one, two or three bedrooms and always have kitchens. Most of the larger complexes have pools and other facilities such as tennis courts and whirlpools.

Often just off the beach, you can rent part of a house or cottage that may not have the ocean view but which will have plenty of charm.

Rates run the gamut. Some places offer daily rentals; others require a week minimum. For the peak summer season, reservations are recommended three months in advance. During the winter, you can often bargain for substantial discounts.

The website www.vrbo.com is a good source of interesting properties being rented by their owners. The CVB has links to rental agents, including:

Island Services (☎ 956-761-2649, 800-527-0294; www.island-services.com) The largest locally owned agency.

Service 24 (☎ 956-761-1487, 800-828-4287; www.service24.com) Reps scores of big condo resorts.

Eating

Except for the peak periods, South Padre Island closes early so unless noted otherwise, plan on dining by 9pm. Condo dwellers will find plenty of markets for all those essential foods you'd never eat at home.

Sunset Cafe & Deli (Map p258; ☎ 956-761-2866; 1004 Padre Blvd; meals from $5; 🕑 7am-3pm; 🔁) Smoothies offer a fresh start to the day as well as breakfast tacos, waffles, eggs Benedict and various Tex-Mex treats. The tuna and avocado sandwich is a lunch fave, as are the salads.

PsychaDeli (Map p261; ☎ 956-772-9770; 3112 Padre Blvd; meals from $7; 🕑 11am-6pm Tue-Sun) Inventive sandwiches are a huge hit with locals at this lime-green bistro. There are veggie options and some fine grilled numbers like the Mexicali Bleu (ham, Swiss and blue cheese, avocado and chipotle sauce on sourdough).

Zeste Cafe & Market (Map p261; ☎ 956-761-5555; 3508 Padre Blvd; meals from $8; 🕑 hours vary, usually 11am-

GULF COAST

9pm) *The* place to assemble that beach picnic that will cause great envy among the weenie-scarfing masses. The deli section has a huge assortment of fine food stuffs. The cafe has Med-accented salads and mains. On some weekend nights they have a long tapas menu until 10pm.

Blackbeard's (Map p261; ☎ 956-761-2962; 103 E Saturn Lane; meals $8-25; 11:30am-10pm) Year after year crowds flock here for an ocean of seafood cooked in myriad ways. Enormous platters have so many options that it may drive you to drink – fortunately the excellent margaritas are cheap. The vast terrace makes the inevitable waits a pleasure.

Daddy's Seafood & Cajun Kitchen (Map p261; ☎ 956-761-1975; 3409 Padre Ave; meals $10-25; 11am-9pm Sun-Thu, to 10pm Fri & Sat) You'll love making a mess with New Orleans–style seafood that includes spicy boiled shrimp and crawfish. Corn, potatoes, oysters and a lot more offer diversions.

Amberjack's Bayside Bar & Grill (Map p258; ☎ 956-761-6500; 209 W Amberjack St; meals $12-30; 11am-11pm) Lagoonside Amberjack's has a popular bar that's more classy than a lot of its neighbors – drinks even come in containers made of real glass. The long menu concentrates on fresh seafood and steaks. Romantic platters for two are best enjoyed on the huge covered patio.

GULF COAST

SAND CASTLES

If you've always dreamed of having your own castle, you can build one on South Padre Island – out of sand. And not just some humdrum, upended-bucket-and-garnished-with-a-seagull-feather affair either, but an honest-to-goodness castle, standing about 8ft tall, with towers, moats, a keep and anything else your heart desires.

Of course, such a creation doesn't come easy. That's where Lucinda 'Sandy Feet' Wierenga and 'Amazin' Walter' McDonald come in. Longtime SPI residents, they've carved out a lucrative living teaching people how to build vast creations that live only until the next dawn – or whenever the tide comes in. All you need is a shovel, a bucket and a few household tools.

Their school, **Sons of the Beach** (☎ 956-761-6222, 956-761-5943; www.sonsofthebeach.com), offers lessons for one to 15 people at $75 per hour. You choose which beach for your lessons. They also have group lessons in the summer at set times for $20 per person – call for times and locations.

Drinking & Entertainment

There's a long stretch of bars and clubs on the lagoon side along Laguna Blvd between Tarpon and Red Snapper Sts.

Coconuts (Map p261; ☎ 956-761-4218; 2301 Laguna Blvd) The clichés start with the thatched roof over the deck but that doesn't stop the mixed crowd of tourists and locals from cutting loose from before the sun sets until well after midnight. Live music rocks the house.

Louie's Backyard (Map p261; ☎ 956-761-6406; 2305 Laguna Blvd) Spring break central, Louie's serves a mere 3000 to 4000 every night. There are multiple stages, big name rappers, a dance floor overlooking the water, cheap booze and snacks, and a minimalist dress code that allows for just about anything.

Chaos (Map p258; ☎ 956-772-1922; 1601 Padre Blvd) Seven venues in one, it's, well, chaotic! Wander amid karaoke, rap, rock, a sports bar (where nerds somehow never meet women) and much more. Get liquored up and shed your clothes for the tattoo parlor or the cameras.

Padre Island Brewing Company (Map p261; ☎ 956-761-9585; 3400 Padre Blvd) A microbrewery treat on an island where the national breweries sponsor constant promotions emphasizing quantity over quality. Burgers and other bar food are popular.

Boomerang Billy's Beach Bar & Grill (Map p261; ☎ 956-761-2420; 2612 Gulf Blvd) Billy's is behind the shambolic Surf Motel and is one of the few bars right on the sand on the gulf side.

Mellow sounds a bit too energetic for this ultimate crash pad.

Getting There & Around

If you can get out to SPI, you won't necessarily need a car. The developed area is fairly compact, easy for walking or cycling, and there's a shuttle.

TO/FROM THE AIRPORTS

Brownsville South Padre Island International Airport (p267) is 26 miles southwest. You can catch the **Rio Gulf Coast Express** (☎ 800-574-8322; www.flybrownsville.com) to Port Isabel ($2, 7am to 5pm Monday to Saturday, no service on holidays) and transfer to the Wave (p262).

Harlingen's Valley International Airport (p255) is 43 miles northwest. The **South Padre Shuttle** (☎ 877-774-0050; www.southpadreshuttle.com) offers door-to-door service; book in advance (per person one way/round-trip $20/35).

BUS

The **Wave** (☎ 956-761-1025; www.sopadre.com; ☯ 7am-7pm), a free shuttle service, serves the island as far north as the convention center and all the way south to Isla Blanca County Park and over the causeway to Port Isabel. During spring break service ends at 5pm.

TAXI

SPI cab companies include **BB's Taxi** (☎ 956-761-7433), charging $35 to $40 to Brownsville airport, $45 to $55 to Harlingen airport.

Rio Grande Valley

The Rio Grande (Big River; the Mexicans call it the Río Bravo, or Brave River) forms a natural border between Texas and Mexico. And nowhere during its 2000-mile course from Colorado's San Juan Mountains to the Gulf of Mexico is it more fraught with drama.

Immigration – legal and otherwise – drug wars and free trade are just some of the hot-button issues that dominate dialogue on either side. And where many of the twinned border towns like Laredo and Nuevo Laredo seemed on the verge of melding into one just a few years ago, the separation between the nations is far greater now than just the width of the river.

Certainly it's easy to define the border as a multibillion-dollar fence goes up on the US side. Meanwhile, it's sadly possible to (literally) lose sight of some of the region's great beauty. But under the guise of the World Birding Center, a string of parks and natural locations makes every effort to both woo and accommodate bird-watchers. Trails in places like the Santa Ana National Wildlife Refuge quickly remove visitors from the bustle of the east end of the valley and deposit them amid deeply wooded wetlands on the river, where trees drip with Spanish moss and birds chirp with abandon.

West along the valley, the Rio Grande passes sleepy burgs like Zapata and Langtry that seem like the fading sets of old westerns, while in Del Rio, as in other border towns, you can enjoy Mexican food that's as good as anywhere.

HIGHLIGHTS

Best Border Town
Stroll the old center and atmospheric, tree-lined avenues of Del Rio (p275)

How to Leave the US without Trying
Brownsville (p265) has a downtown with buildings dating back to 1848 and shops that are pure Mexico

Most Evocative Battlefield
Learn how today's politics were shaped on the sunburned expanse of the Palo Alto Battlefield National Historical Site (p267)

Where Birds Rule Your Roost
The headquarters of the World Birding Center, Bentsen-Rio Grande Valley State Park (p270), has beautiful trails for finding feathered friends

Walk on the Wild Side
Day trips to Mexico's counterparts (boxed text, p266) to US border towns can be richly rewarding, but consider issues about safety and bureaucracy first

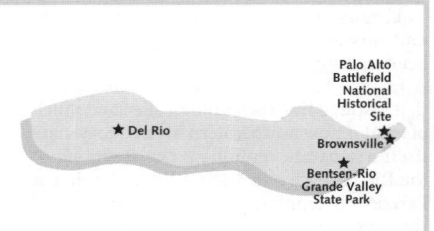

Palo Alto Battlefield National Historical Site
★ Del Rio
★ Brownsville
★ Bentsen-Rio Grande Valley State Park

RIO GRANDE VALLEY

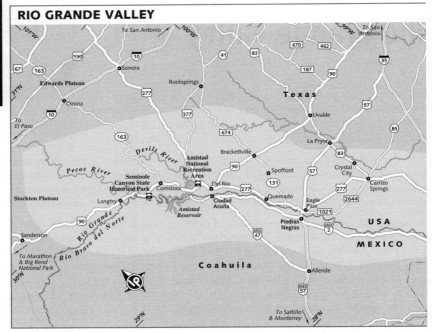

History

The Laredo border area was sparsely populated with nomadic Native American groups until Don Tomás Sánchez, a captain in the Spanish royal army, was given a grant of land here in 1775.

The first non-Indian settlers were ranchers, and missionaries passed through the area, heading into the interior of Texas.

In 1836 Texas seceded from Mexico, an act that inspired the Rio Grande Valley and much of what is now northeastern Mexico to declare itself a separate republic – the Republic of the Rio Grande – in 1840. With its capital at Laredo, the republic lasted just 283 days, until the Mexican army regained control.

The Treaty of Guadalupe Hidalgo, which ended the Mexican War, ran the new border of the USA down the Rio Grande. Like much of Texas, the next century was largely about cattle and then oil.

The valley began a new boom in 1994 with the passage of the North American Free Trade Agreement (Nafta), which opened up trade across the border.

RIO GRANDE VALLEY

The semitropical southern border area of Texas is much wetter than the arid west, thanks to the moisture-laden winds off the Gulf of Mexico. This lush environment is perfect for farming; much of the winter produce sold in the USA comes from Texas.

The temperate winter climate attracts hordes of migratory creatures. A breed known as 'Winter Texans' – American retirees from the north – arrives in flocks (see the boxed text, p273), as do more than 500 species of birds, who in turn attract flocks of bird-watchers to scores of natural spots.

The valley begins at the mouth of the Rio Grande, which meets the gulf in vast palm-studded wetlands, lagoons and remote beaches.

Further west in the valley, most of the land is given over to farming. In the lands west of McAllen, the gulf winds diminish and the land becomes more arid and unpopulated.

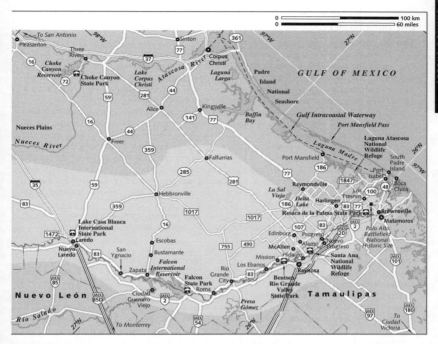

BROWNSVILLE

pop 173,800

Matamoros, Brownsville's Mexican counterpart across the Rio Grande, grew to prominence in the 1820s as the Mexican port closest to then-booming New Orleans. After the Mexican War (1846–48), American merchants and traders thought it wise to cross the Rio Grande to Texas, where they established Brownsville. The town was named for Major Jacob Brown, the US commander of Fort Taylor (later renamed Fort Brown), who died during a Mexican raid.

During the rest of the 19th century, the fast-growing town was filled with ornate brick structures that drew their architectural inspiration from Mexico and New Orleans. Many survive today and help make Brownsville an atmospheric stop. Its authentic and slightly gritty culture make it an excellent day trip from South Padre Island (SPI).

Orientation & Information

Brownsville lies at the southern end of US 77, the spine of the southern Gulf Coast. The downtown area, near the Gateway International Gateway Bridge/Puente Nuevo, E Elizabeth St and International Blvd is a busy place.

Brownsville Convention & Visitors Bureau (☎ 956-546-3721; 650 Ruben M Torres Sr Blvd/FM 802; ⏲ 8am-5pm Mon-Fri, 9am-4pm Sat & Sun) On the west side of US 77/83 at the FM 802 exit; an excellent source of information on the entire area.

Sights

DOWNTOWN

One of the best things you can do in Brownsville is simply go wandering around the downtown area. Streets such as E Washington and E Elizabeth are still busy with the kinds of small shops that once lined main streets across the USA, although ironically, most of the customers are day-trippers from Mexico.

The 1850 home of Brownsville founder Charles Stillman houses the **Brownsville Heritage Complex** (☎ 956-541-5560; www.brownsville history.org; 1325 E Washington St; adult/child $4/2; ⏲ 10am-4pm Tue-Sat, 1-5pm Sun) on his life. This is a good

DAY TRIPS TO MEXICO
Should You Visit?
Time was when no visit to the Rio Grande Valley was complete without a jaunt across the border into one of the towns like Nuevo Laredo, which is twinned with Laredo on the US side. Good and cheap Mexican food (and tequila), mariachis, cheap tatty souvenirs as well as cut-rate dental work and prescription drugs were just some of the lures. Plus there was the thrill of entering a dramatically different culture, just by strolling across a bridge spanning the Rio Grande.

But several years of lurid headlines caused by the carnage of Mexico's drug wars have put a big question mark over border-town day trips. Although tourists are not the targets, fear of getting caught up in the violence is a real concern. Meanwhile, businesses that have delighted generations of Americans (or simply sold them cheap pharmaceuticals) have suffered greatly.

Should you visit? The best answer is to ask locally on the Texas side of the border; conditions change constantly. No matter what, you'll probably feel safest, at least for your first visit, by going during the day. While across, look out for images of La Sante Muerte (Holy Death), an iconic figure of a skeleton with a scythe dressed in robes. It's the symbol of a fast-growing religious cult popular with the gangs.

The US State Department has a useful web page with constantly updated information about Mexican security issues: http://mexico.usembassy.gov/eng/eacs_MexicoSecurityUpdate.html.

Border Details
There are 14 official crossing points along the Texas–Mexico border, most of them open 24 hours daily. Open hours, and estimated waiting times for drivers, are provided by **US Customs and Border Protection** (www.cbp.gov).

Tourists visiting Mexico on a day trip must carry a passport or similar travel document; longer stays may require a visa. They must also obtain a Mexican tourist permit (*forma migratoria para turista*, or FMT) on arrival, unless they are staying within the border zone and not staying more than 72 hours. The border zone generally extends 15 to 20 miles south from the border.

Travelers taking a vehicle into Mexico must obtain Mexican motor insurance and a temporary vehicle importation permit; look for booths at crossings. If you have not obtained the vehicle permit before arrival, you have to do the paperwork at IITV (Importación e Internación Temporal de Vehículos) modules at larger border crossings. All IITV locations are given on the **Banjército** (www.banjercito.com.mx) website – click on 'Red de Módulos IITV.'

Given the hassles of vehicles, most people crossing into Mexico for a day trip from Texas either walk (most of the Mexican cities are right on the Rio Grande) or take a cab – you'll find international taxis near most border crossings. Fares aren't cheap and are open to bargaining; expect to pay $10 to $30. Border bridge tolls are usually under $1 for pedestrians and $3 for vehicles.

place to learn about the downtown area. Be sure to get a copy here (or at the CVB) of the excellent *Guide to Historic Brownsville*, a free brochure detailing the city's heritage. It has superb walking tours.

Among the scores of structures downtown is one of the oldest city halls in continuous use in the US, the **Old Market Place** (12th & Market Sq btwn E Adams & E Washington Sts). Built in 1850, it now also serves as the city's transit center. The **Gem** (400 E 13th St), between E Levee St and E Elizabeth St, is the city's oldest building, dating from 1848. Its projecting balconies once sheltered a saloon.

Other historic buildings easily visited on foot include:

Immaculate Conception Cathedral (1218 E Jefferson St at E 12th St) A late-19th-century Gothic-style example of the artistry of local brick masons.

Russell/Cocke Residence (602 E St Charles St) An 1872 house that shows the wealth of the local traders. Like many downtown buildings it has an interesting historical marker.

V Fernandez Complex (1106 E Adams St) The old trade links to New Orleans are clearly visible in this 1877 building.

FORT BROWN
The University of Texas at Brownsville and Texas Southmost College share a downtown campus that includes the site of Fort Brown, a former US army outpost dating from 1846 (it is named for Jacob Brown who died here that

year fighting the Mexicans). Several buildings from 1868 are restored and used by the campus (older ones were lost in an 1867 hurricane), including the post hospital (Gorgas Hall) and the 1848 Neale Home.

HISTORIC BROWNSVILLE MUSEUM
Housed in the grand Spanish Colonial–style 1928 Southern Pacific Railroad Depot, this small **museum** (☎ 956-548-1313; www.brownsville museum.org; 641 E Madison St; adult/child $5/2; ☼ 10am-4pm Tue-Fri, 10am-2pm Sat) houses historical artifacts and an 1872 steam locomotive. The museum is part of the Mitte Cultural District. Other nearby facilities include an art gallery and a children's museum.

GLADYS PORTER ZOO
This 31-acre **zoo** (☎ 956-546-2177; www.gpz.org; 500 W Ringgold St at E 6th St; adult/child $10/7; ☼ 9am-5:30pm) displays more than 1500 animals in large areas that replicate their natural habitats. Among the crowd-pleasing exhibits are pink flamingos flanking the entrance, a feed-the-giraffe experience (you climb the stairs), and Butterflies, Bugs and Blooms, a walk-through, up-close greenhouse.

Sleeping
Motels are along US 77/83 and there's nothing to recommend right in downtown. Unless you are getting an early start for bird-watching, you might want to stay amid the beachy charms of South Padre Island, an easy 28 miles northeast (see p259).

Best Western Rose Garden Inn (☎ 956-549-5501; www.bestwestern.com; 845 N Expwy exit US 77/83 at Price Rd; r $55-80; ▯ ⊚ ▣) The rose garden is notional but the 121 rooms are large and have microwaves and fridges. Although this is an older property, it is reasonably close to downtown and attractions.

Holiday Inn Express (☎ 956-550-0666; www.hiex press.com; 1985 N Expwy exit US 77/83 at Ruben Torres Sr Blvd; r $100-200; ▯ ⊚ ▣) Fairly comfortable but also generic, the HI has 74 rooms across three floors with inside corridors. The pool is outside near nascent palms; guests enjoy a large breakfast buffet.

Eating
Fans of Mexican food will need a week to sample just some of the excellent local eateries.

ourpick Taco Palenque (☎ 956-546-8172; 1803 Boca Chica Blvd; meals from $5; ☼ 7am-1am) Flagship of a small Rio Grande Valley chain run by a famous local family, you may find yourself here more than once. Order tacos at the counter and then start drooling over the best salsa bar ever. Almost 10 kinds of salsas, cilantro, cabbage, chilis and much more await.

Brownsville Coffee Shop #2 (☎ 956-542-9650; 3230 International Blvd; meals from $5; ☼ 24hr) Want lovely chicken tacos bursting with freshness at 3am? Come here. The tortillas are always fresh and this cheery little family-run place never closes.

Vermillion (☎ 956-542-9893; 115 Paredes Line Rd; meals from $8; ☼ 11am-midnight) It may just seem to be as old as Brownsville, but actually this venerable family-run restaurant dates back to 1934. Both the Tex (sublime chicken fried steak) and the Mex (amazing fajita nachos) are good.

Getting There & Away
Brownsville South Padre Island International Airport (BRO; ☎ 956-542-4373; www.flybrownsville.com; 700 S Minnesota Ave), 4 miles east of downtown, has service on American Eagle to Dallas–Fort Worth and Continental to Houston. For details on ground transport to South Padre Island, see p262.

Greyhound (☎ 956-546-7171; www.greyhound.com; 1134 E St Charles St) has a station just three blocks west of the Gateway International Bridge. There is frequent service to McAllen ($22, 70 minutes) and several busses daily to Corpus Christi and beyond ($42, 3½ hours).

AROUND BROWNSVILLE
US 281 hugs the border and is an interesting route to see sugar cane, the Rio Grande and the vast border fence (see the boxed text, p272). This 60-mile route to McAllen goes via Hidalgo.

Palo Alto Battlefield National Historic Site
On May 8, 1846, General Zachary Taylor and his troops defeated a larger Mexican army on this site in the first major battle of the Mexican

---

DRIVING DISTANCES

Brownsville to Laredo	199 miles, 3 hours
Corpus Christi to Brownsville	159 miles, 2½ hours
Del Rio to Big Bend	253 miles 4 hours
Laredo to Del Rio	179 miles, 3 hours
Laredo to San Antonio	154 miles, 2½ hours

MEXICO: MATAMOROS

While Matamoros (population 430,000) could hardly be described as a cultural mecca, it has the most to offer of all the gritty Mexican border towns that dot the frontier with Texas, with a cluster of historic buildings, a decent contemporary art museum and some stylish restaurants. The touristed areas here are generally safe during the day.

Matamoros lies across the Río Grande from downtown Brownsville. The best day-trip crossing is the **Puente Nuevo** (International Gateway Bridge; ☯ 24hr). From the bridge's southern end, tourist-friendly Avenida Obregón heads down to the town's central grid, 1 mile to the southwest. Abasolo, a pedestrianized shopping street, and **Plaza Hidalgo** are at the city's heart.

Near where Avenida Obregón meets Hidalgo, the excellent **Museo de Arte Contemporáneo de Tamaulipas** (☎ 868-813-1499; cnr Calles 5 & Constitución; adult/student M$15/10; ☯ 10am-2pm & 3-6pm Tue-Sat) showcases quality exhibitions of photography, sculpture and painting. The budget-minded food stalls in Plaza Allende are good places to sample a variety of local fare. Bars kept in business by young Texans are spread out along Avenida Obregón.

The Puente Nuevo is right at the end of International Blvd in the old downtown of Brownsville. There are guarded parking lots and it is a quick stroll over the Rio Grande to Avenida Obregón.

War. The 3400-acre **site** (☎ 956-541-2785; www.nps.gov/paal; admission free; ☯ 8am-5pm) has been preserved from developers (just in the nick of time) and the result is a surprisingly evocative and moody place. It's easy to imagine the soldiers of both sides toiling in the heat, firing cannons and wondering how they ended up in such a desolate place. The visitor center does an excellent job of putting the battle into context: were the Americans invaders or defenders? (Note the display showing what conservative Texas commentators of the day called Abraham Lincoln – a war and slavery critic – and contrast it to the politics of today.)

The site is near the intersection of FM 1874 (Paredes Line Rd) and FM 511, 5 miles north of Brownsville, 2 miles east of US 77/83 and 3.5 miles south of TX 100, the main road to SPI.

Sabal Palm Audubon Center & Sanctuary

The only palm tree native to Texas grows at this 557-acre **sanctuary** (☎ 956-541-8034; www.tx.audubon.org/Sabal.html; Sabal Palm Rd), operated by the National Audubon Society. Tragically, however, the sanctuary is a victim of border politics as the Dept of Homeland Security wants to run the border wall in a way that cuts off all access. Until the matter is resolved, this lush, beautiful and peaceful place will be closed.

Sabal palms reach 20ft to 48ft high and have feathery crowns and thick, bristly trunks. They once lined the Rio Grande, covering an area of nearly 63 sq miles. In the past 150

years, most have been cut down, first by early settlers who needed lumber and later by those clearing land for agriculture.

The preserve is 6 miles east of Brownsville off FM 1419 (also called Southmost Rd). If it reopens, it will be a highlight of your visit.

Resaca de la Palma State Park

Part of the World Birding Center, this new 1200-acre **park** (☎ 956-350-2920; www.worldbirdingcenter.org; 1000 New Carmen Rd; adult/child $4/free; ☯ 8am-5pm) is far from the border. Old courses of the Rio Grande have left several coil-shaped lakes which are ideal for birds and their spotters. Trails wander through this semitropical landscape making this a lovely – and bug-filled – stop even if your interest in birds is flighty. You can rent bikes ($5 to $8) and binoculars ($3). The park is 7 miles northwest of Brownsville and is easily reached via US 77/83 or US 281.

MCALLEN
pop 131,900

McAllen is not just near the Mexican border; it is also near a natural border. To the east are the lush and green lands of the Rio Grande Valley, with its farms, palm trees and fast-growing population. To the west is the beginning of the Chihuahuan Desert, where the land becomes more barren due to the increasingly arid climate.

McAllen is the center of two Texas industries: grapefruits and Winter Texans (see the boxed text, p273). The former are picked when ripe and juicy, the latter are, well, ripe.

Highlight of the season for many is the huge Texas Square Dance Jamboree held each February.

Although McAllen may be short on attractions, its many hotels and restaurants and central location make it a good base for exploring the natural delights of the surrounding area, including the sites of the World Birding Center (see the boxed text, p64).

Orientation & Information
US 83 passes south of the center as a freeway; the business route is more interesting. The main retail spine is 10th St, running north and south.

McAllen Convention & Visitors Bureau (☎ 956-682-2871; www.mcallencvb.com; 1200 Ash Ave; ☯ 8am-5pm Mon-Fri) Just off US Business 83, the CVB is focused on business rather than tourist needs.

Sights
Just 7 miles north of McAllen in Edinburg, the **Museum of South Texas History** (☎ 956-383-6911; 200 N Closner Blvd; adult/child $7/4; ☯ 10am-5pm Tue-Sat, 1-5pm Sun) covers cross-border history from the Ice Age when mammoths roamed the area to the 19th century when soldiers and settlers fought for the region's future.

Sleeping
Fast-growing McAllen has myriad chain motels along 10th St and the two iterations of US 83. For camping, try the lovely natural lands at Bentsen-Rio Grande Valley State Park (p270).

La Copa Hotel (☎ 956-686-1741; www.lacopamcallen.com; 2000 S 10th St; r $55-90; ☯ 🖳) A rare indie motel that is both affordable and really clean, the La Copa is an older 150-room motel that's had a faux Spanish makeover.

Embassy Suites (☎ 956-686-3000; www.embassysuites.com; 1800 S 2nd St at US 83; r $80-160; 🖳 ☯ 🖳) The large rooms at this chain are popular with families, or people who sleepwalk and need room to roam. The free cooked breakfasts, large pool and other amenities keep folks smiling.

Renaissance Casa de Palmas Hotel (☎ 956-631-1101; www.marriott.com; 101 N Main St; r $120-200; 🖳 ☯ 🖳) The classiest place in town dates from 1918 and is lovingly managed by Marriott's upscale brand. Right downtown, the restored Spanish-style hotel is perfectly elegant without being pretentious. The 165 rooms surround a beautiful central courtyard and pool.

Eating & Drinking
As elsewhere throughout the borderlands, Mexican food is the most common cuisine here, but there are good alternatives.

Ms G's Tacos n' More (☎ 956-668-8226; 2263 Pecan Blvd; meals from $3; ☯ 7am-3pm Mon-Sat) Ms G herself arrives every morning at 4:30am to make the region's best flour tortillas for her deceptively simple tacos. Options are many, but you'll never go wrong with *carne guisada* (spicy beef), beans and avocado.

Country Omelette (☎ 956-687-6461; 2622 N 10th St; meals from $5; ☯ 6am-3pm) A hard-day of birdwatching calls for a hearty breakfast and the namesake omelettes here are fluffy and jammed with fillings. Guzzle the coffee and consider the irony of eating eggs.

ourpick Roosevelt's at 7 (☎ 956-928-1994; 821 N Main St; meals from $8; ☯ 11am-2am; ☏) In a land where miserable watery domestic beers rule, the over 40 taps here are like a vision, a glorious vision. In the midst of a modest arts district, Roo's has a large patio with a pool table and lots of casual food like excellent pizza, sandwiches and salads.

Republic of the Rio Grande (☎ 956-994-8385; 1411 S 10th St; meals $12-30; ☯ 11am-11pm Mon-Sat, to 4pm Sun) This place has a casual, upscale atmosphere and a menu of burgers and steaks with a Tex-Mex accent. Dine inside or out on the nice patio. The bar is popular.

Getting There & Away
Busy **McAllen Miller International Airport** (MFE; ☎ 956-681-1500; www.mcallenairport.com) is just south of US 83, off S 10th St. American flies to Dallas–Fort Worth, Continental serves Houston and Delta Connection links to its hub in Memphis.

Greyhound (☎ 956-686-5479; www.greyhound.com; 1501 W US Business 83) has frequent service to Brownsville ($22, 70 minutes) and San Antonio ($38, 4½ hours). There's one bus daily up the valley to Laredo ($30, 3½ hours).

WHAT THE...? GRAPEFRUIT

So unattractive it's compelling, the bizarre **World's Largest Grapefruit** (La Placita Park, 801 Conway Ave) could be a model for a fatal internal growth if it weren't a highly stylized citrus fruit. It's 6 miles west of McAllen in Mission, just south of US Business 83.

RIO GRANDE VALLEY

AROUND McALLEN

There are a number of natural sights along the Rio Grande that are reason enough to make McAllen your base. You can go on **kayak tours** (☎ 956-587-5967; www.loscaminos.org; adult/student $40/20) on some weekends with Los Caminos Real, a group dedicated to preserving the river's heritage. Call for reservations; trips start at Anzaldua County Park, about 7 miles southwest of McAllen, on FN 494 off FM 1016.

Santa Ana National Wildlife Refuge

A birder's heaven, this 2088-acre **refuge** (☎ 956-787-3079; www.fws.gov; off US 281; per vehicle $3; ✆ gates dawn-dusk, visitor center 8am-4pm) run by the US Fish and Wildlife Service is one of the valley's most beautiful spots. Lakes, wetlands, thorny bushes and palms combine for a bucolic setting where the only noises come from birds. The refuge is the seasonal home to almost 400 avian species, and hundreds of butterfly species have been spotted here as well.

Tram tours (adult/child $3/1; ✆ Dec-Apr, call for schedules) are popular, but to really experience the place, head out on foot on some of the 12 miles of trails. Short, looping wooden boardwalks are a breeze for the time-challenged; Spanish moss-draped ash, cedar and elm trees shade the lovely trail, which leads to Willow Lakes. Note that bugs here can make vultures seem tame, but repellents are effective.

Bentsen-Rio Grande Valley State Park

Spot some of over 300 bird species in this serene 760-acre **park** (☎ 956-584-9156; www.world birdingcenter.org; 2800 S Bentsen Palm Dr; adult/child $5/free), which is headquarters for the World Birding Center. Much of the park surrounds several *resacas* – water-filled former river channels that support lush foliage.

The **visitor center** (✆ 8am-5pm) at the entrance has excellent trail guides and many books on birds. You can borrow binoculars here and inquire about a variety of special programs like bird walks and tram tours. The site is good for bikes, which make getting to key attractions, like the 1.8-mile Rio Grande loop trail easy.

The park's widely spaced **tent sites** (per site $12) rarely fill up and have water. Surrounded by thorny brush and shaded by trees, the pastoral experience is described as 'waking up with the birds.' The neighboring **Bentsen Palm Village RV Resort** (☎ 956-585-5568; www.bentsenpalm.com; 2500 S Bentsen Palm Dr; RV sites from $40, cabins from $110; ✆ ⚓) is part of a growing retirement village.

To get here, take the Bentsen Palm Dr (FM 2062) off Business US 83, 3 miles west of Mission. Drive south 5 miles to the park.

National Butterfly Center

Who isn't enchanted by butterflies? This 100-acre **park** (☎ 956-583-9009; www.naba.org; adult/child $5/1; ✆ 9am-5pm Tue-Sun) is being developed both as a learning center and a sanctuary for butterflies and endangered plants. More than 300 species of the little winged jewels have been spotted here. Much of the site – right on the river – is a work in progress but it's worth a stop as it is only 1 mile east of Bentsen-Rio Grande State Park along Military Rd.

THE UPPER VALLEY

The semiarid scrublands between McAllen and Laredo are sparsely populated northwest of Rio Grande City and have a certain desolate beauty. Falcon International Reservoir is favored by fishers.

Los Ebanos Ferry

This small **barge** (☎ 956-485-2855; car with driver $2.75; ✆ 8am-3:50pm), the only hand-pulled ferry across the Rio Grande, carries people over an

---

MEXICO: REYNOSA

Reynosa (population 510,000) is more attractive and less intimidating than Nuevo Laredo, but with less appeal than Matamoros. The tourist trade is geared to Texan day-trippers, many of whom are in town to visit the city's surfeit of dentists, doctors and pharmacists.

The area just below the Puente Internacional and the international bridge is an unfortunate introduction to the city, but things get much nicer very quickly. The **Plaza Principal**, on a rise a few blocks southwest of the bridge, is the site of the town hall and a modern cathedral. Extending south of the plaza, **Hidalgo** is a pedestrianized shopping lane.

Reynosa is 9 miles south of the center of McAllen via US 281. The easiest way to visit is to park in a guarded lot on the US side and then make the short walk over the bridge.

isolated section of the river west of McAllen. The ferry can carry three cars and several people on each five-minute journey.

Privately operated since 1742, the ferry isn't a vital transportation link. Even in these tense border times it can be delightfully tranquil here. The local village is quite poor and tourists are the only real color. It's 6 miles south of US 83 on FM 886.

Rio Grande City
pop 14,600

Fifty-two miles west of McAllen in arid Starr County, Rio Grande City is in the heart of border patrol efforts to stem drug and people smugglers. The territory to the west is desolate, although to the east Winter Texans and other developments are spreading from McAllen.

The town was once a busy trading center, and several brick buildings dating from the 19th century do a slow burn in the sun around town.

La Borde House (☎ 956-487-5101; 601 E Main St; r $60-70) is an 1893 villa designed by a French architect; it has been restored and converted into a small B&B. It has a pleasant, shady courtyard and a small restaurant serving Mexican food. The rooms are filled with period furniture that seem like a time capsule. Nothing here is posh, and service and details can be rather ragged, so stay here for the adventure.

Stop into the hotel at least to pick up one of the brochures detailing the town's historical buildings.

Roma
pop 11,800

Unlike neighboring Rio Grande City, Roma has actively preserved its heritage, which dates back to 1770. The downtown, one block south of US 83, was designated a National Historic Landmark and is such a perfect representation of an early-1900s border town that the 1952 movie *Viva Zapata* was filmed here.

Although hours can be erratic, try stopping into the **Roma Historical Museum** (☎ 956-849-4335; Portscheller & Lincoln Sts; admission free) for one of the handouts detailing the town's several dozen listed historical structures.

Birds, however, are a real draw in Roma. The **Roma Bluffs** (☎ 956-849-4930; www.worldbirding center.org; 610 N Portscheller St; admission free; ⏰ 8am-4pm Tue-Sat) is right downtown and includes 3 acres of lush nature preserve along the banks of the

---

WHAT THE...? KILLER BEE

The **World's Largest Killer Bee statue** (704 E Texano Dr) is in Hidalgo. A classic example of a town's efforts to make lemonade from lemons – or in this case honey from imminent peril – the statue dates to the early 1990s. Hidlago spent $20,000 on this statue. It all seems quaint now as 'killer bees' turned out not to represent a grave threat to society.

Rio Grande. A lookout of the namesake bluff has great views of birds (!), Mexico and the thinly populated countryside.

Falcon International Reservoir

This 136-sq-mile lake was formed by the Falcon Dam (1953) on the Rio Grande. The 500-acre **Falcon State Park** (☎ 956-848-5327; www. tpwd.state.tx.us; admission $2), 3 miles west of US 83 off FM 2098, lines the US side of the lake, which is popular for fishing. The land is mostly covered by cactus and shrubs – no trees – so the park has shaded shelters and picnic areas.

Although seemingly tranquil, the lake has also suffered from the border tensions: fishing boats have been beset by pirates and a Mexican drug cartel was caught planning to blow it up, which might have caused a massive catastrophe.

On the lake's northeast side are the hamlets of **Zapata** and **San Ygnacio**. Zapata was named for Emiliano Zapata, land reformer and freedom fighter during the Mexican Revolution (1911–17). Six miles west of town, a scenic overlook off US 83 provides views of an archetypal Western landscape, complete with mesas on the horizon. San Ygnacio, 30 miles southeast of Laredo on US 83, was founded as a ranching outpost in 1830. Time stands still on its oak-shaded central square, dominated by Our Lady of Refuge Church (1875).

CENTRAL RIO GRANDE

The central Rio Grande region is mostly a sparsely inhabited desert with a few bright lights like Laredo and to a lesser extent Del Rio. On the many little-traveled roads, it's easy to feel the same sense of desolation surely felt by generations of immigrant settlers.

PLEASE FENCE ME IN

After spending close to $3 billion since 2005, the US Department of Homeland Security has a fence along the Mexican border that is still far from complete. But travelers to the eastern end of the Rio Grande Valley will see plenty of tax dollars at work. From the Gulf of Mexico, a new 20ft-tall fence runs along the Rio Grande for over 200 miles. Built of heavy steel and with slats to allow small animals through (but certainly not people!) it is impossible to miss as you drive US 281.

The work has caused plenty of controversy. Some ranchers have complained that the fence runs too far inland from the border and the river, cutting off vital access. Environmentalists' fears that it would disrupt bird migratory paths are still not proven, but areas of natural beauty including the Sabal Palm Audubon Center and Sanctuary (p268) have suffered greatly. The blog Border Wall As Architecture (borderwallsarchitecture.blogspot.com) covers the wall's visual impact, both good and bad.

Meanwhile, no one is sure if the wall is even restricting the flow of immigrants and drugs into the US. Tunnels, ladders and more exotic schemes have all been used to circumvent it. Repairs are constant, even as the arguing over how – or if – it should be finished continues. Wall or no wall, you will constantly see border patrols when you drive near the border. And checkpoints are common, even relatively far inland.

LAREDO
pop 225,600

Even more than other Texas border towns, Laredo has always been tightly entwined with its sister city to the south, the fittingly named Nuevo Laredo (see the boxed text, p274). So the outbreak of drug violence and subsequent tighter border controls have severely crimped a place where Mexico and the US seemed to blend the most seamlessly, even just a few years ago.

While the border situation remains unsettled, Laredo makes for a good stop on any Rio Grande itinerary. Its historic old downtown is beguiling and has two good museums. And in many ways, starting with the strong Hispanic culture, Laredo's like a trip south of the border without the customs inspection.

Orientation & Information

Historic downtown Laredo occupies a compact area on the Rio Grande's north bank, at International Bridges Nos 1 and 2. I-35 ends right at the border.

Laredo Convention & Visitors Bureau (☎ 956-795-2200, 800-361-3360; www.visitlaredo.com; 501 San Agustín Ave at Lincoln St; ☯ 8am-5pm Mon-Fri) Basic but useful.

Texas Travel Information Center (☎ 956-417-4728; I-35 & US 83 exit 18; ☯ 8am-5pm) About 16 miles north of Laredo, this comprehensive center is a showplace and worthy of a stop just for the Southwestern architecture and gardens.

Sights
SAN AGUSTÍN PLAZA

Parts of this plaza, right downtown and the oldest in town, date from 1767. The streets surrounding it are cobblestoned and lined with ancient oaks where you can escape the sun. For details about the historic buildings throughout downtown, pick up a copy of the brochure Heritage Walking Tour of Historic Laredo at the CVB or at area hotels. Nearby streets are interesting for all the traditional shops catering to day-tripping Mexicans. Step behind the La Posada Hotel (p273) for views of the fortified border area, the trickle of the Rio Grande and the omnipresent huge Mexican flag (see the boxed text, p274).

SAN AGUSTÍN CHURCH

This is the third church that has stood on this site at the plaza's east end. Vaguely Gothic-Revival, the church was erected in 1872 and has thick whitewashed walls. The decoration inside and out is simple, and the church hops with large, traditional weddings all weekend long.

REPUBLIC OF THE RIO GRANDE MUSEUM

Housed in the 1840 capitol of the short-lived Republic of the Rio Grande, this excellent **museum** (☎ 956-727-3480; www.webbheritage.org; 1005 Zaragoza St; admission $2; ☯ 9am-4pm Tue-Sat, 1-4pm Sun) brings that turbulent period to life with displays about the confused politics plus items from everyday life. Be sure to head to the back (or rather, stoop), where the oldest part of the building dates to the 1830s.

Nearby and also operated by the Webb County Heritage Foundation, the **Border Heritage Museum** (810 Zaragoza St) may be open with a special exhibition; check at the main museum. It's housed in the restored 19th-century Villa Antigua.

Sleeping

Most of Laredo's lodgings are on San Bernardo and Santa Ursala Aves, which parallel I-35 right to downtown and the border.

Super 8 Motel (☎ 956-722-6321; www.super8.com; 2620 Santa Ursala Ave at I-35 exit 2; r $50-90; 🛜 📺) The better of the two properties of this ubiquitous budget chain is also closer to the center. The 76 rooms are off outside corridors over two floors and all come with microwaves and fridges.

Courtyard by Marriott (☎ 956-725-5555; www.marriott.com; 2410 Santa Ursula Ave at I-35 exit 3; r $70-120; 🖥 🛜 📺) Two miles north of downtown, this place's amenities include a health club and whirlpool (after a day touring in 100°F weather, there's nothing like relaxing in a vat of near-boiling water). Rooms reflect an upscale business-motif, with large desks and easy chairs.

ourpick La Posada Hotel & Suites (☎ 956-722-1701; www.laposada.com; 1000 Zaragoza St, San Agustín Plaza; r $110-200; 🖥 🛜 📺) Far and away the best choice in Laredo, this hacienda-style hotel occupies a complex of buildings dating from 1916 (originally a high school). The stylish rooms surround two large pools and gardens; the deeply shaded verandahs are a world away from the city bustle just outside. Some rooms have patios overlooking the action of the river and border area.

Eating

During the day, numerous street vendors ply the streets of Laredo, offering tacos, ice cream and other cart-distributed treats.

Las Cazuelas (☎ 956-723-3693; 303 Market St; meals from $4; 🕙 6:30am-2:30pm) Looking like the run-down former gas station that it is from the outside, things only get a bit better inside (although the tired decor is scrupulously clean). Various soups and stews meld their flavors in large pots all day long while the tortillas – especially the flour ones – couldn't be fresher.

Taco Palenque (☎ 956-725-9898; 4515 San Bernardo Ave, off I-35 at exit 3; meals from $4; 🕙 24hr) The Laredo outlet of the phenomenal Rio Grande Valley mini-chain (p267) is ready to please around

WINTER TEXANS

Every fall, 150,000 creatures begin their annual migration to the Rio Grande Valley from points throughout the US and Canadian Midwest. But they aren't wildlife. Not even close. They're retired folks drawn to the south end of Texas by the bone-warming climate and the low prices.

Affectionately dubbed 'Winter Texans' by grateful civic boosters, they add at least $400 million to the local economies during the prime season from October to March. They come in huge slow-moving RVs, SUVs or large sedans and stay in the more than 500 senior-citizen parks from Brownsville to McAllen, where they find accommodations for both RVs and mobile homes.

Most Winter Texans return to the same parks every year, where they are part of a close and friendly seasonal society. The communities bustle with activity, including square dancing, cycling, water sports, bingo, craft classes and much, much more. While many folks engage in sedate matches of shuffleboard, others indulge in rougher pursuits, such as water polo.

Many make regular treks to Mexico, where they can obtain economical medical and dental care as well as cheap pharmaceuticals. Most restaurants do a big dinner business from 4pm to 6pm, which is the traditional suppertime in the Midwestern towns that are home to many of these retirees.

The valley's museums, parks and attractions benefit from the Winter Texans who volunteer in droves to staff information desks in visitor centers. They are invariably well informed and anxious to not only help but to chat for a while. Residents and tourists also benefit from the value-conscious Winter Texans, who know a good deal when they see it and know how to stretch fixed incomes. Prices are generally low everywhere.

Come spring, when the snow-blanketed lands they hail from begin to thaw, the Winter Texans head back north for the summer.

MEXICO: NUEVO LAREDO

Nuevo Laredo (population 350,000) is Mexico's busiest border town with a significant percentage of the country's trade passing through, but it's much more famous as 'Narco' Laredo, a reference to brazen violence between rival drug cartels that has sullied the city's reputation. But it isn't the fear of getting caught in the crossfire that should cause you to reconsider a visit; it's that the city has little to offer other than the usual cheap trinkets, tequila and tricks found in most border towns. The city's greatest landmark, the huge **flag** (164ft X 94ft flag on a 320ft-tall pole) just across the border, is an arresting and at times mesmerizing sight. It's easily seen from much of Laredo, especially when heading south on San Bernardo Ave.

Nuevo Laredo's main thoroughfare, Avenida Guerrero, leads seven blocks south from the border to **Plaza Hidalgo**, a pleasant, well-kept square with a bandstand, clock tower and the Palacio Federal. Most bar-hopping Texans stick to the large clubs on and east of Avenida Guerrero; the bars west of Avenida Guerrero tend to draw a rough, local crowd.

Two international bridges link the Laredos. You can do the short walk (or drive) over Puente Internacional No 1 from Convent Ave and Laredo's old town right onto the north end of Avenida Guerrero. Puente Internacional No 2 is vehicles-only. For specific details on the border situation and formalities, see the boxed text, p266.

the clock. The vast salsa bar awaits and there's beer available.

La Unica De Nuevo Laredo (☎ 956-717-4089; 4500 San Bernardo Ave; meals from $7; ⏰ 8am-9pm) It's sit-down simple at this family-run classic that got its start across the border in Nuevo Laredo. Fans of Mexican food will find all the stand-ards, it's just that they're better here. The flautas come with a guacamole that will spoil you for others.

Zaragoza Grill (☎ 956-753-4444; 1000 Zaragoza St; meals $12-40; ⏰ 11am-10pm) In the beautiful lobby of the La Posada Hotel, the Zaragoza offers some of Laredo's finest dining. Needless to say there's a long list of vintage tequilas and wines as well as a creative menu that starts with Mexico and then ranges far.

Shopping

Prowl San Bernardo Ave heading north from downtown for scores of Mexican shops sell-ing everything from housewares to outdoor sculpture to your basic, albeit colorful, junk. Choices include:

Basket & Pottery Alley (☎ 956-724-2415; 3519 San Bernardo Ave) An exuberant cliché selling everything from pots to piñatas in a fiesta-like setting.

Vega's Imports (☎ 956-724-8251; 4002 San Bernardo Ave) Classy merchandise set among lovely grounds.

Getting There & Around

Laredo International Airport (LRD; ☎ 956-795-2000; www.ci.laredo.tx.us/airport) has service by American Eagle and Continental Express to and from their respective hubs at Dallas–Fort Worth

and Houston. The airport is off Bob Bullock Loop, 1.2 miles north of US 59 on the town's northeast side.

Greyhound (☎ 956-723-4324; www.greyhound.com; 610 Salinas Ave) operates right downtown. It of-fers frequent service to San Antonio ($30, from 2¾ hours) and Houston ($42, 6½ hours) plus once daily down the Rio Grande Valley to McAllen ($30, 3½ hours).

CARRIZO SPRINGS

A little burst of life amid the empty lands of the Central Rio Grande, Carrizo Springs is an important junction on Rio Grande journeys. Laredo is 80 miles of sagebrush south on US 83 while Eagle Pass is 44 miles northwest on US 277. There's a smear of fast-food joints and you can admire the stolid 1927 limestone **Dimmit County Courthouse** as you drive past.

EAGLE PASS
pop 22,400

Eagle Pass may be the most Mexican town in the USA. About 97% of its residents are of Mexican origin, and Spanish is spoken far more often than is English. In fact, the main reason most travelers come to Eagle Pass is to get to its sister city – Piedras Negras, in Mexico – and beyond. The town itself is al-most immediately forgettable. Most people on the streets seem to be on their way to some-place else.

From the downtown area, US 277 swings north along Ceylon St (an area of a few beauti-ful homes), 2nd St and Del Rio Blvd.

Eagle Pass Chamber of Commerce (☎ 830-773-3224; www.eaglepasstexas.com; 400 Garrison St; ☺ 9am-5pm Mon-Fri) has information on both Eagle Pass and Piedras Negras.

For centuries, the favored crossing of the Rio Grande in this area was 30 miles south at Guerrero, Coahuila. The route was used by everyone from 17th-century Spanish explorers to Antonio López de Santa Anna as he led his troops to the Alamo. After the Texas War for Independence, the Mexican government prohibited direct trade with Texans, but Mexican villagers near the Rio Grande continued to use a clandestine road that ran north of the old San Antonio Rd, crossing the river near what was called Paso del Águila (Eagle Pass) for the many eagles' nests perched in the nearby pecan trees. The US Army established Fort Duncan at the Paso del Águila in 1849 to protect emigrants heading west in the California gold rush, as well as the flow of trade from Mexico.

Sights

Fort Duncan Museum (☎ 830-773-1714; Fort Duncan Park, Bliss St; admission by donation; ☺ 1-4pm Mon-Sat), housed in the old fort headquarters building, has exhibits and artifacts from the Spanish colonial period through the early 20th century. Note that the museum's hours may be erratic.

Sleeping & Eating

There's no good reason to spend the night in Eagle Pass, however should Del Rio or Laredo seem too far you'll find a half-dozen chains at either end of town along US 277. Not surprisingly, the best food here is Mexican.

Best Western Eagle Pass (☎ 830-758-1234; www.bestwestern.com; 1923 Veterans Blvd; r $65-100; ☺ ☒) This older motel has a pleasant outdoor pool area surrounded by palm trees. The 40 rooms are in two-story wings with outside corridors so you can park outside your door. The large rooms are unexceptional except for the fridges and microwaves.

Morales Tacos (☎ 830-773-5634; 1885 E Main St; meals from $4; ☺ 7am-9pm) Right on US 277 near the center of town, you can't help but pass this little taco drive-through – by all means stop. It doesn't look like much but that's because all the effort goes into the fresh tortillas and their array of fillings.

Parilla de San Miguel (☎ 830-757-3100; 408 S Texas Dr; meals from $6; ☺ 11am-9pm) Many customers at first think they have discovered a new up-

scale Mexican chain when they walk into this well-polished restaurant that evokes the look of a sidewalk cafe. Salsas are varied and are good over the various marinated steaks. It's two blocks southwest of where E Garrison St meets E Main St.

DEL RIO
pop 37,200

If you have time to visit only one Tex-Mex border community, Del Rio is an excellent choice. It's big enough to offer a selection of appealing restaurants and culture, but small enough that its ambience is relaxed. It has an attractive downtown and historic neighborhoods and there's recreation aplenty at nearby Amistad National Recreation Area (p277) and Seminole Canyon State Historical Park (p278).

Laughlin Air Force Base, 6 miles east of town, is a major presence, as are growing numbers of Winter Texans, who migrate to the area from November to March for the mild weather. Also, watch out for sudden and severe thunderstorms – moody yes, but also the reason there are so many hail-damage repair places.

Orientation & Information

In Del Rio, US 90/277/377 becomes Veteran's Blvd (formerly Ave F), the main north–south street through town. US 90 then heads east as E Gibbs St. Southwest of downtown, Garfield St becomes Las Vacas St and then Spur 277 as it approaches the international bridge into Mexico. Another crossing is west of town, over Lake Amistad.

For a fine selection of books, go to the Emporium (p276).

MEXICO: PIEDRAS NEGRAS

The border crossing between Piedras Negras (population 140,000) and Eagle Pass is a major commercial route. Piedras Negras is not an attractive city and not somewhere you'll want to linger long. It has that small-border-town roughness to it.

Walking there is popular – it's just four short blocks from downtown Eagle Pass to downtown Piedras Negras on the main international bridge. For specific details on the border situation and formalities, see the boxed text, p266.

Del Rio Chamber of Commerce (☎ 830-775-3551, 800-889-8149; www.drchamber.com; 1915 Veteran's Blvd; 8:30am-5pm Mon-Fri) Simple but useful.

Sights & Activities
WALKING & DRIVING TOUR
Ask the chamber of commerce or your motel for *A Guide to Historic Del Rio,* a free pamphlet that outlines a walking tour of the historic downtown area and a driving tour of the rest of town.

A couple of highlights downtown:
Courthouse (400 Pecan St) An imposing 1887 local limestone classic.
Roswell Hotel (cnr Garfield & Griner Sts) The top floor was used by quack Dr James Brinkly in the 1930s as a surgery where he used goat glands as an early form of Viagra on men with too much money and not enough sense. The doc's mansion still stands at 512 Qualia Dr.

WHITEHEAD MEMORIAL MUSEUM
Judge Roy Bean (see the boxed text, p279) is buried at **Whitehead Memorial Museum** (☎ 830-774-7568; www.whiteheadmuseum.org; 1308 S Main St; adult/child $5/2; 9am-4:30pm Tue-Sat, 1-5pm Sun), an idiosyncratic and endlessly fascinating place. Check out the room devoted to border radio (legendary '50s DJ Wolfman Jack got his start here in the late 1940s) and a 1287-item nativity-scene collection amassed by the late Beatriz Cadena. Have a picnic on the grounds.

FIREHOUSE ARTS CENTER
Headquarters for the **Del Rio Council for the Arts** (☎ 830-775-0888; www.delrioarts.com; 120 E Garfield St; admission free; 9am-5:30pm Tue-Fri, 10am-2pm Sat), the 1922 Firehouse includes a visual-arts gallery and a great little gift shop. This is HQ for the **First Friday Art Walk** (7-10pm) which covers the growing number of downtown galleries.

SAN FELIPE SPRINGS
Even though *del río* means 'of the river' in Spanish, the missionaries who named the area in the 17th century weren't referring to the Rio Grande but to San Felipe Springs, which gush forth at the rate of over 90 million gallons a day. Although the springs can be viewed by taking San Felipe Springs Rd off US 90 to the San Felipe Country Club, they're really not much to see. Instead, stroll along San Felipe Creek in town, especially at Moore Park, Spur 77 at S Bedell Ave. Swans, ducks and splashing kids make the scene on warm days.

VAL VERDE WINERY
This family-owned **winery** (☎ 830-775-9714; www.valverdewinery.com; 100 Qualia Dr; 10am-5pm Mon-Sat) was established in 1883, making it the state's oldest continually operating vintner. The winery rode out Prohibition by making sacramental wine for church communion use.

Val Verde is best known for its tawny port; discovering the vines growing so close to downtown is a delight.

Sleeping
Chain motels can be found all along Veterans Blvd. For camping, try Amistad NRA (p278).
La Quinta Inn (☎ 830-775-7591; www.laquinta.com; 2005 Veterans Blvd; r $45-90;) A standard motel-style outlet for this usually reliable budget chain. The cheapest of the 100 rooms are pretty basic, but for just a bit extra you can get your room with a fridge and microwave.
Ramada Inn (☎ 830-775-1511; www.ramada.com; 2101 Veterans Blvd; r $70-115;) This older business-oriented place is probably the town's most-posh motel, which doesn't actually mean a whole lot. Over 180 large rooms (with fridges and microwaves) are spread across two wings, some with doors onto the parking lot, others with doors inside halls.
ourpick Villa Del Rio (☎ 830-768-1100; www.villadelrio.com; 123 Hudson Dr; r $100-210;) Surrounded by stately palms and magnolias, this impressive B&B in an 1887 home has an elegant yet updated feel. It's just around the corner from Val Verde Winery and surrounded by bucolic roads fine for strolling. The owner is a talkative local expert.

Eating & Drinking
Del Rio has the best selection of eats west of Laredo.
ourpick Emporium (☎ 830-774-0962; 800 S Main St; snacks from $2; 9am-7pm Mon-Sat) Betty Sanders scoured antiques stores to recreate this authentic 1920s soda fountain. Real ice cream is used for sodas, malts (when's the last time you had one, if ever?), banana splits and more. The shop has a huge range of creative gifts, while the book section excels at stocking local authors and local-internet books.
Brown Bag (☎ 830-768-4837; 44 S Main St; meals from $5; 8am-3pm Mon-Fri, 11am-3pm Sat) Excellent sandwiches and salads right downtown. Get everything to go and have a picnic at the Whitehead Memorial Museum or in Moore Park.

Manuel's Steakhouse (☎ 830-488-6044; 1312 Veterans Blvd; meals from $8; ⏰ 11am-11pm) A Del Rio branch of a Ciudad Acuña original, Manuel's is an excellent place for a meal that goes beyond the enchilada cliché. It's an attractive place with a hopping bar (open until 2am weekends) and tables out front. The dark-fried flour tortilla chips are beyond addictive, the steaks sublime and classics like the *chile rellenos* (mild peppers stuffed with a ground beef mixture and then fried) top-notch.

Herald Martini Bar (☎ 830-774-2845; 321 S Main St; meals from $10; ⏰ 11am-11pm Tue-Thu, to 2am Fri & Sat) In a vintage building downtown, this large and lively bar is the classiest digs in town (which doesn't mean it's still not casual). Expert bartenders pour the namesake cocktail, which you can absorb with excellent steaks, seafood, salads and sandwiches.

Getting There & Away

Greyhound (☎ 830-775-7515; www.greyhound.com; 1 N Main St) through Kerrville Bus Co has regular service to San Antonio ($25, 4½ hours) and connections beyond.

Amtrak's **Sunset Limited** (☎ 800-872-7245; www.amtrak.com; 100 N Main St) runs several times a week west to LA via Alpine (Big Bend National Park; five hours) and east to New Orleans via San Antonio (four hours) and Houston (12 hours). See p357 for more information.

AMISTAD NATIONAL RECREATION AREA

'Amistad' means friendship in Spanish, and Mexican-US cooperation was the spirit in which a dam and reservoir transformed this area of the Rio Grande in the late 1960s. The other word often used to describe Amistad is 'big': at normal levels, the reservoir covers 105 sq miles spanning two nations, with 850 miles of shoreline – 540 in the USA. Amistad Dam itself is 6 miles long, with about two-thirds of its length in Mexico.

Amistad NRA has two major recreational access points: Diablo East and Rough Canyon. Diablo East is 10 miles northwest of Del Rio on US 90; facilities include a marina, beach, fishing dock, picnic areas and a nature trail. Many privately run services are nearby.

Rough Canyon is 23 miles north of Del Rio via US 277/377 and Recreation Rd 2. Known for its multicolored 150ft cliffs, which are visible only from the water, Rough Canyon has a marina, boat ramp, beach and picnic area.

The National Park Service **Visitor Information Center** (☎ 830-775-7491; www.nps.gov/amis; ⏰ 8am-5pm) is 10 miles north of Del Rio on US 90W, after US 90W and US 277/377 split. This is a worthwhile stop for general information on Lake Amistad, visitor services and interpretive programs, which are sometimes held at the Governors Landing amphitheater and at various campgrounds in the NRA. There is no admission fee for land-based day use at Amistad, but camping and boating fees and permits apply.

Rock Art

Indians who lived in the region 3500 to 4500 years ago were drawn to what is now Lake Amistad by the convergence of the Rio Grande and the Devils and Pecos Rivers. They left behind a wealth of rock art, fashioned in what archaeologists call the Lower Pecos River Style (see the boxed text, p278).

The best pictograph sites are along the Rio Grande just downriver from the Pecos confluence. Visitors must boat to the Panther Cave dock and then climb a steep stairway to the

MEXICO: CIUDAD ACUÑA

Ciudad Acuña (population 130,000), a small frontier city just across from Del Rio, Texas, is a fairly busy but hassle-free border crossing, open 24 hours a day. As far as border towns are concerned, this is one of the more mild in respect to grittiness and dubiousness. The city's main claim to fame is that the movie *El Mariachi* and its big-budget sequel *Desperado* were filmed here.

A couple of blocks from the plaza, the main 'tourist' drag, **Hidalgo**, running west from the border, is chock-full of tired souvenir shops, bars and dentists.

It's 4 miles between downtown Del Rio and downtown Acuña, so most people drive and park at one of the pay lots on the US side. Note that it is a hike across the international bridge over the river and marshlands, so some opt for a taxi. For specific details on the border situation and formalities, see the boxed text, p266.

cave. The cave's highlight, a 9ft-long drawing of a mountain lion, accompanies many other animal and human figures. Parida Cave is also best reached by boat, but when the water is low, diehards could access it via a strenuous 3-mile round-trip bushwhack through tall brush.

Activities

The lake is hugely popular with boaters and there's quite a weekend scene of partying whenever it's not cold.

Lake Amistad Resort & Marina/Forever Resorts (☎ 830-774-4157; www.lakeamistadresort.com), at Diablo East, rents a variety of boats, from fishing and ski boats ($40 to $70 per hour) to large and quite comfortable houseboats that sleep four or more ($400 to $900 per day).

Lake Amistad is one of the state's top fishing areas. Its approximately 30 resident species include various bass, sunfish, catfish, crappie, perch, walleye and gar. The NPS has lists of guides online.

Sleeping

Amistad NPS has five scenic but very basic **campgrounds** (sites $4-8) with a total of 79 sites. Only Governors Landing has potable water. All operate on a first-come, first-served basis; they only usually fill up at Easter.

Amistad Lake Resort (☎ 830-775-8591; www.amistadlakeresort.com; 11207 US 90; r $45-65; ☎ ☒) is the place to stay if you want to go bass fishing. The owner, Byron Velvick, is fishing champion and celebrity (including a gossipy stint on the reality TV show *The Bachelor*). The rooms are comfy, clean and come in various sizes.

BRACKETTVILLE
pop 1900

Thirty-one miles east of Del Rio on I-90, Brackettville is a major destination for Winter Texans thanks to Fort Clark Springs, an historic army post that's been recycled as a haven for retired sun-seekers.

Travelers, movie buffs and pilgrims can see John Wayne's legacy at **Alamo Village** (☎ 830-563-2580; www.alamovillage.com; FM 674; admission $10; ☯ 9am-5pm Jun-Aug, call for other times), 7 miles north of Brackettville. The Duke had it built in the late 1950s for his epic (and some would say endless) production of *The Alamo*. Since then it has been used for countless more movies, TV shows and ads. The scenic drive on FM 674 is worth the trip itself.

SEMINOLE CANYON STATE HISTORICAL PARK

The best art galleries in south central Texas are right here along the Rio Grande, and their works of rock art have been on view for at least 4000 years.

Seminole Canyon State Historical Park (☎ 915-292-4464; www.tpwd.state.tx.us; off US 90; adult/child $3/free), 9 miles west of Comstock, is famous for Fate Bell Shelter, a natural canvas of ancient rock art. If the art here were merely decorative, it would be magnificent. But the pictographs are more than drawings: They're windows into their creators' daily routines, dreams, hopes and fears. For more information, see the boxed text, p278.

Tours (☎ 888-762-5278; free; ☯ 10am year-round, 3pm Sep-May, no tours Mon & Tue) are led by volunteers for the Rock Art Foundation (which also organizes Saturday

---

PECOS RIVER ROCK ART

Although humans visited the Rio Grande region 12,000 years ago, they were wanderers, hunting the mammoth and bison that once lived here in abundance. By 7000 years ago, the climate had changed into the arid desert it is today, and a new culture appeared. Although these people lived amid harsh conditions, they possessed a creative spark and produced a distinctive style of art seen only along the Lower Pecos River, Devils River and Rio Grande. It has come to be known as the Pecos River Style.

The defining characteristic of Pecos River Style art is a towering shaman who usually holds an atlatl, or ancient spear, in his hand. According to rock-art expert Solveig Turpin, 'The figure may be headless or crowned with antlers, feline ears, radiant hair or horns. The body is rectangular, often tapering to stubby legs…the shaman can be surrounded by miniature replicas of itself, sometimes inverted as if falling from the sky, or herds of deer, often pierced by spears.'

You can see fine examples of this work at Fate Bell Shelter in Seminole Canyon State Historical Park (p278) and Amistad NRA (p277).

JUDGE ROY BEAN

Judge Roy Bean has been called the West's most colorful justice of the peace. He called himself the 'Law West of the Pecos,' and he ruled the frontier from his combination courthouse, saloon and pool hall in Langtry. Bean was named the local JP in August 1882 to help bring order to the towns and tent camps that had sprung up in the wake of the Southern Pacific's new Sunset Route. There was no other legal authority within 100 miles, so Bean did things his own way, holding court at his bar or on the front porch in good weather. His punishments were unusual and good for business: he'd often order a defendant to pay $30 or $45 and buy a round of drinks.

Bean was a character and his legal exploits were just a few of his adventures. The 1972 film, *The Life and Times of Judge Roy Bean,* is an entertaining primer. It was directed by John Huston and stars Paul Newman. The eponymous visitor center in Langtry (p279) has much more, including his star-crossed romance with British singer and actor Lillie Langtry. He's buried on the grounds of the Whitehead Memorial Museum in Del Rio (p276).

tours to other, more remote, sites in the region). The tours last up to 90 minutes and include a fairly strenuous hike down and up a canyon. Before or after the hike, stop by the visitor center to see excellent exhibits on the area's human history from prehistoric times to more recent railroading and ranching days. There's also a short nature trail and longer trails through the often scorching but fascinating desert terrain.

The park's 31-site **campground** (sites $12-17) has showers and makes a good base for exploring the Seminole Canyon area. It's on a hill, surrounded by beautiful desert vegetation. The nearest town along US 90, Comstock, has limited services. Del Rio, 40 miles southeast, is a good base.

LANGTRY
pop 30

Langtry is a long way from anywhere, but it has managed to parlay its principal claim to fame into a major tourist attraction on US 90: the **Judge Roy Bean Visitor Center** (☎ 432-291-3340; www.traveltex.com; US 90; ☽ 8am-5pm, until 6pm Jun-Aug), an official state visitor center. Displays cover the life of the legendary Lone Star lawman and include the .41-caliber Smith & Wesson revolver he used as his gavel. For more, see the boxed text.

Big Bend & West Texas

West Texas is the land of wide open spaces. If you've ever wondered whether we're going to run out of places to put people, west Texas is like a big sigh of relief. There are places where you can drive for hours and see few signs of other people. That's not to say it's the land of nothing: two national parks, one large city and a handful of interesting small towns offer worthwhile stops between your long stretches of solitude.

Along I-10 there's not much to look at, just scrub brush and open skies. But dip below the interstate and you'll find a landscape that, while perhaps not traditionally beautiful, is captivating and unusual enough that you may find yourself staring out the windows for hours at a time. Sometimes the rugged terrain looks just like a backdrop for an old Western movie (more than a few have been filmed here) and at other times it looks like an alien landscape, with huge rock formations suddenly jutting out of the endless desert.

There is a slowness here that gets under your skin. You may try to keep up with your email and cell phone for a day or two, but spend a week and you'll feel less of a need to keep apace with the modern world. Moving to west Texas means dropping out, and a lot of visitors drawn to the laid-back lifestyle have been inspired to do just that. Even if you don't buy a pair of boots, pack up your things, and relocate to the desert, odds are good you'll come away from west Texas with a new outlook.

HIGHLIGHTS

Most Surprising Nightlife
Music, margaritas and mixing with the locals at the Starlight Theater (p291) in Terlingua ghost town

Quirkiest Art Installation
The Marfa Prada (p295), in between Marfa and Valentine

Most Increasingly Scenic
Big Bend's Lost Mine Trail (p286), which just gets better and better as you climb

Best Taxidermy
The Gage Hotel in Marathon (p300), both for quantity and for having a unique white buffalo

Most Fun Learning Experience
A late-night Star Party at McDonald Observatory (p293) in Fort Davis

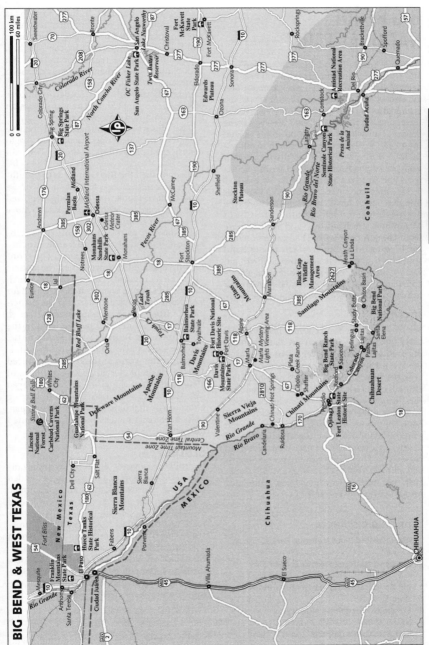

BIG BEND & WEST TEXAS

BIG BEND NATIONAL PARK

Everyone knows Texas is big. But you can't really appreciate just how big until you visit this **national park** (☎ 432-477-2251; www.nps.gov/bibe; 7-day pass vehicle incl occupants/pedestrian or bicycle $20/10), which is almost as big as Rhode Island. When you're traversing Big Bend's 1252 sq miles, you come to appreciate what 'big' really means. It's a land of incredible diversity, vast enough to allow a lifetime of discovery, yet laced with enough well-placed roads and trails to permit short-term visitors to see a lot in two to three days.

Like many popular US parks, Big Bend has one area – the Chisos Basin – that absorbs the overwhelming crunch of traffic. The Chisos Mountains are beautiful, and no trip here would be complete without an excursion into the high country. But any visit to Big Bend should also include time in the Chihuahuan Desert, home to curious creatures and adaptable plants, and the Rio Grande, providing a watery border between the US and Mexico.

HISTORY

Settlement of Big Bend country began 10,000 to 12,000 years ago, when nomadic hunters pursued game into the region at the end of the last ice age. Once the glaciers melted, the area became a searing desert in which few animals could survive. They disappeared, and the hunters soon followed. When humans and animals returned several thousand years later, conditions, although still harsh, allowed a bountiful lifestyle for those who understood the desert's ways. These native peoples lived close to the Rio Grande and harvested plants and animals from the desert. Eventually, however, they were either routed by or assimilated into other nearby cultures.

A Mexican band of Indians known as Chisos came north each summer to live in the mountains that now carry their name, and they were soon joined by the Apaches, who dominated the region for most of the 18th century. The Comanches were very much a presence as well; every fall, the Big Bend country shook with the thundering hooves of horses carrying Comanche war parties on their autumn raids into Mexico.

The desert environment and Native American presence long discouraged Anglo Americans from settling in the Big Bend. In the 1850s, after the Mexican War (1846–48) had established the Rio Grande as the southern border of the USA, federal survey crews came to have a look, and US troops followed soon afterward, ordering the Indians to move toward reservations.

By the end of the 19th century, Anglos had established sheep and cattle ranches throughout the Big Bend region. The economy diversified in a hurry when the settlers discovered cinnabar. This substance, which the region's native peoples had long used for war paint and rock art, was also the principal ore from which mercury was extracted. Before long, some 2000 people lived in the boomtowns of Terlingua and Study Butte, and the Chisos Mining Company – second-largest in the world at the time – produced 100,000 flasks of mercury between 1900 and 1940. But when the cinnabar veins played out, the boom ended with a thud, leaving ghost towns that have only recently and partially been reclaimed by recreation-oriented businesses.

GEOLOGY

For millions of years, Big Bend lay at the bottom of the sea, part of a trough that extended into what is now Arkansas and Oklahoma. Over time, the sea became shallower and eventually disappeared, leaving a wondrous fossil record of marine life and beds of limestone, both thick (the Sierra del Carmen and Santa Elena formations) and thin (the Boquillas formation). Once the sea was gone, the dinosaurs took over; Big Bend was especially favored by pterosaurs, the largest flying creatures ever, with a wingspan of 35ft or more.

About 65 million years ago, the 'mountain building' Cenozoic era began, and tectonic forces produced the Rocky Mountains and

---

DRIVING DISTANCES

Alpine to Big Bend National Park 70 miles, 1¼ hours

Big Bend National Park to El Paso 290 miles, 5 hours

Big Bend National Park to Midland 204 miles, 3¾ hours

El Paso to Guadalupe Mountains National Park 109 miles, 2¼ hours

Fort Stockton to Alpine 67 miles, 1¼ hours

WHEN TO GO

Most travelers consider spring and fall the best times of year to visit Big Bend National Park. Summer (June through August) is very hot, with typical daytime temperatures around 100°F; late summer can be rainy, too. Spring means moderate temperatures and lots of wildflowers (and lots of people), and fall is also quite pleasant, especially for white-water rafting.

Some park-fanciers believe winter is the best time of all to come; it's usually relatively mild, although temperatures in the Chisos can fall below freezing and Basin Rd typically closes two or three times each winter, sometimes for several days. But the snow is never deep enough to preclude hiking, and the touch of frost makes the trees and cacti a beautiful sight. At all times of the year, it's wise to layer your clothes in the morning and peel off the top layers if you get too warm.

the Sierra Madre. Volcanic activity followed, spreading ash and lava over thousands of miles in the region. Increased tensions in the earth's crust created faulting, dropping the central portion of the park and creating what geologists call the Sunken Block, while further elevating the Chisos Mountains. Meanwhile, the Rio Grande – perhaps working in tandem with the Rio Conchos from Mexico – carved the great canyons that define the river today.

ORIENTATION

Park headquarters and the **main visitor center** (☎ 432-477-2251; ☻ 8am-6pm) are at Panther Junction, which is on the main park road 29 miles from the Persimmon Gap entrance and 22 miles from the Maverick entrance near Study Butte. A Chevron service station is nearby, offering fuel, repairs and a small stock of snacks and beverages.

From Panther Junction, another major road leads 20 miles southeast to Rio Grande Village. Two other principal roads, the 7-mile Basin Rd and 30-mile Ross Maxwell Scenic Dr, take off from the main park road west of Panther Junction. Sharp curves and steep grades make Basin Rd unsuitable for recreational vehicles (RVs) longer than 24ft and trailers longer than 20ft.

Maps

The free National Park Service Big Bend map, available at the entrances and visitor centers, is adequate for most visitors to the park. Highly recommended for hiking on the lesser developed trails and backpacking is the *National Geographic Trails Illustrated Big Bend National Park* topographic map ($9.95), available at the visitor centers and gateway town bookstores.

INFORMATION
Emergency & Medical Services

To report an emergency day or night in the park, call the **main park number** (☎ 432-477-2291). After the automated telephone system answers, press 9. If there's no answer, hang up and dial ☎ 911.

Big Bend National Park is no place to get seriously injured or gravely ill. The closest hospital is in Alpine, 108 miles from Panther Junction. The nonprofit **Terlingua Medics** (☎ emergencies 432-371-2222, otherwise 432-371-2536) have a first-aid station that's 26 miles west of Panther Junction, where trained paramedics can offer some assistance. **Big Bend Family Health Center** (☎ 432-371-2661) also has a clinic on FM 170 in Study Butte, where a certified physician assistant sees patients for nonemergencies on an appointment and walk-in basis.

Money

Just when you thought there was nowhere in the USA without an ATM, you've found that place at Big Bend. The closest money machine is in Terlingua, 24 miles west of Panther Junction.

Tourist Information

In addition to the park headquarters at Panther Junction, **visitor centers** (☻ 8am-3:30pm) are found in Chisos Basin and at Persimmon Gap. There are also seasonal visitor centers open November through April at Castolon and the Rio Grande Village. Find out how to make the most of your visit from park rangers, and check the bulletin boards for a list of upcoming interpretive activities, which are held daily November through April, less often the rest of the year. Check the bulletin boards at the visitors centers for

BIG BEND NATIONAL PARK

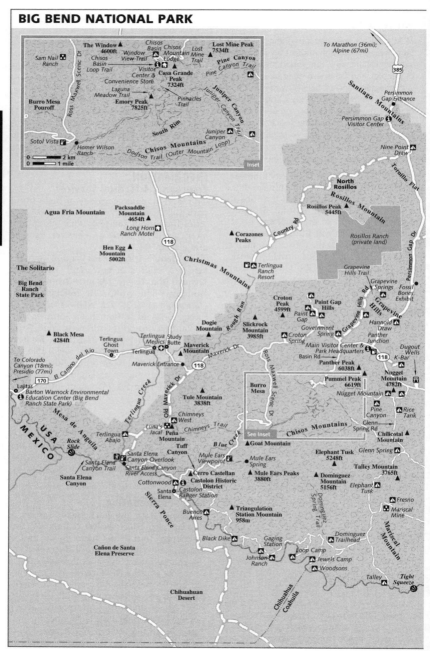

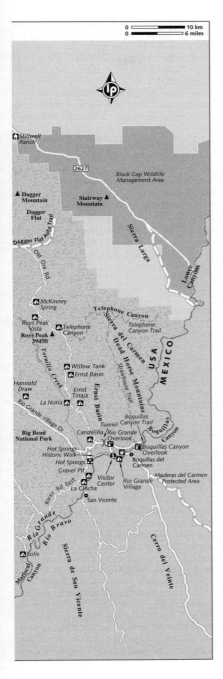

a variety of free leaflets on special-interest topics, including biological diversity, hiking and backpacking, geology, archaeology and dinosaurs.

DANGERS & ANNOYANCES

Big Bend National Park is one of the most remote spots in North America, set amid wild country with all kinds of potential hazards. This doesn't mean it's an inherently dangerous place, but it does mean precautions should be taken.

Don't take the heat for granted; this is the desert, after all. Drink lots of water, and take plenty with you when you hike. To protect against sunburn, wear a hat, sunscreen, long pants and a long-sleeved shirt. And take a cue from the animals: do your hiking early in the morning or in the evening, not at midday when the unrelenting sun turns Big Bend into one big Easy-Bake Oven.

Big Bend's poisonous snakes and tarantulas won't attack unless provoked. Simple rule of thumb? Don't provoke them. Most snakes keep a low profile in daylight, when you're unlikely to see them. Night hikers should stay on the trail and carry a flashlight. Big Bend's scorpions are not deadly, but you should still get prompt attention if you're stung. Shake out boots or shoes before putting them on.

SIGHTS & ACTIVITIES
Castolon Historic District

Dwarfed by the looming Sierra Ponce, the clustering of buildings that make up the Castolon Compound were built in 1920. A half-mile historic stroll offers a brief look at life on the frontier in the Castolon Historic District. Start at the famous La Harmonia Store, which is a mainstay for locals on both sides of the river as well as an ice-cream vending oasis for tourists. A pamphlet ($1) sold in the store serves as a guide.

Hiking

Big Bend has 150 miles of trails amid the largest area of roadless public land in Texas. The slim booklet *Hiker's Guide to Trails of Big Bend National Park* ($1.95 at park visitor centers) gives short descriptions of three dozen trails ranging from easy walks to primitive backpacking routes. Pets are not allowed on park trails, nor are they permitted in the backcountry.

BIG BEND & WEST TEXAS

BEAR IN MIND...

There's a slim chance you might encounter a black bear in the park. If you do, don't run away; instead make lots of noise and look as big as possible by waving your hands above your head. If you see cubs, back away slowly so the mother won't fear an attack. To keep bears from joining you for dinner, store all food, coolers, cooking utensils and toiletries in the trunk of your car or in the special bear-proof lockers, and discard trash in the bear-proof containers provided at campsites and near trailheads.

CHISOS MOUNTAINS

The Chisos has the park's densest concentration of trails, including several of the park's most popular.

The absolute lowest amount of commitment is the short **Window View Trail** that leaves from behind the basin's convenience store. It's only a third of a mile, it's paved and it's wheelchair-accessible – perfect for nonhikers or for anyone who wants to watch the sunset over the Window, a narrow opening in the rock that surrounds the Chisos Basin that provides the perfect frame for the setting sun.

For a bit more of a stretch, take the pleasant **Chisos Basin Loop Trail**, an easy 1.6-mile round-trip hike from the visitors center. This trail enjoys a relatively large amount of shade provided by the Mexican piñons and alligator junipers.

The **Window Trail** is a bit more strenuous, but it has a great payoff: after descending into scrub brush, you enter a shady canyon and scramble around on some rocks, then the trail suddenly ends with a narrowed pass and a 200ft drop-off. This is a clear sign it's time to turn around, but not before admiring the view through the Window. It's 5.5 miles round-trip if you leave from the Basin Trailhead, but you can shave off 1.5 miles if you leave from the campground, and you won't be missing a thing in terms of scenery.

The **Lost Mine Trail** is all about views, which, as you climb over 1000ft in elevation, just get better and better. You'll be right up there with Casa Grande, Lost Mine Peak and, from the highest point, the Sierra del Carmen. It's 4.8 miles total, but you can get a partial payoff by catching the views from about a mile in then turning around and coming back.

Sturdy hikers can bag the highest peak at Big Bend, **Emory Peak**, on the 9-mile portion of the Pinnacles Trail complex. The 1-mile spur trail to the 7825ft peak leaves the main trail after Pinnacles Pass, 3.5 miles from the Basin Trailhead. It ends with a short scramble up a sheer rock wall. Although the mountaintop is dominated by communications equipment, this doesn't detract much from the wide-angle views.

Many serious hikers say the **South Rim** is their favorite Big Bend trek, mainly because of the view at the end: from the South Rim at the southwestern edge of the High Chisos, the vista includes Santa Elena Canyon and the Sierra del Carmen. On clear days, it's even possible to see the mountains of Mexico up to 80 miles away. This is a 13- to 14.5-mile round-trip hike, depending on the route taken, so plan on either a very long day or an overnight outing. Before you go, check with the visitor center, as part of the trail is closed from February 1 to July 15, during peregrine falcon nesting season.

DESERT & RIVERSIDE HIKES

These hikes range from short introductions to the Chihuahua Desert to trails leading to the Rio Grande. Don't forget to drink plenty of water, and wear a hat and sunscreen.

Beginning at campsite 18 at the main Rio Grande Village campground (not the RV park), the three-quarter-mile **Rio Grande Village Nature Trail** passes through dense riparian vegetation before emerging in the desert for a view of the Rio Grande. When you reach the promontory, look across the river toward the village of Ojo Caliente for donkey trains picking their way along invisible paths. This is a good short trail for birding and photography.

Although it's only 1.4 miles round-trip, the **Boquillas Canyon Trail** is rated as moderately difficult because of a short climb at the start followed by a descent to the Rio Grande. Leave time to play on the sand slide and enjoy the sunlight dancing on the canyon walls. The trail begins at the end of the Boquillas Canyon spur road, east of Rio Grande Village.

A hike on **Santa Elena Canyon Trail** is a must if you don't have time to float the Rio Grande. The 1.7-mile round-trip trek from the end of Ross Maxwell Scenic Dr takes hikers upriver into the amazingly steep, narrow Santa Elena Canyon. The trail crosses Terlingua Creek near its start, so pack along some old shoes in case you need to wade.

The 2-mile-round-trip **Hot Springs Historic Walk** offers an easy stroll into the past. JO Langford homesteaded here in 1909 and built a small health resort centered on the hot springs nearby. The site includes remains of the town, and just past the ruins you will find Native American pictographs painted on rock walls. Soakers will find a stone bathtub brimming with 105°F spring water at the river's edge. The trailhead is at the end of a narrow 1.5-mile dirt road leading south from Rio Grande Village Dr, not far west of the village. You can also access the hot springs on the 3-mile (one-way) **Hot Springs Canyon Trail** from Rio Grande Village.

If Boquillas Canyon is the sandbox of giants, the boulders of **Grapevine Hills** are their building blocks. The 2.2-mile round-trip hike off Grapevine Hills Rd (6 miles from Maverick Dr) leads through a sandy wash rimmed by huge hunks of granite. One famous sight, another Big Bend window (this one of boulders) can be seen by following the trail 100 yards along a ridge to the right of the low pass at the south end of the wash.

Backpacking

Big Bend's primitive backpacking routes range from well-traveled desert washes to the truly challenging limestone uplifts of Mesa de Anguila and the Dead Horse Mountains. Rangers say that because of the constantly changing trail and spring conditions, it's pretty much impossible to plan an extended backpacking trip before you actually get to the park. What you can do instead is figure out how much time you have and the distance you'd like to cover; based on that information, park staff will help you plot a trip. Many trails require use of topographical maps and a compass.

Bird-Watching

Prime birding sites at Big Bend include Rio Grande Valley, the Sam Nail Ranch, the Chisos Basin and Castolon near Santa Elena Canyon. **Big Bend Birding Expeditions** (☎ 432-371-2356, 888-531-2223) in Terlingua offers trips in and around the park and on the Rio Grande.

The Big Bend region may be best known for its peregrine falcons, which, while still endangered, have made a comeback as of late. A dozen known nests are found within or near the park. Among other Big Bend bird celebrities, the Colima warbler has its only US nesting spot in the Chisos Mountains, where it lives from April through mid-September. More common Big Bend species include golden eagles, cactus wrens, ravens, Mexican jays, roadrunners, acorn woodpeckers, canyon towhees and a whole bunch of warblers and hummingbirds.

River Trips

Originating in southern Colorado, the Rio Grande is an insignificant trickle by the time it enters Texas. It wouldn't be floatable if not for the Rio Conchos, a Mexican river that flows into the Rio Grande, giving it new life and power for its 118-mile run along the southern border of Big Bend.

SCENIC DRIVES

Big Bend National Park has 110 miles of paved road and 150 miles of dirt road, and scenic driving is easily the park's most popular activity. Booklets are available for $1.95 from the visitor centers to help you make the most of it.

- **Maverick Dr** The 22-mile stretch between the west entrance and park headquarters is notable for its desert scenery and wildlife. Just west of Basin Junction, a side trip on the gravel Grapevine Hills Rd leads to fields of oddly shaped, highly eroded boulders.

- **Ross Maxwell Scenic Dr** This 30-mile route leaves Maverick Dr midway between the west entrance and park headquarters. The Chisos Mountains provide a grand panorama along the way, and the big payoff is the view of Santa Elena Canyon and its 1500ft sheer rock walls.

- **Rio Grande Village Dr** This 20-mile drive leads from park headquarters toward the Sierra del Carmen range, running through the park southeast toward Mexico. The best time to take this drive is at sunrise or sunset, when the mountains glow brilliantly with different hues of reds and oranges.

The Rio Grande has earned its place among the top North American river trips for both rafting and canoeing. Rapids up to Class IV alternate with calm stretches that are perfect for wildlife viewing, photography and just plain relaxation.

Trips on the river can range from several hours to several days. **Boquillas Canyon** is the longest and most tranquil of the park's three canyons and is best for intermediate to advanced boaters and canoeists with camping skills; it lasts three to four days. **Colorado Canyon** is just upriver from the park and, depending on the water level, has lots of white water. It's a popular day-trip option, especially if water levels at Santa Elena aren't favorable for floating. Colorado Canyon is also a good run for experienced canoeists.

Lower Canyons is downriver from the park; unescorted rafters and canoeists should have wilderness skills; the trip lasts seven to 10 days. **Mariscal Canyon** is noted for its beauty and isolation and lasts one or more days. **Santa Elena Canyon** is a classic float featuring the Class IV Rock Slide rapid and lasts at least six to eight hours.

GUIDED TRIPS

Guided floats cost about $120 per person per day, including all meals and gear (except a sleeping bag for overnighters, and your personal effects). Three companies offer guided river rafting trips in and around Big Bend:
Big Bend River Tours (☎ 432-424-3219, 800-545-4240; www.bigbendrivertours.com; Terlingua)
Desert Sports (☎ 432-371-2727, 888-989-6900; www.desertsportstx.com; Terlingua)
Far Flung Adventures (☎ 432-371-2489, 800-359-4138; www.farflung.com; Terlingua)

All have been in business a long time and have solid reputations. Desert Sports is generally known for its reputable guides, and Far Flung is known more for creative trips, such as their 'Paddle and Saddle' or 'Rock and Raft' trips.

GEAR RENTAL & PERMITS

Rafts and other river gear can be rented from **Rio Grande Adventures** (☎ 432-371-2567, 800-343-1649) and **Desert Sports** (☎ 432-371-2727, 888-989-6900; www.desertsportstx.com), both in Terlingua. Both outfits rent canoes and organize shuttle service.

Although the Rio Grande is better known for rafting, travelers looking for a more active adventure should consider canoeing or kayaking, a more hands-on experience. Rio Grande Adventures rents kayaks and offers guided canoe trips starting at $50.

Floaters boating on their own must obtain a free permit at Panther Junction within 24 hours before putting in. Permits for the Lower Canyons of the Rio Grande are available at the Persimmon Gap visitor center and the Stillwell Store at Stillwell Ranch, on FM 2627.

Horseback Riding

Although horses are permitted on many trails at Big Bend, no animals can be rented inside the park. If you bring your own, get the required stock use permit, available free at any visitor center. Government Spring, a primitive campsite near Panther Junction, caters to parties with between four and eight horses. It can be reserved up to 10 weeks in advance by calling ☎ 432-477-2251 ext 158.

SLEEPING & EATING
Camping

For tent campers or smaller RVs that don't require hookups, there are three main campgrounds, some of which can be reserved, some of which are first-come, first-served. Sites typically fill up during spring break, Thanksgiving and Christmas. When everything's full, rangers direct tent campers into primitive sites throughout the Big Bend backcountry.

The most centrally located of the main campgrounds is **Chisos Basin Campground** (☎ reservations 877-444-6777; sites $14) a 60-site campground that has sites with stone shelters and picnic tables. The **Basin Store** (☼ 7am-9pm, reduced hours in summer) carries basic camping supplies, batteries, canned food and some perishables.

Set beneath cottonwood trees near Castolon, the 31-site **Cottonwood Campground** (no reservations; sites $14) provides a subdued and shady environment along the river with no generators or idling vehicles to ruin the ambience. And on the southeast edge of the park, **Rio Grande Village Campground** (☎ reservations 877-444-6777; sites $14) offers 100 sites with water and flush toilets. Generators may only be used from 8am to 8pm; mercifully, there is also a no-generator zone available. The **Village Store** (☼ 9am-6pm) has some groceries.

If you have a larger RV, Rio Grande Village is the only facility with hookups within the park. (Trailers over 25ft have trouble navigating the winding roads down into the Chisos Basin.) There are 25 sites at the concessionaire-operated **Rio Grande Village RV Campground** (☎ 432-477-2293; $29 for 2 people, $3 per extra person). Since there aren't any restrooms, your rig will need water and electrical hookups, as well as a 3in sewer connection.

Chisos Mountains Lodge

This concessionaire-operated **complex** (☎ 432-477-2291, reservations 877-386-4383; www.chisosmountainslodge.com) in the basin gets good, if not great, marks for accommodations and food service. You can do better on both counts if you stay outside the park, but the scenery here is a lot better, and it offers easy access to many of the popular trails. It's also nice to know that you can go straight to your room post-hike, instead of having to drive 45 minutes to rest.

The lodge complex includes the **Roosevelt Stone Cottages** (d $137, extra person $11), which are the choicest accommodations available in the park. Each one has three double beds, so you could sleep six people comfortably. There are only four of these cottages, so they're hard to come by.

Or, you can choose one of the modest, motel-style rooms at the **Casa Grande Lodge & Rio Grande Motel** (d $108-113), which have private balconies and good views of the basin and surrounding mountains. Most rooms have two double beds; a few have one double and one single. The guest rooms here don't have TVs or telephones. Reservations are a must, but management says there are often cancellations.

Talk about a captive audience. It's a 45-minute drive to the next closest restaurants in Study Butte and Terlingua. Still, the lodge **dining room** (breakfast $2-7, dinner $5-10; 7-10am, 11am-4pm, 5-8pm) has decent food, with plenty of options, and the staff, for the most part, are surprisingly cheery and attentive. Try to get a window table, since the sublime Chisos Basin view is the best thing about this place.

GETTING THERE & AWAY

There is no public transportation to, from or within the park. The closest buses and trains run through Alpine, 108 miles northwest of Panther Junction. The nearest major airports are in Midland (230 miles northeast, with shuttle service available to Alpine) and El Paso (325 miles northwest).

WEST OF BIG BEND NATIONAL PARK

Small towns. Ghost towns. Towns that aren't even really towns. Throw in lots of dust and a scorching summer heat that dries out the stream of visitors until it's just a trickle. This isn't everyone's idea of a dream vacation. But if you can't relax out here, then you just plain can't relax. Whatever concerns you in your everyday life is likely to melt away (along with anything you leave in your car). Throw in some rugged natural beauty and some offbeat destinations, and you can see why this un-likely corner of the country is actually fueled almost entirely by tourism.

This is the land that public transportation forgot. You'll need a car, not just to get to Terlingua, but to get around once you're there.

TERLINGUA & STUDY BUTTE
pop 267

A former mining boomtown in the late 19th and early 20th centuries, Terlingua went bust when they closed down the mines in the 1940s. The town dried up and blew away like a tumbleweed, leaving buildings that fell into ruins and earning Terlingua a place in Texas folklore as a ghost town.

But slowly the area has become repopulated, thanks in large part to its proximity to Big Bend National Park, to which it supplies housing for park employees, as well as services to the more than 300,000 park visitors each year. Several businesses make their homes in and around the ghost town; many of the old adobes have been reclaimed by river guides, artists and others who relish the solitude of the outback.

Orientation & Information

You'll hear people talk about Terlingua, Study Butte (pronounced 'stoody byoot'), and Terlingua ghost town as if they're three different towns, but the only real town here is Terlingua; the other two are just areas of the town. Addresses are a relative and fluid thing out here; have patience if you're using a GPS, but take comfort knowing the town's not all that big.

Study Butte refers to a cluster of buildings on Hwy 118 immediately outside the west gate of Big Bend. One mile up the road, at the junction of Hwy 118 and FM 170, things pick up a bit; that's where you'll find the Terlingua **post office** (☎ 432-371-2269) and a 24-hour ATM at **West Texas National Bank** (☎ 432-371-2211). Head west on FM 170 for more of the town's business district. And keep going five miles to reach the historic area called the **Terlingua ghost town**, where you'll find old ruins and new businesses built on top of old ruins.

To get more information on the area, visit the **Big Bend Chamber of Commerce** (☎ 432-317-3949; www.bigbendchamberofcommerce.org).

Activities

Terlingua sits amid prime mountain-biking territory. **Desert Sports** (☎ 432-371-2727, 888-989-6900; www.desertsportstx.com) provides rental bikes, along with advice on the best places to ride. It also offers thrilling raft, canoe, bike and combo trips throughout the Big Bend area.

For horseback riding, call **Big Bend Stables** (☎ 432-371-3064; 800-887-4331; www.lajitasstables.com), where rates run $40 for one hour, $60 for two hours and $75 for three hours. (They don't actually go into Big Bend, which doesn't allow commercial outfitters, but they do host a trail ride in the Terlingua area.) **Big Bend Touring Society** (☎ 432-371-2548) is another local guide service handling a variety of activity trips. If a walking tour is more your speed, pick up a map at the Terlingua Trading Co (see p291).

Sleeping

You'd think lodging would be inexpensive out here; quite the opposite. Expect to pay a little more than you think you ought to.

THE CHAMPIONS OF CHILI

Every November, Terlingua is invaded by thousands of visitors with a hankering for homemade chili. This is no small-town festival; the **Terlingua Chili Cookoff** is such a big deal that they actually have two events to accommodate the hundreds of entrants: the **International Chili Championship** held by the Chili Appreciation Society International (CASI; www.chili.org), which you have to qualify for, and the **Original Terlingua International Frank X Tolbert-Wick Fowler Championship Chili Cookoff** (www.abowlofred.com), which is less competitive and more like a big, spicy party. Don't expect to enjoy quality time with the locals during these events; they mostly go into hiding.

BJ's RV Park (☎ 432-371-2259; www.bjrvpark.com; FM 170; RV sites $22) Sure it's dry and dusty. The whole town is dry and dusty. But this utilitarian park, 5 miles west of Hwy 118, provides a handy alterative when everything's full up in Big Bend.

Chisos Mining Co Motel (☎ 432-371-2430; FM 170; s/d $57/$76, cabins from $97) You'll recognize this quirky little place less than a mile west of Hwy 118 when you spot the oversized Easter eggs on the roof. The rooms are minimalist, but as cheap as you'll find.

Big Bend Motor Inn & Mission Lodge (☎ 432-371-2218, reservations 877-386-4383; Hwy 118/FM 170 junction; d $92-107) At the Hwy 118 and FM 170 intersection, these two properties across the highway from each other don't have much character, but they do have all sorts of sleeping options, including motel rooms, duplex units, apartments, tent camping and RV sites.

Upstairs at the Mansion (☎ 360-713-3408; 1 Perry Mansion Dr in Terlingua ghost town; d $95) Ready for an adventure? Rent a room at the ruins of the old Perry Mansion, which upon approach you will swear is a crumbling, old, abandoned building. Well, here's the thing: it kind of is. But the owners are slowly fixing it up, one charming room at a time. This is Terlingua at its most authentic.

our pick **La Posada Milagro** (☎ 432-371-3044; www.laposadamilagro.net; 100 Milagro Rd, Terlingua ghost town; d $185-210) Built on top of and even incorporating some of the adobe ruins in the historic ghost town, this guesthouse pulls off an amazing feat of providing stylish rooms that blend in perfectly with the surroundings. The decor is west-Texas chic, and there's a nice patio for enjoying the cool evenings. Budget travelers can book a simpler room with four bunk beds for $145 a night.

Eating

Espresso...Y Poco Mas (☎ 432-371-3044; 100 Milagro Rd; food $2.50-6.50; ☼ 8am-2pm) This walkup counter at La Posada Milagro is a refreshing surprise, where you can find pastries, breakfast burritos, lunches and what might just be the best iced coffee in all of west Texas.

Roadrunner Deli (☎ 432-371-2364; Study Butte Mall; menu items $3.50-7; ☼ daily spring through fall) This deli, east of the Hwy 118/FM 170 intersection, specializes in packing tasty picnics for the Big Bend–bound, and they also serve breakfast and lunch. There's also a grocery store next door if you need to supplement your supplies.

Kathy's Kosmic Kowgirl Kafe (☎ 432-371-2164; Hwy 170; barbecue & sandwiches $4-9; ☺ 6:30am-3pm Thu-Mon) Part food stand, part roadside attraction, (and about a mile west of Hwy 118), this hot-pink trailer with hot pink lawn decor sometimes shows movies and has campfires at night.

Tivo's Restaurant (☎ 432-371-2133, Hwy 118; meals $8-14; ☺ 5-9pm Wed-Sun) This family-run Mexican restaurant gets nothing but kudos from locals. Try the spicy chile rellenos. They also serve gringo fare.

our pick **Starlight Theater** (☎ 432-371-2326; 100 Ivey St; mains $9-18; ☺ 5pm-midnight, to 1am Sat) You'd think a ghost town would be dead at night (pardon the pun) but the Starlight Theater keeps things lively. This former movie theater had fallen into roofless disrepair (thus the 'starlight' name) before being converted into a local event space and then eventually a restaurant. There's live music nearly every night in spring and fall, and if there's no entertainment inside, there's usually someone strumming a guitar outside on the porch. To get there, take Hwy 170 to the ghost town turnoff, then follow the road to the end.

La Kiva Restaurant & Bar (☎ 432-371-2250; Hwy 170; mains $9-18; ☺ 5pm-midnight) Talk about your underground restaurant. This quirky place specializing in barbecue is, literally, underground. If things get too smoky inside, the airy patio is a breath of fresh air. There's frequent live music, including an open-mike night every Wednesday 8pm to midnight. It's about 3 miles west of Hwy 118.

Shopping

Terlingua Trading Co (☎ 432-371-2234; 100 Ivey St) This store in the ghost town has great gifts, from hot sauces and wines to an impressive selection of books. Pick up a brochure on the walking tour of historic Terlingua here; it's published by the Terlingua Foundation, a nonprofit group striving to restore the ghost town.

LAJITAS GOLF RESORT & SPA

About half an hour west from the junction in Terlingua, you can trade funky and dusty for trendy and upscale (but still dusty) at **Lajitas Golf Resort & Spa** (☎ 877-525-4827; www.lajitas.com; d from $149). What used to be small-town Texas got bought up and revamped into a swanky destination. The old Trading Post is gone and in its place is a new General Store. (The former Trading Post was the stuff of folk leg-

---

SCENIC DRIVE: EL CAMINO DEL RIO

West of Lajitas, Rte 170 (also known as River Rd, or *El Camino Del Rio* in Spanish) hugs the Rio Grande through some of the most spectacular and remote scenery in Big Bend country. Relatively few Big Bend visitors experience this driving adventure, even though it can be navigated in any vehicle with good brakes. Strap in and hold on: you have the Rio Grande on one side and fanciful geological formations all around, and at one point there's a 15% grade – the maximum allowable. When you reach Presidio, head north on US 67 to get to Marfa. Or, if you plan to go back the way you came, at least travel as far as Colorado Canyon (20 miles from Lajitas) for the best scenery.

---

end, as it was the home of a beer-drinking goat who got elected mayor of the town. Alas, no more.)

The nine-hole course that included a shot over the river into Mexico has now moved to drier ground to escape flooding, and now it's the 18-hole **Black Jack's Crossing**. The resort has a pool and lighted tennis courts. There are also some well-run stables that are open to local visitors whether they're staying at the resort or not. The **Lajitas Equestrian Center** offers horseback trail rides by the hour ($70) as well as full-day rides to the Buena Suerte Mine and Ghost Town.

As for lodging, you can choose from a range of different experiences around the resort, from motel rooms to condos to RV camps. Among the nicest guest rooms are those in the high-ceilinged **Officers' Quarters**, a complex modeled after the original at Fort Davis.

BIG BEND RANCH STATE PARK

At 433 sq miles, this **state park** (☎ 432-229-3416; adult/under 12yr $3/free) is more than 11 times larger than Texas' next biggest state park (Franklin Mountains in El Paso). Taking up almost all the desert between Lajitas and Presidio, Big Bend Ranch reaches north from the Rio Grande into some of the wildest country in North America. It is full of notable features, most prominently the Solitario, formed 36 million years ago in a volcanic explosion. The resulting caldera measures 8 miles east to west and 9 miles north to south. As massive as it is, this former ranch is one of the best-kept secrets in Big Bend country.

Since the park has few facilities and much fewer visitors, you should come prepared. Make sure you have spare tires, a full tank of gas, a gallon of water per day per person, sunscreen, a hat, mosquito repellent and a well-stocked first-aid kit.

You can reach the park's **main office** (☺ 8am-5pm) about a quarter of a mile west of Fort Leaton on FM 170. Access to the park is limited and a permit is required, even when doing hikes along the well-traveled FM 170. Visitors planning to hike or drive into the park's interior must obtain instructions, the gate combination and maps from the main office or, if you're coming from the west, at the restored adobe fortress of **Fort Leaton State Historic Site** (☎ 432-229-3613; FM 170; adult/6-12yr $2/1; ☺ 8am-4:30pm), 3 miles south of Presidio.

If you stop at only one Chihuahuan Desert exhibit in Big Bend country, make it the **Barton Warnock Environmental Education Center** (☎ 432-424-3327; warnock@brooksdata.net; FM 170; adult/child $3/1.50; ☺ 8am-4:30pm), 1 mile east of Lajitas. This education center is staffed by some of the most knowledgeable folks in the region. Admission buys you a lifetime of information on this diverse desert. Call for a schedule of interpretive programs ranging from desert wild flowers to the habits of bats.

CENTRAL WEST TEXAS

The small towns of west Texas have become more than just the gateway to Big Bend National Park. Fort Davis, Marfa, Alpine and Marathon have a sprawling, easy-going charm and plenty of ways to keep a road-tripper entertained.

FORT DAVIS & DAVIS MOUNTAINS
pop 1050

More than 5000ft above sea level, Fort Davis has an altitudinal advantage over the rest of Texas, both in terms of elevation and the cooler weather it offers. That makes it a popular oasis during the summer, when west Texans head towards the mountains to escape the searing desert heat.

The area is part of both the Chihuahuan Desert and the Davis Mountains, giving it a unique setting where wide-open spaces are suddenly interrupted by rock formations springing from the earth. As for the town of

Fort Davis, it sprang up near the actual fort of the same name, built in 1854 to protect the pioneers and gold rushers who were heading out west from the attacks of Comanche and Apache warriors. The town retains an Old West feel befitting its history.

Orientation & Information

Of the towns in this region, Fort Davis is the closest to I-10. The main street through town is a stretch of Hwy 118 that's officially named State Street, but everyone around here calls it Main Street. The town is so small that, when you turn off Main Street, you might well end up on a dirt road. Just a few miles west of town on Hwy 118 is Davis Mountains State Park.

On Sundays, this sleepy little town takes a full day of rest; most of the businesses are closed till Monday. To find out what's going on, visit the **Fort Davis Chamber of Commerce** (☎ 432-426-3015; www.fortdavis.com; 4 Memorial Sq; ☺ 9am-5pm Mon-Fri) at the junction of Hwys 118 and 17.

You can get cash (even on Sundays) at **Fort Davis State Bank** (☎ 432-426-3211; 100 S State St), which has a 24-hour ATM. Hook up to free wi-fi at the **Jeff Davis County Library** (☎ 432-426-3802; 100 Memorial Sq; ☺ 10am-6pm Mon-Fri) – housed in the former county jail between the town square and the courthouse – or at the **Fort Davis Drug Store** (☎ 432-426-3118; 113 N State St; ☺ 8am-4pm).

Sights
FORT DAVIS NATIONAL HISTORIC SITE

A remarkably well-preserved example of a frontier military post, **Fort Davis** (☎ 432-426-3224; www.nps.gov/foda; Hwy 17; adult/15 & under $3/free; ☺ 8am-5pm except major holidays) was established in 1854 and abandoned in 1891. More than 20 buildings remain – five of them restored with period furnishings – as well as 100 or so ruins. It's easy to picture the fort as it was in 1880, especially with bugle calls sounding in the background. It's even easier in the summer months, when interpreters dressed in period clothing are on hand to describe life at the fort.

The fort sits at the foot of Sleeping Lion Mountain and Hospital Canyon, a strategic placement that also makes an impressive backdrop. The site serves as trailhead for several hikes, ranging from the 1-mile Tall Grass Loop to the more ambitious 3-mile trek to Davis Mountain State Park. Ask for a trail map in the fort's visitor center.

MCDONALD OBSERVATORY
Away from all the light pollution of the big cities, the middle of west Texas has some of the clearest and darkest skies in North America. So what better place to put the University of Texas' **McDonald Observatory** (☎ 432-426-3640; www.mcdonaldobservatory.org; daytime pass adult/6-12yr $8/7, star parties adult/6-12yr $10/8; visitor center 10am-5:30pm, tours 11:30am & 2pm). It has some of the biggest telescopes in the world, perched on the peak of 6791ft Mt Locke and so enormous you can spot them from miles away. A day pass gets you a guided tour (including close-up peeks at – but not through – the 107-inch Harlan J Smith Telescope and the 430-inch Hobby-Eberly Telescope) as well as a solar viewing, where you get to stare at the sun without scorching your eyeballs. See the boxed text, p293, for information on Star Parties.

The observatory is 19 miles northwest of Fort Davis on Hwy 118. Allow 30 minutes to drive from town, and get there early because tours fill up fast – especially in March when they're packed with spring breakers. And remember: it gets cold up there at night. Bring extra layers – unless you want to join the masses dropping $30 in the gift shop for blankets and jackets.

DAVIS MOUNTAINS STATE PARK
Just a few miles northwest of Fort Davis on Hwy 118, set amid the most extensive mountain range in Texas, is **Davis Mountains State Park** (☎ 432-426-3337; Hwy 118; adult/12yr $5/free). Hiking, mountain biking, horseback riding (BYO horse) and stargazing are all big attractions here, as is bird-watching. Pick up a bird

---

A STAR-STUDDED EVENT
On Tuesday, Friday and Saturday nights, about half an hour after sunset, **McDonald Observatory** shows off its favorite planets, galaxies and globular clusters at its popular **Star Parties**, where professional astronomers guide you in some heavy-duty stargazing. Using ridiculously powerful laser pointers, they give you a tour of the night sky, and you'll get to use some of the telescopes to play planetary peeping tom.

---

checklist from park headquarters so you know what you're looking at, or, if you already know what you're looking at, use it to impress your bird-watching friends.

With mountains come views, and there's no better place to enjoy your position than at an overlook at the top of Skyline Dr. In daylight, you can check out the surrounding area and neighboring mountain ranges. Dusk brings majestic sunsets, and after dark – and boy does it get dark – you can test your knowledge of the constellations.

Overnighters can camp within the park or bunk down at Indian Lodge (see p294).

OTHER SIGHTS
Can't get enough of pioneer style? The **Overland Trail Museum** (☎ 432-426-3904; adult/child $2/1; 1-5pm Tue-Sat) preserves the home of early settler Nick Mersfelter, while displaying historic photos and farm machinery. The scant opening hours gives you some idea as to the crowds to expect.

Snakes, spiders, scorpions…all the things you should check your boots for before you put them on can be seen on display at the funky **Rattlers & Reptiles** (☎ 432-426-2465; 1600 N State St; adult/under 10yr $4/1; 10am-dark). Sure, the critters on display give some people the willies, but better to run into them here then out on the trail or, worse yet, in your tent.

Four miles south of town, the **Chihuahuan Desert Research Institute and Visitor Center** (☎ 432-364-2499; Hwy 118; suggested admission per car $2; 9am-5pm Mon-Fri, plus Sat & Sun Apr 1-Labor Day) exhibits the region's flora in gardens and on trails.

Activities
SCENIC LOOP DRIVE
Pack up the kids or hop on your bikes and head out for 75 miles of paved splendor on this scenic drive through the Davis Mountains. First you go up, up, up, then you come down, down, down. The countryside is gorgeous – no wonder this is considered one of the most scenic drives in the US. It's also tops among cyclists – at least the ones who can handle the climb. Head out on Hwy 118 northwest from town, then turn left on Hwy 166, which loops you back to town. Or go the opposite route; both afford equally appealing views, although the former is better in the morning so you're not driving or riding into the sun, while the latter is better in the afternoon.

CYCLING

Fort Davis is one of Texas' best areas for road cycling. In addition to the aforementioned Scenic Loop Drive, which is as challenging as it is dramatic, there's some nice, gentle terrain just outside of town for casual cyclists. If you didn't bring a bike, try **Heavenly Skies Café** (☎ 432-426-2007; www.heavenlyskiesfd.com; per 2/24hr $15/35; 11:30am-3:30pm Mon-Fri), which rents them out and can even serve you pie after.

HORSEBACK RIDING

Going for a horseback ride is a natural in the Old West setting of Fort Davis. If you find yourself without a trusty steed, try out one of the one-hour guided horseback tours at **Prude Ranch** (☎ 432-426-3202; www.prude-ranch.com; Hwy 118; 1hr ride $30; 9:30am, 11am, 1:30pm & 3pm), 6 miles northwest of town. Or, for longer rides, mosey on over to **Fort Davis Riding Stables** (☎ 432-426-9075; www.fortdavisstables.com; 120 N Painted Trees Rd; 1hr ride $35; hourly rides from 9am-sunset, closed Wed). They offer hourly rides, sunset rides, all-day rides and overnight rides at the 10,000-acre Sproul Ranch.

Sleeping

Davis Mountains State Park (☎ 432-426-3337; Hwy 118; tent sites/full hookups $10/15) Pitch your tent here and the stargazing can go on till the wee hours. The campsites are in a lush, tree-shaded environment and include picnic tables and grills. Backcountry camping and RV hookups are also available.

Fort Davis Motor Inn & RV Campground (☎ 432-426-2112; www.texbesthotels.com/fort_davis.htm; Hwy 17 N; campsites $18.50, s/d $60/70) Just north of town on Hwy 17 near the fort, this motor lodge has Southwestern-style rooms, as well as RV hookups. It's nothing fancy, but not bad for the price.

Stone Village Tourist Camp (☎ 432-426-3941; www.stonevillagetouristcamp.com; 509 N State St; camp rooms $44, d $69-89;) This renovated motor court is a fun little bargain. The 14 regular rooms are cheery and comfortable, and the six camp rooms are perfect for the budget traveler. Located in the former garages, the camp rooms have concrete floors, stone walls, a roof, electricity and even wi-fi. The only catch – a small one at that – is that one end of the room has a screen and privacy curtain instead of a wall.

Old Schoolhouse Bed & Breakfast (☎ 432-426-2050; www.schoolhousebnb.com; 401 Front St; s with/without bathroom $89/79, d with/without bathroom $101/93;) You can't really tell it used to be the town's schoolhouse, but you can tell the owners put a lot of work into being great hosts, from the comfy rooms to their wonderful homemade breakfasts.

Indian Lodge (☎ 512-389-8982; Davis Mountains State Park; d $90-110, ste $120-135;) Located in the Davis Mountains State Park, this handsome, historic 39-room inn was built in the 1930s by the Civilian Conservation Corps. It has 18 inch–thick adobe walls, hand-carved cedar furniture and ceilings of pine viga and latilla that give it the look of a Southwestern pueblo – that is, one with a swimming pool, gift shop and restaurant. The comfortable guest rooms are a steal, so reserve early.

Hotel Limpia (☎ 432-426-3237; www.hotellimpia.com; 100 State St; r $99-160;) Built in 1912, this historic hotel leans heavily on antiques and floral prints, in a Victorian-meets-Old West kind of way, like the womenfolk came along and gussied up the place. There are few finer places to kick back than on the rocking chairs on the back porch.

Eating & Drinking

Jeff Davis is a dry county, which means no hooch for you. Well, you can always buy a six-pack at the local grocery, but the only place you can imbibe while you dine is at the Hotel Limpia dining room, and that's after paying a $3 membership fee to their private club.

Drug Store Restaurant (☎ 432-426-3118; 113 N State St; items $3-8; 8am-3pm Wed-Mon) No one can do old-fashioned soda fountain quite like a small west Texas town. This place has been open since the 1950s and serves breakfast, lunch, banana splits and purple cows (ice-cream floats made with grape juice).

Chuck Wagon (☎ 432-426-2900; 1300 N State St; mains $3-17; 7am-9pm) Fill up for the trail with steaks, burgers and barbecue; the Big Haul gets you four kinds of meats (because five would just be excessive). The atmosphere doesn't live up to the name: on the plus side, meals are served on tin plates; on the minus side, the booths and ceiling tiles look like they were rescued from a Dairy Queen.

Murphy's Pizzeria & Cafe (☎ 432-426-2020; 107 Musquiz Dr; mains $6-20; 11am-8pm Mon-Sat) Plenty of choices, including thin-crust pizza, sandwiches and salads, make this casual cafe an easy sell when you need to grab a bite.

Cueva de Leon (☎ 432-426-3801; 100 W 2nd St; mains $8-10; ⏲ 11am-3pm & 5-9pm Mon-Sat) While El Paso has a Mexican restaurant on practically every street corner, they're harder to find in central west Texas, so grab some decent enchiladas and chile rellenos while you can. Remember, this is a dry county, so if you were hoping for a margarita or cerveza, you'll have to look elsewhere.

ourpick **Hotel Limpia Dining Room** (☎ 432-426-3241; Main St; mains $10-20; ⏲ lunch 11:30am-2pm, dinner 5:30pm-9:30pm Tue-Sun) The house specialty is (and has been for years) the burgundy-marinated pot roast, and we're not saying everyone keeps eating the broth like soup even after the meat is gone, but you wouldn't blame us if we did, would you? Throw in some cream-cheese mashed potatoes and house-baked bread and you've got yourself a pretty memorable meal.

Getting There & Around
No regularly scheduled public transportation serves Fort Davis or the Davis Mountains. You can get to nearby Alpine (24 miles) by train or bus then rent a car. The closest airports are Midland International Airport (about 160 miles away) and El Paso International Airport (194 miles).

MARFA
pop 2121
The first thing you might wonder about Marfa is, 'Where did all these New Yorkers come from?' and the second, 'Why all the James Dean?'.

Founded in the 1880s, Marfa's two major cultural influences came in the latter part of the 20th century. It got its first taste of fame when Rock Hudson, Elizabeth Taylor and, yes, James Dean came to town to film the 1956 Warner Brothers film *Giant*.

And as for those New Yorkers: tiny, dusty Marfa has become a bit of a pilgrimage for art lovers thanks to one of the world's largest installations of minimalist art. This, in turn, has attracted a disproportionate amount of art galleries, quirky lodging options and interesting restaurants. Throw in some mysterious lights that may or may not be aliens (OK, probably not, but it's fun to pretend) and Marfa has become a majorly buzzed-about destination.

Orientation & Information
Yep, it's small. One mile in any direction from the center of town, and you've just left town.

San Antonio St (the in-town stretch of Hwy 90) is the main east–west thoroughfare, and Dean St bisects the town north–south.

Marfa is on its own schedule, which is pretty much made up according to whim. Plan on coming late in the week or on a weekend, because more than half the places you'll want to visit are closed early in the week.

To get started and pick up some handy maps, stop by the **Marfa Chamber of Commerce** (☎ 432-729-4942; www.marfacc.com; Hotel Paisano, 207 N Highland Ave; ⏲ 9am-6pm Mon-Fri, 10am-2pm Sat). For free internet access, stop by the **Marfa Public Library** (☎ 432-729-4631; 115 E Oak St) and if you need to restock your wallet, **Marfa National Bank** (☎ 729-4344; 301 S Highland) has a 24-hour ATM.

A book lover's oasis in the middle of desolate west Texas, **Marfa Book Company** (☎ 432-729-3906; 105 S Highland) stocks art books, guidebooks and a large selection of Texas literature.

Sights & Activities
CHINATI FOUNDATION
This is it. This is what all the fuss is about. Minimalist artist Donald Judd single-handedly put Marfa on the art-world map when he created the **Chinati Foundation** (☎ 432-729-4362; www.chinati.org; 1 Calvary Row; adult/student $10/5; ⏲ by guided tour only 10am & 2pm Wed-Sun). Judd moved to Marfa from New York City in the 1970s and took over a former army post, using the abandoned buildings to create and display one of the world's largest permanent installations of minimalist art.

This is great news if you like minimalist art. But the tour draws equal numbers of people who look like they're gazing upon works of genius and people who look like they're going to say 'What the hell was that about?' as soon as they get in their car. (It's also a bit of a commitment, taking up the better part of a day: the

---

WHAT THE...? PRADA

So you're driving along a two-lane highway in dusty west Texas, out in the middle of nowhere, when suddenly a small building appears up in the distance like a mirage. As you zip past it you glance over and see...a Prada store? Known as the **'Marfa Prada'** (although it's really closer to Valentine) this art installation doesn't sell $1700 handbags, but it does get your attention as a tongue-in-cheek commentary on consumerism.

tour is broken into two parts and goes from
10am to noon and 2pm to 4pm, though you
don't have to take both). Not sure if you're in
their demographic? It's worth a gander at the
website to make sure you're a fan.

GALLERY HOPPING
If you didn't come to Marfa for the art, you
might be surprised to find the amazing concentration of galleries in town. We're not
talking about rustic cowboy art framed in
barbed wire and old barn wood. And we're
not just talking about Donald Judd-esque
minimalism, either. The town has all sorts
of art to explore, most of it contemporary,
and you can pick up a list of galleries at the
chamber of commerce downstairs at the
Hotel Paisano.

Be sure to find out what's happening at
Ballroom Marfa (☎ 432-729-3600; www.ballroommarfa.
org; 108 E San Antonio; ☼ noon-6pm Thu-Sun), a nonprofit art space located in a former dance hall.
The focus on offbeat projects (including film
and music) means you could wander into a
room filled with red balloons or find yourself
chilling in a simulated living room listening
to vinyl and discussing music with some dude
from Austin.

MARFA MYSTERY LIGHTS
Ghost lights, mystery lights…call them what
you want, but the real mystery of the **Marfa
Lights** that flicker on the horizon at night
seems to be how many of the sightings are
actually just car headlights. There are con-
vincing enough accounts of mysterious lights
that appear and disappear – accounts that go
all the way back to before there was such a
thing as cars. In fact, the cowboy who first
reported seeing them in 1883 thought they
were Apache signal fires.

But, as it turns out, many of the all-too-
willing lights that appear from the viewing
center actually are headlights. And because
the Marfa Lights are one of west Texas' top
tourist attractions, no one wants to be too
specific about how to tell the real thing from
common cars, probably because the number
of satisfied customers would immediately
drop.

Try your luck at the **Marfa Lights Viewing Area**
about 8 miles east of Marfa on Hwy 90/67.
One thing's for sure, if the light is red and
starts to chase you, it's definitely a Marfa
Light.

MARFA AND PRESIDIO COUNTY MUSEUM
Wandering around this homegrown **museum**
(☎ 432-729-4140; 110 W San Antonio St; ☼ 1-5pm Thu-Sat)
is kind of like exploring your grandmother's
attic: lots of old stuff to look at that gives you
a glimpse into the past, but not necessarily
organized in any majorly prescriptive way.
The one area where the museum beats out
grandma is with its excellent collection of
black-and-white photography documenting
west Texas in the early 19th century.

Festivals & Events
Every May Marfa puts on the **Marfa Film Festival**
(www.marfafilmfestival.org), screening features and
shorts – including some of the Texas-centric
films that have used Marfa as a location. And
September brings the **Marfa Lights Festival** –
which has little to do with the lights and is
really just a good excuse to throw a town-wide
street party.

Sleeping
El Cosmico (☎ 432-729-1950; www.elcosmico.com; 802 S
Highland Ave; yurts $60, trailers $90-125; ☼) One of the
funkiest choices in all of Texas, El Cosmico
lets you sleep in a stylishly converted travel
trailer, a tepee or a yurt. It's not for everyone:
the grounds are dry and dusty, you might have
to shower outdoors, and there's no AC (luckily, it's cool at night). But, hey, how often do
you get to sleep in a Kozy Coach?

Riata Inn (☎ 432-729-3800; www.riatainn.com; Hwy
90 E; s/d $65/71; ☼ ☒) With all the interesting
choices in town, the main reason to choose
this motel is the low price – but the superfriendly manager is a nice plus. The parking
lot is also a prime viewing area for the Marfa
Lights.

Stay Marfa (☎ 888-627-3246; San Antonio & Dean
Sts; apt $79-119; ☒ ☼) For the price of a room,
you can enjoy a whole apartment decorated
in a cool, modern style that's one part Ikea,
one part art gallery. The apartments come
about their aesthetic rightly: they're owned
and decorated by the fellows at local gallery
inde/jacobs.

Hotel Paisano (☎ 432-729-3669; www.hotelpaisano.
com; 207 N Highland Ave; d $99-220; ☒ ▯ ☼ ☒)
Marfa's historic hotel has a unique claim to
fame: it's where the cast of the movie *Giant*
stayed. James Dean's room and Elizabeth
Taylor's suite are oft requested. Some of the
rooms could stand a little updating, but the
place does have a dignified charm, along with

a snazzy indoor pool and a touch of taxidermy for good measure.

Thunderbird (☎ 432-729-1984; www.thunderbird marfa.com; 601 West San Antonio Street; d $120-150; 🛜 🖥) This classic 1950s motel was reopened in 2005 as a small boutique with a spiffy new look. The rooms are hip and minimalist, and the grounds and common areas are as cool as the desert air at night.

Cibolo Creek Ranch (☎ 432-229-3737; www.cibolo creekranch.com; d/ste $325/500; ⊠ 🛜 🖥) If you just really want to get away from it all, this luxurious private ranch is definitely *away*. Marfa is the closest town, but it's still a 45-minute drive (part of the reason the ranch offers a meal plan for an additional $75 a day). They even have a private airstrip, and, if for some reason you don't have your own plane, arrangements can be made.

Eating & Drinking

Padre's (☎ 432-729-4425; 209 W El Paso St; meals $3-8; ⏰ 11:30am-10:30pm Mon-Sat) Thank goodness for Padre's. With the fickle schedules of so many local restaurants, you need a place that will actually stay open and feed you. Sure, it's bar food, like burgers and Frito pie, but the plus side of that is, there's also a bar – something else that's hard to come by in Marfa.

Cochineal (☎ 432-729-3300; 107 W San Antonio St; breakfast $4-10, dinner $22-34; ⏰ 8:30am-12:30pm Thu-Sun & 6-10pm daily) The menu changes regularly, due to a focus on local, organic ingredients, but Cochineal is where foodies get their fix at dinnertime. It's also one of the few places you can get a proper breakfast, which is a treat.

Squeeze Marfa (☎ 432-729-4500; 215 N Highland Ave; mains $5-8; ⏰ 9am-4pm Tue-Sat) This cute little cafe serves breakfast, lunch and smoothies, all the better to enjoy on the pleasant, shady patio. The address is on Highland, but the entrance is on Lincoln.

ourpick **Food Shark** (☎ 432-386-6540; 105 S Highland; meals $5-8; ⏰ 11:30am-3pm Tue-Fri) See that battered old food trailer pulled up under the open-air pavilion where the weekend farmer's market is? You do? Lucky you! That means Food Shark is open for business. If you're lucky enough to catch them, you'll find incredibly fresh food like pulled-pork tacos and the specialty, the Marfalafel. Daily specials are excellent, and sell out early.

Blue Javelina (☎ 432-729-1919; 1300 W San Antonio; meals $18-32; ⏰ 6-10pm Fri-Sun, closed summer)

GODDESS OF JUSTICE

High atop the **Presidio County Courthouse** dome is the Goddess of Justice, one hand holding a sword and the other holding – hey, wait, where are her scales? Her empty left hand, which lingers in the air almost like she's checking her watch, probably did once hold a set of scales, as Goddesses of Justice so often do. But legend has it that a gun-slinging cowboy back in the late 1800s shot them out of her hand with a rifle, saying, 'There is no justice in Presidio County.' One way or the other, it makes a good story, and when the courthouse was restored in 2001 no attempt was made to restore the scales.

Embracing the local zeitgeist, Blue Javelina has minimalist hours (only 12 a week), a minimalist menu (only six entrees) and a minimalist decor (inside a former gas station). The innovative dishes don't hold back though.

Getting There & Away

There is an airport in Marfa, but you can't catch a flight there unless you actually charter one. Closest airports for the non–Howard Hughes set are Midland (156 miles) and El Paso (190 miles). You can, however, catch a Greyhound. The **bus station** (☎ 432-729-8174; 3988 Hwy 90 W) is at the old Jimenez Chevron Station, and Amtrak serves nearby Alpine (26 miles).

ALPINE
pop 5786

Centrally located as the hub between Fort Davis, Marfa and Marathon, Alpine is about a half-hour drive from any of them. And it's not just a hub, geographically speaking: it's the seat of Brewster County and the biggest of the four towns, offering services and amenities the others don't. It may not have the unique draws of the other towns, but it's the only city of more than 5000 people, and it also has the area's sole four-year college and its only modern hospital.

Orientation

Alpine is at the junction of Hwy 90 and Hwy 118, 26 miles east of Marfa, 31 miles west of Marathon, 26 miles southeast of Fort Davis and 78 miles north of Terlingua. In town, Hwy 90 breaks up into two one-way streets: Ave E, which travels southwest toward Marfa, and Holland Ave, which heads northeast toward Marathon.

Information
BOOKSTORES
Front Street Books (☎ 432-837-3360; 121 E Holland Ave) The best bookstore in town is open daily and has a smart selection of new, used and out-of-print titles – and the *New York Times* and *Wall Street Journal,* rare commodities out this way. Sometimes national papers come in a day late, providing customers with 'USA Yesterday,' according to the shop assistant.

LIBRARIES
Alpine Public Library (☎ 432-837-2621; 203 N 7th St) Free internet access.
Bryan Wildenthal Library (☎ 432-837-8123) At Sul Ross State University, it's open to the public, too. Free internet access.

MEDICAL SERVICES
Big Bend Regional Medical Center (☎ 432-837-3447; 2600 Hwy 118 N) One of the region's most state-of-the-art hospitals, offering basic care and an emergency room.

MONEY
Fort Davis State Bank (☎ 432-837-1888; 1102 E Holland Ave) A 24-hr ATM service near Sul Ross State University.
West Texas National Bank (☎ 432-837-3375; 101 East Ave E) A 24-hour ATM service right in the middle of town.

POST
Post office (☎ 432-837-9565; 901 Holland Ave W)

TOURIST INFORMATION
Alpine Chamber of Commerce (☎ 432-837-2326; www.alpinetexas.com; 106 N 3rd St) Alpine's Main St organization has put together a 'Historic Walking & Windshield Tour' brochure featuring 39 stops in the downtown area plus a few notable spots further out. Get a copy of the brochure at the chamber office or many local businesses.

Sights & Activities
MUSEUM OF THE BIG BEND
This interesting little **museum** (☎ 432-837-8143; admission free, donation accepted; ☽ 9am-5pm Tue-Sat, 1-5pm Sun) has been around since 1937, but a complete renovation in 2006 makes it a great place to brush up on the history of the Big

Bend region. Learn about how Big Bend was once under the sea, and find out how camels fit into the region's history. The museum is designed for maximum visual appeal, incorporating broad and impressive recreations rather than cases full of relics. Reading is kept to a minimum, but, when called for, the beautifully designed signage draws you right in.

Most impressive? The enormous wing bone of the Texas Pterosaur found in Big Bend National Park – the largest flying creature ever found, with an estimated wing span of more than 50ft – along with the intimidatingly large recreation of the whole bird that's big enough to snatch up a fully grown human and carry him off for dinner.

ROCK HUNTING
Hunt for red plume and pom-pom Texas agate, jasper, labradorite feldspar, calcite, opal and other minerals at the **Woodward Ranch** (☎ 432-364-2271; adult/under 6yr $5/free). This 100-year-old cattle ranch is 16 miles south of town on Hwy 118 and has 2400 acres open to rock hounds. It's $2 a pound for whatever you keep, or, if you prefer easy pickings, visit its **rock shop** (admission free; ☽ 9am-5pm).

SWIMMING
Sul Ross State University's **swimming pool** (☎ 432-837-8236; admission $1; ☽ 4-8pm Mon-Fri, 2-6pm Sat & Sun) is open to the public late afternoons when classes are in session.

Festivals & Events
Preserving the oral tradition of the American West, the annual **Cowboy Poetry Gathering** (www.cowboy-poetry.org) is held every year in late February or early March. This down-home event takes over most of town, from university classrooms to Kokernot Park. Poetry recitations, gun-twirling pistolero demonstrations and chuck-wagon breakfasts are just some of the activities.

Sul Ross State University is the birthplace of intercollegiate rodeo, and many members of the Sul Ross Rodeo Club have gone on to win national championships. Watch these collegiate cowboys strut their stuff each fall at the **Sul Ross National Intercollegiate Rodeo Association Rodeo**.

Sleeping
You must book hotel rooms several months in advance if you plan on attending the Cowboy

Poetry Gathering in March. If everything below is booked, visit the chamber of commerce website at www.alpinetexas.com for more lodging options.

Antelope Lodge (☎ 432-837-2451, 800-880-8106; www.antelopelodge.com; 2310 W Hwy 90; d $49-65) You'd think from the name you were getting a hunting lodge, but it's nothing like that. Rustic stucco cottages with Spanish tile roofs – each one holding two guest rooms – sit sprinkled about a shady lawn. There's a casual, pleasant vibe, and the rooms have kitchenettes, making this a great value for your money.

Oak Tree Inn (☎ 432-837-5711; www.oaktreeinn.com; 2407 E Hwy 90; d $55-89) It doesn't have a ton of personality, but this motel covers the basics in a clean, dependable and generic style, and it's convenient to Sul Ross State University.

our pick Holland Hotel (☎ 432-837-3844, 800-535-8040; www.thehollandhoteltexas.com; 209 W Holland Ave; d $90-110, ste $110-210) Some renovations suck all the original charm out of a historic property, and some don't go far enough in updating it. But sometimes they get it just right. Built in 1928 and beautifully renovated in 2009, the Holland is a Spanish Colonial building furnished in an understated, hacienda-style decor that retains all of its 1930s charm, but with just the right contemporary touches. Add in a lovely (and free!) breakfast, and you'll feel downright pampered.

Maverick Inn (☎ 432-837-0628; www.themaverickinn.com; 1200 E Holland Ave; d $95-145;) The maverick road-tripper will feel right at home at this retro motor court that's been smartly renovated to include luxury bedding and flat-screen TVs. We can't help but love this place, from the west Texas–style furnishings to the cool neon-art sign to the resident cat. Plus, the pool is mighty nice after a hot, dusty day.

Eating
Alicia's Burrito Place (☎ 432-837-2802; 708 East Ave G; mains $4-9; 8am-8pm Mon-Fri, 9am-3pm Sat & Sun) Alicia's is known for its quick and hot breakfast burritos, which, yes, is a Texas thing. Eggs, bacon and the like get rolled up in a portable meal you can eat with your hands – known to cure a hangover or two in their time.

Bread & Breakfast (☎ 432-837-9424; 114 W Holland Ave; mains $5-9; 7am-2pm Mon-Sat) The name is kind of misleading in that they also have lunch, but that's just not as alliterative. This pleasant little bakery/cafe is adept at the baked goods; if nothing else, stop in for a brownie.

La Casita (☎ 432-837-2842; 1104 East Ave H; mains $5-10; 11am-8:30pm Mon-Sat) This Mexican restaurant is one of the most popular places in town. If you can get a seat, join the locals over a plate (and be careful, the plate is hot) of spicy, cheesy specialties.

Penny's Diner (☎ 432-837-5711; 2407 E Hwy 90; mains $6-8; 24hr) Chrome, neon, those little spinny counter stools – Penny's may not be an authentic 1950s diner, but it sure plays up the rock-around-the-clock style. Not many towns the size of Alpine can boast a 24-hour restaurant, and you may thank us if you roll into town after the town's rolled up the sidewalks.

Reata (☎ 432-837-9232; 203 N 5th St; lunch $8-14, dinner $14-32; 11:30am-2pm daily & 5-10pm Mon-Sat) Named after the ranch in the movie *Giant*, Reata does turn on the upscale ranch-style charm – at least in the front dining room, where the serious diners go. Step back into the lively bar area or onto the shady patio and it's a completely different vibe where you can feel free to nibble your way around the menu and enjoy a margarita. The tortilla soup brought us back the next day for seconds.

Entertainment
It may be a small town, but it's a college town, which means Alpine does have a thing or two going on after dark.

Harry's Tinaja (☎ 432-837-5060; 412 E Holland Ave) It's a bit of a dive, but it's a fun one, with pool, darts and live music, plus plenty of outdoor seating.

Railroad Blues (☎ 432-837-3103, 504 W Holland Ave) This is the place to go in Alpine for live music and the biggest beer selection in Big Bend Country. The club frequently draws Austin-based musicians who are heading west on tour.

Getting There & Around
There's no scheduled flights round these parts, but Alpine's airport, north of town along Hwy 118, can accommodate charter flights.

There is, however, an **Amtrak station** (☎ 800-872-7245; www.amtrak.com; 102 W Holland Ave). The train frequently runs anywhere from one to eight hours late in both directions, so it's important to call Amtrak to get an update before setting out for the train station. Check the website for prices and schedules.

BIG BEND & WEST TEXAS

Alpine is served by **Greyhound** (☎ 432-837-5302; 804 W Holland Ave) with service to and from El Paso, San Antonio and beyond.

Rental cars are available from **Alpine Auto Rental** (☎ 432-837-3463; www.alpineautorental.com; 2501 E Hwy 90).

MARATHON
pop 455

Just don't show up and call it 'Mar-a-THON' like it's a race. If you want to fit in 'round these parts you have got to say 'Mar-a-thun,' and it helps if you're wearing a hat and give a friendly nod each time you say it.

This tiny railroad town has two claims to fame: it's the closest town to Big Bend's north entrance, providing a last chance to fill up your car and your stomach before immersing yourself in the park. And it's got the Gage Hotel, a true Texas treasure that's a worthwhile reason to stay a while – at least overnight.

If you want to know more about Marathon, you can get in touch with the **Marathon Chamber of Commerce** (☎ 432-386-4516; www.marathontexas.com; 105 Hwy 90 W) in Front Street Books and they'll help you explore all your options.

Sights & Activities
There's not a whole lot do in Marathon for the average tourist. If you're into bird-watching or feel in the mood for a picnic, you could head 5 miles south of town on Ave D, west of 385, to **Fort Peña Colorado** – a former military outpost that's now a public park known locally as 'the Post.'

Festivals & Events
Pronunciation aside, with a name like Marathon, this was bound to happen. The **Marathon2Marathon** (www.marathon2marathon.net) is a 26.2 mile run through the desert from Alpine to Marathon, and it's a qualifying race for the Boston Marathon, which, after west Texas, should be a cinch. Runners and nonrunners alike mark the occasion with a street festival.

Sleeping
For such a small town, there are actually several interesting lodging options, including rental houses. Check out the listings on www.marathontexas.com.

Marathon Motel (☎ 432-386-4241; W Hwy 90; s/d $70/80;) A lot of places in Texas seem to have their claim to fame, and this little old motor court got its 15 minutes when it was used as a location for the filming of Wim Wenders' film, *Paris, Texas* – although, if you know the movie, you'll be glad to know it's been fixed up.

our pick **Gage Hotel** (☎ 432-386-4205, 800-884-4243; www.gagehotel.com; 101 US 90 W; d $90-97, with bathroom $115-198) This Old West hotel has a fabulous style that's matched only by its love of taxidermy. Each room at this property is individually (though similarly) decorated with Indian blankets, cowboy gear and leather accents. The original building was designed by Henry Trost and built in 1927, and the Los Portales annex has more expensive rooms that surround the lovely pool.

Eating & Drinking
French Co. Grocer (☎ 432-386-4522; 206 N Ave D; 7:30am-9pm Mon-Fri, from 8am Sat, from 9am Sun) Stock up on picnic supplies for the road or enjoy them at the tables outside at this charming little grocery – formerly the WM French General Merchandise store, established in 1900.

Famous Burro (☎ 432-386-4100; cnr Hwy 90 & Post Rd; mains $12-22; restaurant 6-9pm Wed-Sat, bar 5pm-midnight Wed-Sun) This bar-restaurant in a funky old filling station changes its upscale comfort-food menu weekly. Sometimes there's live music, sometimes it's movie night, but it's a fun and laid-back place to hang out any old time.

Ranch 616 (☎ 432-386-4205; 101 US 90 W; dinner mains $28-42; lunch & dinner) This restaurant at the Gage has the same kind of upscale Western comforts as the hotel, and the food is fresh and delectable. Lunch is served seasonally but nobody could seem to agree what that season was.

White Buffalo Bar (☎ 432-386-4205; 101 US 90 W) Guess what's on the wall of this upscale bar located in the Gage Hotel? Not just taxidermy but *rare* taxidermy. Enjoy a margarita, and try to ignore his glassy stare.

Getting There & Away
There is no public transportation to Marathon. Amtrak serves Alpine, 32 miles west on Hwy 90.

EL PASO

pop 609,400

Well, you've made it. You're just about as far west in Texas as you can go. Surrounded mostly by New Mexico to the north and Mexico to the south, El Paso is wedged between the two like a splinter. In fact, at times the city seems to have more in common with its non-Texas neighbors than it does with Texas itself.

Sadly, El Paso and its sister city – Ciudad Juárez, Mexico, which is right across the river – have had a bit of a falling out. At one time, the two cities were inextricably linked, with tourists streaming back and forth across the Good Neighbor International Bridge all day long. But with the rise in gang- and drug-related violence, Juárez has become so dangerous that there is now little traffic between the two sides.

Even with Mexico out of the equation, there's still plenty to do. Outdoorsy types can enjoy cycling in the largest urban park in the US, with over 24,000 acres to explore, and the warm weather makes nearby Hueco Tanks an ideal destination for wintertime rock climbing. Or you can go the culture route and enjoy some of El Paso's excellent museums, most of which are free. Ride the gondola to a mountain peak, buy handcrafted boots and, by all means, eat some of the city's famous red enchiladas.

HISTORY

Although Indians of the Tampachoa tradition lived in El Paso area a thousand or more years ago, Europeans first found El Paso in the 16th century – either in the 1530s when Álvar Núñez Cabeza de Vaca traveled from the Gulf Coast at present-day Galveston to the Pacific Coast of Mexico, or during the 1581 Rodriguez-Chamuscado party.

The first El Paso del Norte was built at what is now Juárez in 1659; the Mexican city kept that name until 1888, when the new name was given to honor Mexican president Benito Juárez. In 1680, a pueblo Indian revolt in New Mexico launched a wave of refugees – some Tigua, some Spaniards and some of uncertain origin – southeast along the Rio Grande. In their new home of Ysleta del Sur and in nearby Socorro, the refugees established what are now the oldest permanent settlements in Texas.

The town now known as El Paso started in 1827; early on, it was named Franklin, after a prominent Anglo settler. A US Army post, the first Fort Bliss, was established in 1849 to protect US interests after the end of the Mexican War. Franklin voted to join Texas in 1850, and the city incorporated as El Paso in 1873. The last 20 years of the 19th century proved to be El Paso's Wild West era, as gunfighters followed the railroads to town. John Wesley Hardin, among the most famous, lived and died here.

Juárez was the scene of one of the first major battles of the Mexican Revolution, an event of major importance on both sides of the border. Mexicans fled to safety in El Paso, and even Pancho Villa briefly took refuge here before turning against the US government for its support of his foe, Venustiano Carranza. In 1916, US President Woodrow Wilson dispatched an expedition led by General John J 'Black Jack' Pershing to search for Villa. The mission proved unsuccessful, but it strengthened Fort Bliss' position as a major military post, a role it still has today.

The mid-20th century was marked by the resolution of a controversy that had been simmering ever since the Mexican War: fixing the US–Mexico border by channeling the Rio Grande into a concrete ditch between El Paso and Juárez. But even with the border demarcated and separate allegiances, El Paso and

---

FIRST THANKSGIVING

We all know that the first Thanksgiving was celebrated in 1621 at Plymouth, right? Not so fast, says El Paso. In 1598, while traveling from Mexico to Santa Fe with an eye toward settling the Southwest, Don Juan de Oñate led 500 followers to the banks of the Rio Grande at what is now San Elizario, Texas. There, the Spanish colonists met with Native Americans for what many El Pasoans say was the real first Thanksgiving, 23 years before the Pilgrims feasted at Plymouth Rock in Massachusetts. Anyone who loves their traditional Thanksgiving feast should give thanks that we celebrate the 1621 version, since the 1598 event occurred on April 30. (Just try finding fresh pumpkin in April.)

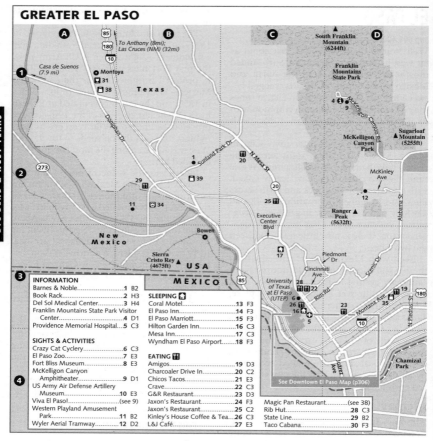

GREATER EL PASO

INFORMATION	
Barnes & Noble	1 B2
Book Rack	2 H3
Del Sol Medical Center	3 H4
Franklin Mountains State Park Visitor	
Center	4 D1
Providence Memorial Hospital	5 C3

SIGHTS & ACTIVITIES	
Crazy Cat Cyclery	6 C3
El Paso Zoo	7 E3
Fort Bliss Museum	8 E3
McKelligon Canyon	
Amphitheater	9 D1
US Army Air Defense Artillery	
Museum	10 E3
Viva El Paso!	(see 9)
Western Playland Amusement	
Park	11 B2
Wyler Aerial Tramway	12 D2

SLEEPING	
Coral Motel	13 F3
El Paso Inn	14 F3
El Paso Marriott	15 F3
Hilton Garden Inn	16 C3
Mesa Inn	17 C3
Wyndham El Paso Airport	18 F3

EATING	
Amigos	19 D3
Charcoaler Drive In	20 C2
Chicos Tacos	21 E3
Crave	22 C3
G&R Restaurant	23 C3
Jaxon's Restaurant	24 F3
Jaxon's Restaurant	25 C2
Kinley's House Coffee & Tea	26 C3
L&J Café	27 E3

Magic Pan Restaurant	(see 38)
Rib Hut	28 C3
State Line	29 B2
Taco Cabana	30 F3

Juárez will always remain tightly connected if for no other reason than because of their geographical proximity.

ORIENTATION

El Paso is wedged between Mexico and New Mexico, so far west that east is the only direction you can drive without leaving Texas. It's a sprawling city of 240 sq miles, but much of that space is taken up by Fort Bliss and the enormous Franklin Mountains State Park. The Franklin Mountains divide the city into a west side and an east side, with downtown sitting due south of the mountains, and the I-10 serving as the primary through-route. Just south of downtown is the Rio Grande and, across the river, Juárez, Mexico.

INFORMATION
Bookstores

Barnes and Noble (Map p302; ☎ 915-581-5353; 705 Sunland Park Dr, West El Paso) Popular with the local literati, with a packed calendar of author signings and special events.

Book Rack (Map p302; ☎ 915-598-2279; 10780 Pebble Hills Blvd) In East El Paso, you can find a huge selection of new and used books.

Bookery (off Map p302; ☎ 915-859-4066; 10167 Socorro Rd) On the Mission Trail, an interesting small shop specializing in Hispanic literature and books for children.

Emergency & Medical Services

Del Sol Medical Center (Map p302; ☎ 915-595-9000; 10301 Gateway Blvd) Provides acute care and emergency services.

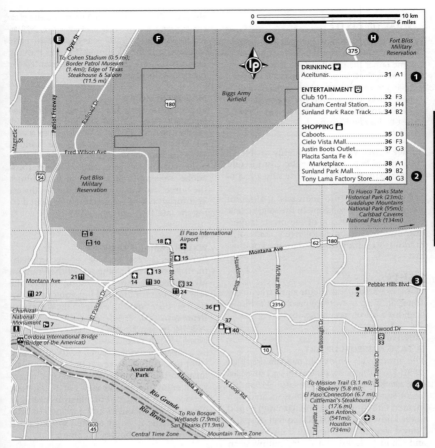

Highway Patrol (☎ 915-855-2105)
Providence Memorial Hospital (Map p302; ☎ 915-577-6011; 2001 N Oregon St)
Sheriff's Department (☎ 915-546-2280)

Internet Access
El Paso Public Library (Map p306; ☎ 915-543-5433; www.ci.el-paso.tx.us/library; 501 N Oregon; ◷ 9am-8pm Mon-Thu, 11am-6pm Fri, 9am-6pm Sat, 1-5pm Sun) Free internet access. Check the website for additional branches.

Money
Bank of America (Map p306; ☎ 915-532-5356; 330 N Stanton St) ATM and currency exchange available.
Bank of the West (Map p306; 500 N Mesa St) Has a 24-hour drive-up ATM.

Post
Post Office (Map p306; ☎ 915-532-8824; 219 E Mills Ave; ◷ 8:30am-5pm Mon-Fri, 8:30am-noon Sat). Call ☎ 800-275-8777 to locate other branches.

Tourist Information
El Paso Convention and Visitors Bureau (Map p306; ☎ 915-534-0601; www.visitelpaso.com; 1 Civic Center Plaza; ◷ 8am-5pm Mon-Sat) Stocks racks and racks of brochures, and the staff is quite helpful. They also have a well-populated website for planning.

DANGERS & ANNOYANCES
El Paso is among the safest cities of its size in the US. This is due in part to Operation Hold the Line, an effort to crack down on illegal immigration into El Paso. Green-and-white

BIG BEND & WEST TEXAS

WHAT TIME IS IT?

When it comes to time zones, El Paso sides with New Mexico, conforming to Mountain Time rather than Central Time like the rest of Texas. Confusing? Occasionally. If you're telling someone in neighboring Van Horn or Fort Stockton what time you'll meet them, be sure to add on the extra hour you'll lose just by leaving El Paso.

Border Patrol vehicles are highly visible all along the El Paso side of the Rio Grande, and the police presence has had the side effect of quelling crime.

Crossing over into Juárez is a different story. While El Paso is one of the safest cities, Juárez has become one of the most dangerous, due to gruesome violence – some of it random – resulting from drug wars. For now, just say no.

SIGHTS

Many of El Paso's museums are free or by donation. Visit www.freeelpaso.com/exhibits.html for a list of free things to do.

Downtown
EL PASO MUSEUM OF ART

This thoroughly enjoyable **museum** (Map p306; ☎ 915-532-1707; www.elpasoartmuseum.org; 1 Arts Festival Plaza; admission free, special exhibits extra; ☿ 9am-5pm Tue-Sat, 9am-9pm Thu, noon-5pm Sun) is located in a former Greyhound station (though you'd never know it) with 104,000 sq feet of space. They'd want us to brag about their Madonna and Child (c 1200), but their Southwestern art is terrific, and the engaging modern pieces round out the collection nicely. All this, and it's free?! Well done, El Paso, well done.

EL PASO MUSEUM OF HISTORY

This **museum** (Map p306; ☎ 915-351-3588; www.elpasotexas.gov/history; 510 N Santa Fe St; admission free; ☿ 10am-5pm Tue-Sat, noon-5pm Sun) has a shiny, new location in the heart of the downtown museum district. It's not huge and sometimes there seems to be a lot of reading, but it's an easy stop-off if you're already at Insights or the Museum of Art.

EL PASO HOLOCAUST MUSEUM

It may seem a little anachronistic in a predominately Hispanic town, but the **Holocaust**

Museum (Map p306; ☎ 915-351-0048; www.elpasoholocaustmuseum.org; 715 N Oregon St; admission free; ☿ 9am-4pm Tue-Fri, 1-5pm Sat & Sun) is as much a surprise inside as out for its thoughtful and moving exhibits that are imaginatively presented for maximum impact.

MAGOFFIN HOME

One of Texas' best kept secrets, this El Paso **landmark** (Map p306; ☎ 915-533-5147; www.visitmagoffinhome.com; 1120 Magoffin Ave; adult/student or senior with ID $2/1; ☿ guided tour 9am-4pm) was built in 1875 for Joseph Magoffin, an early El Paso politician and businessman. With 4ft-thick adobe walls and many original furnishings, the home is a fine example of the Southwest Territorial style of architecture prevalent during the late 19th century.

North
WYLER AERIAL TRAMWAY

Sure, you'd feel a sense of accomplishment if you hiked to the top of the Franklin Mountains. We're not suggesting you take the easy way out (or are we?) but you can get instant gratification with a ride on the **Wyler Aerial Tramway** (Map p302; ☎ 915-566-6622; McKinley Ave; adult/child $7/4; ☿ noon-5pm Wed-Mon, later on weekends & in summer). It only takes about four minutes in the Swiss-made gondolas to glide 2400ft, gaining 940ft in elevation, to reach the viewing platform on top of Ranger Peak (5632ft), where you'll enjoy spectacular views of Texas, New Mexico and Mexico. For maximum enjoyment, bring binoculars and a jacket – maybe even a picnic to enjoy at the top (but leave alcohol and glass bottles at home).

BORDER PATROL MUSEUM

At first, this may seem like a weird little niche **museum** (off Map p302; ☎ 915-759-6060; 4315 Transmountain Rd; donation suggested; ☿ 9am-5pm Tue-Sat), but the more time you spend in west Texas, the more you recognize the Border Patrol as an integral part of the culture. There's not much nuance to the exhibits – it feels like they just stuck some of the more interesting stuff they had in storage into one big room, with some rather big and intimidating chase vehicles at the other end. But there are some interesting artifacts representing both sides of the river. As for the gift shop: what little girl wouldn't be thrilled with a plush pink pony with a Border Patrol logo embroidered on it?

FORT BLISS

As the largest air defense training center in the Western world, Fort Bliss consumes much of the desert northeast of El Paso, and trains troops from all the NATO-allied nations. The **Fort Bliss Museum** (Map p302; ☎ 915-568-4518; 5054 Pleasanton Rd; admission free; 9am-4:30pm) is housed in a reconstruction of the fort's 1854–68 location. It depicts life at the post in 1857, right down to the 31-star flag hanging outside.

One block south, the **US Army Air Defense Artillery Museum** (Map p302; ☎ 915-568-5412; 5000 Pleasanton Rd; admission free; 9am-4:30pm) is the only one of its kind in the US. Its exhibits focus on the history of air defense artillery since 1917, including an outdoor weapons park.

FRANKLIN MOUNTAINS STATE PARK

At 23,863 acres, **Franklin Mountains State Park** (admission $4; 8am-5pm Sep-May, 8am-8pm Jun-Aug) is the largest urban park in the US, capped by 7192ft North Franklin Peak. Although it's in the middle of a city, it's home to ringtail cats, coyotes and a number of other smaller animals and reptiles.

Head to the **visitor center** (Map p302; ☎ 915-566-6441; 1331 McKelligon Canyon Rd) to get a basic park map, written descriptions of the hiking trails, mountain-bike trail maps, or maps of the 17 different rock-climbing routes. The park has 118 miles of mountain-bike, hiking and equestrian trails. The most popular hike, the Ron Coleman Trail, takes off from Smuggler's Pass and winds 3.5 miles to McKelligon Canyon.

VIVA EL PASO!

For a lively introduction to local history, head for **Viva El Paso!** (Map p302; ☎ 915-565-6900; Thu-Sat), an outdoor theatrical extravaganza held every summer in McKelligon Canyon Park's amphitheater. Singing! Dancing! History! Exclamation points!

East
SCENIC DRIVE

Popular at night for viewing city lights, Scenic Dr offers great views of El Paso, Juárez and the surrounding mountains. To get there, take N Mesa St to Kerbey Ave (across from the University), head east til Kerbey becomes Rim Road, then turn right on Scenic Dr. En route, keep an eye out for little Murchison Park – at 4222ft, a fine spot for sunrises.

MISSION TRAIL

Ready for some local history? This 9-mile trail (off Map p302) links two mission churches and a presidio chapel, all of which are on the National Register of Historic Places. Privately owned by the Catholic Diocese, they're not always as visitor-friendly as you might like, but you can arrange a tour or get more information from the **El Paso Mission Trail Association** (☎ 915-851-9997; www.elpasomissiontrail.com; 1 Civic Center Plaza).

The best known of the three is **Mission Ysleta** (☎ 915-859-9848; 131 S Zaragoza Rd; 7am-6pm Mon-Sun), Texas' oldest continually active parish. Although the original structure from 1682 is long gone, the current church built from adobe bricks, clay and straw dates back to 1851, and a beautiful, silver-domed bell tower was added in the 1880s.

The surrounding community of **Ysleta del Sur Pueblo** is sovereign home to the Tigua tribe and is recognized by many as the oldest town in Texas. Despite Spanish influences, the Tigua have strived mightily to retain their identity as the oldest identifiable ethnic group in Texas. A visit to the **Tigua Cultural Center**

GAY & LESBIAN EL PASO

The scene is certainly more under-the-radar than in cosmopolitan Dallas or laid-back Austin, but there are still some organizations and bars ready to welcome you to town. The most gay-friendly businesses are downtown near the Camino Real Hotel (p308).

Travelers can find gay-friendly businesses at **GayCities** (http://elpaso.gaycities.com), including bars, shops, restaurants and hotels. To find out what's going on around town, check out the events calendar at **Rio Grande Adelante** (http://rgadelante.org).

Old Plantation (Map p306; ☎ 915-533-6055; 301 S Ochoa St) has been around forever. It's definitely the main gay bar and one of the best dance clubs in town.

Nearby, **Whatever Lounge** (Map p306; ☎ 915-533-0215; 701 E Paisano Dr) has a predominantly Spanish-speaking gay clientele.

BIG BEND & WEST TEXAS

DOWNTOWN EL PASO

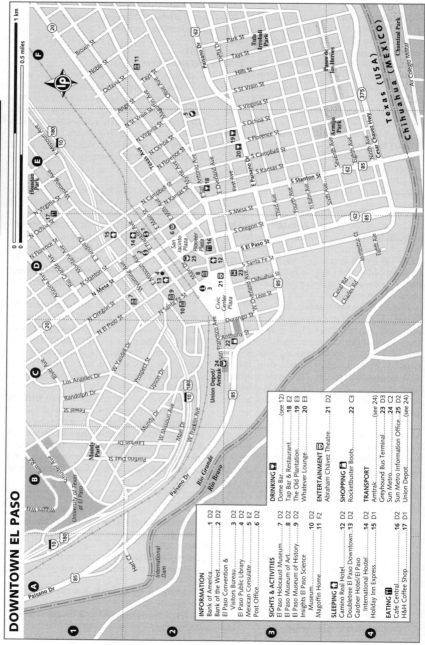

(☎ 915-859-5287; 305 Yaya Lane; admission free; ☯ 10am-4pm Wed-Sun) proves the struggles have not been in vain.

Two miles from Ysleta is **Socorro Mission** (☎ 915-859-7718; 328 S Nevarez Rd; ☯ 10am-3pm Mon-Fri, 10am-6pm Sat, 9am-1pm Sun). Originally built in 1681 by the Piro Indians, who later assimilated into the Tiguas, the church was repeatedly rebuilt after Rio Grande flooding. Although the outside is fairly plain, the inside has some impressive decorative touches, including beautifully hand-painted roof beams rescued from the 18th-century mission.

Last stop is the presidio chapel of **San Elizario** (☎ 915-851-2333; 1556 San Elizario Rd, San Elizario; ☯ 7-11am Mon-Fri), located on a military fort established for the Spanish government in 1684. Today, peaceful San Elizario is notable for its 1882 church and the adjacent town plaza where de Oñate issued his 1598 proclamation claiming the region for Spain.

ACTIVITIES

Crazy Cat Cyclery (Map p302; ☎ 915-577-9666; 2625 N Mesa St; bike rental half/full day $10/40; ☯ 10am-8pm Mon-Sat to 6pm Sun) is the best source of local cycling information and equipment. Some of the city's best mountain biking is five minutes away, and they'll point you in the right direction and sell you a map if you'd like one. They also offer scheduled group rides led by enthusiastic cyclists.

Out in the lower valley, **Rio Bosque Wetlands Park** (off Map p302; ☎ 915-747-8663; Ave of the Americas at Pan American Dr; ☯ dawn-dusk) offers walking tours several times a month. A network of natural surface trails weaves through the wetlands and a fully paved loop trail is in the works. It is really hard to find, so call to get directions, but it's worth the adventure because of the birds to see.

EL PASO FOR KIDS

El Paso Zoo (Map p302; ☎ recorded information 915-544-1928, business line 915-521-1850; 4001 E Paisano Dr; adult/ 3-12yr/senior $10/6/7.50; ☯ 9:30am-5pm) Home to a large number of endangered animals, including the Asian elephant, Sumatran orangutan, Indo-Chinese tiger and the rare Amur Leopard. All told, 700 animals represent 240 species packed into 35 acres. It's not the biggest or most impressive you've ever seen, but it's worth a visit. And it's mercifully shady for both the animals and you.

Insights El Paso Science Museum (Map p306; ☎ 915-534-0000; www.insightselpaso.org; 505 N Santa Fe St; adult/4-11yr/student $6/4/5; ☯ 10am-5pm

Tue-Sat, noon-5pm Sun) Play scientist for a day at this fun, hands-on museum, which brings science to life with interactive exhibits. Needless to say, it's a hit with the kids, but adults can get into it, too (especially if they show up after all the school buses depart).

Western Playland Amusement Park (Map p302; ☎ 575-589-3410; www.westernplayland.com; 1249 Futurity Dr, Sunland Park, NM; admission $5, per ride $2, full access $16; ☯ hours vary, check website) Small but fun, this old-school amusement park is just over the border in New Mexico, and it's a great way to burn off the pent-up kid energy.

TOURS

Border Sights Tours (☎ 915-533-5454; www.bordersights-tours-of-elpaso.com; pick-up at your location; adult/under 18yr $45/20) Tours of the city, Mission Trail and more, as well as specialty tours (extra charge) like wine-tasting – all north of the border.

El Paso Convention and Visitors Bureau (Map p306; ☎ 915-534-0601; www.visitelpaso.com; 1 Civic Center Plaza; ☯ 8am-5pm Mon-Sat) Has a plethora of downloadable walking tours available on its website; click on 'Itineraries' in the 'Things to See & Do' section. Or stop by the center for a hard copy. The self-guided pamphlet, 'El Paso Downtown Historic Walking Tour,' takes about 90 minutes to complete. It's an excellent brochure, and it's free.

Si El Paso Tours (☎ 915-541-1308; www.sielpasotours. com) Offers tours of the town and sometimes sponsors tours led by special guests.

FESTIVALS & EVENTS

Southwestern International Livestock Show and Rodeo Takes over the El Paso County Coliseum for the first two weeks of each February.

Don Juan de Oñate's First Thanksgiving Reenactment (see the boxed text, p301) is staged on the last weekend of April, with festivities at Chamizal National Monument and San Elizario.

LOS MURALES

They're not always mentioned in guidebooks – maybe because they're primarily in the poorest areas of town – but Los Murales, the murals of El Paso, are perhaps the city's preeminent cultural treasure. Of the more than 100 murals in the city, the greatest concentrations are south of downtown between Paisano Dr and the Border Hwy and north of Paisano Dr near Douglass Elementary School. Stop by the convention and visitors bureau (p303) for a map.

International Mariachi Festival In September, El Paso and Juárez team up to celebrate in downtown El Paso.

Amigo Airsho (www.amigoairsho.org) Flying performers of all sorts gather in Biggs Field for this October event. Most of the action takes place up in the air, but there's also entertainment down on the ground.

Sun Bowl College Football Classic (☎ 800-915-2695; www.sunbowl.org) Takes place the last week in December at Sun Bowl Stadium, with many pre-game events held throughout the holiday season.

SLEEPING

El Paso has two main clusters of budget motels; one on N Mesa St around the university and the other on Montana Ave near the airport and Fort Bliss. Most of the top-end hotels cater to the business world. This makes weekday stays at these places rather pricey, but most offer good deals Friday through Sunday. Almost everything is a chain, and there isn't a bed-and-breakfast in town.

Downtown

Gardner Hotel/El Paso International Hostel (Map p306; ☎ 915-532-3661; www.gardnerhotel.com; 311 E Franklin Ave; dm $15; s/d $22/35, with bathroom $42.50/47.50) El Paso's oldest continually operating hotel is also the only real downtown bargain. It probably hasn't changed a whole lot since John Dillinger stayed here in the 1930s, but it has a certain ragtag charm, and the dormitory rooms are an economical choice for the single traveler.

Doubletree El Paso Downtown (Map p306; ☎ 915-532-8733; 600 N El Paso St; d $89-169; ⊠ 🛜 🏋) Freshly remodeled from top to bottom in 2009, the former International Hotel is one of the nicest places in town. The rooms are luxuriously smart, with pleasing color palettes and all the little niceties you could want.

Holiday Inn Express (Map p306; ☎ 915-544-3333; www.hiexpress.com; 409 E Missouri Ave; d $96-125; ⊠ 🖥 🛜 🏋) Sure, it's wedged between a freeway and train tracks, but it still manages to be surprisingly quiet and calm inside. The rooms are cheerful and up to date, and breakfast is included.

Camino Real Hotel (Map p306; ☎ 915-534-3000, 800-769-4300; www.caminoreal.com; 101 S El Paso St; d $99-129; 🖥 🛜 🏋) The only US location of an upscale Mexican hotel chain, the Camino Real has a prime location steps from the convention center and downtown museums; a gorgeous bar with an art glass dome; large, comfortable

rooms; and pretty friendly service, even when they're swamped.

West El Paso

Mesa Inn (Map p302; ☎ 915-532-7911; 4151 N Mesa St; r $31; 🏋) If your answer to the question, 'Well, what did you expect for 30 bucks a night?' would be 'not much,' then this is the place for you. The decor is straight out of the 1970s and the halls are a little creepy, but there's a pool, and you could do worse for the price.

Hilton Garden Inn (Map p302; ☎ 915-351-2121; www.hiltongardeninn.com; 111 W University Ave; r $80-109; ⊠ 🖥 🛜 🏋) Right on the edge of UTEP, the Garden Inn was built to blend with campus architecture, so it resembles a Bhutanese *dzong*, or religious fortress. OK, not that anyone would confuse it for one, but it blends nicely with its surroundings, and the rooms are tasteful and modern.

Casa de Suenos (off Map p302; ☎ 575-874-9166; www.casaofdreams.com, 405 Mountain Vista Rd S, La Union, NM; d $100-105; ⊠ 🛜) El Paso may not have a bed-and-breakfast, but New Mexico does, and it's just 20 miles from downtown. The decor is uber-Southwestern, but it's a serene retreat from the city.

East El Paso

Coral Motel (Map p302; ☎ 915-772-3263; fax 915-779-6053; 6420 Montana Ave; s/d $34/38) Anyone who loves 1950s roadside nostalgia will feel right at home at this funky little motel that mixes genres wildly, from the Spanish-style barrel tile roof to the Jetsons-esque sign to the mish-mash interiors.

El Paso Inn (Map p302; ☎ 915-772-4264; 6210 Montana Ave; s/d $39/45) The outside doesn't look like much at all – just a one-story strip of rooms along a parking lot – but you can tell they put some thought into the interiors, which you don't often find at this price point.

Wyndham El Paso Airport (Map p302; ☎ 915-778-4241; 2027 Airway Blvd; d $90-124; ste $102-154; ⊠ 🖥 🛜 🏋) Late arrival? Early departure? Staying 200 yards from the airport has its advantages. But this place has more to offer than just proximity: it also has the biggest and best hotel pool in town.

El Paso Marriott (Map p302; ☎ 915-779-3300; 1600 Airway Blvd; d $90-205; ⊠ 🛜 🏋) Just down the street a few blocks from the airport, the Marriott has the plushest rooms outside of downtown, although they're on the generic side of lovely.

EATING

El Paso has long proclaimed itself the Mexican food capital of the US, and there certainly are dozens of good restaurants in that category. Ask three different El Pasoans who serves the best Mexican cuisine and you'll get three (or maybe six!) different answers. The area is also known for its steak houses, several of them are just far enough out of town to make dinner feel like an adventure.

Budget

Taco Cabana (Map p302; ☎ 915-775-1460; 6345 Gateway W; tacos $1-3, plates $3-6; ☒ 24hr) In El Paso, even the fast-food Tex-Mex is great. In addition to this central location on I-10, this chain has locations all over town; keep an eye out for the big, pink neon sign. El Paso's not a late-night kind of town, so you'll especially appreciate it in the wee hours.

Chicos Tacos (Map p302; ☎ 915-772-7777; 5305 Montana Ave; tacos $1-4; ☒ 9am-2am Sun-Thu, to 3:30am Fri & Sat) With several locations, Chicos Tacos specializes in its namesake fare – with lots of garlic. Expect a crowd from about 10pm to midnight, when El Pasoans citywide experience a collective craving.

Charcoaler Drive In (Map p302; ☎ 915-581-0660; 5837 N Mesa St; burgers $2-3; ☒ 11am-10pm) If we hadn't pointed this burger joint out, your nose would probably have found it anyway; you can smell their charcoal-grilled burgers from the street. Drive through, place your order, then pull up to a carport and enjoy the 1950s ambience.

Kinley's House Coffee & Tea (Map p302; ☎ 915-838-7177; 2231 N Mesa St; meals $3-7; ☒ 7am-11:30pm Mon-Sat, from 8am on Sun) This cheery and bustling little coffee shop near the UTEP campus has lattes and macchiatos galore, and you can also score sandwiches, crepes and even Japanese noodles. Parking is scarce; there's a drive-through if you need it quick.

G&R Restaurant (Map p302; ☎ 915-546-9343; 401 E Nevada; mains $5-10; ☒ 8am-8pm Mon-Thu, to 9pm Fri & Sat) Family-owned since 1960, G&R is a local favorite. The colonial-style dining room is fun and colorful, all the better to enjoy their authentic and super-affordable enchiladas, rellenos and burritos.

Midrange

H&H Coffee Shop (Map p306; ☎ 915-533-1144; 701 E Yandell Dr; mains $5-8; ☒ 7:30am-3pm) It doesn't look like much, but don't be scared off. This hole

in the wall – which, curiously, is attached to a car wash – is a well-known breakfast hangout that's authentic and friendly.

Jaxon's Restaurant (www.jaxons.com; mains $6-16; ☒ 11am-10pm Sun-Thu, 11am-11pm Fri & Sat; Airway Blvd Map p302; ☎ 915-778-9696; 1135 Airway Blvd; N Mesa St Map p302; ☎ 915-544-1188, 4799 N Mesa St) Tired of Tex-Mex and barbecue? Craving a salad or burger? Jaxon's serves up great American food, and plenty of it. There are some yummy vegetarian options too. What's that word we're looking for? Dependable. Yes, that's it.

L&J Cafe (Map p302; ☎ 915-566-8418; 3622 E Missouri St; mains $7-11) This El Paso staple is located next to the Concordia Cemetery. It's a great place to cure a hangover on Saturday morning when they serve their famous menudo.

Rib Hut (Map p302; ☎ 915-532-7427; 2612 N Mesa St; mains $7-18; ☒ 11am-10pm Mon-Sat, noon-8pm Sun) Go all caveman-like and join the UTEP crowd over a serious plate of ribs in this funky little A-frame building with typical campus-adjacent decor. Wednesday night is packed for rib night, when ribs are $1.75 each.

Crave (Map p302; ☎ 915-351-3677; 300 Cincinnati Ave; mains $7-28; ☒ 7am-11pm Mon-Sat, 7am-6pm Sun) Winning extra points for style – from their cool sign to the forks hanging from the ceiling – this hip little eatery serves up comfort food and classics with a little extra flair. Although dinner goes up to $28, there's still plenty to munch on in the $12-and-under category.

Amigos (Map p302; ☎ 915-533-0155; 2000 Montana Ave; mains $8-11; ☒ 6:30am-9pm Tue-Sun, 6:30am-3pm Mon) Can't get your enchiladas spicy enough? Jolt your taste buds from their ennui at this reliable favorite. The friendly owner can let you know which dishes really bring on the *fuego* (fire), or help you pick something suited for a more moderate palate.

State Line (Map p302; ☎ 915-581-3371; 1222 Sunland Park Dr; mains $8-21; ☒ 11:30am-9:30pm Mon-Thu, to 10pm Fri & Sat, to 9pm Sun) Vegetarians, plug your ears: it's hard to say what we like better, the groovy roadhouse-style decor, or the mounds and mounds of delicious, steaming brisket, sausage and ribs.

Top End

our pick **Magic Pan Restaurant** (Map p302; ☎ 915-581-2121; 5034 Doniphan Dr; lunch $9-11, dinner $18-28; ☒ 11am-2pm Tue-Sun, 5-10pm Wed-Sat) Not to be confused with the crepe chain of the same name, this cute little courtyard cafe is a treat. By day,

THE BEST BLOCK IN EL PASO

If you're looking for variety – perhaps an area where you can restaurant-hop from one place to another for appetizers, entrées, desserts, drinks and live music – look no farther than Cincinnati Ave between Stanton St and Mesa St near UTEP. Always lively with students, Old Kern Pl offers a smorgasbord of good food and conviviality.

enjoy ultrafresh soups, salads and sandwiches under the shade trees on the breezy patio. At night, it takes on more of a fine-dining tone, with twinkle lights illuminating said shade trees and an upscale menu ranging from paella to tenderloin.

Cattleman's Steakhouse (Map p302; ☎ 915-544-3200; Indian Cliffs Ranch; mains $15-33; 5pm-10pm Mon-Fri, 12:30-10pm Sat, 12:30-9pm Sun) This place is 20 miles east of the city, but local folks would probably drive 200 miles to eat here. The food is good, and the scenery is even better. Come early and wander around the grounds of the Indian Cliffs Ranch, then catch the sunset either before or after your meal. It's 4.5 miles north of the I-10 at Fabens.

Edge of Texas Steakhouse & Saloon (Map p302; ☎ 915-822-3343; 8690 Edge of Texas St; lunch $8-12, dinner $16-31; 11am-10pm Wed-Thu & Sun, 11am-11pm Fri & Sat) North of El Paso, nearly on the New Mexico border, this steakhouse is located on an 88,000-acre working cattle ranch. What better place to rustle up a T-bone, rib eye or buffalo steak; they also have plenty of chicken and fish dishes.

Cafe Central (Map p306; ☎ 915-545-2233; 109 N Oregon St; lunch $9-$28, dinner $13-45; 11am-10:30pm Mon-Thu, 11am-11:30pm Fri & Sat) If you've got someone to impress, this is *the* place to go in town, the kind of place where, if you drop your napkin, someone will have picked it up, folded it and handed it back to you before you even notice. The seasonal cuisine is stellar, and the small but elegant dining room attracts El Paso's finest diners.

DRINKING

Dome Bar (Map p306; ☎ 915-534-3000; Camino Real Hotel, 101 S El Paso St; 3-11pm Sun-Wed, 3pm-midnight Thu, 3pm-2am Fri & Sat) Gaze up at the elegant stained-glass dome, sip a martini and enjoy an intimate conversation at this low-key place inside the Camino Real Hotel.

Tap Bar & Restaurant (Map p306; ☎ 915-532-1848; 408 E San Antonio Ave; 9am-2am Mon-Sat, noon-2am Sun) If you prefer dive bars, duck in to the Tap. It has a jukebox with a country and Latin music selection and a pool table that may or may not have all its components.

Aceitunas (Map p302; ☎ 915-581-3260; 5200 Doniphan Dr; 3pm-2am) A unique spot in El Paso, this open-air beer garden is a great place to wind down after a long day of hiking or mountain biking in the Franklin Mountains. The folks here are some of the friendliest you will meet. Many west-side locals call this place home. There's live music Tuesday and Thursday through Saturday.

ENTERTAINMENT

El Paso has a lively fine arts scene and plenty going on in the bars and nightclubs, too, though compared to Austin, there's little in the way of local original music. But if you look hard enough and ask around, you can find live music almost any night of the week. To learn what's going on in town, try the Tiempo Friday supplement to the **El Paso Times** (http://calendar.elpasotimes.com).

Nightclubs

Club 101 (Map p302; ☎ 915-544-2101; www.club101.com; 1148 Airway Blvd) This is *the* reigning dance club in town, with live shows, DJ nights and music that ranges from electronica to pop to even, yes, death metal, depending on the night. Check the website to see what's happening.

Graham Central Station (Map p302; ☎ 915-599-2553; Vista Hills Shopping Center, 1840 Lee Trevino Dr) This five-clubs-in-one venue is El Paso's biggest party place. For one cover, guests can wander from a country/Tejano club to a karaoke lounge to a pool hall, a Top-40 dance hall and a '70s disco. A dress code is strictly enforced.

Performing Arts

The sombrero-shaped **Abraham Chávez Theatre** (Map p306; ☎ 915-534-0609; 1 Civic Center Plaza) is host to most of El Paso's major performing organizations and many touring concerts and plays. These include **El Paso Symphony Orchestra** (☎ 915-534-3776, 915-532-3776), **El Paso Community Concert Association** (☎ 915-544-2022) and **El Paso Opera Company** (☎ 915-581-5534).

Sports

UTEP is part of the Western Athletic Conference, which is the largest collegiate conference in the US. Basketball is especially popular, but the football team has played well in recent years, too. Call ☎ 915-747-5330 or ☎ 915-747-5347 for schedules.

El Paso Diablos (☎ 915-755-2000; www.diablos. com) play Double A Texas League baseball April to September at **Cohen Stadium** (off Map p302; 9700 Gateway Blvd N). There's live and simulcast horse races just over the New Mexico border at **Sunland Park Race Track** (Map p302; ☎ 575-589-1131).

SHOPPING
Placita Santa Fe & Market Place (Map p302; 5034 Doniphan Dr; ☺ 10am-5pm Tue-Sat, 12:30pm-4:30pm Sun) One of the most pleasant places to browse in El Paso and dedicated to local artists and craftspeople selling antiques, silver and handmade jewelry. It has a tranquil shopping atmosphere with flowing fountains that almost make you forget that you're in the desert.

El Paso Connection (off Map p302; ☎ 915-852-0898; 14301 Gateway W; ☺ 9am-7pm) Consists of several showrooms and warehouses that are crowded with antique and imported goods, such as lampshades made from cowhide and large pieces of Southwestern-motif furniture.

Like most major US cities, El Paso has its share of malls where the shopper can find anything from books to socks. **Cielo Vista Mall** (Map p302; ☎ 915-779-7070; 8401 Gateway Blvd W) is located off I-10 on the east side; **Sunland Park Mall** (Map p302; ☎ 915-833-5595; 750 Sunland Park Dr) is the major west-side shopping center.

Feel like you're missing out on south-of-the-border bargains? For an experience not altogether unlike shopping in Juárez, head to the Golden Horseshoe area between Stanton and El Paso Sts and San Antonio Ave in El Paso's downtown area, where cheap clothing, jewelry and housewares abound. It's fairly scruffy, but avoids the danger of crossing over.

GETTING THERE & AWAY
Air
El Paso International Airport (ELP; Map p302; ☎ 915-772-4271; www.elpasointernationalairport.com) is 8 miles northeast of downtown El Paso. It's accessible by bus, taxi and shuttles; see the Getting Around section for more information.

Southwest Airlines (☎ 800-435-9792; www. southwest.com) is the biggest carrier at El Paso International, with about 60% of the domestic flights. Other airlines include **American Airlines** (ww.aa.com) and **Delta** (www.delta.com), and El Paso is a hub for **New Mexico Airlines** (www.pacificwings.com/nma/nm).

Bus
The terminal for **Greyhound** (Map p306; ☎ 915-542-1355; www.greyhound.com; 200 W San Antonio Ave) is four blocks from the center of downtown.

Car
El Paso is on the I-10 just 12 miles from the New Mexico line, but a long day's drive or more from any other major city in Texas. Stay on I-10 eastbound for San Antonio or

BIG BEND & WEST TEXAS

GET THE BOOT

Maybe you've always wanted a pair of cowboy boots. Maybe it's a side effect of your Texas travels. Sure you could pick up a pair of mass-produced boots, but nothing beats a custom-made pair for a mighty fine fit. Even if you can't round up the $800 to $3500 a custom pair costs, make an appointment to visit **Rocketbuster Boots** (Map p306; ☎ 915-541-1300; www.rocketbuster.com; 115 S Anthony St; ☺ by appointment) and you'll see what all the fuss is about. As boot-maker for the stars, Rocketbuster has shod such celebrities as Julia Roberts, Dwight Yoakam, Emmylou Harris and Oprah Winfrey. Their over-the-top designs include everything from wild floral prints to 1950s-era pin-up cowgirls to Day of the Dead skeletons. Owner-designer Nevena Christi will gladly show you around, and you can pick up leather pillows and boot-shaped Christmas stockings for just $75 to $300.

Numerous other custom boot–makers work around town, including **Caboots** (Map p302; ☎ 915-309-4791; www.caboots.com; 2100 Wyoming St; ☺ 9am-5pm Mon-Fri), which also sells a few pre-made pairs (about $300). Bargain shopping? Check out the local outlet centers along I-10, such as **Justin Boots Outlet** (Map p302; ☎ 915-779-5465; 7100 Gateway Blvd E; ☺ 9am-8pm Mon-Fri, to 6pm Sat, noon-5pm Sun) and **Tony Lama Factory Store** (Map p302; ☎ 915-772-4327; 7156 Gateway Blvd E; ☺ 9am-7pm Mon-Fri, to 6pm Sat, noon-5pm Sun).

Houston; I-20, the route to Fort Worth and Dallas, leaves I-10 about 150 miles east of El Paso. The only other major highways are Hwy 54, which runs north to I-40, and Hwy 62/180, the route to Guadalupe Mountains and Carlsbad Caverns National Parks and eventually to Lubbock.

Train

You can catch Amtrak at **Union Depot** (Map p306; ☎ 915-545-2247; www.amtrak.com; 700 San Francisco Ave), which serves both the *Texas Eagle,* which runs from Los Angeles to Chicago with stops in San Antonio, Austin and Dallas, and the *Sunset Limited,* which runs from Los Angeles to New Orleans with stops in San Antonio and Houston. Check the website for fares and schedules.

GETTING AROUND
To/From the Airport

Many hotels and motels provide free shuttles from the airport; call to see if yours does. All the major car-rental companies, as well as ground transportation options, can be found near baggage claim. Sun Metro's bus No 33 and No 57 will get you from the airport to downtown, which is about an 8-mile trip. A taxi to downtown costs between $23 and $25.

Bus

Sun Metro (Map p306; ☎ 915-533-3333; www.ci.el-paso. tx.us/sunmetro; Union Depot, 700 San Francisco Ave) is El Paso's bus service, operating 47 routes citywide. Routes are extensive, but most services stop running early in the evening, including the airport bus (the last one leaves around 9pm). Exact change is required. Check their website for route maps and schedules.

Bus fares are $1.25 for adults and 75¢ for children aged six to 18. Transfers cost 25¢ and should be requested when you board your original bus.

Car

Downtown can be tricky, because there are one-way streets laid out at weird angles, but the outlying commercial areas and neighborhoods are easy to find via I-10 and the major surface streets. As in many larger US cities, drivers tend to run red lights, so beware. I-10 is frequently under construction, so watch for slowdowns. I-10 drivers should

keep an eye peeled for furtive pedestrians who occasionally dart across the freeway at night.

Taxi

Look for taxi stands at the airport and the Greyhound and Amtrak depots. Rates are $1.65 at flag fall, $2.25 each additional mile. We've been warned about unscrupulous cabbies charging extortionate rates downtown (such as $5 for the seven-block ride from the bus station to the Gardner Hotel), so double-check rates before boarding and make sure the meter's on. Larger companies include **Yellow Cab** (☎ 915-532-9999) and **United Independent Cab** (☎ 915-590-8294).

AROUND EL PASO

About 32 miles east of El Paso is **Hueco Tanks State Historical Park** (☎ 915-857-1135; 6900 Hueco Tanks Rd/FM 2775; adult/child/senior $4/free/2; ☼ 8am-6pm Oct-Mar, 7am-7pm Fri-Sun, 8am-6pm Mon-Thu Apr-Sep). The 860-acre park contains three small granite mountains that are pocked with depressions (*hueco* is Spanish for 'hollow') that hold rainwater, creating an oasis in the barren desert. The area has attracted humans for as many as 10,000 years, as evidenced by pictographs. Park staff estimate there are more than 2000 pictographs at the site, some dating back 5000 years.

If you're a rock climber, the chances are that you already know about the park. From October through to early April, Hueco Tanks ranks among the world's top rock-climbing destinations during the winter months, when other prime climbs become inaccessible (although in summer, the desert sun generally makes the rocks too hot to handle).

To minimize human impact, a daily visitor quota is enforced; make reservations 24 hours in advance to gain entry. **Park Headquarters** (☎ 915-849-6684, central reservations 512-389-8900; www.tpwd.state.tx.us; Rte FM 2775; day pass $5, campsites $12-16; ☼ 8am-6pm) has a small gift shop, a nearby interpretive center and 20 campsites. You can explore the North Mountain area by yourself, but to hike deeper into the park – where the more interesting pictographs are – you have to reserve and join one of the free **pictograph** or **bouldering/hiking tours** (☎ 915-857-1135; ☼ call for schedule).

THE I-10 CORRIDOR
Van Horn
pop 2689

Van Horn is notable mainly as a travelers' overnight spot on the long desert that is I-10 in west Texas. Sitting at the crossroads of the interstate, Hwy 54 (which runs north to Guadalupe Mountains National Park) and Hwy 90 (a major route to Big Bend country), Van Horn has about 600 motel rooms, 200 campsites and about 15 restaurants. If you are looking for a good place to stretch your legs, wander over to **Fancy Junk**, right next to Chuy's on Broadway. It's a junkyard that has taken the shape of an art exhibit.

Most people on the interstate truck on through to El Paso, which is just two more hours away, but if you're ready to bunk down for the night, there are a few motels right off the interstate. Better yet, try the historic **Hotel El Capitan** (☎ 877-283-1220; 100 E Broadway; d $69-139; ✗ ⊛), a richly decorated Spanish hacienda–style lodging which has considerably more charm than the chains.

Hungry? Stop off for a little Tex-Mex at **Chuy's Spanish Inn** (☎ 915-283-2066; 1200 W Broadway St; Mexican plates $6-11; ⌚ 10am-10pm). It's right on the highway, so you can't miss it. Chuy's has earned a place in 'Madden's Haul of Fame,' so named by US football broadcaster John Madden. Because he won't fly, the well-traveled Madden spends a lot of time crossing the US by bus, and this is one of his favorite restaurants.

Fort Stockton
pop 8680

Fort Stockton snags a spot on many Texas travelers' itineraries by virtue of its location. Despite having fewer than 10,000 people, it is by far the biggest town on I-10 between El Paso, 238 miles west, and San Antonio, 310 miles east. It's also a major gateway to Big Bend National Park, which is 100 miles south. So it's little surprise that Fort Stockton has more than 800 motel rooms, about 320 campsites and several dozen restaurants.

SIGHTS
Historic Fort Stockton

You can view several original and reconstructed buildings of a 19th-century fort on the Texas frontier at **Historic Fort Stockton** (☎ 432-336-2400; 300 E 3rd St; adult/6-12yr/senior $2/1/1.50; ⌚ 10am-5pm Mon-Sat fall to spring; 10am-5pm Mon-Sat, 1-5pm Sun

---

DETOUR: BALMORHEA STATE PARK

Swimming, scuba diving and snorkeling are the attractions at the 46-acre **Balmorhea State Park** (☎ 432-375-2370; Hwy 17; www.tpwd.state.tx.us; day pass adult/under 12yr $7/free), a true oasis in the west Texas desert. The swimming pool covers 1.75 acres, making it the largest spring-fed swimming facility in the US, 25ft deep and about 75°F year-round. The park is at Toyahvale, 5 miles south of the town of Balmorhea (pronounced bal-mo-ray), which itself is just off I-10 and midway between Pecos and Fort Davis on Hwy 17.

---

summer). The site includes Barracks No 1, a reconstructed building, houses the **Fort Museum** where exhibits and a short video describe the post's history. Living History days are held the first weekend of each November, with demonstrations, encampments and entertainment.

Annie Riggs Memorial Museum

Housed in a former hotel and boarding house, this **museum** (☎ 432-336-2167; 301 S Main St; adult/6-12yr/senior $2/1/1.50; ⌚ 10am-6pm Mon-Sat, 1:30-6pm Sun Jun-Aug, 10am-5pm Mon-Sat Sep-May) is named for the frontier woman who owned and ran the hotel for many years. The building is a documented example of Territorial architecture and is featured in some trade books. It is unusual in that the walls are made only of adobe and no stucco has ever been added to preserve it. Historic photographs and Texas memorabilia line the walls.

SLEEPING & EATING

We'll keep this brief. While there are plenty of options, they're fairly interchangeable. Nothing glamorous, just lots of chains.

Atrium West Inn Hotel & Suites (☎ 432-336-6666; www.atriumwestinn.com; 1305 US 285 N; s/d $70/80; ⊛ 🏊) One of the nicer hotel options in town is this business-oriented hotel, which does indeed have a pretty spiffy atrium with a pool, making it a great place to stop if you want to splash around a bit.

Bienvenidos (☎ 432-336-3615; 405 W Dickinson Blvd; plates $6-10; ⌚ 11-9.30pm Mon-Sat) This local favorite is there to welcome you with heaping plates of Tex-Mex. The food is average but the staff is friendly, and it beats resorting to the International House of Pancakes.

314 GUADALUPE MOUNTAINS NATIONAL PARK •• History

GUADALUPE MOUNTAINS NATIONAL PARK

We won't go so far as to call it Texas' best-kept secret, but the fact is that a lot of Texans aren't even aware of the **Guadalupe Mountains National Park** (www.nps.gov/gumo; 7-day pass adult/under 16yr $5/free). It's just this side of the Texas–New Mexico state line and a long drive from practically everywhere in the state.

Despite its low profile, it is a Texas high spot, both literally and figuratively. At 8749ft, Guadalupe Peak is the highest point in the Lone Star State. The fall foliage in McKittrick Canyon is the best in west Texas, and more than half the park is a federally designated wilderness area.

The National Park Service has deliberately curbed development to keep the park wild. There are no restaurants or indoor accommodations and only a smattering of services and programs. There are also no paved roads within the park, so whatever you want to see, you're going to have to work for it. But if you're looking for some of the best hiking and high-country splendor Texas can muster, you should put this park on your itinerary.

HISTORY

Until the mid-19th century, the Guadalupe Mountains were used exclusively by Mescalero Apaches, who hunted and camped in the area. Members of this tribe, who called themselves Nde, became the hunted starting in 1849 when the US Army began a ruthless three-decade campaign to drive them from the area. The mid-19th century also marked the brief tenure of the Butterfield Overland Mail Route (see the boxed text, p316). Guadalupe Mountains National Park was established in 1972.

GEOLOGY

A geologist's dream, Guadalupe Mountains National Park sits amid the world's most extensive exposed fossil reef. In fact, the mountains contain the world's best example of a 260- to 270-million-year-old exposed rock layer, the Guadalupian Global Stratotype. The reef began to grow 250 million years ago when an immense tropical ocean covered parts of Texas, New Mexico and Mexico. Over a period of five million years, lime-secreting marine organisms built the horseshoe-shaped reef to a length of 400 miles. After the sea evaporated, the reef was buried in sediment for millions more years, until a mountain-building geological uplift revealed part of it as the Guadalupe Mountains.

INFORMATION

Information, rest rooms and drinking water are available at McKittrick Canyon and Dog Canyon, in addition to the **Park Headquarters and Visitor Center** (☎ 915-828-3251; www.nps.gov/gumo; ❂ 8am-4:30pm, to 6pm in summer) at Pine Springs. Visit the website if you want to download a map of the park before you visit.

McKittrick Canyon's fall colors are glorious from early October through mid-November, and while nights can be chilly, daytime is warmly sublime. But be aware that autumn weekends are by far the busiest time and there may be a several-hour wait to enter the canyon.

There are no restaurants, accommodations, gas or other supplies in the park, so some planning is in order. Keep your gas tank full

BIG BEND & WEST TEXAS

DETOUR: CARLSBAD CAVERNS

If you've made it all the way out to the Guadalupe Mountains, you're not too far from another excellent natural attraction: **Carlsbad Caverns National Park** (☎ 877-444-6777; www.nps.gov/cave; cave entry adult/under 15yr $6/free, audio guide $3; ❂ visitor center 8am-5pm, till 7pm in summer). Although the park is over the border in New Mexico, it's only 40 miles from the Guadalupe Mountains National Park, making it closer than, well, almost everything else in the state of Texas.

Cave entrance fees are good for three days and get you access to the one-hour self-guided tour of the Big Room, the seventh largest cave chamber in the world. There are additional fees, and reservations are required, for six different **ranger-led tours** (☎ 800-967-2283; adult $7-20, child half price), including the King's Palace and the Hall of the White Giant. Please note that each of the guided tours has an age limit of anywhere from four to 12 years, depending on difficulty (of the route, not the child), so plan accordingly if you're traveling with a little one.

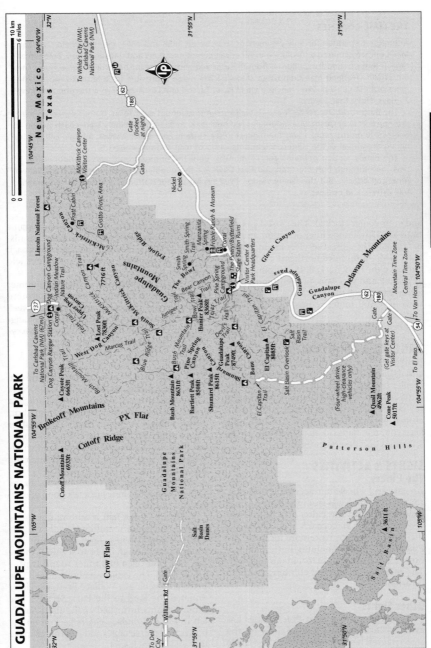

THE MAIL COACHES

Although it operated for only 2½ years or so between 1858 and 1861, the Butterfield Overland Mail Company spurred a revolution in American communications and transportation. Before that time, a letter bound for California from the east was sent via steamship around Cape Horn. The Butterfield Overland Mail Company's stagecoaches made it possible for a letter to move 2700 miles from St Louis to San Francisco via El Paso, Tucson and Los Angeles in a then-breathtaking 25 days. (Take that, FedEx.)

The Butterfield Overland's legacy is well known throughout west Texas, but it's especially well preserved here at Guadalupe Mountains National Park. At 5534ft, the Pinery stagecoach station – one of 200 on the route – was the highest in the system. Four times a week, a bugle call would herald the arrival of the stagecoach and its cargo of mail and passengers.

The Pinery station operated for 11 months, until the original route was abandoned for a new road through Fort Stockton and Fort Davis – a thoroughfare better protected from Native American attacks. But the Pinery station lived on for decades after as a refuge for emigrants, trail drivers and outlaws.

and your cooler stocked. The closest gas stations are 35 miles in either direction on Hwy 62/180 and the closest services are in Whites City, NM, 45 minutes northeast of the park entrance on Hwy 62/180. If camping is not appealing and you want to spend more than a day exploring the park, this resort town with over 100 motel rooms, two RV parks and a couple of mediocre restaurants is your best bet.

DANGERS & ANNOYANCES

Dehydration is the park's main danger. Carry and drink plenty of water – the park recommends one gallon per person per day. Five rattlesnake species live in the park, but rangers say no one has ever been bitten in the park's almost 40-year history. If you're camping, keep your tent flaps closed to keep out snakes, scorpions and desert centipedes.

SIGHTS & ACTIVITIES
The Pinery

An easy and wheelchair-accessible 0.75 mile round-trip trail leads from the Pine Springs visitor center to the ruins of a Butterfield Overland Mail stagecoach stop known as the Pinery. Despite its remote location, the Pinery is the only remaining Butterfield station ruin standing close to a major highway. The ruins are fragile and climbing on them is forbidden.

Other Sights

The main visitor center at Pine Springs has extensive exhibits and a slide show on the area's natural history and geology. The **Frijole**

Ranch & Museum (admission free; ⏰ 8am-4:30pm), a mile or so northeast of Pine Springs, has historical exhibits, including an 1858 stagecoach similar to the kind used on the Butterfield Overland route.

Interpretive programs are held on summer evenings in the Pine Springs campground amphitheater, as well as several times a week during the spring. Topics depend on the rangers' interests, but they have included everything from stargazing to geology.

Hiking

With more than 80 miles of trails and no real designated scenic drives through the park, Guadalupe Mountains National Park is a hiker's oasis, with trails ranging from short nature walks to strenuous climbs. The weather can be unpredictable out here. Thunderstorms are likely on summer afternoons, and winds frequently blow 40mph to 50mph in spring and early summer.

To find the hike that's right for you, try the visitor center, but here are a few good ones to get you started:

McKittrick Canyon Trail is among the park's most popular trails, and deservedly so. The 6.8-mile round-trip is level and scenic any time of year, though never so scenic as in the fall. The **Pratt Cabin** (4.8 miles round-trip) is a highlight. The cabin was built in 1932 by petroleum geologist Wallace Pratt, who later donated the land to the Park Service. The cabin remains furnished as the Pratt family left it. Big Adirondack chairs beckon on the porch, and picnic tables and rest rooms make this a good lunch spot.

Want to stand on the highest spot in Texas? Needless to say, you'll have to work for it on the 8.5-mile round-trip hike up **Guadalupe Peak**. No rock climbing is necessary, but there's a 3000ft elevation gain, so go easy if you've just driven in from the lowlands.

If you're looking for something a little easier, try the **Smith Spring Trail** starting at Frijole Ranch. This path, shaded by Texas madrone and alligator juniper, is a perfect spot to get out of the desert heat without too much exertion. The 2.3-mile loop takes you to Manzanita Spring and gradually climbs up to the refreshing Smith Spring, both precious watering holes for wildlife.

Other Activities

Bird-watchers flock to the park, especially McKittrick Canyon, for excellent viewing opportunities. There are no formal programs, but a checklist of the park's 260 species is available at the park headquarters.

Although many park trails are open to **horseback riding**, no horses are available in or near the park, and no overnight pack trips are permitted. For people bringing their own horses, corrals and campsites are available at Dog Canyon and Frijole Ranch; reserve them by calling the visitor center.

Note, rock climbers shouldn't confuse El Capitan here with the more famous granite formation in California's Yosemite National Park. Guadalupe Mountains' limestone and sandstone formations are ill-suited for climbing.

SLEEPING & EATING

If you're planning on sticking around for a night or two, there aren't a lot of options. You can drive 45 minutes to Whites City, NM, or you can camp in the park and bring your own food. Aaaaand…that's it.

The park **campgrounds** (☎ 915-828-3251; per night $8) are first-come, first-served, (unless you have a group of 10 or more, in which case you can reserve a group camping spot up to 60 days in advance for $3 per person).

The campsites fill up during spring break as well as several nights a week in the summer, although visitors arriving by early afternoon will usually find a site. The most convenient campgrounds are at Pine Springs, right along Hwy 62/180 near the visitor center; if it looks full, look for the 'campground host' sign for directions to overflow RV spots. If all the sites are full, RVs are permitted to park overnight at the nearby state highway picnic areas. There are also campgrounds at Dog Canyon, but those are more suited to visitors entering from the New Mexico side of the park.

There are even fewer eating options than sleeping options – in other words, zero. Plan on bringing food, either to hold you over till you can get to Whites City, or to sustain you throughout your stay without having to cross state lines. And just to make it even more challenging, there are no wood or charcoal fires allowed within the park. (Bring on the trail mix!)

GETTING THERE & AWAY

Guadalupe Mountains National Park is on Hwy 62/180, 110 miles east of El Paso and 55 miles southwest of Carlsbad, New Mexico. Although there is no scheduled public transportation to the park, **Greyhound** (☎ in El Paso 915-542-1355; www.greyhound.com) bus drivers on the El Paso–Carlsbad route will drop you off or make a whistle-stop pickup if you make arrangements in advance.

BIG BEND & WEST TEXAS

Panhandle & Central Plains

The Panhandle and Central Plains may be the part of Texas that most typifies the state to outsiders. This is a land of sprawling cattle ranches, a place where people can still make a living on horseback. Its landscape appears endlessly flat, punctuated only by utility poles and windmills, until a vast canyon materializes, seeming to plunge into another world.

It's a region of long drives on lonely two-laners. Its cities are few and small. But Midland was an important waypoint in the lives of two US presidents, Lubbock embodies the region's rich music heritage in its favorite son, Buddy Holly, and Amarillo keeps cattle kings of the Panhandle. Natural wonders include America's second-largest canyon at Palo Duro, where the Comanche fought on long after other tribes gave in. But the greatest assets are the tiny towns seemingly lost in the past. Slumbering in the sun are forgotten architectural gems and small-town cafes that have you itching for the next mealtime.

The scope and scale make this a place where people tend to think big, but some of the area's purest pleasures are in its details: the scent of sage after rainfall, a flint quarry plied by Texas' first inhabitants thousands of years ago, or the wistful love songs written by young troubadours whose legacies ultimately reached far beyond the plains.

PANHANDLE & CENTRAL PLAINS

HIGHLIGHTS

Best Place to Get Wired
The barbed wire exhibit at the Devil's Rope Museum (p338) in the old Route 66 town of McLean

Biggest Pair of Spectacles
A statue of Buddy Holly's iconic glasses outside his namesake museum in Lubbock (p329)

Where You'll Wish the Road Never Ends
Texas Hwy 70 (p333) wanders through forgotten small towns, lush ranchlands and classic wide open spaces

Food to Die For
Only the foolhardy take the challenge at Amarillo's Big Texan Steak Ranch (p339): eat a huge steak and sides in under an hour and it's free; don't and pay

Where to Get Your Spurs
Wander the old streets and beautiful river trails of San Angelo (p324), then get outfitted Texas-style in a Western gear store

PANHANDLE PLAINS

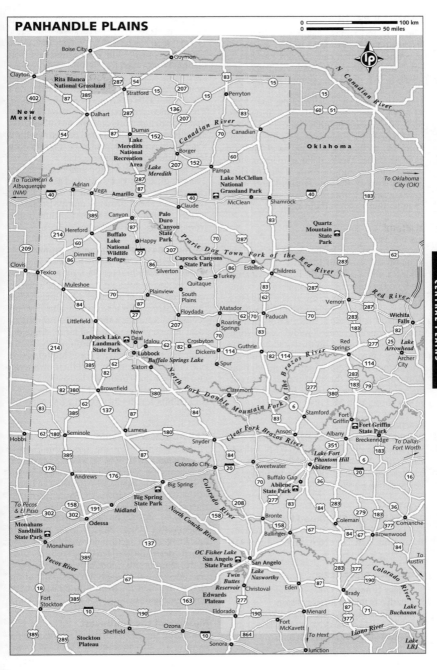

PERMIAN BASIN

The Permian Basin is a flat, physically charmless region of Texas with a lack of vegetation so pronounced that early settlers named one small town Notrees. Instead, you'll see (and smell) forests of oil rigs, pump jacks and petroleum tanks, which have ruled the boom-and-bust economy here since the late 1920s. This is a place where all those testosterone-fueled pickup ads could be filmed.

Although it will never make a top destinations list, the basin's twin towns of Midland and Odessa are excellent places to learn about the oil industry and the roots of an American political dynasty, the Bush family. The growing towns are edging towards each other across the 15 miles that separate them along busy I-20.

Midland
pop 103,100

'Experienced Gang Pusher Wanted' read the signs on the way into Midland. They're not talking about a new vendor for the Crips and the Bloods, rather it's just another of the countless pleas for workers in the local oil industry, which seems to know no economic downturn.

Midland is the more dudelike of the twin cities, a sprawling series of middle class, white-collar subdivisions, with mirrored high-rises towering above a nearly lifeless downtown. The oil industry is conservative, and Midland County has one of the most conservative voting records in the country: in 2008 78% of voters chose John McCain.

INFORMATION
Midland Visitors Center (☎ 432-683-3381, 800-624-6435; www.visitmidlandtexas.com; 1406 W I-20, northside frontage road; ☼ 9am-5pm) Near the Permian Basin Petroleum Museum and I-20 exit 136, this large facility is filled with genial volunteers.

SIGHTS
George W Bush Childhood Home
George and Barbara Bush moved to west Texas from patrician New England in 1948.

DRIVING DISTANCES

Abilene to Austin 213 miles, 3½ hours
Amarillo to Odessa 268 miles, 4 hours
Amarillo to San Angelo 293 miles, 4½ hours
Lubbock to Fort Worth 292 miles, 4½ hours
Odessa to El Paso 274 miles, 4¼ hours

A growing family, the Bushes lived in this **house** (☎ 432-685-1112; www.bushchildhoodhome.com; 1412 W Ohio St; adult/child $5/3; ☼ 10am-5pm Tue-Sat, 2-5pm Sun) from 1952 to 1956, when their son George W was aged five to nine. What's most surprising about this modest house is that even a rising oil exec like George HW didn't live in the 1950s equivalent of a McMansion. There's plenty of material on the life of W that may delight fans and irritate others, but all will find this well-curated museum within a perfectly restored house to be a fascinating look at life in a simpler era.

The museum gift shop has pretty much every book about W by aids and acolytes you can imagine, plus material on W's wife, Laura, who writes about growing up in Midland in *Spoken from the Heart*. (An earlier Bush house from the area is in Odessa, see p322).

Permian Basin Petroleum Museum
This **museum** (☎ 432-683-4403; www.petroleummuseum.org; 1500 I-20 W exit 136, north side; adult/child $8/5; ☼ 10am-5pm Mon-Sat, 2-5pm Sun) is worth a stop even if you're not utterly fascinated with the oil business, for it's as much a history and geology museum as a shrine to the prominent local industry (it has a hall of fame). Outside, there's a big collection of antique oil-drilling equipment. Inside, interactive exhibits include one in which players can drill their own wells and another that simulates the roar of a blow-out, an oil well gone wild (there are as yet no exhibits for the 2010 Gulf of Mexico BP disaster).

CAF Airpower Museum
Historic warplanes are the stars at this impressive **museum** (☎ 432-563-1000; www.airpowermuseum.org; 9600 Wright Dr; adult/child $10/7; ☼ 9am-5pm Tue-Sat) at Midland International Airport. The home of the Commemorative Air Force (formerly the politically incorrectly named Confederate Air Force), this sizable museum has a large collection of planes, mostly from WWII. It has an excellent section devoted to that war, which doesn't flinch from tough subjects such as the atom bomb. Most moving is the nose art collection: the bawdy images painted on aircraft by men far from home tasked with unspeakable duties.

Museum of the Southwest
Housed in the 1937 Turner Mansion, itself a work of art, this **museum** (☎ 432-683-2882; www.

museumsw.org; 1705 W Missouri Ave; ☉ 10am-5pm Tue-Sat, 2-5pm Sun) has an art gallery (free), planetarium (shows adult/child $6/4) and a children's museum (admission $3). Larger-than-life sculptures from the permanent collection dot the tree-shaded grounds, which were built by oil baron Fred Turner.

SLEEPING
Midland offers many more selections than Odessa, even if they're all chains. Budget choices are north of I-20 exit 134; more upscale brands can be found on the TX 250 Loop where it meets TX 158 west of the center.

Super 8 (☎ 432-689-6822; www.super8.com; 3828 W Wall Ave; r $50-100; 🛜 🖭) A tidy two-story version of the ubiquitous budget chain. The neighborhood is charmless except for other cheap motels – and industry. It's north of I-20 exit 134, off Midkiff Rd.

Residence Inn (☎ 432-689-3511; www.residence inn.com; 5509 Deauville Blvd; r $120-200; 🖥 🛜 🖭) Amidst a plethora of brightly lit franchise restaurants, this extended-stay hotel has 131 units in an attractive, if generic, complex. All come with kitchen facilities and are ideal for families.

EATING
Burgers, Fries and Cherry Pies (☎ 432-617-2327; 5210 W Wadley; meals from $5; ☉ 10am-8pm) The name leaves little to the imagination at this modern version of a burger joint up north off the TX 250 loop amidst various malls. The burgers come in myriad forms, many remarkably creative, such as the newly famous French Connection (béarnaise sauce). Best is the option for onion rings *and* tater tots with your meal.

`our pick` **KD's Bar-B-Q** (☎ 432-683-4013; 3109 Garden City Hwy/TX 158; meals from $9; ☉ 11am-8pm Tue-Sat) If you had to go to one Texas 'cue joint, this would do. Line your platter with wax paper and tell the cook what to pile on (the brisket is divine). Add sides such as potato salad, then head to the amazing works bar where you can get beans, pickles and an ocean of sauces. And the peach cobbler? Dang! This rambling place is east of town, just off I-20 at exit 138.

Garlic Press (☎ 432-570-4020; 2200 W Wadley Ave; meals $10-30; ☉ lunch Tue-Fri, dinner Tue-Sat) In an upscale little shopping plaza north of town, the Garlic Press is one of the more stylish places in town. Med-style fare is best enjoyed outside under the shady trees. But this being Midland, a seared ahi tuna appetizer rapidly gives way to an array of steaks with myriad preparations.

GETTING THERE & AROUND
Fittingly for oil towns, Midland and Odessa are nearly impossible to navigate without a car.

Midland International Airport (MAF; ☎ 432-560-2200; www.flymaf.com) sits midway between Midland and Odessa near exit 126 on I-20 and TX 191. The airport is served by American Eagle (Dallas–Fort Worth), Continental Express (Houston), Southwest (Dallas, Houston and Las Vegas) and United Express (Denver).

For long-distance bus service, you need to use Greyhound in Odessa (p322).

Odessa
pop 97,400
In contrast to somewhat prim Midland, hardscrabble Odessa has a downbeat feel. It's the classic split between management and workers, with the latter making homes here. The low-rise downtown has some barely perceptible glories left over from the original boom; mostly, however, it has a very big rabbit.

INFORMATION
Odessa Convention and Visitors Bureau (☎ 432-333-7871, 800-780-4678; www.odessacvb.com; 700 N Grant Ave, Suite 200; ☉ 9am-5pm Mon-Fri) In the Bank of America building.

SIGHTS
White-Pool House
Built in 1887, this is the oldest existing **house** (☎ 432-333-4072; 112 E Murphy St; admission free; ☉ 10am-3pm Wed-Sat) in Ector County. It had just two owners for nearly a century before the Pool family deeded it to the county for preservation in 1973. It shows the change in local fortunes from ranching in the 1880s to the oil boom of the 1920s.

WHAT THE...? JACKRABBIT
Odessa claims to have the world's largest **jackrabbit statue**. The 10ft-tall photo op is at 802 N Sam Houston Ave and was built in honor of the first Championship Jackrabbit Rodeo in 1932.

FRIDAY NIGHT LIGHTS

In 1990 the book *Friday Night Lights* was published to much critical acclaim. In it, journalist HG 'Buzz' Bissinger followed the Panthers football team of **Permian High School** (1800 W 42nd St) during the team's 1988 season. No fawning bit of fluff, the book delved deeply into the lives of the young players and their coaches. It showed teenage angst and portrayed a community where academic excellence was ridiculed in favor of success on the playing field. Many locals were horrified at its exposure of racism and other social ills in Odessa. The book later became a 1994 movie and was used as a basis for a TV series that ran in fits and starts from 2006 to 2011.

The huge Ratliff Stadium, which seats nearly 20,000, is next to the school. Signs, emblazoned with the nickname 'Mojo,' show the team's long history of victory, which coincidentally went into decline when the book was published. (Archrival Midland Lee High School has been doing much better.) But fall Friday nights here under the lights are still *the* place in Texas to watch high school football (www.mojoland.net).

Presidential Museum

This much-lauded **museum** (4919 E University Ave) shut down after going broke in 2009. The prospects of it reopening are doubtful, which is a shame given its even-handed coverage of every presidential election. However, it is still possible to see the 1948 home of the Bush family, which was moved here and sits forlornly out back.

EATING

White House Meat Market (☎ 432-367-9531; 200 E 52nd St; meals from $5; ☺ 6am-6pm Tue-Sat) Hidden amongst some industrial buildings north of the center, the White House is the place to get a great burger, cooked or uncooked. Besides fine Texas beef in deli cases, it serves up fab burgers in simple surrounds and great barbecue.

Ben's Little Mexico (☎ 432-333-4529; 1351 E 8th St; meals from $5; ☺ 11am-8pm Mon-Sat) Like the rest of Odessa, Ben's doesn't look like much. But from this humdrum strip mall location comes some of the best *chile verde* in the region: succulent chunks of marinated pork in a piquant green sauce. Yum!

Barn Door Steak House (☎ 432-337-4142; 2140 Andrews Hwy; meals $14-30; ☺ 11am-2pm daily, 5-9pm Mon-Sat) The Barn Door has been serving Odessa's best steaks for more than 40 years. The restaurant incorporates the old railroad depot from Pecos, moved to this site in 1972. Among the highlights is the fresh bread and hunk of cheddar cheese given to each diner – before the rest arrives.

GETTING THERE & AWAY

Odessa is about 12 miles west of Midland International Airport (p321). The **Greyhound** **bus terminal** (☎ 432-332-5711; www.greyhound.com; 2624 E 8th St) is served by regular buses along the I-20 corridor between El Paso ($46, five hours) and Fort Worth ($62, 6½ hours).

Big Spring

pop 25,700

The relentlessly flat Permian Basin landscape starts to show signs of a change 40 miles east of Midland. Big Spring is on the edge of the Edwards Plateau Caprock Escarpment, the defining topographical feature of the Texas Panhandle. The spring for which the town is named sits in Comanche Trail Park. Nearby, 380-acre **Big Spring State Park** (☎ 432-263-4931; www.tpwd.state.tx.us; admission free) has a fine nature trail with labels describing the hearty plants, such as the spiky argarita bush. A short drive around the top of the park has sweeping views out across the basin and plateau.

There are few west Texas dancehalls more authentic than the **Stampede** (☎ 432-267-2060; 1610 E TX 350), a barebones, early 1950s affair a couple miles northeast of Big Spring. It's the home of Jody Nix and the Cowboys, a legendary family band that has been fueling two-steppers for years. Schedules are loose, although there's something many weekend nights.

SAN ANGELO

pop 89,800

Situated on the fringes of the Hill Country, San Angelo is the kind of place where non-poser men in suits ride motorcycles and women in pickups look like they could wrestle a bull and then hit the catwalk. It's a purely Western place with an appealing overlay of gentility. The Concho River scenically runs through it, and there are numerous walks along its wild, lush banks.

Orientation & Information

Located just a bit west of Texas' geographical center, San Angelo is at the intersection of US 67, US 87 and US 277. Within town, US 87 becomes Bryant Blvd, which – along with Chadbourne St – is the city's main north–south road.

Cactus Book Shop (☎ 325-659-3788; 6 E Concho Ave) Right downtown, carries new and used books plus a good selection of Texana titles.

San Angelo Convention and Visitors Bureau (☎ 325-655-4136, 800-375-1206; www.visitsanangelo. org; 418 W Ave B; ☷ 9am-5pm Mon-Sat, 10am-4pm Sun) A stunning (and helpful) center in a stunning location on the Concho River near downtown. A pedestrian bridge links to a groovy kids' playground.

Sights

FORT CONCHO NATIONAL HISTORIC LANDMARK

No matter how many forts you've seen in your Texas travels, **Fort Concho National Historic Landmark** (☎ 325-481-2646; www.fortconcho.com; 630 S Oakes St; adult/child $3/1.50; ☷ 9am-5pm Mon-Sat, 1-5pm Sun) is likely to be a highlight. Many folks claim it's the best-preserved Western frontier fort in the USA, and much of it has been restored by the city over the decades.

Designed to protect settlers and people moving west on the overland trails, the fort went up in 1867 on the fringes of the Texas frontier and saw service until 1889. Among the highlights are the Headquarters Building, which includes the Fort Concho Museum, and the Post Hospital.

EL PASEO DE SANTA ANGELA

Santa Angela was San Angelo's original name, and El Paseo de Santa Angela marks the route that soldiers stationed at Fort Concho once used to visit the wanton town in its heyday. In 1870, the post surgeon at the fort wrote that 'the village across the Concho…is attaining an unenviable distinction from the numerous murders committed there… Over 100 murders have taken place in the radius of 10 miles.' And then there were the 35 bordellos and saloons that lined Santa Angela's sidewalks.

Today's El Paseo is a (family-friendly) pleasure-filled stroll that is part of the river walk that follows more than 6 miles of the Concho from just west of downtown east to

Bell St. Celebration Bridge links San Angelo's main street, Concho Ave, to the main attractions south of the river, which include a collection of historic buildings along Orient St.

SAN ANGELO MUSEUM OF FINE ARTS

This **museum** (SAMFA; ☎ 325-653-3333; www.samfa.org; 1 Love St; adult/child $2/1; ☷ 10am-4pm Tue-Sat, 1-4pm Sun) is best known for its ceramics collection. Run in partnership with Angelo State University, SAMFA is on the El Paseo and often has compelling special exhibits.

RAILWAY MUSEUM OF SAN ANGELO

The beautifully renovated Santa Fe Depot is home to the **railway museum** (☎ 325-486-2140; adult/child $2/1; ☷ 10am-4pm Sat). The station, on the El Paseo, is the main attraction; when open the museum has models of 1920s San Angelo and old rail cars.

CONCHO AVENUE HISTORIC DISTRICT

At the heart of downtown, the Concho Ave Historic District is a good place to dine or shop. The most interesting section, known as Historic Block One, is between Chadbourne and Oakes Sts. Be sure to pick up a historic walking tour brochure at the visitor center and don't miss the elegant and restored lobby of the 1929 **Cactus Hotel** (36 E Twohig Ave).

Few can resist the come-on of **Miss Hattie's Bordello Museum** (☎ 325-653-0112; www.misshatties. com; 18 E Concho Ave; admission free, tours $5; ☷ 10am-4pm Tue-Sat, tours 1-4pm Thu-Sat) operated as a house of pleasure from 1896 until the Texas Rangers shut it down in 1946. Rooms re-create the plush velvet look considered essential back in the day, but the best feature are the stories of the women and their clients.

SAN ANGELO STATE PARK

This **state park** (☎ 325-949-4757; www.tpwd.state. tx.us; admission $3) is on the western outskirts of town, accessible via FM 2288 (Loop 2288) off W Ave N (which becomes Arden Rd west of downtown), US 87 or US 67. The 7600-acre park surrounds the 1950s reservoir, OC Fisher Lake. More than 50 miles of trails are popular with animal- and bird-watchers.

PRODUCER'S LIVESTOCK AUCTION

No one has a baaad time at the largest sheep auction in the USA, the **Producer's Livestock Auction** (☎ 325-653-3371; www.producersandcargile. com; 1131 N Bell St; admission free). Sheep are sold on Tuesday and cattle on Thursday. The fun begins at 9am; the auctioneers' banter is the most fascinating aspect of the whole deal – it's totally incomprehensible.

Festivals & Events

The big annual **San Angelo Stock Show & Rodeo Cowboys Association Rodeo** (www.sanangelorodeo.com) runs over 10 days in February. It is one of the largest in the Southwest.

Sleeping

Most motels are situated on the major highways on the periphery of town.

San Angelo State Park (☎ 325-949-4757; www.tpwd.state.tx.us; campsites $8-18) Offering the best camping, San Angelo State park has beautifully located backpacker's tent sites; the sites with hookups have some shade.

Inn of the Conchos (☎ 325-658-2811, 800-621-6041; www.inn-of-the-conchos.com; 2021 N Bryant Blvd; r $50-70; 🐾) On the northwest edge of downtown US 87, this is an older, modest 125-room motel that is valiantly hanging on in the face of the chains. Free hot breakfast buffet, high-speed internet plus microwaves and fridges in the rooms are its ammo.

Inn at the Art Center (☎ 325-658-3333; www.innattheartcenter.com; 2503 Martin Luther King; r $75-125; 🐾) Funky is an understatement for this three-room B&B at the back of the bohemian Chicken Farm Art Center. Rooms are as artful as you'd expect at a 1970s chicken farm turned artists' co-op.

Staybridge Suites (☎ 325-653-1500; www.staybridge.com; 1355 Knickerbocker Rd; r $145-180; 🐾 🐾) Families like the large studio and one-bedroom apartments at this extended stay chain motel. It's near US87/277 south of the center.

Eating

Choose from top west Texas produce until it's all gone at the **Concho Valley Farmers Market** (☎ 325-658-6901; El Paseo de Santa Angela; 🕑 7:30am Tue, Thu & Sat late May-Oct).

Charcoal House (☎ 325-657-2931; 1205 N Chadbourne St; meals from $4; 🕑 7am-9pm) The name raises great hopes for the burgers, and they deliver. Options abound at this traditional drive-in with in-car (or truck) service. Details such as the thick bacon win raves as do the breakfasts.

Chef Jason's Deli (☎ 325-227-4432; 23 S Park St; meals from $6; 🕑 lunch Mon-Sat) Jason Helfer, the talented chef behind Peasant Village Restaurant (p324), assembles the best sandwiches and

salads in town. With the lavish desserts (bread pudding, key lime pie et al), you can have a picnic across the street in the beautiful surrounds of the water lily and rose gardens of Civic League Park on the Concho.

Miss Hattie's Café & Saloon (☎ 325-653-0570; 26 E Concho Ave; meals from $6; 🕑 11am-8pm Mon-Sat) This place tips its hat to the bordello museum up the block, with early-20th-century decor featuring tapestries and gilt-edged picture frames. However, the tasty meat is the main attraction, especially the hunk of seasoned beef grilled into a hamburger and then topped with an array of yummies.

Franco's Cafe (☎ 325-653-8010; 2218 Martin Luther King Dr; meals from $8; 🕑 8am-11pm) Franco's is plain as a flour tortilla on the outside but, just like a good burrito, it's what's on the inside that counts. San Angelo's favorite Mexican fare is served through the day. Fajitas win raves, as do the enchiladas.

Peasant Village Restaurant (☎ 325-655-4811; 23 S Park St; dinner from $25; 🕑 lunch Tue-Fri, dinner Tue-Sat) Located in a beautiful 1920s house near downtown, this refined restaurant is just the place if you'd like some fine wine to go with a meal from a seasonally changing menu. Creative mains of steak and seafood are always listed and there's a touch of the Mediterranean throughout. The desserts are simply fab.

Shopping

San Angelo is well known for the namesake pearls formed in the Concho River. These precious orbs occur naturally – and they're not just any pearls. They come in shades of pink and purple, usually in pastels but occasionally in vivid shades. Although most San Angelo jewelers carry Concho pearls, the best selection is at **Legend Jewelers** (☎ 325-653-0112; 18 E Concho Ave).

For Western wear, **JL Mercer & Son** (☎ 325-658-7634; 224 S Chadbourne St) is noted for its custom boots, spurs and other gear. Texas legends like Lyndon Johnson got their boots here (as did cowboy-on-the-screen John Wayne). Custom boots start at $600, but with options (there are many!) you can ride right past $2000 without breaking stride.

Historic Concho Ave has antique shops, vintage clothing stores and **Eggemeyer's General Store** (☎ 325-655-1166; 35 E Concho Ave), an old-style place with penny candy and lots of gift-item nonsense. (Okay, we like the fudge.)

Getting There & Away

Kerrville Bus Co (☎ 325-655-4159; www.iridekbc. com; 55 E 6th St), in the Union Bus Center, provides long-distance bus service out of San Angelo. Routes include San Antonio ($60, five hours), Fort Worth ($60, 5½ hours) and northwest to Big Spring for connections with Greyhound.

AROUND SAN ANGELO
X Bar Ranch

Near Eldorado, a town best known for its wool mills, this 7100-acre **ranch** (☎ 325-853-2688, 888-853-2688; www.xbarranch.com; 5 N Divide, Eldorado) may be just what you're looking for if you're hankering for a real Western holiday. There's horseback riding, of course, plus stargazing, hikes to view Indian mounds, bird-watching and ranch activities. Accommodation at the ranch ranges from campsites (from $10) to comfortable cabins (from $100). The ranch is 40 miles south of San Angelo, off US 277.

Fort McKavett State Historical Park

General William Tecumseh Sherman once called this fort along the San Saba River 'the prettiest post in Texas.' Today, **Fort McKavett State Historical Park** (☎ 325-396-2358; www.visitfortmc kavett.com; FM 864; adult/child $4/3; ☒ 8am-5pm), about 75 miles southeast of San Angelo, preserves the striking ruins of a once-important fort.

Fort McKavett was established by the Eighth Infantry of the US Army in 1852 as a bulwark against Comanche and Apache raids. The fort saw its peak in the mid-1870s, when it housed more than 400 troops and many civilians. Some of the 25 buildings have been restored; the grounds are alive with wildflowers for much of the year.

Sonora
pop 3200

Go underground in the famous local caverns and then squint your eyes in the bright of day in the compact and well-preserved center of diminutive Sonora, a worthy stop on either I-10 or US 277.

Marvel at geological splendor at the **Caverns of Sonora** (☎ 325-387-3105; www.cavernsof sonora.com; RM 1989; adult/child $20/16; ☒ tours 8am-6pm Mar-Aug, 9am-5pm Sep-Feb) on a two-hour tour that covers 2 miles underground. Oddities include everything from sound-absorbing cave sponges to hollow 'soda straw' tubular stalactites and foodlike formations: dumplings, beef jerky, apple sauce, bunches of grapes etc.

The caverns are located 7 miles south of I-10 exit 392, which is 8 miles west of Sonora. The temperature inside the caverns is always about 70°F, with 98% humidity. Tours include about 360 steps.

FUNDAMENTALIST WORRIES

The Mormon Church has spawned many offshoot sects which have broken with the main church over its disavowal of polygamy. In recent years none has been more notorious than the Fundamentalist Church of Jesus Christ of Latter Day Saints (FLDS).

Under the auspices of imprisoned sex offender, Warren Jeffs, the FLDS has secretive communities across North America, including Arizona, Utah and British Columbia. In 2003, the sect purchased a ranch 4 miles northeast of Eldorado, in a spot as isolated as any in Texas (San Angelo, the nearest city, is 40 miles north).

Named the Yearning for Zion Ranch (YFZ Ranch), the property has housed 700 or more people at various times and is rumored to be the current headquarters of the church. In 2008 the ranch made headlines when the Texas Department of Child Protective Services removed more than 400 children from the ranch and placed them in protective custody in San Angelo after a phone tip claimed children had been sexually abused at the ranch. A legal (and media) circus ensued, during which it was established that the original phone call had been a hoax. But allegations that the FLDS was a front for middle-aged men looking for multiple underage brides have swirled around the sect for years.

Eventually, almost all of the children were returned to their mothers, but a number of men at the YFZ Ranch have been indicted and convicted of a variety of sex crimes with underage girls.

Visitors to Eldorado, the namesake of the John Wayne movie, are unlikely to see any of the very plainly dressed and reclusive FLDS members. However, locals are quick to assert that they wish the sect would pack up and move on.

Stop by the **Sonora Chamber of Commerce** (☎ 325-387-2880; 707 NE Crockett Ave; ✹ 9am-5pm Mon-Fri) for a free **walking tour** brochure. Highlights include the handsome Sutton County Courthouse and the site where Will Carver, a member of Butch Cassidy's Hole in the Wall Gang, was shot to death in 1901.

The perfect antidote to chain restaurants, the **Sutton County Steakhouse** (☎ 325-387-3833; 1306 N Service Rd; meals from $6; ✹ 7am-9pm) is close to the I-10 and US 277. Like many places across west Texas, it excels at chicken-fried steak as well as other comfy faves such as cheeseburgers and catfish.

Junction
pop 2700

Winding through the lush and beautiful South Llano River valley, US 377 is light on traffic but big on vistas on its 100-mile route southwest from the pretty little town of Junction towards the border and Del Rio.

Junction proper has a few places where you can get organized for a rafting trip on the river. Or you can go hiking and spot deer, squirrels and the iconic Rio Grande turkey in **South Llano River State Park** (☎ 325-446-3994; www.tpwd.state.tx.us; admission $3). It's also ideal for a picnic or a stroll.

If you are at all near to Junction, don't miss **Isaacks** (☎ 325-446-2629; 1606 Main St; meals from $6; ✹ 6am-9pm Mon-Sat, to 2pm Sun), an old cafe with picture-perfect chicken-fried steak and onion rings worthy of a painting. It's basic chow, but everything is done just right, including the salad bar.

ABILENE
pop 119,500

Abilene is frequently called the 'buckle of the Bible Belt,' and not without reason (it has three bible colleges, for one). This is a buttoned-down town where nonconformists can feel seriously out of place. About 150 miles from either Midland or Fort Worth, the cow-dotted plains barely seem to yield to the city. However, Abilene makes for a good stop owing to one sensational museum and some traditional places to eat that will have you happy that modernity seems in short supply.

Orientation & Information
Abilene is circled by US 83 on the west side of town, by Loop 322 on the southeast side

and I-20 on the northeast. Treadway Blvd (Business Route 83D) is the main north–south street running through downtown; it is marked by little of architectural merit.
Abilene Bookstore (☎ 325-672-6657; 174 Cypress St) This downtown independent bookstore is a gem.
Abilene Convention and Visitors Bureau (☎ 325-676-2556, 800-727-7704; www.abilenevisitors.com; 1101 N 1st St; ✹ 9am-5pm Mon-Fri) Has its offices in the restored Texas & Pacific Railway Depot. Info also available at Frontier Texas! (p326).

Sights
All the sights below, except for the zoo, are within a few blocks of each other downtown.

FRONTIER TEXAS!
Reason enough to stop if you're anyplace near Abilene, **Frontier Texas!** (☎ 325-437-2800; www.frontiertexas.com; 625 N First St; adult/child $8/4; ✹ 9am-6pm Mon-Sat, 1-5pm Sun) makes 100 years of frontier history (1780–1880) possibly more interesting than the real thing. Life-size holograms and other special effects take you inside a buffalo stampede, next to a conniving card shark, at home on a firefly-filled range and much more. Hairs will raise on your arms at the appearance of Comanche chief Esihabitu.

GRACE MUSEUM
This fine **museum complex** (☎ 325-673-4587; www.thegracemuseum.org; 102 Cypress St; adult/child $6/3; ✹ 10am-5pm Tue-Sat, to 8:30pm Thu) includes three distinct museums housed in the former Grace Hotel, once the grandest in Abilene. The art museum features periodically changing exhibitions. The historical museum focuses on Abilene's history from 1900 through 1950. It's heavy on railroad and military memorabilia plus what home life was like in a simpler time. The children's museum has fun science experiments, including one where you can ponder gravity.

NATIONAL CENTER FOR CHILDREN'S ILLUSTRATED LITERATURE
This small **museum** (☎ 325-673-4586; www.nccil.org; 102 Cedar St; admission free; ✹ 10am-4pm Tue-Sat) has a small permanent exhibition of works by William Joyce and other well-known children's book illustrators. The real attractions are the constant special exhibits, which highlight the works of individual artists.

CENTER FOR CONTEMPORARY ARTS

Anchoring Abilene's most interesting district with the sights above, this **gallery** (☎ 325-677-8389; Grissom Bldg, 220 Cypress St; admission free; ⏰ 11am-5pm Tue-Sat) features exhibits by noted artists and is home to numerous studios.

PARAMOUNT THEATRE

Stars twinkle and clouds drift across the velvet blue ceiling of this magical movie and performing-arts palace. You can tour the beautifully restored **Paramount** (☎ 325-676-9620; www.paramount-abilene.org; 352 Cypress St; admission free; ⏰ noon-5pm Mon-Fri) or take in a movie, concert or other performance many nights.

ABILENE ZOO

Jaguars, ocelots, elephants and giraffes are among the more than 800 animals of several hundred species making their home at the **Abilene Zoo** (☎ 325-676-6085; www.abilenetx.com/zoo; 2070 Zoo Lane; adult/child $4/2; ⏰ 9am-5pm), located in Nelson Park in southeast Abilene near the junction of Loop 322 and Highway 36. Highlights include the self-descriptive Creepy Crawly Center and the Discovery Center, which compares plants and animals of the Southwest USA and Central America to similar areas in Africa and Madagascar.

Festivals & Events

The **Western Heritage Classic** (www.westernheritageclassic.com), held the second weekend of May, is a big rodeo featuring working cowboys from ranches across the USA, complete with campfire cook-offs, a Western art show, dances and more.

Sleeping

It's chain city in Abilene. Exits 285, 286 and 288 off I-20 are dotted with motels. Older indie operations south of the center on South 1st St are mostly dubious.

For camping, Abilene State Park (p328) is the best choice.

Knights Inn Civic Plaza (☎ 325-676-0222; www.knightsinn.com; 505 Pine St; r $50-85; 🛜 📷) The only real motel choice near the sights downtown, this former Quality Inn is showing its age. Some 115 units are spread over two floors in this motel-style building.

Vintage House (☎ 325-677-8386; www.thevintagehouse.com; 1541 N 4th St; r $85-110) Far from the roar of the interstate, this stately two-story brick home from 1927 is in an elegant neighborhood close to downtown. The four rooms are large and plushly furnished. There's high-speed internet in each; the hosts are pure charmers.

Courtyard by Marriott (☎ 325-695-9600; www.marriott.com; 4350 Ridgemont Dr; r $100-200; 📷 🛜 📷) Within sight of the Mall of Abilene, this corporate hotel is one of many slathered across these flatlands of national franchises. The three-story building has 100 sizable units, some with slivers of balconylike diversion.

Eating

Abilene has some excellent restaurants that are as casual and timeless as a big-sky sunset on the wide open plains.

La Popular Bakery (☎ 325-672-2670; 1533 Pine St; meals from $3; ⏰ 7am-8:30pm) North of downtown, look for the vibrant yellow building with a mural of fighting cocks. The breakfast burritos are reason enough to bounce out of bed. The bakery is vast and La Popular also makes its own tortillas and *pan dulce*.

Larry's Better Burger Drive-in (☎ 325-677-6801; 1233 N Treadway Blvd/US 83 Business; meals from $4; ⏰ 10am-9pm) The turquoise neon sign could use a sprucing up, as could the view (a tombstone dealer and a busy road), but there's nothing tired about the food, which is top-notch from the drippy cheeseburger to the tasty steak sandwich.

Beehive (☎ 325-675-0600; 442 Cedar St; meals from $5; ⏰ 11am-1pm Tue-Fri, dinner Tue-Sat) Abilene's most gracious restaurant is the place for a cultured lunch or dinner after the high culture of the sights downtown. The menu takes supperhouse standards such as shrimp cocktail and steaks and does them up just right. The cocktails are renowned in teetotaling Abilene for not only *having* alcohol but being made just right.

our pick **Harold's Pit Bar-B-Q** (☎ 325-672-4451; 1305 Walnut St; meals from $6; ⏰ 11am-8pm Tue-Sat) Wow! That's what we said between mouthfuls of fabulous barbecue at this little gem of a place north of town. Everyone seems to be a regular (parents were getting some to-go for their hospitalized child – 'no charge!' said the owner). Besides perfect oak-smoked meats, the corn fritters and berry cobbler amazed.

Joe Allen's Barbecue (☎ 325-672-6082; 1233 S Treadway Blvd; meals from $6) Besides the headline 'cue, this plain-fronted cafe has mesquite-grilled rib-eye steaks cut to order. Lunch specials include pork chops (Tuesday) and catfish (Friday). Expect to wait here, a few blocks on the south side of the tracks south of downtown.

Entertainment

Check to see what's on at the beautiful Paramount Theatre (p327).

Abilene Dragstrip (☎ 325-673-7223; 5601 W Stamford St) Racing cars is a Texas tradition and this ribbon of asphalt is open to everyone. Watch dudes in their pickups challenge each other or go nuts and trash your minivan. It's generally open Friday nights and all day weekends from spring to fall. It's just off I-20 exit 281, Shirley Rd.

Shopping

Hickory St, between 5th and 8th Sts near downtown Abilene, has a good selection of antique and gift shops selling everything from fudge to stained glass to vintage clothing.

Abilene has several noted small manufacturers of custom-made Western gear.

James Leddy Boots (☎ 325-677-7811; 1602 N Treadway Blvd; ☒ 8:30am-5pm Mon-Fri) A legendary maker of custom boots, this family-run store has prices ranging from $500 to five figures. You can usually get a tour of the shop and work area. Breath deep.

Art Reed Custom Saddles (☎ 325-677-4572; 361 East S 11th St; ☒ 9am-5pm Mon-Fri) Art Reed has a month-long waiting list for saddles that start at about $2000. Chaps can also be had, perfect for a starring role as a cowpoke on the range or in some urban leather bar.

Getting There & Away

Greyhound (☎ 325-677-8127; www.greyhound.com; 535 Cedar St) is downtown. Abilene is on the I-20 line running west from Fort Worth ($36, 2½ hours).

AROUND ABILENE
Buffalo Gap
pop 490

Bison used this natural pass in the Callahan Divide for many centuries; later on, it became an outpost on the Dodge Cattle Trail. Today's Buffalo Gap seems to have stolen any charm not claimed by Abilene (which is quite a bit actually). It's a fine detour from Abilene and I-20, just 14 miles southwest via FM 89. Besides the historic village, antique shops abound on the old main drag.

Step back to a time long before the invention of air conditioning made the plains safe for city slickers at **Buffalo Gap Historic Village** (☎ 325-572-3365; www.buffalogap.com; 133 William St; adult/child $7/4; ☒ 10am-5pm Mon-Sat, noon-5pm Sun). This living history museum has almost two dozen buildings, themed for the 1880s, 1905 and 1925. Volunteers bring the past to life, although everybody smells too fresh. Check out the old courthouse, the log cabin that's the oldest structure in the area, a train station, church, doctor's office, filling station and more.

our pick **Perini Ranch Steak House** (☎ 325-572-3339; www.periniranch.com; FM 89 W; meals from $12; ☒ lunch Fri-Sun, dinner Wed-Sun) is frequently named among Texas' best steak houses. Enter under the trees and through the screen door. Try an amazing rib eye at a picnic table outside or sample specialties such as one of the state's best cheeseburgers (get it with chiles). The Sunday brunch draws folks from miles around. Although the county is dry, you can buy a cheap club membership and imbibe like a cowboy.

Abilene State Park

Play Wile E Coyote and go looking for road runners at 529-acre **Abilene State Park** (☎ 325-572-3204; www.tpwd.state.tx.us; 150 Park Rd 32, Tuscola, off FM 89; admission $4), which is 4 miles southwest of Buffalo Gap. Attractions include hiking, bird-watching and wildlife viewing (armadillos, white-tailed deer, Mississippi kite, hummingbirds and more).

The campground has 102 campsites ($12 to $18 per night) including the most atmospheric: 12 tent-only sites. Reserve in advance.

Fort Phantom Hill

Boredom rather than combat doomed this 1851 fort along the Clear Fork of the Brazos River. Fort Phantom Hill was among the outposts constructed to protect settlers on the Texas frontier; it was abandoned just three years later after droves of bored soldiers left it (and the service). Time and fires have taken their toll on the fort and the nearby ghost town – by 1880, 546 people had moved to the settlement, but a letter written to the San Antonio Daily Express in 1892 indicated the town had dwindled to 'one hotel, one saloon, one general store, one blacksmith shop and

10,000 prairie dogs.' Today, visitors find only a handful of buildings and about a dozen chimneys among the windy, lonely ruins.

Fort Phantom Hill is on private land but it's open daily and is free to the public. The grounds are 11 miles north of I-20 on FM 600. Nearby Lake Fort Phantom is popular for fishing, boating, picnicking and camping.

Albany
pop 2000

Albany ranks among the most interesting small towns in Texas. Sitting 35 miles northeast of Abilene, the Shackleford County seat of about 2000 people is a bit off the beaten path on TX 180. It's a worthy 25-mile detour off I-20 or a highlight of one of the loneliest roads in Texas, US 283.

A remarkable facility, the 1877 **Old Jail Art Center** (☎ 325-762-2269; www.theoldjailartcenter. org; 201 S 2nd St; admission free; ◷ 10am-5pm Tue-Sat, 2-5pm Sun) houses a surprising collection that includes ancient terra-cotta Chinese tomb figures and art by such masters as Pablo Picasso, Amedeo Modigliani, Henry Moore and Grant Wood.

Each June, several hundred Albany townspeople get together and put on a show, **Fort Griffin Fandangle** (☎ 325-762-3838; www.fortgriffin fandangle.org; ◷ Thu-Sat, last two weeks of Jun). This energetic musical tells the story of the area's pioneer days, complete with a cattle drive, stagecoach chase and plenty of Old West tomfoolery. Meals are available before the shows.

Fort Griffin State Park

Just 15 miles north of Albany, this **park** (☎ 325-762-3592; www.tpwd.state.tx.us; admission $2) showcases a handful of restored buildings and the ruins of a fort that served the frontier during the Comanche wars from 1867 through 1881. Today, the park is probably best known as a principal home of the official Texas longhorn herd.

LUBBOCK
pop 220,200

'Lubbock or leave it' sing the Dixie Chicks, but this seemingly characteristic bit of Texas bravado isn't what it seems, as the song includes sardonic lines such as 'Got more churches than trees.' And while you'll see plenty of steeples on the horizon, what will really strike you about west Texas' liveliest city is its celebration of life beyond cotton and cows.

Buddy Holly grew up in Lubbock and the town celebrates his legacy in both attractions and an entire entertainment district. It's possible to still find the rockabilly sound that Holly made famous. The other big sound happens on fall weekends when the roar of fans at sport-mad Texas Tech football games can stop a tumbleweed in its tracks.

Orientation & Information

Lubbock is known as 'Hub City' because so many major highways meet here.

The Texas Tech campus sprawls all over the city's near-northwest side, but is mainly centered between 4th and 19th Sts north and south and University and Quaker Aves east and west. The Depot District, Lubbock's liveliest dining and nightlife area, is centered on Buddy Holly Ave (formerly known as Ave H) and 19th St.

Barnes & Noble (☎ 806-793-1061; 6002 Slide Rd; ◷ 9am-10pm) The best of a poor choice, given this is a university town.

KDAV AM 1590 Buddy Holly had a live show here in the 1950s. It still plays music from the era.

Visit Lubbock (☎ 806-747-5232, 800-692-4035; www. visitlubbock.org; 1500 Broadway St, 6th fl; ◷ 9am-5pm Mon-Fri) Small selection of brochures; not a vital stop.

Sights

Buddy Holly's roots in Lubbock (p331) are reason enough to visit.

BUDDY HOLLY CENTER

A huge version of Holly's trademark horn-rims mark the **Buddy Holly Center** (☎ 806-767-2686; www.buddyhollycenter.org; 1801 Crickets Ave; adult/child $5/2; ◷ 10am-5pm Tue-Sat, from 1pm Sun). The center is home to the Buddy Holly Gallery; a room devoted to the Man with those glasses and pristine teeth. The gallery includes some of his schoolbooks, shoes, records and other such items, but best of all are Buddy's Fender Stratocaster and hallmark glasses. It delves into his life and gives a good idea of all the rock musicians he inspired, including Bob Dylan, the Beatles and the Rolling Stones.

The center also houses a fine arts gallery, the Texas Musicians Hall of Fame, which features ever-changing exhibitions on the music and musicians of Texas, and a gift shop.

BUDDY HOLLY STATUE & WALK OF FAME

In front of the Civic Center, at the corner of 8th St and Ave Q, a larger-than-life-size statue of Holly is surrounded by plaques honoring him and other west Texans who made it big in arts and entertainment. Honorees include musicians Joe Ely, Roy Orbison, Bob Wills, Tanya Tucker and Mac Davis.

BUDDY HOLLY'S GRAVE

The headstone in the Lubbock City Cemetery reads 'In Loving Memory of Our Own Buddy Holley. September 7, 1936 to February 3, 1959.' Musical notes and an electric guitar are engraved on the marker, too. Some visitors leave guitar picks, coins and other tokens. The cemetery is located on the eastern edge of town at E 34th St and Martin Luther King Jr Blvd. Once inside the gate, turn down the lane to your right.

TEXAS TECH UNIVERSITY

About 30,000 students attend **Texas Tech University** (☎ 806-742-1299; www.ttu.edu). Established in 1925, this is not the place to see Gothic treasures of academic architecture, but it is a big and busy place during school terms.

For alumni and most locals, the school's sports teams, the Red Raiders, are a huge deal. The football team has been a powerhouse in the old Big 12 Conference of late, including going 11-2 in 2008. However, Coach Mike Leach left under a cloud at the end of 2009 and the team's future is the subject of much Lubbock chatter. Controversy also surrounded the men's basketball program, which the volatile Bobby Knight coached from 2001 to 2008.

Tech sites worth a visit include the following.

National Ranching Heritage Center

This open-air **museum** (☎ 806-742-0498; www.nrhc. com; admission free; ☼ 10am-5pm Mon-Sat, 1-5pm Sun), part of the Texas Tech museum complex, tells a detailed story of what life was like on the Texas High Plains from the late 1700s until the Dust Bowl era of the 1930s. Nearly 50 preserved ranch structures are arrayed on 16 acres. The displays are engrossing, even to those without the urge to bust sod or wax poetic about a doggie.

Museum of Texas Tech University

Art, natural history and science are showcased at this campus **museum** (☎ 806-742-2490; www. depts.ttu.edu/museumttu; 3301 4th St & Indiana Ave; admis-

sion free; ☼ 10am-5pm Tue-Sat, to 8:30pm Thu, 1-5pm Sun), which has more than five million items in its rather eclectic collection. Special exhibits are usually the highlights.

Lubbock Lake Landmark

Another Tech-run attraction, this **site** (☎ 806-742-1116; www.museum.ttu.edu/lll; 2401 Landmark Dr; admission free; ☼ 9am-5pm Tue-Sat, 1-5pm Sun) is a sort of time capsule for all the cultures that have inhabited the South Plains for the last 12,000 years. Bones of critters such as wooly mammoths were first unearthed here when agricultural irrigation caused Lubbock Lake's water table to decline in the 1930s, and excavations have gone on here since 1939.

Four miles of trails now wend through the site, where digs are ongoing. A visitor center provides context on long-gone species such as the giant short-faced bear.

To get there, follow Loop 289 to Clovis Rd west of I-27 on the northwest side of town.

AMERICAN WIND POWER CENTER

A squeaky windmill is part of the iconic opening to *Once Upon a Time in the West*, and you can see more than 90 examples of these Western icons at the **American Wind Power Center** (☎ 806-747-8734; www.windmill.com; 1701 Canyon Lake Dr; admission $5; ☼ 10am-5pm Tue-Sat, from 2pm Sun in summer), located on a 28-acre site at E Broadway St south of MacKenzie Park.

MACKENZIE PARK

Located off I-27 at Broadway St and Ave A, 248-acre Mackenzie Park has two dynamite highlights amidst what's otherwise a mundane urban park.

Prairie dogs are the eponymous stars of **Prairie Dog Town**, a hugely popular 7-acre habitat for the winsome rodents who keep busy excavating their 'town' and watching for groundskeepers.

The irresistibly named **Joyland** (☎ 806-763-2719; www.joylandpark.com; admission $10-18; ☼ varies mid-Mar–Oct, until 10pm Jun-Aug) has three roller coasters, 30 other rides and an array of carnival arcades and games that are little changed from Holly's time.

Festivals & Events

September is a big time in Lubbock, with returning Tech students and the **National Cowboy Symposium and Celebration** (☎ 806-798-7825; www. cowboy.org), a huge gathering of cowboys, cow-

BUDDY HOLLY, A REAL LEGEND

Lubbock native Charles Hardin 'Buddy' Holley was just five years old when he won a local talent contest playing a toy violin. By the time he was a teen, Buddy became a regular performer on local radio in a band that blended country-and-western with rhythm and blues. But Holly (the 'e' was dropped by an early concert promoter) soon became a leading pioneer of a new kind of music – rock and roll. Together with his backup band, the Crickets, Holly drove to Clovis, New Mexico, in early 1957 to record a demo of a song called 'That'll Be the Day.' Within months, Holly had a Top 10 record to his credit, with many more hits to follow, including 'Peggy Sue,' 'Not Fade Away,' 'Maybe Baby,' 'It's So Easy,' 'Rave On,' 'Fool's Paradise' and 'Oh, Boy!'.

Buddy Holly was among the first rock performers to write his own material, and he was among the first to experiment with multitrack overdubbing and echo in the studio. An accomplished guitarist and pianist, Holly also used his voice as an instrument, employing a hiccup here and falsetto there to distinctive effect. He and the Crickets were the real deal. In Texas, they often served as a warm-up act to visiting stars (including a young Elvis Presley), and when they hit it big they were among the first white performers to perform at the legendary Apollo Theater in Harlem, New York City.

If his talents weren't enough, Holly was guaranteed immortality by dying young – he was killed in a plane crash on February 3, 1959, near Clear Lake, Iowa. (Fellow rockers JP 'The Big Bopper' Richardson and Ritchie 'La Bamba' Valens were also on board.) His legend continues to grow and his songs and style are emulated endlessly.

The Buddy Holly Story, a 1978 film that starred Gary Busey and which won an Oscar for its music, is a highly fictionalized account of his life. In a classic bit of melodrama, Holly's parents are falsely shown opposing his music career while the mountains behind the 'Lubbock' bus station are pure Hollywood, literally.

boy wannabes, cowboy scholars, cowboy musicians and cowboy cooks. Yee-haw!

Sleeping

There are a score of motels on Ave Q just south of US 82. They are close to downtown and a reasonable 1.3-mile-walk southeast to the Depot District. There's another cluster of chains south of the center at exit 1 off I-27 and still more scattered along TX 289, the ring road, southwest of town.

BUDGET

Buffalo Springs Lake (☎ 806-747-3353; www.buffalospringslake.net; FM 835 & E 50th St; tent sites $15-35) The lake is 5 miles southeast of Lubbock and is big on fun (think ATV trails) as opposed to natural splendor. Sites vary from basic tent-only ones to those with full hookups.

Rodeway Inn (☎ 806-765-6307; www.rodewayinn.com; 910 Ave Q; r $50-90; ☎) A standard two-story motel with a mere 25 units, this motel is the closest cheapie to nightlife, and with a good night out you won't even mind staying here.

KoKo Inn (☎ 806-747-2591, 800-782-3254; www.lubbockhospitality.net/koko; 5201 Ave Q; r $50-100; ☎ ☎) This locally owned nonchain motel is a real find. You can lounge around on a large red-

wood deck surrounding the indoor pool – perfect during a winter blast. Rooms are nicely equipped and there is a cafe.

Super 8 Civic Center (☎ 806-762-8726; www.super8.com; 501 Ave Q; r $55-95; ☎) Across from a Super Wal-Mart, so you have quick access to cheap pizza (which you can heat up in the rooms with microwaves), the 35 basic rooms are arranged over two floors, with outside walkways. Wi-fi reception is best near the office.

MIDRANGE

Lubbock Inn (☎ 806-792-5181, 800-545-8226; www.lubbockinn.com, 3901 19th St; r $60-120; ☎ ☎) Near the southwest side of Texas Tech, Lubbock Inn has a restaurant and an unusual dogbone-shaped outdoor pool. The 116 rooms are midrange motel standard and are a good size. Interior corridors on the three floors provide shelter from the extremes of local weather.

Broadway Manor Bed & Breakfast (☎ 806-749-4707, 877-504-8223; www.broadwaymanor.net; 1811 Broadway; r $80-150; ☎) Ideally located between downtown and Tech, this stately 1926 brick house has five plush theme rooms. Stay in Bali, Siam or simply travel back to the old West in the Wild West room (you supply the chaps). Some have Jacuzzi tubs.

Holiday Inn Hotel Civic Center (☎ 806-763-1200; www.holidayinn.com; 801 Ave Q; r $90-160; 🛜 🐾) Something of a tower by local standards, the 70 rooms here are arrayed over six stories. Business travelers appreciate the large work desks; anyone in need of a dip will appreciate the indoor pool.

Eating

Good restaurants are scattered around town, although you won't go wrong basing yourself in the Depot District and browsing. An organic **farmers market** (cnr Ave A & 19th St; 🕑 9am-5:30pm Mon-Sat Jun-Nov) sells the region's best produce.

Freebirds World Burrito (☎ 806-741-0900; 1201 University Ave; meals from $4; 🕑 10am-10pm) At the Tech entrance, this popular joint has four sizes of burritos. The 'super monster' will keep you in beans for a week.

Ranch House Restaurant (☎ 806-762-3472; 1520 Buddy Holly Ave; meals from $6; 🕑 6am-4pm Mon-Sat) Formica tables and waiters who know what you want before your morning mouth can form the words help make this huge old diner a classic. Eggs fuel the breakfast hordes, while lunchers vie for pot roast and Red Top stew (beef, carrots and chiles).

Tom & Bingos Bar-B-Que (☎ 806-799-1514; 3006 34th St; meals from $6; 🕑 lunch Mon-Sat) Calling this place a shack is an insult to decrepit buildings everywhere, but appearances are forgotten when you taste the smoked ham and brisket sandwiches (have the latter chopped). Sides are few: use the fries to mop up the tangy, sweet sauce.

Orlando's (☎ 806-747-5998; 2402 Ave Q; meals from $9; 🕑 11am-10pm) This local, family-run Italian institution has introduced pasta to generations of ranch folk – this may explain why, of all things, the sensational burger is an eye-popper. Otherwise dive into the hearty red sauce and make your chin glisten.

Triple J Chop House (☎ 806-771-6555; 1807 Buddy Holly Ave; meals from $12; 🕑 11am-11pm Mon-Sat) The airy, exposed brick dining room has a glass wall looking into a microbrewery. The White Gold Cream and Sip-O-Whit outclass any of the domestic swills favored by locals. Steaks live up to west Texas standards and there are also tasty alternatives with a Southwestern flair.

Entertainment

Go!, a free weekly by the town's wonderfully named newspaper, the *Lubbock Avalanche-Journal*, has full listings of what's on.

DEPOT DISTRICT

The Depot District is Lubbock's nightlife HQ (fittingly, the namesake building at the Buddy Holly Center looks hungover), it covers a few blocks adjoining Buddy Holly Ave between 17th and 19th Sts.

Blue Light (☎ 806-762-3688; www.thebluelightlive.com; 1806 Buddy Holly Ave) This legendary club has plenty of live Texas country and rock. Watch for hall-of-famer Gary P Nunn. Have a smoke at the sidewalk tables.

Cactus Courtyard (☎ 806-535-5610; www.cactus courtyard.com; 1801 Buddy Holly Ave; 🕑 Apr-Oct) Huge open-air venue with west Texas music and all the domestic beers you can quaff.

END OF THE COMANCHE TRAIL

Until 1871, the Comanches were the most feared of the Plains Indian tribes. While others had been beaten by the US Army and forced into camps and reservations, the Comanches were undefeated and had actually expanded their territory, Comancheria, which encompassed what is today everything in Texas and Oklahoma north and west of Austin. Beginning that September, cavalry led by Col Raynald S Mackenzie fought a series of running skirmishes with bands of Comanches in and around the Blanco Canyon (other battles had taken place in Caprock and Palo Duro Canyons). Although at first seemingly indecisive, the conflict proved to be the beginning of the end for the Comanches, who lost much of their goods and wealth in addition to having the heart of their territory invaded by the army for the first time. By 1875 the last free band of Comanches had surrendered.

The pivotal battles were fought in the Blanco Canyon, which can be easily seen just 3 miles east of Crosbyton on US 82, itself 38 miles east of Lubbock. Various paved farm roads running north of here penetrate into the canyon, which remains windy and largely desolate today. As you follow the White River, try to imagine Comanches and cavalry troops eyeing each other from the valley and escarpments.

Cactus Theater (☎ 806-747-7047; www.cactustheater. com; 1812 Buddy Holly Ave) This handsome 1938 theater mostly presents variety shows, including the *Buddy Holly Story*, *Always...Patsy Cline* and *Honky Tonk Angels*.

La Diosa Cellars (☎ 806-744-3600; 901 17th St; ☺ 11am-midnight Tue-Sat) One of several local wineries (see p333), La Diosa uncorks a range of Texas wines beyond its own label. There's inventive Mediterranean-style snacks and meals as well as a coffee bar.

TEXAS TECH

Raucous bars, cheap burrito joints and plasma dealers mark the classic college neighborhood where Broadway crosses University Ave into the campus.

Bash Riprock's (☎ 806-762-2274; 2491 Main St) It's dark and grungy, and the huge beer selection gets a workout on Mondays when the $5 cover gets you $2 pints.

Chimy's Cerveceria (☎ 806-763-7369; 2417 Broadway) A sprawling party house that appeals to students of all ages; the patio is a delight.

Shopping

Dollar Western Wear (☎ 806-793-2818; 5011 Slide Rd) Lubbock has lots of Western-gear shops; this place is among the biggest.

Getting There & Around

Lubbock International Airport (LIA; ☎ 806-775-3126; www.flylia.com) is situated 7 miles north of town, at exit 8 off of I-27. Airlines include American Eagle (Dallas–Fort Worth), Continental (Houston) and Southwest (Dallas, Houston and Las Vegas).

Lubbock is a hub for **Greyhound** (☎ 806-687-4501; www.greyhound.com; 801 Broadway), with buses serving most major Texas cities including Dallas ($66, 6½ hours).

Citibus (☎ 806-762-0111; www.citibus.com; adult/child $1.50/1) provides basic public transportation. Most routes originate from the Downtown Plaza at Broadway St and Buddy Holly Ave downtown.

AROUND LUBBOCK
Wineries

Down in the Texas Hill Country, wine seems to make sense. Up here on the boot-scootin,' teetotalin' High Plains, it sounds like a joke. But hold those 'yucks,' as the Lubbock region has near-ideal wine grape-growing conditions: sandy soil, hot days and cool nights.

Cabernets are the local specialty and more than 20 vineyards are now producing bold reds. You can try many of these while in Lubbock at La Diosa Cellars, a welcoming wine bar run by its namesake winery. Several others are good for a visit, and tours are generally free.

LLANO ESTACADO WINERY

This **winery** (☎ 806-863-2704; www.llanowine.com; 3426 E FM 1585 east of US 87; ☺ 10am-5pm Mon-Sat, noon-5pm Sun) was founded in 1976, making it the oldest – and largest – of the modern Texas wineries. Among the 22 wines produced, the chardonnays have won plaudits.

Llano's (pronounced *yah*-no's) shop features its wines (most $10 to $20, although a gulpable blush is $8) and myriad gourmet items, such as jalapeño mustard, that find their way to the back of the fridge.

CAPROCK WINERY

About 4 miles southwest of Llano Estacado, **CapRock Winery** (☎ 806-863-2704; www.caprockwinery. com; 408 E Woodrow Rd south of FM 1585, half a mile east of US 87; ☺ 10am-5pm Mon-Sat) is worth a visit for its beautiful mission-style headquarters, a showplace both inside and out. CapRock makes about a dozen wines.

PHEASANT RIDGE WINERY

Located 14 miles north of Lubbock near the town of New Deal, this **winery** (☎ 806-746-6033; www.pheasantridgewinery.com; 3507 E County Rd 5700; ☺ noon-6pm Fri & Sat, 1-5pm Sun) is known for its range of wines, including the expected cabs but also a zesty chenin blanc.

Apple Country Hi-Plains Orchards

The sweet smell of apple blossoms in spring perfumes the air as you head east of Lubbock on US 62/82. Some 16 miles east of the city, **Apple Country Hi-Plains Orchards** (☎ 806-892-2961; 12206 E US 62/82; ☺ 9am-6pm Mon-Sat, to 4pm Sun) has pick-your-own apple orchards, a popular lunch cafe and a shop with produce, including wild honey.

ALONG HWY 70

Evocative small towns – some thriving, others nearly gone – are found throughout west Texas. One little burg after another seems ripped from the pages of a Larry McMurty novel. Texas Hwy 70 manages to link a string of these nearly forgotten places: a drive along this road puts you further than simple geography from the 21st century.

Begin in the south in **Sweetwater**, along I-20, some 40 miles west of Abilene. Long and lonely vistas of lush ranchland await as you drive north on Hwy 70. About 55 miles north, turn west at the T-junction with US 380 and drive 5 miles to the nearly evaporated ghost town of **Claremont**. About all that remains is a red stone jail, which could be a movie set.

Return east and rejoin Hwy 70. Some 40 miles of occasional rivers, scattered annuities (oil wells) and countless cattle later, you're in the modestly named hamlet of **Spur**. Most of the once-proud brick structures downtown are barely hanging on, like a chimney with bad grout. But the **Turnaround Cafe** (☎ 806-271-3983; 202 Burlington St; meals from $5; ☻ 5:30am-8:30pm Tue-Sun) is a lively spot for huge omelettes and burgers, cheerfully served in an old filling station.

Just another 11 miles north brings you to the seat of Dickens County: **Dickens**. Another fading burg, you can still sense the pride of the original settlers in the massive courthouse built from carved limestone. Catch up on all the gossip at **TC's Ponderosa** (☎ 806-623-5260; 136 US 82; meals from $5; ☻ 7am-8pm), which is inside the Fina gas station. Superb barbecue is served up simply on Formica tables. Try the hot links and nab a pickled egg and sausage for the road.

From here it is nearly 57 miles almost due north through verdant cattle and cotton country to your ultimate goal, Turkey (p334). Pause in towns such as **Roaring Springs** in Motley County for smatterings of tiny shops that will never attract the attention of Wal-Mart.

TURKEY
pop 400

The lovely lady in city hall told us that 'people are dying too quick.' And indeed like the flight path of its namesake bird, Turkey has been descending for decades. But amidst the grizzled streets is a not-to-be-missed cultural attraction.

Bob Wills Museum

'As heaven would miss the stars above. With every heartbeat I still think of you,' sang Bob Wills in his iconic 'Faded Love.' One of the most important Texas musicians, his life is recalled at the eponymous **museum** (☎ 806-423-1146; www.turkeytexas.net; admission free; ☻ 9am-11:30am

& 1-4pm Mon-Fri). Located in the old elementary school (which also has the tiny city hall and library), the displays cover much of Wills' adventurous life, which included a string of B-movie Westerns. But it's the music that survives. Wills was a major creator of a genre of music known as Western Swing, described by David Vinopal in the *All-Music Guide* like this:

Take fiddle-based old-time stringband music from the '20s and '30s, move it to a city such as Tulsa or Fort Worth, add jazz and blues and pop and sacred music, back it with strings and horns played by a dozen or so musicians, add an electric steel guitar along the way, and you have Western swing; and when you talk Western swing, you start with Bob Wills.

Wills reached his greatest fame in the 1940s with his band the Texas Playboys, with whom he recorded such hits as 'San Antonio Rose' and 'Faded Love.'

The museum includes lots of artifacts from the musician's life, including his fiddles, scrapbooks, movie-posters, a gazillion photos and more. In the halls outside are haunting class photos from the adjoining high school, which closed in 1972. They tell stories of a time when the future of Turkey looked much different.

Turkey celebrates Wills' legacy with **Bob Wills Days** (www.bobwillsday.com) late each April, when 10,000 or more people stuff themselves into Turkey for a weekend of pickin' and grinnin', with jam sessions galore.

QUITAQUE
pop 370

Quitaque has been a rival of Turkey's for decades; the latter never forgave the former for getting the town's combined schools in the 1970s. But this small town isn't doing much better than Turkey, although the beauty of Caprock Canyons brings a steady stream of travelers.

The town of Quitaque's website (www.quitaque.org) lists guesthouses in the area, but many people choose to camp in the Caprock Canyons State Park.

Cafe, bar and de facto community center, **Sportsman** (☎ 806-455-1200; 204 Main St; meals from $6; ☻ 11am-8pm) is a popular place serving excellent Tex-Mex food that lures in regulars with chicken-fried steaks, burgers, enchiladas, nachos and more. Options in these parts are limited, so it's a real find. You can also try asking for B&B lodging, which is sometimes on offer.

CAPROCK CANYONS STATE PARK & TRAILWAYS

Although it's not as well known as Palo Duro Canyon State Park, **Caprock Canyons** (☎ 806-455-1492; www.tpwd.state.tx.us; admission $3) shares the same kind of stunning topography and abundant wildlife. Even the casual visitor is likely to see mule deer, roadrunners and aoudad, the North African barbary sheep transplanted to the Panhandle in the 1950s. The sunsets are stupendous, but the trail system here is what makes Caprock Canyons one of Texas' best state parks: 90 miles of outstanding and diverse hiking, mountain biking and horseback riding, including 26 miles in the park proper and another 64 miles on the Trailways System, a rails-to-trails project. Many visitors are just content to drop a line in the serene waters of little Lake Theo.

The park is home to a donated bison herd from the JA Ranch – the very herd started by pioneer rancher Charles Goodnight in 1876. Take well-marked FM 1065 from Quitaque 3 miles to the park headquarters. Here you can also rent an audio tour for use with a vehicle or arrange for a trail bike.

CAPROCK CANYONS TRAILWAYS

Running through three counties from Estelline to the northeast to South Plains to the southwest, the 64-mile abandoned railroad bed Trailways opened in 1993. Highlights of the trailways include some 50 bridges and the 742ft Clarity Tunnel, a historic railroad passage. It's popular with hikers, bikers and riders. The route runs across the fertile plains and drops into the appropriately named Red River Valley.

Trail access points and parking lots can be found along TX 86 at Estelline, Parnell, Tampico Siding, Turkey and Quitaque. On this section, the trail runs parallel to, but a good distance from, the highway. At Quitaque, the trail swings south then west for the final 23 miles to South Plains – the portion that includes the tunnel. Access points on this part of the trail are at Monk's Crossing and South Plains.

Primitive campsites are available along the route for $8; get a permit from the state park

before setting out. Day users can pay their fees at the self-pay station at each trailhead. Trail users should carry drinking water; in summer it gets hot as blazes and unwise hikers regularly get ill from dehydration. Cyclists and hikers can use the services of **Caprock Home Center** (☎ 806-455-1193; 126 W Main St, Quitaque), where the owner, Roland Hamilton, can arrange shuttles to/from various parts of the Trailways.

PARK TRAILS

The state park also has outstanding trails. Stop at the park headquarters for a map showing trailheads and distances. For an easy trail of about 2.5 miles round-trip, follow the hikers-only Upper Canyon Trail from the South Prong tent camping area trailhead to the South Prong primitive camping area and back. Beyond the primitive camping area, the Upper Canyon Trail becomes increasingly steep and rugged; the cliffs and bluffs are not for the foolhardy. It won't be hard to imagine what it was like for the Comanche people in their final days on the run from the US Army here in the early 1870s (p332).

SLEEPING

Besides the simple campsites along the Trailways, the park has more developed campgrounds as well. Reserve through the **state park reservation system** (☎ 512-389-8900; www.texasstateparks.org).

Walk-in campsites are the most atmospheric. Primitive ones (per site $8) and slightly more developed – but still walk-in – sites (per site $12) can be found in the more remote reaches of the park.

Honey Flat is the park's most developed camping area, with 35 sites with water and electricity (per site $20). It's an easy walk to Lake Theo.

Other options are few: most motels are along I-27 in Tulia, Canyon and Amarillo.

AMARILLO
pop 192,700

Long a vital stop, roughly halfway between Chicago and LA on old Route 66, Amarillo continues to figure in travel plans, simply by being the brightest light on the 543-mile stretch if I-40 between Oklahoma City, Oklahoma, and Albuquerque, New Mexico.

And though the town may seem as featureless as the surrounding landscape, there's plenty here to sate even the most attention-challenged during a road respite. Beef, the big local industry, is at the heart of Amarillo and it features in many of its attractions, including a star role at the Big Texan Steak Ranch (p339).

Like a good steak, Amarillo is marbled – only with railroad tracks. Running south of town, I-40 is especially charmless. Instead, follow SE 3rd Ave from the east to SW 6th Ave through the comatose center and decaying west side to SW 6th Ave. Locally dubbed the San Jacinto District, the strip between Georgia St and Western St was once part of Route 66 and is Amarillo's best shopping, dining and entertainment district.

Information

The *Amarillo Independent* is a frisky free weekly with full local event info and an alternative viewpoint.

Amarillo Convention and Visitor Council (☎ 806-374-1497, 800-692-1338; www.visitamarillotx.com; Amarillo Civic Center, 401 S Buchanan St; �)9am-5pm Mon-Fri, noon-4pm Sat Sep-May, 10am-4pm Sat & Sun Jun-Aug) The staff will be mighty glad you stopped.
Texas Travel Information Center (☎ 806-335-1441; 9700 E I-40 exit 76; ☉ 8am-5pm, to 6pm summer; ☎) Excellent resource, with vast amounts of info.

Sights
CADILLAC RANCH

To millions of people whizzing across the Texas Panhandle each year, the **Cadillac Ranch** (I-40 W, btwn exits 60 & 62; admission free; ☉ 24hr), also known as Amarillo's 'Bumper Crop,' is the ultimate symbol of the US love affair with wheels. A salute to Route 66 and the spirit of the American road, it was created by burying, hood first, 10 west-facing Cadillacs in a wheat field outside town.

In 1974 Amarillo businessperson and arts patron Stanley Marsh 3 funded the San Francisco-based Ant Farm collective's 'monument to the rise and fall of the Cadillac tail fin.' The cars date from 1948 to 1959 – a period in which tail fins just kept getting bigger and bigger – on to 1963, when the fin vanished. Marsh relocated the cars in 1997 to a field 2 miles west of its original location due to urban sprawl.

The cars are easily spotted off the access road on the south side of I-40. The accepted practice today is to leave your own mark on the art by drawing on the cars, which gives them an ever-changing patina. Bring spray

paint in case other visitors haven't left any around.

More cars spring from the ground 18 miles east of Amarillo in Conway, where five stripped-down VW bugs form **Bug Ranch** (I-40 at TX 207), a failed 2002 effort to promote a convenience store. Again, feel free to leave your spray-painted signature.

AMARILLO LIVESTOCK AUCTION

A slice of the real West is on display every Tuesday morning at the **Amarillo Livestock Auction** (☎ 806-373-7464; www.amarillolivestockauction.com; 100 S Manhattan St), just north of SE 3rd Ave on the city's east side. The auction is still one of the state's largest, moo-ving more than 100,000 animals annually (from its 1970s peak of 715,000). The auction starts at 10am and things happen fast: cattle are herded in through one pneumatic gate and out through another, and most animals sell within about 30 seconds. The auctions draw few tourists, but all are welcome. Grab lunch at the Stockyard Cafe (p339).

AMERICAN QUARTER HORSE HALL OF FAME & MUSEUM

Quarter horses, favored on the Texas range, were originally named for their prowess at galloping down early American racetracks, which were a quarter-mile long. These beautiful animals are celebrated at this **museum** (☎ 806-376-5181; www.aqha.com; 2601 I-40 E exit 72A; adult/child $6/2; ☉ 9am-5pm Mon-Sat), which fully explores their roles in ranching and racing.

DON HARRINGTON DISCOVERY CENTER

Sadly you can't snort any helium and talk like Donald Duck, but the lighter-than-air gas that was an Amarillo industry is honored at the **Don Harrington Discovery Center** (☎ 806-355-9547; www.dhdc.org; 1200 Streit Dr; adult/child $7/5; ☉ 9:30am-4:30pm Tue-Sat, from noon Sun). Aquariums, a planetarium and science exhibits round out a visit.

WILDCAT BLUFF NATURE CENTER

Stretch those road legs at this 600-acre **nature center** (☎ 806-352-6007; www.wildcatbluff.org; 2301 N Soncy Rd; adult/child $3/2; ☉ 9am-5pm Mon-Sat), which has trails winding through grasslands, cottonwoods and bluffs. Spy on a prairie dog town and try to spot a burrowing owl or porcupine while avoiding rattlesnakes and tarantulas. The center is just northwest of town, off TX 335.

AMARILLO

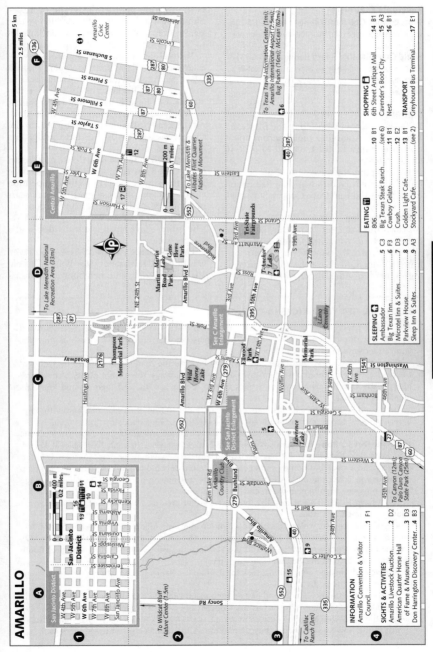

INFORMATION
Amarillo Convention & Visitor
Council..1 F1

SIGHTS & ACTIVITIES
Amarillo Livestock Auction.............2 D2
American Quarter Horse Hall
of Fame & Museum.......................3 D3
Don Harrington Discovery Center...4 B3

SLEEPING
Ambassador....................................5 C3
Big Texan Inn.................................6 F3
Microtel Inn & Suites......................7 D3
Parkview House...............................8 C3
Sleep Inn & Suites..........................9 A3

EATING
806..10 B1
Big Texan Steak Ranch.............(see 6)
Cowboy Gelato..............................11 B1
Crush...12 E2
Golden Light Cafe..........................13 B1
Stockyard Cafe.........................(see 2)

SHOPPING
6th Street Antique Mall..................14 B1
Cavender's Boot City......................15 A3
Nest...16 B1

TRANSPORT
Greyhound Bus Terminal................17 E1

Festivals & Events

Coors Cowboy Club Ranch Rodeo (☎ 806-378-3096; www.coorsranchrodeo.com) Huge rodeo and ranch trade show in June.

World Championship Ranch Rodeo (☎ 806-374-9722; www.wrca.org) No dudes allowed at this real-deal event that crowns the world champion cowboy in November.

Sleeping

With the notable exception of the Big Texan Inn, most of Amarillo's motel accommodations are chains. Exits 64, 65 and 71 off I-40 all have clusters.

For camping, the most natural sites can be found at Lake Meredith National Recreation Area (p340) and Palo Duro Canyon State Park (p341).

Big Texan Inn (☎ 800-657-7177; www.bigtexan.com; 7700 I-40 E exit 74; r $50-90;) The hotel part of Amarillo's star attraction has 55 surprisingly modest rooms behind a faux Old West facade. The real highlight – besides the modest prices –

is the outside pool in the shape of Texas. Should you try the huge steak challenge (see p339), even crawling across the parking lot to collapse in your room may be beyond you.

Microtel Inn & Suites (☎ 806-372-8373; www.microtelinn.com; 1501 Ross St, off I-40 at exit 71; r $60-120;) A typical outlet for this high-scoring budget chain. Rooms are spread over two stories and have interior hallways. 'Suites' are really just larger rooms, but for a small rate increase (often just $10) you get a room that sleeps four easily plus has a fridge and microwave.

Sleep Inn & Suites (☎ 806-242-7777; www.sleepinn.com; 6915 I-40 W, near exit 65; r $70-140;) New in 2009, this simple motel beats the competition simply because it doesn't yet bear the scars of a million road-trippers. The 65 rooms all have fridges, microwaves and plasma TVs. The 'suites' have small room dividers and a sleeper-sofa.

Parkview House (☎ 806-373-9464; www.parkviewhousebb.com; 1311 S Jefferson St; r $85-135;) This old Victorian B&B is in a neighborhood of his-

ROUTE 66: GET YOUR KICKS IN TEXAS

The Mother Road arrows across Texas for a mere 178 miles. The entire route has been replaced by I-40, but through frontage and access roads plus detours through towns such as Amarillo, you can recreate most of the old route.

Given the featureless landscape, one can only imagine the road ennui suffered by scores of travelers as they motored past the brown expanses. As always, there were plenty of entrepreneurs ready to offer diversions for a buck or two. Going east to west, here's some Route 66 highlights in Texas.

Follow old Route 66 which runs immediately south of I-40 from the Oklahoma border through barely changed towns such as Shamrock, with its restored 1930s buildings.

About 33 miles from the border, cross I-40 to the north side and the battered town of McClean. There the **Devil's Rope Museum** (☎ 806-779-2225; www.barbwiremuseum.com; 100 Kingsley St, McLean; admission free; 10am-4pm Tue-Sat) has vast barbed wire displays (where hipsters look for new tattoo patterns) and a small but homey and idiosyncratic room devoted to Route 66. The detailed map of the road in Texas is a must. Also worth a look are the moving portraits of Dust Bowl damage and the refugees from human-made environmental disaster.

You'll have to join I-40 at exit 132, but just west of here on both sides of the freeway are Route 66-themed rest stops.

At exit 78 leave I-40, which runs just south of Amarillo, and follow SE 3rd Ave and SW 6th Ave through town. Here you'll find a plethora of Route 66 sites: the Big Texan Steak Ranch (p339), the historic livestock auction (p336) and the San Jacinto District, which still has original Route 66 businesses such as the Golden Light Cafe (p339).

Just west of Amarillo after exit 62, look for the Cadillac Ranch (p336), where 10 road veterans have met a colorful end.

Use the old highway north of I-40 or exit 36 to reach Vega, an old road town that seems little changed in decades, but which still has some decent cafes. Some 14 miles west, Adrian clings to fame as the purported historic Route 66 midpoint, with LA and Chicago each 1139 miles distant.

Just at the New Mexico border, tiny Glenrio makes the moniker 'ghost town' seem lively.

toric homes dating to the cattle baron days. In addition to five guest rooms and a cottage, it has music and world-travel themed common rooms. There's a hot tub and a hammock in the yard and genial Elwood Park is a short stroll away.

Ambassador (☎ 806-358-6161, 800-817-0521; www.ambassadoramarillo.com; 3100 I-40 W near exit 68; r $90-160; 🖥 🛜 🐾) Ignore the stark exterior of this 10-story hotel (unless you're fascinated by the grain silos) and concentrate on the multitude of services offered at this independent hotel aimed at business travelers. The 263 rooms have numerous plush touches and those in the 'Cattle Baron' class give you extras so you can feel your oats.

Eating & Drinking

At first burp, Amarillo seems awash in chain eateries along the I-40 frontage roads, but delve a little deeper to find some gems, especially along SW 6th Ave. However, don't close your eyes to everything on I-40, as Amarillo's top attraction, the Big Texan, awaits.

Cowboy Gelato (☎ 806-376-5286; 2806 SW 6th Ave; treats from $2; 🕙 11am-8pm Mon-Sat) The Texas plains are flat as a frying pan and often just as hot. Escape the heat in this cute little cafe which makes its own creamy gelatos. Barbecue sandwiches and fried green beans fill out a meal.

Golden Light Cafe (☎ 806-374-0097; 2908 SW 6th Ave; meals $4-8; 🕙 11am-10pm Mon-Wed, to 11pm Thu-Sat) Classic cheeseburgers, home-cut fries and cold beer have sated travelers on Route 66 at this modest brick dive since 1946. On some nights there's live music; when Sean McConnell plays it's packed and hotter than the ancient grill.

806 (☎ 806-322-1806; 2812 SW 6th Ave; meals from $5; 🕙 8am-midnight; 🛜) Wobbling, mismatched chairs define the funky vibe at this coffeehouse, where local slackers ponder moving to New York. Beer in bottles plus lots of tasty, healthy snacks such as chili and hummus provide fuel for thought. There's live acoustic music some nights.

Crush (☎ 806-418-2011; 701 S Polk St; meals $7-20; 🕙 11am-9pm Mon-Thu, to midnight Fri & Sat) Folks in suits and skirts and cowboy boots flock here for Amarillo's best beer and wine selection plus fare that breaks with the ALL BEEF ALL THE TIME local vibe. Salads, tapas and creative light fare are ideally enjoyed outside on the patio. Crush anchors a small nightlife district downtown.

Stockyard Cafe (☎ 806-374-6024; 100 S Manhattan St; meals $8-20; 🕙 9am-2pm Mon-Thu, to 8pm Fri) This cafe in the Amarillo Livestock Auction building (p336) is where the cattlemen sit down for some beef. The steaks are ideal – thick and perfectly charred – but most have the plate-swamping chicken-fried steak. Follow your nose here, past corrals and railroad tracks.

Big Texan Steak Ranch (☎ 800-657-7177; www.bigtexan.com; 7700 I-40 E exit 74; meals $8-35; 🕙 7am-10:30pm; 🛜) A classic, hokey Route 66 roadside attraction, the Big Texan made the move when I-40 opened in 1971 and has never looked back. Stretch-Cadillac limos with steer-horn hood ornaments wait out front, marquee lights blink above, a shooting arcade pings inside the saloon, and a big, tall Tex road sign welcomes you (after taunting billboards for miles in either direction). The legendary come-on: the 'free 72oz steak,' a devilish offer as you have to eat this enormous portion of cow plus a multitude of sides in under one hour, or you pay for the entire meal ($72). Contestants sit at a raised table to 'entertain' the other diners and you can watch anytime via a live webcam (we watched one beefy guy who started out all cocky but by the 45-minute mark was less than half done and staring glumly at the door).

Less than 20% survive the challenge, although one lunatic wolfed it all down in 8 minutes 52 seconds in 2008. Insane eating aside, the ranch is a fine place to eat, the steaks are excellent – and still huge – and we had a very fine prime rib. Adding to the fun are strolling cowboy troubadours, a beer garden, buzzing bar and the willfully schticky vibe. In a word, it's a hoot!

Shopping

The stretch of SW 6th Ave west of Georgia St has numerous antique and junk shops that recall the old Route 66 beat. The **6th Street Antique Mall** (☎ 806-374-0459; 2715 SW 6th Ave) anchors a strip of antique stores. **Nest** (☎ 806-418-2317; 2900 SW 6th Ave) eschews retro funk for a hip collection of local art, sun-powered gadgets and other bits of intrigue.

Cavender's Boot City (☎ 806-358-1400; 7920 I-40 W exit 64) If you're looking for Western wear, you'll love this place that's an easy stop even if you're whizzing past on I-40. This warehouse-sized outpost of the regional chain has about 12,000 pairs of boots in stock at all times.

Getting There & Around

Amarillo International Airport (AMA; ☎ 806-335-1671) is located on the eastern edge of town north of I-40 via exit 76. It's served by American Eagle (Dallas–Fort Worth), Continental (Houston) and Southwest (Dallas and Denver).

Greyhound (☎ 806-374-5371; www.greyhound.com; 700 S Tyler St) runs buses east and west on I-40 plus major cities in Texas such as Dallas ($85, six hours).

Amarillo City Transit (☎ 806-378-3095; adult/child $1.50/1) runs a barebones bus service.

AROUND AMARILLO

The best sights near Amarillo are Palo Duro Canyon (p340) and the little towns along Route 66 (p338). But you can also find some natural escapes to the north.

Lake Meredith National Recreation Area

Some 35 miles northeast of Amarillo, **Lake Meredith National Recreation Area** (☎ 806-857-3151; www.nps.gov/lamr; admission free) is a result of the Sanford Dam water project on the Canadian River. It's a recreation area popular for boating and fishing.

Boat rentals are available at the lake through **Marina at Lake Meredith** (☎ 806-865-3391). Rates for powerboats start at $27 per hour and get cheaper the longer you rent. Deck cruisers are also available.

For **fishing**, Lake Meredith is home to largemouth, small-mouth and white bass, catfish, white crappie, sunfish, carp and walleye.

Camping at Lake Meredith is free, mainly because amenities are limited: there are no reservations, no hookups or showers, but there are generally picnic tables, grills and pit toilets. Sites include spots overlooking the reservoir and more remote locations back in the canyons.

Alibates Flint Quarries National Monument

It's not every day you can pick up a hammer stone used to make tools 10,000 years ago or hold discarded shards of beautifully colored flint left behind by ancient peoples. But at **Alibates Flint Quarries** (☎ 806-857-3151; www.nps.gov/alfl; Fritch; admission free; tours 10am & 2pm by advance reservation only) visitors can touch the past and learn what it was like to live off the land when mammoths roamed the plains.

Tours – the only way to visit – involve 1.5 miles of walking. They leave from a small ranger station, 5 miles west of TX 136 on Alibates Rd, next to Lake Meredith.

PALO DURO CANYON

The pancake-flat Texas plains have some real texture at Palo Duro Canyon, it's just that all the drama is below the horizon rather than above it. Second only to the Grand Canyon in terms of size, the meandering gorge is a place of brilliant colors and vibrant life (the name means 'hard wood' for the groves of mesquite). The nearby town of Canyon, 20 miles south of Amarillo, makes for a comfy base.

Canyon
pop 14,100

Small, yet cultured, Canyon is in many ways more interesting than Amarillo to the north. Georgia O'Keeffe once taught art at what is now west Texas A&M University, and today's campus is home to what many people figure is the best history museum in Texas – the Panhandle-Plains Historical Museum. Moreover, this is an ideal starting spot for Palo Duro Canyon State Park, one of the state's natural showpieces.

SIGHTS

The many ways to skin a buffalo is but one of the myriad highlights of the magnificent **Panhandle-Plains Historical Museum** (☎ 806-651-2244; www.panhandleplains.org; 2401 4th Ave; adult/child $10/5; 🕑 9am-6pm Mon-Sat, 1-6pm Sun, until 5pm Sep-May), a Texas plains must-see.

Collections and displays include: the Panhandle's oil heyday as seen through the prism of the boomtown of Borger and an old-time filling station; life-size casts of dinosaurs; the oldest assembly-line auto in the world (a 1903 Ford); world-class art from Texas painters and photographers; and the previously mentioned role of the buffalo in the rich cultures of Native Americans. You can hit the highlights in an hour or easily lose a day.

SLEEPING

The drive south from Amarillo can be a chore at busy times, so it's better to stay in Canyon for a visit to the park. Campers should head straight to the park (p341).

Buffalo Inn (☎ 806-655-2124, 800-526-9968; www.buffaloinncanyontx.com; 300 23rd St/US 87; r $50-75; 🛜)

This classic 1960s single-story motel is centrally located by the west Texas A&M campus. It's well maintained and has the charm lacking in new chains.

Best Western Palo Duro Canyon (☎ 806-655-1132; www.bestwestern.com; 2801 4th Ave; r $70-180; ⊒ 🖨 🕾 🛎) As tidy inside as the white paint is outside, this recently built 51-unit motel lacks any regional charm but is convenient to the canyon and I-27.

EATING
Canyon has good eats, but choices in the canyon itself are basic.

Ranch House Cafe (☎ 806-655-8785; 810 23rd St; meals from $6; ⏱ 7am-9pm) Look for the classic trapezoidal red sign along the old US 87 strip. Chicken-fried steak, chicken-fried chicken(!) and more lead the long list of diner specials. Ponder the posies on the spare yellow exterior and then enter a kingdom of fresh north Texas chow.

Feldman's Wrong Way Diner (☎ 806-655-2700; 1701 5th Ave; meals from $7; ⏱ 11am-9pm) As the menu says, this classy diner is dedicated to anyone who has made a wrong turn, wrong decision or wandered off the beaten path. Here, at least, you'll know you've done the right thing. Steaks, chicken and pork chops star and are supported by a cast of sides including perfect okra and lovely broccoli. Lots of salads too.

GETTING THERE & AROUND
Canyon (and the actual canyon) are car country.

Palo Duro Canyon State Park
At 120 miles long and about 5 miles wide, Palo Duro Canyon is second in size in the USA only to the Grand Canyon (also in Arizona, naturally). The cliffs striated in yellows, reds and oranges, rock towers and other geologic oddities are a refreshing surprise amongst the seemingly endless flatness of the plains, and are worth at least a gander.

The multihued canyon was created by the Prairie Dog Town Fork of the Red River, a long name for a little river. The great gorge has sheltered and inspired people for a long time. Prehistoric Indians lived in the canyon 12,000 years ago, and Coronado may have stopped by in 1541. Palo Duro was the site of an 1874 battle between Comanche and Kiowa

warriors and the US Army. The over 26,000 acres that make up the park attract hikers, horseback riders and mountain bikers eager for recreation and artists and photographers drawn by the magnificent blend of color and desert light.

The **park** (☎ 806-488-2227; www.tpwd.state.tx.us; adult/child $5/free; ⏱ main gate 6am-8pm Mon-Thu, to 10pm Fri & Sat, shorter in winter) is at the end of TX 217, 12 miles east of Canyon and 24 miles southeast of Amarillo. The best time to visit is in the fall or winter because it gets dang hot here in the summertime (carry lots of water!). A small but pretty 1934 visitors center overlooks the canyon, has interpretive exhibits on the area's geology and history, the region's best bookstore and good tourist info.

ACTIVITIES
Palo Duro's most popular **hiking** trail leads to the Lighthouse, a hoodoo-style formation that's nearly 300ft tall. Almost all of the nearly 6-mile round-trip Lighthouse Trail is flat and easily traversed. The floodplain to the southwest of the Lighthouse Trail has perhaps the park's greatest concentration of wildlife including aoudad sheep, white-tailed mule deer and wild turkeys.

The **Old West Stables** (☎ 806-488-2180; www.oldweststables.com; rides from $35) offers a variety of trips in Palo Duro Canyon.

There are plenty of great mountain-biking trails throughout the canyon, but nowhere to rent bikes.

SLEEPING & EATING
For motels and restaurants, you'll need to be in Canyon or Amarillo. Inside the park, the **Trading Post** (☎ 806-488-2180; ⏱ 6am-8pm Mon-Thu, to 10pm Fri & Sat, shorter in winter) has supplies and simple meals.

Campsites (sites $12-25) range from some attractive and remote ones aimed at backpackers to regular sites with full hookups. **Cabins** (☎ 512-389-9000; www.texasstateparks.org; per night $60-125) are a treat but there are only seven, so reserve.

ENTERTAINMENT
Hokey, jingoistic, over-the-top, effervescent and loud are just some of the adjectives for **Texas** (☎ 806-655-2181; www.texas-show.com; tickets $10-30; ⏱ 8:30pm Tue-Sun early Jun–mid-Aug), an open-air

DETOUR: CANADIAN

Named for the local river, Canadian has few links with the cheery country far to the north (although with locally popular Coors being owned by Molsen, you could say the convenience stores are filled with Canadian beer). Rather, it is a once-dying Texas plains town (one of dozens) that uniquely saved itself by embracing tourism. Main St – often a place to watch out for falling bricks in other small Texas towns – has been much-restored; antique stores, cafes and a beautifully renovated movie theater are among the highlights. There's also an excellent museum, the **River Valley Pioneer Museum** (☎ 806-323-6548; 118 N 2nd St; admission free; ☼ 9am-4pm Tue-Fri, 1-3pm Sat) and an art gallery.

Outside of town, a series of nature trails wander through the fertile countryside. In spring, people come from all over to see the rather comical mating habits of the prairie chicken – antics worthy of an Animal Planet special.

Look for an excellent visitor's guide online (www.canadiantx.org). Rest yourself from the excitement of prairie chicken breeding at the restored vintage **Canadian Inn** (☎ 806-323-6402; www.thecanadianinn.com; 502 N 2nd; r $50-60; ☏). Canadian is 100 miles northeast of Amarillo on US 60/83.

musical show in the natural beauty of the park's Pioneer Amphitheatre. From 6pm on show nights, there's an extra-cost dinner catered by the Big Texan Steak Ranch.

Texas 207 Highway Scenic Drive

Many Panhandle locals say the best views of Palo Duro Canyon aren't in the park but along TX 207 between Claude and Silverton in the south. This quiet 48-mile stretch enters the canyon lands about 13 miles south of Claude (where the 1963 Paul Newman classic *Hud* was filmed). Some of the most dramatic scenery is at the crossings of the Prairie Dog Town Fork of the Red River and Tule Creek. From Silverton both Turkey (p334) and Caprock Canyons (p335) are short drives.

Directory

CONTENTS

ACCOMMODATIONS

Motel and hotel prices vary tremendously from urban to rural areas and from season to season. B&B rates vary less dramatically, although they're typically higher on weekends and holidays. Prices in this book can only be an approximate guideline at best. Also, be prepared to add room tax of about 15% to all rates quoted here. Online discounters such as www.orbitz.com and www.priceline.com can save you quite a bit of money off chain motel and hotel rates, even at the very last minute.

Festivals and conventions can fill accommodations quickly and prices soar, so call ahead to find out what will be going on during your visit. Reservations are always a good idea during Texas' busy periods (most of March for spring break, May through August and the Christmas–New Year's holidays), and they are essential during special events. Better motels and all hotels will take reservations days or months ahead of time. Most chains have toll-free reservations numbers, but it sometimes pays to call the motel or hotel direct

to learn of any manager's specials. Be sure to let the hotel know if you plan a late arrival – many motels will give your room away if you haven't arrived or called by 6pm, unless you've guaranteed it on a credit card. Cancellation policies vary, so ask to avoid being charged a penalty fee later.

As a rule of thumb, the price ranges for our accommodations listings are as follows: budget is less than $80 per night, top end is more than $150 per night, and midrange is everything in between.

B&Bs

European visitors should be aware that North American B&Bs are rarely the casual, inexpensive sort of accommodations found on the continent or in Britain. While they are usually family-run, many B&Bs require advance reservations, though some will be happy to oblige the occasional drop-in (call first). Most B&Bs prohibit smoking. Nearly all have hot breakfasts included in their rates, but light continental breakfasts are not unheard of. The cheapest establishments, with rooms starting at $50, may have clean but unexciting rooms with shared bathrooms. More expensive places have rooms with private bathrooms, perhaps in historical buildings, quaint country cabins or luxurious urban townhouses. Most of these B&Bs charge $80 to $150 for two people, but more luxurious digs might be more. The best are distinguished by a friendly attention to detail by hosts who can provide you with local sightseeing information and added amenities, such as internet access, DVD player and, if you're lucky, a swimming pool.

Camping

Private and public campgrounds and RV parks charge $10 to $25 per night, or even less for primitive tent camping. Sites are often on a first-come, first-served basis, so plan on an early arrival, preferably during the week, as sites fill up fast on Fridays and weekends. More popular campgrounds may accept or require reservations, in which case you'll need a major credit card. Smaller campgrounds usually only accept cash as payment upon entry.

Developed camping areas usually have toilets, drinking water, fire pits (or charcoal grills) and picnic benches. Some have electricity, showers and full RV hookups. Primitive walk-in sites are exclusively for tents and require campers to pack out all trash; some don't have any drinking water.

Most private campgrounds are designed with RVs in mind; tenters can camp, but fees are several dollars higher than at public campgrounds. In addition, state and city taxes apply. Facilities may include hot showers, coin laundry, internet access and a swimming pool. **Kampgrounds of America** (KOA; ☎ 406-248-7444; www.koakampgrounds.com) is a national network of private campgrounds that are expensive, but are among the most reliable for service and amenities.

Hostels

The US hostel network is less widespread than in the rest of the world, and the Texas hostel network is smaller than that of most states. **Hostelling International USA** only has facilities in Austin; you can check its website at www.hiusa.org to see if any more have sprung up or to make reservations online.

Hotels

Texas has a variety of excellent historic hotels, including the Menger (p161) in San Antonio, the Driskill (p128) in Austin, the Gage (p300) in Marathon, the Hotel Limpia (p294) in Fort Davis and many more. Most have been completely updated with modern plumbing and amenities, but they still have plenty of quirks and charm. Rates may start at just $100 per night, even for the big-city classics.

The state also has many hotel chains, where the level of quality and style tends to be standard. Chains in the $95-and-up category include Radisson, Doubletree and Hilton. Many are full-service hotels with room service, fitness facilities and other niceties.

Top-tier chains, like Four Seasons, Omni and Wyndham, can easily run $200 or more a night during the week; rates often fall dramatically on weekends. These luxury hotels will likely have bellhops and a concierge, restaurants and bars, exercise rooms, business centers, room service and more.

Prices advertised by hotels are called 'rack rates' and are by no means written in stone. If you simply ask about specials and discounts, you can often save quite a bit of money. Booking through a travel agent or online can also mean big savings.

Lodges

In national parks, accommodations are limited to either camping or park lodges operating as a concession. Lodges are often rustic looking but usually quite comfortable inside. Restaurants are on the premises and tour services are often available. National-park lodges are not cheap, with most rooms going for close to $100 for a double during the high season, but they are your only option if you want to stay inside the park without camping. If you are coming during the high season, make a reservation months in advance. Big Bend National Park has a lodge, but Guadalupe Mountains National Park does not.

Motels

Motels with $45 rooms are found mostly in small towns along major highways and near the airports and outlying interstate loops in major cities. Rooms are usually small, and although a minimal level of cleanliness is maintained, expect scuffed walls, thin towels, old furniture and strange noises from your shower. Even these rooms normally have a private bathroom, air-conditioning and a TV. The cheapest budget places may not accept reservations, but at least phone from the road to see what's available.

All of the national chain motels accept reservations by phone or online. Chains like Red Roof Inn, Travelodge and Econo Lodge are typically just a few dollars more than your basic Motel 6, which costs from around $35 per night. At the slightly more expensive Super 8 Motels and Days Inns, expect firmer beds and free continental breakfast. Stepping up, chains in the $55-to-$85 range have more spacious rooms, indoor swimming pools and other niceties; La Quinta is a major player in this category, as are Ramada Inn, Best Western, Hampton Inn, Marriott-owned Fairfield Inn and some Holiday Inn properties.

Ranches

Dude ranches and guest ranches welcome visitors as paying guests. All offer horseback riding; some are working cattle ranches where you may also learn how to rope and herd cattle. Many are pretty rustic, though others (like Cibolo Creek in Big Bend) are quite upscale. Bandera, just outside of San Antonio, is home to several options; check the San Antonio & Hill Country chapter for a few possibilities.

ACTIVITIES

The Texas tourism slogan claims that Texas 'is like a whole other country,' and there are certainly a nation's worth of activities available. There are 600 miles of beaches, more than 800 golf courses, and at least 70 working ranches. For an introduction to all the places you can hike, bike, backpack, ride horses, swim, surf, dive, snorkel, kayak, canoe, fish, golf, skydive and more, turn to the Texas Outdoors chapter (p65). There you'll find all kinds of information to help you have fun in Texas.

BUSINESS HOURS

Businesses usually stay open from 9am to 5pm, but there are certainly no hard-and-fast rules. In any large city, a few supermarkets, restaurants and the main post office's lobby are open 24 hours. Shops are usually open from 9am or 10am to 5pm or 6pm (often until 9pm in shopping malls), except Sunday when stores don't open till noon and will mostly be closed by 6pm (even in the malls). Bars usually open in the late afternoon around 4pm or 5pm, but some unlock their doors before noon. Live-music clubs open in the early evening around 6pm or 7pm, but rarely get busy before 9pm. Bars serve liquor until 2am; a few dance clubs stay open until 4am.

Post offices are open from 8am to 5pm or 6pm Monday to Friday, and some are open from 8am to 3pm on Saturday. Banks are usually open from either 9am or 10am to 5pm or 6pm Monday to Friday. A few banks are open from 9am to 2pm or 4pm on Saturday. Hours are decided by individual branches, so if you need specifics, give the branch you want a call. Tourist attractions often keep longer hours during summer, but some also close in the winter.

CHILDREN
What to Expect

Texans love little cowpokes, and kids will usually get fussed over aplenty. There are several theme parks in Texas, including Sea World in San Antonio and Six Flags parks in Arlington (near Dallas), San Antonio and Houston. Many cities have museums, parks, playgrounds, zoos and other attractions specifically aimed at the younger set.

If you take the kids away from urban areas and into the wide-open spaces, you'll see the Texas of your imagination: working cowboys, cool geology and unusual animals. Texas has one of the best state park systems anywhere, and there are usually several parks within easy reach. Ideal destinations include Big Bend National Park, with its scenic beauty, and Caprock Canyons State Park up in the eastern Panhandle, where you can do everything from horseback riding and paddle-boating to taking extended trips on the 64-mile Caprock Canyons Trailways.

In this book we list as often as possible attractions that kids might like, as well as the discounted prices for children. There's rarely an extra charge for kids staying with their parents at motels and hotels. Ask hotel staff or the concierge about licensed babysitting services. Public restrooms often have diaper-changing tables, usually on the women's side,

---

PRACTICALITIES

- Major daily newspapers in Texas include the *Austin-American Statesman*, the *Dallas Morning News*, the *Fort Worth Star-Telegram*, the *Houston Chronicle* and the *San Antonio Express-News*.

- *Texas Monthly* (www.texasmonthly.com) is easily one of the best regional magazines in the USA, with strong reporting, heaps of attitude and excellent photography.

- National Public Radio (NPR) is an excellent source for balanced news coverage.

- Electrical voltage is 110/120V, 60 cycles.

- Distances are in feet, yards and miles; weights are tallied in ounces, pounds and tons.

but it's rare to see women breastfeeding in public. Rental-car companies will rent car seats, which are legally required for young children, for about $5 per day or $25 per week. AAA members may be entitled to reimbursement for car-seat rentals.

Lonely Planet's *Travel with Children* has more information on what to do when on the road with little ones. If you're stuck for ideas, contact the nearest convention and visitors bureau, which can help you work out an itinerary.

Sights & Activities

The open beaches of the barrier islands such as Padre Island are a delight for children and adults alike. However, be alert: the very hard-packed white sand that gives the beaches their allure also means that they are suitable for driving on. Except for limited areas around some park entrances, the beaches are wide open for cars and trucks. Most drivers stay back from the surf and use well-traveled routes along the shore, but you never know when someone might drive a vehicle faster than the speed limit and right along the surf line where sandcastle-builders may be caught unaware.

There are public playgrounds in almost every city, and most have public toilets and water fountains.

Every sizable Texas city has a municipal swimming pool with organized programs; many also have free swim periods. Check with the local visitor center for locations and schedules.

CLIMATE CHARTS

Generally speaking, Texas enjoys a mild southern climate year-round, with statewide average temperatures of 50°F (11°C) in January and 85°F (30°C) in July. (Be aware, though, that average temperatures can be a bit misleading, as daytime temperatures often get up into the 90s in the summer, and, when you factor in humidity, can feel like more.)

But weather varies throughout this large state. In much of the year, evenings in the mountainous regions of west Texas and the Texas Hill Country are cool enough for a jacket or even a coat in winter. And areas of east Texas and the Rio Grande Valley are among the hottest in the country, with summer daytime temperatures averaging 100°F (38°C).

Throughout the state, the weather is very temperamental and, like much of the central part of the United States, the state is susceptible to tornadoes, in fact, Texas leads the nation in tornadoes, with an average of almost 130 per year. Its proximity to the Gulf of Mexico also makes Texas susceptible to hurricanes near the coast, though far less so than, say, Florida and Georgia. (That sounds scarier than it is: the odds of you experiencing either phenomenon are not particularly high.) See the boxed text p348 for more on tornadoes, and p17 for more general weather information.

CUSTOMS REGULATIONS

US Customs allows each person over 21 years old to bring 1L of liquor and 200 cigarettes duty free into the USA. US citizens are allowed to import, duty free, $400 worth of gifts from abroad, while non-US citizens are allowed to bring in $100 worth.

US law permits you to bring in, or take out, as much as $10,000 in US or foreign currency, traveler's checks or letters of credit without formality. Larger amounts of any or all of the above – there are no limits – must be declared to customs.

See p356 for information on crossing the border between Texas and Mexico.

DANGERS & ANNOYANCES
Personal Security & Theft

Although street crime is a serious issue in large urban areas, visitors need not be obsessed with security. Just remember your street smarts:

- Always lock cars and put valuables out of sight.
- Avoid walking alone at night.
- Only use ATMs in well-trafficked areas.
- Avoid carrying your wallet in a back pocket; in fact, consider using a money belt under your clothes.

Guns

The USA has a widespread reputation, partly true but also propagated and exaggerated by the media, as a dangerous place because of the availability of firearms. And while the rifle rack is as much a Texas tradition as the pickup truck, the main danger is from concealed handguns.

In 1995, Texas passed a state law granting a permit to carry a concealed weapon to

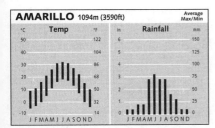

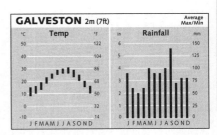

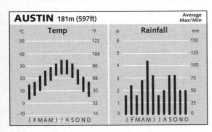

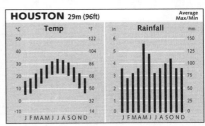

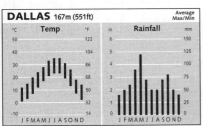

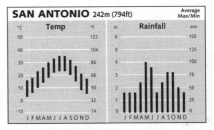

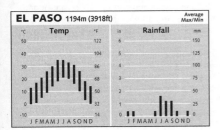

any Texan who has never been convicted of a felony and who passes a course in handgun use and safety. It's likely you won't notice anything at all, since public offices and private businesses are permitted to ban the carrying of concealed weapons on their premises (which is why you'll see signs forbidding firearms in places like post offices, restaurants, movie theaters, theme parks and at the Alamo). But you should still avoid stepping into the line of

fire. Never argue with or make rude gestures at other motorists. If pulled over by a police car, keep both your hands in plain sight at all times (preferably atop the steering wheel) so the officer doesn't mistake your movements for a 'reach' (as in reaching for a weapon).

Recreational Hazards
In wilderness areas the consequences of an accident can be very serious, so inform someone of your route and expected return.

MOSQUITOES
The swampy southern and coastal regions of Texas are perfect breeding grounds for a form of mosquito that deserves inclusion in the boast that 'everything's bigger here.' Seemingly immune to seasonal change, these bugs attack in swarms whether the temperature is in the 90s or down in the 50s. And they are especially resilient.

The best way to combat these bugs is to keep yourself covered (wear long sleeves, long pants, hats, and shoes rather than sandals) and apply a good insect repellent, preferably one containing DEET, to exposed skin and clothing. (Children between two and 12 years of age should use preparations containing no more than 10% DEET, and DEET-containing compounds should not be used on children under the age of two.) For more tips visit the West Nile page at the **Center for Disease Control** (www.cdc.gov/westnile).

JELLYFISH

Jellyfish abound in the mild waters of the Gulf of Mexico. They're around throughout the year and often float in schools. Two varieties pack powerful stings: the Portuguese man-of-war, which is a translucent blue with long tentacles dangling from the center; and the sea nettle, which is also translucent but has tentacles attached to the edge of its bell-shaped central mass.

One good clue that jellyfish are in the area is if you find a dead one on the beach. Look, but don't touch; the venom stings even after a jellyfish dies. If you are stung, quickly remove the tentacles and treat the injured area with vinegar or a supermarket-bought unseasoned meat tenderizer containing a fruit enzyme called papain. For serious reactions, including chest pains or difficulty breathing, seek medical attention.

WILDLIFE

As more people spend time in the backcountry or impinge on wildlife habitat, wildlife attacks on humans and pets are becoming more common. Bears and cougars (mountain lions) pose the most serious hazards, but seemingly placid and innocuous beasts such as bison and mule deer are equally capable of inflicting serious injury on unsuspecting tourists. Also, some animals carry rabies. Keep your distance from all wild animals – even prairie dogs.

You're unlikely to see a mountain lion, but if you do, take the following precautions: hold your ground – don't run; shout and wave your arms above your head; stand close with the others in your group, and pick up small

HURRICANES, TORNADOES & FLOODS, OH MY

A hurricane is a concentrated system of very strong thunderstorms with high circulation. The winds of 74 to 160mph created by a hurricane can extend for hundreds of miles around the eye (center) of a hurricane system. Happily, they're generally sighted well in advance and there's time to prepare. Listen to the National Weather Service (shortwave radio listeners can tune to 162.55 MHz), and dismiss anything else as a rumor.

The Panhandle, Red River Valley on the Texas–Oklahoma border and northeast Texas are among the areas most prone to tornadoes. If you're in an area where a tornado watch is called, there's not much you can do except be aware of the situation and follow the instructions of local radio and TV stations and police.

Low-lying southern and eastern Texas have a propensity to flood, sometimes so severely that entire communities are evacuated and billions of dollars in damage occur. Flash floods, like tornadoes, are inherently impossible to predict, so follow the same advice you would for tornadoes: stay aware of changes in the weather and follow emergency instructions when provided.

If you're determined to sit out a severe weather warning – and we do not recommend that you do – you will need at the very least the following supplies:

- Flashlight
- As much fresh drinking water as possible (storms knock out water supplies)
- Butane lighter and candles
- Canned food, peanut butter, powdered or UHT milk
- Cash (ATMs don't function)
- Portable, battery-powered radio
- Stay in a closet or other windowless room. Cover yourself with a mattress to prevent injury from flying glass. Taping windows does not stop them from breaking, but it does reduce shatter.

children; and if the lion starts behaving aggressively, throw stones – not to hit it, but to scare it away.

SNAKEBITES

In the unlikely event of a bite by a poisonous snake, the main thing to do is stay calm. No matter what you've seen in the movies, snakebites don't cause instantaneous death; but they are dangerous and you need to keep a good, clear head on your shoulders. If you can get to a telephone, call 911, where they can connect you with the nearest Poison Information Center or hospital. If you can, find a ranger.

Place a light, constricting bandage over the bite, keep the wounded part below the level of the heart, and move the wound as little as possible. If it's at all possible, bring along the dead snake for identification – but do not attempt to catch the snake if there's any chance of being bitten again. Sucking out the poison has been widely discredited as treatment for snakebites, since it causes more damage to snakebite victims than the bite itself.

DISCOUNT CARDS
Student & Youth Cards

An ISIC or official school or university ID card often entitles students to discounts on museum admission, theater tickets and other attractions.

Senior Cards

People over the age of 65 (sometimes even 50) typically qualify for the same discounts as students, and then some. Be sure to inquire about such rates at hotels, museums and restaurants. Any photo ID is usually sufficient proof of age. The **American Association of Retired Persons** (AARP; ☎ 888-687-2277; www.aarp.org; 1yr membership $16) is an advocacy group for US residents 50 years and older and is a good resource for travel bargains. Citizens of other countries can also join.

AAA Membership Cards

For its members, the **American Automobile Association** (AAA; ☎ 800-765-0766; www.aaa-texas.com; annual fee $54) provides great travel information, distributes free road maps and driving guides, and sells American Express traveler's checks without commission. The AAA membership card will often get you discounts on motel and hotel accommodations, car rental and admis-

sion charges. AAA also provides emergency roadside service to members in the event of an accident, breakdown or locking your keys in the car. Service is free within a given radius of the nearest service center, and service providers will tow your car to a mechanic if they can't fix it. The nationwide toll-free roadside assistance number is ☎ 800-222-4357.

EMBASSIES & CONSULATES

As a tourist, it's important to realize what your own embassy – the embassy of the country of which you are a citizen – can and can't do.

Generally speaking, an embassy won't be much help if the trouble you're in is remotely your own fault. Remember that you are still bound by the laws of the USA. Your embassy will not be sympathetic if you end up in jail after committing a crime locally, even if such actions are legal in your own country.

In genuine emergencies you might get some assistance, but only if other channels have been exhausted. For example, if you need to get home urgently, a free ticket home is exceedingly unlikely – the embassy would expect you to have insurance. If you have all your money and documents stolen, it might assist in getting a new passport, but a loan for onward travel is out of the question.

Embassies used to keep letters for travelers or have a small reading room with home newspapers, but these days the mail-holding service has been stopped and even newspapers tend to be out of date.

There are many consulates in Dallas and Houston, and Mexican consulates are also peppered throughout border towns. Houston has the most consulates, with about 70; the **Houston International Protocol Alliance** (☎ 713-227-3395) can offer contact details for them all should you be in need of assistance. Check the *Yellow Pages* for a complete listing of the consulates in the area in which you are traveling.

Foreign consulates in Texas include:
Australia (off Map p196; ☎ 713-782-6009; 4623 Feagan St, Houston) Honorary consulate.
Canada (Map p82; ☎ 214-922-9806; 500 N Akard, Suite 2900, Dallas)
France Austin honorary consulate (Map p118; ☎ 512-480-5605; 401 Congress Ave); Dallas honorary consulate (☎ 972-789-9305; 12720 Hillcrest Rd, Suite 730); Houston (off Map p196; ☎ 713-572-2799; 777 Post Oak Blvd, Suite 600)
Germany Dallas honorary consulate (Map p82; ☎ 214-748-8500; 325 N St Paul St, Suitte 2300, Dallas); Houston (☎ 713-627-7770; 1330 Post Oak Blvd, Suite 1850)

Japan (Map p193; ☎ 713-652-2977; 909 Fannin St, Suite 3000, Houston)

Mexico Austin (Map p118; ☎ 512-478-2803; 800 Brazos St, Suite 330); Brownsville (☎ 956-542-4431; 301 Mexico Blvd, Suite F-3); Dallas (Map p78; ☎ 214-932-8670; 1210 River Bend Dr); El Paso (Map p306; ☎ 915-533-3644; 910 E San Antonio Ave); Houston (Map p196; ☎ 713-271-6800; 4507 San Jacinto St); Laredo (☎ 956-723-6369; 1612 Farragut St); San Antonio (Map p152; ☎ 210-227-9145; 127 Navarro St)

New Zealand (☎ 713-973-8680; 246 Warrenton Dr, Houston) Honorary consulate.

UK Houston (Map p193; ☎ 713-659-6270; 1000 Louisiana, Suite 1900); San Antonio honorary consulate (☎ 713-973-8680; 245 Spencer Lane)

FOOD

For Texas' regional cuisine, see p47 and p52. In this book our restaurant reviews are usually sorted by geographical area, then arranged by price. 'Budget' diners, cafes and coffee shops generally cost around $5 for a meal, or up to $10 including taxes and a tip. 'Midrange' restaurants charge $8 to $15 just for the main dish (often called an entrée). At 'Top End' dining establishments, expect to pay from $45 per person for an appetizer, a main course, drinks and dessert, all inclusive.

GAY & LESBIAN TRAVELERS

The larger cities in Texas have gay, lesbian, bisexual and transgender community centers (or at least a gay chamber of commerce) that offer tips on everything from gay-owned businesses to medical care to information on bars, clubs and accommodations. As you travel into the boondocks, it is often much harder to be open. In some rural areas, public displays of affection may land you in serious trouble.

Statewide publications, such as *This Week in Texas* (www.thisweekintexas.com), have guides to the bar and club scene, as well as special events calendars, directories of gay-friendly businesses, personal ads and news. The *Gay & Lesbian Yellow Pages* (www.glyp.com) publishes separate phone directories to Austin, Dallas, Galveston, Houston and San Antonio; browse them online or pick up a copy at local businesses.

The following national resources may also prove useful:

Gay and Lesbian National Hotline (☎ 888-843-4564; www.glnh.org; ☺ 4pm-midnight Mon-Fri, noon-5pm Sat) Referrals to local doctors, attorneys and other professionals.

National Gay and Lesbian Task Force (☎ 202-393-5177; www.thetaskforce.org; 1325 Massachusetts Ave NW, Suite 600, Washington, DC 20005) A civil rights and political advocacy group for GLBT issues. Great national news coverage is found on its website.

HOLIDAYS

National public holidays are celebrated throughout the USA. Banks, schools and government offices (including post offices) are closed on major holidays. Most businesses are closed on Christmas Day. Private businesses and restaurants may also close or have reduced hours on the 4th of July, Thanksgiving and New Year's Day. Public holidays that fall on a weekend are often observed on the following Monday.

New Year's Day January 1
Martin Luther King Jr Day 3rd Monday in January
President's Day 3rd Monday in February
Texas Independence Day March 2
Easter Sunday March/April
Memorial Day last Monday in May
Independence Day July 4
Labor Day 1st Monday in September
Columbus Day 2nd Monday in October
Veterans Day November 11
Thanksgiving 4th Thursday in November
Christmas Day December 25

INSURANCE

Taking out a travel insurance policy to cover theft, lost tickets and medical problems is a good idea, especially in the USA, where some privately run hospitals refuse care without evidence of insurance. (Public hospitals must treat everyone, though standards are lower and, except in the most serious of cases, waits can last for hours.) There are lots of different insurance policies, and your travel agency will have recommendations, but always check the fine print. International policies handled by STA Travel and other student-travel organizations are usually good value. Worldwide travel insurance is available at www.lonelyplanet.com/travel_services. You can buy, extend and claim online anytime – even if you're already on the road.

INTERNET ACCESS

It's always good to get local dial-up numbers from your internet service provider, but nowadays most motel and hotel rooms have phones equipped with data ports or high-speed internet access, and many have wi-fi access in their lobbies, if not their rooms. Deluxe hotels often have fully equipped business centers with computers, photocopiers, fax and internet services. Copy centers, such as **FedEx Office** (☎ 800-463-3339 for nationwide locations), offer internet access, open 24 hours, seven days a week. Coffee shops may also offer internet access, either via free wi-fi for laptop users or, less frequently, pay kiosks. Logging on at public libraries is usually free.

LEGAL MATTERS

Speed limits in smaller towns are strictly enforced, so you should get used to driving a bit slower than usual. Watch for school zones, which can have strictly enforced speed limits as low as 15mph during school hours. Speeding tickets are expensive, and could easily land you a fine of more than $100. Littering is illegal, too. For information on road rules, car rental, insurance and automobile-related concerns, see p359.

If you are stopped by the police for any reason, bear in mind that there is no system of paying fines on the spot. For traffic offenses, the police officer will explain your options to you. Attempting to pay the fine to the officer is frowned upon at best and may compound your troubles by resulting in a charge of bribery.

There is no legal reason to speak to a police officer if you don't wish, but never walk away from an officer until given permission. If you are arrested for any offense, the law says you are innocent until proven guilty. All persons who are arrested are legally allowed to make one telephone call. You're also given, as viewers of any cop show can tell you, the right to remain silent and to refuse to answer questions and the right to representation by an attorney, which will be appointed to you free if you request it from the office of the public defender. If you don't have a lawyer or family member to help you, call your embassy; the police will give you the number upon request.

MAPS

Universal Map (☎ 800-829-6277; www.universalmap.com) publishes a huge array of detailed Mapsco maps and atlases of major Texas cities.

The **Texas Department of Transportation** (☎ 800-452-9292) produces the helpful *Texas Official Travel Map,* available free at many visitor centers and tourist offices across the state. The **American Automobile Association** (AAA; www.aaa.com) offers good driving maps. Other city and regional map products are available in bookstores (especially large ones like Barnes & Noble), pharmacies and gas stations.

MONEY

The US dollar ($) is divided into 100 cents (¢). Coins come in denominations of 1¢ (penny), 5¢ (nickel), 10¢ (dime), 25¢ (quarter), the seldom seen 50¢ (half dollar) and $1 (the 'golden dollar,' which hasn't really caught on, though you may get them as change from stamp and ticket vending machines). Quarters are the most commonly used coins in vending machines and parking meters, so it's handy to have a stash of them.

Bills (banknotes) come in $1, $2, $5, $10, $20, $50 and $100 denominations – $2 bills are rare, but perfectly legal. True to the American spirit of adventure, all the bills are the same size and color – make sure to check the denomination before handing someone $100 for a pack of gum.

ATMs

Automated Teller Machines, or ATMs, are a convenient way of obtaining cash from a bank account back home (within the USA or from abroad). Even small-town banks have ATMs, and they are common everywhere: at grocery stores, malls, convenience stores and even gas stations. Being able to get as much cash as you want whenever you want eliminates the need for traveler's checks, but watch out for surcharges. Both your bank and the owner of the ATM you use will typically charge a small fee for each transaction (usually about $1.50). The ATM must display the fee it will charge you, but how much your bank charges is something you'll have to check before you go.

Cash

Though carrying cash is more risky than carrying traveler's checks or credit cards, it's still a good idea to travel with some cash for convenience; it's useful to help pay all those tips, and some smaller, more remote places may not accept credit cards.

Credit Cards

Major credit cards are accepted at most hotels, restaurants, shops, gas stations and car-rental agencies throughout the USA. In fact, you'll find it hard to perform certain transactions, such as renting a car or purchasing tickets, without one. Visa and MasterCard are the most widely accepted, and where one is accepted, both usually are.

Carry copies of your credit-card numbers separately from the cards. If you lose your credit cards or they are stolen, contact the company immediately. Following are toll-free numbers for the main credit-card companies.

American Express (☎ 800-528-4800)
Diners Club (☎ 800-234-6377)
Discover (☎ 800-347-2683)
MasterCard (☎ 800-627-8372)
Visa (☎ 800-847-2911)

Tipping

Tipping is expected in restaurants and better hotels, and by taxi drivers, hairdressers and baggage carriers. In restaurants, waitstaff are paid minimal wages and rely on tips for their livelihoods. Tip 15% to 20%, but never tip in fast-food, take-out or buffet-style restaurants where you serve yourself.

Taxi drivers expect 10% and hairdressers get 15% if their service is satisfactory. Baggage carriers (skycaps in airports, attendants in hotels) get $1 to $2 per bag. In hotels, leave a few dollars in the room for the housekeeping staff for each day of your stay when you check out.

Traveler's Checks

Traveler's checks offer protection from theft or loss. Foreign visitors will save trouble and expense if they buy traveler's checks in US dollars. For refunds on lost or stolen traveler's checks, call the issuer; for example **American Express** (☎ 800-221-7282) or **Thomas Cook** (☎ 800-223-7373). Keeping a record of the check numbers and the checks you have used is vital when it comes to replacing lost traveler's checks. Keep this record separate from the checks themselves.

SOLO TRAVELERS

Travel, including solo travel, is usually safe and easy. In general, you need to exercise more vigilance in large cities than in rural areas. Women traveling alone should have few problems, though some men may interpret a woman drinking alone in a bar as a bid for male company, whether intended that way or not. Everyone should avoid hiking, cycling long distances or camping alone, especially in unfamiliar places.

TELEPHONE

In many areas, local calls have moved to a 10-digit calling system. This means you must dial the area code even when making a local call.

With the prevalence of cell phones, pay phones are harder to find, but most shopping centers and some gas stations have them. Calls are usually 25¢ to 50¢.

To make an international call direct, dial 011, then the country code, followed by the area code and the phone number. (An exception is to Canada, where you dial 1 + area code + number. International rates apply to Canada.)

For international operator assistance, dial 0. The operator can provide specific rate information and tell you which time periods are the cheapest for calling.

If you're calling Texas from abroad, the international country code for the USA is 1.

Cell Phones

In the USA, cell phones operate on different frequencies from other countries, so check with your service provider to make sure yours will work – and ask if roaming charges will apply, since they can be pricey. You may be able to take the SIM card from your phone and install it in a rented mobile phone compatible with the US system, or rent a phone with prepaid call time, but neither option is very cheap.

Phone Cards

Phone cards are now almost essential for travelers using the US phone system. There are two basic types. A phone credit card bills calls to your home phone number. Some cards issued by foreign phone companies work in the USA; inquire before you leave home. A prepaid phone card is a good alternative for travelers and widely available in big cities and from major retailers. Always check the card's connection fees (see if it has a toll-free access number from pay phones) in addition to the rate. AT&T sells a reliable phone card that's available at many retailers.

TIME

Most of Texas is in the Central time zone, an hour behind New York (Eastern time) and two hours ahead of Los Angeles (Pacific time). When it's noon in Austin, it's 6pm in London, 7pm in Paris, Berlin and Madrid, 9pm in Moscow and 3am/5am in winter/summer

Sydney. Parts of extreme west Texas are in the Mountain time zone, one hour behind Central time; when it's noon in Austin, it's 11am in El Paso. Keep in mind that clocks are set ahead during daylight savings time, which takes place from early March to early November; clocks 'spring forward' one hour in March and 'fall back' one hour in November.

TOURIST INFORMATION

Larger cities and towns have tourist information centers run by local convention and visitor bureaus (CVBs). They're good sources of information, offering details on attractions and events and sometimes providing free trip-planner kits, reservation services for hotels and B&Bs, and tickets for tours, transport and other activities. In smaller towns, local chambers of commerce often perform the same functions.

State tourist offices give out free maps and vacation planners. The free *Texas State Travel Guide* is a glossy magazine-style guidebook that lists information offices and major sights and attractions for almost every city and town in the state. It's available online at www.travel-tex.com or at one of the many, many **Texas Travel Information Centers** (☎ 800-452-9292) sprinkled across the state.

TRAVELERS WITH DISABILITIES

Public buildings (including hotels, restaurants, theaters and museums) are required by the Americans with Disabilities Act (ADA) to be wheelchair accessible and have available restroom facilities. Public transportation services (buses, trains and taxis) must be made accessible to all, including those in wheelchairs. Texas has gone a long way toward ensuring accessibility at kid-friendly attractions. Telephone companies are required to provide relay operators for the hearing impaired. Many banks now provide ATM instructions in Braille, and you will find audible crossing signals as well as dropped curbs at busier roadway intersections. Guide dogs may legally be brought into restaurants, hotels and other businesses.

Larger private and chain hotels have suites for disabled guests. Most local buses are wheelchair-accessible, and some bus companies offer paratransit services in addition to regular service for those with disabilities. Many car-rental agencies offer hand-controlled vehicles or vans with wheelchair lifts at no extra charge, but only with advance reservations. Disabled parking at blue-colored curbs and specially designated spots in public lots is by permit only. All major airlines, Greyhound buses and Amtrak trains allow service animals to accompany passengers and frequently sell two-for-one packages when seriously disabled passengers require attendants. Airlines will also provide assistance for connecting, boarding and deplaning the flight; ask for assistance when making your reservation. (Note: airlines must accept wheelchairs as checked baggage and have an onboard chair available, though advance notice may be required.)

A good website listing resources for the disabled is www.access-able.com, or try the following useful organizations:

Mobility International USA (MIUSA; ☎ 541-343-1284; www.miusa.org; 132 E Broadway, Suite 343, Eugene, OR 97401) Advises disabled travelers on mobility issues and runs an educational exchange program.

Society for Accessible Travel & Hospitality (SATH; ☎ 212-447-7284; www.sath.org; 347 Fifth Ave, Suite 610, New York, NY 10016) Has information on a wide range of destinations around the world.

VISAS

After several years of upheaval, US entry requirements are becoming pretty well established again. However, all travelers should double-check current visa and passport regulations before coming to the USA because things change.

The main portal for US visa information is the **US State Department** (www.travel.state.gov), which maintains the most comprehensive information, including downloadable forms, lists of US consulates abroad and even visa wait times.

Visa Applications

Apart from Canadians and those entering under the Visa Waiver Pilot Program (see p354), all foreign visitors need to obtain a visa from a US consulate or embassy. In most countries, you must now schedule a personal interview, to which you must bring your documentation and proof of fee payment. Afterward, barring problems, visa issuance takes from a few days to a few weeks.

Your passport must be valid for at least six months longer than your intended stay in the USA (some countries have exemptions from this), and you'll need to submit a recent photo (2in by 2in) with the application; there is a $140 processing fee (check the website at http://travel.state.gov/visa for details, as fees change).

Visa applicants are required to show documents of financial stability (or evidence that a US resident will provide financial support), a round-trip or onward ticket and 'binding obligations' that will ensure their return home, such as family ties, a home or a job.

There are numerous grounds for exclusion: see the State Department website for a full list. The most important concern is whether you have a criminal record or a communicable disease. If you are tempted to fudge the truth here, don't.

The most common visa is a Non-Immigrant Visitors' Visa (B1 for business purposes, B2 for tourism). A visitors' visa is good for one or five years with multiple entries, and it specifically prohibits the visitor from taking paid employment in the USA. The validity period depends on your country of origin. The length of time you'll be allowed to stay in the USA is determined by US immigration at the port of entry.

If you're coming to the USA to work or study, you will need a different type of visa, and the company or institution to which you're going should make the arrangements.

Visa Waiver Program

Currently, under the US Visa Waiver Program (VWP), visas are not required for citizens of 36 countries for stays up to 90 days (no extensions) if you have a machine-readable passport (MRP). If you don't have an MRP, you'll need a visa to enter the USA.

Citizens of VWP countries *must* register with the Electronic System for Travel Authorization (ESTA) online (https://esta.cbp.dhs.gov) at least 72 hours before their trip begins. Once approved, ESTA registration is valid for up to two years.

Visa Extensions & Reentry

If you want to stay in the USA longer than the time indicated on your Form I-94, you must contact the Department of Homeland Security's **Bureau of Citizenship and Immigration Services** (www.uscis.gov) at least 45 days before your authorized stay expires and file a request. The decision to grant or deny a request for extension of stay is made solely by the Bureau of Citizenship and Immigration Services.

Transportation

CONTENTS

GETTING THERE & AWAY

Most travelers arrive in Texas by air or car, with buses running a distant third and trains an even more distant fourth. Flights, tours and rail tickets can be booked online at www.lonelyplanet.com/travel_services.

ENTERING THE REGION

If you're arriving from outside the USA, you must carry out immigration and customs formalities at the first airport you land in. So even if your luggage is checked from, say, London to Dallas, you will still have to take it through customs if you first land in New York, at which point your luggage may be inspected. The **Transportation Security Administration** (TSA; www.tsa.gov) keeps an ever-changing list of prohibited items that cannot be brought through security checkpoints; check its website for the current status.

AIR

Unless you live in or near Texas, flying to the region and then renting a car is the most time-efficient option.

Airports & Airlines

The main international gateways to Texas are Dallas/Fort Worth International Airport (DFW) from Europe and Houston's George

Bush Intercontinental Airport (IAH) from Latin America and some Pacific points. Houston and Dallas are the major hubs as well for US domestic carriers, though some also have direct flights into Austin-Bergstrom International Airport and San Antonio International Airport. San Antonio's airport also offers some flights to Mexico.

The following airports are the major international airports in Texas.

Austin-Bergstrom International Airport (AUS; ☎ 512-530-2242; www.ci.austin.tx.us/austinairport)

Dallas/Fort Worth International Airport (DFW; ☎ 972-574-8888; www.dfwairport.com)

Dallas Love Field (DAL; ☎ 214-670-6073; www.dallas-lovefield.com)

El Paso International Airport (ELP; ☎ 915-780-4700; www.elpasointernationalairport.com)

Houston Airport System: George Bush Intercontinental Airport (IAH; ☎ 281-443-4551; www.fly2houston.com/iah)

Houston Airport System: William P Hobby Airport (HOU; ☎ 713-641-7770; www.fly2houston.com/hobbyHome)

Lubbock Preston Smith International Airport (LBB; ☎ 806-775-2044; www.flylia.com)

Midland International Airport (MAF; ☎ 432-560-2200; www.flymaf.com)

Rick Husband Amarillo International Airport (AMA; ☎ 806-335-1671; www.ci.amarillo.tx.us/departments/airport.html)

San Antonio International Airport (SAT; ☎ 210-207-3411; www.sanantonio.gov/aviation)

AIRLINES FLYING TO/FROM TEXAS

Several major airlines fly in and out of Texas:

AeroMexico (AM; ☎ 800-237-6639; www.aeromexico.com)

American Airlines (AA; ☎ 800-433-7300; www.aa.com)

Continental (CO; ☎ 800-523-3273; www.continental.com)

Delta (DL; ☎ 800-221-1212; www.delta.com)

JetBlue Airways (JBU; ☎ 800-538-2583; www.jetblue.com)

Frontier Airlines (FFT; ☎ 800-432-1359; www.frontierairlines.com)

Mexicana (MX; ☎ 800-531-7921; www.mexicana.com)

Southwest (SWA; ☎ 800-435-9792; www.southwest.com)
United Airline (UAL; ☎ 800-864-8331; www.ual.com)
US Airways (AWE; ☎ 800-428-4322; www.usairways.com)

Tickets

Your plane ticket will probably be the single most expensive item in your budget, so it pays to research fares thoroughly. The best-known sites include www.expedia.com and www.travelocity.com, though it's worth noting that neither handles tickets for Southwest Airlines, a popular discount carrier with extensive service to Texas from many US markets. Check out www.southwest.com. For other special internet-only airfares, try www.orbitz.com and other online travel discounters. Websites like www.travelzoo.com and www.smarterliving.com do not sell air tickets, but can link you to a wealth of internet-based flight deals.

US domestic airfares vary tremendously depending on the season you travel, the day of the week you fly, the length of your stay and the flexibility the ticket allows for flight changes and refunds. Still, nothing determines fares more than demand, and when things are slow, airlines lower their fares to fill empty seats. There's a lot of competition, and at any given time any one of the airlines could have the cheapest fare. Southwest often seems to have some of the best deals, however (see Air under Getting Around, p358).

Cheap tickets are available in two distinct categories: official and unofficial. Official ones have a variety of names including advance-purchase fares, budget fares, Apex and super-Apex. Unofficial tickets are simply discounted tickets that the airlines release through selected travel agents, traditional or online (they

aren't available through airline offices). The cheapest tickets are often nonrefundable and require an extra fee for changing your flight. Many insurance policies will cover this loss if you have to change your flight for emergency reasons.

Round-trip (return) tickets usually work out cheaper than two one-way fares – often much cheaper. Airport departure taxes are usually included in the cost of tickets bought in the USA. Tickets purchased abroad may not have these included, but they're minimal. Check with a travel agent in the USA to see if you may need to pay any departure taxes before leaving and, if so, how much.

Travelers coming from the UK will probably find the cheapest flights are being advertised by obscure bucket shops whose names haven't yet reached the telephone directory. Many are honest and solvent, but there are a few rogues who will take your money and disappear, to reopen elsewhere a month or two later under a new name. If you feel suspicious about a firm, don't pay all the money at once – leave a deposit of 20% or so and pay the balance on receiving the ticket. If they insist on cash in advance, go elsewhere. And once you have the ticket, telephone the airline to confirm that you are booked on the flight.

LAND
Border Crossings

There are 26 border crossings into Mexico, many of which are in El Paso, Laredo and Brownsville. Check the US State Department's travel warnings at travel.state.gov for updates and advisories.

Note that the US Border Patrol also maintains several checkpoints at scattered locations throughout the Texas interior. If you see one, have your passport or other documents ready for presentation in case you're asked.

Should you decide to cross the border despite the government's warnings, know that US citizens must carry proof of citizenship – a passport, birth certificate or voter registration card plus a photo ID such as a driver's license – when crossing into Mexico. Canadians should carry a passport or birth certificate. Other foreign nationals should have a passport and appropriate visas before entering Mexico and returning to the USA.

On returning to Texas from Mexico, a stop at US Customs is required. Be prepared to state your nationality and declare any purchases made in Mexico.

Bus

Greyhound (☎ 800-229-9424; www.greyhound.com), the only nationwide bus company, has reduced local services considerably but still runs cross-country. It has extensive fixed routes and its own terminal in major cities, albeit often in undesirable parts of town. Buses are generally comfortable, the company has an exceptional safety record and buses usually run on time. Still, schedules are often inconvenient, fares are relatively high and bargain airfares can undercut buses on long-distance routes; in some cases, for shorter routes, it can be cheaper to rent a car than to ride the bus. However, there is one other benefit to riding the bus: fewer cars on the road means reduced carbon emissions.

Long-distance bus trips are often available at rock-bottom prices by purchasing or reserving tickets at least a week in advance. Keep in mind travel times can vary dramatically depending on the time of day and the route you take.

Car & Motorcycle

Drivers of cars and motorcycles will need to carry the vehicle's registration papers, proof of liability insurance and a driver's license. US, Canadian and Mexican driver's licenses are accepted. Other drivers should carry an International Driving Permit in addition to a domestic license.

Interstate 35 runs south from the Dallas–Fort Worth metro area past Austin, San Antonio and eventually Laredo, where you can cross into Mexico. Customs officials along the entry points between the USA and Mexico can be strict and often wary of anyone who doesn't look straitlaced. The transcontinental interstate for the southern USA is I-10, and it runs from Florida to California, passing through much of Texas.

Train

Amtrak (☎ 800-872-7245; www.amtrak.com) provides cross-country passenger services, stopping in many cities across Texas. Train travel is fairly comfortable, even in its reclining coach seats (though if you can spring for a sleeper, it's worth it). Trains have lounge and dining cars, and there's usually plenty of entertainment. Amtrak generally costs a little more than Greyhound, but, if the trip itself is just as important as getting from point A to point B, Amtrak usually delivers a nicer experience. The frequent service delays are the only real downside to US train travel.

Schedules usually vary from published timetables the further you are from your starting point. Amtrak services through Texas are on the *Sunset Limited,* which runs between Florida and Los Angeles, and the *Texas Eagle,* between Los Angeles and Chicago. Fares for train travel vary greatly, depending on different promotional fares and destinations. Tickets can be purchased by credit card over the phone, via the website, from a travel agent or at an Amtrak depot. Most small train stations don't sell tickets; they must be booked with Amtrak over the telephone or through its website. Some small stations have no porters or other facilities, and trains may stop there only if you have bought a ticket to that station in advance.

CLIMATE CHANGE & TRAVEL

Every form of transport that relies on carbon-based fuel generates CO_2, the main cause of human-induced climate change. Modern travel is dependent on aeroplanes and while they might use less fuel per kilometre per person than most cars, they travel much greater distances. It's not just CO_2 emissions from aircraft that are the problem. The altitude at which aircraft emit gases (including CO_2) and particles contributes significantly to their total climate change impact. The Intergovernmental Panel on Climate Change believes aviation is responsible for 4.9% of climate change – double the effect of its CO_2 emissions alone.

Lonely Planet regards travel as a global benefit. We encourage the use of more climate-friendly travel modes where possible and, together with other concerned partners across many industries, we support the carbon offset scheme run by ClimateCare. Websites such as climatecare.org use 'carbon calculators' that allow people to offset the greenhouse gases they are responsible for with contributions to portfolios of climate-friendly initiatives throughout the developing world. Lonely Planet offsets the carbon footprint of all staff and author travel.

TOURS

Tours of the USA are so numerous that it is impossible to attempt any kind of comprehensive listing. Probably those of most interest to the general traveler are coach tours that visit the national parks and make guest ranch excursions. For those with limited time, package tours can be an efficient and relatively inexpensive way to go. **Green Tortoise** (☎ 415-956-7500, 800-867-8647; www.greentortoise.com; 494 Broadway, San Francisco, CA 94133) offers alternative bus transportation with stops at places like hot springs and national parks. Your meals are cooperatively cooked and you sleep on bunks on the bus or camp. This is not luxury travel, but it is fun. Its 14-day Cross-Country USA: Southern Dream package runs from August to October. The trip from Boston to San Francisco stops in Texas, where you swim in Austin's Barton Springs and tour Carlsbad Caverns. See the website for details, and last-minute deals.

GETTING AROUND

Texas is big, but it's not hard to get around. The easiest way is to rent a car, but you can get to most larger destinations by Greyhound bus. Flying is often a fine option as well if time is short; with Southwest's special fares, it sometimes beats the bus, so check before assuming that flying is going to cost you an arm and a leg. There's also limited train service within Texas.

AIR

Most larger domestic airlines have connecting services to larger Texas cities through either Dallas or Houston as a Texas hub; you can fly within the state on these flights as well, but the price will probably be higher than with a regional carrier. Over the past several years, the best deals have come consistently from Southwest – which serves Amarillo, Austin, Corpus Christi, Dallas (Love Field), El Paso, Harlingen, Houston (William P Hobby Airport), Lubbock, Midland-Odessa and San Antonio – including frequent $35 one-way fares between Texas destinations. Southwest also offers internet special fares from its website at www.southwest.com.

Whenever you're quoted airfares, remember that they may not include airport-assessed passenger facility charges (PFCs) of up to $12 round-trip.

BICYCLE

Cycling is a feasible way of getting around within some regions, but remember that Texas is spread out, and cities are connected by major interstates, so traveling from city to city on a bike is trickier. There are bicycle rental shops in most major cities, but the rates for each 24 hours can be as high as renting a car. If you're planning on cycling the whole time, it would pay to bring your bike with you from home.

Bicycles can be transported by air. Your best bet is to disassemble or partially disassemble them and put them in a bike bag or box. You may have to remove the pedals and front tire so that it fits in your box or bag. Check all this with the airline well in advance, preferably before you pay for your ticket. Be aware that some airlines will welcome bicycles, while others will treat them as an undesirable nuisance and do everything possible to discourage them.

Greyhound buses will accept bicycles as checked baggage for a fee. Amtrak usually accepts bicycles as part of regularly checked baggage, although a carrying case is required and a nominal fee may be charged on smaller trains.

Cyclists should carry at least two full bottles of water and refill them at every opportunity. Spare parts are widely available and repair shops are numerous, but it's still important to be able to do basic mechanical work, like fixing a flat, yourself.

BUS

Greyhound bus lines (☎ 800-231-2222; www.greyhound.com) is the main line serving Texas. It's generally more cost-effective than flying or taking the train, especially if you're traveling last minute (airlines are typically only a bargain when you have the luxury of advanced planning). Of course, you'll spend a lot more time reaching your destination. If you're traveling to multiple cities, check into a Greyhound **Discovery Pass** (www.discoverypass.com), which includes unlimited travel for seven, 15, 30 or 60 days.

The best fares are found on its website, although tickets can also be bought over the phone with a credit card (MasterCard, Visa or Discover) and mailed if purchased 10 days in advance or picked up at the terminal with proper identification. Greyhound terminals also accept American Express, traveler's checks and cash. All buses are nonsmoking, and reservations are made with ticket purchases only.

Greyhound has its own terminal in most central cities, albeit often in shady parts of town. Greyhound has reduced or eliminated services to smaller rural communities it once served efficiently. In many small towns Greyhound no longer maintains terminals, but merely stops at a given location, such as a fast-food restaurant (which may be the only choice for meal). In these unlikely terminals, boarding passengers usually pay the driver with exact change.

CAR & MOTORCYCLE

By far the most convenient and popular way to get around Texas is by car. Speed limits in smaller towns are strictly enforced, and rural Texans don't usually hurry, so you should get used to driving a bit slower than usual. Motorcycles are also very popular, and, with the exception of rainy days, conditions are perfect: good, flat roads and generally warm weather. There are lots of trucks and SUVs in Texas, so you'd have to get used to being

the smallest thing on the road and give way to vehicles larger than you (which is most of them).

To avert theft, do not leave expensive items, such as purses, compact discs, cameras, leather bags or even sunglasses visibly lying about in the car. Tuck items under the seat, or even better, put items in the trunk and make sure your car does not have trunk entry through the back seat; if it does, make sure that it is locked. Don't leave valuables in the car overnight.

Automobile Associations

If you plan on doing a lot of driving in the USA, it might be beneficial to join the **American Automobile Association** (AAA; ☎ 800-765-0766; www. aaa-texas.com; annual fee $54). AAA provides emergency roadside service to members in the event of an accident, breakdown or locking your keys in the car. Service is free within a given radius of the nearest service center, and service providers will tow your car to a mechanic if they can't fix it. The AAA has reciprocal agreements with other motoring associations; members of some foreign auto

TRANSPORTATION

ROAD DISTANCE CHART (miles)

	Amarillo	Austin	Corpus Christi	Dallas	El Paso	Fort Worth	Galveston	Houston	San Antonio
Austin	507								
Corpus Christi	655	217							
Dallas	364	199	415						
El Paso	438	577	696	638					
Fort Worth	342	187	403	36	608				
Galveston	657	218	226	291	798	319			
Houston	601	161	220	242	743	270	54		
San Antonio	510	80	143	278	552	266	251	196	
South Padre Island	803	366	179	563	844	551	411	368	292

clubs are entitled to AAA services, so bring your membership card and/or a letter of introduction from home. The nationwide toll-free roadside assistance number is ☎ 800-222-4357.

Driver's License

US, Canadian and Mexican driver's licenses are accepted. Other drivers should carry an International Driving Permit in addition to a domestic license. Local traffic police are more likely to accept it as valid identification than an unfamiliar document from another country, though it's wise to carry both documents. Your national automobile association can provide one for a small fee. They're usually valid for one year.

Fuel & Spare Parts

Gas stations are ubiquitous and many are open 24 hours a day. Small-town stations may be open only from 7am to 8pm or 9pm. Most gas stations in larger cities let you pay at the pump with built-in credit- or debit-card readers. At some small-town stations where pumps haven't been outfitted with credit card readers, you must pay before you pump; at others, you may pump before you pay. You might even encounter a full-service station, where an attendant pumps your gas for you, but those are increasingly rare.

If you break down in a privately owned vehicle, check in the *Yellow Pages* under 'Towing,' or if you're on the road without a phone book, get to a pay phone and call **directory assistance** (☎ 411) and ask an operator to call a towing company for you. If the operator says he or she can't, ask to speak to a supervisor and explain your situation; they'll usually look one up in the *Yellow Pages* for you.

Most rental cars are covered for breakdown; see your rental agreement for a toll-free number to call in case this happens. If the company can't get to you until the next day, ask if your motel costs can be covered.

Insurance

Note that in Texas (as well as the United States as a whole) any car you drive must have liability insurance, which means that you won't have to pay for damages if you hit someone. If you're driving a private vehicle, the owner of the car should already have private insurance. If you're renting a car, the liability insurance is called Loss/Damage Waiver (LDW) or Collision/Damage Waiver (CDW), and it's not automatically included in the cost of the rental.

There are three ways you can get the proper coverage for your rental car. In some cases, the credit card you charge your rental on might offer it automatically. Or, if you own a car and have insurance at home, your liability insurance may extend to coverage of rental cars. And when you rent the car, you will be given the option to purchase liability coverage, which costs from $10 to $25 a day in addition to the cost of the car. If you think you might be covered through one of the first two methods, make absolutely sure before you decline the LDW at the car counter. Some people still take the optional LDW just for the additional coverage, even if they're already covered elsewhere.

Rental

All major car-rental companies in the USA have offices throughout Texas. Typically a small car costs at minimum $25 per day and $130 a week. On top of that there will be a 10% state rental tax, plus a heap of local taxes, and additional daily fees for each insurance option you take.

Rates go up and down like the stock market, and it's always worth phoning around to see what's available. Generally speaking, the best deals come on weekly or weekend rental periods. Reserving ahead of time usually ensures the best rates – and reserving ahead can even mean calling from the pay phone in the rental office to the company's toll-free reservation line before you approach the counter. Sometimes the head office can

---

DRIVERS BEWARE

Uninsured drivers are a widespread epidemic in Texas. Your chances of being hit by someone here who doesn't carry liability insurance, even though it is legally required for all drivers, is higher than in any other state in the USA. By some estimates, at least one out of every five drivers in Texas is uninsured. Be sure your own insurance policy covers damages and medical injuries caused by uninsured motorists, and also that the deductible isn't unreasonably high. A thousand dollars can be a lot of money to pay out for a fender-bender that wasn't your fault in the first place.

get you a better price than the branch office, so always call ahead, or check the website for internet-only offers.

Most car-rental companies include unlimited mileage at no extra cost – be sure to check this point, because you can rack up hundreds of miles even just in the city, and at 25¢ per mile, this could lead to an unhappy surprise when you get the bill. If you plan to drop off the car at a different location from the one where you originally rented it, check that there won't be any penalty.

The following national car-rental agencies have locations in Austin and San Antonio:

Advantage (☎ 800-777-5500; www.advantage.com)
Alamo (☎ 800-462-5266; www.alamo.com)
Avis (☎ 800-230-4898; www.avis.com)
Budget (☎ 800-527-0700; www.budget.com)
Dollar (☎ 800-800-4000; www.dollar.com)
Enterprise (☎ 800-736-8222; www.enterprise.com)
Hertz (☎ 800-654-3131; www.hertz.com)
National (☎ 800-227-7368; www.nationalcar.com)
Thrifty (☎ 800- 847-4389; www.thrifty.com)

AGE & CREDIT REQUIREMENTS

Most operators require that you be at least 25 years old and have a major credit card in your own name. Some will rent to younger drivers (minimum age 21), but you must pay outrageous surcharges. Renting without a credit card – if you can even accomplish it – will require a large cash deposit, and you'll have to work things out well in advance with the company. The minimum age for renting motorcycles is usually 21 years old; you'll need to show a valid motorcycle license. The minimum age for renting a scooter or moped (scooters are OK at highway speeds, while mopeds are only for around town) is 16.

Road Rules

The minimum age for driving a car in Texas is 16. Americans drive on the right side of the road and pass on the left. A right turn on a red light is permitted after a full stop unless signs indicate otherwise. Speed limits are posted *and* enforced. Speed limits are 70mph daytime, 65mph nighttime on interstates and freeways unless otherwise posted. (In urban areas, the speed limit often dips to 55mph.) Speed limits in cities and towns can vary from 25mph to 45mph. Watch for school zones, which can have strictly enforced speed limits as low as 15mph during school hours. Speeding tickets are expensive; going 10mph

ROADSIDE HAZARDS

In rural Texas, folks sometimes drive on the shoulder of the road. We asked around and it seems some do it just because they plan to turn soon, even though 'soon' may be 5 miles down the road. Some drivers seem to do it out of courtesy to faster drivers. Whatever the reason, bicyclists and pedestrians traveling on smaller roads would do very well to stay aware and watch out for shoulder drivers.

above the limit could land you a fine of more than $100.

Texas requires the use of seat belts for drivers and front-seat passengers. Children under age four, or under 36 inches tall, must be secured in a federally approved child safety seat; kids between four and 17 must wear regular safety belts.

Texas also requires those riding motorcycles to wear helmets. Exceptions are only granted for those who are at least 21 years old and have applied for a state helmet exemption sticker.

DRINKING & DRIVING

The drinking age is 21, and you need an ID (driver's license or other identification with your photograph and date of birth on it) to prove your age. Undercover agents from the Texas Alcoholic Beverage Commission pose as employees or consumers in shops that sell alcohol, trawling for underage buyers. You could incur stiff fines, jail time and penalties if caught driving under the influence of alcohol. Statewide the blood-alcohol limit is 0.08%, which is reached after just two 12oz bottles of beer for a 135lb woman or three for a 175lb man. If you're younger than 21 years old it is illegal to drive after you have consumed any alcohol – zero tolerance. During holidays and special events, roadblocks are sometimes set up to deter drunk drivers.

HITCHHIKING

Hitchhiking is never entirely safe in any country in the world, and we don't recommend it. Travelers who decide to hitchhike should understand that they are taking a small but serious risk. You may not be able to identify the local rapist, murderer, thief – or even a driver

---

ACCIDENTS DO HAPPEN

Accidents do indeed happen – especially in such a car-dependent country as the USA. It's important that a visitor knows the appropriate protocol when involved in a 'fender-bender.'

- Don't try to drive away. Remain at the scene of the accident; otherwise you may spend some time in the local jail.
- Call the police (and an ambulance, if needed) immediately and give the operator as much specific information as possible (your location, if there are any injuries involved etc). The emergency phone number is ☎ 911.
- Get the other driver's name, address, driver's license number, license plate number and insurance information. Be prepared to provide any documentation you have, such as your passport, international driver's license and insurance documents.
- Tell your story to the police carefully. Refrain from answering any questions until you feel comfortable doing so (with a lawyer present, if need be – see Legal Matters in the Directory chapter, p351). That's your right under the law. The only insurance information that you need to reveal is the name of your insurance carrier and your policy number.
- Always comply with an alcohol Breathalyzer test. If you take the option not to, you'll almost certainly find yourself with an automatic suspension of your driving privileges.
- If you're driving a rental car, call the rental company promptly.

---

who has just had too much to drink – before you get into the vehicle. And in Texas, the chances are hitchhikers won't get picked up anyway – odds of catching a lift from someone here are next to nothing.

People who do choose to hitchhike will be safer if they travel in pairs and let someone know where they are planning to go.

Universities often have ride-sharing programs, as well as bulletin boards that advertise ride-sharing possibilities, especially at the ends of semesters and during school holidays.

LOCAL TRANSPORTATION

Local bus service is available only in larger cities. Transfers – slips of paper that allow you to change buses – are sometimes free, sometimes a few cents extra, but usually no more than 25¢ more than the regular adult fare. Pay as you board (always board through the front doors); exact change is usually required, though some buses accept $1 bills. Operating hours differ from city to city, but in general, buses run from about 6am to 10pm. Dallas,

Houston and Austin also have light rail to speed things up a bit.

Passengers using wheelchairs should contact the local bus company to inquire about special transport services. Most local buses in Texas are wheelchair-accessible, though some bus companies offer individual transit services in addition to regular service for those with physical or mental disabilities.

TRAIN

Amtrak (☎ 800-872-7245; www.amtrak.com) fares for travel within Texas vary greatly, depending on different promotional fares and destinations. Tickets can be purchased by credit card over the phone, from a travel agent or at an Amtrak depot. Amtrak has two train routes that cross the state. The Texas segment of the *Sunset Limited* stretches from El Paso to San Antonio to Houston. The *Texas Eagle* runs between Los Angeles and Chicago, but earns its name with stops in El Paso, Alpine, Del Rio, San Antonio, San Marcos, Austin, Fort Worth and Dallas, among others.

The Authors

MARIELLA KRAUSE
Coordinating Author, Austin, San Antonio & Hill Country, Big Bend & West Texas

Mariella first fell in love with Austin when she checked out the UT (University of Texas) campus during her junior year of high school. After college she intended to live 'everywhere,' but felt so at home in Austin that she accidentally stayed for 15 years, during which time she took lots of road trips to the places she would one day write about in this book. Mariella is now a freelance writer living in San Francisco, but still sprinkles her language with Texanisms whenever possible, much to the amusement of those who don't consider 'y'all' a legitimate pronoun. No matter where she lives, she will always consider Texas home.

SARAH CHANDLER
Dallas–Fort Worth Metroplex, Houston & East Texas

Sarah is now based in New York City but hails from the chilly Nordic lands of Minneapolis, where she had never seen a breakfast taco. A live-music junkie, at 19 she took an epic train trip to Austin and was thrilled to discover rock bands playing *outside* in the dead of winter. Since then, life's been Texas-sized. After the Michener Center for Writers lured her to A-town for grad school, Sarah spent seven years screenwriting, performing Shakespeare in Zilker Park and teaching a few now-famous Longhorn players. Austin coaxes her back for SXSW, evening swims at Barton Springs, and margaritas (frozen, no salt). Some of her exes live in Texas.

RYAN VER BERKMOES
Gulf Coast, Rio Grande Valley, The Panhandle & Central Plains

Ryan grew up in Santa Cruz, California, the sort of goofball beach-town that made him immediately love Port Aransas. An itinerant wanderer, he was most at home on the miles of backroads he traversed for this book. Whether discovering a forgotten town on Hwy 70 or driving to the literal end of the road to (happily!) check out another empty Gulf Coast beach, he relished every click on the odometer. Prowling Galveston's Strand caused Ryan to show that sure sign of geographic affection: ponderings of real estate agent windows. When not searching out the freshest shrimp or perfect onion ring, Ryan lives in Portland, Oregon.

LONELY PLANET AUTHORS

Why is our travel information the best in the world? It's simple: our authors are passionate, dedicated travelers. They don't take freebies in exchange for positive coverage so you can be sure the advice you're given is impartial. They travel widely to all the popular spots, and off the beaten track. They don't research using just the internet or phone. They discover new places not included in any other guidebook. They personally visit thousands of hotels, restaurants, palaces, trails, galleries, temples and more. They speak with dozens of locals every day to make sure you get the kind of insider knowledge only a local could tell you. They take pride in getting all the details right, and in telling it how it is. Think you can do it? Find out how at **lonelyplanet.com**.

Behind the Scenes

THIS BOOK

The 3rd edition of *Texas* was researched and written by Mariella Krause (coordinating author), Sarah Chandler and Ryan Ver Berkmoes, with Sara Benson contributing text across the book. This guidebook was commissioned in Lonely Planet's Oakland office, and produced by the following:

Commissioning Editor Suki Gear
Coordinating Editor Kirsten Rawlings, Daniel Corbett
Coordinating Cartographers Hunor Csutoros, Sam Sayer
Coordinating Layout Designer Paul Iacono
Managing Editor Bruce Evans
Managing Cartographers Alison Lyall, David Connolly, Shahara Ahmed
Managing Layout Designers Indra Kilfoyle, Celia Wood
Assisting Editors Helen Koehne, Charlotte Harrison, Fionnuala Twomey, Kate James, Jackey Coyle, Helen Yeates, Averil Robertson, Angela Tinson, Ali Lemer
Cover Research Sabrina Dalbesio
Internal Image Research Sabrina Dalbesio
Thanks to Raphael Richards

THANKS
MARIELLA KRAUSE

It was no secret around the Lonely Planet office that I wanted to work on Texas, so my biggest thanks is to Suki Gear for calling me up and saying, 'It's time, little lady.' (OK, that's not exactly how she phrased it, but she made it happen.) Another big thanks to Gene Brenek and Michael Helferich for the use of their spare bedroom, their trucks and their cat while they were gallivanting around Buenos Aires. Thanks to Angela Otey and Bill Gundry, who put me up in San Antonio and helped me rescue Guapo the dog. And for the last leg of my trip, muchas gracias to the Fowlers – Pat, Jeff, Leigh Ann and Jeff Schmidt – for welcoming me to El Paso.

RYAN VER BERKMOES

Working on this edition of Texas was my own version of Groundhog Day. I worked on the first edition back in 1997 and, some 60-plus guidebooks later, I was back wondering just what the secret is of a perfect chicken-fried steak. Thanks to Lonely Planet's Suki Gear for giving me the chance to relive (continue living?) my misspent youth. Huge thanks

THE LONELY PLANET STORY

Fresh from an epic journey across Europe, Asia and Australia in 1972, Tony and Maureen Wheeler sat at their kitchen table stapling together notes. The first Lonely Planet guidebook, *Across Asia on the Cheap*, was born.

Travelers snapped up the guides. Inspired by their success, the Wheelers began publishing books to Southeast Asia, India and beyond. Demand was prodigious, and the Wheelers expanded the business rapidly to keep up. Over the years, Lonely Planet extended its coverage to every country and into the virtual world via lonelyplanet.com and the Thorn Tree message board.

As Lonely Planet became a globally loved brand, Tony and Maureen received several offers for the company. But it wasn't until 2007 that they found a partner whom they trusted to remain true to the company's principles of traveling widely, treading lightly and giving sustainably. In October of that year, BBC Worldwide acquired a 75% share in the company, pledging to uphold Lonely Planet's commitment to independent travel, trustworthy advice and editorial independence.

Today, Lonely Planet has offices in Melbourne, London and Oakland, with over 500 staff members and 300 authors. Tony and Maureen are still actively involved with Lonely Planet. They're traveling more often than ever, and they're devoting their spare time to charitable projects. And the company is still driven by the philosophy of *Across Asia on the Cheap*: 'All you've got to do is decide to go and the hardest part is over. So go!'

365

SEND US YOUR FEEDBACK

We love to hear from travelers – your comments keep us on our toes and help make our books better. Our well-traveled team reads every word on what you loved or loathed about this book. Although we cannot reply individually to postal submissions, we always guarantee that your feedback goes straight to the appropriate authors, in time for the next edition. Each person who sends us information is thanked in the next edition and the most useful submissions are rewarded with a free book.

To send us your updates – and find out about Lonely Planet events, newsletters and travel news – visit our award-winning website: **lonelyplanet.com/contact**.

Note: we may edit, reproduce and incorporate your comments in Lonely Planet products such as guidebooks, websites and digital products, so let us know if you don't want your comments reproduced or your name acknowledged. For a copy of our privacy policy visit lonelyplanet.com/privacy.

to my dear friend Justin Marler and his wonderful family; even ignoring the world's freshest eggs, it was too long. And Alex Hershey? You never looked better. To that fine Texas lawman who stopped me going 82 in a 60 zone, your mere warning kept my late schedule from becoming my own Alamo.

SARAH CHANDLER

Big thanks to Suki Gear for taking a chance on a 'Yankee by birth, Texan by choice.' Julia Peek, you were the kind of pardner-in-crime every cowgirl needs, whether hitting the bars in Waco or chaining out in Huntsville. Thanks to Andrea and Scott Ginder in Austin for rocking out with me at SXSW

– it's now a tradition! Jennifer and Bryan Lockett, y'all took wonderful care of me in Fort Worth. Dreya Johannsen, gratitude for the lovely condo where I began this manuscript. Thanks to my parents for your support. Mariella Krause, I owe you infinite drinks at the San Jose Motel. Finally, to the people of Jefferson: you proved that east Texas really is one of the friendliest places on earth.

ACKNOWLEDGMENTS
Many thanks to the following for the use of their content:

Globe on title page ©Mountain High Maps 1993 Digital Wisdom, Inc.

BEHIND THE SCENES

Index